The Legal Writing Handbook

The Legal Writing Handbook

Research, Analysis, and Writing

Second Edition

Laurel Currie Oates
Director, Legal Writing Program
Seattle University School of Law

Anne Enquist
Writing Advisor,
Seattle University School of Law

Kelly Kunsch
Reference Librarian,
Seattle University School of Law

Aspen Law & Business
A Division of Aspen Publishers, Inc.

Printed in the United States of America

10 9 8 7 6 5 4 3 2

ISBN 1-56706-695-X

Library of Congress Cataloging-in-Publication Data

Oates, Laurel Currie, 1951–
    The legal writing handbook : analysis, research, and writing /
Laurel Currie Oates, Anne Enquist, Kelly Kunsch.—2nd ed.
        p.   cm.
    Includes index.
    ISBN 1-56706-695-X
    1. Legal composition.   2. Legal research—United States.
I. Enquist, Anne, 1950–   .   II. Kunsch, Kelly, 1958–   .
III. Title.
KF250.O18   1998
808′.06634—dc21   97-49350
                                                                                CIP

About Aspen Law & Business, Law School Division

In 1996, Aspen Law & Business welcomed the Law School Division of Little, Brown and Company into its growing business — already established as a leading provider of practical information to legal practitioners.

Acquiring much more than a prestigious collection of educational publications by the country's foremost authors, Aspen Law & Business inherited the long-standing Little, Brown tradition of excellence — born over 150 years ago. As one of America's oldest and most venerable publishing houses, Little, Brown and Company commenced in a world of change and challenge, innovation and growth. Sharing that same spirit, Aspen Law & Business has dedicated itself to continuing and strengthening the integrity begun so many years ago.

ASPEN LAW & BUSINESS
A Division of Aspen Publishers, Inc.
A Wolters Kluwer Company

To my parents, Bill and Lucille Currie,
my husband, Terry, and my children, Julia and Michael.
Thank you.

To my family, Steve, Matt, and Jeff Enquist,
and my parents, Arthur and Agnes Meiering,
for their love, support, and patience.

To my parents, blame them.
—K²

Summary of Contents

Section I

A Course in Legal Analysis, Research, and Writing   *1*

Part I

A Foundation for Legal Writing   *3*

Chapter 1   An Overview of the United States   5
             Legal System
Chapter 2   An Introduction to Common and   21
             Enacted Law
Chapter 3   An Introduction to Legal Analysis   31

Part II

The Legal Writing Process   *63*

Chapter 4   The Objective Memorandum: Its Purpose,   65
             Audience, and Format
Chapter 5   The First Memorandum   79
Chapter 6   The Second Memorandum   177
Chapter 7   The Opinion Letter   241
Chapter 8   Writing an Appellate Brief   253
Chapter 9   Oral Advocacy   369

Section II

Resources in Legal Research, Style, and Grammar   *385*

Part III

A Guide to Legal Research   *387*

Chapter 10	Introduction to Legal Research	389
Chapter 11	Constitutions and Charters	393
Chapter 12	The Legislative Branch	397
Chapter 13	The Executive Branch and Administrative Agencies	413
Chapter 14	The Judicial Branch	421
Chapter 15	Secondary Sources	439
Chapter 16	Shepard's *Citators*	457
Chapter 17	Computer-Assisted Legal Research	467
Chapter 18	How to Approach a Legal Research Problem: Sample Research Plans	495

Part IV

A Guide to Effective Writing   *505*

Chapter 19	Effective Writing—The Whole Paper	507
Chapter 20	Connections Between Paragraphs	527
Chapter 21	Effective Paragraphs	535
Chapter 22	Connections Between Sentences	565
Chapter 23	Effective Sentences	587
Chapter 24	Effective Words	623
Chapter 25	Eloquence	683

Part V

A Guide to Correct Writing   *701*

Chapter 26	Grammar	703
Chapter 27	Punctuation	761
Chapter 28	Mechanics	827
Chapter 29	Legal Writing for English-as-a-Second-Language Students	861

Glossary of Usage	*905*
Glossary of Terms	*915*
Index	*923*

Table of Contents

Section I

A Course in Legal Analysis, Research, and Writing   *1*

Part I

A Foundation for Legal Writing   *3*

Chapter 1

An Overview of the United States Legal System   *5*

§1.1	The Three Branches of Government	6
	§1.1.1 The Executive Branch	6
	§1.1.2 The Legislative Branch	6
	§1.1.3 The Judicial Branch	7
	a. The Hierarchical Nature of the Court System	7
	b. The Federal Courts	9
	c. State Courts	12
	d. Other Courts	12
§1.2	The Relationship Between the Federal and State Governments	13
	§1.2.1 A Short History	13
	§1.2.2 The Relationship Between Laws Enacted by Congress and Those Enacted by the State Legislatures	14

§1.2.3   The Relationship Between Federal and   16
          State Courts
§1.2.4   The Relationship Among Federal, State,   17
          and Local Prosecutors
§1.3   A Final Comment   19

Chapter 2

An Introduction to Common and Enacted Law   *21*

§2.1   Common Law   21
§2.2   Enacted Law   23
§2.3   Mandatory versus Persuasive Authority   25
        §2.3.1   Which Jurisdiction's Law Applies?   26
        §2.3.2   What "Law" Will Be Binding on   28
                  the Court?

Chapter 3

An Introduction to Legal Analysis   *31*

§3.1   Meeting the Clients   31
§3.2   Obtaining the Facts   32
§3.3   Locating the Applicable Statute   32
§3.4   Analyzing the Statute   35
§3.5   Locating and Analyzing the Cases   36
§3.6   Synthesizing the Law   40
§3.7   Gathering Additional Information   42
§3.8   Identifying the Legally and Emotionally   49
        Significant Facts
§3.9   Formulating Arguments   51
        §3.9.1   Arguing the Law   51
                  a. Plain Language Arguments   51
                  b. Legislative Intent   52
                  c. Public Policy   54
        §3.9.2   Arguing the Application of the Law   55
                  to the Facts
                  a. Factual Arguments Based on the Plain 55
                      Language of the Law
                  b. Arguments Based on Analogous Cases   60
                  c. Policy Arguments   61

Part II

The Legal Writing Process 63

Chapter 4

The Objective Memorandum: Its Purpose, Audience, and Format 65

Chapter 5

The First Memorandum 79

§5.1   Getting the Assignment   80
A. Prewriting   **82**
§5.2   Preparing a Research Plan   82
    §5.2.1   Determining What Law Applies   82
    §5.2.2   Drafting a Preliminary Statement   83
    §5.2.3   Preparing a List of Search Terms   83
    §5.2.4   Selecting the Sources You Want to Check 84
§5.3   Researching the Problem   86
§5.4   Keeping Track of What You Have Found   103
§5.5   Understanding What You Have Found   103
B. Drafting   **109**
§5.6   Drafting the Heading   110
§5.7   Drafting the Statement of Facts   111
    §5.7.1   Deciding What Facts to Include   111
        a. Legally Significant Facts   111
        b. Emotionally Significant Facts   112
        c. Background Facts   113
        d. Unknown Facts   113
    §5.7.2   Selecting an Organizational Scheme   114
    §5.7.3   Presenting the Facts Accurately and   116
        Objectively
§5.8   Drafting the Issue Statement or Question Presented   118
    §5.8.1   Deciding How Many Issue Statements You 118
        Should Have and the Order in Which They
        Should be Listed
    §5.8.2   Selecting a Format   118
        a. Reference to the Applicable Law   119
        b. The Legal Question   119
        c. Legally Significant Facts   120
§5.9   Drafting the Brief Answer   123
§5.10   Drafting the Discussion Section: An Introduction   124
    §5.10.1   Selecting an Organizational Plan   125

	§5.10.2	Presenting the General Rule	126
		a. Single Statutory Section	127
		b. Multiple Statutory Section	128
		c. Statutes Plus Cases	129
	§5.10.3	Raising and Dismissing the Undisputed Elements	131
	§5.10.4	Discussing the Disputed Elements	132
		a. Presenting the Specific Rule	133
		b. Describing the Analogous Cases	134
		c. Presenting Each Side's Arguments	137
		d. Predicting How the Court Will Decide the Element	143
§5.11	Avoiding the Common Problems		144
	§5.11.1	Speak for Yourself	144
	§5.11.2	Lay It Out	144
	§5.11.3	Show How You Reached Your Conclusions	146
	§5.11.4	Use Terms Consistently	148
	§5.11.5	See More than the Obvious	148
§5.12	Drafting the Conclusion		150
C.	**Revising**		**152**
§5.13	Checking Content		152
	§5.13.1	Have You Given the Attorneys the Information That They Need?	152
	§5.13.2	Is the Information Presented Accurately?	153
	§5.13.3	Is the Information Well-Organized?	154
	§5.13.4	Are the Connections Explicit?	157
D.	**Editing**		**160**
§5.14	Editing and Proofreading		161
	§5.14.1	Editing	161
		a. Writing Effective Sentences	161
		b. Writing Correctly	169
	§5.14.2	Proofreading	169
§5.15	A Note About Citations		170
§5.16	Final Draft of Memo		170

Chapter 6

The Second Memorandum — 177

§6.1	Receiving the Assignment		177
§6.2	Preparing a Research Plan		179
	§6.2.1	Drafting the Preliminary Issue Statement	179
	§6.2.2	Determining What Law Applies	180
	§6.2.3	Preparing a List of Search Terms	181
	§6.2.4	Deciding Which Sources to Check	181
§6.3	Understanding What You Have Found		184

§6.4	Constructing the Arguments	195
§6.5	Drafting the Statement of Facts	198
§6.6	Drafting the Question Presented	199
§6.7	Drafting the Brief Answer	200
§6.8	Drafting the Discussion Section	201
	§6.8.1 Planning the Discussion Section	201
	§6.8.2 Using the Integrated Format	203
	§6.8.3 Presenting the General Rules	207
	§6.8.4 Presenting the Analogous Cases	214
	a. Integrating the Discussion of Analogous Cases into the Argument	214
	b. Using Parentheticals	219
	c. Other Reminders	222
	§6.8.5 Presenting Each Side's Argument	225
	a. Organizing the Arguments	225
	b. Introducing the Arguments	225
	§6.8.6 Avoiding the Common Problems	230
§6.9	Revising for Conciseness and Preciseness	236
	§6.9.1 Writing Concisely	237
	§6.9.2 Writing Precisely	238

Chapter 7

The Opinion Letter   *241*

§7.1	Audience	241
§7.2	Purpose	242
§7.3	Conventions	243
	§7.3.1 The Introductory Paragraph	243
	§7.3.2 Statement of the Issue	244
	§7.3.3 Opinion	245
	§7.3.4 Summary of the Facts	245
	§7.3.5 Explanation	245
	§7.3.6 Advice	246
	§7.3.7 Concluding Paragraph	247
	§7.3.8 Warnings	247
§7.4	Writing Style	247
§7.5	Tone	248

Chapter 8

Writing an Appellate Brief   *253*

A.	***Introduction to Appellate Practice***	***253***
§8.1	Introduction to Advocacy	253
§8.2	Appellate Practice	255
	§8.2.1 Types of Appellate Review	255

	§8.2.2	Scope of Review	256
	§8.2.3	Filing the Notice of Appeal or Notice for Discretionary Review	257
	§8.2.4	Preparing the Record on Appeal	258
	§8.2.5	Types of Briefs	258
§8.3		The Appellate Brief: Its Audience and Purpose	259
	§8.3.1	Audience	259
	§8.3.2	Purpose	260
	§8.3.3	Conventions	260

B. Drafting an Appellate Brief — **263**

§8.4		*State v. Strong*	263
§8.5		Preparing to Write the Brief	264
	§8.5.1	Reviewing the Record for Error	264
	§8.5.2	Selecting the Issues on Appeal	265
		a. Was There Error?	266
		b. Was the Error Preserved?	266
		c. Was the Error Harmless?	266
		d. What Is the Standard of Review?	267
	§8.5.3	Preparing an Abstract of the Record	268
	§8.5.4	Preparing the Record on Appeal	269
§8.6		Researching the Issues on Appeal	269
§8.7		Planning the Brief	270
	§8.7.1	Analyzing the Facts and the Law	270
	§8.7.2	Developing a Theory of the Case	271
	§8.7.3	Selecting an Organizational Scheme	272
		a. Deciding on the Number of Questions and Headings	272
		b. Ordering the Issues and Arguments	275
§8.8		Preparing the Cover	275
§8.9		Preparing the Table of Contents	276
§8.10		Preparing the Table of Authorities	276
§8.11		Drafting the Assignments of Error	276
§8.12		The Issues Pertaining to Assignments of Error (Questions Presented)	277
	§8.12.1	Selecting a Format	278
	§8.12.2	Making the Issue Statement Subtly Persuasive	279
		a. State the Question So That It Suggests the Conclusion You Want the Court to Reach	280
		b. Present the Legally Significant Facts in the Light Most Favorable to Your Client	280
		c. Emphasize or De-emphasize the Standard of Review	281
	§8.12.3	Make Sure That the Issue Statement Is Readable	282
§8.13		Statement of the Case	283
	§8.13.1	Checking the Rules	283
	§8.13.2	Drafting the Procedural History	284
	§8.13.3	Drafting the Statement of Facts	285

		a.	Selecting the Facts	285
		b.	Selecting an Organizational Scheme	286
		c.	Presenting the Facts in the Light Most Favorable to the Client	286
§8.14	Summary of the Argument			300
§8.15	Drafting the Argumentative Headings			300
	§8.15.1	Use the Argumentative Headings to Provide the Court with an Outline of the Argument		300
	§8.15.2	Use the Argumentative Headings to Persuade		301
		a.	Write Your Headings as Positive Assertions	301
		b.	Provide Support for Your Assertions	302
		c.	Make the Headings as Specific as Possible	303
		d.	Make Your Headings Readable	304
	§8.15.3	Use the Conventional Formats for Headings		305
§8.16	Drafting the Arguments			307
	§8.16.1	Knowing What You Need, and Want, to Argue		307
	§8.16.2	Selecting an Organizational Scheme		308
	§8.16.3	Presenting the Rules, Descriptions of Analogous Cases and Arguments in the Light Most Favorable to Your Client		315
		a.	Presenting the Rule in the Light Most Favorable to Your Client	315
		b.	Presenting the Cases in the Light Most Favorable to Your Client	318
		c.	Presenting the Arguments Effectively	323
		d.	Don't Ignore the "Weaknesses" That are Inherent in Your Argument	324
		e.	Respond to Your Opponent's Arguments but Do Not Emphasize Them	327
§8.17	The Conclusion or Prayer for Relief			329
§8.18	Signature			330
§8.19	Appendix			330
§8.20	Revising, Editing, and Proofreading			330
			Appellant's Brief	332
			Respondent's Brief	352

Chapter 9	

Oral Advocacy **369**

| §9.1 | Audience | 369 |
| §9.2 | Purpose | 370 |

§9.3		Preparing for Oral Argument	370
	§9.3.1	Deciding What to Argue	370
	§9.3.2	Preparing an Outline	370
	§9.3.3	Practicing the Argument	371
	§9.3.4	Reviewing the Facts and Law	371
	§9.3.5	Organizing Your Materials	371
		a. Notes or Outline	371
		b. The Briefs	372
		c. The Record	372
		d. The Law	372
§9.4		Courtroom Procedures and Etiquette	372
	§9.4.1	Seating	372
	§9.4.2	Before the Case Is Called	372
	§9.4.3	Courtroom Etiquette	373
	§9.4.4	Appropriate Dress	373
§9.5		Making the Argument	373
	§9.5.1	Introductions	373
	§9.5.2	Opening	374
	§9.5.3	Statement of the Issues	374
		a. The Moving Party	374
		b. The Responding Party	374
	§9.5.4	Summary of Facts	374
		a. The Moving Party	374
		b. The Responding Party	375
		c. References to the Record	375
	§9.5.5	The Argument	375
	§9.5.6	Answering Questions	376
	§9.5.7	Closing	377
	§9.5.8	Rebuttal	377
§9.6		Delivering the Argument	378
	§9.6.1	Do Not Read Your Argument	378
	§9.6.2	Maintain Eye Contact	378
	§9.6.3	Do Not Slouch, Rock, or Put Your Hands in Your Pockets	379
	§9.6.4	Limit Your Gestures and Avoid Distracting Mannerisms	379
	§9.6.5	Speak So That You Can Be Easily Understood	379
§9.7		Making Your Argument Persuasive	379
§9.8		Handling the Problems	380
	§9.8.1	Counsel Has Misstated Facts or Law	380
	§9.8.2	You Make a Mistake	380
	§9.8.3	Not Enough Time	380
	§9.8.4	Too Much Time	381
	§9.8.5	You Don't Know the Answer to a Question	381
	§9.8.6	You Didn't Understand the Question	381
	§9.8.7	You Become Flustered or Draw a Blank	382
	§9.8.8	You're Asked to Concede a Point	382
§9.9		A Final Note	382

Section II

Resources in Legal Research, Style, and Grammar　*385*

Part III

A Guide to Legal Research　*387*

Chapter 10

Introduction to Legal Research　*389*

§10.1　What Lawyers Research　389
§10.2　Legal Research as Part of a Process　390
§10.3　Outline of the Legal System of the United States　390

Chapter 11

Constitutions and Charters　*393*

§11.1　The United States Constitution　393
§11.2　State Constitutions　396
§11.3　Charters　396

Chapter 12

The Legislative Branch　*397*

§12.1　Locating Statutes　397
　　　§12.1.1　Session Laws　397
　　　§12.1.2　Codes　400
　　　　　　a.　Official versus Unofficial Codes　400
　　　　　　b.　Annotated versus Unannotated Codes　401
　　　　　　c.　Updating Annotated and Unannotated　401
　　　　　　　　Codes
　　　　　　d.　Research Strategies　401
　　　§12.1.3　Statutes Available on Computer Databases　405
§12.2　Compiling a Legislative History　409
　　　§12.2.1　The Legislative Process　409
　　　　　　a.　Introduction of a Bill　409
　　　　　　b.　Consideration by a Committee　409
　　　　　　c.　Floor Debates　409
　　　　　　d.　Consideration by the Other House　410
　　　　　　e.　Approval or Veto by the President or　410
　　　　　　　　the Governor

§12.2.2   Compiled Legislative Histories   411
§12.2.3   Sources for Federal Legislative Histories   411
§12.2.4   Sources for State Legislative Histories   411

Chapter 13

The Executive Branch and Administrative Agencies   **413**

§13.1   Presidential Documents   413
§13.2   Administrative Agencies   414
         §13.2.1   Delegation of Power   414
         §13.2.2   Federal Regulations   415
         §13.2.3   The Federal Register   415
         §13.2.4   The Code of Federal Regulations   415
                    a.   Search Tools   417
                    b.   Updating the C.F.R.   417
§13.3   State Regulations   420
§13.4   Administrative Decisions   420

Chapter 14

The Judicial Branch   **421**

§14.1   Court Decisions   421
         §14.1.1   Slip Opinions   421
         §14.1.2   Advance Sheets   422
         §14.1.3   Bound Reporters   422
         §14.1.4   The National Reporter System   423
         §14.1.5   Other Reporters   425
         §14.1.6   Online Court Decisions   431
§14.2   Court Rules   431
§14.3   Digests   432

Chapter 15

Secondary Sources   **439**

§15.1   Sources for Background Reading   439
         §15.1.1   Legal Encyclopedias   440
         §15.1.2   Hornbooks   440
         §15.1.3   Practice Books   445
§15.2   Sources That Can Be Used as Finding Tools   445
         §15.2.1   *American Law Reports*   445
         §15.2.2   Looseleaf Services   451

§15.3	Sources That Can Be Cited as Persuasive Authority	453
	§15.3.1 Treatises and Other Books	453
	§15.3.2 Law Reviews and Other Legal Periodicals	453
	§15.3.3 Uniform Laws and Model Acts	455
	§15.3.4 Restatements	455
§15.4	Other Secondary Sources	456
	§15.4.1 Legal Dictionaries	456
	§15.4.2 Words and Phrases	456
	§15.4.3 Form Books	456

Chapter 16

Citators 457

§16.1	How Citators Work	457
§16.2	*Shepard's* Citators	458
§16.3	Coverage of Different Citators	458
	§16.3.1 Differences in Coverage of State and Regional Reporters	458
	§16.3.2 Differences in Coverage for Various Supreme Court Citators and Reporters	459
§16.4	Tips on Using *Shepard's*	463
§16.5	*Shepard's* Online	464
§16.6	KeyCite	465

Chapter 17

Computer-Assisted Legal Research 467

§17.1	Indices and Full-Text Searching	468
§17.2	LEXIS and Westlaw	468
	§17.2.1 Similarities and Differences in the Two Systems	468
	§17.2.2 Composition of LEXIS and Westlaw Services	469
	§17.2.3 Search Words	470
	§17.2.4 Truncation and Root Expansion	472
	§17.2.5 Hyphenation	474
	§17.2.6 Plurals and Capitalization	475
	§17.2.7 Noise Words (Stop Words)	475
	§17.2.8 Connectors	475
	a. Or	476
	b. And	476
	c. Proximity Connectors	477
	d. Not	479
	§17.2.9 Search Order of Connectors	480
	§17.2.10 Segment/Field Searching	481
	§17.2.11 Natural Language Searching	483

§17.2.12   Cite-Checking Online   483
    a.   *Shepard's* Online   483
    b.   KeyCite   484
    c.   AutoCite and InstaCite   484
§17.2.13   Costs of Computer-Assisted Research   485
    a.   Subscription   485
    b.   Search Costs   486
    c.   Printing   486
§17.3   Other Computerized Research Services   487
§17.4   Research on the Internet   487
    §17.4.1   Overview of the Internet   487
    §17.4.2   Finding Information on the Internet   488
    §17.4.3   Internet Research Benefits and Problems 490
§17.5   Online Search Strategies   491

Chapter 18

How to Approach a Legal Research Problem: Sample Research Plans   *495*

Research Plan 1   Statutory Research: When the Governing
    Statute Is Known   496
Research Plan 2   Statutory Research: When the Governing
    Statute Is Not Known   497
Research Plan 3   Statutory Research: Federal Legislative
    Histories   498
Research Plan 4   Federal Administrative Law   499
Research Plan 5   Common Law Research: When the Name
    of the Case Setting Out the Common Law
    Rule Is Known   500
Research Plan 6   Common Law Research: When the Name
    of the Case Setting Out the Common Law
    Rule Is Not Known   501
Research Plan 7   Procedural Issues   502
Research Plan 8   International Law   503

Part IV

A Guide to Effective Writing   *505*

Chapter 19

Effective Writing— The Whole Paper   *507*

§19.1   The Psychology of Writing   507

§19.2	Outlines, Writing Plans, and Ordered Lists	509
	§19.2.1 Read It All; Mull It Over	510
	§19.2.2 Don't Overlook the Obvious	510
	§19.2.3 Find Order Using a Three-Column Chart	510
	§19.2.4 Talk to a Colleague	513
	§19.2.5 Try a New Analogy or Format	513
	§19.2.6 Consider Your Reader, Purpose, and How You View the Case	514
§19.3	Drafting the Document	516
	§19.3.1 Give Yourself Optimum Writing Conditions	516
	§19.3.2 Trick Yourself into Getting Started	516
	§19.3.3 Write What You Know Best First	516
	§19.3.4 "Get the Juices Flowing"	517
	§19.3.5 Take It One Step at a Time	517
	§19.3.6 Reward Yourself	517
§19.4	Revising	518
	§19.4.1 Develop a Revision Checklist	518
	§19.4.2 Write an After-the-Fact Outline	518
	§19.4.3 Do a Self-Critique	519
	§19.4.4 Check for Unity and Coherence	519
§19.5	Editing	520
§19.6	Proofreading	521
§19.7	Myths About Writing	522

Chapter 20

Connections Between Paragraphs 527

§20.1	Headings	527
§20.2	Roadmaps and Signposts	530
	§20.2.1 Roadmaps	530
	§20.2.2 Signposts	532

Chapter 21

Effective Paragraphs 535

§21.1	The Function of a Paragraph	535
§21.2	Unity and Coherence in Paragraphs	536
	§21.2.1 Paragraph Unity	536
	§21.2.2 Paragraph Coherence	537
	a. Using Familiar Organizational Patterns	537
	b. Using Key Terms	539
	c. Using Sentence Structure and Other Coherence Devices	540
§21.3	Paragraph Patterns	542
§21.4	Paragraph Length	544

§21.5   Topic and Concluding Sentences   547
         §21.5.1   Stated Topic Sentences   548
         §21.5.2   Implied Topic Sentences   551
         §21.5.3   Concluding Sentences   552
§21.6   Paragraph Blocks   557

Chapter 22

Connections Between Sentences   **565**

§22.1   Generic Transitions   565
         §22.1.1   Using Generic Transitions   565
         §22.1.2   Problems with Generic Transitions   568
§22.2   Orienting Transitions   570
§22.3   Substantive Transitions   574
         §22.3.1   The Structure of Substantive Transitions   574
         §22.3.2   The Content of Substantive Transitions   581
                    a.   Bridging the Gap Between Law and   582
                          Application
                    b.   Applying Another Court's Rationale   583
                    c.   Gathering Together Several Facts   584
                    d.   Gathering Together Several Ideas   585
                    e.   Bridging the Gap Between Sections   586
                          of a Document

Chapter 23

Effective Sentences   **587**

§23.1   Active and Passive Voice   587
         §23.1.1   Identifying Active and Passive Voice   587
         §23.1.2   Effective Use of Active Voice   588
         §23.1.3   Effective Use of Passive Voice   590
§23.2   Concrete Subjects   593
§23.3   Action Verbs   595
§23.4   Distance Between Subjects and Verbs   597
§23.5   Sentence Length   599
         §23.5.1   The Reader   599
         §23.5.2   The Context   603
         §23.5.3   The Power of the Short Sentence   605
§23.6   Emphasis   606
         §23.6.1   Telling the Reader What Is Important   607
         §23.6.2   Underlining   608
         §23.6.3   Using Positions of Emphasis   608
         §23.6.4   Using Punctuation for Emphasis   612
         §23.6.5   Using Single-Word Emphasizers   614
         §23.6.6   Changing the Normal Word Order   616

§23.6.7   Repeating Key Words   617
§23.6.8   Setting Up a Pattern   618
§23.6.9   Variation: Deliberately Breaking a Pattern   619
§23.6.10   Strategies for Emphasis in Context   619

Chapter 24

Effective Words   *623*

§24.1   Diction and Precision   623
§24.1.1   Colloquial Language   625
§24.1.2   Reader Expectations and Idioms   625
§14.2.3   Not-Really-Synonymous Synonyms   627
§24.1.4   Same Term for the Same Idea   628
§24.1.5   Apples and Rutabagas   630
§24.1.6   Subject-Verb-Object Mismatch   630
§24.1.7   Grammatical Ambiguities   635
§24.2   Conciseness   638
§24.2.1   Don't State the Obvious   639
§24.2.2   Don't Start Too Far Back   640
§24.2.3   Don't Overuse Quotations   641
§24.2.4   Create a Strong Subject-Verb Unit   643
§24.2.5   Avoid Throat-Clearing Expressions   645
§24.2.6   Don't Use Pompous Language   647
§24.2.7   Don't Repeat Yourself Needlessly   648
§24.2.8   Clean Out the Clutter   651
§24.2.9   Focus and Combine   653
§24.2.10   Avoid Excessive Conciseness   659
§24.3   Plain English v. Legalese   660
§24.3.1   Archaic Word Choice   663
§24.3.2   Foreign Phrases   665
§24.3.3   Use of Terms of Art and Argot   667
§24.3.4   Use of "Said" and "Such" as Articles   668
§24.3.5   Omission of the Article "The"   669
§24.3.6   Use of "Same" as a Pronoun   669
§24.3.7   Absence of First- and Second-Person   670
           Pronouns
§24.3.8   Some Final Words About Legalese   673
§24.4   Gender-Neutral Language   673
§24.4.1   Generic Use of "Man"   674
§24.4.2   Generic Use of "He"   675
         a.   Revise the Sentence So That the   675
               Antecedent and Its Pronoun are Plural
         b.   Revise the Sentence So That a   675
               Pronoun Is Not Needed
         c.   Replace the Masculine Noun and   676
               Pronoun with "One," "Your," "He" or
               "She," as Appropriate

		d.	Alternate Male and Female Examples and Expressions	676
		e.	Repeat the Noun Rather Than Use an Inappropriate Masculine Pronoun	677
	§24.4.3		Gender-Neutral Job Titles	677
	§24.4.4		Sexist Modifiers	678
	§24.4.5		Other Sexist Language	678
§24.5	Bias-Free Language			679
	§24.5.1		Stay Abreast of the Preferred Terminology	680
	§24.5.2		Avoid Irrelevant Minority References	681
	§24.5.3		Use Racial, Ethnic, and Religious Terms Precisely	681
	§24.5.4		Choose the More Specific Term	681
	§24.5.5		Choose Words That Emphasize the Person, Not the Disability	682

Chapter 25

Eloquence   **683**

§25.1	Purple Prose		684
§25.2	Common Features of Eloquent Writing		685
	§25.2.1	Alliteration and Assonance	685
	§25.2.2	Cadence	687
	§25.2.3	Variety in Sentence Length	690
	§25.2.4	Variety in Sentence Openers	692
	§25.2.5	Parallelism	694
	§25.2.6	Onomatopoeia	696
	§25.2.7	Simile and Metaphor	697
	§25.2.8	Personification	698

Part V

A Guide to Correct Writing   **701**

Chapter 26

Grammar   **703**

§26.1	Basic Sentence Grammar		703
	§26.1.1	Sentence Patterns	703
	§26.1.2	Single-Word Modifiers	706
	§26.1.3	Phrases	707
		a. Gerunds	708
		b. Participles	708

	c.	Infinitives	709
	d.	Absolutes	709
§26.1.4		Clauses	709
§26.1.5		Appositives	711
§26.1.6		Connecting Words	711
	a.	Coordinating Conjunctions	712
	b.	Correlative Conjunctions	713
	c.	Conjunctive Adverbs	713
§26.2		Fragments	714
§26.2.1		Missing Main Verb	714
§26.2.2		Subordinate Clauses Trying to Pose as Sentences	715
§26.2.3		Permissible Uses of Incomplete Sentences	718
	a.	In Issue Statements Beginning with "Whether"	718
	b.	As Answers to Questions	718
	c.	In Exclamations	719
	d.	For Stylistic Effect	719
	e.	As Transitions	719
§26.3		Verb Tense and Mood	720
§26.3.1		Tense	720
§26.3.2		Mood	724
§26.4		Agreement	727
§26.4.1		Subject-Verb Agreement	727
§26.4.2		Pronoun-Antecedent Agreement	737
§26.5		Pronoun Reference	742
§26.5.1		Each Pronoun Should Clearly Refer Back to Its Antecedent	742
§26.5.2		Avoid Use of "It," "This," "Such," and "Which" to Refer Broadly to a General Idea in a Preceding Sentence	743
§26.5.3		Pronouns Should Refer Back to Nouns, Not Adjectives	746
§26.6		Modifiers	747
§26.6.1		Misplaced Modifiers	747
§26.6.2		Dangling Modifiers	750
§26.6.3		Squinting Modifiers	753
§26.7		Parallelism	754

Chapter 27

Punctuation *761*

§27.1		The Comma	761
§27.1.1		Critical Commas: Those That Affect Meaning and Clarity	765
§27.1.2		Basic Commas: Those That Educated Readers Expect	774

	§27.1.3	Esoteric Commas: Those That Are Required in Sophisticated Sentence Structures	785
	§27.1.4	Unnecessary Commas: Those That Should Be Omitted	787
§27.2	The Semicolon		792
	§27.2.1	Use of the Semicolon with "Yet" or "So"	795
	§27.2.2	Use of the Semicolon with Coordinating Conjunctions	796
	§27.2.3	Use of the Semicolon with Citations	796
§27.3	The Colon		797
§27.4	The Apostrophe		799
§27.5	Other Marks of Punctuation		803
	§27.5.1	Quotation Marks	803
		a. Identification of Another's Written or Spoken Words	803
		b. Block Quotations	805
		c. Effective Lead-ins for Quotations	806
		d. Quotations Within Quotations	808
		e. Quotation Marks with Other Marks of Punctuation	809
		f. Other Uses for Quotation Marks	809
	§27.5.2	Ellipses	810
	§27.5.3	Brackets	813
	§27.5.4	Parentheses	815
		a. To Enclose Short Explanations of Cases Within Citations	815
		b. To Refer Readers to Attached or Appended Documents	816
		c. To Confirm Numbers	816
		d. To Enclose Numerals That Introduce the Individual Items in a List	817
		e. To Announce Changes to a Quotation That Cannot Be Shown by Ellipses or Brackets	817
		f. To Introduce Abbreviations After a Full Name Is Given	817
	§27.5.5	The Hyphen	818
		a. Word Division	818
		b. Compound Modifiers and Compound Nouns	818
	§27.5.6	The Dash	821
§27.6	Comma Splices and Fused Sentences		823
	§27.6.1	Comma Splices	823
	§27.6.2	Fused Sentences	826

Chapter 28

Mechanics 827

§28.1	Spelling		827
	§28.1.1	Getting Motivated	827
	§28.1.2	Spelling Crutches	828
		a. Computer Software	828
		b. Dictionaries	829
		c. Legal Spellers	829
		d. Secretaries and Typists	829
	§28.1.3	Spelling Strategies	829
		a. Spelling Rules	831
		b. Spelling Lists	840
§28.2	Capitalization		842
	§28.2.1	General Rules	842
		a. Beginning of a Sentence	842
		b. Proper Nouns and Adjectives	844
	§28.2.2	Headings	849
	§28.2.3	Miscellaneous Rules for Capitalization	849
§28.3	Abbreviations and Symbols		852
	§28.3.1	General Rules for Abbreviations	852
	§28.3.2	Miscellaneous Rules for Abbreviation	853
	§28.3.3	Inappropriate Abbreviations	855
	§28.3.4	General Rules for Symbols	856
§28.4	Italics		856
§28.5	Conventions of Formal Writing		858
	§28.5.1	Use of First-Person Pronouns	858
	§28.5.2	Use of Contractions	859
	§28.5.3	Numbers	859
	§28.5.4	Use of Questions and Exclamations	859

Chapter 29

Legal Writing for English-as-a-Second-Language Students 861

§29.1	Grammar Rules for Non-Native Speakers of English		862
	§29.1.1	Articles	862
		a. "A" and "An"	862
		b. "The"	867
		c. No Article	872
	§29.1.2	Verbs	874
		a. Verbs with Auxiliary, or Helping, Verbs	874
		b. Verb Tense in Conditional Sentences	878

		c.	Verb Tense in Speculative Sentences	878
		d.	Verbs + Gerunds, Infinitives, or Objects	880
		e.	Two- or Three-Word Verbs	886
	§29.1.3	Prepositions	887
		a.	Prepositions That Follow Verbs Commonly Used in Law	888
		b.	Prepositions That Follow Adjectives Commonly Used in Law	889
		c.	Prepositions That Follow Nouns Commonly Used in Law	890
		d.	Prepositions in Idioms	890
§29.2	Rhetorical Preferences in Writing	890
	§29.2.1	Cultural Assumptions about Readers and the Purposes for Writing	892
		a.	Assumptions and Expectations in the United States and in the United States Legal Culture	892
		b.	Assumptions and Expectations in Other Cultures	897
	§29.2.2	Culturally Determined Patterns in Writing	899
		a.	Preferences in the United States	899
		b.	Preferences in Other Cultures	900
	§29.2.3	Conciseness v. Repetition	901
		a.	Preferences in the United States	901
		b.	Preferences in Other Cultures	902

Glossary of Usage   **905**
Glossary of Terms   **915**

Index   *923*

Preface

Legal writing is both simple and complex. On the one hand, it is simply a matter of organizing information into well-established formats and following well-established patterns of analysis. It is being methodical about research and correct about citation, grammar, and punctuation when the document is written. That much is a big job, but a fairly simple job.

On the other hand, legal writing is complex. Part of the complexity is keeping all those simple tasks organized. Beyond that, however, legal writing is complex because it requires creativity, insight, and judgment.

Within the parameters of accepted formats and types of argumentation, for example, legal writers must create an organization where one did not previously exist and create arguments that, at least in some cases, have not been made before.

But that is not all. In addition, legal writers must have the insight and ability to cut to the heart of a matter. They must be able to see what is really at stake in a case; they must be able to look at the big picture and know where to focus their and their reader's attention.

And that is still not all. At all times, legal writers must exercise judgment: They must know what matters most and what matters least, what is effective, what is persuasive, what is extraneous, and what is just plain irrelevant.

This book, then, is about both the simple skills of legal writing and the complex art of legal writing. For the law student or the practicing lawyer, it brings together the three major components of legal writing—research, writing, and analysis—and discusses each from the most basic level to the more advanced, sophisticated levels.

Part I of the *Handbook* provides background information about the United States legal system and introduces legal analysis and argumentation. Part II uses a step-by-step approach to take the reader through the process of writing an objective office memorandum, an opinion letter, and a trial and an appellate brief. Throughout the process, it shows the integration of research, writing, and analysis.

Most important, all of this is done in context. That is, the points about research, analysis, and writing are presented within the structure of realistic cases. Further, each point is illustrated and reinforced by numerous examples from memoranda and briefs.

Parts III, IV, and V are all resource materials. Part III provides more in-depth information about research and citation; Parts IV and V provide more in-depth information about writing. Parts III, IV, and V also include references to *The Practice Book for the Legal Writing Handbook*.

In short, *The Legal Writing Handbook* is three books in one: It is a complete book about research, a complete book about analysis, and a complete book about writing. Thus, just about everything a law student needs to know about legal writing is here, in one book.

Laurel Currie Oates
Anne Enquist
Kelly Kunsch

January 1998

Acknowledgments

This book has truly been a collaborative effort. It is the result of the work of many colleagues and students, all of whom deserve recognition.

Mary Beth Harney was critical to the book's development in the early stages. She helped conceptualize the book and allowed us to use many examples of her own writing. Our friend and colleague, Marilyn Berger, introduced us to the people at Little, Brown (now Aspen Law and Business) and encouraged us to persevere. Former Dean Fred Tausend was also a significant supporter of this project in its early years. Thanks to him and our current dean, Jim Bond, we had the institutional support and their personal encouragement, both of which were necessary to complete this project.

We have been fortunate throughout this process to have had the critiques and counsel of numerous colleagues who have taught legal writing. A heartfelt thank you to Barbara Barker, Deborah Dowd, Mary Beth Harney, Margaret Morgan, Jill Ramsfield, Chris Rideout, Barry Shanks, Michael Charneski, Crystal Crawford, Bill Tuthill, John Nivala, Julie Monfils, Martha Schaeffer, Janet Dickson, Steve Bernheim, Nancy Bradburn-Johnson, Linda Dyckman, Irene Scharf, Tim Bakken, Jeff Ramsdell, David Walter, Marc Lampson, Nancy Soonpaa, Susan McClellan, Ed Raftis, Jennie Zavatsky, Bob Chang, Connie Krontz, Judi Maier, Henry Wigglesworth, Lori Bannai, Nancy Jones, and Jessie Grearson.

In addition, we have also benefited from the knowledge and advice of many other faculty members at the Seattle University of Law: Janet Ainsworth, David Boerner, Melinda Branscomb, Annette Clark, Sid De-Long, John Mitchell, Mark Reutlinger, John Strait, and John Weaver. One other faculty member who deserves a special note of appreciation is our friend Paula Lustbader.

Perhaps the most important collaborators in this project have been our students. Their writing appears throughout the book, and they were our first readers. So many made recommendations and allowed us to use their writing that we cannot mention them all, but we want them to know how much we appreciate their part in what we think of as "their book."

Some students made substantial contributions and deserve special recognition. Thank you to Susan McClellan, Annette Clark, Luanne Coachman, Mary Lobdell, Eileen Peterson, Lance Palmer, Edwina Martin-Arnold, Vonda Sargent, Melissa May, Kevin Dougherty, Cindy Burdue, Amy Blume, and Chris Fredrikson.

The new chapter on "Legal Writing for English-as-a-Second Language Law Students" would not have been possible without the help of several colleagues and students. Thanks to Donn R. Callaway for his guidance as we first began to explore this topic, to Dana Yaffee and Linda Chu for their excellent research, and to Jessie Grearson and Jeffrey Gore for their comments and suggestions on early drafts. Thanks too to our many ESL law students who inspired us with their dedication and hard work. We are particularly grateful to Stephanie Ko, Neli Espe, Nicolay Kvasnyuk, Masha Fartoutchnaia, Linda Chu, Meihuei Hu, and Julian Lin for allowing us to use their writing as examples and for reading early drafts of the chapter and suggesting changes.

Finally, and undoubtedly most important, is our secretary, Lori Lamb. Besides her hard work and patience, we want to acknowledge her special contribution to this book: She kept us sane.

The Legal Writing Handbook

Section I

A Course in Legal Analysis, Research, and Writing

Part I

A Foundation for Legal Writing

All knowledge builds on prior knowledge. The ability to understand concept B depends on prior knowledge of concept A; the ability to understand concept C depends on prior knowledge of both A and B.

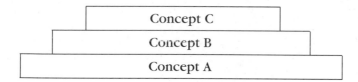

This is particularly true in legal writing. Before you[1] can do legal research, you must know what resources are available and the weight given to each; before you can write, you must possess not only basic writing skills but also an understanding of your audience, your purpose, and the conventional formats.

Underlying this knowledge, though, must be an understanding of the system in which you are operating. You must understand the United

---

1. Throughout this book, the authors have deliberately used a somewhat more informal writing style than that which is recommended for legal writing itself. Writing a textbook, like writing anything else, is governed by who the reader is, what the writing's purpose is, what the conventions are for that type of writing, and what relationship the writer wants to have with the reader. Thus, a slightly more informal style seemed appropriate for this textbook. Notice, for example, that the authors use both first and second person, some contractions, some colloquial phrases, and more dashes than they recommend for legal writing.

The primary danger in using a more informal style is that students may consciously or unconsciously emulate the authors' style in their legal writing. As a precaution against this possibility, the authors suggest that students read section 28.5 before beginning to write a legal memorandum or brief and, as always, consider the audience, purpose, and conventions of the type of writing they are doing.

States system of government and, within that larger system, the United States system of law. In addition, you must begin developing the ability to think like a lawyer. The three chapters in Part I lay the foundation for legal writing.

Chapter 3
An Introduction
to Legal Analysis

Chapter 2
An Introduction to Common
and Enacted Law

Chapter 1
An Overview of the United States
Legal System

An Overview of the United States Legal System

The United States system of government. For some, it is the secret to democracy, the power to elect one's leaders and the right to speak freely. For others, it is a horrendous bureaucracy, a maze through which one must struggle to obtain a benefit, to change a law, or to get a day in court. For still others, it is more abstract, a chart in a ninth-grade civics book describing the three branches of government and explaining the system of checks and balances.

For lawyers, the United States system of government is all of these things and more. It is the foundation for their knowledge of the law, the stage on which they play out their professional roles, the arena for the very serious game of law.

No matter which metaphor you prefer—foundation, stage, arena— the point is the same. To be successful as a law student and a lawyer, you must understand the system. You must know the framework before you can work well within it.

Like most complex systems, the United States system of government can be analyzed in a number of different ways. You can focus on its three branches—the executive branch, the legislative branch, and the judicial branch—or you can focus on its two parts, the federal government and the state governments.

In this chapter, we do both. We look first at the three branches, examining both their individual functions and their interrelationships. We then examine the relationship between state and federal government, again with an eye toward their individual functions and powers.

§1.1   THE THREE BRANCHES OF GOVERNMENT

Just as the medical student must understand both the various organs that make up the human body and their relationship to each other, the law student must understand both the three branches of government and the relationships among them.

§1.1.1   The Executive Branch

The first of the three branches is the executive branch. In the federal system, the executive power is vested in the President; in the states, it is vested in the governor. (See Article II, Section 1 of the United States Constitution and the constitutions of the various states.) In general, the executive branch has the power to implement and enforce laws. It oversees public projects, administers public benefit programs, and controls law enforcement agencies.

The executive branch also has powers that directly affect our system of law. For example, the President (or a governor) can control the law-making function of the legislative branch by exercising his or her power to convene and adjourn the Congress (or state legislature) or by vetoing legislation. Similarly, the President or a governor can shape the decisions of the courts through his or her judicial nominations or by directing the attorney general to enforce or not to enforce certain laws.

§1.1.2   The Legislative Branch

The second branch is the legislative branch. Congress's powers are enumerated in Article I, Section 8 of the United States Constitution, which gives Congress, among other things, the power to lay and collect taxes, borrow money, regulate commerce with foreign nations and among the states, establish uniform naturalization and bankruptcy laws, promote the progress of science and the useful arts by creating copyright laws, and punish counterfeiting. Powers not granted Congress are given to the states or left to the people. (See the Tenth Amendment to the United States Constitution.) The state constitutions enumerate the powers given to the state legislatures.

Like the executive branch, the legislative branch exercises power over the other two branches. It can check the actions of the executive by enacting or refusing to enact legislation requested by the executive, by controlling the budget and, at least at the federal level, by consenting or refusing to consent to nominations made by the executive.

The legislative branch's power over the judicial branch is less obvious. At one level, it can control the judiciary through its power to establish courts (Article I, Section 8 grants Congress the power to establish inferior federal courts) and its power to consent to or reject the executive branch's judicial nominations. However, the most obvious control it has over the judiciary is its power to enact legislation that supersedes a common law or court-made doctrine or rule.

The legislative branch also shares its lawmaking power with the executive branch. In enacting legislation, it sometimes gives the executive branch the power to promulgate the regulations needed to implement or enforce the legislation. For example, although Congress (the legislative branch) enacted the Internal Revenue Code, the Internal Revenue Service (part of the executive branch) promulgates the regulations needed to implement that code.

§1.1.3   The Judicial Branch

The third branch is the judicial branch. Article III, Section 1, of the United States Constitution vests the judicial power of the United States in one supreme court and in such inferior courts as Congress may establish. The state constitutions establish and grant power to the state courts.

a.   The Hierarchical Nature of the Court System

Both the federal and the state court systems are hierarchical. At the lowest level are the trial courts, whose primary function is fact-finding. The judge or jury hears the evidence and enters a judgment.

At the next level are the intermediate courts of appeals. These courts hear the majority of appeals, deciding (1) whether the trial court applied the right law and (2) whether there is sufficient evidence to support the jury's verdict or the trial judge's findings of fact and conclusions of law. Unlike the trial courts, these courts do not conduct trials. There are no witnesses, and the only exhibits are the exhibits that were admitted during trial. The decisions of the appellate courts are based solely on the written record and the attorneys' arguments.

At the top level are the states' highest court and the Supreme Court of the United States. The primary function of these courts is to make law. They hear only those cases that involve issues of great public import or cases in which different divisions or circuits have adopted or applied conflicting rules of law. Like the intermediate courts of appeals, these courts do not hear evidence; they only review the trial court record. See Exhibit 1.1.

An example illustrates the role each court plays. In *State v. Strong* (see Chapter 8), the defendant was charged with possession of a controlled substance. At the trial court level, both the state and the defendant presented witnesses and physical evidence. On the basis of this evidence, the trial court decided the case on its merits, the trial judge deciding the questions of law (whether the evidence should be suppressed), and the jury deciding the questions of fact (whether the state had proved all of the elements of the crime beyond a reasonable doubt).

Both issues were decided against the defendant: The trial court

---

| EXHIBIT 1.1 | The Roles of the Trial, Intermediate, and Supreme Courts |

Trial Court

- The trial court hears witnesses and views evidence.
- The trial court judge decides questions of law; the jury decides questions of fact. (When there is no jury, the trial court judge decides both the questions of law and the questions of fact.)

Intermediate Court of Appeals

- The intermediate court of appeals reviews the written record and exhibits from the trial court.
- When an issue raises a question of law, the intermediate court of appeals may substitute its judgment for the judgment of the trial court judge; when an issue raises a question of fact, the appellate court must defer to the decision of the finder of fact (the jury or, if there was no jury, the trial judge).

Supreme, or Highest, Court

- Like the intermediate court of appeals, it reviews the written record and exhibits from the trial court.
- Like the intermediate court of appeals, it has broad powers to review questions of law: It determines whether the trial court and intermediate court of appeals applied the right law correctly. Its power to review factual issues is, however, very limited. Like the intermediate court of appeals, it can determine only whether there is sufficient evidence to support the decision of the jury or, if there was no jury, the decision of the trial court judge.

judge ruled that the evidence was admissible, and the jury found that the state had met its burden of proof. Disagreeing with both determinations, the defendant filed an appeal with the intermediate court of appeals.

In deciding this appeal, the appellate court could consider only two issues: whether the trial court judge erred when he denied the defendant's motion to suppress and whether there was sufficient evidence to support the jury's verdict.

Because the first issue raised a question of law, the appellate court could review the issue *de novo.* It did not need to defer to the judgment of the trial court judge; instead, it could exercise its own independent judgment to decide the issue on its merits.

The appellate court had much less latitude with respect to the second issue. Because the second issue raised a question of fact and not law, the appellate court could not substitute its judgment for that of the jury.

It could only review the jury's findings to make sure that they were supported by the evidence. When the question is one of fact, the appellate court can decide only (1) whether there is sufficient evidence to support the jury's verdict or (2) whether the jury's verdict is clearly erroneous — not whether it would have reached the same conclusion.

Regardless of the type of issue (law or fact), the appellate court must base its decision on the written trial court record and exhibits and the attorneys' arguments. Consequently, in *Strong,* the intermediate court of appeals did not see or hear any of the witnesses. The only people present at the appeal were the judges and the attorneys. Not even the defendant, Strong, was present.

If Strong lost his first appeal, he could petition the state supreme court (through a writ of certiorari), asking it to hear his case. If the state supreme court granted the petition, its review, like that of the intermediate court of appeals, would be limited. Although the supreme court would review the issue of law *de novo,* it would have to defer to the jury's decision on the questions of fact.

Most of the cases that you will read in law school are appellate court decisions, decisions of the state or federal intermediate court of appeals or Supreme Court. These cases, however, represent only a small, and perhaps not representative, percentage of the disputes that lawyers see during the course of the year. See Exhibit 1.2.

Thus, as you read the cases in your casebooks, remember that you are seeing only the proverbial tip of the iceberg. For a case to reach the Supreme Court, the parties must have had the financial means to pursue it, and the Court must have found that the issue raised was significant enough to grant review.

b.   The Federal Courts

In the federal system, most cases are heard initially in the federal district courts, the primary trial court in that system. These courts have original jurisdiction over most federal questions and have the power to review the decisions of some administrative agencies. Each state has at least one district court, and many have several. For example, Indiana has the District Court for Northern Indiana and the District Court for Southern Indiana. Cases that are not heard in the district court are usually heard in one of several specialized courts: the United States Tax Court, the United States Court of Federal Claims, or the United States Court of International Trade.

The intermediate court of appeals is the United States Court of Appeals. There are currently thirteen circuits: eleven numbered circuits, the District of Columbia Circuit, and the Federal Circuit. See Exhibit 1.3. The Federal Circuit, which was created in 1982, reviews the decisions of the United States Court of Federal Claims and the United States Court of International Trade, as well as some administrative decisions.

The highest federal court is the United States Supreme Court. Al-

---

| EXHIBIT 1.2 | **Number of Cases That Move Through the Court System** |

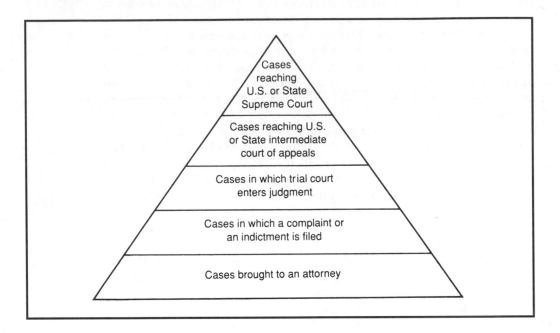

though many people believe that the Supreme Court is all-powerful, in fact it is not. As with other courts, there are limits on the Supreme Court's powers. It can play only one of two roles.

In its first role, the Supreme Court plays a role similar to that of the state supreme courts. In the federal system, it is the highest court, the court of last resort. In contrast, in its second role, it is the final arbiter of federal constitutional law, interpreting the United States Constitution and determining whether the federal government or a state has violated rights granted under the United States Constitution.

Thus, although people often assert that they will take their case all the way to the Supreme Court, they may not be able to. The Supreme Court can hear the case only if it involves a question of federal constitutional law or a federal statute. The Supreme Court does not have the power to hear cases involving only questions of state law. For example, although the United States Supreme Court has the power to determine whether a state's marriage dissolution statutes are constitutional, it does not have the power to hear purely factual questions, such as whether it would be in the best interests of a child for custody to be granted to the father or whether child support should be set at $300.00 rather than $400.00 per month.

Each year the United States Supreme Court receives more than 7,000 requests for review (writs of certiorari). Of the approximately 100 cases

EXHIBIT 1.3	The Thirteen Federal Judicial Circuits*

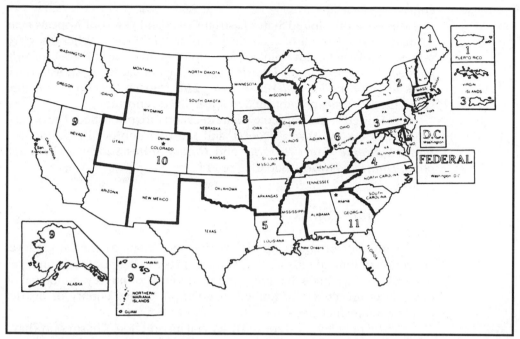

*Reprinted from *Federal Reporter* (West's National Reporter System) with permission of West Publishing Company.

EXHIBIT 1.4	The Federal Court System

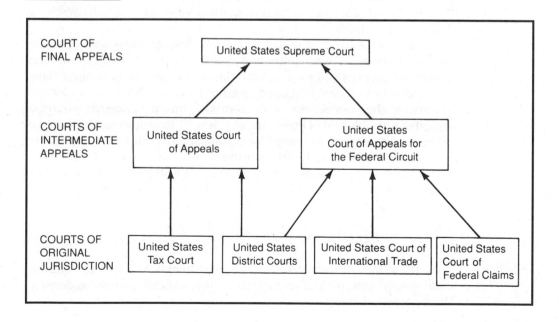

that it actually hears, the overwhelming majority are appeals from the federal courts.

Exhibit 1.4 illustrates the relationships among the various federal courts.

Because the United States District Court and Court of Appeals hear so many cases, not all of their decisions are published. When they are published, district court opinions are published in either the *Federal Supplement* or *Federal Rules Decisions,* and current Court of Appeals decisions are published in *Federal Reporter, Third Series.* (Decisions from the specialized courts are published in specialized reporters.)

All United States Supreme Court decisions are published. The official reporter is *United States Reports,* and the two unofficial reporters are West's *Supreme Court Reporter* and *United States Supreme Court Reports, Lawyer's Edition.* See Chapter 14.

c.   State Courts

A number of courts operate within the states. At the lowest level are courts of limited jurisdiction. These courts can hear only certain types of cases or cases involving only limited amounts of money. Municipal or city courts are courts of limited jurisdiction, as are county or district courts and small claims courts.

At the next level are courts of general jurisdiction. These courts have the power to review the decisions of courts of limited jurisdiction and original jurisdiction over claims arising under state law, whether it be under the state constitution, state statutes, or state common law.

About three-quarters of the states now have an intermediate court of appeals. These courts hear appeals as of right from the state courts of general jurisdiction, and the bulk of their caseload is criminal appeals. Because of the size of their workload, many of these courts have several divisions or districts.

Every state has a state supreme court. These courts review the decisions of the state trial courts and courts of appeals and are the final arbiters of questions of state constitutional, statutory, and common law.

Decisions of state trial courts are not usually published. In addition, because of the volume, not all decisions of intermediate state courts of appeals are published. Those that are, and all decisions of the state supreme court, appear in one of West Publishing Company's regional reporters and the state's official reporter, if one exists. See Chapter 14.

Exhibit 1.5 illustrates the typical relationship among the various state courts.

d.   Other Courts

There are also several other court systems. As sovereign entities, many Native American tribes have their own judicial systems, as does the United States military.

EXHIBIT 1.5	The State Court System

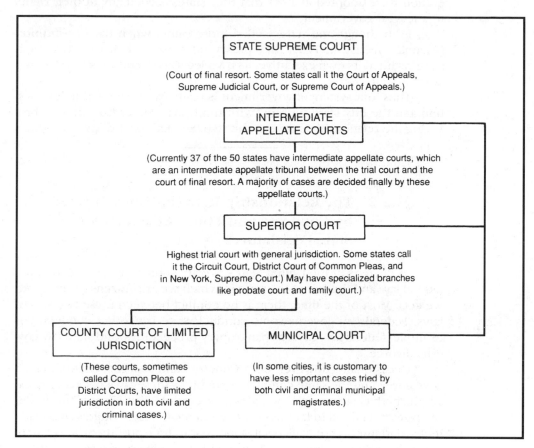

STATE SUPREME COURT

(Court of final resort. Some states call it the Court of Appeals,
Supreme Judicial Court, or Supreme Court of Appeals.)

INTERMEDIATE
APPELLATE COURTS

(Currently 37 of the 50 states have intermediate appellate courts, which
are an intermediate appellate tribunal between the trial court and the
court of final resort. A majority of cases are decided finally by these
appellate courts.)

SUPERIOR COURT

Highest trial court with general jurisdiction. Some states call
it the Circuit Court, District Court of Common Pleas, and
in New York, Supreme Court.) May have specialized branches
like probate court and family court.)

COUNTY COURT OF LIMITED
JURISDICTION

(These courts, sometimes
called Common Pleas or
District Courts, have limited
jurisdiction in both civil and
criminal cases.)

MUNICIPAL COURT

(In some cities, it is customary to
have less important cases tried by
both civil and criminal municipal
magistrates.)

§1.2   THE RELATIONSHIP BETWEEN THE FEDERAL AND STATE GOVERNMENTS

It is not enough, however, to look at our system of government from only the perspective of its three branches. To understand the system, you must also understand the relationship between the federal and state governments.

§1.2.1   A Short History

Like most things, our system of government is the product of our history. From the early 1600s until 1781, the "United States" were not united. Instead, the "country" was composed of independent colonies, all operating under different charters and each having its own laws and legal system. Although the colonies traded with each other, the relationship among the colonies was no closer than the relationship among the European countries prior to 1992. It was not until the Articles of Confederation were adopted in 1781 that the "states" ceded any of their rights to a federal government.

Even though the states ceded more rights when the Constitution became effective in 1789, they preserved most of their own law. Each state retained its own executive, its own legislature and laws, and its own court system.

Thus, our system of government is really two systems, a federal system and the fifty state systems, with the United States Constitution brokering the relationship between the two. See Exhibit 1.6.

---

§1.2.2   The Relationship Between Laws Enacted by Congress and Those Enacted by the State Legislatures

As citizens of the United States, we are subject to two sets of laws: federal law and the law of the state in which we are citizens (or in which we act). Most of the time, there is no conflict between these two sets of laws: Federal law governs some conduct; state law, other conduct. For example, federal law governs bankruptcy proceedings, and state law governs divorce.

Occasionally, however, both Congress and a state legislature enact laws governing the same conduct. Sometimes these laws coexist. For example, both Congress and the states have enacted drug laws. Acting under the powers granted to it under the Commerce Clause, Congress has made it illegal to import controlled substances or to transport them across state lines; the states, acting consistently with the powers reserved to them, have made the possession or sale of controlled substances within the state illegal. In such instances, citizens are subject to both laws. A defendant can be charged under federal law with transporting a drug across state lines and under state law with possession.

There are times, however, when federal and state law do not complement each other and cannot coexist. An act can be legal under federal law but illegal under state law. In such instances, federal law supersedes state law, provided that the federal law is constitutional. As provided in the Supremacy Clause (Article VI, Clause 2), laws enacted by Congress under the powers granted to it under the Constitution are the "supreme Law of the Land; and the Judges in every State shall be bound thereby. . . ."

The answer is different when the conflicting laws are from different states. Although there are more and more uniform laws (the Uniform Child Custody Act, the Uniform Commercial Code), an activity that is legal in one state may be illegal in another state. For instance, although prostitution is legal in Nevada as a local option, it is illegal in other states.

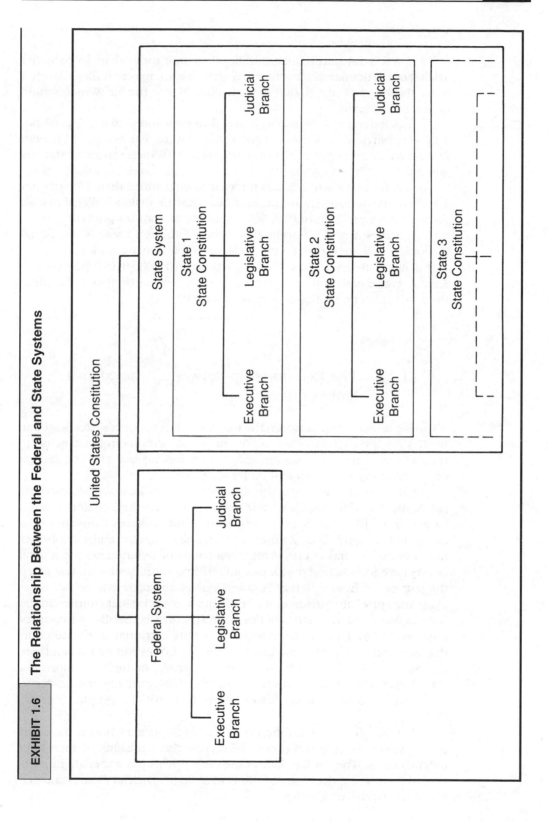

EXHIBIT 1.6   **The Relationship Between the Federal and State Systems**

Questions

1. A federal statute makes it illegal to emit more than 15 parts per 10,000 of particulate X into the air. A state statute makes it illegal to emit more than 5 parts per 10,000 of particulate Y into the air. Which statute or statutes govern?

2. A federal statute makes it illegal to emit more than 15 parts per 10,000 of particulate X into the air. A state statute makes it illegal to emit more than 25 parts per 10,000 of particulate X. Which statute or statutes govern?

3. A federal statute makes it illegal to emit more than 15 parts per 10,000 of particulate X into the air. A state statute makes it illegal to emit more than 5 parts per 10,000. Which statute or statutes govern?

4. States A and B border each other. Although there is no federal law or law in State B making the emission of particulate X illegal, in State A it is illegal to emit more than 5 parts per 10,000. If the factory is in State A, is the emission of 10 parts per 10,000 of particulate X illegal? Is the result the same if the factory is in State B?

---

§1.2.3   The Relationship Between Federal and State Courts

The relationship between the federal and state court systems is complex. Although each system is autonomous, in certain circumstances the state courts can hear cases brought under federal law and the federal courts can hear cases brought under state law.

For example, although the majority of cases heard in state courts are brought under state law, state courts also have jurisdiction when a case is brought under a provision of the United States Constitution, a treaty, and certain federal statutes. Similarly, although the majority of cases heard in the federal courts involve questions of federal law, the federal courts have jurisdiction over cases involving questions of state law when the parties are from different states (diversity jurisdiction).

The appellate jurisdiction of the courts is somewhat simpler. In the state system, a state's supreme, or highest, court is usually the court of last resort. The United States Supreme Court can review a state court decision only when the case involves a federal question and when there has been a final decision by the state's supreme, or highest, court. If a state has an intermediate court of appeals, that court has the power to review the decisions of the lower courts within its geographic jurisdiction.

In the federal system, the United States Supreme Court is the court of last resort, having the power to review the decisions of the lower federal courts. The United States Court of Appeals has appellate jurisdiction to review the decisions of the United States District Courts and certain administrative agencies.

Questions

1. Which courts have subject matter jurisdiction over cases arising under the Social Security Act (a federal statute)? The federal courts? The state courts?

2. Which courts have subject matter jurisdiction in a child custody case brought under your state's Marriage and Divorce Act? The federal courts? Your state's courts?

3. Defendant Smith believes that the sentence imposed by your state's trial court violates the Eighth Amendment's prohibition against cruel and unusual punishment. Which courts have subject matter jurisdiction? Your state's appellate courts? The United States Supreme Court?

4. State A has enacted a statute making all abortions illegal. Which courts have the power to determine whether the statute is constitutional? State A's courts? The United States Supreme Court?

---

§1.2.4 The Relationship Among Federal, State, and Local Prosecutors

The power to prosecute cases arising under the United States Constitution and federal statutes is vested in the Department of Justice, which is headed by the Attorney General of the United States, a presidential appointee. Assisting the United States Attorney General are the United States Attorneys for each federal judicial district. The individual United States Attorneys' offices have two divisions: a civil division and a criminal division. The civil division handles civil cases arising under federal law, and the criminal division handles cases involving alleged violations of federal criminal statutes.

At the state level, the system is slightly different. In most states, the attorney for the state is the state attorney general, usually an elected official. Working for the state attorney general are a number of assistant attorney generals. However, unlike the United States attorneys, most state attorney generals do not handle criminal cases. Their clients are the various state agencies. For example, an assistant attorney general may be assigned to the department of social and health services, the department of licensing, the consumer protection bureau, or the department of worker's compensation, providing advice to the agency and representing the agency in civil litigation.

Criminal prosecutions are handled by county and city prosecutors. Each county has its own prosecutor's office, which has both a civil and a criminal division. Attorneys working for the civil division play much the same role as state assistant attorney generals. They represent the county and its agencies, providing both advice and representation. In contrast, the attorneys assigned to the criminal division are responsible for prosecutions under the state's criminal code. The county prosecutor's office decides whom to charge and then tries the cases.

EXHIBIT 1.7   **Federal, State, and Local Prosecutors**

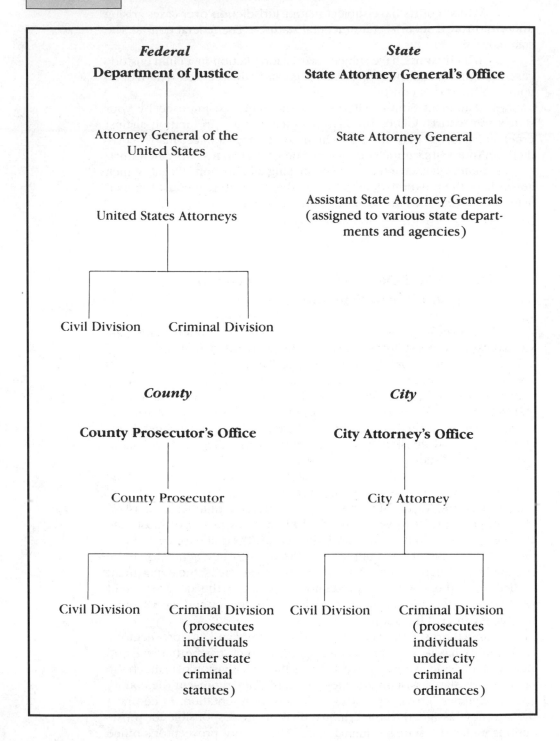

Federal
Department of Justice

Attorney General of the
United States

United States Attorneys

Civil Division   Criminal Division

State
State Attorney General's Office

State Attorney General

Assistant State Attorney Generals
(assigned to various state departments and agencies)

County
County Prosecutor's Office

County Prosecutor

Civil Division   Criminal Division
(prosecutes
individuals
under state
criminal
statutes)

City
City Attorney's Office

City Attorney

Civil Division   Criminal Division
(prosecutes
individuals
under city
criminal
ordinances)

Like the counties, cities have their own city attorney's office which, at least in large cities, has civil and criminal divisions. Attorneys working in the civil division advise city departments and agencies and represent the city in civil litigation; attorneys in the criminal division prosecute criminal cases brought under city ordinances. State, county, and city prosecutors do not represent federal departments or agencies, nor do they handle cases brought under federal law. See Exhibit 1.7.

§1.3   A FINAL COMMENT

Although there are numerous other ways of analyzing the United States system of government, these two perspectives—the three branches perspective and the federal-state perspective—are the foundation on which the rest of your study of law will be built. Without such a foundation, without a thorough understanding of the interrelationships among the parts of the system, many of the concepts that you will encounter in law school would be difficult to learn.

This is particularly true of legal writing. Without understanding both the role each branch plays and the relationship between state and federal government, you cannot be an effective researcher or an effective legal analyst. You must understand the United States system of government so that you can determine which sources to look at in the library. In addition, you must understand the United States system of government before you can tackle the topic of the next chapter, determining whether a particular case or statute is mandatory or persuasive authority.

Chapter 2

An Introduction to Common and Enacted Law

As you saw in Chapter 1, our system of government is complex. To some extent, each of the three branches has the power to create law. The legislative branch enacts statutes, the executive branch promulgates regulations, and the judicial branch both interprets the statutes and regulations and, in the absence of enacted law, creates its own common law rules.

In this chapter we explore further the relationship between the three branches and the law that they create.

§2.1 COMMON LAW

Historically, most of our law was common law, or law created by the courts. Rights to property (Property), the rights of parties to enter into and enforce contracts (Contracts), and the right of an individual to recover from another for civil wrongs (Torts) were all governed by common law doctrines developed originally in England and adopted in this country by the states.

This common law relies on a system of precedent. Each case is decided not in isolation, but in light of the cases that have preceded it. In other words, instead of creating new rules for each case, the courts apply the rules announced and developed in earlier cases. The system works as follows.

Assume for the moment a blank slate. You are in a state with no statutes and no common law rules.

In the first case to come before your state's courts, Case A, a mother asks the court to grant her custody of her two children, a 2-year-old son and a 4-year-old daughter. There are no statutes or earlier cases to which the court can look for guidance. The court must make its own law. Looking at the facts of the case before it, the court must decide whether the mother should be awarded custody.

Assume that the court grants the mother's request for custody because, given the ages of the children, the court believes that it is in the children's best interest to remain with their mother. The Tender Years Doctrine is born.

Not long after, another mother requests custody of her children, a 4-year-old son and a 14-year-old daughter.

Unlike Case A, in Case B the slate is not blank. In deciding Case B, the court will be guided by the court's decision in Case A. The reasoning in Case A (that given the ages of the children it is in the children's best interest to remain with their mother) now becomes the "rule" in Case B.

Applying this rule, the court grants the mother custody of her 4-year-old son: Given his age, it is appropriate that he remain with his mother. It also grants the mother custody of her 14-year-old daughter, relying on the daughter's gender. It is most appropriate, the court reasons, that a teenage daughter remain with her mother.

In deciding the next case, Case C, the court applies the rule announced in Case A (that it is in the best interest of young children to remain with their mother) and in Case B (that it is appropriate that teenage daughters remain with their mother), granting a mother custody of 5- and 10-year-old daughters even though the mother has a history of abusing alcohol. Because the mother is not currently drinking, the court holds that it is in the girls' best interest to remain with their mother.

Thus, each case builds on past cases, the reasoning in one case becoming the rule in the next.

Case A

The court's reasoning:	It is in the best interest of young children to remain with their mother.

Case B

Rule that the court applies:	It is in the best interest of young children to remain with their mother (cites Case A).
Additional reasoning:	It is in the best interest of teenage daughters to remain with their mother.

Case C

Rules that the court applies:	(1) It is in the best interest of young children to remain with their mother (cites Cases A and B).
	(2) It is in the best interest of teenage daughters to remain with their mother (cites Case B).

Additional reasoning: It is appropriate to grant custody to
                               mother despite her history of alcohol
                               abuse because mother is not currently
                               drinking.

Of course, not all of the rules announced in earlier cases are applied
in subsequent cases. (If Case D involves the custody of a 1-year-old girl
whose mother does not have a history of alcohol abuse, the court would
apply only the rule announced in Case A; it would not need to consider
the additional rules set out in Cases B and C.) Nor does each case add to
the existing law. (The court could decide Case D without giving additional
reasons to support its conclusion.)

In addition, in certain circumstances, the courts are not bound by
rules from earlier cases. Because the law is court-made, a higher court
can overrule the rules set out either in its own decisions or in the decisions of lower courts within its jurisdiction, substituting a new rule for
the common law rule announced and applied in the earlier cases.

§2.2   ENACTED LAW

Although historically most of our law was common law, today much of it
is enacted law. Acting under the authority granted to them, the legislative
and executive branches have enacted and promulgated numerous statutes
and regulations, some of which have superseded the common law. For
example, state statutes have replaced common law rules governing the
relationship between landlords and tenants, and the Uniform Commercial
Code has replaced the common law rules governing commercial contracts.

Enacted law, however, seldom stands on its own. In the process of
interpreting and applying statutes, the courts often announce new rules.
Although these rules are not common law rules, they are rules nonetheless, and unless the legislature enacts legislation changing the rule, they
will be followed by the courts in subsequent cases.

The relationship between common law, statutes, and cases interpreting and applying statutes becomes clearer if we look once again at
the example begun in the preceding section.

This time presume that not long after the court decided Case D the
state legislature enacted a statute rejecting the Tender Years Doctrine.
Instead of giving preference to mothers, the statute now requires that the
courts grant custody "in accordance with the best interest of the children." No longer is the mother to be given preference; instead, in determining custody, the court is to consider a number of factors including
the parents' wishes; the children's wishes; the interaction and interrelationship of the child with parents and siblings; the child's adjustment to
his or her home, school, and community; and the mental and physical
health of all of the individuals involved.

EXHIBIT 2.1	The Types of Law

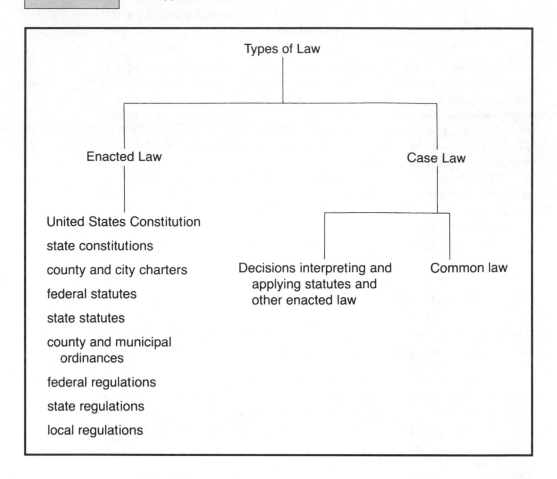

This statute supersedes the common law doctrine set out in Cases A, B, C, and D. To the extent that these cases are inconsistent with the statute, they are no longer good law. Thus, when Case E comes before the court, the court applies the statute and not the common law doctrine.

The application of a statute is not, however, always clear. For example, in Case E the mother contends that she should be given custody not because the children are young but because she has always been their primary caretaker. Although the statute does not specifically address this argument, the court agrees with the mother, holding that because the mother has always been the primary caretaker, it would be in the children's best interest to remain with her.

Because this "rule" (that the court can consider which parent has been the primary caretaker) is not inconsistent with the statute, it can be used by the courts in subsequent cases. In deciding Case F, the court will apply not just the statute but also the rule announced in Case E. Similarly, in deciding Case G the court will consider not only the statute but the rule in Case E and any rules announced in Case F. Just as the courts look to precedent in deciding a case involving a common law rule, they also look to precedent in deciding a case brought under a statute.

Thus, in our legal system, there are two types of law: enacted law and case law. Enacted law, when broadly defined, includes any law that has been adopted, enacted, or promulgated by either the people or a legislative body. The United States Constitution, the constitutions of each of the states, federal statutes, state statutes, city and county ordinances, and regulations promulgated by federal, state, and local agencies are all considered enacted law. In contrast, case law is law that has not been promulgated by the people or by a legislative body. It is law that has been created and announced by the courts in written opinions. See Exhibit 2.1.

The trick is in knowing which law to apply.

Note: Although the terms "case law" and "common law" are sometimes used interchangeably, they are not synonyms. The term "common law" refers to law created by the courts in the absence of enacted law. For example, most of tort law and much of property law are based not on statutes, but on common law doctrines created by the courts. In contrast, the term "case law" is broader. It refers to the written decisions of the courts and encompasses not only decisions announcing and applying common law, but also decisions interpreting and applying enacted law.

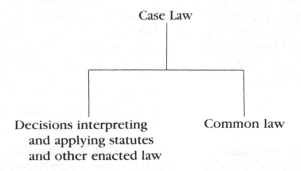

Case Law

Decisions interpreting
and applying statutes
and other enacted law

Common law

§2.3   MANDATORY VERSUS PERSUASIVE AUTHORITY

Not all enacted and common law is given equal weight. In deciding which law to apply, courts distinguish between mandatory and persuasive authority.

Mandatory authority is law that is binding on the court deciding the case. The court must apply that law. In contrast, persuasive authority is law that is not binding. Although the court may look to that law for guidance, it need not apply it.

Determining whether a particular statute or case is mandatory or persuasive authority is a two-step process. You must first determine which jurisdiction's law applies (that is, whether federal or state law applies and, if state law applies, which state's law); you must then determine which of that jurisdiction's statutes and cases are binding on the court that will be deciding the case.

§2.3.1   Which Jurisdiction's Law Applies?

Sometimes determining which jurisdiction's law applies is easy. For example, common knowledge (and common sense) tells you that federal law probably governs whether a federal PLUS loan constitutes income for federal income tax purposes. Similarly, you would probably guess that a will executed in California by a California resident would be governed by

---

EXHIBIT 2.2 | **Ranking of Authorities**

United States Constitution

State Constitution
Cannot take away rights granted by
the U.S. Constitution

Federal Statutes
Cannot take away rights granted by
U.S. Constitution; in addition, Congress can only enact laws that are
consistent with the grant of power
given to Congress under the Constitution.

State Statutes
Cannot take away rights granted by
the state constitution; in addition, a
state legislature can only enact
laws that are consistent with the
power retained by the states under
the U.S. Constitution and power
granted to that particular state legislature by that state's constitution.

United States Supreme Court
Bound by the United States Constitution and United States Code insofar as the code is constitutional.
Not bound by its own prior decisions, decisions of state courts, or
decisions of lower courts.

State Supreme Court
Bound by the United States and the
state's constitution, decisions of
the U.S. Supreme Court interpreting the U.S. Constitution or relating
to a dispute involving that state,
and state statutes insofar as those
statutes are constitutional. Not
bound by its own prior decisions,
decisions of federal courts not
related to federal constitutional
questions or involving the state,
the decisions of other states, or
decisions of lower courts within the
same state.

(continued on next page)

EXHIBIT 2.2   *(continued)*

United States Court of Appeals
(13 circuits)
Bound by U.S. Constitution, United States Code, and United States Supreme Court decisions. Not bound by decisions issued by the United States District Court, nor is any given circuit bound by its own prior decisions or the decisions of another circuit.

United States District Courts
(These are the trial courts in the federal system.) Each court is bound by the U.S. Constitution, the United States Code and decisions of the United States Supreme Court, and the Court of Appeals for the circuit in which the district court if located. The opinions of the district court may or may not be published, and, although they have some persuasive authority, no court is bound by them.

State Court of Appeals
Bound by the U.S. and state constitution, decisions of the State Supreme Court and the U.S. Supreme Court relating to federal constitutional questions. Not bound by its own prior decisions, decisions by the courts of any other state, or by the decisions of any lower court within the same state.

State Trial Courts
Courts bound by the U.S. and state constitutions, state statutes, decisions of the United States Supreme Court relating to federal constitutional issues, and decisions of the state supreme court and state court of appeals for the geographic area in which the trial court is located. In most states decisions of the trial courts are not published. Whether or not such decisions are published, no court is bound by them.

California state law. At other times, though, the determination is much more difficult. You probably would not know what jurisdiction's law governs a real estate contract between a resident of New York and a resident of Pennsylvania for a piece of property located in Florida.

Although the rules governing the determination of which jurisdiction's law applies are beyond the scope of this book (they are studied in Civil Procedure, Federal Courts, and Conflicts), keep two things in mind.

First, remember that in our legal system, federal law almost always preempts state law. Consequently, if there is both a federal and a state statute on the same topic, the federal statute will preempt the state statute to the extent that the two are inconsistent. For example, if a federal statute makes it illegal to discriminate in the renting of an apartment on the basis of familial status but under a state statute such discrimination is lawful, the federal statute governs—it is illegal to discriminate on the basis of familial status. There are a few instances, however, when a state constitutional provision or a state statute will govern: If the state constitution gives a criminal defendant more rights than does the federal constitution, the state constitution applies. States can grant an individual more protection. They cannot, however, take away or restrict rights granted by the federal constitution or a federal statute.

Second, although legal scholars still debate whether there is a federal common law, in the federal system there is not the same body of common law as there is in the states. Unlike the state systems, in the federal system, there are no common law rules governing adverse possession or intentional torts such as assault and battery, false imprisonment, or the intentional infliction of emotional distress. Thus, if the cause of action is based on a common law doctrine, the case is probably governed by state and not federal law.

§2.3.2   What "Law" Will Be Binding on the Court?

Within each jurisdiction, the authorities are ranked. The United States Constitution is the highest authority, binding both state and federal courts. Under the Constitution is other state and federal law.

In the federal system, the highest authority is the Constitution. Under the Constitution are the federal statutes and regulations, and under the federal statutes and regulations are the cases interpreting and applying them.

In the state system, the ranking is similar. The highest authority is the state constitution, followed by (1) state statutes and regulations and the cases interpreting and applying those statutes and regulations and (2) the state's common law.

In addition, the cases themselves are ranked. In both the federal and state systems, decisions of the supreme court carry the most weight: When deciding a case involving the same law and similar facts, both the court of appeals and the trial courts are bound by the decisions of the supreme, or highest, court. Decisions of intermediate courts of appeals come next; the trial courts under the jurisdiction of the intermediate court of appeals are bound by the court of appeals' decisions. At the bottom are the trial courts. Trial court decisions are binding only on the parties involved in the particular case.

Statutes and cases are also ranked by date. More recent statutes supersede earlier versions, and more recent common law rules supersede early rules by the same level court. Courts are bound by the highest court's most recent decision. For example, if there is a 1967 state intermediate court of appeals decision that makes an activity legal and a 1986 supreme court decision that makes it illegal, in the absence of a statute, the 1986 supreme court decision governs. The 1986 decision would be mandatory authority, and all of the courts within that jurisdiction would be bound by that decision.

Questions

1. In 1930, in Case A, the supreme court of your state set out a common law rule. In 1956, in Case B, the supreme court of your state

changed that rule. In your state, which case would be binding on a trial court: Case A or Case B?

Case A	State Supreme Court	1930
Case B	State Supreme Court	1956

2. Same facts as in #1 except that in 1971, in Case C, your state supreme court modified the test set out in Case B, adding a requirement. In your state, what test would a trial court use: the test set out in Case A, the test set out in Case B, or the test set out in Case C?

Case A	State Supreme Court	1930
Case B	State Supreme Court	1956
Case C	State Supreme Court	1971

3. Same facts as in #2 except that in 1976 your state legislature enacted a statute that completely changed the common law rule. What is now mandatory authority: the statute or the case(s)?

Case A	State Supreme Court	1930
Case B	State Supreme Court	1956
Case C	State Court of Appeals	1971
State Statute		1976

4. Same facts as in #3 except that in 1980, in Case D, a case involving the application of the 1976 statute, the court of appeals gives one of the words in the statute a broad interpretation. (The word was not defined in the statute itself.) In applying the statute, which courts are bound by the court of appeals' decision in Case D: A trial court within the court of appeals' geographic jurisdiction? A trial court outside the court of appeals' geographic jurisdiction? The division of the court of appeals that decided Case D? A division of the court of appeals other than the division that decided Case D? The state supreme court?

State Statute		1976
Case D	State Court of Appeals	1980

5. In 1985, in Case E, a different division of the court of appeals applies the 1976 statute. In reaching its decision, the court declines to follow the decision in Case D: Instead of interpreting the word broadly, the court interprets it narrowly. The losing party disagrees with this decision and files an appeal with the state supreme court. In deciding this appeal, is the state supreme court bound by the decision in Case D? The court of appeals' decision in Case E?

Case D	State Court of Appeals	1980
Case E	State Court of Appeals	1985

6. Same facts as in #5 except that in 1989 the state legislature amends the statute, explicitly defining the word that was the subject of debate in Cases D and E. The legislature elects to give the word a very narrow meaning. In Case F, brought before a state trial court in 1990, what would be controlling: the 1976 version of the statute? the 1989 version of the statute? Case D? the court of appeals' decision in Case E? the supreme court's decision in Case E? (In Case E the Court of Appeals defined the word narrowly; the supreme court defined it broadly.)

State Statute		1976
Case D	State Court of Appeals	1980
Case E	State Court of Appeals	1985
Case E	State Supreme Court	1986
Amended version of statute		1989

Chapter 3

An Introduction to Legal Analysis

"Think like a lawyer." By now, you have heard this phrase numerous times. During law school orientation, it was a mantra: "In law school, you will learn to think like a lawyer"; "Our job is to teach you how to think like a lawyer"; "Law school will change you. When you leave, you will think like a lawyer."

But what does it mean to think like a lawyer? Do lawyers think differently than accountants, doctors, and stockbrokers do? The answer is yes and no. Although each group must be able to think critically, it is only the lawyers who think dialectically. Accountants, doctors, and lawyers collect and use information; lawyers collect, use, and argue.

This chapter introduces you to the dialectical mode of thinking. In it, you will see in the context of a sample case how lawyers argue both the law and the application of that law to a particular set of facts.

§3.1 MEETING THE CLIENTS

Law is about people. Consequently, we begin this chapter with the parties to this dispute: Mr. and Mrs. Greenbaum.

Mr. Greenbaum

Four weeks ago, Mr. Greenbaum left his wife of twelve years and moved into an apartment. Today he is in the office of his attorney, Julia Michael, talking about divorce.

Mr. Greenbaum begins the interview by telling Ms. Michael that he has decided to file for divorce. On hearing this, Ms. Michael encourages Mr. Greenbaum to talk. She asks Mr. Greenbaum how long he and Mrs. Greenbaum have been separated, whether Mr. Greenbaum is interested in talking to Mrs. Greenbaum about reconciliation, whether Mr. Greenbaum is interested in meeting with a counselor, and whether Mr. Greenbaum has talked to Mrs. Greenbaum about the custody of the children or the division of property.

In doing this, Ms. Michael has two goals. First, she wants to make sure that Mr. Greenbaum actually wants to file for divorce. Many people go to an attorney not because they want a divorce but because they want someone to talk to or because they want to put pressure on their spouse. Second, she wants to begin identifying the issues. Is there a dispute over the custody of the children? Over the division of the property? Over child or spousal support?

In this case, Mr. Greenbaum tells Ms. Michael that he does, in fact, want a divorce. He and his wife have gone through counseling, and reconciliation does not seem likely.

He also tells her that his primary goal is to get custody of the children.

Mrs. Greenbaum

At about the same time, Mrs. Greenbaum is in the office of her attorney, Matthew Jeffrey. Mrs. Greenbaum tells Mr. Jeffrey that her husband left home four weeks earlier without telling her that he was moving out and without making arrangements for the children or for the disposition of the property. The children are currently with Mrs. Greenbaum, and she wants to keep them and the couple's home.

§3.2   OBTAINING THE FACTS

What the attorney does at this point depends on how much he or she knows about custody actions. An attorney who practices family law will know what questions to ask; one who doesn't, may not. In the latter case, the attorney will be able to ask only general questions. Instead of getting all of the information, his or her goal is to get the information that is needed to find the applicable statute or common law doctrine.

For the purposes of this section, let's assume that the attorneys know very little about child custody. As a consequence, during this initial interview, they find out only that Mr. and Mrs. Greenbaum have two children, Tom, age 9, and Mary, age 7; that Mr. Greenbaum, the CEO of a small family business, thinks that he should have custody because his wife is inconsistent in her dealings with the children; and that Mrs. Greenbaum, a high school teacher, thinks that she should get custody because she has, since the birth of the children, been their primary caretaker.

§3.3   LOCATING THE APPLICABLE STATUTE

An attorney who practices family law will know, from memory, both the number of the applicable statute and its language. Our attorneys, however, know only that custody actions are governed by state statute. They do not know the number of the applicable statute, and it has been several years since either one has read it.

As a result, they must locate the applicable statute. They do this by looking in their state's code, using the subject or topic index to locate the number of the applicable section and then locating the text of that section in the main volumes.

For the purposes of this problem, let's assume that the attorneys locate the following statute.

Uniform Marriage and Divorce Act*

Section 402: Best Interests of Child

The court shall determine custody in accordance with the best interests of the child. The court shall consider all relevant factors including:

(1) the wishes of the child's parent or parents as to his custody;

(2) the wishes of the child as to his custodian;

(3) the interaction and interrelationship of the child with his parent or parents, his siblings, and any other person who may significantly affect the child's best interest;

(4) the child's adjustment to his home, school, and community; and

(5) the mental and physical health of all individuals involved.

The court shall not consider conduct of a proposed custodian that does not affect his relationship to the child.

The next step is to determine whether this section is, in fact, the applicable section. Is section 402 the section that the court will use in determining which parent will be granted temporary and permanent custody?

The answer to this question is often in the title of the statute. In codifying a statute, the code revisor indicates the scope of the section in its title. Unfortunately, in this case, the title is of little help: It does not indicate whether the statute applies to temporary custody decisions, permanent custody decisions, or modification proceedings. The attorneys must look further.

The next place they look is the text of the statute. In the first sentence, the legislature states that "[t]he court shall determine custody. . . ." Although this phrase tells the attorneys that the statute governs child custody, it does not tell them whether it governs initial custody decisions.

The next place that the attorneys look is the other sections in the same chapter or act. The table of contents is set out below.

---

*This Act has been reprinted through the permission of the National Conference of Commissioners on Uniform State Laws, and copies of the Act may be ordered from them at a nominal cost at 676 N. St. Clair St., Ste. 1700, Chicago, IL 60611, (302) 915-0195.

CUSTODY*

401.   Jurisdiction; Commencement of Proceeding
402.   Best Interests of Child
403.   Temporary Orders
404.   Interviews
405.   Investigation and Reports
406.   Hearings
407.   Visitation
408.   Judicial Supervision
409.   Modification
410.   Affidavit Practice

From this list, it appears that there are two other sections that potentially apply to child custody actions: section 403, Temporary Orders, and section 409, Modification.

When the attorneys examine these sections, they find that they do relate to child custody. Section 403 gives the court the power to award temporary custody.

Section 403: Temporary Orders*

(a) A party to a custody proceeding may move for a temporary custody order. The motion must be supported by an affidavit as provided in Section 410. The court may award temporary custody under the standards of Section 402 after a hearing or, if there is no objection, solely on the basis of the affidavits.

(b) If a proceeding for dissolution of marriage or legal separation is dismissed, any temporary custody order is vacated unless a parent or the child's custodian moves that the proceeding continue as a custody proceeding and the court finds, after a hearing, that the circumstances of the parents and the best interest of the child require that a custody decree be issued.

(c) If a custody proceeding commenced in the absence of a petition for dissolution of marriage or legal separation under subsection (1)(ii) or (2) of Section 401 is dismissed, any temporary custody order is vacated.

In contrast, section 409 deals only with the modification of existing child custody orders.

Thus, although there is nothing in the Uniform Act that specifically states that section 402 governs temporary and permanent custody decisions, the attorneys determine that section 402 is the applicable section by reading the title, the language of section 402, and the other related statutes.

---

*This Act has been reprinted through the permission of the National Conference of Commissioners on Uniform State Laws, and copies of the Act may be ordered from them at a nominal cost at 676 N. St. Clair St., Ste. 1700, Chicago, IL 60611, (302) 915-0195.

Question

Is section 402 mandatory or persuasive authority?

§3.4 ANALYZING THE STATUTE

Having determined that section 402 is the applicable section, the attorneys begin to analyze it, taking it apart and examining each part closely. Who determines which parent gets custody, and how is that decision made?

The answer to the first question is in the first sentence of the statute. The legislature states that it is the court that determines which parent gets custody: "The court shall determine . . . ." The statute does not say, however, who has the "burden of proof." Is it the father who has the burden? The mother? The parent with custody? The parent without custody?

Question

What does the phrase "burden of proof" mean? If you don't know, where can you find the answer?

———————————

The answer to the second question is also in the first sentence of the statute. The legislature states that "[t]he court shall determine custody in accordance with the best interests of the child."

At this point, the attorneys stop and think about what the legislature has done. In enacting this statute, has the legislature set out a list of elements, or has it created a standard?

Question

As a practical matter, what is the difference between a statute that sets out a list of elements, or requirements, and one that sets out a standard or a general principle? Why would the legislature select one approach in some instances and another approach in other instances?

———————————

After looking at the statute more carefully, the attorneys determine that the legislature has set out a standard. In determining which parent gets custody, the court will consider "the best interests" of the children. Although the five-item list looks like a list of elements, it is not. A parent does not have to prove each item in the list. Instead, the legislature has listed the factors that it wants the courts to consider in deciding what would be in the best interests of the children. Thus, in enacting section 402, not only has the legislature set out the standard, but it has also provided the court with instructions for applying it.

In reading a statute, you need to look at every word in the statute. For example, note that in the second sentence the legislature has used the word "shall" rather than "may" or "can." Because the legislature has used "shall," the court has no discretion. It must do what the legislature says.

Also note that the legislature tells the court not to consider all factors but only those factors that are "relevant." Finally, look at the word "including." Through its use of this word, the legislature tells the court that it considers the five factors set out in the statute to be relevant. The courts must, therefore, consider each of them. The legislature does not, however, tell the court to look only at those five factors. If there are other relevant factors, the court must also consider them.

Question

Is each parent's occupation a relevant factor? Who would decide, and how would they make their decision?

Exercise

Write a one-page letter to your client in which you paraphrase and explain section 402.

§3.5   LOCATING AND ANALYZING THE CASES

The attorneys have identified and analyzed the applicable statute. Their search for the "law," however, is not over. Even though custody decisions are governed by statute and not common law, the attorneys still need to locate and read the applicable cases. To understand why, you must understand the relationship between the common law, section 402, and the cases interpreting and applying section 402.

Historically, custody decisions were governed by common law. Because there was no statute, the courts were free to create their own common law rules. Although the rule was not the same in every state, in most states the courts adopted the Tender Years Doctrine, a rule that granted the custody of young children to the mother unless the court found her to be unfit.

The common law has, however, been superseded by statute. Acting under the authority granted to them by the federal and state constitutions, state legislatures have enacted statutes setting out the rules to be used in deciding child custody. In some instances, these statutes codified the common law rule. The legislature simply adopted and put into statutory form the common law rule. In other instances, the legislature abolished the common law rule, replacing it with a different rule or standard.

In those states in which the legislature simply codified the common

EXHIBIT 3.1   **Statute Codifies Common Law Rule**

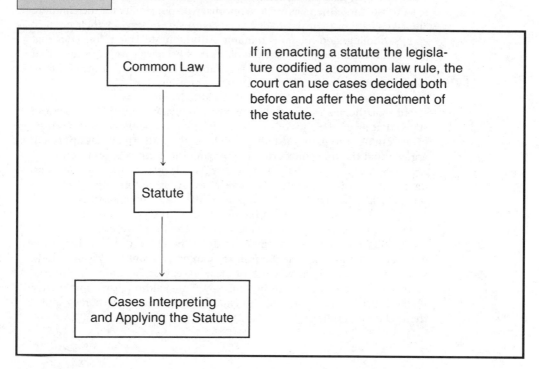

law rule, the cases setting out or applying the common law rule are still "good law," and the courts can look to them to find the policy underlying the common law rule and statute or to see how the rule was applied in analogous cases. See Exhibit 3.1. This is not, however, the case in those states in which the legislature abolished the common law rule and enacted a new rule or standard. In these states, the cases decided before the enactment of the statute are not good law and should not, as a general rule, be used in interpreting or applying the statute. The courts can use only those cases decided after the enactment of the statute. See Exhibit 3.2.

The attorneys find cases interpreting and applying the statute using the annotations, or notes of decision, that follow the text of the statute in an annotated code. In this instance, assume that the attorneys locate only the following two hypothetical cases: *In re Marriage of Huen* and *In re Marriage of Nabrinski.*

In re Marriage of Huen

24 Official Rep. 9, 678 Reg. Rep. 68 (1989)

This is an appeal from an order granting the mother custody of her two sons. The facts are as follows.

Deana and Daniel Huen were married in 1984. Both worked until 1986, at which time Mrs. Huen quit work to care for the couple's twin sons. Since 1986, Mrs. Huen has assumed primary responsibility for the children. She takes care of their day-to-day needs, and she supervises their medical care, schooling, and religious training. Although Mr. Huen concedes that Mrs. Huen has been providing the children's primary care, he argues that he is equally able to provide such care, and, given the sex of the children, that it would be in their best interests to grant him custody.

The trial court granted custody to Mrs. Huen. In so doing, the court stated that the sex of the child was not a relevant factor. The court also stated that given the ages of the children, it would be in the best interests of the children to grant custody to their mother. Mr. Huen has appealed, arguing that the trial court erred in applying the Tender Years Doctrine.

We find that the trial court did err. The Tender Years Doctrine is no longer the law in this state. The legislature abolished it when it enacted section 402. The standard now applied is the "best interests of the child."

We do, however, uphold the decision of the trial court. If a child is too young to express his or her preference, the best interests of the child dictate that the trial court award custody of the child to the primary caregiver, absent a finding that the primary caregiver is unfit to have custody. In this case, Mrs. Huen was the primary caregiver; accordingly, the trial court did not err in granting her custody. Thus, although we might have reached a different result had the children been older, we hereby affirm the trial court's ruling.

EXHIBIT 3.2   **Statute Changed Common Law Rule**

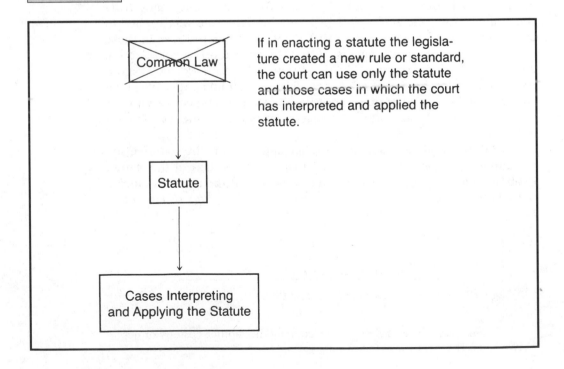

Common Law

If in enacting a statute the legislature created a new rule or standard, the court can use only the statute and those cases in which the court has interpreted and applied the statute.

Statute

Cases Interpreting and Applying the Statute

In this case, the court does two things. First, it states that the statute supersedes the common law rule. There is no longer a presumption that the mother should be granted custody of young children. The courts must follow the statute and award custody in accordance with the best interests of the child. Second, it creates a new rule. The court states that when "the child is too young to express his or her preference, the best interests of the child dictate that the trial court award custody of the child to the primary caregiver absent a finding that the primary caregiver is unfit to have custody." The court then applies this new rule, holding that because the mother had been the primary caregiver, the trial court did not err in granting her custody.

Questions

1. Is the trial court's statement that "the sex of the child is not relevant" a rule, part of the court's holding, or dicta? See Glossary of Terms.

2. Is the trial court's statement that it might have reached a different result had the children been older a rule, part of the court's holding, or dicta?

Exercise

In one paragraph, summarize the rules set out in *In re Marriage of Huen.*

IN RE MARRIAGE OF NABRINSKI
38 Official Rep. 501, 489 Reg. Rep. 66 (1988)

This case arises as the result of a trial court order granting custody of a girl, age 7, and a boy, age 11, to their father.

In deciding which parent should be awarded custody, the court must consider the best interests of the children. Section 402, Uniform Marriage and Divorce Act. In deciding what would be in the best interests of the children, the court must consider the wishes of the parents and child as to custody; the interaction and interrelationship of the child with his or her parent or parents, siblings, and any other person who may significantly affect the child's best interest; the child's adjustment to home, school, and community; and the mental and physical health of all individuals involved. *Id.*

In addition, the court must look to see which parent has been the primary caregiver. *In re Marriage of Huen,* 24 Official Reporter 9, 678 Regional Reporter 68 (1986). Absent evidence that the primary caregiver is an unfit custodian, custody will be given to that parent. *Id.*

In determining which parent is the primary caregiver, the court will look to see who was the primary caregiver at the time the parents separated. The parent who provided for the daily needs of the children will be deemed to be the primary caregiver, and to ensure continuity in the lives of the children, except in exceptional circumstances, custody will be granted to him or her.

In this case, the mother was providing the primary care for both children. She took them to school and picked them up after school, and she supervised their after school activities and homework. She is also the one who maintained the home: she cleaned the house, did the laundry, did the shopping, and prepared the meals. We do, therefore, find that the trial court erred in granting custody of the children to their father. Consequently, even though we might have reached a different result if the mother were still involved with other men, because these indiscretions were in the past, this court finds that it would be in the best interests of the children to grant custody to the mother. We, therefore, reverse the holding of the trial court.

In this case, the court repeats the statute and the rule set out in *In re Marriage of Huen*. It also creates an additional rule. In determining which parent is the primary caregiver, the court will look to see which parent was the primary caregiver at the time the couple separated. The court also explains the rationale for this rule. The court states that by granting custody to the parent who was the primary caregiver at the time the couple separated, it is trying to ensure continuity in the children's lives.

Question

In *Nabrinski,* what is the court's holding? Are any of the court's statements dicta?

Exercise

In one paragraph, summarize the rules set out in *In re Marriage of Nabrinski*. In writing your paragraph, make clear the relationship between the factors set out in the statute and the rules set forth in the case.

Question

Are *Huen* and *Nabrinski* mandatory or persuasive authority?

---

§3.6 Synthesizing the Law

The attorneys now have before them both the text of the statute and the cases in which the courts have interpreted and applied the statute. The next step is to put the pieces together.

In many instances, this is done by a legal intern or an associate. The intern or associate researches the law and then prepares an in-house memorandum in which he or she summarizes and applies the law to the facts of the client's case. The beginning of the discussion section would look like this.

EXAMPLE

Discussion

Section 402 of the Uniform Marriage and Divorce Act sets out the standard that the trial court must use in awarding custody.

Section 402: Best Interests of Child

The court shall determine custody in accordance with the best interests of the child. The court shall consider all relevant factors including:

(1) the wishes of the child's parent or parents as to his custody;

(2) the wishes of the child as to his custodian;

(3) the interaction and interrelationship of the child with his parent or parents, his siblings, and any other person who may significantly affect the child's best interest;

(4) the child's adjustment to his home, school, and community; and

(5) the mental and physical health of all individuals involved.

The court shall not consider conduct of a proposed custodian that does not affect his relationship to the child.

The state supreme court has held that this statute supersedes the common law in effect at the time the statute was enacted. *In re Marriage of Huen,* 24 Official Reporter 9, 678 Regional Reporter 68 (1986). Consequently, there is no longer a presumption that the custody of young children should be awarded to the mother. *Id.* at 11, 678 Regional Reporter at 69. The supreme court has, however, held that if "the child is too young to express his or her preference, the best interests of the child dictate that the trial court award custody of the child to the primary caregiver absent a finding that the primary caregiver is unfit to have custody." *Id.*

In determining which parent is the primary caregiver, the courts look to see which parent was acting as the primary caregiver at the time the parents separated. *In re Marriage of Nabrinski,* 38 Official Reporter 501, 489 Regional Reporter 66 (1988). By awarding custody to the primary caretaker, the courts seek to ensure, to the extent possible, continuity of care. *Id.*

In reading this excerpt, note several things. First, look at the organizational scheme. The writer has set out first the statute and then the rules from the cases. This is correct. Because child custody actions are governed by statute, the analysis must begin with the statute and not the cases. Second, note the focus of the discussion. Although the rules are presented in date order (the statute first, the rule from *Huen* second, and the rule from *Nabrinski* last), neither the dates nor the names of the cases are the focus. Instead, the writer has focused on the decisionmaking process:

1.   In awarding child custody, the standard is best interests of the child;
2.   If the child is young, it is usually in the best interests of the child to grant custody to the child's primary caretaker;
3.   In determining which parent is the primary caretaker, the courts look to see which parent was the primary caretaker at the time the parents separated.

Finally, note that the writer has done more than just quote from the cases. He or she has summarized the rules, putting them into his or her own language.

There may, however, be a problem with the way in which the rules are presented. Has the writer accurately explained the relationship between the factors listed in the statute and the rules set out in the cases?

Exercise

Now that you have all of the law, rewrite the client letter from Exercise on page 36. In doing so, do not quote either the statute or cases verbatim.

---

§3.7   GATHERING ADDITIONAL INFORMATION

After receiving the letters from their attorneys, Mr. and Mrs. Greenbaum decide to file for divorce. In his Petition for Dissolution of Marriage, Mr. Greenbaum requests sole custody of the children. In her Answer, Mrs. Greenbaum counters, also asking for sole custody. Because the parties do not agree on custody, a hearing is scheduled.

For both attorneys, the next step is to collect more information. Now that they know the law, they know what types of information they need to make their case to the court.

For purposes of this exercise, let's assume that the attorneys obtain the following information.

**CITY
MEDICAL CENTER**

PSYCHOLOGICAL EXAMINATION REPORT

Mr. Greenbaum   Mrs. Greenbaum
Date of Birth: Date of Birth:
January 15, 1964   January 12, 1965

Examination Dates: Examination Dates:
July 27 & 28, 1998   July 25 & 26, 1998

Examination Procedures:

Draw-a-Person Test, Wechsler Adult Intelligence Scale, Story Recall, Bender-Gestalt (five-second delay, copy, memory), Rorschach Test, Thematic Apperception Test, Word Association Test, Concept Sorting Test, Minnesota Multiphasic Personality Inventory, Sentence Completion Test, Diagnostic Interviews.

IDENTIFICATION AND REFERRAL: This examination is being completed at the request of Dr. Herbert Modlin, who was requested to do a comprehensive evaluation by Mrs. Greenbaum's attorney for the purpose of aiding and assisting in the determination of appropriate child custody. The parties have been married for 12 years and the children in question are a son, Tom, age nine, and a daughter, Mary, age seven. Tom is in the fourth grade, and Mary is in the first grade. Mrs. Greenbaum is a school teacher. Mr. Greenbaum is a business executive. Both parties are seeking custody of their children, and both have alleged that they would be fit to have custody of the children.

Both parties are college graduates and married just prior to Mrs. Greenbaum's completing her education. She taught school after they married until her first child was born. They have been typically upwardly mobile with Mr. Greenbaum advancing in his business career. They report usual social and recreational activities, at least at the beginning and middle of their marriage. More recently, they have moved in separate directions with different interests, and this has contributed to and is part of the marital discord.

Each continues to relate to his or her parental family and both have living parents who are active and supportive. They have been financially stable, and both are responsible in terms of money management.

Neither reports intense quarreling but rather a drifting apart.

Mr. Greenbaum is seeking custody of his children and alleges that his relatively flexible schedule will facilitate parenting the children. Mrs. Greenbaum is also seeking custody, and because she teaches school, her schedule is compatible with the children's school on a daily basis as well as at vacation times. She would require childcare assistance on school mornings.

The children are presently residing with Mrs. Greenbaum. Appropriate arrangements for childcare have been maintained by Mrs. Greenbaum consistent with her employment schedule.

EXAMINATION PROCESS: Both parties cooperated fully and completely with the examination. Although the examination was requested by the wife and her attorney, the husband was more than willing to cooperate and believed that all parties would benefit from the examination. No unusual mannerisms or behaviors were noted in either of these individuals. Both were appropriate in affect, mood, and behavior during the examination. Both dressed appropriately for the examination. There are no indications of manipulative or other types of behavior that might tend to taint the results. There is every indication that the results of this examination are a valid and reliable estimate of both of their intellectual and emotional functioning. Neither of these parents was using any medication at the time of the examination on a regular basis. Both are right-handed and wear corrective glasses.

EXAMINATION FINDINGS: <u>Mrs. Greenbaum</u>: The patient's cognitive functioning is intact. Overall she functions within the Bright-Normal range of intellectual abilities. She does somewhat better on verbal as opposed to nonverbal tasks. Her memory is intact, and she shows good judgment. There are no indications of organic brain syndrome.

This examination does not reveal any gross dysfunction or indications of extreme, acute, or chronic psychopathology. The patient is sensitive to a wide range of feelings but somewhat emotionally liable. Although she is likely to become excited with little provocation, she is able to regain control of herself relatively quickly. She does integrate positive feelings into her life but occasionally has difficulty managing depression. She is the kind of person who would rely on chemicals and perhaps alcohol to relieve such depression. To some extent her use of alcohol is situational—her way of medicating herself. Her desire for custody may also be, at least at some level, motivated by her desire to punish her husband.

She is the kind of person who may be mildly inconsistent in discipline and likely to give in to demands that children make on her rather than dealing with some of the attending emotional stress. She can be flexible, however, and will not allow those tendencies to go too far before she is able to regroup and appropriately and consistently provide direction as well as discipline. Her discipline practices are lenient and rely on more abstract use of love and affection as opposed to structure. She is the kind of person who values individual differences and supports persons in achieving their potential as opposed to forcing persons to fit into preconceived roles. Her expectations, however, are high, and she expects a great deal from herself as well as others.

The patient is capable of forming and maintaining intimate and genuine relationships. She is slightly inconsistent in relationships as her mood shifts and she becomes somewhat emotionally liable; this causes her difficulties in maintaining relationships at a high level. This is much more likely to be a problem in her relationships with adults (and men in particular) as opposed to how she relates to young children.

Mr. Greenbaum: This patient is a hard-driving, achievement-oriented person. He manages his life and life circumstances in a relatively compulsive, routine, scheduled manner. His interactions with people are managed in the same way. He has the potential to be sensitive to feelings but in many instances will avoid or make an effort to disguise sensitive feelings. To some extent, he is a hyper-masculine person who bolsters himself with excessive displays of masculinity. He does have the potential to be a nurturing and sensitive person, but this is not the primary way that he ordinarily functions.

This man's parenting skills reflect his overall personality development and character traits. He is rigid in his discipline and overly consistent. He does not show a great deal of flexibility, and his expectations are that his desires, orders, and mandates will be carried forward without question and without compromise. This is not done by him in any harsh or brutal fashion, but rather calmly and with assertiveness. He adheres to very structured moral and ethical standards and expects people to fit into a mold that will satisfy societal and cultural expectations. His expectation, for example, would be that his children behave in ways that are normally expected for boys and girls, and it would be difficult for him to tolerate deviations.

To some extent this man expects more adultlike behavior from children than may be appropriate. He does not always attempt to put himself in the child's place to understand desires, motivations, and needs of the child. These last comments are subtle and not reflective of any gross misunderstanding he has of children and their behavior.

DIAGNOSTIC IMPRESSION: No formal psychiatric diagnosis is provided for either of these individuals at the present time. Neither shows symptomatology at the time of this examination. The personality characteristics described above can be encapsulated in summary fashion by viewing Mr. Greenbaum as a compulsive type of individual and Mrs. Greenbaum as a mildly hysterical and emotionally effervescent person. In both instances, however, these personality characteristics are not debilitating, nor do they in any way impair functional capacity.

EXPLANATORY FORMULATION: Both of these parents are fit to have custody of their children. Neither of them is harmful to the children, nor would they be damaging to the children in any way.

Certain predictable outcomes, however, are possible based on this psychological evaluation. If the children were placed with Mrs. Greenbaum, it is very likely that their life would be less structured but more emotionally exciting, and there would be more responsiveness, at least at their present ages, to their emotional needs and individual differences. Mrs. Greenbaum is less concerned with form and more interested in the substance of relationships. If the children were placed with Mr. Greenbaum, there would be more routine and regularity to their life, slightly less responsiveness to emotional and nurturing needs, and more concern with behavior fitting into well-defined and prescribed standards.

There are, of course, advantages and disadvantages to both modes of childrearing and understanding of the nurturing parenting process. Actually, the styles of these two parents complement each other and in an intact family would provide the best of both dimensions. Where custody is an issue, however, either of these parents can provide adequate and sufficient custodial parenting but with the differences suggested above.

R. E. Schulman, Ph. D.

R.E. Schulman, Ph.D.
Certified Psychologist

RES/vw

Date: August 2, 1998

M The
Menninger
Foundation

August 17, 1998

Dear Mr. Skoloff:

I have completed my clinical evaluation of the four members of the Greenbaum family. I assume you have received a report of the psychological test results from Doctor Schulman. As you know, I have utilized Doctor Schulman's findings in my evaluations.

I understand that the court will need to make a decision concerning child custody and, to the extent that it may be helpful, I have a contribution to make. In my opinion, Mrs. Greenbaum is the preferred parent for custody of the two children at the present time for the following reasons:

1. As a trained and experienced schoolteacher, Mrs. Greenbaum has above average knowledge of growth and development in children and age-appropriate management of children.
2. Mrs. Greenbaum is able to experience and react to the two children as separate individuals with different needs because of the age, sex, and personality characteristics.
3. Mrs. Greenbaum is warm, outgoing, and appropriately emotional.
4. Mrs. Greenbaum's motives in seeking custody are pure. She wants custody because she believes that only she can provide the loving and nurturing environment that young children need.
5. Mr. Greenbaum tends to some rigidity concerning standards of behavior and is a bit lacking in flexibility. He emphasizes efficiency and reason at the expense of feelings. He is uncomfortable with emotional expressions and may inadvertently discourage normal emotional development of the children.

I am strongly in favor of visitation rights for the noncustodial parent. Although under some circumstances such visitation can be destructive, in this case I do not find in the parents a degree of bitterness, vindictiveness, and desire to continue warfare which would make visitation a trying experience for the children. Both parents may well continue to express some disapproval of the other, but probably not to a degree which the children cannot handle.

I am strongly opposed to joint custody for children of this age. In our culture, the latency period (ages six to twelve) is a period for defining and consolidating basic personality traits which will determine significant coping devices of that individual for years to come. These traits are selected, tried out, modified, and developed into efficient, stress-handling techniques, chiefly within the family: security and safety notably influence psychological development of a child at this age. He needs a place to belong, and home should be a place of trust where there are predictable, trustworthy people with whom the child can interact meaningfully without unnecessary fear of disruption and unpredictability. If one has a home base that is secure and consistent, then one can venture into the wide, wide world without undue apprehension.

If I can be of further assistance in this case, please feel free to call upon me.

Sincerely yours,

Herbert C. Modlin, M.D.

HCM:gn

Enclosures

§3.8   IDENTIFYING THE LEGALLY AND
EMOTIONALLY SIGNIFICANT FACTS

The next step is to go through the affidavits, identifying the legally and emotionally significant facts.

A fact is legally significant if the court would consider it in determining whether the legal requirements are, or are not, met. For example, in the *Greenbaum* case, any fact that the court would consider in determining the "best interests" of the children is legally significant. Other facts, and in particular those facts that relate to the behavior of the parent but do not affect the parent's relationship to the child, are not legally significant and will not (or should not) be argued by the attorneys or considered by the court.

Notice the circular nature of legal analysis. The attorneys could not determine which statute applied until they had at least some of the facts. However, it wasn't until they knew which statute applied that they knew which facts were legally significant.

Question

Under section 402 of the Uniform Marriage and Divorce Act, which of the following facts are legally significant? Explain your answers.

a.   the amount that each parent earns
b.   a parent's tendency to gamble
c.   a parent's sexual practices
d.   a parent's relationship with his or her own parents
e.   the child's academic, artistic, or athletic abilities

In our case, the attorneys determine which facts are legally significant by going through the affidavits, identifying the facts that the court would consider in evaluating each factor. Do the same in the following chart.

Legally Significant Facts	
Factor	*Legally Significant Facts*
1. Preference of parents	
2. Preference of children	
3. Interaction & interrelationship	
4. Adjustment to home, school, and community	
5. Physical and mental health	
6. Other factors	
7. Conduct that court will not consider	

Question

Are the facts that you listed next to number 7 legally significant? Why or why not?

_____

The attorneys also identify those facts that are emotionally significant.

An emotionally significant fact is a fact that, although not legally significant, may sway the court. For example, although in a criminal action the defendant's age and reasons for committing the crime are usually not legally significant, a judge may be more inclined to rule in favor of a 90-year-old widow who stole a loaf of bread because she was hungry than a 20-year-old junkie who stole to support a drug habit. Remember, judges are people, and they will find some cases more emotionally appealing than others.

Questions

In a child custody action, which of the following facts would be emotionally significant?

a. a grandparent's statements about how much one of the parents loves his or her children
b. information indicating that in the past one of the parents had a drug or alcohol problem
c. the fact that one of the parents is a well-known personality in the community
d. the fact that one of the parents is well educated and the other never graduated from high school
e. the fact that one parent regularly attends church and the other attends church only on major religious holidays

In the *Greenbaum* case, which facts, if any, are emotionally significant?

Emotionally Significant Facts	
Facts That Favor *Mr. Greenbaum*	*Facts That Favor* *Mrs. Greenbaum*

_____

§3.9   FORMULATING ARGUMENTS

The next step is to formulate the arguments. Given the law and the facts, what arguments can the attorneys make in trying to persuade the court to grant their client custody?

There are three types of cases: cases in which the law itself is in dispute; cases in which the application of the law is in dispute; and cases in which both the law and its application are disputed. In the first type, the parties argue the law itself. The plaintiff asks the court to apply Rule A, and the defendant asks the court to apply Rule B. In the second type, the parties agree that Rule C applies. What they disagree about is (1) what the facts are or (2) how Rule C should be applied to the facts. In the third type, the parties disagree both about the law and about how the law should be applied to the facts of the case.

The *Greenbaum* case falls into the third category. Although both sides agree that the standard is best interests of the children, they disagree about what test the court should apply. While Mrs. Greenbaum's attorney wants the court to apply the rules set out in *Huen* and *Nabrinski,* Mr. Greenbaum's attorney wants the court to disregard those rules. She thinks that because the rules are inconsistent with the statute, they should not be applied. In addition, both sides will argue the facts, arguing both about what the facts are and about how the law should be applied to them.

Questions

How much latitude do the courts have in interpreting and applying a statute? Who decides whether a court has exceeded its power and changed the law instead of interpreting it?

———————

§3.9.1   Arguing the Law

In the first type of case, the law itself is in dispute. The parties disagree about which statute or common law rule applies or about how the statute or rule should be interpreted.

As in the other types of cases, in this type of case it is not enough to simply state your position. You cannot just state that the court should interpret the statute in a manner that supports your client's position. You must make arguments.

In the *Greenbaum* case, the attorneys can make several types of arguments: They can support their position by arguing the plain language of the statute, legislative intent, or public policy.

a.   Plain Language Arguments

In arguing that the plain language of the statute supports the position being advocated, an attorney emphasizes what the statute does, and does not, say. For example, in the case that we are working on, Mr. Green-baum's attorney would argue that rules set out in *Huen* and *Nabrinski* are inconsistent with the plain language of the statute. The statute does not tell the court to award custody to the parent who was the primary caregiver at the time the couple separated. It tells the court to consider all relevant factors.

Exercise

Write out what the father's attorney, Ms. Michael, would say in arguing that the rules set out in *Huen* and *Nabrinski* are inconsistent with the plain language of the statute. After you have written out the father's argument, think about how the mother's attorney would respond. Can Mr. Jeffrey also make an argument based on the plain language of the statute? If you think that he can, write out that argument.

---

b.   *Legislative Intent*

Attorneys also use legislative intent to support their interpretation of the law. In enacting the statute, did the legislature intend result A or did it intend result B? Before our attorneys can make an argument based on legislative intent, they need to do more research.

Evidence of the legislature's intent can be found in several different places. Sometimes the legislature explains its intent in the statutory section itself or in an introductory section that precedes the act. At other times, legislative intent can be found in the comments, if there are any, that accompany the statute or in the records of the legislature (the transcripts of legislative hearings on the statute or act, committee reports discussing the statute or act, or transcripts of floor debate).

In our problem case, the attorneys begin their search with the section of the Marriage and Divorce Act that explains the Act's purpose.

Section 102 Purposes: Rules of Construction*

This Act shall be liberally construed and applied to promote its underlying purposes, which are to:
    (1) provide adequate procedures for the solemnization and registration of marriage;
    (2) strengthen and preserve the integrity of marriage and safeguard family relationships;
    (3) promote the amicable settlement of disputes that have arisen between parties to a marriage;

---

*This Act has been reprinted through the permission of the National Conference of Commissioners on Uniform State Laws, and copies of the Act may be ordered from them at a nominal cost at 676 N. St. Clair St., Ste. 1700, Chicago, IL 60611, (302) 915-0195.

(4) mitigate the potential harm to the spouses and their children caused by the process of legal dissolution of marriage;

(5) make reasonable provision for spouse and minor children during and after litigation; and

(6) make the law of legal dissolution of marriage effective for dealing with the realities of matrimonial experience by making irretrievable breakdown of the marriage relationship the sole basis for its dissolution.

The phrases in this section that are potentially applicable are those stating (1) that the Act is to be liberally construed to promote its underlying purposes, (2) that in enacting the Act the legislature sought to mitigate the potential harm to the children caused by the process of legal dissolution of marriage; and (3) that the legislature sought to make reasonable provisions for spouses and minor children during and after litigation. These statements are, however, so broad that they are of little use to either side.

The next thing that the attorneys look for is a legislative history, that is, the records from legislative hearings, committee reports, and floor debate. Unfortunately, none are available: The hearings and floor debate have not been transcribed, and there was no written committee report.

In the absence of such information, the attorneys turn to the Uniform Act itself, locating and reading the Commissioners' Notes that follow section 402. Although these comments were written by the commissioners who drafted the Uniform Act and not the state legislature, they are of some value. If the state legislature had the comments before it when it adopted the Uniform Act, the attorneys can argue that the Commissioners' Notes reflect not only the intent of the commissioners but also the intent of the legislature.

The following notes follow section 402 of the Uniform Act.

COMMISSIONERS' NOTES TO SECTION 402

This section, excepting the last sentence, is designed to codify existing law in most jurisdictions. It simply states that the trial court must look to a variety of factors to determine what is the child's best interest. The five factors mentioned specifically are those most commonly relied upon in the appellate opinions; but the language of the section makes it clear that the judge need not be limited to the factors specified. Although none of the familiar presumptions developed by the case law are mentioned here, the language of the section is consistent with preserving such rules of thumb. The preference for the mother as custodian of young children when all things are equal, for example, is simply a shorthand method of expressing the best interest of children — and this section enjoins judges to decide custody cases according to that general standard. The same analysis is appropriate to the other common presumptions: a parent is usually preferred to a nonparent; the existing custodian is usually preferred to any new custodian because of the interest in assuring continuity for the child; preference is usually given to the custodian chosen by agreement of the parents. In the case of modification, there is also a specific provision designed to foster continuity of custodians and discourage change. See Section 409.

The last sentence of the section changes the law in those states which continue to use fault notions in custody adjudication. There is no reason to encourage parties to spy on each other in order to discover marital (most commonly, sexual) misconduct for use in a custody contest. This provision makes it clear that unless a contestant is able to prove that the parent's behavior in fact affects his relationship to the child (a standard which could seldom be met if the parent's behavior has been circumspect or unknown to the child), evidence of such behavior is irrelevant.

These notes seem to support the mother's request for custody. For, even though there is nothing in the statute itself that states that there is a presumption that it would be in the best interests of the children to give custody to the mother, the commissioners state that "the preference for the mother as custodian of young children when all things are equal . . . is simply a shorthand method of expressing the best interests of the children . . . ."

Exercise

Write out what Mrs. Greenbaum's attorney, Mr. Jeffrey, would say in arguing that the rules set out in *Huen* and *Nabrinski* accurately reflect the legislature's intent in enacting section 402. After you have written out Mrs. Greenbaum's argument, think about how Mr. Greenbaum's attorney might respond. Can Ms. Michael make an argument based on legislative intent? If you think that she can, write out her argument.

----

c. *Public Policy*

Closely related to arguments based on legislative intent are arguments based on public policy. When attorneys make this type of argument, they argue that Rule A is more consistent with public policy than is Rule B or that, as a matter of public policy, Rule A and not Rule B should be adopted.

The question, of course, is what is public policy? In general, policies reflect societal values. As a society, we want to protect the rights of the innocent, compensate those who have been injured, and conserve judicial resources.

In setting out the purposes of the Act (look once again at section 102 on page 52), the legislature listed some of the policies underlying the Uniform Child Custody Act. There may, however, be others. Can Mr. Greenbaum argue that, as a matter of public policy, the court should protect the rights of fathers, giving them an equal opportunity for custody?

Exercise

1. If you represent Mrs. Greenbaum, write out the arguments that her attorney might make in arguing that the rules set out in *Huen* and *Greenbaum* are consistent with public policy. If you represent Mr. Greenbaum, do the opposite. Write out the arguments that Mr. Greenbaum's attorney would make in arguing that the rules set out in those cases violate public policy.

2. Working with your group, prepare a five-minute oral argument. If you represent Mrs. Greenbaum, argue that the court should apply the rules set out in *Huen* and *Nabrinski;* if you represent Mr. Greenbaum, argue that the rules set out in those two cases are inconsistent with the statute and should not, therefore, be applied.

---

§3.9.2   Arguing the Application of the Law to the Facts

In addition to arguing the law, our attorneys can argue the application of the law to the facts. They can make factual arguments based on the plain language of the statute and rules; arguments based on analogous cases; and, once again, arguments based on policy.

a.   Factual Arguments Based on the Plain Language of the Law

The first type of argument, a factual argument based on the plain language of the law, is the most common. The attorney simply applies the law to the facts of the case.

Law	+	**Facts**	=	**Legal Conclusion**
Speed limit is 55 mph		Plaintiff was driving 65 mph		Plaintiff has violated the law

In our sample case, the attorneys can make a number of factual arguments. They can make arguments based on each of the factors, and they can apply the rules set out in the cases.

We begin with the first of the five factors. In this case, both parents want custody.

Law	+	**Facts**	=	**Legal Conclusion**
Parents' wishes as to custody		Father wants custody		Factor favors father
		Mother wants custody		Factor favors mother

Because both parents want custody, an evaluation of this factor results in a draw. Both parents can use this factor to support their arguments.

However, there may be a way in which Mr. Greenbaum's attorney, Ms. Michael, can use this factor to her client's advantage. Look carefully at the psychologist's report. In it, the psychologist states that he thinks that the mother's desire to get custody may be based, at least at some level, on her desire to "punish" the children's father. This is an opening, and, if the father wants it, an opportunity to make an argument.

EXAMPLE

Mr. Greenbaum's Argument

It would not be in the best interests of the children to grant custody to Mrs. Greenbaum. Although Mrs. Greenbaum has requested custody of Tom and Mary, she wants custody not because she believes that such an award would be in the best interests of the children but because she wants to punish her husband. She feels rejected, and to counter this rejection, she has resorted to self-medication. Although Mrs. Greenbaum is a good parent, her desire for custody is motivated at least in part by her desire to punish Mr. Greenbaum.

EXAMPLE

Mrs. Greenbaum's Response

The children's mother asks this court to grant her custody of her two children, Tom, age 9, and Mary, age 7. Both children have lived with their mother since Mr. Greenbaum moved out of the house without making arrangements for them.

Mrs. Greenbaum has not asked for custody to punish Mr. Greenbaum. She has requested custody because she wants to keep the children and because she believes that such a grant would be in the best interest of the children. As Dr. Modlin stated in his report:

> Mrs. Greenbaum's motives in seeking custody are pure. She wants custody because she believes that only she can provide the loving and nurturing environment that young children need.

Affidavit of Dr. Modlin.

As you read these two arguments, note several things. First, each side has applied law to fact. They have not talked about just the law, and they have not talked about just the facts. Instead, they have used both the law and the facts to support their requests for custody.

Second, in making arguments, each attorney has presented the facts in the light most favorable to his or her client. The attorneys have emphasized those facts that support their arguments and de-emphasized those that do not. Also note that Mrs. Greenbaum's attorney has included facts that do not directly relate to the first factor. For example, he has stated that it was the father who left the family home.

Questions

1. Why did the attorney include the statement that it was the father who left home? Is it, in the context of the first factor, legally significant? If not, is it an emotionally significant fact? What inference is Mrs. Greenbaum's attorney asking the court to make?

2. In addition to including the statement that it is the father who left the family home, the mother's attorney has also included the names and ages of the children. Why did Mr. Jeffrey include these facts? Are they legally significant? Emotionally significant?

Finally, look at the language that each side uses. The packaging of an argument can be almost as important as the content. For example, note that while Mr. Greenbaum's attorney refers to Mrs. Greenbaum as "Mrs. Greenbaum," Mrs. Greenbaum's attorney refers to her as "the children's mother." This choice of labels was calculated. Although times are changing, many judges are still predisposed to grant the custody of young children to their mother. Consequently, while Mr. Greenbaum's attorney wants to de-emphasize the fact that Mrs. Greenbaum is the mother of young children, Mrs. Greenbaum's attorney wants to emphasize it.

Now let's look at the second factor. Neither child has stated a preference as to which parent he or she would like to live with, and there is nothing in the record that seems to support a finding that the children prefer, secretly or otherwise, one parent over the other.

Question

Because neither child has expressed a preference, how should the attorneys handle this factor? Should they discuss it, ignore it, or argue it?

We now move to the third factor, "the interaction and interrelationship of the child with his parent or parents, his siblings, and any other person who may significantly affect the child's best interests." For the moment, assume that Mr. Greenbaum's attorney has prepared the following drafts of her argument relating to the third factor.

EXAMPLE   **VERSION 1**

MR. GREENBAUM'S ARGUMENT

In deciding custody, the court must also consider "the child's interaction and interrelationship with his parent or parents, his siblings, and any other persons who may significantly affect the child's best interest." In this case, this factor weighs in favor of Mr. Greenbaum. It would, therefore, be in the best interests of the children to grant him custody.

EXAMPLE   **VERSION 2**

MR. GREENBAUM'S ARGUMENT

As the head of his own business, Mr. Greenbaum is able to set his own schedule. He can, therefore, stay at home with the children until they leave for school, and he can take time off to stay with the children when they are ill or to take them to the doctor or dentist. If granted custody, he would hire a housekeeper to care for the children in the afternoon and to clean the house, do the laundry, and prepare the evening meal.

Mr. Greenbaum sets high standards for both himself and his children. In addition, unlike Mrs. Greenbaum, he is consistent. He sets reasonable rules, and he enforces them calmly. Mr. Greenbaum also plays with the children on a regular basis, and he takes them camping and fishing.

In each of the versions set out above, Ms. Michael gives the judge only "half the package." In version 1, she sets out the law and her conclusion but does not give the judge the facts. In version 2, she sets out the facts but not the law or her conclusion.

Recognizing what she has done wrong, Ms. Michael writes another draft.

| EXAMPLE | VERSION 3 |

MR. GREENBAUM'S ARGUMENT

In deciding custody, the court must also consider "the child's interaction and interrelationship with his parent or parents, siblings, and any other person who may significantly affect the child's best interests." In this case, Mr. Greenbaum has an excellent relationship with his children. He interacts with both children: He frequently plays with both children, and he takes them camping and fishing. He has also established a good parent-child relationship.

He has also set high standards for both of his children, and he works to help them meet those standards. He is also a consistent disciplinarian. He has established fair rules and, unlike Mrs. Greenbaum, enforces those rules consistently and calmly.

In addition, Mr. Greenbaum has a flexible work schedule. In the morning, he can stay at home until the children leave for school, and when necessary, he can take time off to take them to the doctor or dentist. If granted custody, Mr. Greenbaum also plans to hire a housekeeper. The housekeeper would care for the children after school and, so that he could spend more time with the children, the housekeeper would also clean the house, do the laundry, and prepare the evening meal.

Because Mr. Greenbaum interacts well with his children and has a good parent-child relationship, this factor supports a finding that it would be in the best interests of the children to grant custody to Mr. Greenbaum.

This version is much better than the first two. Not only has Mr. Greenbaum's attorney set out the rules and facts, but she has also tied, or applied, specific parts of the rule to specific facts. For example, she has taken the word "interaction" from the statute and identified the facts that could be used to prove that Mr. Greenbaum interacts well with his children. "He interacts with both children: He frequently plays with both children, and he takes them camping and fishing." Similarly, she has taken the word "interrelationship" and identified the facts that could be used to prove that Mr. Greenbaum has a good relationship with his children.

Questions

Mr. Greenbaum's attorney talks about the statute in terms of the parent-child relationship. Is this what the legislature meant when it instructed the court to look at the child's interrelationship with his parent or parents? If you were Mrs. Greenbaum's attorney, how would you argue this portion of the statute?

You should also note that in arguing this factor, Mr. Greenbaum's attorney discusses Mr. Greenbaum's ability to care for the children. Although the statute does not explicitly call for such information, most judges want it and, because it relates to and perhaps determines a parent's interaction and relationship to the children, Ms. Michael decided to put the information here.

As an attorney, you will be required to make numerous tactical decisions. For example, in arguing the third factor, you would have to decide whether you wanted to discuss only Mr. Greenbaum's interaction and interrelationship with the children or whether you wanted to compare his interaction and interrelationship with that of Mrs. Greenbaum.

Questions

How would you have argued this factor? As Mr. Greenbaum's attorney, would you have discussed only Mr. Greenbaum's strengths? Only Mrs. Greenbaum's weaknesses? Both sides' strengths and weaknesses? What would you do if you were the attorney representing Mrs. Greenbaum?

We now turn to the rules set out in *Huen* and *Nabrinski.* What arguments would each side make? Are the ages of the children significant?

b.   Arguments Based on Analogous Cases

Because our system is one based on precedent, cases can be used in two ways: as the source, or authority, for a rule and as an example of how that rule has been applied in similar cases. If the earlier case is favorable, supporting the client's position, the attorney will emphasize the similarities between the two cases, arguing that because the client's case is like the earlier case, the court should reach the same result. In contrast, if the earlier case is unfavorable, the attorney will try to distinguish the earlier case, arguing that because the facts are different, the court should reach the opposite conclusion. See Exhibit 3.3.

In our sample problem, the cases seem to support Mrs. Greenbaum's position. Accordingly, in comparing her case to *Huen* and *Nabrinski,* her attorney emphasizes the similarities and de-emphasizes the differences.

EXAMPLE

MRS. GREENBAUM'S ARGUMENT

Our case is like *In re Marriage of Huen* and *In re Marriage of Nabrinski.* In both of these cases, the mother was the primary caregiver at the time of separation. In *Huen,* the mother took care of the children's day-to-day needs and supervised their medical care, schooling, and religious training. In *Nabrinski,* the mother supervised the children's after-school activities and homework and maintained the home, doing the cooking, cleaning, and shopping.

In our case, it is Mrs. Greenbaum, and not Mr. Greenbaum, who is the primary caregiver. Like the mothers in *Huen* and *Nabrinski,* Mrs. Greenbaum prepares the children for school and is with them after school and on school holidays. In addition, it is Mrs. Greenbaum who takes the children to the doctor and the dentist, attends school conferences, and shops for the children. Finally, it is Mrs. Greenbaum who maintains the home. Mrs. Greenbaum is the one who does the cleaning, the laundry, and the shopping.

In contrast, Mr. Greenbaum's attorney wants to distinguish the cases.

Exercise

Can Mr. Greenbaum use the analogous cases to his advantage? Write out the arguments that you think his attorney might make.

---

c.　Policy Arguments

The final type of argument is a policy argument. In addition to using policy in arguing the law, attorneys use policy in arguing the application

---

EXHIBIT 3.3	**Arguments Based on Analogous Cases**

The court reached the result that you want the court to reach in your case	*The court did not reach the result that you want the court to reach in your case*
• Emphasize similarities • De-emphasize similarities • Argue that because the cases are similar, the court should reach the same result	• De-emphasize similarities • Emphasize differences • Argue that because the differences are significant, the court need not reach the same result

of the law to the facts. Given the facts of this case, and our values, who should get custody? As a matter of public policy, should custody be given to a father who left the home without making arrangements for the children?

Exercise

1. Write out the policy arguments that you could make on behalf of your client.

2. Working with your group, prepare a five-minute oral argument in which you apply the law to the facts of the sample case. If you are representing the mother, argue that, given the facts, she should get custody. If you represent the father, argue that he should get custody. Note: Some groups will also be asked to play the role of the judge, asking questions and issuing a decision.

A Final Note

You now have at least some idea of what it means to think like a lawyer. You have seen how lawyers analyze statutes and cases and what types of arguments they make in arguing on behalf of their clients. The following chapters will help you develop these skills, explaining in more detail how lawyers research, analyze, argue, and write about legal problems.

Part II

Objective Memoranda, Client Letters, and Briefs

It is the side of lawyering that is seldom portrayed in novels or T.V. dramas. It is, however, how most lawyers spend most of their time. Instead of spending their days in court, they spend their days behind their desks, researching and writing.

In this part of the *Handbook,* we introduce you to three of the kinds of writing you will do as a lawyer. In Chapters 4, 5, and 6, we describe objective writing; in Chapter 7, advisory writing; and in Chapter 8, persuasive writing. In particular, we walk you through the process of writing three types of "documents": an objective in-house memorandum, a client letter, and an appellate brief. In the final chapter in this part, Chapter 9, we introduce you to oral advocacy.

Chapter 4

The Objective Memorandum: Its Purpose, Audience, and Format

If you work as a legal intern after your first year of law school, you will probably spend most of your time researching and writing objective memoranda, also known as office memos. An attorney will ask you to research a question, you will research it, and then you will present your research and analysis to the attorney in a written memo. The attorney who assigned the project will then read through your memo and, using the information contained in it, advise a client, negotiate with an opposing party, or prepare a brief or oral argument.

Thus, office memos are in-house memoranda that have as their primary audience attorneys in the office and that have as their primary purpose providing those attorneys with information. In addition, sometimes a copy of the memo is sent directly to the client, who will read it to determine what his or her options are.

Although the format of a memo will vary from law firm to law firm, most attorneys want the following sections: a heading, a statement of facts, a formal statement of the issue, a brief answer, a discussion section, and a formal conclusion.

Set out below are two memos written by first-year law students. As you read through them, ask yourself the following questions.

- What types of information are contained in the memos?
- In what order is that information presented?
- In presenting the information, what role did the students assume? Did they simply play the role of a "reporter," summarizing what they had found, or did they do more?

- What types of authority did the students cite? How did they use those authorities?
- Are the memos well written? Why or why not?

EXAMPLE 1

To: Connie Krontz

From: Thomas McMurty

Date: September 28, 1997

Re: Beaver Custom Carpets, File No. 97-478

Whether oral contract for three rugs is enforceable under Colorado's UCC Statute of Frauds exception for specially manufactured goods when the rugs have the Reutlinger family flower woven into them at one-foot intervals.

Statement of Facts

Our client, Beaver Custom Carpets (BCC), a Colorado corporation doing business in Colorado, wants to know whether it can enforce an oral contract for three rugs that were manufactured to the buyers' specifications.

The buyers, Mr. and Mrs. McKibbin, first contacted BCC in June of this year, asking whether BCC could replicate the original rugs in the Reutlinger Mansion, which Mr. and Mrs. McKibbin were refurbishing and turning into a bed and breakfast. Around the perimeter of each rug was a twelve-inch maroon strip; in the center was beige carpet with the Reutlinger family flower woven into the carpet at one-foot intervals.

After examining a picture of the rugs, BCC called its manufacturer. The manufacturer told BCC's sales representative that it could produce the rugs. Although the looms would have to be specially set, standard dyes could be used. On June 19, the sales representative sent the McKibbins a proposal setting out the specifications and the price, $16,875.

On June 29, Mrs. McKibbin called the sales representative and told him that she and her husband wanted to purchase the rugs. The next day, the salesperson ordered the rugs from the manufacturer. A written contract was not sent to the McKibbins.

On August 4, Mrs. McKibbin called BCC and told the sales representative that because her husband had fallen from the roof of the mansion, they were canceling their order. BCC called its manufacturer the same day. Unfortunately, the rugs had already been completed, and BCC was forced to accept delivery of the rugs at a cost of $13,500.

On August 15, BCC sent the McKibbins a bill for the proposal price of the rugs. Last week, BCC received a letter from the McKibbins' attorney stating that because the contract was not in writing, it was not enforceable under the UCC Statute of Frauds.

BCC sold the rugs to a wholesaler on September 1 for $10,000. BCC has done business with this wholesaler on one prior occasion. Similar rugs are not available from other carpet stores.

BCC is a specialty carpet firm that specializes in custom work. It has been in business for only one year and is in financial trouble.

Question Presented

Under Colorado's UCC Statute of Frauds exception for specially manufactured goods, Colo. Rev. Stat. § 4-2-201(3)(a), is an oral contract for the sale of rugs enforceable when (1) the rugs were manufactured to the buyers' specifications, (2) the same rugs are not available at other outlets, (3) the buyers told the seller that they did not want the rugs after the rugs had been completed, and (4) the seller sold the rugs to a wholesaler with whom it had done business on one prior occasion?

Brief Answer

Probably. Although the formal requirements of the Statute of Frauds are not met, the contract is probably enforceable under the exception for specially manufactured goods: To produce the rugs, the manufacturer had to specially set its looms, and the rugs were sold not to a retail customer but to a wholesaler at a loss.

Discussion

Specially manufactured goods are exempt from the writing requirement because the very nature of the goods serves as a reliable indication that a contract was indeed formed. When the goods conform to the special needs of a particular buyer and are not, therefore, suitable for sale to others, not only is the likelihood of a perjured claim diminished, but denying enforcement of such a contract would impose a substantial hardship on the aggrieved party. *See Colorado Carpet Installation, Inc. v. Palermo,* 668 P.2d 1384, 1390 (Colo. 1983). *Accord Impossible Electronics Techniques, Inc. v. Wackenhut Protective Systems, Inc.,* 669 F.2d 1026, 1037 (5th Cir. 1982).

Thus, even if the formal requirements of the UCC Statute of Frauds are not met, a contract is enforceable if the goods were specially manufactured. The applicable portion of the Colorado statute reads as follows.

(3) A contract which does not satisfy the requirements of subsection (1) but which is valid in other respects is enforceable

    (a) if the goods are to be specially manufactured for the buyer and are not suitable for sale to others in the ordinary course of the seller's business and the seller, before notice of repudiation is received and under circumstances which reasonably indicate that the goods are for the buyer, has made either a substantial beginning of their manufacture or commitments for their procurement; . . .

Colo. Rev. Stat. § 4-2-201(3)(a).

In our case, two of the elements are not likely to be in dispute. The rugs had been completed before notice of repudiation was received, and the flower woven into the rugs indicates that the rugs were made for the McKibbins. Two elements will, however, be in dispute. The parties will disagree about whether the rugs were specifically manufactured and about whether BCC was able to resell the rugs in the ordinary course of its business.

Specially Manufactured for the Buyer

Although the term "specially manufactured" is not defined in the statute, the Colorado Supreme Court has held that it refers to the nature of the goods and not to whether the goods were made in the usual course of the seller's business. *Colorado Carpet Installation, Inc. v. Palermo,* 668 P.2d 1384, 1390 (Colo. 1983).

In the only Colorado case discussing the exception for specially manufactured goods, the Colorado Supreme Court held that carpeting that was available from other carpet outlets and that had not been cut to unusual shapes or subjected to special dyeing, weaving, or other procedures was not specially manufactured. *Id.* In contrast, in a Virginia case, the Virginia Supreme Court held that wrapping material imprinted with the buyer's name and unique artwork and cut to the buyer's specifications was "specially manufactured because the wrapping material was personalized and of little value to a third party." *Flowers Baking Co. of Lynchburg, Inc. v. R-P Packaging, Inc.,* 329 S.E.2d 462, 464 (Va. 1985). *Accord Smith-Scarf Paper Co. v. P.N. Hirsch & Co. Stores, Inc.,* 754 S.W.2d 928 (Mo. Ct. App. 1988) (holding that cellophane imprinted with the defendant's logo and cut to the size specified by the defendant was specially manufactured.)

In the present case, BCC can argue that the rugs were specially manufactured for the buyer. Relying on the plain language of the statute, it argues that the rugs were in fact specially manufactured: BCC had to make special arrangements with the manufacturer and, to produce the rugs, the manufacturer had to specially set its looms.

BCC can also contrast the facts in its case to the facts in *Colorado Carpet.* Unlike *Colorado Carpet,* in this case, identical rugs are not available from other carpet outlets. The rugs in question are one-of-a-kind: They were made to fit specific rooms, and special weaving was required. The case is more like *Flowers*. Like the wrapping material, the rugs were personalized. The Reutlinger family flower is as distinctive as any company name or logo and, as a consequence, rugs with such a flower woven into them are of little value to a third party.

Finally, BCC can argue policy. In this instance, the rugs themselves are evidence that a contract was formed. BCC probably would not have produced rugs matching the original rugs in the Reutlinger Mansion had there not been a contract. In addition, if the court does not enforce the contract, BCC, a small business which is already in financial trouble, will suffer a substantial loss.

The McKibbins will argue that the rugs were not specially manufactured. Unlike *Flowers,* in this case it is only the Reutlinger family flower and not the Reutlinger name that is woven into the rugs. Furthermore, the flower is not particularly unusual; BCC was able to sell the rugs to a wholesaler with little or no difficulty.

The McKibbins' best argument is, however, a policy argument. They can argue that under the UCC, oral contacts should be the exception rather than the rule. Thus, a seller whose only business is custom or specially manufactured goods should not be exempt from the Statute of Frauds simply because its goods are specially manufactured. For, if all of such a seller's goods are custom, a written contract will never be necessary, and written contracts will become the exception and not the rule. In addition, the McKibbins can argue that a seller who deals in only custom goods is just as likely to fabricate a contract for custom goods as is a seller who deals in ready-made merchandise.

BCC can respond to such an argument by citing *Wackenhut,* a case in which the seller sold custom closed-circuit television cameras. In holding that the cameras were specially manufactured, the court said the fact that the seller is in the business of manufacturing custom-designed and -made goods does not necessarily preclude a finding that the goods are specially manufactured. *Id.* at 1037.

The court will probably find that the rugs were specially manufactured for the McKibbins. The rugs were not available from other outlets and, to produce the rugs, the manufacturer had to specially set its looms. Although BCC is in the business of producing custom carpets, it is not likely that it would have produced rugs with the Reutlinger family flower woven into them unless it had been requested to do so.

Not Suitable for Sale to Others in the Ordinary Course of the Seller's Business

In determining whether goods are suitable for sale to others in the ordinary course of the seller's business, the courts look first at the nature of the seller's business and then at whether the seller could reasonably be expected to find a buyer for the goods. *See*

Colorado Carpet Inc., 668 P.2d at 1391. For example, in *Colorado Carpet,* the court first identified the nature of Colorado Carpet's business, finding that its business was to purchase carpet from wholesalers and then to resell the carpet to retail purchasers at a price that included a labor charge for installation. It then looked at whether it was reasonable to expect that Colorado Carpet could resell the carpets. In holding that it was reasonable, the court considered three factors: (1) that Colorado Carpet dealt in similar carpets on a regular basis, (2) that the carpets were large enough that they could be cut to other dimensions, and (3) that Colorado Carpet had in fact been able to resell the carpets. It returned some of the carpet to the manufacturer and sold the rest to a local purchaser. *Id.* at 1391. Thus, the court found that the goods were suitable for sale to another in the ordinary course of Colorado Carpet's business and that the exception for specially manufactured goods did not apply.

BCC can argue that it was not able to sell the goods in the ordinary course of its business. Unlike Colorado Carpet, BCC does not deal in standard carpets in standard sizes and shapes. The individuals with whom BCC does business are looking for rugs designed to their specifications. In addition, the rugs cannot be altered to make them suitable for another customer. The rugs cannot be cut to another size or shape, and the colors and flower design cannot be changed. Finally, BCC can argue that it was not able to sell the goods to a retail customer. It had to resell them to the manufacturer.

The McKibbins will respond by arguing that BCC was able to resell the goods. While it did not resell them to a retail customer, it did resell them to a wholesale dealer with whom it had done business in the past. In addition, the facts do not indicate that BCC made any attempt to resell the rugs to a retail customer.

Because BCC's ordinary course of business is selling to retail customers and not wholesale companies, a court is likely to find that the rugs were not suitable for sale to others in the ordinary course of BCC's business. It is not reasonable to expect that BCC could find a retail customer that would want rugs in those sizes and colors and with that particular design.

Conclusion

Although the formal requirements of the UCC Statute of Frauds are not met, the contract between BCC and the McKibbins is probably enforceable under the exception for specially manufactured goods.

BCC should be able to prove the first element, that the rugs were specially manufactured for the McKibbins. The rugs were made to the McKibbins' specifications: The manufacturer specially set its looms to weave the Reutlinger family flower into the rugs.

BCC should also be able to prove the second element, that

the goods are not suitable for sale to others in the ordinary course of BCC's business. BCC's ordinary course of business is selling carpets to retail customers, not wholesalers.

The third element, that there had been a substantial beginning prior to repudiation, and the fourth element, that the evidence reasonably indicates that the goods were for the McKibbins, are not likely to be in dispute. The rugs had been completed at the time Mrs. McKibbins canceled the order, and the family flower is evidence that the goods were for the McKibbins.

Because it is likely that a court would enforce the contract, we should advise BCC to pursue this action. We can either contact the McKibbins' attorney and attempt to settle the matter or file a complaint.

EXAMPLE 2

To: Senior Partner

From: Summer Intern

Date: August 22, 1994

Re: Possible law suit against Martha and Marshall Erikson

Statement of Facts

Our clients, John and Ann Murray, want to know if they have a cause of action against Martha and Marshall Erikson for the death of their son, Peter, age 8.

The Murrays and Eriksons attend the same church. In late June of this year, the Eriksons invited church members to come to their property to picnic and pick raspberries. On July 2, 1994, the Murrays decided to accept the Eriksons' invitation and went, with their two children, to the Eriksons' property. When they arrived, they went to the house and talked for a few minutes with Mrs. Erikson. Mrs. Erikson then showed them the path that led to a small stream and the berry patch. Mrs. Erikson did not tell the Murrays that there was an abandoned apiary on the property or warn them that bees might be in the hives.

The Murrays walked to the raspberry patch, and all four members of the family picked together for about an hour. The family then went to the stream and ate a picnic lunch and played in the water. While the parents were resting alongside the stream, the children wandered into an open field and discovered the apiary.

Neither of the children had ever seen an apiary, and they did not know that bees might be inside. Peter began throwing rocks at the apiary and the bees began swarming, stinging both Peter and his then 10-year-old sister Laura.

When Mr. and Mrs. Murray heard their children's cries, they ran toward them. Although the Murrays were concerned, at this point they did not think that the stings were life-threatening. Five minutes later, though, Peter began having trouble breathing. Mr. Murray began carrying Peter to the house while Mrs. Murray ran ahead to call 911. Although the paramedics arrived within about 10 to 15 minutes, Peter died at the hospital from a severe allergic reaction. Because Peter had never been stung before, the Murrays did not know that he was allergic to bees and did not carry any medication.

The Eriksons own five acres of land in a rural area outside a small town. Until about five years ago, the Eriksons maintained the berry patch, orchard, apiary, and large gardens, using some of the produce for themselves and donating the surplus to the local food bank. Because of declining health, five years ago Mr. and Mrs. Erikson gave away the bees and started planting a much smaller garden. They had not been to the area where the apiary was located for at least a year and were not aware that bees had nested in it. The Eriksons did not charge the Murrays to use their land.

Mr. Erikson is 82 and a retired doctor, and Mrs. Erikson is 76 and a retired school teacher.

Question Presented

Whether the owners of five acres of land containing an orchard, berry patch, abandoned apiaries, and small stream are protected by Oregon Recreational Use of Private Lands Act when the owners did not warn a family that they invited onto the land to picnic and pick berries about an abandoned apiary and one of the family's children dies after being stung by bees that had, unbeknownst to the owners of the land, nested in the apiary.

Brief Answer

Probably. A court is likely to find that the Eriksons are protected under the Oregon Recreational Use of Private Lands Act. The Eriksons' land probably meets the definition of agricultural land and it is unlikely that the Eriksons' conduct in not warning the Murrays about the apiaries was willful, wanton, and reckless.

Discussion

Oregon's Public Recreational Use of Private Lands Act, Or. Rev. Stat. §§ 105.665-105.680 (1991), limits the liability of private landowners who allow the public to use their land for recreational purposes. In enacting this Act, the Oregon legislature hoped to encourage private landowners to make their lands available for public use. Or. Rev. Stat. § 106.660. The two sections that are applicable in this case are sections 105.665(2) and 105.675(1). The sections read as follow.

Or. Rev. Stat. § 105.665(2):

Except as provided in ORS[1] 105.675:

***

(2) An owner of land who either directly or indirectly invites or permits any person to use the land for any recreational purpose without charge does not thereby:
   (a) Extend any assurance that the land is safe for any purpose;
   (b) Confer upon such person the legal status of an invitee or licensee to whom a duty of care is owed; or
   (c) Assume reponsibility or incur liability for any injury, death or loss to any person or property caused by an act or omission of that person.

Or. Rev. Stat. § 105.675(1)

Nothing in ORS 105.655 to 105.680 limits in any way any liability to an owner of land
(1) for the willful, wanton and reckless failure of an owner of land to guard or warn against a known dangerous structure or other improvement or a known dangerous activity on the land.

In our case, several elements of Ore. Rev. Stat. § 105.665(2) are not likely to be in dispute. The Eriksons are the owners of the land, and they invited members of their church, including the Murrays, onto their land. In addition, the Murrays fall within the definition of persons, and they used the land for a recreational purpose—picnicking and picking berries—without charge. There is, however, likely to be a dispute as to whether the Eriksons' land falls within the definition of land and whether section 105.675(1) applies.

Does the Eriksons' Property Fall Within the Statutory Definition of Land?

Although some of the older cases indicate that the word "land" should be narrowly construed, in 1991, the legislature amended the statute expanding the definition. "Land" is now defined as follows.

(2) "Land" means agricultural land, range land, forest land, and land adjacent or contiguous to any bodies of water, watercourses, or the ocean shore . . . including roads, bodies of water, water-

---

1. While the *Bluebook* uses the abbreviation "Ore. Rev. Stat." for Oregon statutes, the Oregon Legislature uses ORS.

courses, private ways, private buildings and structures on such lands and machinery or equipment on the land when attached to the realty. . . .

Or. Rev. Stat. § 105.655(2) (Supp. 1992).

Unfortunately, the only Oregon case that discusses the definition of land is one decided prior to the most recent amendment. In that case, *Tijerina v. Cornelius Church,* 273 Or. 58, 539 P.2d 634 (1975), the defendant argued that its land was agricultural land because it produced vegetation normally grown for agricultural purposes, the vegetation was harvested, and the property was suitable for commercial farming. The plaintiff responded by arguing that the land was not agricultural land because the vegetation that grew on the land was not planted and was harvested not for agricultural reasons but to comply with fire regulations. The court agreed with the plaintiff, holding that because the land was not used for commercial farming, it did not fall within the definition of agricultural land. In doing so, the court stated that it is not enough that the land could be used for agricultural purposes; most of the land in Oregon could be put to such use. The statute should only apply when the land has recreational value "but may not be susceptible to adequate policing or correction of dangerous conditions." *Id.* at 636–37. There are no cases involving watercourses.

The Eriksons can make two arguments: that their land is agricultural land and, in the alternative, that their land is contiguous to a watercourse, specifically, a small stream. In arguing that their land is agricultural land, the Eriksons will distinguish *Tijerina.* Unlike the land in that case, their land is used for agricultural purposes. The land has fruit trees and a berry patch and until relatively recently it had a large garden and an apiary. In addition, unlike *Tijerina* in which the vegetation was harvested to comply with fire codes, in this case the fruit and berries are harvested and used by either the Eriksons or members of the community. In the alternative, the statute defines land as any land contiguous to "any watercourse." Because a stream runs through the Eriksons' land, it is contiguous to a watercourse.

In response to the Eriksons' first argument, the Murrays will respond that the land does not meet the definition of agricultural land because it is not being used for commercial farming, something that the court in *Tijerina* required. Like the defendants in *Tijerina,* the Eriksons have never sold what their land produces. Either they used the fruit, berries, and produce themselves, or they gave it away. What the Eriksons have is a large home garden and not a farm. In response to the Eriksons' second argument, the Murrays will argue that the small stream is not a waterway. Although the Act does not define waterway, the common definition of a waterway is "any body of water wide and deep enough for boats, ships, etc. . . ." *Webster's New World Dictionary* (3rd College Ed. 1988). There is nothing in the facts that indicates that the stream is wide or deep enough for a boat, let alone a ship. Finally, the Murrays will argue that the Act applies only when the land is not susceptible to adequate policing or correction of dangerous conditions. Because the Eriksons own only five acres either they, or someone acting on their behalf, could police the land and correct any dangers.

The Eriksons will counter by arguing that it should not, as a matter of public policy, matter whether they sell or give away the fruit, berries, and vegetables that their land produces. What should matter is that their land is being used for agricultural purposes. Thus, if their land is used to produce food, which it is, it falls within the statutory definition. In addition, the Eriksons will argue that the Murrays' definition of a waterway is too narrow. The first definition listed in *Webster's New World Dictionary* is "a channel or runnel along which water runs," *id.* at 1510, and a runnel is "a small stream, little brook, or rivulet," *id.* at 1175. Thus, the stream that runs through the Eriksons' property meets the definition of a waterway. Finally, the Eriksons will argue that because of their advanced age they are not able to police their land. It has been several years since they have been able to go to that portion of the land where the apiary is located.

Because the recent amendments to the statute indicate that the legislature intends that the definition of land be broadly construed, it is likely that a court would find that the Eriksons' property falls within the statutory definition of land. Although the Eriksons do not sell the fruit and berries that are grown on their land, the land is being used for agricultural purposes. In addition, although the stream is small, there is a good chance that the court would find that it falls within the definition of a waterway.

Does Section Or. Rev. Code § 105.675(1) Apply?

As initially enacted, Section 105.675(1) made landowners liable when their conduct was reckless.

> Or. Rev. Stat. § 105.675(1)
>
> Nothing in ORS 105.655 to 105.680 limits in any way any liability of an owner of land
> (1) for the reckless failure of an owner of land to guard or warn against a known dangerous structure or other improvement or a known dangerous activity on the land
>
> 1971 Or. Laws c. 780 § 5.

The statute was, however, amended in 1987 and the words "willful, wanton, and reckless" were substituted for the word "reckless."

Although there have been no cases since the statute was amended, in a case decided prior to the amendment the court held that the correct test for recklessness is the one set out in Restatement (Second) of Torts § 500 (1975). *Van Gordon v. Portland General Electric,* 294 Or. 763, 764, 662 P.2d 716, 717 (1983). Under the Restatement, conduct is reckless

> if a person does an act or intentionally fails to do an act which it is his duty to do, knowing or having reason to know of facts which would lead a reasonable man to realize, not only that his conduct creates an unreasonable risk of physical harm to another, but also that such risk is substantially greater than that which is necessary to make his conduct negligent.

The Murrays must, however, do more than prove recklessness. They must also prove that the Eriksons' conduct was willful and wanton. Although there are no current cases defining willful and wanton, in an early case, *Falls v. Mortensen,* 207 Or. 130, 295 P.2d 182 (1956), the court adopted the definition of "willful, wanton, or reckless" set out in 38 Am Jur. 855, Negligence § 178.

> A defendant's act is properly characterized as willful, wanton, or reckless only when it was apparent, or reasonably should have been apparent, to the defendant that the result was likely to prove disastrous to the plaintiff, and he acted with such an indifference toward, or utter disregard of, such a consequence that it can be said he was willing to perpetrate it. The elements necessary to characterize an injury as wantonly or willfully inflicted are (1) knowledge of a situation requiring the exercise of ordinary care and diligence to avert injury to another, (2) ability to avoid the resulting harm by ordinary care and diligence in the use of the means at hand, and (3) the omission of such care and diligence to avert the threatened danger, when to the ordinary mind it must be apparent that the result is likely to prove disastrous to another.
> *Id.* at 131.

In the only case applying the "reckless" test, the court held that the defendant was reckless in not warning the plaintiff about the dangers posed by hot springs. *Van Gordon v. Portland General Electric,* 294 Or. 761, 662 P.2d 714 (1983). Specifically, the court found (1) that defendant knew that a dangerously hot pool could be adjacent to a warm pool and that people, unaware of the dangerously high temperatures of some of the pools, had been, in the past, burned; (2) that the danger could have been eliminated by educating the public and posting additional warning signs, and (3) that the plaintiff, a child, was severely burned. *Id.* at 764, 662 P.2d at 717–718. There are no cases applying the willful and wanton test.

In the Eriksons' case, the Murrays will argue that the Eriksons' conduct was willful, wanton, and reckless. Just as the defendant in *Van Gordon* knew that some of the pools were dangerously hot, the Eriksons knew that the abandoned apiary was near the raspberry patch and, having kept bees in the past, the Eriksons either knew or should have known that there was a good chance the bees would nest in the hives. In addition, just as the defendant in *Van Gordon* could have eliminated the danger by warning the public, the Eriksons could have avoided the danger by warning the Murrays. Finally, as in *Van Gordon,* the Eriksons should have known that failure to warn could have disastrous results.

The Eriksons can respond by arguing that their conduct was not reckless, let alone willful and wanton. Unlike *Van Gordon* in which the defendants knew that others had been injured, in this case the Eriksons did not even know that there were bees in the hives. Furthermore, in this case it would have been almost impossible to avoid the harm. Even if the Eriksons had removed the hives, bees would have been on the property. It is not uncommon for wild bees to nest in the ground or in a tree stump. In addition, warning the Murrays that there might be bees on the land would have had little value given the fact that the Murrays did not know that their son was allergic to bees. Finally, as a matter of public policy, this is not a case in which liability should be imposed. If landowners are going to open their land to the public, they must not be held liable for injuries resulting from objects naturally on the land, particularly when those objects do not usually pose a danger to an individual.

A court is not likely to find that the Eriksons' conduct was willful, wanton, and reckless. Although the Eriksons should have known that bees were on their land, they did not know that they posed a danger to the Murrays. In addition, there is little that the Eriksons could have done to prevent the harm given that bees are common on agricultural land. Because no one knew that Peter was allergic, a warning that there were bees would not have prevented his death.

Conclusion

More likely than not the Eriksons are protected under Oregon's Recreational Use of Private Lands Act. The Eriksons invited the Murrays onto their land, the Murrays used the land for recreational purposes, and the Eriksons did not charge the Murrays. In addition, a court is likely to find that the Eriksons' land is agricultural land. Although the land is not being used for commercial farming, it is being used to produce food. In the alternative, even if the court does not find that the land is agricultural land, it may find that it falls within the protection of the statute because a small stream runs through the property. Finally, it is unlikely that a court would find that the Eriksons' conduct was willful, wanton, and reckless. The Eriksons did not know about the bees and, even if they did, their failure to remove the hives or warn the Murrays is not likely to have prevented the harm given the fact that bees are common on agricultural land and no one knew that Peter was allergic to bees.

Chapter 5

The First Memorandum

In this chapter we show you how to write a relatively simple objective memorandum. Specifically, we show you how to locate the applicable statutes and cases, how to analyze and synthesize those statutes and cases, and how to draft, revise, and edit the statement of facts, question presented, brief answer, discussion section, and formal conclusion. A copy of the completed memo is set out at the end of the chapter.

As you read through the chapter, keep several things in mind. First, remember that the process of researching and writing an objective memorandum is a recursive one. Thus, although we show you how to write the sections in the order that they will appear in the final draft, they do not need to be written in that order. Many attorneys write the question presented, brief answer, or discussion section before drafting the statement of facts. Second, remember to use the other chapters in this book. Chapters 1 through 3 explain our legal system, how attorneys create arguments, and how to read and analyze statutes and cases; Chapters 10 through 18 provide additional information about legal research; and Chapters 19 through 29 show you how to write effectively and correctly. In addition, the next chapter, Chapter 6, provides additional information about writing memos.

Finally, remember that writing an objective memorandum is a difficult task that can take years to master. To do a good job, you must know not only the law itself but also how attorneys and judges think and talk about that law. While we can teach you some of the standard moves, much of what you need to know can be learned only through practice. Just as it takes years to become an expert physician, musician, or athlete, it takes years to become an expert lawyer.

§5.1   Getting the Assignment

For the purposes of this chapter, presume that you are a legal intern at a mid-sized general practice firm in Boston, Massachusetts. On your first day on the job, the attorney to whom you have been assigned hands you the following memo.

EXAMPLE

To: Legal Intern

From: William Pariso

Date: September 1, 1998

Re: Case No. 98-478
        Eliza Johnson v. Elite Insurance

One of our long-time clients, Elite Insurance, has been contacted by an attorney representing one of its former employees, Eliza Johnson. Elite Insurance referred the call to me, and this morning I talked with Ms. Kim, the attorney representing Ms. Johnson.

Ms. Kim alleges that Elite Insurance violated the Electronic Communications Privacy Act of 1986 when it recorded telephone conversations between her client, Ms. Johnson, and another individual, Mark Porter. Specifically, Ms. Kim alleges that Elite Insurance violated 18 U.S.C. § 2511 when it recorded Ms. Johnson's conversations without her consent. The facts, as related to me by Ms. Kim, are as follows:

- On August 19, 1998, one of Elite Insurance's office managers, Tom Wilson, called Ms. Johnson into his office and told her that she was being fired because she had violated company policy by using the office telephones for personal business. He then disclosed the fact that he had been monitoring Ms. Johnson's phone calls for the last four or five weeks and had overheard conversations between Ms. Johnson and an individual named Mark Porter that indicated that the two were having an affair.
- Ms. Johnson did not explicitly consent, either orally or in writing, to the monitoring of her phone calls and did not know that her phone calls with Mr. Porter were being monitored. Had she known, she would not have had the same conversations.
- As of this date, Johnson has not found another position. In addition, Ms. Johnson's husband has left her and is considering filing for divorce.

I have also talked to Eric Wilson at Elite Insurance. He gave me the following information.

- Mr. Wilson did, in fact, monitor and record Ms. Johnson's phone calls by attaching a recorder to an extension phone. He began recording them in mid-July and stopped a day or two before he fired Ms. Johnson.
- Mr. Wilson began monitoring Ms. Johnson's phone calls because he had information that indicated that Ms. Johnson was part of an insurance fraud scheme.
- At the time that Ms. Johnson was hired, she was told that the phones and computers should be used for business purposes only. In addition, she was told that Elite would periodically monitor her phone calls to ensure that she was providing good service.
- When customers call Elite, they hear a message that tells them that their phone call may be monitored.
- Mr. Wilson says that, because he is so busy, he seldom monitors his employees' phone calls. Once an employee is trained, he usually listens in only two or three times a year, usually immediately before their annual performance evaluation. Although he does not tell employees which calls he will be monitoring, he usually discusses the calls with them immediately afterwards. Before the monitoring in question, Ms. Wilson had last monitored two or three of Ms. Johnson's calls in January 1998 as part of her annual performance review.
- Mr. Wilson also said that despite the company policy, employees regularly use the phones for personal business, for example, to check on their children or to make doctor appointments. As long as these calls are short, they are tolerated.
- Ms. Johnson worked for Elite Insurance from January 1996 until she was terminated. Her performance evaluations were average or slightly below average. In listening to Ms. Johnson's phone calls, Mr. Wilson did not hear anything that led him to believe that Ms. Johnson was engaged in insurance fraud. He did, however, overhear conversation indicating that Johnson was having an affair.
- Elite Insurance employs about 250 people in eight states. The company is doing well financially.

Although it appears that Elite Insurance did willfully use a mechanical device to intercept a wire communication, see § 2511(1)(a), one of the exceptions may apply. I would like you to research the consent exception. I'll have someone else research the business use exception. If Ms. Johnson files suit, it would be in the United States District Court for the District of Massachusetts.

A. PREWRITING

Just as the artist begins "painting" long before paint is put on canvas, the writer begins "writing" long before the first word is put on paper. The artistic process begins with an image, an idea, or an insight that is shaped and then reworked many times before the project is finished. The writing process begins with a question that is focused and refocused through research and analysis.

In both instances, the process takes place in context. The artist's work is influenced by training, by the expectations of the artistic community, and by the reactions of viewers to past works. Similarly, your work will be shaped by your knowledge of the law, the conventions governing both the format and content of a legal memorandum, and your understanding of your readers and how they will use the memo.

Thus, like the artist, you begin work with a vision, although it may be a preliminary one. Although you do not yet know what the final product will look like, you have an idea of where you want to go. You know the attorney's question, the types of information the attorney needs, and how the memo will be used. All of this information is your touchstone, your point of reference, and as such can guide most if not all of the decisions you make throughout the writing process.

§5.2 PREPARING A RESEARCH PLAN

Upon receiving a memo like the one set out above, you should do three things. First, read the memo carefully, making sure that you understand both the facts and what it is that the attorney wants you to do. Second, ask questions. For example, ask the attorney how much time you should spend on the project and when it is due. Third, prepare a research plan.

Although a research plan can be either written or "in your head," at first it is a good idea to have it in writing. The first step in preparing such a plan is to determine whether the problem is governed by state or federal law and by enacted or common law. You should then draft a preliminary issue statement, a list of search terms, and a list of the sources that you plan to check and the order in which you plan to check them.

§5.2.1 Determining What Law Applies

The first step is to determine whether the issue is governed by state or federal law and by enacted or common law. In our sample case, this step is easy: opposing counsel has told us that her client is seeking relief under a federal statute, 18 U.S.C. § 2511.

In other cases, this step may be more difficult. For example, you might not know whether a case involving employment discrimination is governed by state or federal law or whether a case involving a claim of adverse possession is governed by enacted or common law. In such instances, start by asking questions. For example, ask the assigning attorney whether he or she knows what law governs. If he or she doesn't, either do some general background reading to familiarize yourself with the area of law, see section 15.1, or begin your research by looking for a federal statute, second for a state statute, and third for state common law.

§5.2.2   Drafting a Preliminary Issue Statement

Good research begins with a good preliminary issue statement. Although you will not be able to draft the final version of the issue statement until after you have completed your research, by drafting a preliminary one now, you force yourself to focus. What is it that you have been asked to research?

The issue can usually be stated broadly or narrowly, or it can find its focus somewhere in between.

EXAMPLES

1. Does one of the exceptions to 18 U.S.C. § 2511 apply?
2. Did Ms. Johnson explicitly consent to the monitoring of her phone calls?
3. Under the Electronic Communications Privacy Act, did Eliza Johnson consent to the monitoring of her phone calls when, at the time she was hired, she was told that the phones should be used for business purposes only and that her phone calls would be periodically monitored to ensure good customer service?

The first example is too broad. The attorney did not ask you to research all of the exceptions; he asked you to research only the consent exception. In contrast, the second example is too narrow because it asks only about explicit consent. As you will see when we look at the cases, consent may be either explicit or implied. The final example, example 3, is the best of the three. It is neither too broad nor too narrow, and it identifies the facts that are likely to be important in deciding whether Ms. Johnson consented.

§5.2.3   Preparing a List of Search Terms

After you have drafted your preliminary issue statement, the next step is to prepare a list of search terms, that is, a list of words and phrases that can be used to locate the law.

The major publishing companies suggest two different strategies for developing such lists. One recommends listing words describing (1) the parties involved, (2) the places where the facts arose and the objects and things involved, (3) the acts or omissions that gave rise to the legal action or issue, (4) the defense to the action or issue, and (5) the relief sought. The other recommends looking up descriptive words that suggest the Thing, the Act, the Person, or the Place involved (TAPP).

Using a combination of these two techniques, you might come up with the following list of search terms.

Electronic Communications Privacy Act
consent
phone calls
employer-employee
intercepting phone calls
monitoring phone calls
recording phone calls

§5.2.4   Selecting the Sources You Want to Check

The final step is to determine which sources you are going to check and the order in which you are going to check them.

When you are asked to research a statutory question, you will usually want to start your research by locating the statute itself.[1] After you have found the statute, you will then want to locate cases that are factually similar to yours that have applied or interpreted the statute. Finally, you will want to "cite check" the cases to determine whether they are still good law and to locate additional cases that are on point. The following research plan shows the sources that you would want to look at in researching our sample problem and the order in which you would want to consult them.

---

1. There are times, however, when you may want to start your research by doing some background reading in a secondary source. For example, you may want to do background reading if you do not know whether an issue is governed by federal or state law or by enacted or common law. In addition, even when you know the answers to these questions, you may want to do background reading when the problem is complex and you are unfamiliar with the area. See Chapter 15 for a description of sources you could consult.

EXAMPLE

SAMPLE RESEARCH PLAN

Jurisdiction: Federal

Type of Law: Enacted law

Preliminary Issue Statement:

Under the Electronic Communications Privacy Act, did Eliza Johnson consent to the monitoring of her phone calls when, at the time she was hired, she was told that the phones should be used for business purposes only and that her phone calls would be periodically monitored to ensure good customer service?

Search Terms:

Electronic Communications Privacy Act
consent
phone calls
employer-employee
intercepting phone calls
monitoring phone calls
recording phone calls

Step 1: Locate 18 U.S.C. § 2511.

Step 2: Locate version of 18 U.S.C. § 2511 in effect at the time cause of action arose.

Step 3: Locate that portion of 18 U.S.C. § 2511 that deals with consent and determine which elements are likely to be in dispute.

Step 4: Look for statutory definitions.

Step 5: Read through the notes of decision following section 2511, identifying the cases that appear to be most useful.

Step 6: Locate the cases in the appropriate federal reporter, and read the relevant portion(s) of each case.

Step 7: Cite check the cases to determine (1) whether the cases are still good law and (2) whether there are any additional cases.

Step 8: Look up and, if appropriate, cite check any additional cases.

Step 9: Locate law review articles and other commentaries that might be on point.

---

§5.3   Researching the Problem

Research plan in hand, you can now head for the library.

Step 1: Locate 18 U.S.C. § 2511

Federal statutes can be found in one of four print sources: the Statutes at Large, the United States Code (U.S.C.), the United States Code Annotated (U.S.C.A.), and the United States Code Service (U.S.C.S.) In addition, federal statutes are available on several CD-ROM products, on LEXIS and Westlaw, and on the internet.

In the Statutes at Large, federal acts are set out in the order that they were enacted. For example, an act signed into law on January 24, 1998, precedes an act signed into law on January 25, 1998. Because the Statutes at Large use a chronological rather than a topical organizational scheme, they are not usually the best source. Unless you are doing a legislative history or looking for a statute that is no longer in effect, the better source is a code.

In a code, the statutes that are currently in effect are grouped by topic. For example, all the statutes relating to the military are placed under one title, those relating to the federal tax code under another, and those relating to education or social and health services under still another. As legislation is passed relating to one of these topics, the code is revised to show the changes.

The official version of the federal code is the United States Code, which is published by the United States Printing Office. In it are the text of all the federal statutes, arranged by title and section numbers, and legislative history notes. There are also two unofficial versions of the code: United States Codes Annotated and United States Code Service. Both sets have the following: the text of the United States Constitution, the text of the federal statutes currently in effect, historical notes for each statute, notes of decision, and tables of cases. In addition, the United States Code Annotated contains references to West's key number system and cross-references to other West materials, and United States Code Service contains references to applicable A.L.R. annotations and other books in the American Jurisprudence series. See section 12.1.2.

If you are using the print versions of these codes, you can locate a particular statutory section in one of three ways. If you know the number of the applicable statute, you can go directly to the volume that contains that title and section number. If you don't know the section number, you can locate that number using either the popular names table or the subject index. If you are using a CD-ROM product or an online source, you can search either by typing in the statutory number or, if you do not know the number, terms and product-appropriate connectors.

In our example case, you decide to use the print version of the United States Code Annotated because it is the set that is in the firm library. Because you know the citation to the applicable statute, you go

---

EXHIBIT 5.1 | United States Code 18 § 2511

Ch. 119   WIRE INTERCEPTION, ETC.   **18 § 2511**

Library References

Telecommunications ☞491 et seq.

C.J.S. Telegraphs, Telephones, Radio, and Television §§ 287, 288.

Notes of Decisions

Generally 2
Retroactive effect 1

Sanitary Corp., D.C.Pa.1968, 288 F.Supp. 701.

---

1. Retroactive effect

This chapter applies only prospectively. U. S. v. American Radiator & Standard

2. Generally

This chapter is directed to reliability components of confession-exclusion rules, not to extrinsic policy components. U. S. v. Schipani, D.C.N.Y.1968, 289 F.Supp. 43.

§ 2511. Interception and disclosure of wire or oral communications prohibited

(1) Except as otherwise specifically provided in this chapter any person who—

(a) willfully intercepts, endeavors to intercept, or procures any other person to intercept or endeavor to intercept, any wire or oral communication;

(b) willfully uses, endeavors to use, or procures any other person to use or endeavor to use any electronic, mechanical, or other device to intercept any oral communication when—

(i) such device is affixed to, or otherwise transmits a signal through, a wire, cable, or other like connection used in wire communication; or

(ii) such device transmits communications by radio, or interferes with the transmission of such communication; or

(iii) such person knows, or has reason to know, that such device or any component thereof has been sent through the mail or transported in interstate or foreign commerce; or

(iv) such use or endeavor to use (A) takes place on the premises of any business or other commercial establishment the operations of which affect interstate or foreign commerce; or (B) obtains or is for the purpose of obtaining information relating to the operations of any business or other commercial establishment the operations of which affect interstate or foreign commerce; or

(v) such person acts in the District of Columbia, the Commonwealth of Puerto Rico, or any territory or possession of the United States;

EXHIBIT 5.1   *(continued)*

.h. 119   **WIRE INTERCEPTION, ETC.**   **18 § 2511**

.ttack or other hos ile acts of a foreign power, to obtain foreign
ntelligence information deemed essential to the security of the Unit-
·d States, or to protect national security information against foreign
:ntelligence activities.   Nor shall anything contained in this chapter
·e deemed to limit the constitutional power of the President to take
·uch measures as he deems necessary to protect the United States
..zainst the overthrow of the Government by force or other unlawful
:~eans, or against any other clear and present danger to the struc-
·ure or existence of the Government.   The contents of any wire or
·ral communication intercepted by authority of the President in the
.xercise of the foregoing powers may be received in evidence in any
·rial hearing, or other proceeding only where such interception was
·easonable, and shall not be otherwise used or disclosed except as
:s necessary to implement that power.

Added Pub.L. 90–351, Title III, § 802, June 19, 1968, 82 Stat. 213.

Historical Note

References in Text.   Chapter 5 of title
4.7 of the United States Code, referred to
in par. (2) (b), is chapter 5 of Title 47,
Telegraphs, Telephones, and Radiotele-
graphs.   Such chapter 5, set out as section 151 et seq. of Title 47, is the Communications Act of 1934.

Section 605 of the Communications Act
of 1934 (48 Stat. 1143; 47 U.S.C. 605), re-

ferred to in par. (3), is section 605 of Title
47, Telegraphs, Telephones, and Radiotel-
egraphs.

Legislative History.   For legislative
history and purpose of Pub.L. 90–351, see
1968 U.S.Code Cong. and Adm.News, p.
2112.

Library References

Telecommunications ⬳491, 493, 494.

C.J.S. Telegraphs, Telephones, Radio,
and Television §§ 122, 252, 287, 288.

Notes of Decisions

Crimes   3
Enforcement   2
Probable cause   1

_____

1. Probable cause

General rule, under this chapter prohibiting unauthorized electronic surveillance,
is that eavesdropping and wiretapping
are permitted only with probable cause
and a warrant. Alderman v. U. S., Colo.
& N.J.1969, 89 S.Ct. 961, 394 U.S. 165, 22 L.
Ed.2d 176, rehearing denied 89 S.Ct. 1177,
394 U.S. 939, 22 L.Ed.2d 475.

2. Enforcement

Without experience showing the contrary Supreme Court should not assume

that this chapter prohibiting unauthorized electronic surveillance will be cavalierly disregarded or will not be enforced
against transgressors. Alderman v. U. S.,
Colo. & N.J.1969, 89 S.Ct. 961, 394 U.S. 165,
22 L.Ed.2d 176, rehearing denied 89 S.Ct.
1177, 394 U.S. 939, 22 L.Ed.2d 475.

3. Crimes

Telephone subscriber is not authorized
to use his telephone to commit a crime.
State v. Holliday, Iowa 1969, 169 N.W.2d
768.

EXHIBIT 5.1   *(continued)*

CRIMES AND CRIMINAL PROCEDURE   18 § 2511

Note 5

Where telephone company maintained testboard where trouble reports from customers were handled and use of board by employees was monitored by supervisors for purpose of service quality control checks and, in plaintiff employee's case, for purpose of preventing his persistent use of testboard phone for personal calls, against which he had been warned several times, company's legitimate interest in maintaining quality control and availability of lines brought its monitoring activities within exception from prohibition against interception of wire communications, contained in this section. Simmons v. Southwestern Bell Tel. Co., W.D.Okla. 1978, 452 F.Supp. 392, affirmed 611 F.2d 342.

Homeowners could not amend trespass complaint to allege violation of wiretapping statutes by television broadcaster, where broadcaster's employee purportedly entered home as veterinary student and secretly videotaped events in home which were subsequently broadcast, as broadcaster intercepted communication for commercial purposes, not purpose of committing tortious act or trespass. Copeland v. Hubbard Broadcasting, Inc., Minn.App.1995, 526 N.W.2d 402, review denied.

3e. Willfully

For purposes of provision of statute making it crime to willfully intercept any wire or oral communication, person acts "willfully" if he knowingly or recklessly disregards known legal duty. Farroni v. Farroni, C.A.6 (Ohio) 1988, 862 F.2d 109.

Civil liability for allegedly unlawful wiretapping required proof of criminal willfulness; "willfully" within meaning of criminal prohibition against interception of wire or oral communication required employee in civil action to show intentional or reckless disregard of legal obligations by employer. Malouche v. JH Management Co., Inc., C.A.4 (S.C.) 1988, 839 F.2d 1024.

Term "willfully" as used in this section has the same meaning whether liability is imposed criminally or civilly; thus, neither civil nor criminal liability can be established against any defendant without showing that he acted with intentional or reckless disregard of his legal obligations. Citron v. Citron, C.A.2 (N.Y.) 1983, 722 F.2d 14, certiorari denied 104 S.Ct. 2350, 466 U.S. 973, 80 L.Ed.2d 823.

Wife's allegation that husband, caused electronic recording device to be installed on her phone and took tape recordings of conversation between wife and third parties was sufficient to raise question as to whether husband acted intentionally or in reckless disregard of his legal obligations and thus sufficiently pleaded "willfulness" of husband's conduct to survive motion to dismiss action pursuant to electronic surveillance provisions of Omnibus Crime Control and Safe Streets Act, where complaint alleged that husband played tapes thus obtained for persons other than his attorney. Nations v. Nations, W.D.Ark.1987, 670 F.Supp. 1432.

Civil action under federal statutes prohibiting illegal wiretaps or other electronic surveillance could be brought against media defendants who, although they did not participate in illegal surveillance, allegedly knew that recorded conversations they were given had been illegally obtained. Natoli v. Sullivan, N.Y.Sup.1993, 606 N.Y.S.2d 504, 159 Misc.2d 681, affirmed 616 N.Y.S.2d 318, 206 A.D.2d 841, leave to appeal denied.

3f. Intent

Criminal and civil liability is imposed under federal-wiretapping statute upon proof that defendant intentionally intercepted oral communications at issue, without showing of disregard of known legal duty, at least to those communications to which he was not party. Earley v. Smoot, D.Md.1994, 846 F.Supp. 451.

Husband's record of telephone conversations of his wife violated federal wiretapping law, even though husband claimed that he was not aware that interception was illegal; law required only that act of recording be intentional, without regard to motive. Young v. Young, Mich.App. 1995, 536 N.W.2d 254, 211 Mich.App. 446.

3g. Knowledge

Attorney for fire insurer was not liable in damages to insureds, under federal wiretap statute, for having made use of allegedly illegally obtained tape recording in attempt to establish that insureds had committed fraud in connection with their claim; attorney had no knowledge of facts tending to show that tape recording was illegally obtained and federal court presiding over insurance claim had allowed recording into evidence. Hamed v. Pfeifer, Ind.App. 3 Dist. 1995, 647 N.E.2d 669.

4. Discovery

In civil action for allegedly intercepting, tape recording, and threatening to disclose contents of plaintiffs' personal telephone conversations in violation of this chapter, admission by one defendant to intercepting and recording some of plaintiffs' telephone conversations did not establish the illegality of the interception and recording so as to prohibit, under this section, disclosure of recordings to defendants' attorney, as it could not be determined whether he might effectively invoke a statutory exception to the recording, such as consent. McQuade v. Michael Gassner Mechanical & Elec. Contractors, Inc., D.C.Conn.1984, 587 F.Supp. 1183.

5. Consent

U. S. v. Merritts, E.D.Ill.1975, 387 F.Supp. 807, [main volume] reversed 527 F.2d 713.

Pretrial detainee impliedly consented to audiotaping of his telephone calls from detention center, and, thus, consent exception applied under provision of Title III of Omnibus Crime Control and Safe Streets Act prohibiting intentional use of any electronic, mechanical, or other device to intercept any oral communication; detainee signed consent form and was given prison manual a few days after his arrival, and detention center posted signs above telephones warning of monitoring and taping. U.S. v. Van Poyck, C.A.9 (Cal.) 1996, 77 F.3d 285, certiorari denied 117 S.Ct. 276.

Consent to have telephone communications intercepted should not casually be inferred, but rather surrounding circumstances must convincingly show that party knew about and consented to interception in spite lack of formal notice or deficient formal notice, in determining whether

EXHIBIT 5.1   *(continued)*

---

18 § 2511   CRIMES AND CRIMINAL PROCEDURE
Note 5

intercepted telephone conversations are admissible. U.S. v. Lanoue, C.A.1 (R.I.) 1995, 71 F.3d 966.

Employer's interception of employee telephone calls did not come within consent exception to federal and Maine wiretapping laws; although intercepted corporate officer was told that employee calls would be monitored, officer was not told of manner in which monitoring was conducted or that he himself would be monitored. Williams v. Poulos, C.A.1 (Me.) 1993, 11 F.3d 271.

"Consent to use" defense did not apply to defendant who represented husband in divorce action and who allegedly improperly used wife's recorded telephone conversations in connection with divorce action. U.S. v. Wuliger, C.A.6 (Ohio) 1992, 981 F.2d 1497, rehearing denied 999 F.2d 1090, certiorari denied 114 S.Ct. 1298, 510 U.S. 1191, 127 L.Ed.2d 647, rehearing denied 114 S.Ct. 1872, 128 L.Ed.2d 492.

Employee's consent to tape recording of intercepted telephone calls could not be implied, so as to exempt employer from liability for violating wire and electronic communications interception provisions of the Omnibus Crime Control and Safe Streets Act, merely because employer warned employee that calls may be monitored to cut down on personal use of telephone, or because extension telephone was located in owners' residence. Deal v. Spears, C.A.8 (Ark.) 1992, 980 F.2d 1153.

District court, ruling on suppression motion, did not clearly err in its factual finding that police informant's consent to recording of his telephone conversation with drug supplier was not coerced; police officer denied threatening informant with prosecution of his girlfriend, and DEA agent's testimony furnished evidence that informant cooperated out of desire for leniency for himself. U.S. v. Wake, C.A.5 (Tex.) 1991, 948 F.2d 1422, certiorari denied 112 S.Ct. 2944, 504 U.S. 975, 119 L.Ed.2d 569.

Consent required for admissibility of tape recording is question of fact to be determined from totality of circumstances, and court need not submit consent issue to jury after making initial determination of admissibility. U.S. v. Gomez, C.A.5 (Tex.) 1991, 947 F.2d 737, certiorari denied 112 S.Ct. 1504, 503 U.S. 947, 117 L.Ed.2d 642.

Although right at stake in an exclusionary hearing to prevent admission of conversations recorded in violation of federal wiretapping restrictions is statutory, not constitutional, Fourth Amendment precedents determine whether party to communication consented to an interception within meaning of statute. U.S. v. Antoon, C.A.3 (Pa.) 1991, 933 F.2d 200, rehearing denied, certiorari denied 112 S.Ct. 300, 502 U.S. 907, 116 L.Ed.2d 243.

Where Government made recording of conversation between defendant and government informant with consent and cooperation of informant, there was no need to inform defendant or to obtain court order. U.S. v. Barone, C.A.2 (N.Y.) 1990, 913 F.2d 46.

Tenant consented to his landlady's recording of his telephone calls and, therefore, her interception of calls did not violate federal wiretapping statute; landlady repeatedly informed tenant that all of her incoming calls were being monitored and that blanket admonishment left no room for tenant to wonder whether his calls would be intercepted. Griggs-Ryan v. Smith, C.A.1 (Me.) 1990, 904 F.2d 112.

Absent evidence that arrestee who agreed to telephone defendant knew that call was being monitored, Government failed to carry burden of establishing consent to taping of call, as required for admission of tape under federal wiretap statute. U.S. v. Gomez, C.A.5 (Tex.) 1990, 900 F.2d 43, rehearing denied.

Electronic surveillance of attorney did not violate federal communications interception statute where one of parties to conversation had consented to interception; accordingly, police officers could not be held liable in civil rights action brought by attorney arising out of interception. Lewellen v. Raff, C.A.8 (Ark.) 1988, 843 F.2d 1103, rehearing denied 851 F.2d 1108, certiorari denied 109 S.Ct. 1171, 489 U.S. 1033, 103 L.Ed.2d 229.

Inmates impliedly consented to interception of their telephone calls by using prison telephones when they were on notice of the prison's interception policy from at least four sources. U.S. v. Amen, C.A.2 (N.Y.) 1987, 831 F.2d 373, certiorari denied 108 S.Ct. 1573, 485 U.S. 1021, 99 L.Ed.2d 889.

Where defendant knew that third party would monitor his phone calls by listening in periodically and agreed to let her do so and did not object when she broke in and participated in conversations, he did not consent only to "mechanical" interceptions of his calls, but also gave her right to record calls. U.S. v. Tzakis, C.A.2 (N.Y.) 1984, 736 F.2d 867.

Government agent, a party to conversation between agent and defendant, testified that he gave his voluntary consent to have the conversation monitored, and therefore tape-recorded conversation was admissible pursuant to this section. U.S. v. Boley, C.A.10 (Okla.) 1984, 730 F.2d 1326.

Communication is not unlawfully intercepted within meaning of this section where one of parties to conversation is acting under color of law or has given prior consent to interception; this section permits introduction of consensual recordings and thus controls over conflicting state eavesdropping regulations. U.S. v. McNulty, C.A.10 (Colo.) 1983, 729 F.2d 1243.

Employee's knowledge of employer's capability of monitoring her private telephone conversations, by itself, could not be considered implied consent to such monitoring. Watkins v. L.M. Berry & Co., C.A.11 (Ala.) 1983, 704 F.2d 577.

Where paid informer gave his consent before recording conversations in which he was involved, the conversations were free from warrant requirement. U.S. v. Davanzo, C.A.11 (Fla.) 1983, 699 F.2d 1097.

Trial court properly admitted tapes of defendant's telephone conversations, where the tapes were made with the consent of the other party to the conversations. U.S. v. Jones, C.A.5 (La.) 1982, 693 F.2d 343.

Conspirator, who requested private detective to install electronic equipment on him in order directly to the main volumes, locating first those volumes that contain Title 18 of the United States Code and then, within those volumes, the volume that contains section 2511. In the bound portion of the volume, you find the text of the statute and, following the text of the statute, historical notes, references to other West materials, and notes of decisions. See Exhibit 5.1.

Exercise

In your library, locate 18 U.S.C. § 2511 in each of the following sources:

(a) the print version of the United States Code
(b) the print version of United States Code Annotated
(c) the print version of United States Code Service
(d) a CD-ROM version of either United States Code Annotated or United States Code Service
(e) LEXIS or Westlaw
(f) the internet

Which of these sources is easiest to use? Which source is most reliable? What are the cost factors associated with each source?

Step 2: Locate Version of 18 U.S.C. § 2511 in Effect at the Time Cause of Action Arose.

The next step is to determine whether you have the version of the statute in effect at the time the cause of action arose. In our example case, this means that you want to make sure that you have the version of 18 U.S.C. § 2511 in effect in July and August 1998.

When using the print version of a code, locating the applicable version of a federal statute is a multistep process. First, you need to locate the statute in the bound portion of the code. Second, if your cause of action arose after the dates covered in the bound volume, you need to check the pocket part at the back of the bound volume to determine whether an amended version of your statutory section appears there. Third, if your cause of action arose after the dates covered in the pocket part, you need to check the quarterly and monthly print supplements that are usually shelved at the end of the code, determining whether an amended version of your statute appears there. Finally, if you need even more current information, you need to check an online source, for example, LEXIS or Westlaw.

When using a CD-ROM product or an online source, there are fewer sources to check. If you are using a CD-ROM product, you will usually need to check only two sources: the CD-ROM product itself and an online update service. If you are using an online source, you will usually only need to use the online source. Note, however, that while it may be easier to find the most current version of a statute using a CD-ROM product or online source, it can be difficult, if not impossible, to find an older version. For example, if your cause of action arose in 1997 and the statute was amended in 1998, you may not be able to find the 1997 version of the statute on the CD-ROM or online source.

Exercise

Look again at the versions of the statute that you located in the previous exercise. How current is each version? How would you update the version that you found to find a more current version?

Step 3: Locate that Portion of 18 U.S.C. § 2511 that Deals with Consent and Determine which Elements Are Likely to be in Dispute.

Once you have found the applicable version of 18 U.S.C. § 2511, the next step is to read through the statute, skimming the entire statute and locating the sections that discuss consent. Note that subsection (1) sets out the language that the senior attorney referred to in his memo.

> Except as otherwise specifically provided in this chapter any person—
>   (a) intentionally intercepts, endeavors to intercept, or procures any other person to intercept or endeavor to intercept, any wire, oral or electronic communication . . .
>   shall be punished as provided in subsection (4) or shall be subject to suit as provided in subsection (5).

Also note that two subsections discuss consent. Section (2)(c) applies when the person intercepting the communication is acting under color of law, and section (2)(d) applies when the person intercepting the communication is not acting under color of law.

> Subsection (2)(c):
> It shall not be unlawful under this chapter for a person acting under color of law to intercept a wire, oral, or electronic communication, where such person is a party to the communication or where one of the parties to the communication has given prior consent to such interception.
> Subsection (2)(d):
> It shall not be unlawful under this chapter for a person not acting under color of law to intercept a wire, oral, or electronic communication where such person is a party to the communication or where one of the parties to the communication has given prior consent to such interception unless such communication is intercepted for the purpose of committing a criminal or tortuous act in violation of the Constitution or law of the United States or of any State.

In our case, subsection 2(d) appears to be the applicable section. At least in the memo from Mr. Pariso, the supervising attorney, there is no indication that either Mr. Wilson or Elite Insurance was acting under color of law, that is, there is no evidence that either Mr. Wilson or Elite Insurance was a government employee or agent or was acting under the direction of a governmental employee or agent.

The next step is to re-read the statute, looking carefully at the language. In doing so, note that the subsection sets out both an exception and an exception to the exception and that both the exception and the exception to the exception have several parts or "elements."

Exception

It shall not be unlawful under this chapter

- for a person not acting under color of law
- to intercept a wire, oral, or electronic communication
- where such person is a party to the communication
  or
  where one of the parties to the communication has given prior consent to such interception

Exception to the Exception

unless

- such communication
- is intercepted
- for the purpose of committing any criminal or tortuous act in violation of the Constitution or laws of thc United States or of any State

In our case, the first element of the exception should not be in dispute. As discussed earlier, there is no evidence that either Mr. Wilson or Elite Insurance was acting under color of law. In addition, the second and third elements do not appear to be in dispute. Although additional research is needed, more likely than not a phone call is a wire communication, and a communication was intercepted when Elite Insurance recorded Ms. Johnson's phone conversations. It is, however, likely that the fourth element will be in dispute. Elite will argue that there was prior consent, and Ms. Johnson will argue that there was no prior consent.

If Elite is able to prove all of the elements of the exception, it seems unlikely that Ms. Johnson would argue the exception to the exception. She does not want to contest the fact that there was a communication or that that communication was intercepted. In addition, at least at this point, there does not seem to be any evidence that the communication was intercepted for the purpose of committing a criminal or tortuous act.

Thus, it appears that only one element, prior consent, is likely to be in dispute.

Step 4: Look for Statutory Definitions

In interpreting a statute, courts look first to the definitions section of the act. In enacting the statute, did the enacting body, that is, Congress or the state legislature, define the terms that it used?

Definitions can be located in one of several ways. In text versions, they can be located using the table of contents at the beginning of the act or the cross-references following the text of the statute; with CD-ROM products or online services, they can be located using a boolean search.

In our example problem, definitions are set out in 18 U.S.C. § 2510. Although this section does not define the terms "consent" or "prior consent," it does define "communication," "intercept," and "electronic, mechanical, or other device." Thus, you should read those definitions, checking to make sure that those elements are not likely to be in dispute. A reading of these definitions confirms our earlier decisions. A telephone call seems to fall within the definition of a wire communication and a call is intercepted when it is recorded.

Exercise

Locate 18 U.S.C. § 2510 in each of the following sources:

(a) the print version of United States Code Annotated or United States Code Service
(b) the CD-ROM version of either United States Code Annotated or United States Code Service
(c) LEXIS or Westlaw
(d) the internet

Step 5: Read Through the Notes of Decision Following the Statute, Identifying the Cases that Appear to be Most Useful.

The next step is to look for a case that has defined or interpreted the phrase "prior consent." Although there are a number of ways to locate cases interpreting or applying a statute, one of the easiest and most efficient is to use the notes of decision that follow the text of the statute in an annotated code.

These notes, or annotations, are written by attorneys who work for the company that publishes the set in which the notes appear. These attorneys read the opinions and then prepare a note for each point of law set out in the case. If a case sets out one point of law, the attorney prepares one note; if the case contains twenty points, the attorney prepares twenty notes.

These notes are then placed under the applicable statute. For example, notes relating to 18 U.S.C. § 2511 are placed in the notes of decision following 18 U.S.C. § 2511, and notes relating to 18 U.S.C. § 2510 are placed in the notes of decision following 18 U.S.C. § 2510. If a case sets out only one point of law relating to a particular statute, then that case will be referred to only once in the notes following that statute. If, however, the case sets out several points of law relating to the statute, there will be several notes, all referring to the same case, in the notes of decision section.

If there are only a few notes of decision for a particular statutory section, those notes will be organized only by court and date. Notes from decisions issued by higher courts will appear before notes from decisions of lower courts and notes from more recent opinions will appear before notes from older decisions. If, however, there are a number of notes of decision under a particular statutory section, those notes of decision will be organized by topic and a list of the topics with their corresponding section numbers will precede the notes themselves. Then, within each topic, the notes from higher court opinions will precede notes from lower court opinions and the notes from more recent cases will precede the notes from older cases.

Exercise

Which of the following sources have notes of decision?

(a) the print version of United States Code Annotated
(b) the print version of United States Code Service
(c) CD-ROM products
(d) LEXIS
(e) Westlaw
(f) the internet

For the sources that have notes of decision, how current are the notes? Are the notes of decision in each source the same? Why or why not?

In our example problem, there are five pages of notes under the subheading for consent. Although you could locate and read all of the cases listed under the consent subheading, it is usually better to be more selective, initially locating the four or five "best" cases. The question, of course, is how to determine which cases are best.

While the process of selecting cases is somewhat subjective, there are guidelines that you should follow. First, as a general rule, select cases that are mandatory authority over cases that are only persuasive authority. For instance, in our example case, select United State Supreme Court and, because Massachusetts is in the First Circuit, First Circuit Court of Appeals cases over cases from other circuits and cases from the district courts.

Second, as a general rule, select more recent cases over older cases. For example, if there are ten or fifteen First Circuit cases, select the more recent ones over older ones. Similarly, if you are selecting among cases that are only persuasive authority, you will usually want to select more recent cases over older cases.[2]

Third, select cases that appear to set out the types of information that you are looking for over cases that are more general or that discuss another point. For example, if you are looking for what constitutes implied consent, select a case that specifically mentions implied consent over a case that discusses consent in more general terms. Finally, select cases that are more factually similar over cases that are less factually similar. Thus, in our case, select cases involving the monitoring of phone calls by individuals not acting under color of law over cases involving the monitoring of phone calls by governmental employees or agents, cases involving employers and employees over cases involving family members, and cases that involve the interception of wire communications over cases that involve the interception of electronic communications.

Exercise

Locate the Notes of Decision section following 28 U.S.C. § 2510. In that section, locate the Notes dealing with consent. Read through these Notes, and then, using the guidelines set out above, identify the four or five cases that you would look at first. See Exhibit 5.1.

Step 6: Locate the Cases in the Appropriate Federal Reporter, and Read the Relevant Portion(s) of Each.

Cases are published in sets of books called reporters, each of which publishes opinions from a particular court or group of courts. For example, United States Reporter (U.S.), Supreme Court Reporter (S. Ct.), and United States Supreme Court Reports, Lawyers' Edition, (L.Ed.) publish only opinions from the United States Supreme Court. Similarly, the Federal Reporter (F., F.2d, or F.3d) publishes only opinions from the United States Court of Appeals. In contrast, the Pacific Reporter (P. or P.2d) has intermediate court of appeals and supreme court opinions from fifteen different states. In each set, the opinions are set out in the order in which they were issued and not by topic or, if a reporter contains the opinions of more than one court, by court.

For some reporters, for example, the United States Reporter, there is only one series. For other reporters, however, there is more than one.

---

2. The information that you need to determine whether a case is mandatory or persuasive, that is, the name of the court and the date of the decision can usually be found either at the beginning or end of the annotation. For more on mandatory and persuasive authority, see Chapter 2.

For instance, the Federal Reporter has three series: Federal Reporter (F.), Federal Reporter, Second Series (F.2d), and Federal Reporter, Third Series (F.3d). The Federal Reporter has 300 volumes and opinions issued between 1789 and 1924; Federal Reporter, Second Series has 1000 volumes and opinions issued between 1924 and 1993; and Federal Reporter, Third Series, has opinions from 1993 to present.

To locate a particular case you need its citation.[3] In this citation, the first set of numbers following the case give you the volume number, the letters the reporter, and second set of numbers the page on which the opinion begins.

Williams v. Poulos, 11	F.3d	271.
case name volume	name of reporter	first page of opinion

Once you have found several potentially applicable cases, the next step is to read them. As a general rule, you will want to begin by reading the synopsis and headnotes that precede the text of each decision. Although they are not part of the court's decision and cannot be cited as authority, they can help you determine whether the case might be useful.

If after reading the synopsis and headnotes you determine that a case is not useful, discard it, writing in your research notes that you looked at the case but did not find it useful. If, however, the case appears to be useful, read the opinion itself. When the opinion is short (three to five pages), you will usually want to read all of it. If it is longer, begin by reading the portions (1) stating the issue or issues, (2) summarizing the facts, and (3) discussing the relevant points of law.

In doing this reading, look for a number of different things. First, make sure that the opinion is "on point." For example, does it discuss the section of the statute that you are researching? Second, make sure that you understand the question before the court. Was the court determining whether there was consent, or was it deciding only a procedural issue, such as whether the trial court erred in granting the defendant's motion for summary judgment?

Also determine how you might be able to use the case. Is this a case that you can cite as authority for the general rule? If not, is it a case that you or the other side might be able to use in your arguments? Finally, look at the statutes, cases, and secondary authorities that the court cites. If any of them look promising, copy the citations and look them up later.

The following example shows what went through the mind of an experienced legal researcher as she read *Williams v. Poulos.* The first column is the section of the court's opinion in *Williams v. Poulos* that discusses consent. The second column is our experienced legal researcher's thoughts.

---

3. Although typically these citations are not in proper *Bluebook* form, they do give you the information that you need to locate the case.

Text of Opinion	*What researcher was thinking as she read*

Williams v. Poulos
11 F.3d 271 (1st Cir. 1993)

(First part of opinion not set out.)

OK, this case is mandatory authority and it is relatively recent.

[The researcher began by reading the syllabus set out at the beginning and by noting that the Court of Appeals affirmed the trial court's decision. She then read through the headnotes, locating the one that discussed consent. She then turned to that part of the opinion]

[6] Both the federal and Maine acts specifically exempt from their prohibitions the interception of telephone calls where one or more of the conversants has consented to or, in the case of the Maine act, previously authorized the interception. *See* 18 U.S.C. § 2511(2)(d) and 15 M.R.S.A. § 709(4)(C).

I wonder if there is a Massachusetts statute on point? If there is, why hasn't Johnson's attorney said anything about it? Although I don't need to worry about it now, I should make the attorney aware that the plaintiff might also be able to bring suit under a state statute.

Good. This is a case that discusses the section of the statute applicable to our case.

As we have made clear, consent under Title III need not be explicit; instead it can be implied. *See Griggs-Ryan v. Smith,* 904 F.2d 112, 116 (1st Cir. 1990)

It looks like there are two types of consent: explicit and implied. I probably should take a look at *Griggs*: it is cited as authority for the rule and is mandatory authority.

Implied consent is not, however, constructive consent. *Id.* "Rather, implied consent is 'consent in fact' which is inferred 'from surrounding circumstances indicating that the party *knowingly agreed* to the surveillance.'" *Id.* at 116-17 (quoting *United States v. Amen,* 831 F.2d 373, 378 (2d Cir. 1987), *cert. denied,* 485 U.S. 1021, 108 S.Ct. 1573, 99 L.Ed.2d 889 (1988) (brackets omitted). In light of the prophylactic purpose of Title II, implied consent should not be casually inferred. *See id.* at 117.

I wonder what the court means by constructive consent? How is constructive consent different from implied consent? I'd better look for a definition of that term.

This may be a problem. It appears that to establish consent, we will need to prove that Ms. Johnson knowingly agreed to the surveillance. I wonder if telling her that her phone calls might be recorded is going to be enough or whether she needed to sign something? Because the court is relying so heavily on *Griggs,* I need to make sure that I read it.

Text of Opinion	*What researcher was thinking as she read*
Here the record reflects and the district court found that Ralph Dyer was told of the "monitoring" of CAR employee telephone calls. The record is not clear, however, as to whether Dyer was informed (1) of the manner—i.e., the intercepting and recording of telephone conversations—in which this monitoring was conducted; and (2) that he himself would be subjected to such monitoring. There was testimony tending to indicate that he was so informed, which the district judge apparently chose not to credit, and testimony tending to indicate that he was not.	It seems as if the court may be setting out a two-part test: the employee must be told how his or her calls will be monitored and the employee must specifically know that his or her calls are being monitored. If this is the test, we may be OK. Although we'll have to check it out, my guess is that Ms. Johnson probably knew how the monitoring occurred. In addition, it seems as if she was specifically told that her calls might be monitored.
In our view, the latter testimony, far from incredible, was highly plausible. Thus, there is no basis for us to conclude that the district court clearly erred in finding that Dyer was not told of the manner in which the monitoring was conducted and that he himself was be monitored *Cf. Rodriguez-Morales,* 931 F.2d at 982 (district court's finding should not be disturbed where there are two possible views of the evidence). And without at least this minimal knowledge on the part of Dyer, we do not see how his consent in fact to the monitoring could be inferred from this record. *Cf. Griggs-Ryan,* 904 F.2d 177 (implied consent inferred where defendant was informed (1) that all incoming calls, (2) on a particular line, (3) would be tape recorded.) Accordingly, we reject the contention that the court erred in finding that defendants are not protected by the consent exception.	What was the testimony? I need to go back and read the first part of the opinion to find out what evidence was presented at trial.
	OK, the court is not reviewing the issue de novo. It's just looking to see whether the evidence is sufficient to support the jury's verdict. Because it's only cited for the standard of review, I probably don't need to look at *Rodriguez.*
	I really need to look at *Griggs.* Although we might be able to get past this court's test, I'm not sure that we can get past the *Grigg* test. Which is the right test? We can argue the test set out here, but I'm sure that Ms. Johnson will argue that it's the test set out in *Griggs.* I need to check for some more cases. Probably the easiest thing to do at this point is to cite check *William v. Poulos* looking for cases that refer to headnote 6.

If the first four or five cases that you select answer the question that you were asked to research, you do not need to do look for more cases.

If, however, these cases do not answer the question, you need to do additional research. At this point you have a number of options: (1) You can go back to the notes of decision, identifying and then looking up the next best four or five cases; (2) you can look up cases that were cited in the cases you have already read, for example, the *Griggs* case; or (3) you can run a search in a CD-ROM or online database.

Exercise

Locate and read *Griggs-Ryan v. Smith.* As you do so, write down what you are thinking. Are you interacting with the opinion in the same ways that the experienced legal researcher did in the example set out above?

Step 7: Cite Check to Determine (1) Whether the Cases That You Plan To Use Are Still Good Law and (2) Whether There Are Any Additional Cases.

Attorneys cite check cases for two reasons: to determine whether a particular case is still "good law" and to determine whether there are any other, more recent cases that are on point.

You can cite check a case using either the print version of *Shepard's* or the cite checking services found on LEXIS and Westlaw. If you are cite checking using *Shepard's,* keep in mind the following. First, if you are shepardizing using the print version of *Shepard's,* remember that the volumes are not cumulative. As a result, you will usually need to check one or more bound volumes and one or more supplements. Second, if you are shepardizing online, remember that that the online versions of *Shepard's* are no more current than the print version. As a result, in addition to shepardizing you will also need to use some of the other online update services, for example, Lexcite or Instacite. See section 17.2.12.

To shepardize a case,[4] use the case citation, looking up that citation in the print version of *Shepard's* or entering the citation into LEXIS or Westlaw. For the purposes of this chapter, presume that in shepardizing *William v. Poulos* on LEXIS, we find the following information.

Cite: 11 F.3d 271*

1	SC	Same Case	801 F. Supp. 867	
			Cir 1	
2			22 F.3d 363, 366	
3			29 F.3d 733, 739	
4			43 F.3d 749, 752	3
5			48 F.3d 30, 38	5

---

4. For an explanation of West's "KeyCite," see § 17.2.12.

*Reprinted with the permission of Reed Elsevier, provider of the LEXIS/NEXIS services. Also reproduced with the permission of Shepard's/McGraw Hill, Inc. Further reproduction is strictly prohibited.

6			49 F.3d 830, 836	
			Cir. 3	
7	F	Followed	898 F. Supp. 276, 280	4
			Cir. 4	
8			38 F.3d 736, 740	
			Cir. 5	
9			19 F.3d 1527, 1541	
			Cir. 6	
10	F	Followed	63 F.3d 1391, 1394	
11			90 Nw. U. L. Rev. 1009, 1028	

In this example, the first entry is a reference to an earlier decision in the same case. Before the case was decided by the First Circuit Court of Appeals, the case was heard and decided by the United States District Court; its opinion was published and can be found in volume 801 of the Federal Supplement at page 867.

The next set of entries are to cases that have cited *Williams v. Poulos.* Entries 2 through 6 are citations to opinions from courts within the First Circuit, entry 7 is to a Third Circuit case, entry 8 to a Fourth Circuit case, entry 9 to a Fifth Circuit case, and entry 10 to a Sixth Circuit case. The last entry, entry 11, is a reference to a law review article that cited *Williams v. Poulos.*

For each entry, three different types of information may be given: a history or treatment code, a citation, and a headnote reference. The history or treatment code identifies the action taken by the citing court. For example, if the citing court reversed, overruled, followed, criticized, or explained the cited opinion, the appropriate treatment code will be set out in the first column. If there is no treatment code, the citing court cited the case but did not take one of the actions for which there is a code. In the print version of *Shepard's,* a list of the treatment codes and their meanings is set out at the beginning of each volume. In the online versions, the code is set out in one column and its meaning in the next.

Following the treatment code is a citation that tells you where the case you are shepardizing has been cited. In the online version set out above, you are given both the page number where the opinion begins and the page number on where the case you are shepardizing appears. In the print version of *Shepard's,* the first page of the decision is not given.

The last piece of information is a headnote reference. If in citing your case, a later court referred to a point of law set out in one of the headnotes in your case, a reference to that headnote will appear in the last column. For example, if in a later case, the court cites to the rule of law set out in headnote 1 in *Williams v. Poulos,* a "1" will appear in the last column. If there is no entry in the last column, it means that the cite to the case was more general; the cited case did not specifically refer to a rule of law set out in one of the headnotes. By using the information in this last column, you can save considerable time. Instead of looking up every citation, you need look up only those that deal with the headnotes that are applicable to the issues that you have been asked to research.

For example, in shepardizing *Williams v. Poulos,* you would need to look up only those cases that have cited the case for the rule of law set out in headnote 6, the headnote dealing with consent.[5]

Thus, shepardizing *Williams v. Poulos* tells us that the case is still good law. It has not been reversed or overruled or even questioned by a later court. It does not, however, lead us to any additional cases. Although *Williams v. Poulos* had been cited by other courts, it has never been cited for the rules set out in headnote 6. The only potentially useful cite is the citation to the law review article. Thus, we skip step 8 and move directly to step 9.

Exercise

Shepardize *Griggs-Ryan v. Smith.* For each entry, explain what the entry means.

Step 8: Locate Law Review Articles Or Other Commentaries that Might Be On Point.

Although this final step is not essential, it is often useful. A law review article can help you make sense of the statutory language and cases that you have found, it can help you identify arguments that each side might make, and it can provide you with a check on your research, alerting you to an important case that you may have missed.

Just as there are a number of ways to locate statutes and cases, there are a number of ways to locate law review articles: (1) You can locate articles using a print index, for example, the print version of the *Index to Legal Periodicals;* (2) you can locate articles using a CD-ROM product, for example Wilsondisc, which is based on the *Index to Legal Periodicals,* or LegalTrac, which is based on the *Current Law Index;* or (3) you can use LEXIS or Westlaw, doing either full text searches or searches in one of the available indexes. See section 15.3.2 for the coverage of each of these sources. In addition, you can locate law review articles through cross-references in an annotated code, through *Shepard's* (see above), and through citations that appear in an opinion.

---

5. If an opinion is published in more than one reporter, you can shepardize the case using either citation. You will, however, find different information depending on which citation you use. Because the different sets have different coverage, entries that appear under one cite may not appear under the other. To determine the coverage, use the "Scope" command on Westlaw or check the coverage statements found at the front of the print volumes. Also note that if an opinion is printed in more than one reporter, you must make sure that you use headnote numbers that correspond to the citation that you are using. What may be headnote 3 in the official reporter may be headnote 5 in the unofficial reporter.

In our example case, we decide to look up the law review article that we found when we shepardized *Williams v. Poulos.* Because the firm library does not have the Northwestern University Law Review, we look first for it on Northwestern University's Law Review's homepage. Not finding it there, we then locate it on Westlaw using the Find command.

Exercise

Identify other law review articles that may be on point using the following sources:

1. The print version of the *Index to Legal Periodicals*
2. Wilsondisc or LegalTrac
3. LEXIS or Westlaw

Select one law review article and locate a copy of it either in the print version of the law review or by using LEXIS or Westlaw. In addition, if it is a recent article, try to locate it on the internet.

§5.4   KEEPING TRACK OF WHAT YOU HAVE FOUND

In doing legal research, you must have a system. You must know where you have already looked and what it is that you found, and you must keep track of which statutes and cases you have and have not cite checked.

In addition, you must think as you research. Although it may seem easier to photocopy everything and then read it, it isn't. Read as you go, analyzing each piece and trying to put the pieces together. You won't know what else you need until you know what you already have.

One way of keeping yourself organized is to develop a structured note-taking system. For example, many researchers find it helpful to create a sheet for each element like the one set out below. Others start a notebook with tabs for the general rule section, the elements that are not in dispute, and each element that is in dispute. Still others create their own computer files and databases.

Whichever method you use, make it a practice to write down the full citation for each case and to list the statutes and cases that you have cite checked. There is nothing worse than having to run back to the library to locate a parallel cite or to cite check a case that you aren't sure you've cite checked.

§5.5   UNDERSTANDING WHAT YOU HAVE FOUND

At this point, you may feel overwhelmed. You have spent hours in the library, and your desk is stacked with notes and photocopies or you have dozens of computer files. The question is, now what? Is it time to start drafting the memo? The answer is, not yet. Before you begin drafting, you must put the pieces together.

EXHIBIT 5.2

Research Notes

Element in Dispute
Prior Consent

I. Rule or test that court applies in determining whether element is met:

Cites:

II. Analogous Cases

First Case:

Second Case:

Third Case:

III. Arguments that we can make:

IV. Argument that the other side is likely to make:

Sometimes putting the pieces together is easy. An early court sets out a test, which is repeated verbatim by later courts. At other times, however, the courts set out the rules in slightly different ways and it isn't clear, at least on a quick reading, whether the decisions are consistent or inconsistent. Consider, for example, the following case summaries.

Watkins v. Berry

Court held that there was no consent. Employer told employees that phone calls might be monitored to improve sales techniques. In addition, employees told that they could use phones for personal calls and that these calls would be monitored only to the extent necessary to determine that call was a personal call.

Griggs-Ryan v. Smith

Court found that there was consent. Landlady used an extension phone to listen in on phone calls made by one of her tenants. Landlady had told tenant that she would monitor all calls.

Campiti v. Walonis

Court found that there was no consent. Police officer used an extension phone to listen in on a phone call between two inmates. It was common practice for officers to listen in on phone calls made and received by inmates.

Deal v. Spears

Court found that there was no consent. Employers told employee that her calls might be monitored to reduce number of personal calls. Employers also hoped to uncover information about a burglary suspected to be an inside job.

Williams v. Poulos

Court found that there was no consent. Employer installed monitoring system to reduce misuse of company phones. Employees were told that their calls might be monitored. New CEO was aware of policy but did not know manner in which calls were monitored or that his calls were being monitored.

While these summaries are helpful, they do not go far enough. If you are going to "put the pieces together," you need to look at the cases even more carefully and more systematically. Begin by looking again at the issues before the courts. While the summaries indicate that the issue in each case was whether there was consent, that is not accurate. Instead of deciding for themselves whether there was or was not consent, the appellate courts were only reviewing the trial courts' decisions. For example, in *Watkins v. Berry* the issue was whether the trial court had erred in granting summary judgment; in *Campiti v. Walonis,* whether there was sufficient evidence to support the trial court's finding that there was no consent; and in *Williams v. Poulos,* whether there was sufficient evidence to support the granting of an injunction.

Then look carefully at the rules being set out by the courts and the authority cited for each rule. Are the courts setting out essentially the same rules, citing the same cases as authority for those rules, or are the courts setting out different rules, citing either different authorities or no authority? In our example, although the courts use slightly different language, they seem to be setting out essentially the same rules: (1) implied consent should not be casually inferred and (2) implied consent is consent in fact, which is inferred from surrounding circumstances indicating that the party knowingly agreed to the monitoring of his or her phone calls. Although they do not all cite the same cases as authority, many of the cases cite *Griggs-Ryan v. Smith.*

Finally, if the courts appear to be setting out different rules, look for a pattern. For example, if you put the cases in date order, the earliest case first, does it appear that the rule is evolving? Do the earliest cases set out a broad rule, which through the years has been narrowed by the courts, or do the earliest cases set out a narrow rule, which has been broadened? If it does appear that the rule is evolving, does it appear that one set of jurisdictions has adopted one rule, and a second set of jurisdictions another rule? For instance, have the First and Second Circuits adopted a narrow rule while the Eighth and Eleventh Circuits have adopted a broader one? If neither of these approaches work, can you explain the differences on the basis of some underlying principle, or do the decisions seem to be result-oriented? As a matter of public policy, do the courts want to give employers the right to control their employees' use of the phone? Are the courts likely to find consent when the plaintiff is an inmate but not when the plaintiff is a tenant?

Although there are a number of ways to do this type of analysis and synthesis, many attorneys find it useful to develop a chart like the following one in which the cases are grouped first by jurisdiction, mandatory authority being listed first, and then within each jurisdictional grouping, by date.

Case	Key Facts	Rule Court Applied	Court's Holding and Rationale
Campiti v. Walonis First Circuit, 1979	Action under 2511(2)(c). Police officer used an extension phone to listen in on phone calls between two inmates. The defendant argued that there was implied consent because the prisoner should have known that his call would be monitored: an officer placed the call for the prisoner, and it was common practice to monitor calls.	No rule stated.	First Circuit found that there was sufficient evidence to uphold the trial court's finding that there was no consent.
Griggs-Ryan v. Smith First Circuit, 1990	Action under 2511(2)(d). Landlady repeatedly told tenant that all incoming phone calls would be monitored. All of tenant's incoming calls were in fact monitored.	Consent may be explicit or implied. No all-purpose definition of implied consent. "Implied consent is 'consent in fact' which is inferred 'from surrounding circumstances indicating that the party knowingly agreed to the surveillance.' " p. 116-17 Implied consent should not be casually inferred.	First Circuit upheld the trial court's granting of defendant's motion for summary judgment. The plaintiff did not put forth any evidence indicating that he had some plausible reason for believing that fewer than all of his calls were being recorded.

Case	Key Facts	Rule Court Applied	Court's Holding and Rationale
Williams v. Poulos First Circuit, 1993	Action under 2511(2)(d). Employer had monitoring system installed to reduce its telephone bill and decrease employee theft. After the system was installed, managers were told that all phone calls were subject to random monitoring and that they should inform those under them of this fact. Sometimes monitoring was random; sometimes a particular employee's calls were monitored. Dyer was told about the monitoring system when he assumed the position of CEO and Chairman of the Board.	"Implied consent is 'consent in fact' which is inferred 'from surrounding circumstances indicating that the party *knowingly agreed* to the surveillance. Implied consent should not be casually inferred." p. 117.	First Circuit affirmed trial court's granting of an injunction on the grounds that there was evidence Dyer was not informed (1) of the manner in which the calls would be monitored or (2) that his calls would be monitored.
Deal v. Spears 8th Circuit, 1992	Action under 2511(2)(d). Employers warned employee that they *might* monitor phone calls to reduce number of personal calls. In fact, employers also hoped to gain information about a burglary that they believed had been an inside job.	Consent is not to be "cavalierly implied." p. 1157. Knowledge that employer is capable of monitoring phone calls is not enough.	Court held as a matter of law that under the circumstances there was no consent. The employers only told employee that they might monitor her phone calls, not that they were monitoring them. In addition, fact that employers hoped to catch employee in an admission about burglary indicates that they did not believe that employee knew that her phone calls were being recorded.

Case	Key Facts	Rule Court Applied	Court's Holding and Rationale
Watkins v. Berry 11th Circuit, 1983	Action under 2511(d)(2). Employer told employees that their phone calls will be monitored to improve sales techniques. Employees also told that they may use phones for personal calls and that these calls will only be monitored long enough to determine that the calls are personal. Employer monitored all of personal phone calls received by employee during her lunch hour.	Consent is not be cavalierly implied. Knowledge of capability of monitoring is not sufficient.	Eleventh Circuit reversed and remanded, holding that trial court erred in granting summary judgment for defendant because there was an issue of material fact relating to the scope of the monitoring. It is the task of the trier of fact to determine the scope of the consent and whether the interception exceeded that scope.

Exercise

Imagine that the attorney who assigned our example office memo has called you into his office and has asked you tell him what you have found so far. You tell him that although the cases indicate that constructive consent is not enough, consent may be implied. He then asks you what test the courts use in determining whether there is implied consent. What do you tell him?

B. DRAFTING

With the prewriting stage behind you, it is now time to put pen to paper or fingers to keyboard.

As you begin writing, keep several things in mind. First, remember your audience. In writing an objective memorandum, you are not writing for the other side or even a judge. Your primary audience is an attorney in your firm.

Second, remember how the attorney will use the memo. Your purpose is not to persuade. It is to give the attorney the information that he or she needs to evaluate the case objectively and advise the client. Consequently, in writing the memo, you must present the law objectively. This is not the time to omit or even de-emphasize unfavorable precedent or facts. If the attorney is to evaluate the case accurately, you must present both the favorable and unfavorable information.

Third, remember that unlike briefs, there are no court rules specifying the format of an objective memorandum. There are only conventions. Although these conventions are useful for both the writer and the reader, once you understand them, you should feel free to break them when appropriate. When a convention does not serve its purpose, don't use it.

Finally, and perhaps most importantly, remember that writing a memo is a recursive process. Writing is not just putting completely formed ideas on paper. It is a process of discovery. As a result, as you write you will begin thinking about the problem in new ways, which may require doing more research or rethinking your analysis or synthesis of the law.

Similarly, because the process is recursive, there is no right order in which to write the sections. While some writers draft the sections in the order in which they appear in the memo, others begin with the brief answer, the discussion section, or even the conclusion. Because each section is connected to the others, wherever you start, you will have to go back to that section at the end, revising it in light of what you wrote in the other sections.

§5.6   DRAFTING THE HEADING

The heading is the easiest section to write. It consists of only four entries: the name of the person to whom the memo is addressed, the name of the person who wrote the memo, the date, and an entry identifying the client and the issue or issues discussed in the memo. Although the first three entries are self-explanatory, the fourth needs some explanation.

In some firms, the memo is filed only in the client's file. For such firms, the "Re:" entry can be quite general.

EXAMPLE 1

To: William Pariso

From: Legal Intern

Date: September 8, 1998

Re: Eliza Johnson v. Elite Insurance, File No. 98-478

In other firms, the memo is filed not only in the client's file but also in a "memo bank," that is, a computer or paper file in which all memos are filed by topic. In these offices, the "Re:" section serves two purposes. Within the client's file, it distinguishes the memo from any other memos that may have been or will be written, and in the memo bank, it provides either the database for a word search or topic categories under which the memo will be filed. To serve this last purpose, the heading should include the key terms.

EXAMPLE 2

To: William Pariso

From: Legal Intern

Date: September 8, 1998

Re: Eliza Johnson v. Elite Insurance, File No. 98-478
         18 U.S.C. § 2511: Consent to intercept or monitor phone
         calls.

---

§5.7 DRAFTING THE STATEMENT OF FACTS

In most objective memoranda, the first section is the statement of facts. In it, the intern sets out, clearly, concisely, and objectively, the facts relevant to the issue that he or she has been asked to research.

§5.7.1 Deciding What Facts to Include

In a typical statement of facts, there are three types of facts: the legally significant facts, the emotionally significant facts, and background facts. In addition, the writer usually identifies those facts that are unknown.

a. *Legally Significant Facts*

A legally significant fact is a fact that a court would consider significant either in deciding that a statute or rule is applicable or in applying that statute or rule. In our example case, a court would find legally significant those facts relating to consent. A court would not, however, find legally significant the number of people employed by Elite Insurance.

Either of two techniques can be used to determine whether a fact is legally significant. The first technique, which is used before the discussion section has been written, is to prepare a two-column chart. In the first column, list the elements, and in the second, the facts that the court would consider in deciding whether those elements are met. Facts that are not listed next to an element are not legally significant.

EXAMPLE

Law	Facts
person not acting under color of law	monitoring done by Elite Insurance
intercept	calls recorded using a recorder attached to an extension phone
. . .	. . .

The second technique is used after the discussion section has been completed. To ensure that you have included all of the legally significant facts in your statement of facts, go through your discussion section, listing each fact that you used in setting out each side's arguments; then check this list against your fact statement. If you used a fact in the arguments, that fact is legally significant and should be included in the statement of facts. (Remember, writing a memo is a recursive process. Even though you may write the statement of facts first, you will need to revise it after you have completed the discussion section.)

Exercise

Using one or both of the techniques listed above, determine which facts will be legally significant in deciding whether the element "prior consent" is met.

b.   *Emotionally Significant Facts*

An emotionally significant fact is one that, while not legally significant, may affect the way the judge or jury decides the case.

In our example case, several facts could be considered emotionally significant. For example, although it is not legally significant that Ms. Johnson was having an affair, this fact, if admitted, might influence a jury. The jury might see the case differently if it knew that Ms. Johnson was talking to a lover rather than a sick child. As a consequence, the attorney needs to consider this fact in evaluating the case.

Exercise

Reread the memo from the supervising attorney. What other facts might be considered emotionally significant?

c.　Background Facts

In addition to including the legally and emotionally significant facts, also include those facts that are needed to tell the story and that provide the context for the legally and emotionally significant facts. For example, in our example case, the fact that Johnson began working for Elite Insurance in January 1996 is neither legally nor emotionally significant. The writer has, however, included that fact in the statement of facts because it helps tell the story.

EXAMPLE

Johnson began working for Elite Insurance in January 1996. At the time she was hired, Johnson was told that the phones and computers should be used for business purposes only. In addition, she was told that it was Elite's policy to monitor all of an employee's phone calls during his or her one-month training period and to periodically monitor them after that time to ensure that the employee was providing good service. In accordance with this company policy, clients calling the office heard a message saying that their phone calls might be monitored to ensure good service.

---

d.　Unknown Facts

Sometimes you are not given all of the facts needed to analyze an issue. Because the attorney did not know the law, he or she did not ask the right questions or the documents containing the unknown facts are in the possession of the opposing party. If the unknown facts go to the heart of the issue, try to obtain them before writing the memo. For example, if in our example case Mr. Pariso had not said in his memo that Elite had told Johnson about its monitoring policy, you should obtain that information before writing the memo. If the unknown facts are less important, go ahead and write the memo, but tell the attorney, either in the statement of facts or the discussion section, what facts are unknown.

EXAMPLE

Wilson intercepted the phone calls by attaching a tape recorder to an extension phone. At this point, we do not know whether, when she answered the phone, Johnson heard the message warning incoming callers that their calls might be monitored.

---

§5.7.2   Selecting an Organizational Scheme

As a general rule, begin your statement of facts with an introductory paragraph that identifies the parties and the cause of action. Then present the facts using one of three organizational schemes: a chronological organizational scheme, a topical organizational scheme, or a combination of the two, for example, a scheme in which you organize the facts by topic and then, within each topic, present the facts in chronological order.

The facts themselves usually dictate which organizational scheme will work best. If the case involves a series of events related by date, then the facts should be presented chronologically. If, however, there are a number of facts that are not related by date (for example, the description of several different pieces of property) or a number of unrelated events that occurred during the same time period (for example, four unrelated crimes committed by the defendant over the same two-day period), the facts should be organized by topic.

In our example case, the facts can be presented using either a scheme that is primarily chronological or topical.

EXAMPLE 1   CHRONOLOGICAL ORGANIZATION

STATEMENT OF FACTS

Elite Insurance has contacted our office asking whether it violated the Electronic Communications Privacy Act when it intercepted Eliza Johnson's phone calls without her explicit consent.

Johnson began working for Elite Insurance in January 1996. When she was hired, Johnson was told that the phones and computers should be used for business purposes only. In addition, she was told that it was Elite's policy to monitor all of an employee's phone calls during his or her one-month training period and to periodically monitor them after that time to ensure that employees were providing good service to Elite's clients. In accordance with this policy, clients calling the office heard a message saying that their phone calls might be monitored to ensure good service.

In fact, Elite seldom intercepts its employees' calls. According to Eric Wilson, the office supervisor, after the training period ends, employee calls are only intercepted two or three times a year, usually immediately before the employee's annual performance review. Although Wilson does not tell employees in advance that he will be intercepting their calls, he usually discusses the calls with them immediately after they have been intercepted.

Because he had information indicating that Johnson might be involved in an insurance fraud scheme, Wilson began intercepting her calls in mid-July and stopped intercepting them in mid-August. At no point during this time did Wilson tell Johnson that he was intercepting her calls or discuss the calls with her. Although his intercepting did not produce any evidence that Johnson was involved in any type of illegal activity, he did overhear conversations indicating that Johnson was having an affair. On August 19, 1998, Wilson fired Johnson because she had used the phones for personal business.

Wilson intercepted the phone calls by attaching a tape recorder to an extension phone. At this point, we do not know whether when she answered the phone, she heard the message warning incoming callers that their calls might be monitored. Ms. Johnson did not explicitly agree, either orally or in writing, to the interception of her calls, and she states that she did not know that her calls were being intercepted.

EXAMPLE 2   TOPICAL ORGANIZATION

STATEMENT OF FACTS

Elite Insurance has contacted our office, asking whether it violated the Electronic Communications Privacy Act when it monitored Eliza Johnson's phone calls without her express consent.

As a matter of company policy, Elite Insurance periodically monitors its employees' phone calls to ensure that they are providing good service to Elite's clients. All calls are monitored during the employee's initial one-month training period. After that, employee calls are monitored two or three times a year, usually immediately before the employee's annual performance review. Individuals calling Elite hear a message telling them that their calls may be monitored.

Although Elite tells its employees that the phones and computers should be used for business purposes only, employees do use the phones for personal calls, for example, to check on a child or to make doctor appointments. These calls are tolerated if they are short.

Elite began monitoring Eliza Johnson's calls in mid-July 1998 because it had information indicating that she might be involved in an insurance fraud scheme. It continued monitoring her calls until about mid-August when Johnson was fired for using the phones for personal calls. Although the monitoring did not produce any evidence that Johnson was involved in an insurance fraud scheme, it did reveal that she was having an affair with another individual.

Although Wilson does not tell employees in advance that he will be intercepting their calls, he usually discusses the calls with them immediately after they have been intercepted. Elite intercepted Johnson's phone calls using a recorder attached to an extension phone. At this point, we do not know whether when she answered the phone, she heard the message warning incoming callers that their calls might be monitored. Ms. Johnson did not explicitly agree, either orally or in writing, to the interception of her calls, and she states that she did not know that her calls were being intercepted.

Question

Which of the above examples works best? Why?

§5.7.3   Presenting the Facts Accurately and Objectively

In writing the statement of facts for an objective memorandum, you need to present the facts accurately and objectively. This means that you cannot set out facts that are not in the record, you cannot leave out facts that are legally significant, and you cannot present the facts so that they favor one side over the other.

In the following example, the author has violated all three of these "rules."

EXAMPLE

Beginning in July 1988, Elite Insurance began surreptitiously monitoring Johnson's phone calls in an attempt to find information that it could use to fire her. Although the monitoring did not produce any information indicating that Johnson was involved in an illegal activity, Elite continued monitoring all of her client calls until mid-July, when, without notice, it fired her.

The author violated the first rule when, in the first sentence, she states that Elite began monitoring Johnson's phone calls in an attempt to find information that it could use to fire her. This fact is not in the memo from Mr. Pariso. The memo only says that Elite began monitoring Johnson's calls because it had information that she was involved in an insurance fraud scheme. The author violated the second rule when she fails, in the second sentence, to mention that as a result of the monitoring Elite discovered that Ms. Johnson was using the phones for personal calls, a violation of company policy. Finally, the author violated the third rule by using such words and phrases as "surreptitiously," "in an attempt," and "without notice."

In addition to stating the facts accurately and objectively, you also need to present the facts as facts and not as legal conclusions. For example, in our sample statement of facts, you cannot say that Ms. Johnson consented or did not consent. Although in the context of some cases such a statement would be a statement of fact, given the issue that you have been asked to research, it is a legal conclusion.

Checklist for Critiquing the Statement of Facts

A.   Content

- All of the legally significant facts have been included.
- When appropriate, emotionally significant facts have been included.
- Enough background facts have been included so that a person not familiar with the case can understand what happened.
- The unknown facts have been identified.
- The facts are presented accurately.
- The facts are presented objectively.
- The writer has not included legal conclusions in the statement of facts.

B.   Organization

- The writer has included an introductory sentence or paragraph that identifies the parties and the nature of the dispute.
- The writer has used one of the conventional organizational schemes: chronological, topical, or a combination of chronological and topical.

C.   Writing

- The attorney can understand the facts of the case after reading the statement of facts once.
- The paragraph divisions are logical, and the paragraphs are neither too long nor too short.
- Transitions and dovetailing have been used to make clear the connection between ideas.
- In most sentences, the writer has used the actor as the subject of the sentence, and the subject and verb are close together.
- The writer has varied the length of the sentences and the sentence patterns so that each sentence flows smoothly from the prior sentence.
- The writing is concise and precise.
- The writing is grammatically correct and correctly punctuated.
- The statement of facts has been proofread.

§5.8   DRAFTING THE ISSUE STATEMENT OR QUESTION PRESENTED

The issue statement, also called the question presented, establishes the memo's focus. It identifies the applicable statute or common law rule, it sets out the legal question, and it summarizes the facts that will be significant in deciding that question.

§5.8.1   Deciding How Many Issue Statements You Should Have and the Order in Which They Should Be Listed

By convention, you should have the same number of questions presented as parts to the discussion section. Accordingly, if you have three issue statements — whether service of process was adequate, whether the statute of limitations has run, and whether the defendant was negligent — you should also have three parts to the discussion section, one corresponding to each of the three issues. If, however, you have only one issue statement, for example, whether Ms. Johnson consented to the monitoring of her phone calls, your discussion section will have only one part.

Convention also dictates that in a multi-issue memo you list the issues in the same order in which you discuss those issues in the discussion section. The first issue statement will correspond to the first section of the discussion section, the second will correspond to the second section, and so on.

§5.8.2   Selecting a Format

The two most common formats for an issue statement are the "under-does-when" format and the "whether" format. This chapter discusses the under-does-when format; the next chapter discusses the whether format.

The under-does-when format is easier to use because the format forces you to include all the essential information. After the "under," insert a reference to the applicable law; after "does," "is," or "can," insert the legal question, and after "when," insert the most important of the legally significant facts.

Under (insert reference to applicable law)
does/is/can (insert legal question)
when (insert most important legally significant facts)?

a.   Reference to Applicable Law

If it is to provide the reader with useful information, the reference to the rule of law cannot be too specific or too general. For example, in our sample problem, a reference to just the statutory number would be too specific; very few attorneys would know that 18 U.S.C. § 2511(2)(b) deals with the interception of wire communications. Similarly, a reference to "federal law" is too broad. Hundreds of thousands of cases are filed each year in which the issue is governed by federal law.

References that are too specific:

Under 18 U.S.C. § 2511(2)(a), . . .
Under 18 U.S.C. § 2511, . . .
Under Title 18, . . .

References that are too broad:

Under federal law, . . .
Under the applicable statute, . . .

Appropriate references:

Under the Electronic Communications Privacy Act, . . .
Under the Electronic Communications Privacy Act, 18 U.S.C.
§ 2511, . . .

b.   The Legal Question

After setting out the applicable law, you need to set out the question. Again, in doing so, you want to make sure that your statement is neither too narrow nor too broad. If stated too narrowly, the question will not cover all of the issues and sub-issues in the discussion section; if stated too broadly, the question doesn't serve its function of focusing the reader's attention on the real issue.

Legal questions that are too narrow:

did Ms. Johnson explicitly consent to the monitoring of her phone calls . . .
did Ms. Johnson impliedly consent to the monitoring of her phone calls . . .

Legal questions that are too broad:

were Ms. Johnson's rights violated when . . .
is Elite Insurance liable . . .

Legal questions that are properly framed:

did Ms. Johnson consent to the interception of her phone calls when . . .
is there prior consent to the interception of a wire communication when . . .

c. *Legally Significant Facts*

In our legal system questions are always decided in the context of specific facts. As a consequence, you need to include in your issue statement those facts that the court will consider in answering the legal question.

The problem lies in deciding which facts to include. If there are only two or three facts that are legally significant, the answer is easy. Include them all. If, however, there are five, ten, or even fifteen legally significant facts, it will be difficult, if not impossible, to include them all and still write an issue statement that is readable. In these situations you need to do one of three things: summarize the facts, categorize the facts and then list only the categories, or include only the most significant of the legally significant facts.

In the first example set out below, the issue statement is by far too long. Most attorneys would not take the time to read through it. The second issue statement is much better. Although not all the legally significant facts are included, the most important ones are.

EXAMPLE 1   POOR

Under the Electronic Communications Privacy Act, 18 U.S.C. § 2511, did Ms. Johnson consent to the interception of her phone calls when (1) at the time she was hired she was told that the phone and computers should be used for business purposes only and that it was the company's policy to monitor all of an employee's phone calls during his or her one-month training period and to periodically monitor them after that to ensure good customer service; (2) in fact, after the initial training period Elite only monitored its employees' phone calls two or three times a year, usually immediately before an employee's annual performance evaluation; (3) all incoming callers heard a message telling them that their calls were subject to monitoring; (4) because it had information indicating that Johnson might be involved in an insurance fraud scheme, Elite monitored Johnson's calls for four to five weeks using a recorder attached to an extension phone; (5) although the monitoring did not produce information indicating that Johnson was involved in an insurance fraud scheme it did produce information indicating that Johnson was using the phones for personal calls; and (6) Johnson did not know that her calls were being monitored?

| EXAMPLE 2 | BETTER |

Under the Electronic Communications Privacy Act, 18 U.S.C. § 2511, did Ms. Johnson consent to the interception of her phone calls when she was told that her calls would be periodically monitored to ensure good customer service, but Elite seldom monitored its employees' calls and Ms. Johnson did not know that her calls were being monitored?

There are several other situations that may cause problems. First, you may encounter a situation in which it is not clear which rule of law the court will apply: If the court adopts one rule, one set of facts will be significant, and if it adopts the other rule, another set of facts will be significant. In such a situation, include only those facts that the court would consider significant in determining which rule to apply.

Second, you may encounter a situation in which the facts are in dispute: The plaintiff alleges that things happened one way, and the defendant alleges that they happened another way. In such situations, summarize each side's allegations. If you cannot, simply state the facts that are not disputed and indicate which facts, or categories of facts, are in dispute.

You may also be tempted to state as a fact something that is a legal conclusion. For example, the first time you write a question presented you may write something like the following.

EXAMPLE   STATES A LEGAL CONCLUSION AS A FACT

Under the Electronic Communications Privacy Act, did Ms. Johnson consent to the monitoring of her phone calls when she did not expressly or impliedly consent to such monitoring?

Common sense tells you that the answer to this question must always be no. If she did not expressly or impliedly consent, she did not consent. If your issue statement is to be meaningful, you must set out the facts that the court will consider in determining whether the test is met and not the test itself.

Finally, one of the "facts" that you will usually include in your question presented is the identity of the client. There are two schools of thought about how this fact should be handled. One says that the issue statement should be case-specific and that the client should be referred to by name. The other says that the question presented should be generic. Proponents of this school say that the client should not be referred to by name; instead you should determine what role the client plays and then use that label. Before writing a memo, check with your supervising attorney to determine which approach he or she would like you to take.

Checklist for Critiquing the Question Presented

A.   Content

- The reference to the rule of law is neither too broad nor too narrow.
- The legal question is properly focused.
- The most significant legally significant facts have been included.
- Legal conclusions have not been set out as facts.

B.   Format

- The writer has used one of the conventional formats, for example, the under-does-when format.

C.   Writing

- The reader can understand the question presented after reading it once.
- The writer has used all three slots in the sentence: the opening, the middle, and the end.
- The writer has used a concrete subject and an action verb, and the subject and verb are close together.

- In presenting the facts, the writer has used parallel constructions.
- The sentence is grammatically correct and correctly punctuated.
- The question presented has been proofread.

§5.9   DRAFTING THE BRIEF ANSWER

The brief answer serves a purpose similar to that served by the formal conclusion: It tells the attorney how you think a court will decide an issue and why. It is not, however, as detailed as the formal conclusion.

As a general rule, include a separate brief answer for each question presented. In addition, start each of your brief answers with a one- or two-word short answer. The words that are typically used are "probably," and "probably not." After this one- or two-word answer, explain the answer in one or two sentences.

EXAMPLE

QUESTION PRESENTED

Under the Electronic Communications Privacy Act, 18 U.S.C. § 2511, did Ms. Johnson consent to the interception of her phone calls when she was told that her phone calls would be periodically intercepted to ensure good customer service but Elite Insurance seldom monitored its employees' calls and Ms. Johnson did not know that her calls were, in fact, being monitored?

BRIEF ANSWER

Probably not. Johnson did not explicitly consent to the interception of her phone calls and, under the circumstances, the court probably will not find implied consent. Even though Elite told Johnson that her calls might be intercepted and incoming callers heard a message warning them that their calls might be monitored, Elite did not make a practice of monitoring employees' calls for extended periods of time, and Elite's own reason for intercepting the calls indicates that it did not believe that Johnson knew that her calls were being intercepted.

Checklist for Critiquing the Brief Answer

A.   **Content**

- The writer has predicted but not guaranteed how the issue will be decided.

- The writer has briefly explained his or her prediction, for example, explaining which elements will be easy to prove and which will be more difficult.

B.   Format

- A separate brief answer has been included for each question presented.
- The answer begins with a one- or two-word short answer. This one- or two-word short answer is then followed by a one- or two-sentence explanation.

C.   Writing

- The writer can understand the brief answer after reading it once.
- The writer has used concrete subjects and action verbs, and the subjects and verbs are close together.
- When appropriate, the writer has used parallel constructions.
- The writing is grammatically correct and correctly punctuated.
- The brief answer has been proofread.

§5.10   DRAFTING THE DISCUSSION SECTION: AN INTRODUCTION

In reading the discussion section, attorneys expect to see certain types of information, and they expect to see that information presented in a particular order.

These expectations are not born of whim. Instead, they are based on conventional formats, which are themselves based on the way attorneys approach legal questions. In analyzing a legal problem, the lawyer begins with the law. What is the applicable statute or common law rule? The lawyer then applies that law to the facts of the client's case. Are both sides likely to agree on the conclusion, or will the application of the law be in dispute?

If the application is in dispute, the attorney looks to see how the law has been applied in similar cases. Because our system is a system based on precedent, the courts usually decide like, or analogous, cases in a like manner.

The attorney then considers the arguments that each side is likely to make. What types of factual arguments or arguments based on the analogous cases are each side likely to make? Given the purpose and policies underlying the statute or rule, what type of policy arguments might each side make?

Finally, the attorney makes a prediction. Given the facts, rules, cases, and arguments, how will a court decide the case?

The discussion section reflects this process. It contains the same components — rules, analogous cases, arguments, and mini-conclusions — in the same order. At its simplest, and at its best, it analyzes the problem for the attorney, walking him or her step-by-step through the law, cases, and arguments to the probable outcome.

§5.10.1   Selecting an Organizational Plan

The first step in drafting the discussion section is the selection of an organizational plan. While content always determines form, most issues involve one of three types of analysis and thus, one of three types of organizational plans. In this chapter we discuss one of those plans, the plan for an elements analysis. In the next chapter we discuss the second and third types of plans: the plan for the balancing of competing interests and the plan that is used when the issue is one of first impression.

Plan A: Elements Analysis

The most commonly used plan is the one for an elements analysis. It is used when a statute or common law rule requires that the court determine whether a series of elements or requirements has been satisfied. For example, an elements analysis is used in applying a criminal statute, in determining whether a person has committed an intentional tort or was negligent, and in applying most court rules.

When this plan is used, the discussion begins with a statement of the general rule and a list of the elements. After raising and dismissing the elements that are not in dispute, the writer discusses each of the elements that are in dispute, for each disputed element setting out the applicable rules, the analogous cases, each side's arguments, and a mini-conclusion. The following outline illustrates a basic organizational plan.

ORGANIZATIONAL PLAN FOR AN ELEMENTS ANALYSIS

I.   First Issue
     Statement of general rule
     A.   Undisputed elements
          1.   Identify elements
          2.   Explain why each of these elements are not in dispute
     B.   First disputed element
          1.   Rule
          2.   Analogous cases (if available)
          3.   Arguments
          4.   Mini-conclusion
     C.   Second disputed element
          1.   Rule
          2.   Analogous cases (if available)
          3.   Arguments
          4.   Mini-conclusion

Although sometimes you will be able to use Plan A without any modifications, more often than not some modifications will be necessary. For example, in our sample problem there is only one undisputed element (party to the communication) and one disputed element (consent). The one disputed element has, however, two parts, one of which is undisputed and one of which is in dispute. Thus, we need to modify Plan A, adapting it to our problem.

ORGANIZATIONAL SCHEME FOR SAMPLE PROBLEM

I.   General rule
     Introduce 18 U.S.C. § 2511 and set out applicable portions.
     A.   Element not in dispute
          Paragraph telling the attorney why the element "party to the communication" is not in dispute
     B.   Element in dispute
          Paragraph telling attorney that consent may be explicit or implied but not constructive
          1.   Explicit consent (not in dispute)
               a.   Rules
               b.   Application of rules
          2.   Implied consent (in dispute)
               a.   Rules
               b.   Descriptions of analogous cases
               c.   Ms. Johnson's arguments
               d.   Elite Insurance's arguments
               e.   Mini-conclusion

Exercise

Look again at the sample memos set out in chapter 4. Do any of the problems involve an elements analysis? If they do, has the author used Plan A or a modification of Plan A in organizing the discussion section?

§5.10.2   Presenting the General Rule

Because all legal analysis begins with a rule, which is then applied to the facts of a particular case, you will usually begin the discussion section by setting out the general rule.

OUTLINE OF DISCUSSION SECTION

I.   First Issue
     Statement of the general rule

Sometimes, the general rule will be a statute or a subsection of statute. For instance, in our sample case, the general rule could either be 18 U.S.C. § 2511 or 18 U.S.C. § 2511(2)(d), depending on where we decide to start the discussion. At other times, the general rule may be a constitutional provision, for example, the Fourth Amendment; a common law rule, for example, the test for adverse possession; or a court rule, for example, Civil Rule 56, the rule that governs motions for summary judgment. This chapter discusses the first situation, the situation in which the general rule is a statute. The next chapter discusses the other situations.

a.   Single Statutory Section

When the rule is a single statutory section, introduce the statute and then quote the relevant portions.[6] In the following examples, the first example is poor because the writer has not introduced the statute. She has simply begun the discussion by setting out the text of the statute. The second example is much better. The writer has placed the statute in context, telling the attorney what to look for.

EXAMPLE 1   STATUTE NOT INTRODUCED

(3) A contract which does not satisfy the requirements of subsection (1) but which is valid in other respects is enforceable
(a) if the goods are to be specially manufactured for the buyer and are not suitable for sale to others in the ordinary course of the seller's business and the seller, before notice of repudiation is received and under circumstances which reasonably indicate that the goods are for the buyer, has made either a substantial beginning of their manufacture or commitments for their procurement; . . .

Colo. Rev. Stat. § 4-2-201(3)(a).

EXAMPLE 2   STATUTE INTRODUCED

Even if the formal requirements of the UCC Statute of Frauds are not met, a contract is enforceable if the goods were specially manufactured. The applicable portion of the statute reads as follows:

(3) A contract which does not satisfy the requirements of subsection (1) but which is valid in other respects is enforceable

---

6. Because most attorneys want to see the text of the statute, if the statute is short, quote it in full. If it is longer, choose one of the following options: (1) quote only the applicable portions; (2) quote the entire statute, but italicize or bold the applicable portions; or (3) paraphrase the statute and attach a photocopy of the text of the statute to the end of the memo.

(a) if the goods are to be specially manufactured for the buyer and are not suitable for sale to others in the ordinary course of the seller's business and the seller, before notice of repudiation is received and under circumstances which reasonably indicate that the goods are for the buyer, has made either a substantial beginning of their manufacture or commitments for their procurement; . . .

Colo. Rev. Stat. § 4-2-201(3)(a).

---

b. Multiple Statutory Sections

The approach is similar when there is more than one applicable statutory section: Introduce the statutes and then quote the relevant portions, starting with the more general sections and ending with the more specific. Think of your general rule section as an inverted pyramid: broadest rules first, narrower rules next, specific rules and exceptions last. See section 21.3.

In the following example, the writer has made two mistakes. First, the introductions are weak. The writer identifies the sections but does not place those sections in a larger context, tell the attorney what to look for in reading the statutory sections, or explain how the sections are related. Second, instead of setting out the general rules before the more specific rules, the writer has set out the sections in the order that they appeared in the code.

EXAMPLE   **WEAK INTRODUCTIONS AND GENERAL RULES NOT PRESENTED BEFORE MORE SPECIFIC RULES**

9A.40.010 reads as follows:

(1) "Restrain" means to restrict a person's movements without consent and without legal authority in a manner which interferes substantially with his liberty.
(2) "Abduct" means to restrain a person by either (a) secreting or holding him in a place where he is not likely to be found, or (b) using or threatening to use deadly force.

Section 9A.40.030 states that

(1) A person is guilty of kidnapping in the second degree if he intentionally abducts another person under circumstances not amounting to kidnapping in the first degree.

The following example is much better. The introductions establish a context and explain the relationships among the sections, and the more general rules are set out before the more specific ones.

EXAMPLE   **STRONGER INTRODUCTIONS AND MORE GENERAL RULES SET OUT BEFORE MORE SPECIFIC RULES**

A person is guilty of kidnapping in the second degree if "he intentionally abducts another person under circumstances not amounting to kidnapping in the first degree." 9A.40.030(1).
The term "abducts" is defined in section 9A.40.010(2):

> (2) "Abduct" means to restrain a person by either (a) secreting or holding him in a place where he is not likely to be found, or (b) using or threatening to use deadly force.

"Restrain" is defined in 9A.40.010(1).

> (1) "Restrain" means to restrict a person's movements without consent and without legal authority in a manner which interferes substantially with his liberty.

---

c. Statutes Plus Cases

In some problems you will have to present not only the statute but also rules from cases that have interpreted the statute. In these situations, quote the statute and then set out the rules from the cases.

EXAMPLE

Section 402 sets out the standard that the trial court must use in awarding child custody.

Section 402: Best Interest of Child

> The court shall determine custody in accordance with the best interest of the child after considering all relevant factors including:
> (1) the wishes of the child's parent or parents as to his custody;
> (2) the wishes of the child as to his custodian;
> (3) the interaction and interrelationship of the child with his parent or parents, his siblings, and any other person who may significantly affect the child's best interest;

(4) the child's adjustment to his home, school, and community; and

(5) the mental and physical health of all individuals involved.

The court shall not consider conduct of a proposed custodian that does not affect his relationship to the child.

Because this statute supersedes the common law, there is no longer a presumption that the custody of young children should be awarded to the mother. *In re Marriage of Huen,* 56 Official Reporter 487, 534 Regional Reporter 1985 (1986). The Supreme Court has, however, held that if the child is too young to express his or her preference, the best interests of the child mandate that the trial court award custody of the child to the primary caregiver absent a finding that the caregiver is unfit to have custody. *Id.*

In our example case about intercepted phone calls, we need to do what you will often do: use a variation of one of the basic patterns. Although ultimately we will discuss a single statutory section, subsection 2511(2)(d), we need to let the attorney know how we decided that that subsection was the applicable section.

EXAMPLE

DISCUSSION

18 U.S.C. § 2511 sets out two consent exceptions. Subsection 2511(2)(c) applies when the party intercepting the communication was acting under color of law, and subsection 2511(2)(d) applies when the party intercepting the communication was not acting under color of law. Because there is no evidence that Elite Insurance was acting under color of law when it intercepted Johnson's phone calls, the applicable subsection is 2511(2)(d), which reads as follows:

> (d) It shall not be unlawful under this chapter for a person not acting under color of law to intercept a wire or oral communication where such a person is a party to the communication or where one of the parties to the communication has given prior consent to such interception. . . .

The applicable language of this subsection is "where one of the parties to the communication has given prior consent to such interception."

Questions

Look again at the sample memos set out in Chapter 4, locating the general rule paragraphs. How would you describe these paragraphs? Did the writers set out a single statutory section, multiple statutory sections, or a statutory section plus cases? Is there a way that the general rule paragraphs could be rewritten to make them even better?

§5.10.3   Raising and Dismissing the Undisputed Elements

Although sometimes you will want to discuss the elements in order, integrating your discussion of undisputed and disputed elements, or put your discussion of the undisputed elements at the very end of your discussion section, most of the time you will want to raise and dismiss them "up front."

OUTLINE OF DISCUSSION SECTION

I.   First Issue
     Statement of the general rule
     A.   Dismiss those elements that are not in dispute
          1.   Identify elements that are not in dispute
          2.   Explain why elements are not in dispute

In raising and dismissing the undisputed elements, do three things: identify the elements that are not in dispute, briefly explain why those elements are not in dispute, and provide a transition to the discussion of the disputed elements.[7] In the first of the following examples, the author has identified the undisputed element but has not set out the facts that support her conclusion or provided a transition to the next part of the discussion. In contrast, in the second example, the author has done all three things.

EXAMPLE 1	AUTHOR IDENTIFIES ELEMENT BUT DOES NOT EXPLAIN CONCLUSION OR PROVIDE TRANSITION TO NEXT PART OF DISCUSSION

In our case, both sides will agree that the first element, that the person giving consent be a party to the communication, is not in dispute.

---

7. Even when the reason why the element is not in dispute seems obvious, the better practice is to briefly set out the facts or reasoning that support your conclusion. Sometimes what seems obvious to you will not be obvious to your reader and, at other times, your conclusion may be based on a fact that has not been established or a faulty assumption.

EXAMPLE 2   **AUTHOR IDENTIFIES ELEMENT AND SETS OUT FACTS THAT SUPPORT CONCLUSION**

In our case, both sides will agree that the first element, that the person giving consent be a party to the communication, is not in dispute. In each of the phone calls at issue, Ms. Johnson was one of the parties involved in the call. Thus, the only element that is in dispute is whether Ms. Johnson gave prior consent.

---

§5.10.4   Discussing the Disputed Elements

After dismissing the elements that are not in dispute, you need to move to what is the heart of the discussion, the discussion of the element or elements that are in dispute. In discussing these elements, you need to provide the attorney with four types of information: (1) the rule or test that the court will apply in deciding whether the element is met, (2) descriptions of analogous cases, if such cases are available, (3) each side's arguments, and (4) your prediction about how the court is likely to decide the element. Although there are a number of different ways in which this information can be presented, this chapter presents them in the order discussed above: rules first, analogous cases second, arguments third, and prediction last.

OUTLINE OF DISCUSSION SECTION

    I.   First Issue

         Statement of the general rule

         A.   Dismiss those elements that are not in dispute

             1.   Identify elements that are not in dispute

             2.   Explain why elements are not in dispute

         B.   Discuss first disputed element

             1.   Identify element

             2.   Set out specific rules and tests

             3.   Describe analogous cases

             4.   Set out each side's arguments

             5.   Predict how court is likely to decide element

         C.   Discuss second disputed element

             1.   Identify element

             2.   Set out specific rules and tests

             3.   Describe analogous cases

             4.   Set out each side's arguments

             5.   Predict how court is likely to decide element

a.   Presenting the Specific Rule

In addition to presenting the general rule, you also need to present specific rules for each element. Although sometimes these specific rules are set out in the statute, more often than not they are not. If there is a rule or test, it is one that the courts have developed in applying the statute. For instance, in our example case, the statute does not set out the rule or test that the courts should apply in determining whether there is prior consent. The statute only says that there must be prior consent. The courts have, however, created rules and tests. For example, as we discovered during our research, prior consent may be either explicit or implied but not constructive.

In setting out specific rules, keep the following in mind. First, set out only those rules and tests that are applicable to the particular element that you are discussing. Second, set out the more general rules before more specific rules or exceptions. See sections 5.10.2 and 21.3. Finally, let content dictate organization. Instead of trying to fit the rules into a prescribed format, let the rules themselves determine the format.

What this means in the context of our example case is that we begin our discussion of consent with what is the most general rule, the rule that consent may be explicit or implied but not constructive. We then divide our discussion into two parts. In the first part, we raise and dismiss explicit consent, briefly explaining why there was no explicit consent in our case. In the second part, we discuss implied consent, setting out the rules and tests that the courts apply in determining whether there is implied consent, describing the analogous cases, setting out each side's arguments, and making our prediction.

EXAMPLE

The courts have construed the phrase "prior consent" to include explicit and implied consent but not constructive consent. *See Williams v. Poulos,* 11 F.3d 271, 281 (1st Cir. 1993); *Griggs-Ryan v. Smith,* 904 F.2d 112, 119 (1st Cir. 1990). In our case, there was no explicit consent. Although Ms. Johnson was told that calls were monitored, she did not explicitly agree to the interception of her calls. There may, however, have been implied consent.

Specific rule for consent

Raise and dismiss explicit consent

Transition

Specific rules for implied consent	The courts have repeatedly held that consent should not be "cavalierly" implied. *Deal v. Spears,* 980 F.2d 1153, 1159 (8th Cir. 1992); *Watkins v. L.M. Berry & Co.,* 704 F.2d 577, 581 (11th Cir. 1983). Instead, implied consent should only be found when the circumstances indicate that an individual knowingly agreed to the interception of his or her communications. *Williams v. Poulos,* 11 F.3d at 281; *Griggs-Ryan,* 904 F.2d at 117.
More general rule set out before more specific rule	

b.   Describing the Analogous Cases

If the application of a particular rule to a particular set of facts is clear, analogous case descriptions are not needed. Just set out the rule and then apply that rule to your facts. If, however, the application is not clear, descriptions of analogous cases will help the attorney understand how they might be applied in the client's case.

Selecting Analogous Cases

In selecting analogous cases, try to select at least one case in which the court found that the element was met[8] and one case in which the court held that it was not. In addition, select the cases that you know that you would want to use in arguing your position to the court and the cases that you believe that the other side is most likely to rely on in making its arguments. Do not make the mistake of including just the cases that support your client's position. The attorney also needs to know about the other side's cases.

Sometimes, there are only one or two cases from which to choose. In such circumstances, present those cases, letting the attorney know that they were the only cases on point. At other times, there will be dozens or maybe even hundreds of cases. In these instances, be selective. Using the same criteria that you used in doing your research, select cases from your jurisdiction over cases from other jurisdictions, cases from higher courts over cases from lower courts, more recent cases over older cases, and more factually analogous cases over less factually analogous cases. See section 3.5.

Also keep in mind that you may use different cases to illustrate different points. For example, when several elements are in dispute, you

---

8. In doing an elements analysis, use the language "proved," "met," or "satisfied." For example, say that Johnson "must prove that she did not give implied consent," that "the court will probably find that the first element is met," or "in this case the first element is satisfied."

may use one set of cases in conjunction with one of the disputed elements and a different set of cases in conjunction with another disputed element.

Presenting the Analogous Cases

As a general rule, start your analogous case section with a sentence introducing the cases. Sometimes this sentence will simply let the attorney know that there are only a limited number of analogous cases.

EXAMPLES

To date, only three First Circuit cases have discussed the consent exception. In one of these cases, *Griggs-Ryan v. Smith*, ...

In addition to the three First Circuit cases, there are several cases from other jurisdictions. In the case most factually analogous to ours, *Deal v. Spears*, ...

At other times, the sentence will set out the principle that you are using the cases to illustrate.

EXAMPLES

The courts have repeatedly held that the consent requirement is not met if the individual only knew that his or her phone calls might be monitored. For example, in *Campiti v. Walonis*, 811 F.2d 387 (1st Cir. 1979), ...

The courts have, however, held that there was consent when the plaintiff was told that all of his or her calls would be monitored. For instance, in *Griggs-Ryan v. Smith*, ...

After introducing the cases, describe them. Sometimes, these case descriptions will be very short: you will set out only one or two facts and the court's holding. At other times they may be several paragraphs in length: you will set out not only the facts and holding but also the court's reasoning.

How you introduce the cases and how much you say about them will be determined by how you use those cases in setting out each side's argument. Both your topic sentences and your case descriptions should "set up" the arguments that you ultimately make. Compare, for example, the following examples.

EXAMPLE 1

To date, only three First Circuit cases have discussed the consent exception. In one of these cases, *Griggs-Ryan v. Smith,* the Court of Appeals affirmed summary judgment for the defendant when the plaintiff's landlady had repeatedly told him that all of his phone calls would be recorded and when the plaintiff did not put on any evidence indicating that his landlady had told him that she had stopped recording incoming calls or that she was recording only parts of calls. *Id.* at 119. In the other two cases, the Court of Appeals affirmed decisions finding no consent. In *Campiti v. Walonis,* 811 F.2d 387 (1st Cir. 1979), the Court of Appeals affirmed the district court's decision that there was no consent despite the defendant's argument that the plaintiff, a prisoner, should have known that his phone calls might be monitored. *Id.* at 393. Similarly, in *Williams v. Poulos,* the Court of Appeals affirmed the granting of an injunction because there was evidence in the record indicating that the plaintiff, a CEO, did not know that his phone calls were being intercepted. *Id.* at 282.

In addition to the three First Circuit cases, there are several cases from other jurisdictions. In the case most factually analogous to ours, *Deal. v. Spears,* the Spears, Deal's employers, told Deal that they might be forced to intercept or restrict her telephone privileges if she continued using the store's telephone for personal calls. After the Spears told Deal to limit her calls, the store was burglarized and the Spears suspected that Deal was involved. As a result, they installed a recording device on the extension phone in their mobile home, which was next to the store, in the hopes of catching Deal in an unguarded admission. When turned on, the recorder automatically recorded all conversations made on either the store phone or the extension with no indication to the parties using the phone that their conversations were being recorded. *Id.* at 1155–1156.

The Spears taped and listened to about twenty-two hours of calls over a six-week period. Although they did not hear anything indicating that Deal had been involved in the burglary, they did find out that she had sold a keg of beer at cost in violation of store policy and that she was having an affair with another individual. Deal was fired after Mr. Spears played parts of the tapes for her. Deal brought suit under Title 18, and the district court granted judgment to her, finding that the consent exception did not apply. The Spears appealed, and the Eighth Circuit Court of Appeals affirmed the district court's determination that there was no consent on the grounds (1) that the Spears only told Deal that they might intercept her phone calls and not that they were intercepting the calls and (2) that because the Spears hoped to catch Deal in an admission, it was not reasonable to assume that Deal knew that her calls were being intercepted. *Id.* at 1157.

EXAMPLE 2

The courts have repeatedly held that the consent requirement is not met if the individual only knew that his or her phone calls might be monitored. For example, in *Campiti v. Walonis,* 811 F.2d 387 (1st Cir. 1979), the First Circuit affirmed the trial court's decision that there was no consent despite the defendant's argument that the plaintiff, a prisoner, should have known that his phone calls might be monitored. Similarly, in *Williams v. Poulos,* the First Circuit affirmed the granting of an injunction because there was no evidence in the record indicating that the plaintiff, a CEO, knew that his phone calls were being monitored. *See also Deal v. Spears,* 980 F.2d 1153 (8th Cir. 1992) (court held that there was no consent when employee was only told that her calls might be monitored and defendants' reasons for monitoring the calls indicated that they did not believe that plaintiff knew that her calls were being intercepted).

The courts have, however, held that there was consent when the plaintiff was told that all of his or her calls would be monitored. For instance, in *Griggs-Ryan v. Smith,* the First Circuit upheld the trial court's granting of summary judgment for the defendant when the plaintiff's landlady had repeatedly told the plaintiff that all of his incoming phone calls would be recorded and the plaintiff did not put on any evidence indicating that his landlady had told him that she had stopped recording incoming calls or that she was recording only parts of calls. *Id.* at 119.

Questions

In the above examples, how are the topic sentences and case descriptions different? After reading the case descriptions set out in Example 1, what types of arguments do you expect to see? After reading the case descriptions set out in Example 2, what types of arguments do you expect to see?

c. *Presenting Each Side's Arguments*

It is at this point in writing the memo that your role changes dramatically. No longer are you just a "reporter" telling the attorney what you found in doing your research. If you are going to do a good job presenting each side's arguments, you must become an advocate, using all of your training and resources to construct the arguments that each side is likely to make. You must think like the plaintiff's attorney and then like the defendant's attorney.

Although there is no easy way to come up with each side's arguments, the following two strategies can be useful.

Strategy No. 1: Consider the Standard Moves

Like other disciplines, law has its own set of "standard moves." For example, attorneys make four basic types of arguments: factual arguments in which the attorney applies the plain language of the statute or rule to his or her facts; analogous case arguments in which the attorney compares and contrasts his or her facts to the facts in the analogous cases; policy arguments in which the attorney argues that a particular policy dictates that the court reach a particular result; and legislative history arguments in which the attorney argues that Congress or a state legislative body intended that a statute have a particular effect or be interpreted in a particular way. Thus, one way to determine what each side might argue is to run through these standard moves, completing a chart like the one set out below.

	Plaintiff's argument	*Defendant's argument*	*Plaintiff's rebuttal*
Factual argument			
Analogous case arguments			
Policy arguments			
Legislative history arguments			

Strategy No. 2: Look at the Arguments the Parties Made in Analogous Cases

Although constructing each side's arguments is always a creative act, you just need to improve the wheel, not reinvent it. To come up with what the parties might argue in your case, look at what the parties argued in similar cases. For example, Elite Insurance can probably make the same argument that the defendant made in *Campiti v. Walonis:* given the circumstances, Ms. Johnson should have known that her calls would be monitored. Similarly, Ms. Johnson can make the same argument that the plaintiff made in *Campiti,* that such a rule would distort the plain language of the statute.

At least initially, write down, in order, all of the arguments that come to mind.

Possible Plaintiff's Argument	*Possible Defendant's Arguments*
• Given Elite's past practices, Johnson did not expect that her calls would be monitored in July and August. In the past, they had only been monitored in January, immediately before her annual performance review.	• Johnson was told that her calls would be periodically monitored and they were, in fact, periodically monitored.
• The recording was not sufficient to put Johnson on notice. It was heard by incoming callers and not by Johnson.	• Even though Johnson may not have heard the message telling incoming callers that the conversations might be monitored, she knew about the message.
• This case is like *Deal v. Spears.* Like the defendant in that case, Elite was trying to prove that Johnson was involved in an illegal activity. Thus, it is not reasonable to assume that Elite thought that Johnson knew that her calls were being recorded.	• As a matter of public policy, employers should not have to tell employees that they are going to intercept a particular call or set of calls. If this type of specific notice is required, employers will not be able to adequately monitor their employees' phone calls.
• This case may also be like *Williams v. Poulos* and *Campiti v. Walonis.* It is not clear from the facts whether Johnson knew how her calls were being recorded.	• Our case is different from *Campiti* and *Williams.* In those cases, the plaintiffs were never specifically told that their calls would be monitored. Here, Johnson was told that her calls would be subject to monitoring.
• Unlike the earlier instances when Johnson's calls were monitored, this time her supervisor did not talk to her immediately after the call.	• Our case is similar to *Griggs-Ryan.* As in that case, in our case defendant did what it said it would do: in *Griggs* that was to monitor all calls and in our case it was to periodically monitor calls.
• If Johnson did consent, she consented to the monitoring of her calls to see if she was providing good customer service. She did not consent to the monitoring of calls that were clearly personal in nature or to monitoring designed to catch her in an illegal act.	

Then, after creating your list, go back through the list, crossing off those arguments that don't pass the "giggle" test (a court would laugh if you made the argument), and organizing the arguments. Does the plaintiff have just one assertion that it can support in one or more ways, or does it have several alternative arguments? Similarly, does the defendant have just one assertion, or are there several different arguments that it can make? For each "line of argument," set out the assertion and then the facts, cases, and policies that support that argument.

Exercise

The following chart sets out the plaintiff's two lines of argument and the support for those arguments. Fill in the rest of the chart, setting out Elite's arguments and its support for those arguments.

Johnson's Arguments	*Elite's Arguments*

First Line of Argument:

No implied consent. The circumstances do not indicate that Johnson "knowingly agreed" to the interception of her phone calls.

- Like the plaintiffs in *Williams v. Poulos,* and *Campiti v. Walonis,* Johnson did not know that her calls were being intercepted.
- In addition, given Elite's common practices, Johnson did not expect that her calls would be monitored in July and August. She expected them to be monitored only in January, at the time of her annual performance review, and she expected that her supervisor would talk to her about a call immediately after the call was made.
- The facts also indicate that Elite did not believe that Johnson knew that her calls were being intercepted. Like the defendant in *Deal v. Spears,* it hoped to uncover evidence indicating that Johnson was involved in an illegal activity.

Second Line of Argument:

Even if Johnson did consent to some monitoring of her calls, she only consented to limited monitoring.

- Johnson was told only that her calls would be monitored to determine whether she was providing good customer service.

After determining what arguments each side is likely to make, decide how you want to present those arguments. Although you have a number of options, in this chapter we present only one: the script format.

Like a playwright writing the script for a mock argument to a court, when you use this format, you set out the moving party's arguments first, the responding party's argument's next, and the moving party's rebuttal, if any, last.

The following example shows how to set out each side's arguments using this format. Note that in setting out each side's arguments, the writer has started by setting out the party's assertion. She then sets out her support for that assertion.

EXAMPLE

FIRST DRAFT OF EACH SIDE'S ARGUMENTS

Johnson will argue that the consent element is not met because she did not knowingly agree to the interception of her phone calls. Like the plaintiffs in *Campiti, Williams,* and *Deal,* who did not know that their calls were being intercepted, Johnson did not know that Elite was intercepting her calls. In the past, her phone calls had been monitored only in January, immediately before her annual performance review, and her supervisor had intercepted only two or three of her calls and had talked to her about those calls immediately afterwards. In addition, the facts indicate that Elite did not believe that Johnson knew that her calls were being intercepted. Just as the Spears in *Deal v. Spears* hoped to catch Deal in an admission tying her to a burglary, Elite hoped to catch Johnson in an admission tying her to an insurance fraud scheme.

Johnson's first assertion

Use of cases and facts to support first assertion

In the alternative, Johnson can argue that even if she did consent to the monitoring of her phone calls to determine whether she was providing good customer service, she did not consent to the monitoring of her personal calls.

Johnson's second argument

To win, Elite must distinguish the cases that Johnson will rely on, establishing that the circumstances indicate that Ms. Johnson knowingly agreed to the intercepting of her phone calls. *Campiti* and *Williams* will be relatively easy to distinguish. Unlike *Campiti,* in which the prisoners were never told that their calls would be intercepted, and *Williams,* in which the CEO was never told that his calls might

Elite's first argument

Distinguishing cases that Johnson relied on to support her argument

be intercepted, Johnson was told about the company's monitoring policy. In addition, Elite can distinguish *Deal* on the basis that unlike Deal, who never knew that any of her calls were being intercepted, Johnson knew that her calls had been intercepted in the past and that they were subject to being intercepted in the future. In fact, this case is more like *Griggs-Ryan,* the case in which the landlady repeatedly told her tenants that all incoming calls would be intercepted, than it is any of the other cases. Just as the tenants in *Griggs-Ryan* received regular reminders about their landlady's policy, so did Johnson: the message that incoming callers received telling them that their calls were subject to monitoring should have provided Johnson with a daily reminder about Elite's monitoring policy.

Elite's second line of argument

In addition to distinguishing the cases, Elite can argue that as a matter of public policy employers with monitoring policies like Elite's should be able to intercept employee phone calls without explicitly telling them that a particular call or set of calls will be intercepted. Because employees are likely to act differently when they know a particular call is being intercepted, employers will not be able to effectively monitor the type of service their employees are providing or determine whether an employee is violating a company policy or is engaged in fraud if they must tell an employee that a particular call or set of calls is being intercepted.

Johnson's rebuttal

Johnson is likely to respond to these arguments in two ways. First, it is not clear whether or not she heard the message that incoming callers heard. As a result, although the message may have put incoming callers on notice, it did not put her on notice, particularly given what she knew about Elite's actual practices. Second, the statute specifically requires that an individual give prior consent. Thus, even though an employer may have an interest in intercepting an employee's phone call, that interest is not recognized under the statute.

d. Predicting How the Court Will Decide the Element

The final piece of information that you need to include is your prediction about how a court would decide the element. Is it more likely that it will find the element met or more likely that it will find the element not met?

In writing this section, you must once again change roles. Instead of playing the role of reporter describing the rules and analogous cases or advocate making each side's arguments, you must play the role of judge. You must put yourself in the position of the particular court that would decide the issue—trial court, appellate court, state court, federal court—and decide how that court is likely to rule.

At least initially, you may be uncomfortable making such predictions. How can you, a first-year law student, predict how the court might rule? The good news is that with time, and experience, you will get better and better at predicting how a court will rule. In the meantime, read the statutes and cases carefully and focus as much attention as you can on each side's arguments. Careful reading, careful consideration of arguments, plus common sense will all help you make reliable predictions. Remember too that you are predicting, not guaranteeing, an outcome.

In setting out your conclusion, do two things: set out your prediction and briefly explain why you believe the court will decide the element as you have predicted. In the first example, the author has set out his prediction but not his reasoning. In the second, the author has set out both his prediction and his reasoning.

EXAMPLE 1   AUTHOR HAS SET OUT HIS CONCLUSION BUT NOT HIS REASONING

A court will probably find that there was no implied consent because the test for implied consent is not met.

EXAMPLE 2   AUTHOR HAS SET OUT BOTH HIS CONCLUSION AND HIS REASONING

A court will probably find that there was no implied consent because Johnson did not knowingly agree to the interception of her calls. Although Elite told Ms. Johnson that her calls were subject to periodic monitoring, the interceptions that took place were not consistent with prior company practices. In addition, Elite's own reasons for monitoring Johnson's calls indicate that it did not believe that Johnson knew her calls were being intercepted.

---

§5.11   AVOIDING THE COMMON PROBLEMS

Although the path to writing a good discussion section is filled with pitfalls, if you know what to look for, you can avoid most of them.

§5.11.1   Speak for Yourself

The temptation to string together a series of quotations is always there. Particularly when you are not sure that you understand the law, it can seem easier to quote than to put the rule into your own words.

However, quoting almost always creates more problems than it solves. To write a good memo, you must understand not only each rule but also how the rules fit together and will be applied to the facts of your case. Thus, although quotations may get you past the rule section, they can't help you write the descriptions of analogous cases, each side's arguments, or your prediction as to how the court is likely to rule.

Overquoting can also cause writing problems. In quoting, you inevitably run into problems with verb tenses and pronouns. In setting out the rules, one judge uses the past tense and another the present tense, and instead of using the proper noun, a judge will use a pronoun that does not have, at least in the quoted language, a referent. In addition, each judge usually has his or her own writing style and, when you combine them, your own writing becomes a mishmash of styles.

Because of these problems, use quotations sparingly. Quote statutes but little else. See section 24.2.3.

§5.11.2   Lay It Out

Most attorneys are bright. Given all of the pieces of a puzzle and enough time, they can put the puzzle together. A discussion section is not, however, a puzzle. Attorneys reading a memo don't want you to hand them the pieces in a box; they want you to hand them the completed puzzle. It is you, and not they, who should be doing the work.

Study the following examples.

**EXAMPLE 1   PIECES JUST HANDED TO THE ATTORNEY
IN A BOX**

In *Campiti, Williams,* and *Deal,* the defendants did not know that their calls were being monitored. Johnson did not know that her calls were being intercepted. In *Deal v. Spears,* the defendants taped the plaintiff's calls in the hope of connecting her to a burglary. Elite taped Johnson's calls in the hope of finding out whether she was involved in an insurance fraud scheme. In the past, Elite had only taped Johnson's calls as part of her annual performance review. This time the taping occurred in July and August. In the past, when Johnson's supervisor intercepted her calls, he talked to her immediately after listening in on a call.

Even the brightest attorney would have difficulty understanding this first example. Although the writer has given the attorney all of the pieces, the pieces are not sorted or connected.

EXAMPLE 2   PIECES SORTED, BUT NOT CONNECTED

Like the plaintiffs in *Campiti, Williams,* and *Deal,* Johnson did not know that her calls were being intercepted. The taping occurred well past the end of her initial one-month training period and was done in July and August rather than January at the time of her annual performance review. Her supervisor did not talk to her about the calls immediately after recording them. He taped calls for almost six weeks before telling her that her calls were being intercepted. As in *Deal v. Spears,* in this case, Elite's motive for recording the calls indicates that it did not believe that Johnson knew that her calls were being recorded. Just as the Spears hoped to catch Deal in an admission tying her to a robbery, Elite hoped to catch Johnson in an admission tying her to an insurance fraud scheme.

In this second example, the writer has sorted and ordered the pieces. Although the resulting text is more understandable, because the pieces are not connected, the attorney still has to work to figure out how they go together.

EXAMPLE 3   PIECES PUT TOGETHER

Johnson will argue that the consent element is not met because she did not knowingly agree to the interception of her phone calls. Like the plaintiffs in *Campiti, Williams,* and *Deal,* who did not know their calls were being intercepted, Johnson did not know that Elite was intercepting her calls. In the past, her phone calls had only been monitored in January, immediately before her annual performance review, and her supervisor had only intercepted two or three of her calls and had talked to her about those calls immediately afterwards. In addition, the facts indicate that Elite did not believe that Johnson knew her calls were being intercepted. Just as the Spears hoped to catch Deal in an admission tying her to a burglary, Elite hoped to catch Johnson in an admission tying her to an insurance fraud scheme.

This example is much better than the previous two. By adding topic sentences and transitions, the writer has made the connections between ideas explicit. For more on topic sentences and transitions see sections 21.5 and 22.1.

§5.11.3   Show How You Reached Your Conclusions

After you have spent days researching and thinking about a problem, the answer often seems obvious. The client has a cause of action or it does not, the element is met or it is not. Because the answer is so clear, when it comes time to write the discussion section, the natural tendency is to jump from the rule directly to the conclusion.

You must not do this. Although the attorneys are interested in your conclusion, they are more interested in how you reached that conclusion. They want you to think through the problem for them, rehearsing and evaluating each side's arguments.

The following examples illustrate the difference between analysis that is weak and conclusory and analysis that gives the attorneys what they need.

EXAMPLE 1

Johnson will argue that the consent element is not met because she did not knowingly agree to the interception of her phone calls. In contrast, Elite will argue that Johnson did consent because she knew about its monitoring policy. The court will probably find that there was prior consent.

In above example, the analysis is conclusory. The writer simply sets out her conclusion and each side's assertions. Without knowing what the arguments are, the attorneys have no basis for evaluating either conclusion or the assertions.

EXAMPLE 2

Johnson will argue that the consent element is not met because our case is more like *Campiti, Williams,* and *Deal* than *Griggs-Ryan v. Smith.* Elite will respond by distinguishing *Campiti, Williams,* and *Deal* and by showing how this case is more like *Griggs-Ryan v. Smith.* The court will probably find that this case is more like *Griggs-Ryan v. Smith* than it is *Campiti, Williams,* and *Deal* and find that the consent element is met.

Example 2 is only marginally better. It is not enough to tell the attorney which cases each side will use. You must use them.

EXAMPLE 3

Like the plaintiffs in *Campiti, Williams,* and *Deal,* who did not know that their calls were being intercepted, Johnson did not know that Elite was monitoring her calls. In the past, her phone calls had only been monitored in January, immediately before her annual performance review, and her supervisor had monitored only two or three of her calls and had talked to her about those calls immediately afterwards. In addition, as in *Deal,* in our case, Elite monitored Johnson's calls to try to obtain evidence that she was involved in an illegal activity.

Example 3 is better than the first two. In addition to identifying the cases, the writer has used them, comparing the facts in the analogous cases with the facts in the client's case. The writer has not, however, explained why the factual similarities and differences are significant. Why is it significant that like the plaintiffs in *Campiti, Williams,* and *Deal* Johnson did not know that her calls were being monitored? Similarly, why is it significant that in both *Deal* and our case the defendant was trying to determine whether the plaintiff was involved in an illegal activity?

EXAMPLE 4

Johnson will argue that the consent element is not met because she did not knowingly agree to the interception of her phone calls. Like the plaintiffs in *Campiti, Williams,* and *Deal,* who did not know that their calls were being monitored, Johnson did not know that Elite was intercepting her calls. In the past, her phone calls had only been monitored in January, immediately before her annual performance review, and her supervisor had intercepted only two or three of her calls and had talked to her about those calls immediately afterwards. In addition, the facts indicate that Elite did not believe that Johnson knew that her calls were being intercepted. Just as the Spears in *Deal v. Spears* hoped to catch Deal in an admission tying her to a burglary, Elite hoped to catch Johnson in an admission tying her to an insurance fraud scheme.

This last example is an example of a good argument. The writer begins by setting out his first assertion, which is tied to the legal test. He then uses the analogous cases and the facts from his case to support that assertion. He then sets out a second assertion, once again using the cases and facts to support that assertion.

§5.11.4   Use Terms Consistently

In some types of writing, elegant variation is desirable. While novelists and poets frequently vary the words they use, at different times calling the lake a shimmering pond, a foreboding sea, or an environmental waste, lawyers do not. In law, a lake is a lake. If you use a different word, the attorney (and in interpreting a contract, the court) will assume that you meant something different. See sections 24.1.4.

This means that as a writer, you need to find the right word and then use that word throughout the discussion. For example, you should not use the words like "element" and "factor" interchangeably.

Question

What is the difference between an element and a factor? (See the Glossary of Terms at the end of the book). In the context of our example problem, when would you use the word monitor? When would you use the word "intercept"? In answering the question, think about which word is used by Elite Insurance and which word is used in the statute.

§5.11.5   See More Than the Obvious

Finally, look beyond the obvious. The difference between an acceptable memo and one that wins praise is sophisticated analysis. The exceptional intern is one who sees, and then presents, arguments that other interns don't see. For instance, in our example case, the intern who would win praise is the one who recognized that it is not just Ms. Johnson who could give consent. Mr. Porter was also a party to the communication and, if he called Ms. Johnson, he would have heard the message telling him that the calls were subject to monitoring.

Checklist for Critiquing the Discussion Section

A.　Content

General Rule Section

- The writer has included a sentence or paragraph establishing a context and introducing the statute or common law rule.
- The writer has set out the general rule, quoting the applicable statutory sections and quoting or paraphrasing the common law rule.
- The writer has not included rules or information that the attorney does not need.
- The rules are stated accurately and objectively.
- For each rule stated, the writer has included a citation to authority.

Discussion of Each Element

- For each element, the writer has set out the applicable definitions, rules, and tests.
- When an element is undisputed, the writer has raised and dismissed it.
- When an element is in dispute, the writer has included descriptions of analogous cases, setting these descriptions out before the arguments (script format) or integrating the descriptions into the discussion (integrated format).
- In describing analogous cases, the writer has given the attorney the information that he or she needs: no more and no less.
- The descriptions of the analogous cases are accurate.
- The writer has set out each side's arguments.
- The analysis is not conclusory: The writer has explained why the plain language supports the conclusion, why the factual similarities between the analogous cases and the client's case are significant, why it would be consistent with the policies underlying the statute or rule to decide the case in a particular way.
- The analysis is sophisticated: The writer has addressed more than the obvious arguments.
- The writer has included mini-conclusions in which he or she predicts how the question will be decided and gives reasons to support those predictions.
- In setting out the rules, analogous cases, arguments, and mini-conclusions, the writer has used the language of the law.

B. Large-scale Organization

- The writer has used an organizational scheme that is logical: Threshold questions are discussed first, and when issues build on each other, they are discussed in the appropriate order.
- The writer has presented the information in the order in which the attorney expects to see it. For example, the general rule is stated first, and specific rules are set out before the arguments based on those rules.

C. Writing

- The attorney can understand the discussion section after reading it once.
- The paragraph divisions are logical, and the paragraphs are neither too long nor too short.
- Signposts; topic sentences, transitions, and dovetailing have been used to make clear the connections between ideas.
- In most sentences, the writer has used the actor as the subject of the sentence, and the subject and verb are close together.
- The writer has varied the length of the sentences and the sentence patterns so that each sentence flows smoothly from the prior sentence.
- The writing is concise and precise.
- The writing is grammatically correct and correctly punctuated.
- The discussion section has been proofread.

§5.12   DRAFTING THE CONCLUSION

In a one-issue memo, the conclusion is used to summarize your analysis of that one issue. For example, in our example case, the conclusion is used to tell the attorney why you believe the consent exception applies or does not apply.

EXAMPLE

    A court will probably find that Elite intentionally intercepted Johnson's telephone calls without her prior consent. Johnson did not explicitly agree to the interception of her calls, and the facts do not indicate that Johnson knowingly agreed to such interceptions. Although Elite told Ms. Johnson that her calls were subject to periodic monitoring, the monitoring that took place was not consistent with prior company practices: (1) the monitoring occurred not in January at the time of Ms. Johnson's annual performance review but in July and August; (2) instead of monitoring only two or three calls, Elite monitored calls for four or five weeks; and (3) instead of talking to her about a call immediately after the call, Elite only talked to her about the calls at the very end. In addition, even if Johnson did consent to the monitoring of her calls to determine whether she was providing good customer service, she did not consent to the monitoring of personal calls, which, although against company policy, were tolerated. Even though the court is likely to find that Ms. Johnson did not consent to the interception, we may be able to establish that the other party to the communication, Mr. Porter, consented to the monitoring of any calls that he may have made to Ms. Johnson. Although this may not eliminate Elite's liability, it may lessen it.

While some attorneys will want you to stop at this point, others will want you to go one step further and advise the attorney about what you think should be done next. What should the attorney tell the client? What action should the attorney take next? Is this the type of case that the firm should, or wants to, handle? When you are asked to include this type of information in your conclusion, add a paragraph like the following.

EXAMPLE

Because it does not appear that the consent exception applies, I recommend that we try to settle this case unless another exception applies.

Checklist for Critiquing Conclusion

A. Content

- In a one-issue memorandum, the conclusion is used to predict how the issue will be decided and to summarize the reasons supporting that prediction.
- When appropriate, the writer includes not only the conclusion but also strategic advice.

B.   Organization

- The information is organized logically.

C.   Writing

- The attorney can understand the conclusion after reading it once.
- The paragraph divisions are logical, and the paragraphs are neither too long nor too short.
- Signposts, topic sentences, transitions, and dovetailing have been used to make clear the connections between ideas.
- In most sentences, the writer has used the actor as the subject of the sentence, and the subject and verb are close together.
- The writer has varied the length of the sentences and the sentence patterns so that each sentence flows smoothly from the prior sentence.
- The writing is concise and precise.
- The writing is grammatically correct and correctly punctuated.
- The conclusion has been proofread.

C.   REVISING

§5.13   CHECKING CONTENT

In revising a draft, the first thing that should be checked is its content. If there are problems with content, nothing else matters.

§5.13.1   Have You Given the Attorneys the Information That They Need?

In checking content, the first question to ask yourself is whether you have given the attorney the information requested. Did you research the assigned issue or issues? Did you locate all of the applicable statutes and cases? Did you identify and present the arguments that each side is likely to make? Did you evaluate those arguments and predict how the court is likely to rule?

In our example problem, the intern has given the attorney the information that he requested. The research is complete: The intern found not only the applicable statute but also the key cases. The discussion also begins at the right place. Because the attorney only asked about the exception, the intern did not discuss the underlying offense. The discussion also stops where it should. The attorney did not ask for a discussion of damages. The assignment was to determine whether the exception applied.

Last but not least, the intern included all of the pieces. She included both the general and specific rules and, when appropriate, descriptions of analogous cases. In addition, she applied those rules and cases to the facts of the client's case, anticipating the arguments that each side was likely to make and then evaluating those arguments and predicting how the court was likely to rule.

Thus, when the intern asks herself whether she has given the attorney the information he needs, the answer is yes. She knew the law, and in presenting that law, she used good judgment.

§5.13.2 Is the Information Presented Accurately?

In law, small errors can have serious consequences. An overlooked "o" in *Shepard's,* an omitted "not," or an "or" that should have been an "and" can make the difference between winning and losing, between competent lawyering and malpractice.

As a consequence, in writing the memo, you must exercise great care. Because the attorney is relying on you, your research must be thorough and your presentation accurate. Every statute and case must be cite checked, each quotation copied accurately, and each paraphrase a fair statement of the law. You must also use cases carefully. The facts must be presented accurately, and the holding correctly identified. Unless the attorney reads the statutes and cases that you cite, he may not see an error until it is too late.

In the following example, the intern has made a number of mistakes. If you were the attorney, would you see them?

EXAMPLE

Consent will be implied only when the individual knowingly agrees to the interception of his or her phone calls. *Williams v. Poulos,* 11 F.3d 271, 281 (8th Cir. 1993); *Griggs-Ryan v. Smith,* 904 F.2d 112, 19 (1st Cir. 1990). Thus, while the court found that there was implied consent in *Griggs-Ryan,* a case in which the plaintiff's landlady repeatedly told the plaintiff that she monitored all incoming calls, the court found that there was no implied consent in *Deal v. Spears,* 980 F.2d 1153 (8th Cir. 1992), a case in which the plaintiff's employers only told the plaintiff that they might intercept her calls.

The first mistake is in the first sentence: The writer has not stated the rule accurately. The rule is not that consent will be implied only when the individual knowingly agrees to the interceptions of his or her phone calls. Instead, the rule is that consent is implied only when the *circumstances indicate* that an individual knowingly agreed to the interception of his or her calls. The second error is in the citation to *Williams v. Poulos.* The case is a First Circuit and not an Eighth Circuit case. The last mistake is in the description of *Griggs-Ryan.* The issue in that case was not whether or not there was implied consent but whether the trial court's granting of summary judgment was proper. Thus, it is wrong to say that the court found that there was implied consent.

Questions

Which of the above errors is most serious? Least serious? Why?

§5.13.3   Is the Information Well Organized?

The next step is to check the discussion section's large-scale organization. Has the information been presented in a logical order? Does the information appear in the order that the attorney expects to see it?

One way to check large-scale organization is to prepare an after-the-fact outline. This is done either by labeling the subject matter of each paragraph and then listing those labels in outline form or by summarizing what each paragraph says. See section 19.4.2.

The following example shows how the first type of after-the-fact outline is done using an excerpt from the discussion section from our example problem.

EXAMPLE

Step 1: Identify the subject matter of each paragraph.

Discussion

18 U.S.C. § 2511 sets out two consent exceptions.   **General Rule Section**
Subsection 2511(2)(c) applies when the party intercepting the communication was acting under color of law, and subsection 2511(2)(d) applies when the party intercepting the communication was not acting under color of law. Because there is no evidence that Elite Insurance was acting under color of law when it intercepted Johnson's phone calls, the   • Applicable
applicable subsection is 2511(2)(d), which reads as follows: subsection

(d) It shall not be unlawful under this chapter for a person   • Text of applicable
not acting under color of law to intercept a wire or oral com-   subsection
munication where such a person is a party to the communication or where one of the parties to the communication has given prior consent to such interception. . . .

The applicable language of this subsection is "where one of the parties to the communication has given prior consent to such interception."

- Applicable language in applicable subsection

In our case, both sides will agree that the first element, that the person giving consent be a party to the communication, is not in dispute. In each of the phone calls at issue, Ms. Johnson was one of the parties involved in the call. Thus, the only element in dispute is whether Ms. Johnson gave prior consent.

Undisputed Element

- Facts supporting conclusion

- Transition

The courts have construed the phrase "prior consent" to include explicit and implied consent but not constructive consent. *See Williams v. Poulos,* 11 F.3d 271, 281 (1st Cir. 1993); *Griggs-Ryan v. Smith,* 904 F.2d 112, 119 (1st Cir. 1990). In our case, there was no explicit consent. Although Ms. Johnson was told that calls were intercepted, she did not explicitly agree to the interception of her calls. There may, however, have been implied consent.

Disputed Element

- Specific rule

- No explicit consent

In deciding whether there is implied consent, the courts have stated that such consent should not be cavalierly implied. *Deal v. Spears,* 980 F.2d 1153, 1157 (8th Cir. 1992); *Watkins v. L.M. Berry & Co.,* 704 F.2d 577, 581 (11th Cir. 1983). Instead, implied consent should be found only when the circumstances indicate that an individual knowingly agreed to the interception of his or her communications. *Williams v. Poulos,* 11 F.3d at 281; *Griggs-Ryan v. Smith,* 904 F.2d at 117.

- **Test for implied consent**

To date, only three First Circuit cases have discussed the consent exception. In one of these cases, *Griggs-Ryan v. Smith,* the Court of Appeals affirmed summary judgment for the defendant when the plaintiff's landlady had repeatedly told the plaintiff that all of his phone calls would be recorded and the plaintiff did not put on any evidence indicating that his landlady had told him that she had stopped recording incoming calls or that she was recording only parts of calls. *Id.* at 119. In the other two cases, the Court of Appeals affirmed decisions finding no consent. In *Campiti v. Walonis,* 811 F.2d 387 (1st Cir. 1979), the First Circuit affirmed the district court's decision that there was no consent despite the defendant's argument that the plaintiff, a prisoner, should have known that his phone calls might be monitored. Similarly, in *Williams v. Poulos,* the First Circuit affirmed the granting of an injunction because there was evidence in the record indicating that the plaintiff, the CEO, did not know that his phone calls were being intercepted.

- Discussion of analogous cases

Griggs-Ryan v. Smith

Campiti v. Walonis

Williams v. Poulos

Step 2: Put the labels in outline form and compare the after-the-fact outline with the original outline.

After-the-Fact Outline	*Original Outline*
I. General Rule Section • Applicable subsection • Text of applicable subsection • Applicable language in applicable subsection	I. General Rule Section Introduce 18 U.S.C. § 2511 and set out applicable portions.
II. Undisputed Element • Facts supporting conclusion • Transition	II. Undisputed Element Paragraph telling the attorney why the element "party to the communication" is not in dispute.

III. Disputed Element
• Specific rule
 	
• No explicit consent
 	
• Test for implied consent
• Discussion of analogous cases
Griggs-Ryan v. Smith
Campiti v. Walonis
Williams v. Poulos
	III. Disputed Element
	Paragraph telling attorney that consent may be explicit or implied but not constructive.
	1. Explicit consent (not in dispute)
	  a. Rules
	  b. Application of rules
	2. Implied consent (in dispute)
	  a. Rules
	  b. Descriptions of analogous cases

Step 3: Making the Changes

After comparing the two outlines, the next step is to decide what changes are needed. Sometimes this means changing the draft so that it matches the original outline; at other times it means deciding that the draft is better than the original outline. The goal, however, remains the same: to present the information in a manner that is both logical and that meets the attorney's expectations as a reader.

§5.13.4   Are the Connections Explicit?

Having revised for content and organization, you now need to look at the draft through the reader's eyes. Will the organizational scheme be apparent to the reader? Can the reader determine how paragraphs, sentences, and even the parts of sentences are related? If the connections are not explicit, more roadmaps, signposts, and transitions are needed.

Roadmaps

A roadmap is just what the term implies: a "map" providing the reader with an overview of the document. In some instances, you will need to include a separate roadmap in which you outline the steps in the analysis. At other times, the rule section will provide the outline.

EXAMPLE 1   **SEPARATE ROADMAP OUTLINING THE STEPS IN THE ANALYSIS**

In deciding whether the contract is enforceable, the court will first determine whether the formal requirements of the Statute of Frauds are met. If they are, the contract is enforceable; if they are not, the contract is not enforceable unless one of the exceptions, for example, the exception for specially manufactured goods, applies.

EXAMPLE 2   **RULE SECTION THAT ACTS AS ROADMAP**

The courts have construed the phrase "prior consent" to include explicit and implied consent but not constructive consent. *See Williams v. Poulos,* 11 F.3d 271, 281 (1st Cir. 1993); *Griggs-Ryan v. Smith,* 904 F.2d 112, 119 (1st Cir. 1990). In our case, there was no explicit consent. Although Ms. Johnson was told that calls were periodically monitored, she did not explicitly agree to the interception of her calls. There may, however, have been implied consent.

Note that in both examples, the roadmaps are substantive in nature. Instead of saying, "First I will discuss this and then I will discuss that," the authors have outlined the court's decision-making process. See section 20.2.1.

Signposts, Topic Sentences, and Transitions

Signposts, topic sentences, and transitions serve the same function that directional signs serve on a freeway. They tell the attorneys where they are, what to expect, and how the pieces are connected. See Chapter 22 and sections 20.2.2 and 21.5. While these directional signs may not be particularly important in some types of writing, they are essential in legal writing. Without them, the connections between paragraphs and between sentences are not clear and the attorney has trouble following the analysis.

Compare Example 1, in which the writer has not included topic sentences, signposts, or transitions with Example 2. In Example 2, the topic sentence, signposts, and transitions are in boldface type.

EXAMPLE 1   NO TOPIC SENTENCES, SIGNPOSTS, OR TRANSITIONS

In *Campiti v. Walonis,* 811 F.2d 387 (1st Cir. 1979), the First Circuit affirmed the trial court's decision that there was no consent despite the defendant's argument that the plaintiff, a prisoner, should have known that his phone calls might be monitored. In *Williams v. Poulos,* the First Circuit affirmed the granting of an injunction because there was no evidence in the record indicating that the plaintiff, the CEO, knew that his phone calls were being monitored. *Id.* at 282.

In *Griggs-Ryan v. Smith,* the First Circuit upheld the trial court's granting of summary judgment for the defendant when the plaintiff's landlady had repeatedly told the plaintiff that all of his incoming phone calls would be recorded and the plaintiff did not put on any evidence indicating that his landlady had told him that she had stopped recording incoming calls or that she was recording only parts of calls. *Id.* at 119.

EXAMPLE 2   TOPIC SENTENCES AND TRANSITIONS ADDED

The courts have repeatedly held that the consent requirement is not met if the individual only knew that his or her phone calls might be monitored. For example, in *Campiti v. Walonis,* 811 F.2d 387 (1st Cir. 1979), the Court of Appeals affirmed the trial court's decision that there was no consent despite the defendant's argument that the plaintiff, a prisoner, should have known that his phone calls might be monitored. **Similarly,** in *Wil-*

liams v. Poulos, the First Circuit affirmed the granting of an injunction because there was no evidence in the record indicating that the plaintiff, a CEO, knew that his phone calls were being monitored. *Id.* at 282.

The courts have, however, held that there was consent when the plaintiff was told that all of his or her calls would monitored. For instance, in *Griggs-Ryan v. Smith,* the First Circuit upheld the trial court's granting of summary judgment for the defendant when the plaintiff's landlady had repeatedly told the plaintiff that all of his incoming phone calls would be recorded and the plaintiff did not put on any evidence indicating that his landlady had told him that she had stopped recording incoming calls or that she was recording only parts of calls. *Id.* at 114–115.

Dovetailing

Dovetailing is another technique that can be used to make the connections between ideas clear.

EXAMPLE 1

Johnson was **hired** by Elite Insurance in January 1996. **At the time she was hired,** Johnson was told that the phones and computers should be used for business purposes only. In addition, she was told that it was Elite's **policy** to monitor all of an employee's phone calls during his or her one-month training period and to periodically monitor them after that time to ensure that employees were providing good service to Elite's clients. **In accordance with this company policy,** clients calling the office heard a message saying that their phone calls might be monitored to ensure good service.

In this example, the author has used dovetailing to make clear the connections between the first and second sentences and the third and fourth sentences. The second sentence begins with the phrase, "At the time she was hired," which refers back to the word "hired" in the first sentence, and the fourth sentence begins with the phrase "In accordance with this company policy," which is a reference back to the policy referred to in the third sentence.

EXAMPLE 2

Both sides will agree that the first element, that the person giving consent be a party to the communication, is not in dispute. In each of the phone calls at issue, Ms. Johnson was one of the parties involved in the call. **Thus, the only element in dispute is whether Ms. Johnson gave prior consent.**

The courts have construed the phrase "prior consent" to include explicit and implied consent but not constructive consent. *See Williams v. Poulos,* 11 F.3d 271, 281 (1st Cir. 1993); *Griggs-Ryan v. Smith,* 904 F.2d 112, 119 (1st Cir. 1990). In our case, there was no explicit consent. Although Ms. Johnson was told that her calls might be intercepted, she did not explicitly agree to the interception of them. **There may, however, have been implied consent.**

In deciding whether there is implied consent, the courts have stated that such consent should not be cavalierly implied. *Deal v. Spears,* 980 F.2d 1153, 1157 (8th Cir. 1992); *Watkins v. L.M. Berry & Co.,* 704 F.2d 577, 581 (11th Cir. 1983). Instead, implied consent should only be found when the circumstances indicate that an individual knowingly agreed to the interception of his or her communications. *Williams v. Poulos,* 11 F.3d at 281; *Griggs-Ryan v. Smith,* 904 F.2d at 117.

While in the first example dovetailing was used to make clear the connections between sentences, in the second example it was used to make clear the connections between paragraphs. The first sentence in the second paragraph refers back to the last sentence in the first paragraph and the first sentence in the third paragraph refers back to the last sentence in the second paragraph.

D. EDITING

The work is now almost done. When you step back from the memo and look at it through the attorney's eyes, you are pleased with its content, organization, and presentation.

The last steps in the process are editing and proofreading your work. Like the painter preparing to have his work judged by a critic, you go back through your memo once again, correcting errors in grammar, punctuation, and usage and checking your citations. You also read your memo for style. Does each sentence flow smoothly from the prior sentence? Do the words create vivid images? Does the writing engage the reader? In sum, is the memo the work of an artisan or an artist?

§5.14   EDITING AND PROOFREADING

Although some writers mistakenly believe that revising, editing, and proofreading are all the same skill, they are not. Revising is literally "re-seeing" your creation. It is stepping back and examining the "vision" that you have.

Editing, on the other hand, is more a shaping of the vision, making the vision clearer, more concise, more precise, more accessible to a reader.

Proofreading is different yet again. It is the search for error. When you proofread, you are not asking yourself "Is there a better way of saying this?" Instead, you are looking to see if what you intended to have on the page is, in fact, there.

Although the lines between revising and editing and between editing and proofreading blur at times, the distinctions among these three skills are important to keep in mind, if for no other reason than to remind you that there are three distinct ways of making changes to a draft and that the best written documents undergo all three types of change.

§5.14.1   Editing

Editing, like revising, requires that you look at your work through fresh eyes. At this stage, however, the focus is not on the larger issues of content and organization but on sentence construction, precision and conciseness, grammar, and punctuation. The goal is to produce a professional product that is easy to read and understand. In this chapter, we focus on writing effective sentences and writing correctly; in the next chapter, we focus on precision and conciseness.

a.   *Writing Effective Sentences*

Most writers can substantially improve their sentences by following four simple rules of thumb:

1. Use the actor as the subject of most sentences.
2. Keep the subject and verb close together.
3. Put old information at the beginning of the sentence and new information at the end.
4. Vary sentence length and pattern.

Rule 1	Use the Actor as the Subject of Most Sentences

By using the actor as the subject of most of your sentences, you can eliminate many of the constructions that make legal writing hard to understand: overuse of the passive voice, most nominalizations, expletive constructions, and many misplaced modifiers.

1. Passive Constructions

In a passive construction, the actor appears in the object rather than the subject slot of the sentence, or it is not named at all. For example, in the following sentence, although the jury is the actor, the word "jury" is used as the object rather than the subject.

EXAMPLES   PASSIVE VOICE

> A verdict was reached by the jury.
> A verdict was reached.

To use the active voice, simply identify the actor (in this case, the jury) and use it as the subject of the sentence.

EXAMPLE   ACTIVE VOICE

> The jury reached a verdict.

Now read each of the following sentences, marking the subject and verb and deciding whether the writer used the actor as the subject of the sentence. If the writer did not use the actor as the subject of the sentence, decide whether the sentence should be rewritten. As a general rule, the active voice is better unless the passive voice improves the flow of sentences or the writer wants to de-emphasize what the actor did. For more on the effective use of the active and passive voice see section 23.1.

EXAMPLE

> To date, there have only been three First Circuit cases discussing the consent exception. In one of these cases, *Griggs-Ryan v. Smith,* summary judgment for the defendant was affirmed when the plaintiff's landlady had repeatedly told the plaintiff that all of his phone calls would be recorded and the plaintiff did not put on any evidence indicating that his landlady had told him that she had stopped recording incoming calls or that she was recording only parts of calls. In the other two cases, the Court of Appeals affirmed

decisions finding no consent. In *Campiti v. Walonis,* 811 F.2d 387 (1st Cir. 1979) the Court of Appeals affirmed the district court's decision that there was no consent despite the defendant's argument that the plaintiff, a prisoner, should have known that his phone calls might be monitored. *Id.* at 393–394. Similarly, in *Williams v. Poulos,* the granting of an injunction was affirmed because there was evidence in the record indicating that the plaintiff, a CEO, did not know that his phone calls were being intercepted. *Id.* at 282.

Sentence 1:

To date, there have only been three First Circuit cases discussing the consent exception.

In writing this sentence, the actor has used the passive voice. Instead of using the actor (cases) as the subject of the sentence, the author used an expletive construction (there is). The sentence would have been better if the author had written, "To date, only three First Circuit cases have discussed the consent exception."

Sentence 2:

In one of these cases, *Griggs-Ryan v. Smith,* summary judgment for the defendant was affirmed when the plaintiff's landlady had repeatedly told the plaintiff that all of his phone calls would be recorded and the plaintiff did not put on any evidence indicating that his landlady had told him that she had stopped recording incoming calls or that she was recording only parts of calls. *Id.* at 119.

Sentence 2 is another sentence in which the author did not use the actor (the court) as the subject of the sentence. Because the use of the passive voice does not improve the transition between sentences, it would have been better to say, "In one of these cases, *Griggs-Ryan v. Smith,* the Court of Appeals affirmed summary judgment when the plaintiff's landlady had repeatedly told the plaintiff that all of his phone calls would be recorded and the plaintiff did not put on any evidence indicating that his landlady had told him that she had stopped recording incoming calls or that she was recording only parts of calls."

Sentence 3:

In the other two cases, the Court of Appeals affirmed decisions finding no consent.

In this sentence, the writer uses the active voice: The actor, the Court of Appeals, is used as the subject of the sentence. Here, the use of the active voice is effective. Not only does it result in a strong subject-verb unit (the Court of Appeals affirmed), but it also allows the writer to use dovetailing to make clear the connection between sentences 3 and 4.

Sentence 4:

In *Campiti v. Walonis,* 811 F.2d 387 (1st Cir. 1979), the Court of Appeals affirmed the district court's decision that there was no consent despite the defendant's argument that the plaintiff, a prisoner, should have known that his phone calls might be monitored.

Like sentence 3, this sentence is written in the active voice. The actor (the Court of Appeals) is used as the subject of the sentence.

Sentence 5:

Similarly, in *Williams v. Poulos,* the granting of an injunction was affirmed because there was evidence in the record indicating that the plaintiff, a CEO, did not know that his phone calls were being intercepted.

This sentence is written in the passive voice: the actor, the Court of Appeals, does not appear in the sentence. Although many writers would have written this sentence using the active voice, some would have chosen to use the passive voice for stylistic reasons. If too many sentences in a row have the same actor, for example, the Court of Appeals, the sentences can become monotonous.

For more on active and passive voice, see section 23.1.

2. Nominalizations

You are guilty of using nominalizations if you turn a word that is usually used as a verb into a noun. For example, in the following sentence, the words "application" and "conclusion" are nominalizations.

EXAMPLE

Application of the same principles here dictates the conclusion that there was no implied consent.

To make this sentence better, identify the actor and then, in the verb, specifically state what action that actor has taken or will take. See sections 23.2 and 24.2.4.

EXAMPLE

If it **applies** the same principles to this case, the court will conclude that there was no implied consent.

---

3.   Expletive Constructions

In an expletive construction, the phrase "it is" or "there are" is used as the subject and verb of the sentence. Although it is sometimes necessary to use such a construction (note the use of expletive constructions in this paragraph), such a construction gives the reader almost no information. It is, therefore, much better to use a concrete subject and verb — that is, a subject and verb that describe something the reader can "see" in his or her mind. See sections 23.2 and 24.2.4.

EXAMPLE

Expletive
It is Elite's argument that . . .

Corrected
Elite will argue that . . .

---

4.   Dangling Modifiers

A dangling modifier is a modifier that does not reasonably modify anything in the sentence. For example, in the following sentence, the phrase "Applying this definition" does not reasonably modify anything in the sentence. It is not "it was held" that is doing the applying.

EXAMPLE 1

Applying this test, it was held that there was no implied consent.

The dangling modifier can be eliminated if the actor is used as the subject of the sentence.

EXAMPLE 2

Applying this test, the court held that there was no implied consent.

Now the phrase "Applying this test" modifies something in the sentence: the court. For more on dangling modifiers, see section 26.6.2.

Rule 2   Keep the Subject and Verb Close Together

Researchers have established that readers cannot understand a sentence until they have located both the subject and the verb. In addition, readers have difficulty remembering the subject if it is separated from the verb by a number of words. If there are a number of words separate the subject and the verb, the reader must go back and relocate the subject after finding the verb.

The lesson to be learned from this research is that, as a writer, you should try to keep your subject and verb close together. In the following examples, the subject and verb are in boldface type.

EXAMPLE 1   **SUBJECT AND VERB TOO FAR APART**

Similarly, the **First Circuit** in *Williams v. Poulos,* a case in which there was evidence in the record indicating that the plaintiff, a CEO, did not know that his phone calls were being intercepted, **affirmed** the trial court's granting of an injunction.

Even without the full citation, this sentence is difficult to read.

EXAMPLE 2   **SUBJECT AND VERB CLOSE TOGETHER**

Similarly, in *Williams v. Poulos,* the **First Circuit affirmed** the granting of an injunction because there was evidence in the record indicating that the plaintiff, a CEO, did not know that his phone calls were being intercepted.

The sentence reads more smoothly if the subject (First Circuit) is placed next to the verb (affirmed). For more information on the distance between subjects and verbs, see section 23.4.

| Rule 3 | **Put Old Information at the Beginning of the Sentence and New Information at the End** |

Sentences, and the paragraphs that they create, make more sense when the old information is placed at the beginning of sentences and the new information is placed at the end. When this pattern is used, the development progresses naturally, from left to right, without unnecessary backtracking.

EXAMPLE

The Spears taped and listened to about twenty-two hours of calls over a six-week period. Although during this period they did not hear anything indicating that Deal had been involved in the burglary, they did find out that she had sold a keg of beer at cost in violation of store policy and that she was having an affair with another individual.

In the first sentence the new information is that the Spears taped and listened to calls over a six-week period. Thus, this information is placed at the end of the sentence. The second sentence then starts with a reference back to this information, which is now old information, and ends with new information: what the Spears heard while listening to Deal's conversations. In particular, note the dovetailing. The first sentence ends with a reference to a six-week period, and the second sentence begins with a reference back to that time period. See section 22.3.

Rule 4	Vary Both the Length of Your Sentences and the Sentence Patterns

Even if writing is technically correct, it is not considered good if it isn't pleasing to the ear.

EXAMPLE 1

Johnson began working for Elite Insurance in January 1996. Johnson was told that the phones and computers should be used for business purposes only. She was also told that it was Elite's policy to monitor all of an employee's phone calls during his or her one-month training period. Calls were periodically monitored after that time to ensure that the employee was providing good service. Clients calling the office heard a message saying that their phone calls might be monitored to ensure good service.

In the above example, the writing is not pleasing because the sentences are similar in length and all follow the same pattern (subject-verb-object). Although short, uncomplicated sentences are usually better than long, complicated ones, the use of too many short sentences results in writing that sounds sophomoric. As the following example illustrates, the passage is much better when the writer varies sentence length and pattern.

EXAMPLE 2

Johnson began working for Elite Insurance in January 1996. At the time she was hired, Johnson was told that the phones and computers should be used for business purposes only. In addition, she was told that it was Elite's policy to monitor all of an employee's phone calls during his or her one-month training period and to periodically monitor them after that time to ensure that the employee was providing good service. In accordance with this company policy, clients calling the office heard a message saying that their phone calls might be monitored to ensure good service.

For more on sentence construction see Chapter 23.

b. Writing Correctly

For a moment, imagine that you have received the following letter from a local law firm.

Dear Student:

Thank you for submitting an application for a position as a law clerk with are firm. Your grades in law school are very good, however, at this time we do not have any positions available. Its possible, however, that we may have a opening next summer and we therefore urge you to reapply with us then.

Sincerely,

Senior Partner

No matter how bad the market is, most students would not want to be associated with a firm that sends out a five-line letter containing three major errors and several more minor ones. Unfortunately, the reverse is also true. No matter how short-handed they are, most law firms do not want a law clerk who has not mastered at least the basic rules of grammar and punctuation. Most firms cannot afford a clerk who makes careless errors or one who lacks basic writing skills.

Consequently, at the editing stage you need to go back through your draft, correcting errors. Look first for the errors that potentially affect meaning (misplaced modifiers, incorrect use of "which" and "that") and for errors that the well-educated reader is likely to notice (incomplete sentences, comma splices, incorrect use of the possessive, lack of parallelism). Then look for the errors that you know, from past experience, you are likely to make.

§5.14.2   Proofreading

Most writers learn the importance of proofreading the hard way. A letter, brief, or contract goes out with the client's name misspelled, with an "or" where there should have been an "and," or without an essential "not." At a minimum, these errors cause embarrassment; at worst, they result in a lawsuit.[9]

To avoid such errors, treat proofreading as a separate step in the revising process. After you have finished revising and editing, go back through your draft, looking not at content, organization, or sentence style, but for errors. Have you written what you intended to write?

Proofreading is most effective when it is done on hard copy several days (or when that is not feasible, several hours) after you have finished editing. Force yourself to read slowly, focusing not on the sentence, but

---

9. See, for example, *Emter v. Columbia Health Services,* 63 Wash. App. 378, 819 P.2d 390 (1991).

on the individual words in the sentence. Is a word missing? Is a word repeated? Are letters transposed? You may force yourself to read slowly by covering up all but the line you are reading, by reading from right to left, or by reading from the bottom of the page to the top.

Also force yourself to begin with the sections that caused you the most difficulty or that you wrote last. Because you were concentrating on content or were tired, these sections probably contain the most errors.

Finally, when you get into practice, make it a habit to have a second person proofread your work. Not only will such a person see errors that you did not, he or she is also less likely than you to "read in" missing words. Although you are responsible for every word that goes out under your name, a trusted proofreader is worth his or her weight in chocolate bars.

§5.15   A NOTE ABOUT CITATIONS

As a legal writer, you have an extra burden. In addition to editing and proofreading the text, you must also edit and proofread your citations to legal authorities.

At the editing stage, focus on selection and placement of citations. Is the authority that you cited the best authority? Did you avoid string cites (the citing of multiple cases for the same point)? Have you included a citation to authority for every rule stated? Did you include the appropriate signal? Have you over- or underemphasized the citation? (You emphasize a citation by placing it in the text of a sentence; you de-emphasize it by placing it in a separate citation sentence.)

In contrast, at the proofreading stage focus on the citation itself. Are the volume and page numbers correct? Are the pinpoint cites accurate? Have you included the year of the decision and any subsequent history? Is the spacing correct?

§5.16   FINAL DRAFT OF MEMO

At long last, we are at the end of the process. Having been researched, drafted, revised, edited, and proofread, the final draft of the memo looks like this.

EXAMPLE   **FINAL DRAFT**

To: William Pariso

From: Legal Intern

Date: September 8, 1998

Re: Eliza Johnson v. Elite Insurance, File No. 98-478
         18 U.S.C. § 2511: Consent to intercept or monitor phone
         calls.

STATEMENT OF FACTS

Elite Insurance has contacted our office, asking whether it violated the Electronic Communications Privacy Act when it intercepted one of its employee's phone calls without her explicit consent.

Eliza Johnson began working for Elite Insurance in January 1996. When she was hired, Johnson was told that the phones and computers should be used for business purposes only. In addition, she was told that it was Elite's policy to monitor all of an employee's phone calls during his or her one-month training period and to monitor them periodically after that time to ensure that employees were providing good service to the Company's clients. In accordance with this policy, clients calling the office heard a message saying that their phone calls might be monitored to ensure good service.

In fact, Elite seldom intercepted its employees' calls. According to Eric Wilson, the office supervisor, after the training period has ended, employee calls are only intercepted two or three times a year, usually immediately before the employee's annual performance review. Although Wilson does not tell employees in advance that he will be intercepting their calls, he usually discusses the calls with them immediately after they have been intercepted.

Because he had information indicating that Johnson might be involved in an insurance fraud scheme, Wilson began intercepting her calls in mid-July and stopped intercepting them in mid-August. At no point during this time did Wilson tell Johnson that he was intercepting her calls or discuss the calls with her. Although his intercepting did not produce any evidence that Johnson was involved in any type of illegal activity, he did overhear conversations indicating that Johnson was having an affair. On August 19, 1998, Wilson fired Johnson because she had used the phones for personal business.

Wilson intercepted the phone calls by attaching a tape recorder to an extension phone. At this point, we do not know whether when she answered the phone, Johnson heard the message warning incoming callers that their calls might be monitored. Ms. Johnson did not explicitly agree, either orally or in writing, to the interception of her calls, and she states that she did not know that her calls were being intercepted.

QUESTION PRESENTED

Under the Electronic Communications Privacy Act, 18 U.S.C. § 2511, did Ms. Johnson consent to the interception of her phone calls when she was told that her phone calls would be periodically intercepted to ensure good customer service but when Elite seldom monitored calls, and Ms. Johnson did not know that her calls were being intercepted?

BRIEF ANSWER

Probably not. Johnson did not explicitly consent to the interception of her phone calls and, under the circumstances, a court probably will not find implied consent. Even though Elite told Johnson that her calls might be intercepted and incoming callers heard a message warning them that their calls might be monitored, Elite did not make a practice of monitoring employees' calls and Elite's motive for intercepting the calls indicates that it did not believe that Johnson knew that her calls were being intercepted.

DISCUSSION

18 U.S.C. § 2511 sets out two consent exceptions. Subsection 2511(2)(c) applies when the party intercepting the communication was acting under color of law, and subsection 2511(2)(d) applies when the party intercepting the communication was not acting under color of law. Because there is no evidence that Elite Insurance was acting under color of law when it intercepted Johnson's phone calls, the applicable subsection is 2511(2)(d), which reads as follows:

> (d) It shall not be unlawful under this chapter for a person not acting under color of law to intercept a wire or oral communication where such a person is a party to the communication or where one of the parties to the communication has given prior consent to such interception. . . .

The applicable language of this subsection is "where one of the parties to the communication has given prior consent to such interception."

In our case, both sides will agree that the first element, that the person giving consent be a party to the communication, is not in dispute. In each of the phone calls at issue, Ms. Johnson was one of the parties involved in the call. Thus, the only element in dispute is whether Ms. Johnson gave prior consent.

The courts have construed the phrase "prior consent" to include explicit and implied consent but not constructive consent. *See Williams v. Poulos,* 11 F.3d 271, 281 (1st Cir. 1993); *Griggs-Ryan v. Smith,* 904 F.2d 112, 119 (1st Cir. 1990). In our case, there was no explicit consent. Although Ms. Johnson was told that calls were intercepted, she did not explicitly agree to the interception of her calls. There may, however, have been implied consent.

In deciding whether there is implied consent, the courts have stated that such consent should not be cavalierly implied. *Deal v. Spears,* 980 F.2d 1153, 1157 (8th Cir. 1992); *Watkins v. L.M. Berry & Co.,* 704 F.2d 577, 581 (11th Cir. 1983). Instead, implied consent should only be found when the circumstances indicate that an individual knowingly agreed to the interception of his or her communications. *Williams v. Poulos,* 11 F.3d at 281; *Griggs-Ryan v. Smith,* 904 F.2d at 117.

To date, only three First Circuit cases have discussed the consent exception. In one of these cases, *Griggs-Ryan v. Smith,* the Court of Appeals affirmed summary judgment for the defendant when the plaintiff's landlady had repeatedly told the plaintiff that all of his phone calls would be recorded and the plaintiff did not put on any evidence indicating that his landlady had told him that she had stopped recording incoming calls or that she was recording only parts of calls. *Id.* at 119. In the other two cases, the Court of Appeals affirmed decisions finding no consent. In *Campiti v. Walonis,* 811 F.2d 387 (1st Cir. 1979), the First Circuit affirmed the district court's decision that there was no consent despite the defendant's argument that the plaintiff, a prisoner, should have known that his phone calls might be monitored. *Id.* at 393. Similarly, in *Williams v. Poulos,* the First Circuit affirmed the granting of an injunction because there was evidence in the record indicating that the plaintiff, a CEO, did not know that his own phone calls were being intercepted. *Id.* at 282.

In addition to the three First Circuit cases, there are several cases from other jurisdictions. In the case most factually analogous to ours, *Deal v. Spears,* the Spears, Deal's employers, told Deal that they might be forced to intercept or restrict her telephone privileges if she continued using the store's telephone for personal calls. After the Spears told Deal to limit her calls, the store was burglarized and the Spears suspected that Deal was involved. As a result, they installed a recording device on the extension phone in their mobile home, which was next to the store, in the hopes of catching Deal in an unguarded admission. When turned on, the recorder automatically recorded all conversations made on either the store phone or the extension with no indication to the parties using the phone that their conversation was being recorded. *Id.* at 1155–1156.

The Spears taped and listened to about twenty-two hours of calls over a six-week period. Although they did not hear anything indicating that Deal had been involved in the burglary, they did find out that she had sold a keg of beer at cost in violation of store policy and that she was having an affair with another individual. Deal was fired after Mr. Spears played parts of the tapes for her. Deal brought suit under Title 18, and the District Court granted judgment to her, finding that the consent exception did not apply. The Spears appealed, and the Eighth Circuit Court of Appeals affirmed the District Court's determination that there was no consent on the grounds (1) that the Spears only told Deal that they might intercept her phone calls and not that they were intercepting the calls and (2) that because the Spears hoped to catch Deal in an admission, it was not reasonable to assume that Deal knew that her calls were being intercepted. *Id.* at 1157.

Johnson will argue that the consent element is not met because she did not knowingly agree to the interception of her phone calls. Like the plaintiffs in *Campiti, Williams,* and *Deal,* who did not know that their calls were being intercepted, Johnson did not know that Elite was intercepting her calls. In the past, her phone calls had only been monitored in January, immediately before her annual performance review, and her supervisor had only intercepted two or three of her calls and had talked to her about those calls immediately afterwards. In addition, the facts indicate that Elite did not believe that Johnson knew that her calls were being intercepted. Just as the Spears hoped to catch Deal in an admission tying her to a burglary, Elite hoped to catch Johnson in an admission tying her to an insurance fraud scheme. In the alternative, Johnson can argue that even if she did consent to the monitoring of her phone calls to determine whether she was providing good customer service, she did not consent to the monitoring of her personal calls. Thus, Elite should have stopped recording her calls as soon as it recognized the call as being a personal call.

To win, Elite must establish that the circumstances indicate that Ms. Johnson knowingly agreed to the intercepting of her phone calls. *Campiti* and *Williams* will be relatively easy to distinguish. Unlike *Campiti,* in which the prisoners were never told that their calls would be intercepted, and *Williams,* in which the CEO was never told that his calls might be intercepted, Johnson was told about the company's monitoring policy. In addition, Elite can distinguish *Deal* on the basis that unlike Deal, who never knew that any of her calls were being intercepted, Johnson knew that her calls had been intercepted in the past and that they were subject to being intercepted in the future. In fact, this case is more like *Griggs-Ryan,* the case in which the landlady repeatedly told her tenants that all incoming calls would be intercepted, than it is any of the other cases. Just as the tenants in *Griggs-Ryan* received regular reminders about their landlady's policy, so did Johnson: the message that incoming callers received telling them that their calls were subject to monitoring should have provided Johnson with a daily reminder about Elite's monitoring policy.

Elite can also argue that as a matter of public policy, employers with monitoring policies like Elite's should be able to intercept employee phone calls without explicitly telling them that a particular call or set of calls will be intercepted. Because employees are likely to act differently when they know a particular call is being intercepted, employers will not be able to effectively monitor their employees' activities if they must tell an employee that a particular call or set of calls is being intercepted. Finally, Elite can argue that its warning that it would periodically monitor an employee's calls was broad enough to encompass both business and personal calls. An employee who is using the phone for personal calls is unable to provide as good service as one who only uses the phone for business calls.

Johnson is likely to respond to these arguments in two ways. First, it is not clear whether she heard the message that incoming callers heard. As a result, although the message may have put incoming callers on notice, it did not put her on notice, particularly given what she knew about Elite's actual practices. Second, the statute specifically requires that an individual give prior consent. Thus, even though an employer may have an interest in intercepting an employee's phone call, that interest is not recognized under the statute.

A court will probably find that there was no implied consent because Johnson did not knowingly agree to the interception of her calls. Although Elite told Ms. Johnson that her calls were subject to periodic monitoring, the interceptions that took place were not consistent with prior company practices. In addition, Elite's own reasons for monitoring Johnson's calls indicate that it did not believe that Johnson knew her calls were being intercepted.

CONCLUSION

A court will probably find that Elite Insurance intentionally intercepted Ms. Johnson's telephone calls without her prior consent. Although Elite told Ms. Johnson that her calls were subject to periodic monitoring, the monitoring that took place was not consistent with prior company practices. The monitoring occurred not in January at the time of Ms. Johnson's annual performance review but in July and August. In addition, instead of monitoring only two or three calls, Elite monitored calls for four or five weeks, and instead of talking to her about a call immediately after the call, Elite only talked to her about the calls at the very end. Finally, even if Johnson did consent to the monitoring of her calls to determine whether she was providing good customer service, she did not consent to the monitoring of personal calls, which, although against company policy, were tolerated. Finally, even though the court is likely to find that Ms. Johnson did not consent to the interception, we may be able to establish that the other party to the communication, Mr. Porter, consented to the monitoring of any calls that he may have made to Ms. Johnson. Although this may not eliminate Elite's liability, it may lessen it.

Chapter 6

The Second Memorandum

This chapter builds on Chapter 5. While in Chapter 5 we showed you how to research and write a relatively simple memo, in this chapter we show you how to research and write a more difficult one. In doing so, we review some of the material contained in Chapter 5 and introduce some new techniques: how to organize a memo that does not involve an analysis of elements, how to organize the discussion section using an integrated approach, how to use parentheticals, and how to write more concisely and precisely.

§6.1 RECEIVING THE ASSIGNMENT

It is now the summer after your second year of law school, and you are working for a personal injury firm in Roswell, New Mexico. One of the cases the firm is handling is an electromagnetic field (EMF) case. The facts are set out in the following memo from the senior partner.

EXAMPLE

To: Legal Intern

From: Raymond Sanchez

Re: File No. 123
        Nancy and Alan Flynn

- The Flynns want to know whether they have a cause of action against Pecos Power. Because there are high voltage lines behind their house, they have been unable to sell it.

- The Flynns' house is a four bedroom, three bathroom, 3500 square foot home with a pool and garden in the backyard. From the back of the house, the Flynns have a view of El Capitan Mountain and New Mexico's spectacular sunsets. The Flynns bought the house for $35,000 in 1975.
- When the Flynns bought the house, they knew that the land behind their home was owned by Pecos Power. Nothing was on the land, however, and when the Flynns contacted Pecos Power, they were told that the Power Company had no immediate plans for the land.
- In 1995, high voltage lines were erected on the land that runs behind the Flynns' home. In 1995, the lines were completed, and power began running through them. The lines are within 50 feet of the Flynns' home.
- In the last two years, a number of articles discussing EMFs have appeared in the *Roswell Daily Record,* the local newspaper. Several of the articles indicated that there was at least some evidence that exposure to EMFs increased the risk of cancer or other health problems, and one in the real estate section indicated that buyers should be wary of buying a home next to high voltage lines.
- A year ago, when their youngest child left for college, the Flynns put their house on the market. They did so for three reasons: (1) they wanted a smaller home, (2) the high voltage lines have obstructed their view of the mountain and sunsets, something they value, and (3) they no longer feel comfortable using their backyard pool or maintaining their large vegetable gardens because of the danger posed by the EMFs. In fact, since learning about the alleged dangers posed by EMFs, they almost never use their backyard, and they keep their grandchildren inside when they come to visit.
- Almost a year later, the Flynns have still been unable to sell their house, even though they have lowered the price from $199,000 to $179,000. The Flynns' real estate agent has told them that because of all of the publicity about EMFs, many people will not buy a house near power lines because they fear that either they or their children will get cancer. Even the recent studies that indicate that power lines do not cause leukemia do not seem to have quelled people's fears.
- The Flynns have had their house tested for EMFs. Although the house itself tested within safe limits, unusually high levels (21 milligauss) were found in the pool and garden areas.
- Neither Mr. nor Mrs. Flynn nor their children have, or have had, cancer.
- The Flynns' home is only one of two in the area that back up onto the high voltage power lines.

Because we need to get back to the client quickly, I have

asked several interns to work on the project. For your part, please determine whether the Flynns have a cause of action in nuisance.

---

§6.2　PREPARING A RESEARCH PLAN

Once again, the first step is to prepare a research plan. Before going into the library, you need to draft a preliminary issue statement, determine what law is likely to apply, prepare a list of search terms, and decide what sources you are going to consult and in what order.

§6.2.1　Drafting the Preliminary Issue Statement

Sometimes drafting the preliminary issue statement is difficult. In assigning the project, the attorney has not been clear about what he or she wants you to research. In these situations, you need to do two things. First, ask to see the case file. By reading through the file, you may be able to get a better feel for what you do and do not need to research. Second, ask questions, either at the time that you are given the assignment or after you have read the file or done some initial research. Most attorneys would rather have you ask questions than spend time researching something that they did not want researched.

Fortunately, in this case, drafting the preliminary issue statement is relatively easy. In his memo, the assigning attorney, Raymond Sanchez, set out the question that he wants you to research. All you need to add are the facts. Thus, you prepare the following statement.

Preliminary Issue Statement

Do the Flynns have a cause of action in nuisance against Pecos Power when they have been unable to sell their home, which is located within 50 feet of high voltage power lines?

You quickly realize, though, that to answer this question, you will need to answer a number of other questions. Thinking back to your first year of law school, you remember that there are different types of nuisance. Something can be a public nuisance, a private nuisance, a nuisance per se, or a nuisance in fact. You also remember reading a case that said that actions authorized by law cannot be a nuisance, or at least a nuisance per se. Finally, you know nothing about EMFs. If you are going to be able to analyze the problem, you are going to have to find out what they are.

Thus, in addition to writing the preliminary issue statement, you decide to write down some of the other questions that come to mind. You sketch out the following flow chart.

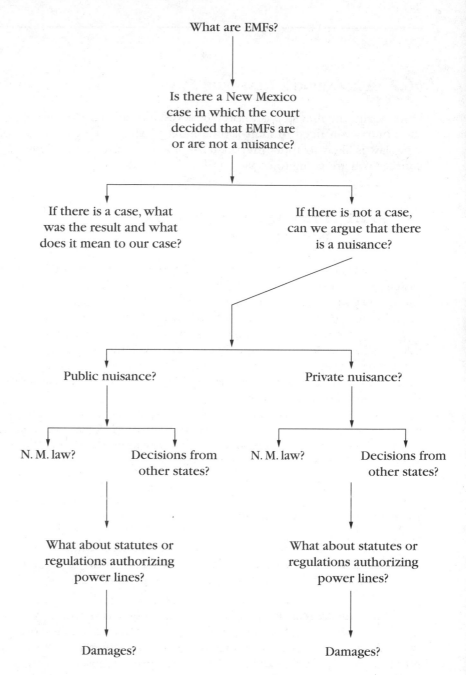

§6.2.2 Determining What Law Applies

In determining what law applies, you think, once again, back to your first-year classes. Your memory tells you that nuisance is governed by state rather than federal law. In addition, it tells you that although traditionally nuisance was a common law doctrine, many states have enacted statutes. Thus, you tentatively determine that the Flynn case will be governed by New Mexico statutes governing nuisance or, if there are no statutes, by New Mexico common law.

§6.2.3   Preparing a List of Search Terms

In preparing your list of search terms, you decide to include broad terms such as "nuisance" and narrower terms like "electromagnetic fields" and "EMFs." In addition, you decide to include terms that are related to some of the sub-questions, for example, "utility companies," "power companies," and "high voltage lines."

§6.2.4   Deciding Which Sources to Check

Like many other problems, there are a number of ways to research this problem. In fact, in thinking about which sources to check, you come up with four possible strategies.

Strategy No. 1: Begin with New Mexico Statutes Annotated

- Using the New Mexico Statutes Annotated, locate the statutes currently in effect relating to nuisance and high voltage power lines.
- Read the statutes, looking for sections that appear to apply.
- If no section or sections appear to apply, move to strategy 2. If section or sections do appear to apply, continue as set out below.
- Read and analyze the applicable statutory section or sections.
- Read the Notes of Decision following the applicable section or sections, looking for cases that appear on point, particularly for cases dealing with EMFs.
- Read the cases that appear on point.
- Cite check the cases that are on point, determining whether they are still good law and whether there are additional cases that are on point.
- Look for law review articles that are on point.

Strategy No. 2: Begin with the Pacific Digest

- Look up "Nuisance" in the Pacific Digest.
- Read through the Notes of Decision, looking both for statutory references and for cases that appear on point.
- Locate and read the cases and statutory sections that appear on point.
- Cite check the cases and statutes that are on point, determining

whether they are still good law and whether there are additional cases that are on point.
- Look for law review articles that are on point.

Strategy No. 3: Begin by Looking for a Law Review Article or an ALR Annotation that Is on Point

- Using either a print, CD-ROM, or online index, locate ALR annotations and law review articles that appear to be on point.
- Locate and skim either the annotations or two or three of the most recent law review articles, looking specifically for information about nuisances and EMFs.
- Look up and read the N.M. statutes and cases cited in the articles or, if no N.M. statutes or cases are cited, the most recent out-of-state cases discussing nuisance.
- Use either strategy 1 or strategy 2 to locate N.M. statutes and analogous cases.

Strategy No. 4: Begin by Running Online Search

- Using either LEXIS or Westlaw, run the following search in the New Mexico cases database: "electromagnetic field" EMF w/10 nuisance.
- Read and cite check any statutes and cases that you locate.
- If nothing is found in the N.M. database, revert to strategy 1, 2, or 3 above, or run same search in an all-states database and then revert to strategy 1, 2, or 3.

In the Flynn case, all four strategies have advantages and disadvantages. If you use Strategy No. 1, you can quickly locate New Mexico's statutes relating to nuisance and high voltage power lines. In addition, by reading the nuisance statutes and Notes of Decision following them, you can quickly eliminate public nuisance as possible cause of action. It is unlikely that the Flynns can prove that Pecos Power maintained the lines without lawful authority or that the lines are injurious to public health, safety, morals, or welfare or that they interfere with the exercise and enjoyment of public rights. Finally, this strategy also leads you to at least some of the cases that discuss private nuisance: Some of the cases listed in the Notes of Decision, for example, *City of Albuquerque v. State* discuss not only the rules relating to public nuisance but also the rules relating to private nuisance. There are, however, some things that you can't find using Strategy No. 1. Because the statutes discuss only public nuisance, the Notes of Decision following them are not a reliable source for finding cases dealing with private nuisance. In addition, the Notes of Decision are not a reliable way of finding EMF cases. Even if a case involved EMFs, the word "EMF" might not appear in the note.

While Strategy No. 1 provided an easy way to find the New Mexico statutes, Strategy No. 2 provides an easy way of finding New Mexico cases. Under "Nuisance" in the Pacific Digest are cases setting out the general rules relating both to private and public nuisance. See section 14.3 for a discussion of digests. Key numbers 1 through 58 discuss private nuisance, and key numbers 59 through 96 discuss public nuisance. Some of these cases provide citations to the New Mexico statutes. What is more difficult to find are cases that discuss EMFs. Like the Notes of Decision following a statute, the Notes of Decision in the digest may not set out the specific facts of a case. In addition, the Notes of Decision do not include citations to out-of-state cases or to law review articles.

Strategy No. 3 has several advantages over Strategies 1 and 2. First, several of the law review articles explain EMFs and provide citations to scientific studies. Second, several of the articles discuss EMFs as a basis for a cause of action in nuisance, providing you with a list of cases in which the courts have ruled on the issue. Finally, a number of the authors have taken a position on the issue, setting out arguments either for or against allowing EMFs as a basis for a cause of action in nuisance. What the articles do not provide, however, are citations to New Mexico statutes or to New Mexico cases that might be used to argue by analogy.

The last strategy has the advantage of providing a quick answer to what is probably the most basic question: Is there a New Mexico case in which the court has decided that EMFs are or are not a nuisance? If there is such a case, it may answer the question and no further research would be needed. If, though, there is no such case, then you will have to run the same search in other jurisdictions to see if they have decided the issue or revert to strategies 1, 2, or 3.

As in most cases, in our example case, all four strategies lead, eventually, to the same information. Thus, in deciding where to start, you should consider the availability of the various sources, the costs associated with using those sources, and the reliability and currency of the sources. Do not, however, automatically eliminate a source because it is not readily available. An hour spent going to the nearest law library to read recent law review articles may be more cost efficient than several hours of other types of research.

For the purposes of our problem, presume that the firm has copies of the New Mexico code and reporters, the Pacific Digest, and a Westlaw subscription that allows unlimited use of the New Mexico database. It does not, however, have ALR, an index to law review articles, any law reviews other than the *New Mexico Law Review,* or reporters from other states. In this situation, you decide to prepare the following research plan.

Research Plan

Preliminary Issue Statement:	Do the Flynns have a cause of action in nuisance against Pecos Power when they have been unable to sell their home, which is located 50 feet from high voltage power lines?
Jurisdiction:	New Mexico

Type of Law:	Statutory and common law
Search Terms:	"nuisance," "electromagnetic fields," EMFs, "utility companies," "power companies," and "high voltage lines"

Step 1: Run the following search in Westlaw's New Mexico databases: "electromagnetic field" EMF w/10 of nuisance.

Step 2: If that search produces no results, run the following search: "electromagnetic field" EMF.

Step 3: Look up "Nuisance," "Power Companies," "Power Lines," and "Utilities" in the General Index of the New Mexico Statutes Annotated. Identify and read the statutes that appear on point and any cases listed in the Notes of Decision that appear to be on point. Cite check both the statutes and cases to make sure that they are still good law.

Step 4: If that search produces no results, look up "Nuisance" in the Pacific Digest. Read the Notes of Decision, identifying the five or six cases that appear most on point. Read and cite check the cases that appear on point. Also read and cite check any cases that you locate through cite checking.

Step 5: Go to county law library and locate and read law review articles and out-of-state cases that appear to be on point. Cite check any of the out-of-state cases that you think that you might use.

Question

What strategy would you use if you were doing the research in a law school library or a large state or county law library? What are the advantages and disadvantages of your proposed search strategy?

_____

§6.3   Understanding What You Have Found

Presume that in doing the research, you found the following:

- Several New Mexico statutes defining public nuisances
- Several New Mexico cases setting out the rules relating to both public and private nuisances
- Several law review articles discussing EMF litigation, including lawsuits in which the plaintiff tried to establish a cause of action in nuisance

You did not find any New Mexico cases discussing EMFs.

Having found the material, you now must make sense of it. Although there are a number of ways of doing this, you decide to start by going back to the flow chart that you made earlier, answering the questions in it.

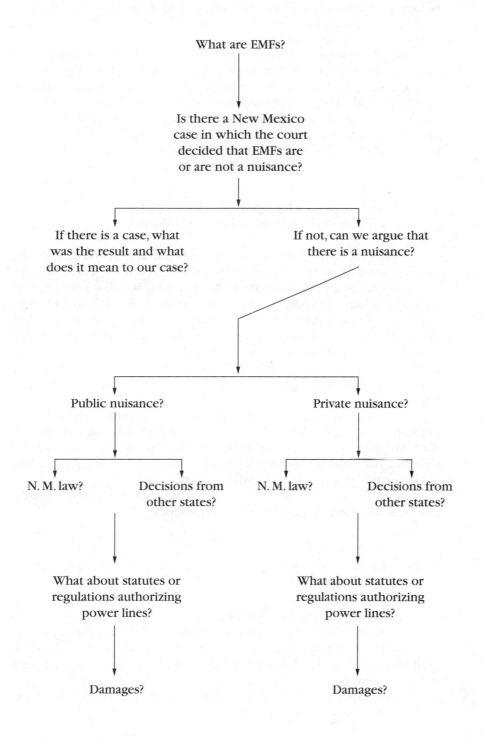

1. What Are EMFs?

As a practicing attorney, you will often need to become an instant "expert" on a particular topic. You will need to learn about a specific accounting procedure, a specific type of injury, or a specific type of technology. As a consequence, you will often need to do "non-legal legal research," locating and reading information in other fields. The trick is in knowing how much you need to know.

In the Flynn case, you don't need to know everything that there is to know about EMFs. You just need to know enough about them to understand the danger that they potentially pose and how they are similar or dissimilar from other "substances" that have been found to constitute a nuisance. Thus, at least at this point, it is enough to read the descriptions of EMFs set out in the law review articles. You don't need to read the reports that they cite or do research in scientific or medical journals.

2. Is There a New Mexico Case in Which the Court Decided that EMFs Are or Are Not a Nuisance?

Having developed a basic understanding of EMFs, you turn to the next question: Is there a New Mexico case in which the court decided that EMFs are or are not a nuisance? Because your Westlaw searches produced no results and you did not see any references to EMFs in reviewing the Notes of Decision in the New Mexico Code and Digest, you are confident that the New Mexico Supreme Court has not decided the issue and that there is no published decision from the New Mexico Court of Appeals. Thus, there is no mandatory authority on the issue and, when the issue reaches the New Mexico appellate courts, it will be an issue of first impression.

What you don't know, though, is whether there is any EMF litigation currently in the New Mexico trial courts. To find out whether there is such litigation, you would need to consult more informal sources, for example, bar bulletins and newsletters, articles in local newspapers, other lawyers, and possibly, various EMF websites.

After checking out some of these informal sources and not finding anything, you turn to the next level of questions.

3. Can the Flynns Argue that the EMFs Constitute a Public Nuisance?

As you discovered in doing the research, public nuisances are defined by statute. Thus, you begin your analysis by re-reading the applicable statutes. The first thing that you do is read through the table of contents at the beginning of the chapter, identifying those sections that are potentially on point.

In the Flynn case, only three sections are general enough to be po-

---

EXHIBIT 6.1

ARTICLE 8
Nuisances

Sec.
30-8-1. Public nuisance.
30-8-2. Polluting water.
30-8-3. Refuse defined.
30-8-4. Littering.
30-8-5. Enforcement.
30-8-6. Posting; notice to public.
30-8-7. Public education.
30-8-8. Abatement of a public nuisance.
30-8-8.1. Abatement of house of prostitution.

Sec.
30-8-9. Abandonment of dangerous containers.
30-8-10. Placing injurious substance on highways.
30-8-11. Illegal prescribing of medicine.
30-8-12. Conduct offensive to public well-being.
30-8-13. Unlawfully permitting livestock upon public highways.
30-8-14. Highway department; agreements with owners or lessees of highway frontage; provisions.

30-8-1. Public nuisance.

A public nuisance consists of knowingly creating, performing or maintaining anything affecting any number of citizens without lawful authority which is either:

    A. injurious to public health, safety, morals or welfare; or

    B. interferes with the exercise and enjoyment of public rights, including the right to use public property.

Whoever commits a public nuisance for which the act or penalty is not otherwise prescribed by law is guilty of a petty misdemeanor.

History: 1953 Comp., § 40A-8-1, enacted by Laws 1963, ch. 303, § 8-1.

Cross references. — For polluting of water being public nuisance, see 30-8-2 NMSA 1978. For provisions on abatement of public nuisance, see 30-8-8 NMSA 1978. For conduct offensive to public well-being, see 30-8-12 NMSA 1978. For house of prostitution being public nuisance, see 30-9-8 NMSA 1978. For gambling and gambling houses being public nuisance, see 30-19-8 NMSA 1978. For provision making forest fire burning without proper precaution a public nuisance, see 30-32-1 NMSA 1978.

Nuisance must affect group of people. — A public nuisance must affect a considerable number of people or an entire community or neighborhood. Environmental Imp. Div. v. Bloomfield Irrigation Dist., 108 N.M. 691, 778 P.2d 438 (Ct. App. 1989).

Acts of municipality under governmental authority. — In the absence of a showing of fraud, collusion, or illegality, a city's constitutional and statutory authority to construct public highways and bridges constitutes a valid defense to a claim of nuisance per se. City of Albuquerque v. State ex rel. Village of Los Ranchos de Albuquerque, 111 N.M. 608, 808 P.2d 58 (Ct. App. 1991).

Acts which the law authorized to be done, if carried out and maintained in the manner authorized by law, where a public entity acts under its governmental

tentially applicable: sections 30-8-1, 30-8-5, and 30-8-8. You begin by reading the most general of the sections, section 30-8-1. See Exhibit 6.1.

30-8-1 Public Nuisance

A public nuisance consists of knowingly creating, performing or maintaining anything affecting any number of citizens without lawful authority which is either

    A. injurious to public health, safety, morals or welfare; or

    B. interferes with the exercise and enjoyment of public rights, including the right to use public property.

Although the Flynns can prove that Pecos Power knowingly created and maintained the high voltage lines, they cannot prove that it did so without lawful authority. The erection of the high voltage lines was approved by the New Mexico Public Utilities Commission. In addition, it seems unlikely that the Flynns can prove that the lines are injurious to public health or that they interfere with the exercise and enjoyment of public rights. Because it does not appear that the Flynns can establish that the lines constitute a public nuisance, you don't spend any additional time on this issue. You don't spend time trying to figure out what the phrase "affecting any number of citizens" means, and you don't try to answer the other questions in this section of the flow chart. Although in reading the cases you will need to make sure that you interpreted the statute correctly, at this point you turn your attention to private nuisance.

4. Can the Flynns Argue that the EMFs Constitute a Private Nuisance?

Because there are no New Mexico statutes dealing with private nuisance, you turn to the cases, looking again at the cases that discussed private nuisance. In particular, you look again at *Padilla v. Lawrence,* a case that appeared under a number of different subsections in the New Mexico Digest and that appears to be one of the key cases in New Mexico.

In reading *Padilla v. Lawrence,* you want to do a number of things. First, you want to put the case in context, determining whether the case is mandatory or persuasive authority and what the social and political context was when it was decided. Second, you want to find the rules. What test or tests did the court apply in determining whether there was a private nuisance? Third, you want to find out how the court applied the rules that it set out. What were the facts in the case, and what conclusion did the court reach when it applied the rules to those facts? Finally, you want to see what types of arguments the parties made and how the courts responded to those arguments.

Thus, you begin your reading of *Padilla v. Lawrence* by reading the caption:

101 N.M. 556

**Atanacio PADILLA and Juanita Padilla
and Johnny E. Padilla, Plaintiffs-
Appellees, Cross-Appellants,**

v.

**Amy LAWRENCE and Sun Country Garden Products,
a New Mexico Corporation, Defendants-Appellants,
Cross-Appellees.**

No. 7348.

Court of Appeals of New Mexico.

June 7, 1984.

Certiorari Denied July 19, 1984.

Because *Padilla* is a Court of Appeals decision, a New Mexico trial court must apply the rules set out in it unless one of the parties can distinguish the case. The decision is not, however, binding on the New Mexico Court of Appeals or the New Mexico Supreme Court. These courts can apply the rules set out in the case or modify or reject those rules.

The next step is to determine how long the case is. If it is only two or three pages long, you will probably want to read it in its entirety; if it is longer, it is better to begin by reading the syllabus and by skimming the headnotes. Because *Padilla v. Lawrence* is relatively long, you choose the second approach, reading the syllabus and headnotes to determine the causes of action, the issues on appeal, and the sections of the opinion that appear to be on point.

Text of Syllabus	**What to Look For**
Class action was brought against manure processing plant and its owner requesting an injunction, money damages based upon theories of trespass, public nuisance, private nuisance, negligence, and personal injury, and also requesting punitive damages. The District Court, Bernalillo County, Frank H. Allen, Jr., D.J., awarded plaintiffs damages for inconvenience, discomfort, and annoyance, defendants appealed, and plaintiffs cross-appealed. The Court of Appeals, Minzner, J., held that: (1) substantial evidence supported trial court's finding of private nuisance; (2) award of damages for annoyance, discomfort, and inconvenience was not abuse of discretion; (3) trial court properly refused to award damages for diminution in property value; (4) trial court properly denied injunctive relief for a continuing nuisance; (5) trial court properly dismissed public nuisance claim; (6) plaintiffs were not entitled to damages for trespass; and (7) plaintiffs were not entitled to punitive damages. Affirmed.	The first thing that you note in reading the syllabus is that the plaintiffs set out causes of action in both public and private nuisance. Although it does not appear that the Flynns have a cause of action for a public nuisance (see pages 187–188), they may have a cause of action for a private nuisance. Thus, the case appears to be on point and you keep reading. The second thing that you note are the types of damages that were awarded. The trial court awarded the plaintiff damages for inconvenience, discomfort, and annoyance but not for diminution in property value. This may not be good news. Although the Flynns may be able to claim damages for inconvenience, discomfort, and annoyance, what they really want is to be compensated for the diminished value of their home.

After reading the syllabus, you begin reading the headnotes, looking most carefully at those that have as their heading "Nuisance." Headnotes 1 and 2, 4 through 16, and 21 set out general rules for private nuisances, and headnotes 22 and 23 set out rules for public nuisances. Because the headnotes related to nuisance are at the beginning of the opinion, you decide to begin reading the opinion at the beginning, quickly reading through the material set out below.

OPINION

MINZNER, Judge.

Atanacio Padilla, Juanita Padilla, and their son, Johnny E. Padilla ("plaintiffs"), long-term residents of Bernalillo, New Mexico, filed a class action complaint against defendant Amy Lawrence and defendant Sun Country Garden Products, a corporation ("the plant"). Lawrence is the owner of the plant, also located in Bernalillo, which processes bark and manure for the purpose of packaging soil conditioner for sale. Plaintiffs requested an injunction against the plant and sought money damages based upon theories of trespass, public nuisance, private nuisance, negligence, and personal injury. Plaintiffs also sought punitive damages.

Prior to trial, the court dismissed the class action count and plaintiffs withdrew the personal injury count. The case was tried before the trial court, which dismissed the negligence and public nuisance claims at the close of plaintiffs' case. Following presentation of all the evidence, judgment was entered for plaintiffs on the private nuisance claim. The court refused to grant injunctive relief but awarded plaintiffs Atanacio and Juanita Padilla $10,000 each for inconvenience, discomfort, and annoyance. The court also awarded Johnny E. Padilla the sum of $2,000 for discomfort and annoyance. Although the trial court found that the value of plaintiffs' residence has been diminished by the operation of the plant, it concluded that plaintiffs failed to prove the amount of the loss. The trial court also concluded that no trespass was established and declined to award punitive damages.

What to Look For

In reading this part of the opinion, you are looking for several things: the identity of the parties, the basis for the nuisance cause of action, and what happened at trial.

When you get to this part of the opinion, the part dealing with damages, you begin reading more slowly. The news isn't as bad as you thought. The reason the plaintiffs weren't awarded damages for the diminuition in the value of their property is they failed to prove the amount of their loss.

Because the heading indicates that this is the section of the opinion that deals with private nuisance, you slow down, reading more carefully. You also begin asking yourself the following questions. How are the facts in this case similar to or different from the facts in our case? What test or tests did the court apply? What arguments did the parties make, and how did the court respond to those arguments?

Text of Opinion	What to Look For

I. LIABILITY FOR PRIVATE NUISANCE

Plaintiffs Atanacio and Juanita Padilla own real property on which their residence is located, which is approximately 600 feet from the nearest boundary of the plant. They have resided in the house for over twenty-five years. The plant has been in operation for approximately five years. It is located in the industrial park of Bernalillo and covers over nine acres. Plaintiffs' house is among several residences near the plant. The record indicates that these residences are outside the industrial park.

The trial court heard testimony from the plaintiffs, from several of their neighbors, from plaintiffs' expert witness, and from a realtor as to the negative physical and aesthetic impact of the plant's operation on plaintiffs' enjoyment of their property. The witnesses testified that the plant's operation has resulted in plaintiffs' exposure to odors, dust, noise, and flies, which were not in evidence prior to construction and operation. The witnesses testified that an odor, variously described as that of a dead animal, of a pig pen, and of rotten fish, permeated the air, and that dust, noise, and flies were also a problem. The odor prohibited cooking in the summer, prevented use of evaporative cooling, and generally interfered with normal residential activities. Plaintiff Atanacio Padilla testified that the odor and dust caused him to have nosebleeds and fits of choking.

Mr. Padilla also testified that he and his wife finally moved from the residence in 1982 because of the problems associated with the plant's operation and that the nosebleeds and choking

As you read the opinion, you note that the facts in *Padilla* are similar to the facts in our case. In both instances, the plaintiffs owned their home for over 25 years and the "nuisance" was built after the plaintiffs had lived in their homes for some time. There are, however, some important differences. While the Padillas were forced to move from their home, the Flynns are still living in theirs. In addition, while everyone agrees that the noise and odors from a bark and manure processing plant are "harmful," not everyone agrees that EMFs are dangerous.

In reading this part of the opinion, you want to compare the testimony that was presented in *Padilla* with the testimony that you might be able to present. Is the evidence in *Padilla* stronger and more compelling than the evidence in the Flynn case, or is the evidence in the Flynn case stronger? You decide that the evidence can be viewed in either of two ways. On the one hand, the evidence in *Padilla* seems stronger than the evidence in the Flynn case. In Flynn, there are no odors, noise, dust, or flies, and the Flynns have not been forced to leave their home. On the other hand, the evidence in Flynn can be viewed as being stronger. While in *Padilla* the plant only caused inconvenience and discomfort, the EMFs might result in cancer and death. The problem, of course, is in establishing a causal link.

Text of Opinion	**What to Look For**

Text of Opinion

have stopped. Plaintiff Johnny E. Padilla testified that he began renting the residence at that time and that the problems continue. The realtor testified that the plant's operation caused problems that affected the property's value as a residence.

A. *The Requirement of Unreasonableness in the Context of a Private Nuisance*

[1, 2] A private nuisance has been defined as a non-trespassory invasion of another's interest in the private use and enjoyment of land. *Scott v. Jordan,* 99 N.M. 567, 661 P.2d 59 (Ct.App.1983). It is a civil wrong based on a disturbance of rights in land. *Jellison v. Gleason,* 77 N.M. 445, 423 P.2d 876 (1967). The elements of proof depend on whether the conduct is intentional or unintentional. Liability for intentional conduct requires that the conduct be unreasonable. *See Restatement (Second) of Torts* [hereinafter cited as *Restatement*] §822(a) (1979).

[3, 4] We must sustain the trial court's findings and conclusions if they are supported by substantial evidence, and we must review the facts and evidence in the light most favorable to the prevailing party. *Scott v. Jordan.* Viewed in this light, the evidence would support a finding that the invasion was intentional because defendants knew or should have known that their conduct in operating the plant

What to Look For

It is at this point that the court begins to set out definitions and rules. Because you will need to include these rules in your memo, you begin to take notes, recording first the definition of a private nuisance. However, when you get to that portion of the opinion that sets out the elements of proof, you stop. In the Flynn case, is the conduct intentional or unintentional? At least part of the answer to this question is in the next paragraph: Conduct is intentional if the defendant knew or should have known that its conduct interfered with the plaintiffs' use and enjoyment of their land.

In applying this rule to the Flynn case, you decide that, more likely than not, a court would find that the conduct was intentional. Just as the defendants in *Padilla* should have known that their plant would interfere with the Padillas' use and enjoyment of their land, in our case Pecos Power should have known that the erection of the high voltage lines would interfere with the Flynns' use and enjoyment of their land. You do, however, decide to check the Restatement sections cited in *Padilla.*

Although this paragraph is not directly on point—the paragraph sets out the standard of review—it provides a good reminder that in *Padilla* the Court of Appeals did not review the evidence *de novo.* It only determined whether there was substantial evidence to support the trial court's findings.

Text of Opinion	What to Look For

interfered with plaintiffs' use and enjoyment of their land. *See Restatement* §825(b). Evidence also supports the finding that the operation of the plant was unreasonable.

[5, 6] Defendants have argued that the trial court's finding of unreasonableness lacks substantial evidence, but they have analyzed "unreasonableness" as if the issue were negligence. Although defendants offered testimony that steps were taken to reduce the plant's negative impact on the area and that they had complied with City Council and Environmental Improvement Division requests and requirements, liability for nuisance, unlike liability for negligence, exists regardless of the degree of care exercised to avoid injury. *Wofford v. Rudick,* 63 N.M. 307, 318 P.2d 605 (1957). In the nuisance context, an intentional invasion is unreasonable if the gravity of the harm outweighs the utility of the actor's conduct, *see Scott v. Jordan; Restatement* § 826(a), or if the harm caused by the conduct is serious and the financial burden of compensating for the harm would not make continuing the conduct unfeasible, *Restatement* §826(b). Section 826(b) of the *Restatement* recognizes that damages may be appropriate even if the utility of the activity outweighs the harm it causes. *Carpenter v. Double R Cattle Co.,* 105 Idaho 320, 669 P.2d 643 (App. 1983).

[7] The unreasonableness of intentional invasions is "a problem of relative values to be determined by the trier of fact in each case in the light of all the circumstances of that case." *Restatement* §826 comment b. The *Restatement,* §§827 and 828, has suggested factors which are relevant in determining the gravity of harm[1] and the utility of conduct.[2] These factors are relevant under both Section 826(a) and Section 826(b). *See Carpenter v. Double R Cattle Co.*

This paragraph presents another hurdle. Presuming that the conduct was intentional, can the Flynns establish that the operation of the power lines is unreasonable? The court sets out a two-prong test: An intentional invasion is unreasonable if the gravity of harm outweighs the utility of the actor's conduct or if the harm caused by the conduct is serious and the financial burden of compensating for the harm would not make continuing the conduct unfeasible. The first prong of the test would be difficult to prove. At this point, there is no direct proof that EMFs cause cancer, and electrical power is of great social utility. The second prong of the test might be a bit easier to establish. If we can establish that the harm is serious, we may be able to prove that the cost of compensating individuals like the Flynns does not make the activity, the providing of electrical power, unfeasible. The good news is that the court did not accept the defendants' argument that there was no nuisance because the defendants had taken steps to reduce the plant's negative impact.

In this paragraph the court discusses the two-prong test in more detail. It sets out the factors from the Restatement and then applies them to the facts of the case. As the Flynns' attorney, we need to do the same thing. We need to go through the factors, determining what each side could argue.

Text of Opinion

[8, 9] The trial court found that the operation of the plant deprived plaintiffs from enjoying the use of their property and caused plaintiffs Atanacio and Juanita Padilla to move away from their residence of twenty-five years. Further, there was evidence that the property would be difficult to sell for residential purposes and the court found that the value of the residence has been diminished. Plaintiffs Atanacio and Juanita Padilla established their home long before defendants began operating the plant, and priority of occupation is a circumstance of considerable weight in determining unreasonableness. *Schlotfelt v. Vinton Farmers' Supply Co.*, 252 Iowa 1102, 109 N.W.2d 695 (1961). Although there was evidence that the conduct was suitable to the character of the locality, and this is relevant to the question of social utility under Section 828, this evidence alone is not sufficient to require a finding of reasonableness. *Scott v. Jordan.* Further, compliance with city and agency requirements is not sufficient to require a finding of reasonableness. *Schlotfelt v. Vinton Farmers' Supply Co.*

There was substantial evidence to support the trial court's finding of unreasonableness. The finding of a private nuisance is affirmed.

1. In determining the gravity of harm, the suggested factors include the extent and character of the harm involved, the social value that the law attaches to the type of use or enjoyment invaded, the suitability of the particular use or enjoyment to the character of the locality, and the burden on the person harmed of avoiding the harm. *Restatement* § 827.

2. In determining the utility of conduct, the suggested factors include the social value that the law attaches to the primary purpose of the conduct, the suitability of the conduct to the character of the locality, and the impracticability of preventing or avoiding the invasion. *Restatement* § 828.

What to Look For

Some of the facts that the trial court relied on in *Padilla* are the same as the facts in our case. In both cases, there is evidence that the property is difficult to sell, and in both cases the plaintiffs had established their homes before the defendants began their conduct. There are, however, some differences. While the Padillas moved from their home, the Flynns have not. In addition, power plants may have more social utility than a bark and manure processing plant.

After reading *Padilla,* you read the other cases that appear to be on point. In doing so, you use similar strategies, that is, you put the cases in context, you identify the rules that the court applied, and you determine what arguments each side made and how the court responded to those arguments.

The next step is to look at the cases as a whole. Have the courts set out and applied the same rules in each case? If they have, more likely than not the court will apply the same rule in your case. If they haven't, you need to look for a pattern. Can the cases be distinguished on their facts? Is the rule evolving? For example, have the courts moved from a broad to a narrow interpretation of the rule? Can the differences be explained on the basis of some underlying policy? What do the cases in which the court found for the plaintiff have in common? Similarly, what do the cases in which the court found for the defendant have in common? Preparing a chart like the one set out in section 5.4 can help you see patterns that you might not otherwise see.

§6.4　CONSTRUCTING THE ARGUMENTS

Experienced attorneys begin constructing arguments almost as soon as they receive a case. They think about what arguments they might be able to make as they talk to the client and read through supporting documents and as they read, analyze, and synthesize the law.

Although each attorney approaches the process in a slightly different way, most attorneys do the following.

1. They Brainstorm

At least initially, most attorneys try to identify as many arguments as possible. To do so, they try to approach the problem from several different perspectives.

(a)　They analyze the law, thinking about how each side would argue each issue and sub-issue and how they would use each rule, test, and analogous case.

(b)　They analyze the facts, thinking about how each side might use each. In addition, they think about the missing or unknown facts, the "what ifs."

(c)　They think about the standard arguments that are made in this type of case. For example, they think about what type of factual, analogous case, and policy arguments they might be able to make.

(d)　They think about the bigger picture. What would be the "right" or "just" way of resolving this case? What are the implications of finding for the plaintiff? for the defendant? What is the social and political context in which the case is being decided?

For example, in *Flynn*, the list might look something like this.

Possible Arguments:

- EMFs create a risk of cancer.
- At this point the evidence is inconclusive; some studies indicate that that there is a link between EMFs and health problems, and others don't.
- Fear of EMFs is unreasonable.
- In no other cases have the courts found that EMFs constitute a nuisance.
- The EMFs have interfered with the Flynns' use of their property.
- The lines obstruct the Flynns' view.
- Because of their fear of cancer, the Flynns no longer use their backyard.
- The Flynns should have expected that Pecos Power might erect power lines on its property.
- Unlike the Padillas, the Flynns have not been forced to move from their house.
- There are no unpleasant odors or flies. Is there noise?
- The burden of compensating Flynns would not be substantial— all they want is to be able to sell their home.
- Any increased costs can be passed on to the ratepayers.
- The Flynns should not have to bear the cost of something that benefits everyone.
- Very few people live close to high voltage lines.
- Almost everyone lives near some sort of power line; finding for the Flynns could open the floodgates.
- It is the media that has created the fear of EMFs.

Some attorneys approach brainstorming in a very systematic way, considering each of the possibilities one by one. Others simply keep lists as they research, read, analyze, and write. Still others need to talk about the case with someone in the firm, relying on an informal oral argument to help them flesh out each side's arguments. The trick is not to stop after coming up with one possible argument, but to keep thinking about additional arguments, both that you might be able to make on behalf of your client and that the other side might make.

2. They Develop Assertions and Arguments to Support Those Assertions

As they brainstorm, most attorneys begin to develop assertions, which are usually based on the legal rules and tests. For example, in brainstorming, you might come up with the following assertions.

Flynns' Assertion:

The harm caused by the high voltage lines is serious, and the financial burden of compensating the Flynns for the harm they have suffered would not make continuing the conduct unfeasible.

Pecos Power's Assertions:

The harm caused by the high voltage line is not serious.

In the alternative, even if the harm caused by the high voltage lines is serious, the burden of compensating everyone who lives near power lines would make continuing to provide low cost power unfeasible.

As they develop these assertions, most attorneys begin to match them with the arguments that they identified while brainstorming. What arguments support the Flynns' assertion? Pecos Power's assertions?

Arguments that Support Flynns' Assertion

Harm is serious because

- like the Padillas, the Flynns are no longer able to fully enjoy their home.
  - the lines interfere with their view
  - they no longer use their backyard
  - they cannot sell their home
- EMFs create a risk of cancer.

Burden of compensating Flynns would not make continuing conduct unfeasible because

- all the Flynns want is to be able to sell their house.
- very few people live close to high voltage lines.
- company can pass costs on to customers through rate increases.
- as a matter of public policy, it is the public and not the Flynns who should bear the cost of the harm.

Arguments that Support Pecos Power's Assertions

The harm caused by the high voltage line is not serious because

- recent studies have not found a link between EMFs and leukemia.
- the harm is a fear of EMFs and not any actual harm from the EMFs.
- there is no reason why the Flynns cannot use their backyard.

- the Flynns knew that the land behind their home was owned by Pecos Power and that it might erect power lines on it.

Even if the harm caused by the high voltage lines is serious, the burden of compensating everyone who lives near power lines would make continuing to provide low cost power unfeasible because

- compensating the Flynns would open the floodgates to a variety of claims, not only based on high voltage lines but on all power lines and power facilities.
- neither Pecos Power nor its customers should have to bear the burden of harms caused by unreasonable fears; if anyone is liable, it should be the media.

3. They Evaluate the Assertions and Arguments in Support of Those Assertions

After coming up with as many assertions and arguments as they can, most attorneys take a step back and evaluate those arguments, deciding which assertions and arguments are worth making and which aren't. While in writing a brief, attorneys are selective, presenting only the strongest arguments, in writing an objective memorandum they err on the side of including rather than excluding an argument. If the memorandum is to serve its purpose, those reading it must know about all of the arguments that each side is likely to make. Thus, in the Flynn case, most attorneys would eliminate from the list only those assertions and arguments that can't pass the giggle test, for example, that it is the media that is liable for any harm that the Flynns have suffered.

Question

Why would you want to know what arguments each side is likely to make before you begin drafting your statement of facts, question presented, and brief answer?

---

§6.5   DRAFTING THE STATEMENT OF FACTS

As you learned in Chapter 5 (see section 5.7), in drafting the statement of facts you want to include all of the legally significant facts and those emotionally significant and background facts that the attorney needs to understand and evaluate the case. In addition, you want to tell the attorney what facts are missing.

There are two ways to determine which facts are legally significant.

Before you begin writing, you can go through the issues and sub-issues one at a time, identifying the facts that a court would consider in deciding those issues. Then, after you have written the first draft of your discussion section, you can go back through it, making sure that you included in your statement of facts each of the facts that you used in your discussion section. To determine which emotionally significant and background facts you need to include, think about which facts might influence the outcome of the case and which facts are needed to tell the story.

Once you have decided which facts need to be included, you can then select an organizational scheme. As a general rule, you will want to present the facts either in chronological or topical order, or you will want to use a topical scheme, presenting the facts in chronological order within each topic. Finally, in writing the statement of facts, you want to make sure that you present the facts accurately and objectively. Although in writing a brief you want to present the facts in the light most favorable to your client, you do not want to do so in an objective memorandum.

In the Flynn case, there is at least one missing fact. Although the Flynns have indicated that people won't buy their house because of its proximity to the high voltage lines, there may be another reason why the house is hard to sell. It is possible that the Flynns have not maintained the home or that there is something else in the neighborhood that makes the property hard to sell.

The only other issue in writing the statement of facts for the Flynn case is whether to include an explanation of EMFs and, if you include one, where to put it. Whether an explanation should be included depends on how much the assigning attorney and others who might work on the case know about EMFs. If they know what EMFs are, it is not necessary to include an explanation. Even though you needed to find out what EMFs were so that you could research and analyze the problem, don't automatically assume that your reader needs the same information. Where to put the explanation is a judgment call: the explanation fits equally well in the statement of facts and the discussion section.

§6.6   Drafting the Question Presented

In Chapter 5, you saw how to draft a question presented using the "under-does-when" format. See section 5.8. After the "under," you inserted a reference to the rule of law; after the "does" or a similar word, the legal conclusion; and after the "when," the most significant of the legally significant facts.

Although the "under-does-when" format is the easiest format to use, many attorneys prefer the more traditional "whether" format. Under this format, the question begins with the word "whether," which is then followed by a statement of the legal question and most significant of the legally significant facts. Although there is not a separate reference to the rule of law, a reference may be incorporated into the legal question.

Whether the Flynns have a cause of action for either public or private nuisance when, because of the proximity of high voltage lines, they have been unable to sell their home.

At first, most writers are bothered by the fact that questions presented written using the whether format are incomplete sentences. If you are one of those writers, remember that the format is shorthand for "The question is whether . . . ." Also remember that because the complete sentence is a statement rather than a question, you need to use a period and not a question mark.

§6.7   DRAFTING THE BRIEF ANSWER

The brief answer answers the question asked in the question presented. By convention, most brief answers begin with a one- or two-word answer, which is followed by a one-, two- or three-sentence explanation.

In writing the brief answer, think about what you would tell the attorney if he or she stopped you and asked you for the bottom line. Do the Flynns have a cause of action in nuisance? The one- or two-word answer to this question is probably not. Why not?

The Flynns do not have a cause of action for public nuisance because Pecos Power's building of the lines was authorized and because there is no evidence that the lines injure the public. In addition, while the case for private nuisance is stronger, it will be difficult to prove that the lines cause serious harm given the most recent EMF studies. Although you could say more, the more detailed explanation should be saved for the discussion section and formal conclusion.

Brief Answer

Probably not. The Flynns do not have a cause of action for public nuisance because Pecos Power was authorized to build the lines and because there is no evidence that the lines injure the public. In addition, the Flynns probably do not have a cause of action for private nuisance: Given the recent EMF studies, it will be difficult to prove that the EMFs are harmful. To prevail, the Flynns would have to establish that Pecos Power is liable for conduct that the public reasonably or unreasonably believes causes harm.

§6.8   DRAFTING THE DISCUSSION SECTION

As you learned in Chapter 5, drafting the discussion section is a multi-stage process involving planning, drafting, revising, editing, and proof-reading. In this chapter, we walk you through the process again, showing you two other organizational plans and ways of integrating your discussion of the rules, analogous cases, and arguments.

§6.8.1   Planning the Discussion Section

In addition to the organizational plan for an elements analysis (see Plan A set out in section 5.10.1), there are two other organizational plans that are commonly used: Plan B, an organizational plan for problems that require the balancing of competing interests and Plan C, an organizational plan for problems that raise issues of first impression.

When the problem requires the balancing of competing interests, one of the following two versions of Plan B usually works well. Note that in the second version, the organizational scheme is very similar to the organizational scheme for an elements analysis.

PLAN B

VERSION 1

A.   Statement of general rules including a description of the interests that are balanced
B.   Description of analogous cases
C.   The plaintiff's or moving party's arguments
D.   The defendant's or responding party's arguments
E.   An evaluation and balancing of each side's arguments

VERSION 2

A.   Statement of general rule including (1) interests that are balanced and (2) factors that are considered in balancing these interests
B.   Factors that are not in dispute
    1.   Identify factors
    2.   Explain why factors are not in dispute
C.   First disputed factor
    1.   Rule
    2.   Analogous cases (if available)
    3.   Plaintiff's arguments
    4.   Defendant's arguments
    5.   Mini-conclusion
D.   Second disputed factor
    1.   Rule
    2.   Analogous cases (if available)
    3.   Plaintiff's arguments
    4.   Defendant's arguments
    5.   Mini-conclusion
E.   Evaluation of factors and balancing of interests

The basic organizational scheme for a problem involving an issue of first impression is as follows.

PLAN C

A.   Status of law in governing jurisdiction
B.   Rules adopted in other jurisdictions
    1.   Rule adopted in majority of jurisdictions and reasons courts have given for adopting that rule
    2.   Rule adopted in minority of jurisdictions and reasons courts have given for adopting that rule
C.   Critical evaluation of each rule and prediction about which rule your jurisdiction is likely to adopt
D.   Application of rule most likely to be adopted by court (Plan A or Plan B, depending on whether rule requires an elements analysis or the balancing of competing interests)
E.   Application of other rules (optional). Plan A or Plan B, depending on whether rule requires an elements analysis or the balancing of competing interests

Because the Flynn case involves both the balancing of competing interests and an issue of first impression, both Plan B and Plan C work. If the problem is viewed as a nuisance problem, Plan B works best. Using Plan B, you can set out the test for nuisance and then apply it to the facts of the Flynn case. If, however, the problem is viewed as an EMF problem, then the better choice is Plan C. Under this plan, you would begin by letting the attorney know that the issue is one of first impression and then explain how the issue has been decided in other jurisdictions.

**EXAMPLE 1   ORGANIZATION OF DISCUSSION SECTION
FOR FLYNN MEMO USING PLAN B**

A.   Introductory paragraph or block of paragraphs identifying the two types of nuisance
    1.   Introductory sentence
    2.   Test for public nuisance
    3.   Application of test for public nuisance to the facts of our case
    4.   Test for private nuisance
B.   Description of analogous private nuisance cases
    1.   No EMF cases in New Mexico
    2.   Description of other New Mexico nuisance cases
    3.   Description of EMF nuisance cases from other jurisdictions
C.   The Flynns' arguments, including factual arguments, arguments based on analogous cases, and policy arguments

D. Pecos Power's arguments, including factual arguments, arguments based on analogous cases, and policy arguments

E. An evaluation and balancing of each side's arguments

EXAMPLE 2	ORGANIZATION OF DISCUSSION SECTION OF FLYNN MEMO USING PLAN C

A. Introductory paragraph identifying the two types of nuisance
    1. Introductory sentence
    2. Test for public nuisance
    3. Application of test for public nuisance to the facts of our case
B. Status of law in New Mexico: New Mexico courts have never decided whether EMFs can constitute a private nuisance
C. Rules adopted in other jurisdictions
    1. Rule adopted in majority of jurisdictions and reasons courts have given for adopting that rule
    2. Rule adopted in minority of jurisdictions and reasons courts have given for adopting that rule or rules
D. Critical evaluation of each rule and prediction about which rule New Mexico is likely to adopt
E. Application of rule most likely to be adopted by court
    1. Rule
    2. Description of analogous cases
    3. The Flynns' arguments
    4. The Pecos Power's arguments
    5. An evaluation and balancing of each side's interests
F. Application of minority rule (optional)

---

§6.8.2 Using the Integrated Format

In each of the plans set out above, the script format was used. The moving party's arguments were set out first, the responding party's arguments second, and an evaluation of those arguments last. Although many attorneys prefer this format because it allows them "to see" each side's arguments, other attorneys prefer a more integrated approach.

The following examples illustrate some of the ways in which the arguments can be integrated. For both Plan A and Plan B, we set out four organizational plans. We begin by showing you how the discussion section would be organized if you used the script format; we then show you three different ways of integrating your discussion of the rules, the analogous cases, and each side's arguments. As you read through the examples, notice that with each example the amount of integration increases.

PLAN A: ELEMENTS ANALYSIS

Script format

I. General rule, including list of elements
  A. Raise and dismiss undisputed elements
  B. First disputed element
    1. Specific rule
    2. Description of analogous cases
    3. Plaintiff's arguments

    4. Defendant's argument

    5. Mini-conclusion
  C. Second disputed element
    1. Specific rule
    2. Description of analogous cases
    3. Plaintiff's arguments

    4. Defendant's argument

    5. Mini-conclusion

Integrated Format: Option 1 (Integrated discussion of each side's arguments)

I. General rule, including list of elements
  A. Raise and dismiss undisputed elements
  B. First disputed element
    1. Specific rule
    2. Description of analogous cases
    3. First line of argument (integrated discussion of both plaintiff's and defendant's arguments)
    4. Second line of argument (integrated discussion of both plaintiff's and defendant's arguments)
    5. Mini-conclusion
  C. Second disputed element
    1. Specific rule
    2. Description of analogous cases
    3. First line of argument (integrated discussion of both plaintiff's and defendant's arguments)
    4. Second line of argument (integrated discussion of both plaintiff's and defendant's arguments)
    5. Mini-conclusion

Integrated Format: Option 2 (Integrated discussion of both sides' arguments; descriptions of analogous cases integrated into the discussion of arguments)

I. General rule, including list of elements
  A. Raise and dismiss undisputed elements

Integrated Format: Option 3 (Integrated discussion of both sides' arguments; rules and descriptions of analogous cases integrated into discussion of arguments)

I. General rule, including list of elements
  A. Raise and dismiss undisputed elements

B. First disputed element
 1. Specific rule
 2. First line of argument
  (integrated discussion of both plaintiff's and defendant's arguments; descriptions of analogous cases integrated into arguments)
 3. Second line of argument
  (integrated discussion of both plaintiff's and defendant's arguments; descriptions of analogous cases integrated into arguments)

 4. Mini-conclusion

C. Second disputed element
 1. Specific rule
 2. First line of argument
  (integrated discussion of both plaintiff's and defendant's arguments; descriptions of analogous cases integrated into arguments)

 3. Second line of argument
  (integrated discussion of both plaintiff's and defendant's arguments; descriptions of analogous cases integrated into arguments)

 4. Mini-conclusion

B. First disputed element
 1. First line of argument
  (integrated discussion of both plaintiff's and defendant's arguments; rules and descriptions of analogous cases integrated into arguments)
 3. Second line of argument
  (integrated discussion of both plaintiff's and defendant's arguments; rules and descriptions of analogous cases integrated into arguments)

 4. Mini-conclusion

C. Second disputed element
 1. Specific rule
 2. First line of argument
  (integrated discussion of both plaintiff's and defendant's arguments; rules and descriptions of analogous cases integrated into arguments)

 3. Second line of argument
  (integrated discussion of both plaintiff's and defendant's arguments; rules and descriptions of analogous cases integrated into arguments)

 4. Mini-conclusion

PLAN B: BALANCING OF COMPETING INTERESTS

Script Format for Version 1 of Plan B

A. Statement of general rules including a description of the interests that are balanced

B. Description of analogous cases

C. The plaintiff's or moving party's arguments

Integrated Format: Option 1 for Version 1 of Plan B (Integrated discussion of both sides' arguments)

A. Statement of general rules including a description of the interests that are balanced

B. Description of analogous cases

C. First line of argument
 (integrated discussion of both plaintiff's and defendant's arguments)

D. The defendant's or responding
party's arguments

E. An evaluation and balancing of
each side's arguments

D. Second line of argument
(integrated discussion of both
plaintiff's and defendant's
arguments)

E. An evaluation and balancing of
each side's interests

**Integrated Format: Option 2 for
Version 1 of Plan B
(Integrated discussion of both
sides' arguments; descriptions of
analogous cases integrated into
arguments)**

A. Statement of general rule
including a description of the
interests that are balanced

B. First line of argument
(integrated discussion of both
plaintiff's and defendant's
arguments; discussion of
analogous cases integrated into
discussion of arguments)

C. Second line of argument
(integrated discussion of both
plaintiff's and defendant's
arguments; discussion of
analogous cases integrated into
discussion of arguments)

D. An evaluation and balancing of
each side's arguments

**Integrated Format: Option 3 for
Version 2 of Plan B
(Integrated discussion of both
sides' arguments; descriptions of
analogous cases integrated into
arguments when rule has factors)**

A. Statement of general rule
including (1) interests that are
balanced and (2) factors that are
considered in balancing these
interests

B. Factors that are not in dispute
1. Identify factors
2. Explain why factors are not
in dispute

C. First Disputed Factor
1. Rule
2. First line of argument
(integrated discussion of both
plaintiff's and defendant's
arguments; descriptions of
analogous cases integrated
into arguments)
3. Second line of argument
(integrated discussion of both
plaintiff's and defendant's
arguments; descriptions of
analogous cases integrated
into arguments)
4. Mini-conclusion

D. Second disputed factor
1. Rule
2. First line of argument
(integrated discussion of both
plaintiff's and defendant's
arguments; descriptions of
analogous cases integrated
into arguments)

3. Second line of argument
   (integrated discussion of both
   plaintiff's and defendant's
   arguments; descriptions of
   analogous cases integrated
   into arguments)
4. Mini-conclusion

E. An evaluation and balancing of
   each side's interests

In deciding whether to use the script format or a more integrated approach, you should consider two factors: your supervising attorney's preferences and the nature of the problem. While some problems lend themselves to a script format, others lend themselves to a more integrated approach. Whichever approach you use, however, the first step is to list each side's arguments and counterarguments. If you don't do so, your analysis is likely to be either conclusory or one-sided.

§6.8.3   Presenting the General Rules

Whether you use the script or an integrated format, you will almost always begin the discussion section by setting out the general rules. In each instance, the goal is the same: to "set the stage" for the rest of the analysis.

As you saw in Chapter 5, sometimes the general rule is a statute. In these instances, you will introduce the statute and then set out the relevant sections.

EXAMPLE 1   **AUTHOR INTRODUCES AND SETS OUT
                APPLICABLE STATUTE**

18 U.S.C. § 2511 sets out two consent exceptions. Subsection 2511(2)(c) applies when the party intercepting the communication was acting under color of law, and subsection 2511(2)(d) applies when the party intercepting the communication was not acting under color of law. Because there is no evidence that Elite Insurance was acting under color of law when it intercepted Johnson's phone calls, the applicable subsection is 2511(2)(d), which reads as follows:

(d) It shall not be unlawful under this chapter for a person not acting under color of law to intercept a wire or oral communication where such a person is a party to the communication or where one of the parties to the communication has given prior consent to such interception. . . .

The applicable language of this subsection is "where one of the parties to the communication has given prior consent to such interception."

At other times, the general rule is a common law rule. In these instances, you will introduce and then set out the common law rule.

EXAMPLE 2   AUTHOR INTRODUCES AND SETS OUT COMMON LAW RULE

To establish title through adverse possession, the party claiming title must establish that its possession was (1) exclusive, (2) actual and uninterrupted, (3) open and notorious, and (4) hostile and under claim of right for the statutory period. *Williams v. Howell,* 108 N.M. 225, 228, 770 P.2d 870, 873 (1989).

Whether the general rule is a statute or common law rule, sometimes you will need to do more than just set out the rule. To set the stage, you will need to explain the policies underlying the statute or common law rule, explain the historical development of the rule, or provide the attorney with other types of background information.

EXAMPLE 3   AUTHOR EXPLAINS POLICIES UNDERLYING STATUTE AND DEVELOPMENT OF RULE

During the 1980s, private hospitals began engaging in what is commonly called "patient dumping." Faced both with the need to control costs and increasing numbers of uninsured and underinsured patients, hospitals responded by refusing to provide emergency room care to patients who could not pay. *Gatewood v. Washington Healthcare Corp.,* 933 F.2d 1037, 1039 (D.C. Cir. 1991).

Because few states imposed a duty upon private hospitals to treat patients, Congress enacted the Emergency Medical Treatment and Active Labor Act (EMTALA), 42 U.S.C. § 1395(dd). Under this Act, hospitals receiving Medicare funds must do two things. First, the hospital must screen patients to determine whether they require emergency medical treatment. Second, if a patient requires emergency medical treatment, the hospital must stabilize that patient before discharging or transferring him or her to another facility. 42 U.S.C. § 1395dd(a)-(c). The relevant portions of the Act are attached.

In writing the general rules section in the *Flynn* case, you could take one of two approaches. If the attorneys who are likely to read the memo understand EMFs and you are treating the problem as a nuisance problem and using Plan B, the first of the following examples works well. In contrast, if the attorneys who are likely to read the memo are not familiar with EMFs and you are treating the problem as involving a question of first impression and using Plan C, the second example works best.

EXAMPLE 1   **APPROACH USED (A) IF ATTORNEYS KNOW WHAT EMFs ARE AND (B) PROBLEM IS TREATED AS A NUISANCE PROBLEM**

Discussion	Explanation of Author's Decisions
While plaintiffs have a cause of action in trespass when their right to exclusive possession is invaded, they have a cause of action in nuisance when an invasion interferes with their right to use the land. W. Page Keeton, *Prosser and Keeton on Torts,* § 13 at 67 (5th ed. 1984).	Because the attorney asked another intern to research trespass, the author of this memo just distinguishes trespass from nuisance. By distinguishing trespass, the author places the discussion of nuisance in context.
In New Mexico, a nuisance can be either public or private. Public nuisances are defined by statute.	This sentence gives the attorney information and acts as a roadmap for the rest of the discussion. Because she can raise and dismiss public nuisance as a cause of action, she discusses it first.

At this point, the author moves from a discussion of the general rules to a discussion of public nuisance, setting out the specific rules. Because most attorneys like to see the text of the applicable statutes, she quotes section 30-8-1.

30-8-1 Public Nuisance

A public nuisance consists of knowingly creating, performing or maintaining anything affecting any number of citizens without lawful authority which is either
A. injurious to public health, safety, morals or welfare; or
B. interferes with the exercise and enjoyment of public rights, including the right to use public property.

N.M. Stat. Ann. § 30-8-1 (Michie 1997).

After setting out the specific rule, the author applies it. Note that she begins the paragraph with a topic sentence that sets out her conclusion.

In our case, a court is unlikely to find that the high voltage lines constitute a public nuisance. The statute is designed to protect rights held in common by the public, not the rights of private individuals to the peaceful enjoyment of their own land. *City of Albuquerque v. State,* 111 N.M. 608, 610, 808 P.2d 58, 61 (1991).

At this point, the author moves from a discussion of public nuisance to a discussion of private nuisance, setting out the specific rules for private nuisance. Once again, she begins the paragraph with a topic sentence that sets out her conclusion. She then sets out the rules, presenting more general rules related to private nuisance before more specific rules. In addition, she raises and then quickly dismisses those legal theories that are not likely to work. For example, she quickly raises and dismisses the theory that the power lines are a nuisance per se.

A court might, however, find that the power lines constitute a private nuisance, that is, a nontrespassory invasion of another's interest in the private use and enjoyment of land. *Padilla v. Lawrence,* 101 N.M. 556, 685 P.2d 964 (1984); *Scott v. Jordan,* 99 N.M. 567, 661 P.2d 59 (1983). Such nuisances can be either nuisances per se or nuisances in fact. A nuisance per se is conduct that is at all times a nuisance; a nuisance in fact is conduct that becomes a nuisance by reason of its circumstances, location, or surroundings. *City of Albuquerque v. State,* 111 N.M. 608, 610, 808 P.2d 58, 61–62 (1991). Because high voltage lines are not a nuisance at all times (for example, high voltage lines running through unpopulated areas are not a nuisance), the Flynns should argue that the lines are a nuisance in fact and not a nuisance per se.

In determining whether conduct constitutes a nuisance in fact, the courts look at whether the conduct was intentional or unintentional. *Padilla*, 101 N.M. at 561, 685 P.2d at 968. Although the courts have not defined unintentional conduct, they have held that conduct is intentional if the actor knew or should have known that the harm was likely to result, *id.* For example, in *Padilla* the court held that the defendants knew or should have known that the operation of the bark and manure processing plant would interfere with plaintiffs' use of their land, and in *Scott v. Jordan,* the court held that the defendant should have known that its cattle feed lot would interfere with the plaintiffs' use of their land. Although the application is not as clear in this case, a court is likely to find that the conduct was intentional. When Pecos Powers erected the power lines, it knew that the lines would obstruct the Flynns' view and produce EMFs.

This paragraph picks up where the last paragraph left off, continuing the discussion of nuisance in fact. In discussing nuisance in fact, the author once again sets out more general rules before more specific rules. Note how the author handles the fact that the courts have never defined (or for that matter, even discussed) unintentional conduct. Instead of hiding that information from the attorney, she tells him that the courts have never defined the phrase. Also note that, when appropriate, she applies a rule. For example, after setting out the test for intentional conduct, she applies it to the facts of our case.

When the conduct is intentional, the courts then determine whether it is unreasonable using one of two tests: An intentional invasion is unreasonable (1) if the gravity of harm outweighs the utility of the actor's conduct or (2) if the harm caused by conduct is serious and the financial burden of compensating for the harm would not make continuing the conduct unfeasible. *Padilla,* 101 N.M. at 561, 685 P.2d at 968 (1984).

In this paragraph the author sets out the two-prong test that will become the focus of the analysis.

| EXAMPLE 2 | **APPROACH USED (A) IF ATTORNEYS DO NOT KNOW WHAT EMFs ARE AND (B) PROBLEM IS TREATED AS AN ISSUE OF FIRST IMPRESSION** |

Explanation	Discussion

Because the attorneys who are likely to read the memo are not familiar with EMFs, the author begins by explaining what EMFs are, where they occur, and how they are measured.

Electricity creates two types of fields. Electrical fields are produced when electrical charges are present, and magnetic fields are produced by the movement of those charges. It is the second of these types of fields, the magnetic fields, to which the term EMFs refers. *See, e.g.*, Margo R. Stoffel, *Electromagnetic Fields and Cancer*, 21 Ohio N.U.L. Rev. 551 (1995).

EMFs appear everywhere that electricity is used. Thus, not only power lines but also electrical appliances such as computers, TVs, radios, hair dryers, and electric blankets emit EMFs. The strength of an EMF is measured in "gauss," or "milligauss," also known as magnetic flux density. Readings taken away from electrical appliances and wires are usually in the range of 0.1 to 4 milligauss. Although readings taken near an electrical source can be very high, they diminish rapidly as one moves away from the source. For example, a reading taken within one inch of an electric can opener might be 20,000 milligauss while a reading taken one foot from the can opener might be 20 milligauss. Similarly, a reading taken near high voltage power lines will be much higher than a reading taken 20 feet away, and one taken 20 feet away will be much higher than one taken 100 feet away. *Id.*

At this point, the research on the effect of short-term and prolonged exposure to different levels of EMFs has been inconclusive. While some studies have linked exposure to EMFs to various types of cancer, other more recent studies have found no such link. U.S. Environmental Protection Agency, Questions and Answers About Electric and Magnetic Fields (EMFs) 2 (1992).

Whether EMFs from high voltage lines constitute a nuisance is an issue of first impression in New Mexico. There are no appellate level decisions and no cases currently pending in the trial or appellate courts. There have been, however, EMF cases in a number of other jurisdictions.

After explaining EMFs, the author tells the attorneys that the issue is one of first impression in New Mexico. She then explains how other jurisdictions have decided the issue.

In the jurisdictions that have decided the issue, the courts have held that high voltage lines, and the EMFs that they produce, did not constitute either a public or private nuisance. *See, e.g., Jordan v. Georgia Power Co.*, 466 S.E. 601 (Ga. App. Ct. 1995); *Borenkind v. Consolidated Edison Co.*, 164 Misc. 2d 808, 626 N.Y. S.2d 414 (N.Y. Sup. 1995). In some of these cases, the court based its decision on the fact that the power lines were authorized by law. In others, it based its decision on the fact that the evidence linking EMFs to cancer was inconclusive. In still others, the court found that the plaintiffs had not proved damages.

In deciding whether New Mexico will allow a cause of action in nuisance, the New Mexico courts are likely to look first at whether EMFs constitute a public nuisance and then at whether they constitute a private nuisance.

At this point, the author picks up the discussion where it began in Example 1, setting out the general rules and then discussing public and private nuisance.

Public nuisances are defined by statute.

30-8-1 Public Nuisance
A public nuisance consists of knowingly creating, performing or maintaining anything affecting any number of citizens without lawful authority which is either
A. injurious to public health, safety, morals or welfare; or
B. interferes with the exercise and enjoyment of public rights, including the right to use public property.

N.M. Stat. Ann. § 30-8-1 (Michie 1997).

In our case, a court is unlikely to find that the high voltage lines constitute a public nuisance. The statute is designed to protect rights held in common by the public, not the rights of private individuals to the peaceful enjoyment of their own land. *City of Albu-querque v. State,* 111 N.M. 608, 610, 808 P.2d 58, 61 (1991).

A court might, however, find that the power lines constitute a private nuisance, that is, a nontrespassory invasion of another's interest in the private use and enjoyment of land. *Padilla v. Lawrence,* 101 N.M. 556, 685 P.2d 964 (1984); *Scott v. Jordan,* 99 N.M. 567, 661 P.2d 59 (1983). Such nuisances can either be nuisances per se or nuisances in fact. A nuisance per se is conduct that is at all times a nuisance; a nuisance in fact is one that becomes a nuisance by reason of its circumstances, locations, or surroundings. *City of Albuquerque v. State,* 111 N.M. 608, 610, 808 P.2d 58, 61–62 (1991). Because high voltage lines are not at all times a nuisance (for example, high voltage lines running through unpopulated areas are not a nuisance), we should argue that the lines are a nuisance in fact and not a nuisance per se.

* * *

§6.8.4   Presenting the Analogous Cases

In Chapter 5, you saw how to set out your descriptions of analogous cases in a separate "analogous case section." Although this technique often works well, sometimes it works better to integrate your description of the analogous cases into your presentation of the arguments. As a general rule, it usually works better to describe the cases in a separate section if you are relying on just one, two, or three cases and you use the same cases in making several different arguments. In contrast, it usually works better to integrate your descriptions of the cases into the arguments if you use different cases to support different arguments. The goal is to give the attorney the information that he or she needs when he or she needs it.

a.   Integrating the Discussion of Analogous Cases into the Arguments

In the first of the following examples, the author has used the script format, setting out the rules first, the descriptions of the analogous cases second, each side's arguments third, and his mini-conclusion last. In the second example, the author has used an integrated approach. After setting out the rule, he sets out the arguments, integrating the discussion of the analogous cases into those arguments. The descriptions of analogous cases are in boldface type.

EXAMPLES

Example 1: Script Format

* * *

When the conduct is intentional, the courts then determine whether it is unreasonable using one of two tests: An intentional invasion is unreasonable (1) if the gravity of harm outweighs the utility of the actor's conduct or (2) if the harm caused by the conduct is serious and the financial burden of compensating for the harm would not make continuing the conduct unfeasible. *Padilla v. Lawrence,* 101 N.M. 556, 561, 685 P.2d 964, 968 (1984).

In the cases in which the New Mexico courts have found that the gravity of the harm outweighed the utility of the conduct, the harm was substantial and the social utility of the activity alleged to be a nuisance was minimal. For example, in *Padilla,* the plaintiffs were forced to move out of their home because of the noise and odors coming from defendant's bark and manure processing plant. *Id.* at 560, 685 P.2d at 967. Similarly, in *Scott v. Jordan,* 99 N.M. 567, 661 P.2d 59 (1983), the plaintiffs could not enjoy their home because of the dust, flies, and noxious odors from

Example 2: Integrated Format (Descriptions of Analogous Cases Highlighted)

* * *

When the conduct is intentional, the courts then determine whether it is unreasonable using one of two tests: An intentional invasion is unreasonable (1) if the gravity of harm outweighs the utility of the actor's conduct or (2) if the harm caused by conduct is serious and the financial burden of compensating for the harm would not make continuing the conduct unfeasible. *Padilla v. Lawrence,* 101 N.M. 556, 561, 685 P.2d 964, 968 (1984).

In the *Flynn* case, it is unlikely that a court would find that harm caused by the building of the high voltage lines outweighs the social utility of the lines. **In the cases in which the New Mexico courts have found a nuisance, the harm was more serious and the social utility of the conduct was not as great. For example, in *Padilla,* the court held that a bark and manure processing plant constituted a private nuisance when, because of the noise and odors coming from the plant, the plaintiffs were forced to move out of their home. *Id.* at 569, 661 P.2d at 60. Similarly, in *Scott v. Jordan,* 99 N.M. 567,** the defendant's cattle feed lot. In both cases, the plaintiffs had established their homes before the conduct alleged to be a nuisance began. *Id.* at 569, 661 P.2d at 60.

In contrast, the courts have usually held that an activity does not constitute a nuisance when it is permitted or authorized by law. For instance, in *State v. Egolf,* 107 N.M. 315, 757 P.2d 371 (1988), one of the factors that the court considered in finding that the building of a trout pond was not unreasonable was that a zoning commission had found that the pond complied with zoning regulations. *Accord, Espinosa v. Roswell Tower, Inc.,* 121 N.M. 306, 910 P.2d 940 (1995) (violation of NESHAP was a public nuisance per se); *City of Albuquerque v. State,* 111 N.M. 608, 808 P.2d 58 (river crossing project not subject to abatement as a public nuisance because it was authorized by law and approved by concerned public agencies). In addition, in the jurisdictions that have decided EMF cases, the courts have held that the plaintiffs did not have a cause of action in nuisance. *See, e.g., Jordan v. Georgia Power Co,* 466 S.E.2d 601 (Ga. App. Ct. 1995) (no cause of action in nuisance because evidence as to whether electromagnetic fields cause harm is inconclusive); *Borenkind v. Consolidated Edison Co.,* 164 Misc. 2d 808, 626 N.Y.S.2d 414 (N.Y. Sup. 1995) (no cause of action in nuisance because no conclusive evidence that EMFs cause harm).

661 P.2d 59 (1983), the court held that a cattle feeding operation constituted a nuisance when, because of the dust, flies, and noxious odors, the plaintiffs could no longer enjoy their home. *Id.* at 569, 661 P.2d at 60.

In addition, in the jurisdictions that have decided EMF cases, the plaintiffs have lost. *See, e.g., Jordan v. Georgia Power Co.,* 466 S.E.2d 601 (Ga. App. Ct. 1995) (no cause of action in nuisance because evidence as to whether electromagnetic fields cause harm is inconclusive); *Borenkind v. Consolidated Edison Co.,* 164 Misc.2d 808, 626 N.Y.S.2d 414 (N.Y. Sup. 1995) (no cause of action in nuisance because no conclusive evidence that EMFs cause harm).

In our case, the Flynns have not been forced to move from their home and show no signs of cancer. Thus, the harm that they have suffered is less than the harm that the plaintiffs suffered in *Padilla* and *Scott.* In addition, high voltage lines have, at least arguably, more social utility than either a bark and manure processing plant or a cattle feed lot.

It is also unlikely that a court would find that the harm that the Flynns have suffered is serious. The Flynns allege three types of harm: that the high voltage lines have interfered with their use and enjoyment of the interior of their home by blocking their western view; that the high voltage lines have interfered with their use and enjoyment of their backyard because they are con-

Because it will be difficult to establish that the harm that the Flynns have suffered is greater than the social utility of the high voltage lines, the Flynns' best argument is that the harm caused by the conduct is serious and that the financial burden of compensating for the harm would not make continuing the conduct unfeasible. Like the plaintiffs in *Padilla* and *Scott,* the Flynns are no longer able to fully use their property. Because of the high readings in their backyard, they are not able to use their pool or maintain their garden without fear of increasing their risk of cancer. In addition, the high voltage lines have destroyed their western view, one of their primary reasons for purchasing their home. Finally, they are not able to sell their home. Although the home has been on the market for more than a year, the Flynns have not received any offers. According to their real estate agent, the recent publicity about the potential dangers of EMFs has made it difficult if not impossible to sell homes near high voltage lines.

While the harm to the Flynns is serious, the financial burden of compensating the Flynns for the harm is minimal. At this point, the Flynns are only asking to be compensated for the loss of their home's value.

Finally, the Flynns can argue that as a matter of public policy they should not be forced to bear the loss caused by the building of the high voltage lines. If the lines are of great social utility, then it is the public and not an individual landowner who should bear the cost. By adjusting the

cerned that exposure to high EMF levels increases their risk of cancer; and that because of high voltage lines, they have been unable to sell their home.

Although the lines do interfere with Flynns' view, a court is unlikely to find that the harm supports an action in nuisance. When they bought the house, the Flynns knew that the property behind the house was owned by the utility company and that the company might erect lines on the property at any time.

It is also unlikely that a court will find that the Flynns' fear of EMFs is reasonable. While the Flynns can cite studies linking EMFs to cancer and other health problems (for example, birth defects, miscarriages, and neurological dysfunctions), Pecos Power can cite studies showing no link.

The more difficult question is who should bear the cost of the public's fear of buying a house near high voltage lines. The Flynns will argue that it is the public that should bear the cost. If the lines are of great social utility, then it is the public and not an individual landowner who should bear the cost. By adjusting the utility company's rate structure, the cost of compensating individuals like the Flynns can be distributed among all those who benefit from the high voltage lines. In contrast, Pecos Power will argue that the public should not have to bear the cost of compensating individuals like the Flynns. The Flynns are having trouble selling their home not because the EMFs are dangerous utility company's rate structure, the cost of compensating individuals like the Flynns can be distributed among all those who benefit from the high voltage lines.

Pecos Power will respond by arguing that because the high voltage lines are authorized by law, they are not a nuisance. Like the river crossing project in *City of Albuquerque v. State,* the lines in this case have been authorized by law and approved by concerned public agencies.

In addition, Pecos Power will argue that any harm that the Flynns have suffered is not serious. Because the most recent studies have established that high voltage lines do not increase the risk of cancer, the Flynns' decision not to use their backyard and pool is unreasonable. In addition, the Flynns knew when they bought their home that the land behind their home was owned by Pecos Power and that the utility could, at any time, erect power lines on the property. Thus, the Flynns cannot complain that the lines interfere with their view.

Pecos Power can also argue that neither it nor its ratepayers should have to bear the cost of the public's unreasonable fears. The Flynns are having trouble selling their home not because the EMFs are dangerous but because the public fears that they might be dangerous. If Pecos Power were forced to compensate individuals for fear of harm, it would open the floodgates to all types of claims based on unreasonable fears, such as claims that regular overhead wires or transformer boxes cause some type of harm.

but because the public fears that they might be dangerous. If Pecos Power were forced to compensate individuals for fear of harm, it would open the floodgates to all types of claims based on unreasonable fears, such as claims that regular overhead wires or transformer boxes cause some type of harm.

The final factor that the court will consider is that the high voltage lines are authorized by law. Although this factor is not dispositive, *see e.g., Padilla v. Lawrence,* the courts typically do not find that conduct constitutes a nuisance when such conduct is authorized by law. **For instance, in *State v. Egolf,* 107 N.M. 315, 317, 757 P.2d 371, 372 (1988), one of the factors that the court considered in finding that the building of a trout pond was not unreasonable and therefore not a nuisance was the fact that a zoning commission had found that the pond complied with zoning regulations. Similarly, in *City of Albuquerque v. State,* 111 N.M. 608, 610, 808 P.2d 58, 60– 61 (1991), the court held that a river crossing project was not subject to abatement as a public nuisance because it was authorized by law and approved by concerned public agencies. *Accord, Espinosa v. Roswell Tower, Inc.,* 121 N.M. 306, 910 P.2d 940 (1995) (violation of NESHAP was a public nuisance per se).** Given the courts' decisions in these cases, in *Flynn* the court is likely to give great weight to the fact that the lines were authorized by law and approved by the New Mexico Public Utilities Commission.

wires or transformer boxes cause some type of harm.

Finally, Pecos Power will remind the court that in other jurisdictions in which the courts have considered the issue, the courts have held EMFs do not constitute a nuisance.

While the Flynns must concede that the lines are authorized by law, they will argue that such a fact does not prevent the court from finding that the lines are a nuisance in fact. In addition, the Flynns will argue that the studies are inconclusive. While some of the recent studies have not found a link between EMFs and childhood leukemia, other studies have found a link. In addition, EMFs may cause other health problems, such as problems with the immune system. Thus, the Flynns are acting reasonably in avoiding those areas of their property with high readings, and others are acting reasonably in deciding not to buy a home near power lines.

Question

What are the advantages and disadvantages of each of the above approaches?

---

b.   Using Parentheticals

While sometimes you will need to use several sentences or even several paragraphs to describe a case, at other times, a phrase or a clause is all that is needed. In these latter instances, instead of describing the case in text, you can use a parenthetical.

As a general rule, you will want to set a case out in text when it is one of your key cases. For example, in the *Flynn* case, you would want to describe both *Padilla* and *Scott* in text. If, however, a case is being offered only as additional support for a proposition or to illustrate a single point, then a parenthetical is appropriate. Thus, in *Flynn,* it was appropriate to discuss *Espinoza v. Roswell Tower, Inc.* and *City of Albuquerque v. State* in a parenthetical.

In using parentheticals, keep several "rules" in mind. First, keep the parentheticals short. If you cannot give the attorney the information that he or she needs in a word, phrase, or clause, do not use a parenthetical. Second, make sure that in trying to present the information concisely, you don't mislead the attorney. For example, in discussing *Espinoza v. Roswell Tower, Inc.,* and *City of Albuquerque v. State,* it is important to let the attorney know that those cases involved public and not private nuisances. Third, if you are citing several cases, use parallel constructions for each of your parentheticals. See section 26.7. Although there is no set format for parentheticals, most take one of the following forms.

word or phrase	(cattle feed lot)
participial phrase	(holding that a cattle feed lot was a nuisance in fact)
clause	(Court held that a cattle feed lot was a nuisance in fact)

As a general rule, do not capitalize the first word of the parenthetical when using only a word, phrase, or participial phrase. Do capitalize the first word when using a complete clause or sentence. In addition, if you use one form for one parenthetical, use the same form for the other parentheticals in the same string. Finally, don't overuse parentheticals. If you use too many parentheticals, particularly with string citations, your memo can become difficult to read.

EXAMPLE   **PARENTHETICALS TOO LONG AND PARALLEL CONSTRUCTION NOT USED**

Accord, Espinosa v. Roswell Tower, Inc., 121 N.M. 306, 910 P.2d 940 (1995) (The court found that the defendant repeatedly knocked down ceilings containing asbestos from buildings it owned and dumped at least some of the debris near an abandoned city landfill and that such actions, which were in violation of NESHAP, constituted a public nuisance per se); *City of Albuquerque v. State,* 111 N.M. 608, 808 P.2d 58 (1991) (holding that a municipal highway project that involved building a bridge over the Montano River that was authorized by law and approved by governmental agencies was not subject to abatement as a public nuisance).

EXAMPLE   **PARENTHETICAL MISLEADING BECAUSE KEY FACTS OMITTED**

Accord, Espinosa v. Roswell Tower, Inc., 121 N.M. 306, 910 P.2d 940 (1995) (violation of NESHAP a nuisance); *City of Albuquerque v. State,* 111 N.M. 608, 808 P.2d 58 (1991) (bridge over river not a nuisance).

EXAMPLE   **EFFECTIVE USE OF PARTICIPIAL PHRASES**

Accord, Espinosa v. Roswell Tower, Inc., 121 N.M. 306, 910 P.2d 940 (1995) (holding that violation of NESHAP was a public nuisance per se); *City of Albuquerque v. State,* 111 N.M. 608, 808 P.2d 58 (1991) (holding that bridge across river was not a public nuisance because it was authorized by law and approved by concerned public agencies).

EXAMPLE   **EFFECTIVE USE OF CLAUSES**

Accord, Espinosa v. Roswell Tower, Inc., 121 N.M. 306, 910 P.2d 940 (1995) (Violation of NESHAP was a public nuisance per se); *City of Albuquerque v. State,* 111 N.M. 608, 808 P.2d 58 (1991) (Bridge across river was not a public nuisance because it was authorized by law and approved by concerned public agencies).

Exercise

Critique the following use of parentheticals. What has the author done well? What changes might you make?

See, e.g., Jordan v. Georgia Power Co, 466 S.E.2d 601 (Ga. App. Ct. 1995) (No cause of action in nuisance because evidence as to whether electromagnetic fields cause harm is inconclusive); *Borenkind v. Consolidated Edison Co.,* 164 Misc.2d 808, 626 N.Y.S.2d 414 (N.Y. Sup. 1995) (No cause of action in nuisance because no conclusive evidence that EMFs cause harm).

c. Other Reminders

In describing analogous cases, also keep the following in mind. First, make sure that your analysis is principle-based rather than case-based. For example, if you are using the script format, begin your analogous case section by setting out the principle that you are using the case to illustrate and not with the name of the case.

EXAMPLE   **POOR EXAMPLE: DESCRIPTION OF ANALOGOUS CASES IS CASE-BASED RATHER THAN PRINCIPLE-BASED**

In *Padilla,* the plaintiffs were forced to move out of their home because of the noise and odors coming from defendant's bark and manure processing plant. Similarly, in *Scott v. Jordan,* 99 N.M. 567, 661 P.2d 59 (1983), the plaintiffs could not enjoy their home because of the dust, flies, and noxious odors from the defendant's cattle feed lot. In both cases, the plaintiffs had established their homes prior to the construction of the activities alleged to be nuisances.

EXAMPLE   **SCRIPT FORMAT: DESCRIPTION OF ANALOGOUS CASES IS PRINCIPLE-BASED**

In the cases in which the New Mexico courts have found that the gravity of the harm outweighed the utility of the conduct, the harm was substantial and the social utility of the activity alleged to be a nuisance was minimal. For example, in *Padilla,* the plaintiffs were forced to move out of their home because of the noise and odors coming from defendant's bark and manure processing plant. Similarly, in *Scott v. Jordan,* 99 N.M. 567, 661 P.2d 59 (1983), the plaintiffs could not enjoy their home because of the dust, flies, and noxious odors from the defendant's cattle feed lot. In both cases, the plaintiffs had established their homes prior to the construction of the activities alleged to be nuisances.

There are several techniques that you can use to come up with a topic sentence like the one set out in the previous example. In this instance, the author began with the rule: "In determining whether a use is unreasonable, the courts balance the gravity of the harm against the utility of the conduct." Because she knew she wanted to illustrate how the court applied this rule, she then wrote the following two sentence openers, the first one to introduce the cases in which the court had found that the activity constituted a nuisance and the second to introduce the cases in which the court found that the activity did not constitute a nuisance.

First Sentence Opener: (To Introduce Cases in Which Court Found that Activity Was a Nuisance)

In the cases in which the New Mexico courts have found that the gravity of the harm outweighed the utility of the conduct, ...

Second Sentence Opener: (To Introduce Cases in Which the Court Found that the Activity Was Not a Nuisance)

In contrast, in the cases in which the New Mexico courts have found that the gravity of the harm does not outweigh the utility of the conduct, ...

Having written the sentence openers, the author stopped and asked herself what each group of cases had in common. Because she did not know the answer to the question, she did what attorneys often do: she went back to the cases, rereading them to find out what the cases in which the court held that there was a nuisance had in common and what the cases in which the court held that there was no nuisance had in common. Then, after rereading them for this specific purpose, she returned to her writing, completing the sentences and making necessary revisions. Thus, to come up with the principle, the author read, wrote, read, and wrote. You can use a similar technique when using the integrated format.

Second, make sure that in doing principle-based analysis you don't end up writing sentences so long that they are difficult to read. Although sometimes you can say everything you need to say about a case in a single sentence, at other times you will need to use two, three, or, occasionally, even a dozen sentences. Try reading example 1 and then, without rereading the paragraph, summarizing what it says.

EXAMPLE 1　　POOR

In the cases in which the New Mexico courts have found that the gravity of the harm outweighed the utility of the conduct, the harm was substantial and the social utility of the conduct alleged to be a nuisance was minimal. For example, in *Padilla,* the court held that the evidence was sufficient to support the trial court's finding that a bark and manure processing plant constituted a nuisance when, because of the noise and odors coming from the plant, the plaintiffs had been forced to move from their residence of twenty-five years and the plaintiffs had established their home long before the defendants began operating their plant.

Because the second sentence is so long (67 words), most readers have a difficult time understanding the paragraph without rereading it. In such situations, it is better to shorten the offending sentence either by deleting unnecessary information or by dividing it into several shorter sentences.

EXAMPLE 2   BETTER

In the cases in which the New Mexico courts have found that the gravity of the harm outweighed the utility of the conduct, the harm was substantial and the social utility of the activity alleged to be a nuisance was minimal. For example, in *Padilla,* the plaintiffs were forced to move out of their home because of the noise and odors coming from defendant's bark and manure processing plant.

EXAMPLE 3   BETTER

In the cases in which the New Mexico courts have found that the gravity of the harm outweighed the utility of the conduct, the harm was substantial and the social utility of the activity alleged to be a nuisance was minimal. For example, in *Padilla,* the court held that the defendant's bark and manure processing plant constituted a private nuisance in fact. In reaching this conclusion, the court considered the fact that the plaintiffs had been forced to leave their home of twenty-five years because of the noise and odors coming from the plant.

Question

Which of the above examples is most effective? Why?

§6.8.5   Presenting Each Side's Arguments

Whether you use the script or the integrated format, your goal in presenting each side's arguments is the same: to tell the attorney what each side is likely to argue and how, given those arguments, a court is likely to rule. Thus, under both formats, the content is essentially the same. The only difference is in the way the arguments are organized.

a.   *Organizing the Arguments*

As you saw in Chapter 5, when the script format is used the arguments are presented in the order that that they would be presented to a judge: the moving party's arguments first, the responding party's arguments second, and the moving party's rebuttal third. In contrast, when an integrated format is used, the arguments appear as they often appear in a judicial opinion: argument by argument.

Script Format	*Integrated Format*

Moving Party's Arguments
• Argument 1
• Argument 2
• Argument 3
	Argument 1
	   Integrated discussion of
	   moving and responding par-
	   ties' arguments

Responding Party's
Arguments
• Argument 1
• Argument 2
• Argument 3
• Argument 4
	Argument 2
	   Integrated discussion of
	   moving and responding par-
	   ties' arguments
	
	Argument 3
	   Integrated discussion of
	   moving and responding par-
	   ties' arguments

Moving Party's Rebuttal
• Counterargument 1
• Counterargument 2
	Argument 4
	   Integrated discussion of
	   moving and responding par-
	   ties' arguments

Thus, while under the script format the organizing principle was the "parties," under the integrated format the organizing principle is the arguments themselves.

b.   *Introducing the Arguments*

Because the arguments are organized differently under the script and integrated formats, the topic sentences that are used to introduce the arguments are also different. When the script format is used, the topic sentences identify the party making the argument and the party's assertion. In contrast, when the integrated format is used, the topic sentence identifies the argument and usually states how a court would decide that particular issue. Look again at the excerpts from the discussion section in the Flynn memo, this time comparing the topic sentences that are used to introduce the arguments in the memo written using the script format with the topic sentences introducing the arguments in the memo written using an integrated approach.

EXAMPLES   **EXCERPTS FROM THE DISCUSSION SECTION IN THE FLYNN MEMO (TOPIC SENTENCES ARE HIGHLIGHTED)**

Example 1: Script Format

* * *

When the conduct is intentional, the courts then determine whether it is unreasonable using one of two tests: An intentional invasion is unreasonable (1) if the gravity of harm outweighs the utility of the actor's conduct or (2) if the harm caused by conduct is serious and the financial burden of compensating for the harm would not make continuing the conduct unfeasible. *Padilla v. Lawrence,* 101 N.M. 556, 561, 685 P.2d 964, 968 (1984).

In the cases in which the New Mexico courts have found that the gravity of the harm outweighed the utility of the conduct, the harm was substantial and the social utility of the activity alleged to be a nuisance was minimal. For example, in *Padilla,* the plaintiffs were forced to move out of their home because of the noise and odors coming from defendant's bark and manure processing plant. *Id.* at 560, 685 P.2d at 967. Similarly, in *Scott v. Jordan,* 99 N.M. 567, 661 P.2d 59 (1983), the plaintiffs could not enjoy their home because of the dust, flies,

Example 2: Integrated Format Integrating Arguments

* * *

When the conduct is intentional, the courts then determine whether it is unreasonable using one of two tests: An intentional invasion is unreasonable (1) if the gravity of harm outweighs the utility of the actor's conduct or (2) if the harm caused by conduct is serious and the financial burden of compensating for the harm would not make continuing the conduct unfeasible. *Padilla v. Lawrence,* 101 N.M. 556, 561, 685 P.2d 964, 968 (1984).

In the Flynn case, it is unlikely that a court would find that harm caused by the building of the high voltage lines outweighs the social utility of the lines. In the cases in which the New Mexico courts have found a nuisance, the harm was more serious, and the social utility of the conduct was not as great. For example, in *Padilla,* the court held that a bark and manure processing plant constituted a private nuisance when, because of the noise and odors coming from the plant, the plaintiffs were forced to move out of and noxious odors from the defendant's cattle feed lot. *Id.* at 569, 661 P.2d at 60. In both cases, the plaintiffs had established their homes before the conduct alleged to be a nuisance began.

In contrast, the courts have usually held that an activity does not constitute a nuisance when it is permitted or authorized by law. For instance, in *State v. Egolf,* 107 N.M. 315, 319, 757 P.2d 371, 374 (1988), one of the factors that the court considered in finding that the building of a trout pond was not unreasonable was that a zoning commission had found that the pond complied with zoning regulations. *Accord, Espinosa v. Roswell Tower, Inc.,* 121 N.M. 306, 910 P.2d 940 (1995) (violation of NESHAP a public nuisance per se); *City of Albuquerque v. State,* 111 N.M. 608, 808 P.2d 58 (1991) (river crossing project not subject to abatement as a public nuisance because it was authorized by law and approved by concerned public agencies). In addition, in the jurisdictions that have decided EMF cases, the courts have held that the plaintiffs did not have a cause of action in nuisance. *See, e.g., Jordan v. Georgia Power Co.,* 466 S.E.2d 601 (Ga. App. Ct. 1995) (no cause of action in nuisance because evidence as to whether electromagnetic fields cause harm is inconclusive); *Borenkind v. Consolidated Edison Co.,* 164 Misc.2d 808, 626 N.Y.S.2d 414 (N.Y. Sup. 1995) (no cause of action in nuisance because no conclusive evidence that EMFs cause harm).

their home. *Id.* at 560, 685 P.2d at 967. Similarly, in *Scott v. Jordan,* 99 N.M. 567, 661 P.2d 59 (1983), the court held that a cattle feeding operation constituted a nuisance when, because of the dust, flies, and noxious odors, the plaintiffs could no longer enjoy their home. *Id.* at 569, 661 P.2d at 60.

In addition, in the jurisdictions that have decided EMF cases, the plaintiffs have lost. *See, e.g., Jordan v. Georgia Power Co.,* 466 S.E.2d 601 (Ga. App. Ct. 1995) (no cause of action in nuisance because evidence as to whether electromagnetic fields cause harm is inconclusive); *Borenkind v. Consolidated Edison Co.,* 164 Misc.2d 808, 626 N.Y.S.2d 414 (N.Y. Sup. 1995) (no cause of action in nuisance because no conclusive evidence that EMFs cause harm).

In our case, the Flynns have not been forced to move from their home and show no signs of cancer. Thus, the harm that they have suffered is less than the harm that the plaintiffs suffered in *Padilla* and *Scott.* In addition, high voltage lines have, at least arguably, more social utility than either a bark and manure processing plant or a cattle feed lot.

It is also unlikely that a court would find that the harm that the Flynns have suffered is serious. The Flynns allege three types of harm: that the high voltage lines have interfered with their use and enjoyment of the interior of their home by blocking their western view, that the high

Because it will be difficult to establish that the harm that the Flynns have suffered is greater than the social utility of the high voltage lines, the Flynns' best argument is that the harm caused by the conduct is serious. Like the plaintiffs in *Padilla* and *Scott,* the Flynns are no longer able to fully use their property. Because of the high readings in their backyard, they are not able to use their pool or maintain their garden without fear of increasing their risk of cancer. In addition, the high voltage lines have destroyed their western view, one of the primary reasons that they purchased the home. Finally, they are not able to sell their home. Although the home has been on the market for more than a year, the Flynns have not received any offers. According to their real estate agent, the recent publicity about the potential dangers of EMFs has made it difficult if not impossible to sell homes near high voltage lines.

While the harm to the Flynns is serious, the financial burden of compensating the Flynns for the harm is minimal. At this point, the Flynns are only asking to be compensated for the loss of their home's value.

Finally, the Flynns can argue that as a matter of public policy they should not be forced to bear the loss caused by the building of the high voltage lines. If the lines are of great social utility, then it is the public and not an individual landowner who should bear the cost. By adjusting the utility company's rate structure, the cost of compensat-

voltage lines have interfered with their use and enjoyment of their backyard because they are concerned that exposure to high EMF levels increases their risk of cancer, and that because of high voltage lines, they have been unable to sell their home.

Although the lines do interfere with Flynns' view, a court is unlikely to find that the harm supports an action in nuisance. When they bought the house, the Flynns knew that the property behind the house was owned by the utility company and that the company might erect lines on the property at any time.

It is also unlikely that a court will find that the Flynns' fear of EMFs is reasonable. While the Flynns can cite studies linking EMFs to cancer and other health problems, for example, birth defects, miscarriages, and neurological dysfunctions, Pecos Power can cite studies showing no link.

The more difficult question is who should bear the cost of the public's fear of buying a house near high voltage lines. The Flynns will argue that it is the public that should bear the cost. If the lines are of great social utility, then it is the public and not an individual landowner who should bear the cost. By adjusting the utility company's rate structure, the cost of compensating individuals like the Flynns can be distributed among all those who benefit from the high voltage lines. In contrast, Pecos Power will argue that the public should not have to bear the cost of compensating individuals like the ing individuals like the Flynns can be distributed among all those who benefit from the high voltage lines.

Pecos Power will respond by arguing that because the high voltage lines are authorized by law, they are not a nuisance. Just as in *City of Albuquerque v. State,* in this case the lines have been authorized by law and approved by concerned public agencies.

In addition, Pecos Power will argue that any harm that the Flynns have suffered is not serious. Because the most recent studies have established that high voltage lines do not increase the risk of cancer, the Flynns' decision not to use their backyard and pool is unreasonable. In addition, the Flynns knew when they bought their home that the land behind their home was owned by Pecos Power and that the utility could, at any time, erect power lines on the property. Thus, the Flynns cannot complain that the lines interfere with their view.

Pecos Power can also argue that neither it nor its ratepayers should have to bear the cost of the public's unreasonable fears. The Flynns are having trouble selling their home not because the EMFs are dangerous but because the public fears that they might be dangerous. If Pecos Power were forced to compensate individuals for fear of harm, it would open the floodgates to all types of claims based on unreasonable fears, such as claims that regular overhead

Flynns. The Flynns are having trouble selling their home not because the EMFs are dangerous but because the public fears that they might be dangerous. If Pecos Power were forced to compensate individuals for fear of harm, it would open the floodgates to all types of claims based on unreasonable fears, such as claims that regular overhead wires or transformer boxes cause some type of harm.

The final factor that the court will consider is the fact that the high voltage lines are authorized by law. Although this factor is not dispositive, *see e.g., Padilla v. Lawrence,* the courts typically do not find that conduct constitutes a nuisance when such conduct is authorized by law. For instance, in *State v. Egolf,* 107 N.M. 315, 319, 757 P.2d 371, 374 (1988), one of the factors that the court considered in finding that the building of a trout pond was not unreasonable and therefore not a nuisance was the fact that a zoning commission had found that the pond complied with zoning regulations. Similarly, in *City of Albuquerque v. State,* 111 N.M. 608, 610, 808 P.2d 58, 61–62 (1991), the court held that a river crossing project was not subject to abatement as a public nuisance because it was authorized by law and approved by concerned public agencies. *Accord, Espinosa v. Roswell Tower, Inc.,* 121 N.M. 306, 910 P.2d 940 (1995) (violation of NESHAP a public nuisance per se). Given the courts' decisions in these cases, in *Flynn* the court is likely to give great weight to the fact that the lines were authorized by wires or transformer boxes cause some type of harm.

Finally, Pecos Power will remind the court that in other jurisdictions in which the courts have considered the issue, the courts have held EMFs do not constitute a nuisance.

While the Flynns must concede that the lines are authorized by law, they will argue that such a fact does not prevent the court from finding that the lines are a nuisance in fact. In addition, the Flynns will argue that the studies are inconclusive. While some of the recent studies have not found a link between EMFs and childhood leukemia, other studies have found a link. In addition, EMFs may cause other health problems, such as problems with the immune system. Thus, the Flynns are acting reasonably in avoiding those areas of their property with high readings, and others are acting reasonably in deciding not to buy a home near power lines.

law and approved by the New Mexico Public Utilities Commission.

Question

In the examples set out above, what types of information have the authors included in the topic sentences?

---

§6.8.6   Avoiding the Common Problems

When you use the script format, it is relatively easy to set out both sides' arguments. The format itself forces you to set out the moving party's arguments, the responding party's arguments, and the moving party's rebuttal. Unfortunately, it is harder to set out both sides' arguments using the integrated format. Once you have stated a conclusion, there is a tendency to set out only those arguments that support that conclusion. As a result, the supervising attorney sees only half of the analysis. Compare the following examples.

EXAMPLE 1   THE AUTHOR HAS INCLUDED ONLY ONE SIDE'S ARGUMENTS

It is not likely that a court would find that the harm that the Flynns have suffered is serious. When they bought their house, the Flynns knew that the property behind the house was owned by the utility company and that the company might erect lines on the property at any time. In addition, at least at this point, there is no conclusive evidence that EMFs pose a health problem. As a consequence, the public's fear of EMFs in buying a house near high voltage lines is unreasonable.

EXAMPLE 2   THE AUTHOR HAS INCLUDED BOTH SIDES' ARGUMENTS

It is also unlikely that a court would find that the harm that the Flynns have suffered is serious and the financial burden of compensating for that harm would not make continuing the conduct unfeasible. The Flynns allege three types of harm: that the high voltage lines have interfered with their use and enjoyment of the interior of their home by blocking their western view, that the high voltage lines have interfered with their use and enjoyment of their backyard because they fear that exposure to high EMF levels increases their risk of cancer, and that because of high voltage lines, they have been unable to sell their home.

Although the lines do interfere with the Flynns' view, a court is unlikely to find that that harm supports an action in nuisance. When they bought the house, the Flynns knew that the property behind the house was owned by the utility company and that the company might erect lines on the property at any time.

It is also unlikely that a court will find that the Flynns' fear of EMFs is reasonable. Although the Flynns can cite studies linking EMFs to cancer and other health problems (for example, birth defects, miscarriages, and neurological dysfunctions), Pecos Power can cite studies showing no link.

The more difficult question is who should bear the cost of the public's fear of buying a house near high voltage lines. The Flynns will argue that it is the public that should bear the cost. If the lines are of great social utility, then it is the public and not an individual landowner who should bear the cost. By adjusting the utility company's rate structure, the cost of compensating individuals like the Flynns can be distributed among all those who benefit from the high voltage lines. In contrast, Pecos Power will argue that the public should not have to bear the cost of compensating individuals like the Flynns. The Flynns are having trouble selling their home not because the EMFs are dangerous but because the public fears that they might be dangerous. If Pecos Power were forced to compensate individuals for fear of harm, it would open the floodgates to all types of claims based on unreasonable fears, such as claims that regular overhead wires or transformer boxes cause some type of harm.

One of the reasons that writers tend not to include both sides' arguments is that it is difficult to find ways to present those arguments without using the language "the plaintiff will argue" and "the defendant will argue." Although sometimes it can be difficult to find language that works, there are some techniques that you can use.

One of the most common techniques that writers use is to put one side's argument in a dependent clause and the other side's argument in the main clause. Thus, they might put one side's argument in a clause that begins with "although," "even though" or "despite" and the other side's argument in the main clause.

EXAMPLES

Although the lines do interfere with the Flynns' view, a court is unlikely to find that that harm supports an action in nuisance.

Even though this factor is not dispositive, *see e.g., Padilla v. Lawrence,* the courts typically do not find that that conduct constitutes a nuisance when such conduct is authorized by law.

The problem, of course, is that if you use this construction too often the writing becomes repetitive. Look, for instance, at the following example.

EXAMPLE

Although the lines do interfere with the Flynns' view, a court is unlikely to find that that harm supports an action in nuisance.

When they bought the house, the Flynns knew that the property behind the house was owned by the utility company and that the company might erect lines on the property at any time.

It is also unlikely that a court will find that the Flynns' fear of EMFs is reasonable. Although the Flynns can cite studies linking EMFs to cancer and other health problems (for example, birth defects, miscarriages, and neurological dysfunctions), Pecos Power can cite studies showing no link.

Thus, you need to use other strategies. The following examples show some of the other techniques that you can use.

EXAMPLE 1

If the court finds that the Flynns' and public's fears of EMFs are reasonable, it is likely to find that the harm is serious. If, however, it finds that the fears are unreasonable, it is likely to reach the other conclusion.

EXAMPLE 2

Thus, to win, the Flynns would have to prove that EMFs are harmful, something that plaintiffs in other jurisdictions have been unable to do. For example, in both *Jordan v. Georgia Power Co.,* 466 S.E.2d 601 (Ga. App. Ct. 1995) and *Borenkind v. Consolidated Edison Co.,* 164 Misc.2d 808, 626 N.Y.S.2d 414 (N.Y. Sup. 1995), the courts held that the plaintiffs did not have a cause of action in nuisance because the evidence did not establish that EMFs were harmful.

EXAMPLE 3

The Flynns allege three types of harm: that the high voltage lines have interfered with their use and enjoyment of the interior of their home by blocking their western view, that the high voltage lines have interfered with their use of their backyard because they are concerned that exposure to high EMF levels increases their risk of cancer, and that because of high voltage lines, they have been unable to sell their home.

Even though the lines do interfere with the Flynns' view, a court is unlikely to find harm that supports an action in nuisance. When they bought the house, the Flynns knew that the property behind the house was owned by the utility company and that the company might erect lines on the property at any time. . . .

Finally, it is not wrong to use the language "the plaintiff will argue" or "the defendant will argue" when you are using the integrated format. Even though you are using the arguments as your organizing principle, you can still use this language to present each side's points. Just remember to include a topic sentence and don't use the technique in every paragraph.

EXAMPLE

The more difficult question is who should bear the cost of the public's fear of buying a house near high voltage lines. The Flynns will argue that it is the public that should bear the cost. If the lines are of great social utility, then it is the public and not an individual landowner who should bear the cost. By adjusting the utility company's rate structure, the cost of compensating individuals like the Flynns can be distributed among all those who benefit from the high voltage lines. In contrast, Pecos Power will argue that the public should not have to bear the cost of compensating individuals like the Flynns. The Flynns are having trouble selling their home not because the EMFs are dangerous but because the public fears that they might be dangerous. If Pecos Power were forced to compensate individuals who fear harm, it would open the floodgates to all types of claims based on unreasonable fears such as claims that regular overhead wires or transformer boxes cause some type of harm.

Even when they use these techniques, some interns still write arguments that are conclusory. They make assertions but then provide only minimal support for them. Once again, compare the following examples.

EXAMPLE 1   ANALYSIS IS CONCLUSORY

In the *Flynn* case, it is unlikely that a court would find that harm caused by the building of the high voltage lines outweighs the social utility of the lines. Although the Flynns have suffered some harm, that harm is not as serious as the harm the plaintiffs have suffered in other cases. *See e.g., Padilla v. Lawrence,* 685 P.2d 964 (1984); *Scott v. Jordan,* 99 N.M. 567, 661 P.2d 59 (1983).

EXAMPLE 2   **ANALYSIS IS BETTER**

In the *Flynn* case, it is unlikely that a court would find that harm caused by the building of the high voltage lines outweighs the social utility of the lines. In the cases in which the New Mexico courts have found a nuisance, the harm was more serious and the social utility of the conduct was not as great. For example, in *Padilla,* the court held that a bark and manure processing plant constituted a private nuisance when, because of the noise and odors coming from the plant, the plaintiffs were forced to move out of their home. *Id.* at 560, 685 P.2d at 967. Similarly, in *Scott v. Jordan,* 99 N.M. 567, 661 P.2d 59 (1983), the court held that a cattle feeding operation constituted a nuisance when, because of the dust, flies, and noxious odors, the plaintiffs could no longer enjoy their home. *Id.* at 569, 661 P.2d at 60. In contrast, in the *Flynn* case, the Flynns are still able to live in their house and they have not become ill. Thus, the harm that they have suffered is less than the harm that the plaintiffs suffered in *Padilla* and *Scott.*

EXAMPLE 3   **ANALYSIS IS BETTER YET**

In the *Flynn* case, it is unlikely that a court would find that harm caused by the building of the high voltage lines outweighs the social utility of the lines. In the cases in which the New Mexico courts have found a nuisance, the harm was more serious and the social utility of the conduct was not as great. For example, in *Padilla,* the court held that a bark and manure processing plant constituted a private nuisance when, because of the noise and odors coming from the plant, the plaintiffs were forced to move out of their home. *Id.* at 560, 685 P.2d at 967. Similarly, in *Scott v. Jordan,* 99 N.M. 567, 661 P.2d 59 (1983), the court held that a cattle feeding operation constituted a nuisance when, because of the dust, flies, and noxious odors, the plaintiffs became ill. *Id.* at 569, 661 P.2d at 60. In contrast, in our case, the Flynns have suffered little harm. Unlike the Padillas, the Flynns have not been forced to leave their home and, unlike the Scotts, they have not become ill. In addition, a court is likely to find that high voltage lines have more social utility than either a bark and manure processing plant or a cattle feed lot. Thus, to win, the Flynns would have to prove that EMFs are harmful, something that plaintiffs in other jurisdictions have been unable to do. For example, in both *Jordan v. Georgia Power Co.,* 466 S.E.2d 601 (Ga. App. Ct. 1995) and *Borenkind v. Consolidated Edison Co.,* 164 Misc.2d 808, 626 N.Y.S.2d 414 (N.Y. Sup. 1995), the courts held that the plaintiffs did not have a cause of action in nuisance because the evidence did not establish that EMFs were harmful.

In the first example, the author states his conclusion — that the court is not likely to find that the harm outweighs the social utility — but provides little support for that conclusion. It is not enough to simply assert that the harm that the Flynns have suffered is less than the harm that the plaintiffs have suffered in other cases. You need to explain what harm the plaintiffs suffered in other cases and how that harm compares to the Flynns' harm. The second example is much better. Instead of just citing the cases, the author has described them and then compared the facts in those cases to the facts in *Flynn*. He has not, however, dealt specifically with what is the Flynns' best argument: that EMFs are harmful or at least potentially harmful. While the author has done some of this in the third example, the arguments are still not as sophisticated as they might be.

Exercise

Rewrite the third example, making the arguments even more sophisticated.

---

§6.9   REVISING FOR CONCISENESS AND PRECISENESS

In addition to revising your memo, you also need to edit it. Thus, in addition to reviewing what you have written to make sure that your content and large-scale organization are good (see section 19.4) and that you have used roadmaps, signposts, and transitions effectively (see sections 20.2 and 22.1), you also need to make sure that your sentences are well constructed (see Chapter 23) and that your writing is both concise and precise. Every word should count, and every word should be the right word.

§6.9.1   Writing Concisely

Although writing sentences with strong subject-verb units eliminates much unnecessary language, you also need to take your red pen to such throat-clearing expressions as "it is expected that . . ." and "it is generally recognized that . . ." and to redundancies like "combined together" and "depreciate in value" (see sections 24.2.5 and 24.2.7). In the following example, the language that should be deleted has been crossed out.

EXAMPLE

In contrast, ~~it is important to note that~~ the courts have usually held that an activity does not constitute a nuisance when it is ~~permitted or~~ authorized by law. For instance, in ~~the case~~ *State v. Egolf,* 107 N.M. 315, 757 P.2d 371 (1988), one ~~of the~~ factors that the court considered in finding that the building of a trout pond was not unreasonable and therefore not a nuisance was ~~the fact~~ that a zoning commission had found that the pond complied with zoning regulations.

In addition, often a sentence can be reduced to a clause, a clause to a phrase, and a phrase to a word.

EXAMPLE   SENTENCE REDUCED TO A CLAUSE

Original

In some New Mexico cases, the courts have found that the gravity of the harm outweighed the social utility of the conduct. In these cases, the harm was substantial and the social utility of the conduct alleged to be a nuisance was minimal. For example, in *Padilla,* . . . .

Rewrite

In the New Mexico cases in which the courts have found that the gravity of the harm outweighed the social utility of the conduct, the harm was substantial and the social utility of the conduct alleged to be a nuisance was minimal. For example, in *Padilla,* . . . .

EXAMPLE	CLAUSE REDUCED TO A PHRASE

Original

For example, in *Padilla,* the plaintiffs were forced to move out of their home because there were odors and noise coming from the bark and manure processing plant.

Rewrite

For example, in *Padilla,* the plaintiffs were forced to move out of their home because of the odors and noise coming from the bark and manure processing plant.

EXAMPLE	PHRASE REDUCED TO A WORD

Original

In both cases, the plaintiffs had established their homes prior to the construction of the activities alleged to be nuisances.

Rewrite

In both cases, the plaintiffs had established their homes before the conduct alleged to be a nuisance began.

§6.9.2   Writing Precisely

In addition to writing concisely, you also want to write precisely, selecting the correct term and then using that term consistently. For example, do not use the word "holding" to refer to something that was not the court's holding and, once you have labeled something as an "element," do not later refer to it as a "requirement," or "factor." See section 24.1.4.

EXAMPLE	"HELD" USED INCORRECTLY

For example, in *Padilla,* the court held that because of the noise and odors coming from the plant, the plaintiffs were forced to move out of their home.

In the above example, the author misuses the word "held." The court's holding is its decision in a particular case and has two components: a reference to a rule of law and a reference to the specific facts to which that rule was applied. Thus, while the court may have **found**, as a finding of fact, that the plaintiffs were forced to move out of their home because of the noise and odors, the court **held** that a bark and manure processing plant constituted a private nuisance when, because of the noise and odors coming from the plant, the plaintiffs were forced to move out of their home.

EXAMPLE	INCONSISTENT USE OF TERMS

In deciding whether the harm outweighs the social utility of the conduct, the courts consider the following factors:

. . .

In this case, the first element favors the . . .

In law, the words "element" and "factor" have very different meanings. If a statute sets out three elements, then all three of those elements must be met; in contrast, if a statute lists three factors, then a court need only consider those factors in deciding the case. Thus, the above example would confuse legal readers. Are the items listed elements, which must be proved, or only factors, things that the court must consider?

In addition to making sure that you have selected the right word and used it consistently, also make sure that the subjects of your sentences "go with" the verbs and objects.

EXAMPLE	SUBJECT AND VERB MISMATCH

While a court might argue that the lines are not a nuisance because they are authorized by law, this factor is not conclusive.

While courts "state," "find," "rule," and "hold," they seldom argue. It is the parties who present arguments. See section 24.1.6. Thus, the above sentence needs to be rewritten as follows:

EXAMPLE

Rewrite

While Pecos Power might argue that the lines are not a nuisance because they are authorized by law, this factor is not conclusive.

For checklists for critiquing a memo, see Chapter 5.

Chapter 7

The Opinion Letter

What happens to an objective memorandum once it is completed? In some instances, the attorney uses it to prepare for a meeting with the client. The attorney reads the memo and then conveys the information to the client orally. More frequently, however, the attorney uses the memorandum to write an opinion letter to the client.

This was the situation in the BCC case discussed in memo 1 in chapter 4. After studying the memorandum, the attorney wrote a letter to Mr. Beaver, the owner of Beaver Custom Carpets.

Question

Why are more and more attorneys putting their advice in writing?

In writing this letter, the attorney took the information contained in the memorandum and repackaged it so that it better met the needs of its new audience: the clients. A memorandum is written to a particular audience (the attorney) for a particular purpose (to help the attorney evaluate the case and advise the client); an opinion letter is written to a different audience for a different purpose.

§7.1 AUDIENCE

Although the primary audience for an opinion letter is the client, there may be a secondary audience. The letter may be read not only by the client but also by an interested third party or, in some cases, by the other side. Consequently, in writing the letter, you must write for both the client and for anyone else who may read the letter.

§7.2 PURPOSE

For a moment, assume that the audience is the client and no one else. In writing to that client, what is your purpose? Is it to inform? To persuade? To justify the bill? To keep the client? Should you be giving the client only your conclusions, or should you be giving the client the information that he or she needs to reach his or her own conclusions?

Your role is determined, at least in part, by your state's Rules of Professional Conduct. The following rules are representative.

Rule 1.4   Communication . . .

(b) A lawyer shall explain a matter to the extent reasonably necessary to make informed decisions regarding the representation.

Rule 1.13   Client Under a Disability

(a) When a client's ability to make adequately considered decisions in connection with the representation is impaired, whether because of minority, mental disability or for some other reason, the lawyer shall, as far as reasonably possible, maintain a normal client-lawyer relationship with the client.

Rule 2.1   Advisor

In representing a client, a lawyer shall exercise independent professional judgment and render candid advice. In rendering advice, a lawyer may refer not only to law but to other considerations such as moral, economic, social, and political factors that may be relevant to the client's situation.

Questions

How would you write the following letters?

1. A letter to a banker who wants to discharge an employee with AIDS. On the basis of your research, you have determined that a discharge based on the fact that the employee has AIDS would violate state law. There may, however, be ways of getting around state law.

2. A letter to a person with Alzheimer's disease who wants to know the tax consequences of giving real estate valued at $400,000 to his son.

3. A letter to a college-educated woman who is divorcing her spouse about her rights to marital property. The woman, who was abused, has told you that she wants you to make the decisions for her. What would you tell the client if you believe the husband's offer is fair? unfair?

---

§7.3　CONVENTIONS

Just as convention dictated the content and form of the objective memorandum, convention also dictates the content and form of the opinion letter. Most opinion letters have (1) an introductory paragraph identifying the issue and, most often, the attorney's opinion; (2) a summary of the facts on which the opinion is based; (3) an explanation of the law; (4) the attorney's advice; and (5) a closing sentence or paragraph. Note the similarities between the objective memorandum and the opinion letter.

Objective Memorandum	*Opinion Letter*
heading	name
	address
	file reference
	salutation
question presented	introductory paragraph
brief answer	opinion
statement of facts	summary of facts on which opinion is based
discussion section	explanation
conclusion	advice
	closing

§7.3.1　The Introductory Paragraph

In writing the introductory paragraph, you have two goals: to establish the appropriate relationship with the reader and to define the issue or goal. In addition, you will often include substantive information. When the news is favorable, you will almost always want to set out your opinion in the introductory paragraph.

Because the introductory paragraph is so important, avoid "canned" openings. Do not begin all of your letters with "This letter is in response to your inquiry of . . ." or "As you requested . . .". Instead of beginning with platitudes, begin by identifying the topic or issue. Compare the following examples.

EXAMPLE 1

This letter is in response to your inquiry of September 10, 1997. I have now completed my research and have formed an opinion. The issue in your case is whether you can enforce your "contract" with the McKibbins. It is my opinion that you can.

EXAMPLE 2

> Since our meeting two days ago, I have researched the Uniform Commercial Code's Statute of Frauds. Based on this research, I believe that your oral contract with the McKibbins is enforceable under the exception for specially manufactured goods.

EXAMPLE 3

> I have researched your potential claim against the McKibbins, and I think that you will be pleased with the results.

The first two sentences of Example 1 could be used to open almost any letter. The sentences could have been typed into the computer, the attorney filling in the blanks with the appropriate information each time that he or she writes a letter. Because these types of sentences subtly suggest to the reader that he or she is just one more client to whom the attorney is cranking out a response, most successful attorneys avoid them. Instead, like the authors of the Examples 2 and 3, they personalize their openings.

§7.3.2   Statement of the Issue

Although you need to identify the issue, you do not want to include a formal issue statement. The under-does-when format used in office memos is inappropriate in an opinion letter.

In deciding how to present the issue, keep in mind your purpose, both in including a statement of the issue and in writing the letter itself. You are including an issue statement because you want the client to know that you were listening and because you want to protect yourself. Thus, you include a statement of the issue for both rhetorical and practical reasons. You use it to establish the relationship with the client and to limit your liability.

Look again at the examples above. In each, how did the writer present the issue?

In Example 1, the attorney was explicit in setting out the issue. He states: "The issue in your case is whether you can enforce your 'contract' with the McKibbins." The issue statement is not as readily identified in Examples 2 and 3. Instead of setting out the issue, the writers simply identify the topic that they researched.

Question

Which approach is better? Why? When?

———————

§7.3.3　Opinion

The client is paying you for your opinion. It is, therefore, essential that you include your opinion, or conclusion, in the letter.

When the news is good, you will usually put your opinion in the introductory paragraph; having had his or her question answered, the client can then concentrate on the explanation. You may, however, want to use a different strategy when the news is bad. Instead of putting your opinion "up front," you may choose to put it at the end, hoping that having read the explanation, the client will better understand the conclusion.

Whatever your opinion, present it as your opinion. Because you are in the business of making predictions and not guarantees, never tell the client that he will or will not win. Instead, present your opinion in terms of probabilities: "The court will probably find that the goods were specially manufactured." "It is not likely that you would win on appeal."

§7.3.4　Summary of the Facts

There are two reasons for including a summary of the facts. As with the statement of the issue, the first is rhetorical: You want the client to know that you heard his or her story. The second is practical. You want to protect yourself. Your client needs to know that your opinion is based on a particular set of facts and that if the facts turn out to be different, your opinion might also be different.

Just as you do not include all of the facts in the statement of facts written for an objective memorandum, you do not include all of the facts in an opinion letter. Include only those that are legally significant or that are important to the client. Because the letter itself should be short, keep your summary of facts as short as possible.

§7.3.5　Explanation

Under the rules of professional responsibility, you must give the client the information that he or she needs to make an informed decision. It is essential, therefore, that you give not only your opinion but also the basis for your opinion. The explanation section is not, however, just a repeat of the discussion section from your memorandum. It is usually much shorter and much more client-specific.

When the explanation requires a discussion of more than one or two issues, you will usually want to include a roadmap. See section 20.2.1. Before beginning your explanation, outline the steps in the analysis.

EXAMPLE 1

As a general rule, only written contracts are enforceable. Because your contract was not in writing, it will be enforceable only if the court finds that the exception for specially manufactured goods applies. For this exception to apply, we must prove that the rugs were "specially manufactured," that they were not suitable for sale in the ordinary course of your business, and that you had . . . .

EXAMPLE 2

If you decide to go to trial, the court must decide two questions. The first is whether your actions constitute an assault. If the court finds that they do, it must then determine whether Mr. Hoage was damaged. For you to be held liable, both questions must be answered affirmatively.

Having outlined the steps, you can then discuss each step in more detail.

The amount of detail will depend on the question, the subject matter, and the client. Although there are exceptions, as a general rule, do not set out the text of the statute or include specific references to cases. Instead, just tell the client what the statutes and cases say, without citations to authority.

After explaining the law, do some basic application of law to fact. If a particular point is not in dispute, explain why it isn't; if it is in dispute, summarize each side's arguments. The difference between the analysis in an objective memorandum and in an opinion letter is a difference in degree, not kind. In each instance, give the reader what he or she needs — nothing more and nothing less.

§7.3.6   Advice

When there is more than one possible course of action, include an advice section in which you describe and evaluate each option. For example, if there are several ways in which your client could change its business operations to avoid liability, describe and evaluate each of those options. Similarly, if your client could choose negotiation over arbitration or arbitration over litigation, describe and evaluate each option. Having described the options, you can then advise the client as to which option you think would be in his or her best interest.

§7.3.7   Concluding Paragraph

Just as you should avoid canned openings, also avoid canned closings. Instead of using stock sentences, use the concluding paragraph to affirm the relationship that you have established with the client and to confirm what, if anything, is to happen next. What is the next step and who is to take it?

§7.3.8   Warnings

Some firms will want you to include explicit warnings. They will want you to tell the client that your opinion is based on current law and on the facts currently available and that your opinion might be different if the facts turn out to be different. Other firms believe that these warnings, when set out explicitly, set the wrong tone. Because practice varies, determine which approach your firm takes before writing the letter.

In writing your letter you can use the modified semi-block format, the full block (the date, the paragraphs, and the signature block are not indented), or the modified block (paragraphs are not indented but the date and signature block are). For examples of each format, see *Webster's Legal Secretaries Handbook* (2d ed., 1996).

§7.4   WRITING STYLE

It is not enough that the law be stated correctly and that your advice be sound. The client must be able to understand what you have written.

As with other types of writing, a well-written letter is one that is well organized. As a general rule, you will want to present the information in the order listed above: an introductory paragraph in which you identify the issue and give your opinion followed by a summary of the facts, the explanation of the law, your advice, and a concluding sentence or paragraph. You will also want to structure each paragraph carefully, identifying the topic in the first sentence and making sure that each sentence builds on the prior one. Transitions are also important. Use them to keep your reader on track and to make the connections between ideas explicit.

Also take care in constructing your sentences. You can make the law more understandable by using concrete subjects and verbs and relatively short sentences. When longer sentences are needed, manage those sentences by using punctuation to divide the sentence into shorter units of meaning.

Finally, remember that you will be judged by the letter you write. Although clients may not know whether you have the law right, they will know whether you have spelled their name correctly. In addition, most will note other mistakes in grammar, punctuation, or spelling. If you want to be known as a competent lawyer, make sure that your letters provide the proof.

§7.5   TONE

In addition to selling competence, you are selling an image. As you read each of the following letters, picture the attorney who wrote it.

EXAMPLE   LETTER A

Dear Mr. and Mrs. McDonald:

This letter is to acknowledge receipt of your letter of February 17, 1997, concerning your prospects as potential adoptive parents. The information that you provided about yourself will need to be verified through appropriate documentation. Furthermore, I am sure that you are cognizant of the fact that there are considerably more prospective adoptive placements than there are available adoptees to fill those placement slots.

Nonetheless, I will be authorizing my legal assistant to keep your correspondence on file. One can never know when an opportunity may present itself and, in fact, a child becomes unexpectedly available for placement. If such an opportunity should arise, please know that I would be in immediate contact with you.

Very sincerely yours,

Kenneth Q. Washburn, III
Attorney at Law

EXAMPLE   LETTER B

Dear Bill and Mary,

Just wanted you to know that I got your letter asking about adopting a baby. I can already tell that you two would make great parents. But, as you probably know, there are far more "would be" parents out there than there are babies.

But I don't want you to lose hope. You might be surprised. Your future little one may be available sooner than you think. It has happened before! And you can be sure that I'll call you the minute I hear of something. Until then, I'll have Marge set up a file for you.

All the best,

Ken Washburn

EXAMPLE   LETTER C

Dear Mr. and Mrs. McDonald:

Your letter about the possibility of adopting a baby arrived in my office yesterday. The information in your letter indicates that you would be ideal adoptive parents. However, I am sure that you realize that there are more couples who wish to adopt than there are adoptable babies. For this reason, you may have to wait for some time for your future son or daughter.

Even so, occasionally an infant becomes available for adoption on short notice. For this reason, I will ask my legal assistant to open a file for you so that we can react quickly if necessary. Because we do not know exactly when an infant will become available, I recommend that we begin putting together the appropriate documentation as soon as possible. In the meantime, please know that I will call you immediately if I learn of an available infant who would be a good match for you.

Sincerely,

Kenneth Washburn

Questions

1. How does your image of Mr. Washburn change from letter to letter? In each letter, which words or phrases are key in creating an image of Mr. Washburn? How might you explain the difference in content among the three letters?

2. How do you think Mr. and Mrs. McDonald will respond to each of the letters? If you were Mr. or Mrs. McDonald, in what types of cases

would you want the Mr. Washburn of letter A to represent you? of letter B? of letter C?

3. Why might an attorney elect to adopt the writing style of letter A? letter B? Does letter C have the "perfect" tone?

Checklist for Critiquing the Opinion Letter

I. Organization

- The information has been presented in a logical order: The letter begins with an introductory sentence or paragraph that is followed, in most instances, by the attorney's opinion, a summary of the facts, an explanation, the attorney's advice, and a concluding paragraph.

II. Content

- The introductory sentence identifies the topic and establishes the appropriate relationship with the client.
- The attorney's opinion is sound and is stated in terms of probabilities.
- The summary of the facts is accurate and includes both the legally significant facts and the facts that are important to the client.
- The explanation gives the client the information that he or she needs to make an informed decision.
- The options are described and evaluated.
- The concluding paragraph states who will do what next and sets an appropriate tone.

III. Writing

- The client can understand the letter after reading it once.
- When appropriate, the attorney has included roadmaps.
- The paragraph divisions are logical, and the paragraphs are neither too short nor too long.
- Signposts and topic sentences have been used to tell the client where he or she is in the explanation and what to expect next.
- Transitions and dovetailing have been used to make clear the connections between sentences.
- In most sentences, the writer has used the actor as the subject of the sentence.
- In most sentences, the subject and verb are close together.
- The writer has used the passive voice when he or she wants to emphasize what was done rather than who did it or when the passive voice facilitates dovetailing.
- In most sentences, the old information is at the beginning of the sentence and the new information is at the end.

- The writer has varied both sentence length and sentence structure so that each sentence flows smoothly from the prior sentence.
- The writing is concise: When appropriate, sentences have been reduced to clauses, clauses to phrases, and phrases to words.
- The writer has used language precisely: The writer has selected the correct term and used that term consistently.

Chapter 8

Writing an Appellate Brief

A. INTRODUCTION TO APPELLATE PRACTICE

§8.1 INTRODUCTION TO ADVOCACY

The brief is one of the attorney's most powerful tools. In an age of crowded dockets, the attorney's voice is most clearly heard in the quiet of the judge's chambers. A good brief can persuade the court to reverse or affirm a lower court's ruling, create a new rule or follow an old one, or change or continue an established policy. If the brief does not persuade, it is unlikely that the oral argument will.

Unfortunately, good briefs are hard to write. Writing one requires knowledge, insight, and hard work. You must understand both your audience and your purpose in writing to that audience; you must have mastered both the facts of your case and the law; and you must put all of the pieces together clearly, concisely, and persuasively.

In writing an appellate brief you are not, however, starting from scratch. You will be using the research, analytical, and writing skills that you have already developed. In addition, you will be using the advocacy skills that you learned as a child and teenager. As the following example illustrates, most of us learned the "standard moves" of advocacy long before we came to law school.

EXAMPLE

Jon, a 17-year-old junior, wants to use his father's sports car for the junior prom. Because he knows that persuading his father will be difficult, Jon plans his strategy carefully. During the week before he makes his request, Jon is on his best behavior. He is easy to get along with, does his homework without being nagged, and even volunteers to mow the lawn.

When he finally approaches his father, he begins by setting the stage. He subtly reminds his father of how mature and reliable he has become and then begins talking about Sarah, his date for the prom, and about the importance of the event. Isn't Sarah beautiful and intelligent? Isn't your junior prom something you remember for the rest of your life?

He then poses the question. He isn't asking for himself; he is asking for Sarah. Wouldn't it be so much nicer for Sarah if he could take her to the prom in his father's sports car rather than the family's other car, which shows the effect of years of hauling kids from one event to another?

When his father doesn't immediately agree, Jon launches into his first argument. Although Jon's father has said that neither Jon nor his older brothers can drive the sports car, Jon knows that there have been exceptions. Both of Jon's older brothers were allowed to drive the car to their proms. Thus, Jon's version of the rule is not that he and his brothers cannot drive the car but that they can drive the car only on prom nights.

Jon's father responds by distinguishing the cases. Both of Jon's brothers had excellent driving records, while Jon has had two speeding tickets. Thus, the father's version is not that the teenagers can drive the sports car only on prom nights but that a teen can drive the car on prom night provided that he has a good driving record.

Instead of accepting defeat and walking away, Jon tries a couple of other approaches. He begins by conceding that in the past he did not have a good driving record. Recently, however, his driving record has been very good. In the last nine months, he has not had any tickets. Thus, his argument is that, in fact, he falls within the rule set out by his father. Because he currently has a good driving record, he should be allowed to use the sports car on prom night. Jon also tries a couple of policy arguments. If his parents want to promote safe driving, he should be rewarded for his recent behavior. In addition, his parents can promote participation in social activities that they approve of by allowing him to use the car. He also refers his father to the decision of the family's neighbors, the Morgans. Although the Morgans' son David has a worse driving record than Jon, the Morgans have told David that he can use their Lincoln Continental for the prom.

In making his argument to his father, Jon does many of the things that you will do as an attorney. He creates a favorable context for his argument, he presents the facts in the light most favorable to his position, he frames the issue carefully, asking his father for the car not for himself but for his girlfriend, and he makes factual arguments, arguments based on both "in-state" and "out-of-state" cases, and policy arguments.

Exercise

The following policy was set out in the course information packet that you received at the beginning of the semester.

> If a paper is turned in after the time it is due, a late penalty of one full letter grade will be imposed for every twenty-four-hour period that the assignment is late. For example, if a paper receiving a grade of B is turned in two hours after it is due, the grade on the paper will be reduced from a B to a C. Extensions will be granted only when requested in advance or when illness or an emergency has substantially interfered with the student's ability to complete the assignment on time.

In explaining this policy, the professor stated that the policy existed for two reasons: She wanted to simulate the constraints that the students would encounter in practice (in practice, sanctions may be imposed if deadlines are not met), and she wanted to be fair to students who met the deadlines. You know of two instances in which students turned in their briefs late. In the first, the student was involved in a serious automobile accident while driving to school to turn in her brief. The accident occurred at 9:00 a.m.; the brief was due at 1:00 p.m.; and the brief was turned in at 3:00 p.m. In this instance, the professor waived the late penalty.

In the second case, the student underestimated the amount of time that it would take to have the brief copied. As a result, the brief was turned in ten minutes late. In this instance, the professor did not waive the late penalty.

You completed writing the brief at 10:00 p.m. on the day before it was due. Unfortunately, when you began to print it out, your hard disk crashed, and you lost your entire 25-page brief. Although you worked all night trying to recreate the brief, your brief was one hour late. Because you thought that you might make the deadline, you did not call the professor to request an extension. You have turned in all of your other assignments on time.

§8.2   APPELLATE PRACTICE

§8.2.1   Types of Appellate Review

In most jurisdictions, court rules provide for two types of appellate review: an appeal as of right and discretionary review. For example, in Washington, Rule on Appeal 2.1(a) (RAP 2.1(a)) reads as follows.

RULE 2.1: METHODS FOR SEEKING REVIEW OF TRIAL COURT DECISION—GENERALLY

(a) **Two Methods for Seeking Review of Trial Court Decisions.** The only methods for seeking review of decisions of the superior court by the Court of Appeals and by the Supreme Court[1] are the two methods provided by these rules. The two methods are:

(1) Review as a matter of right, called "appeal"; and
(2) Review by permission of the reviewing court, called "discretionary review."

RAP 2.2 then lists the decisions of the superior court that may be appealed, and RAP 2.3 describes the conditions under which a court will grant discretionary review. As in many other jurisdictions, final judgments, decisions determining actions, orders of public use and necessity, juvenile court dispositions, orders depriving a person of all parental rights, and orders of incompetency and commitment may be appealed as of right. Other decisions will be reviewed only if the superior court has committed an obvious error that would render further proceedings useless, the superior court has committed probable error and the decision of the superior court substantially alters the status quo or substantially limits the freedom of a party to act, or the superior court has departed so far from the accepted and usual course of judicial proceedings or so far sanctioned such a departure as to call for review by an appellate court.

Exercise

Locate your state's rules on appeal. In your state, what trial court decisions may be appealed as a matter of right? At the discretion of the court?

§8.2.2   Scope of Review

As a general rule, an appellate court reviews only those errors listed in the notice of appeal or notice for discretionary review. For example, in Washington, RAP 2.4 provides as follows.

RULE 2.4: SCOPE OF REVIEW OF A TRIAL COURT DECISION

(a) **Generally.** The appellate court will, at the instance of appellant, review the decision or parts of the decision designated in the notice of appeal or notice for discretionary review and other decisions in the case as provided in sections (b), (c), (d), and (e). The appellate court will, at the instance of the state, review those acts in the proceeding below which if repeated

---

1. The superior court is Washington's general jurisdiction trial court, the Court of Appeals is its intermediate court, and the Supreme Court is its court of last resort.

on remand would constitute error prejudicial to state. The appellate court will grant a respondent affirmative relief by modifying the decision which is the subject matter of the review only (1) if the respondent also seeks review of the decision by the timely filing of a notice of appeal or a notice for discretionary review, or (2) if demanded by the necessities of the case.

In addition, as a general rule, appellate courts review only those errors that were raised, or preserved, at trial. The only types of errors that can be raised for the first time on appeal are claims that the trial court lacked jurisdiction to hear the case, claims that the plaintiff failed to establish facts upon which relief can be granted, and claims that the error was manifest and involves a constitutional right.

RULE 2.5: CIRCUMSTANCES WHICH MAY AFFECT SCOPE OF REVIEW

(a) **Errors Raised for First Time on Review.** The appellate court may refuse to review any claim of error which was not raised in the trial court. However, a party may raise the following claimed errors for the first time in the appellate court: (1) lack of trial court jurisdiction, (2) failure to establish facts upon which relief can be granted, and (3) manifest error affecting a constitutional right. A party or the court may raise at any time the question of appellate court jurisdiction. A party may present a ground for affirming a trial court decision which was not presented to the trial court if the record has been sufficiently developed to fairly consider the ground. A party may raise a claim of error which was not raised by the party in the trial court if another party on the same side of the case has raised the claim of error in the trial court.

Exercise

Locate your state's rules on scope of review. How are they different from the rules set out above?

§8.2.3　Filing the Notice of Appeal or Notice for Discretionary Review

The rules on appeal also set out the procedure for filing a notice of appeal or a notice for discretionary review. In Washington, Title 4 of the Rules on Appeal sets out the jurisdiction of each division of the State's Court of Appeals and the process for seeking direct review by the State's Supreme Court; Title 5 sets out the time limits for filing the notice, what the notice must contain, and where the notice must be filed; and Title 6 explains how the courts notify the parties about the acceptance of review.

Of particular importance to us for our example case (see section 8.4) are RAP 4.1(b)(2), which states that decisions by the Pierce County Superior Court are reviewed by Division II of the Washington Court of Appeals; RAP 5.2(a), which states that the notice of appeal must be filed not with the appellate court but in the trial court and that the notice must be filed within 30 days after entry of final judgment; and RAP 5.3, which states that the notice of appeal must be titled Notice of Appeal, must specify the party or parties seeking review, must designate the decision or part of the decision that the party wants reviewed, and must name the appellate court to which review is taken.

Exercise

Once again, check your state's rules on appeal. Must decisions of a particular trial court be appealed to a particular division of your court of appeals? How much time does a party have to seek review? What information must be included in the notice of appeal and notice for discretionary review?

§8.2.4   Preparing the Record on Appeal

After filing the notice of appeal or notice for discretionary review, the next thing that the appellant or petitioner must do is designate the record on appeal. He or she must identify those clerk's papers, portions of the report of proceedings, and exhibits that are relevant to the issues on review.

After identifying those portions of the trial record that are relevant, the appellant or petitioner must serve on all the parties, the clerk of the trial court, and the clerk of the appellate court a designation of clerk's papers and exhibits and make arrangements to have the relevant portions of the trial record transcribed. The responding party can then elect whether it wants to supplement the record.

Exercise

Once again check your State's rules on appeal. How is the record on review prepared and transmitted to the appellate court?

§8.2.5   Types of Briefs

The next step in the process is the preparation of the brief itself. As a general rule, the appellant or petitioner files its brief first, serving a copy of the brief on the appellate court and the respondent. After reading the appellant or petitioner's brief, the respondent then prepares and files its brief, serving it on both the court and on the appellant or petitioner. The appellant or petitioner then has the opportunity to file a reply brief, answering arguments made by the respondent in its brief. In some jurisdictions, the rules also permit a reply brief by the respondent, a brief by the appellant in a criminal case, and amicus briefs.

Question

What types of briefs do your State's rules on appeal permit?

§8.3 THE APPELLATE BRIEF: ITS AUDIENCE AND PURPOSE

Just as it was important to understand the audience and purpose of an objective memorandum and opinion letter, it is important to understand the audience and purpose of an appellate brief. For, without an understanding of your audience and your purpose in writing to that audience, you will not be able to make good decisions about what to include and exclude or about how to best present your arguments.

§8.3.1 Audience

The primary audience for an appellate brief is the panel of judges who will be deciding the appeal. This means that if you are seeking review in an immediate court of appeals, you will usually be writing to three judges, and if you are seeking review in your state supreme court, you will be writing to nine justices. When you are writing for your intermediate court of appeals, you may or may not know who your judges will be. In many states, there are more than three judges on the court and you are not told which judges will be on your panel until the day of oral argument. In contrast, when you are writing to your state supreme court, you will usually know who will be hearing your case.

Whether or not you know for sure which judges will be hearing your case, you should research your court before you begin to write. You can do this by reading recent decisions issued by the court or by talking with other attorneys who are familiar with it. In addition, you can usually locate information about individual judges on your state court's homepage on the internet. Often these pages will provide pictures of each judge and information about their education and prior experience.

Exercise

Research one or two of your intermediate state court judges. How did you find out about them? What did you learn? How might this information affect the way you frame the issues or present your arguments?

The judges are not, however, your only audience. In most appellate courts, each appeal is assigned to a particular judge who then assigns the case to one of his or her law clerks. After reading the briefs and independently researching the issues, the clerk prepares a memo to the judge (usually called a bench memo) that summarizes the law and each side's arguments and, in some courts, recommends how the appeal should be decided. Because law clerks can shape how the judges view the appeal, they are some of your most significant readers. Finally, you are also writing for your client and for opposing counsel. You want to write your brief in such a way that your client feels that his or her story is being told and that opposing counsel knows that he or she is up against a well prepared, thoughtful, and vigorous advocate.

As you write, you also need to keep in mind that most appellate judges have substantial workloads. Many intermediate appellate judges hear between 100 and 150 cases a year, writing opinions in approximately one-third of those cases. If each party submits a 50-page brief, each judge would read between 10,000 and 15,000 pages in the course of a year. Length is, therefore, an issue. Appellate judges want briefs that are brief.

Also keep in mind that appellate judges must work within certain constraints, the most significant of which is the standard of review. Although in some cases the court's review is *de novo,* in most cases the review is more limited: Instead of deciding the case on its merits, the appellate court only reviews the decisions of the trial court, looking, for example, to see if the trial judge abused his or her discretion or if there is substantial evidence to support the jury's verdict. (For more on standard of review, see section 8.5.2.d.)

In addition, in some cases the appellate court is itself bound by mandatory authority. State intermediate courts of appeal are bound by the decisions of the state's supreme court, and both the state courts and the United States Court of Appeals are bound by decisions of the United States Supreme Court interpreting and applying the United States Constitution.

§8.3.2   Purpose

In writing an appellate brief, your purpose is twofold: to educate and to persuade. In addition to explaining the underlying facts and the law, you must also explain what happened at trial, persuading the appellate court that the decision of the trial court was correct and should be affirmed or that the trial court's decision was wrong and that the case should, therefore, be reversed or remanded to the trial court for further action.

§8.3.3   Conventions

Just as the process of bringing an appeal is governed by rules, so is the format of an appellate brief. These rules are usually quite specific and govern everything from the types of briefs that may be filed to the sections that must be included, the type of paper, and citation form. The following rules are representative.

RULE 10.3: CONTENT OF BRIEF

(a) Brief of Appellant or Petitioner. The brief of the appellant or petitioner should contain under appropriate headings and in the order here indicated:

(1) *Title Page.* A title page, which is the cover.

(2) *Tables.* A table of contents, with page references, and a table of cases (alphabetically arranged), statutes and other authorities cited, with references to the pages of the brief where cited.

(3) *Assignments of Error.* A separate concise statement of each error a party contends was made by the trial court, together with the issues pertaining to the assignments of error.

(4) *Statement of the Case.* A fair statement of the facts and procedure relevant to the issues presented for review, without argument. Reference to the record must be included for each factual statement.

(5) *Argument.* The argument in support of the issues presented for review, together with citations to legal authority and references to relevant parts of the record. The argument may be preceded by a summary.

(6) *Conclusion.* A short conclusion stating the precise relief sought.

(7) *Appendix.* An appendix to the brief if deemed appropriate by the party submitting the brief.

(b) Brief of Respondent. The brief of respondent should conform to section (a) and answer the brief of appellant or petitioner. A statement of the issues and a statement of the case need not be made if respondent is satisfied with the statement in the brief of appellant or petitioner. If a respondent is also seeking review, the brief of respondent must state the assignments of error and the issues pertaining to those assignments of error presented for review by respondent and include argument on those issues.

(c) Reply Brief. A reply brief should be limited to a response to the issues in the brief to which the reply brief is directed.

RULE 10.4: PREPARATION AND FILING OF BRIEF BY PARTY

(a) Typing or Printing Brief. Briefs shall conform to the following requirements:

(1) One legible, clean, and reproducible copy of the brief must be filed with the appellate court. The brief should be printed or typed in black on 20-pound substance 8½- by 11-inch white paper. Margins should be at least 2 inches on the left side and 1½ inches on the right side and on the top and bottom of each page.

(2) The text of any brief typed or printed in a proportionally spaced typeface must appear in print as 12 point or larger type with 3 points or more leading between lines. The same typeface and print size should be standard throughout the brief, except that footnotes may appear in print as 10 point or larger type with 2 points or more leading between lines and quotations may be the equivalent of single spaced. Except for material in an appendix, the typewritten or printed material in the brief shall not be reduced or condensed by photographic or other means.

(3) The text of any brief typed or printed in a monospaced typeface shall be done in pica type or the equivalent at no more than 10 characters per inch. The lines must be double spaced, that is, there may

be at most 3 lines of type per inch. Quotations and footnotes may be single spaced. Except for material in an appendix, the typewritten or printed material in the brief shall not be reduced or condensed by photographic or other means.

(b) Length of Brief. A brief of appellant, petitioner, or respondent, and a pro se brief in a criminal case should not exceed 50 pages. A reply brief should not exceed 25 pages. An amicus curiae brief, or answer thereto, should not exceed 20 pages. For the purpose of determining compliance with this rule appendices, the title sheet, table of contents, and table of authorities are not included. For compelling reasons the court may grant a motion to file an over-length brief.

(c) Text of Statute, Rule, Jury Instruction, or the Like. If a party presents an issue which requires study of a statute, rule, regulation, jury instruction, finding of fact, exhibit, or the like, the party should type the material portions of the text out verbatim or include them by copy in the text or in an appendix to the brief.

(d) Motion in Brief. A party may include in a brief only a motion which, if granted, would preclude hearing the case on the merits.

(e) Reference to Party. References to parties by such designations as "appellant" and "respondent" should be kept to a minimum. It promotes clarity to use the designations used in the lower court, the actual names of the parties, or descriptive terms such as "the employee," "the injured person," and "the taxpayer."

(f) Reference to Record. A reference to the record should designate the page and part of the record. Exhibits should be referred to by number. The clerk's papers should be abbreviated as "CP"; exhibits should be abbreviated as "Ex"; and the report of proceedings should be abbreviated as "RP." Suitable abbreviations for other recurrent references may be used.

(g) Citations. Citations must be in conformity with the form used in current volumes of the Washington Reports. Decisions of the Supreme Court and of the Court of Appeals must be cited to the official report thereof and should include the national reporter citation and the year of the decision. The citation of other state court decisions should include both the state and national reporter citations. The citation of a United States Supreme Court decision should include the United States Reports, the United States Supreme Court Reports Lawyers' Edition, and the Supreme Court Reporter. The citation of a decision of any other federal court should include the federal reporter citation and the district of the district court or circuit of the court of appeals deciding the case. Any citation should include the year decided and a reference to and citation of any subsequent decision of the same case.

(h) Unpublished Opinions. A party may not cite as an authority an unpublished opinion of the Court of Appeals.

In addition to the rules, there may be other, unwritten conventions governing the format of the brief. For example, most attorneys may use a particular format for the table of authorities or for the questions presented or there may be conventions regarding the capitalization of words like "court." Thus, in addition to reading and following the rules, always check with the court clerk and other attorneys to find out what is expected.

Exercise

Check your state rules on appeal. What sections need to be included in the brief? How long can the brief be? What typefaces and margins are required? How should you refer to the parties? Should you use the *Bluebook* or some other citation system?

B.   DRAFTING AN APPELLATE BRIEF

§8.4   STATE V. STRONG

It is your second year in law school, and you have been hired to work in the Office of Assigned Counsel in Tacoma, Washington. One of the cases that the office is handling is *State v. Strong*. The facts of the case are as follows.

On May 17, 1997, Mr. Strong was standing on a street corner in Tacoma, Washington, in an area known for an unusually high incidence of illegal drug activity, when he was approached by Officer Thomas Hanson. Because he did not recognize Mr. Strong, Officer Hanson asked Strong his name and several questions about what he was doing in the area. Mr. Strong cooperated, giving the officer his name.

Officer Hanson then went back to his patrol car and drove about a block to a block and a half down a hill. He then stopped and ran a criminal history check using Mr. Strong's name and description. The check showed that Mr. Strong had prior arrests for drug-related crimes but no outstanding warrants. As he began to drive away, Officer Hanson glanced into his rearview mirror and saw Mr. Strong standing in the middle of the road, staring at his car. His suspicions aroused, Officer Hanson turned his car around, driving back toward Mr. Strong. As he did so, Mr. Strong began walking quickly toward an apartment complex and an adjacent wooded area. Because the area was dark, Officer Hanson turned on his spotlight so that he could see better. After he did so, Mr. Strong walked toward a tree, dropped what appeared to be a package under the tree, and then walked quickly away. Mr. Strong then slowed his pace, eventually stopping. Neither the record nor the findings of facts make it clear when Mr. Strong stopped or how far he walked.

Officer Hanson got out of his car, told Mr. Strong to stop walking, and retrieved the package from behind the tree. In the package he found half of a cola can containing what appeared to be crack cocaine. Officer Hanson read Mr. Strong his *Miranda* warnings and formally placed him under arrest. During the search incident to arrest, Officer Hanson discovered a .38 caliber semi-automatic pistol and a Rolex watch on Mr. Strong. The substance in the cola can was later confirmed to be crack cocaine.

Although Mr. Strong could have sought discretionary review of the trial court's denial of his motion to suppress, he chose not to do so because it would have been difficult to establish that the superior court committed an obvious error that would render further proceedings useless or that the superior court departed so far from the accepted and usual course of judicial proceedings as to call for immediate review by an appellate court. See section 8.2.1 above. As a result, the case proceeded to trial and, after a one-day trial, a jury found Mr. Strong guilty on all three counts. One month later, a sentencing hearing was held, and Mr. Strong was sentenced.

Soon after the entry of judgment and sentence, Ms. Elder, Mr. Strong's attorney and your supervising attorney, met with Mr. Strong to explain his options. She described the appeals process, telling him how long he had to file an appeal (30 days from the date of entry of judgment and sentence), how long it would take for his case to be heard by the court of appeals (about 18 to 24 months), and the provisions for staying his sentence while his case was on appeal. In addition, she also explained that if he did not appeal or if his appeal was denied, his current convictions would be used in calculating his sentence on any future crimes.

After considering his options, Mr. Strong decided that he wanted to appeal. As a result, Ms. Elder prepared a notice of appeal and ordered a copy of the record.

§8.5   PREPARING TO WRITE THE BRIEF

§8.5.1   Reviewing the Record for Error

Elder received her copy of the record on November 16. Several days later, she began reviewing it.

Like most attorneys, Elder reviewed the record for error using a four-step process. She began by reviewing her trial notes, writing down the errors that she identified during the trial. She then began a systematic review of the record, noting

- each motion that she made that was denied,
- each motion that the State made that was granted,
- each objection that she made that was denied,
- each objection that the State made that was granted,
- each request for a jury instruction that she made that was denied, and
- each request for a jury instruction that the State made that was granted.

For example, in going through the transcript for the sentencing hearing, Ms. Elder noted the following objection, which was overruled.

EXCERPT FROM VERBATIM REPORT OF PROCEEDINGS

State's Direct Examination of Officer Hanson
* * *

Q. Officer, why did you stop the defendant after he dropped the object behind the tree?

A. I believed he was trying to dispose of some type of contraband, narcotics or something, that he didn't want me to find in his possession.

Q. At the time that he dropped the item, you didn't know what it was. Is that correct?

A. No I didn't.

Q. How did you describe it in your report?

A. I'll have to review my notes. If I remember right, I described it as some type of package.

Q. And even if it wasn't a controlled substance, were you concerned that—

A. He could have been littering. It could have been—

Ms. Elder: Your Honor, once again I am going to object. Speculation at point.

Mr. Lion: Your Honor, the question was why this officer—

Ms. Elder: The officer has testified as to why he stopped him and to what he believed it was, as far as he knew. Speculation as to anything further about what it could have been is gratuitous and not relevant.

Mr. Lion: Your Honor, it has to do with this officer's basis for stopping someone—

The Court: Overruled.

Mr. Lion: Thank you.

As her third step, Elder looked for the other, less obvious types of errors.

- Were Strong's constitutional rights violated? (Was he read his *Miranda* rights? Was he represented by counsel at all significant stages in the process?)
- Was he tried within the appropriate time period? Was he given the right to confront the witnesses against him? Is his sentence cruel and unusual?
- Is the statute under which Strong was charged constitutional?
- Was there misconduct on the part of the judge, opposing counsel, or the jury?

Finally, she examines her own actions. Did she miss a defense or fail to object to a motion or a piece of evidence? If she did, Strong might be able to argue that he was denied effective assistance of counsel.

Having identified the potential errors, Elder can analyze them and decide which of them she should raise on appeal.

§8.5.2 Selecting the Issues on Appeal

As an appellate judge, whom would you find more credible: the attorney who alleges twenty-three errors or the one who alleges three?

Most appellate judges take the attorney who lists two, three, or four errors more seriously than the attorney who lists a dozen or more. Instead of describing the attorney who lists numerous errors as "thorough" or "conscientious," judges use terms such as "inexperienced," "unfocused," and "frivolous." When so many errors are listed, the appellate court is likely to think that the problem is not the trial court but the attorney bringing the appeal.

But how do you decide which errors to discuss in your brief? Once again, Ms. Elder uses a four-step process. She determines whether there was in fact an error, whether that error was preserved, whether the error was harmless, and the standard of review.

a.   Was There an Error?

The first question is whether there was in fact an error. Does the Constitution, a statute, or case law allow you to make a credible argument that the trial judge's ruling was erroneous? In order to answer this question, you will usually need to do at least some research. For example, in *Strong,* Ms. Elder had you do some preliminary research to determine whether a good faith argument could be made that the search was illegal under either the Fourth Amendment or the Washington Constitution. Because your research indicated that there was an argument under both the Fourth Amendment and the Washington Constitution, she continued with her analysis of those issues. In contrast, the other research that she had you do was not as fruitful. After doing some preliminary research on sentencing, you determined that you could not make a good faith argument that the trial court erred in ruling that possession of a short firearm and possession of a controlled substance are not the same criminal conduct. As a result, Ms. Elder abandoned that issue. Without a good faith basis for raising the sentencing issue, she risked, at a minimum, annoying the court and, at worst, a potential Rule 11 action for making a frivolous claim.

b.   Was the Error Preserved?

It is not enough that there was an error. Unless the error involves an issue of constitutional magnitude, that error must have been preserved. Defense counsel must have objected or in some other manner brought the alleged error to the attention of the trial court.

Thus, in *Strong,* if Ms. Elder had not filed a motion to suppress, she would not have been able to raise the admissibility of the evidence for the first time on appeal. Although the admissibility of the evidence affects an appellant's Sixth Amendment right to a fair trial, the Washington courts have held that it is not an error of constitutional magnitude. Having brought a motion to suppress, however, Ms. Elder did not need to do more to preserve the error.

c.   Was the Error Harmless?

The next question is whether the error was harmless. As the courts have often said, an appellant is entitled to a fair trial, not a perfect one.

The reversal of a conviction entails substantial social costs: it forces jurors, witnesses, courts, the prosecution, and the appellants to expend further time, energy, and other resources to repeat a trial that has already once taken place. . . . These societal costs of reversal and retrial are an acceptable and often necessary consequence when an error . . . has deprived the appellant of a fair determination of the issue of guilt or innocence. But the balance of interest tips decidedly the other way when the error has had no effect on the outcome of the trial.

William Rehnquist, *Harmless Error, Prosecutorial Misconduct, and Due Process: There's More to Due Process Than the Bottom Line,* 88 Colum. L. Rev. (1988).

In determining whether an error is harmless, most courts apply either the contribution test or the overwhelming untainted evidence test. Under the contribution test, the appellate court looks at the tainted evidence to determine whether that evidence could have contributed to the fact finder's determination of guilt. If it could have, reversal is required. The courts that apply the overwhelming untainted evidence test take a different approach: Instead of looking at the tainted evidence, they look at that which is untainted. If the untainted evidence is sufficient to support a finding of guilt, reversal is not required.

Thus, as an advocate, you need to weed out those errors that were harmless. Although the court may have acted improperly when it allowed a particular piece of testimony, you don't have a case if that same testimony was properly elicited from several other witnesses.

d.   What Is the Standard of Review?

The last thing that you need to consider is the standard of review. In deciding whether there was an error, what standard will the appellate court apply? Will it review the issue *de novo,* making its own independent determination, or will it defer to the trial court, affirming the trial court unless the trial court's finding was clearly erroneous or the trial court judge abused his or her discretion?

As a general rule, an appellate court will review questions of law *de novo.* As a consequence, when the issue is whether the jury was properly instructed, the appellate court will make its own independent determination. The standard is much higher when the question is one of fact. In most circumstances, an appellate court will not disturb factual findings unless such findings are "clearly erroneous" or "contrary to law." Similarly, the appellate courts give great deference to the trial court judge's evidentiary rulings, not reversing unless the judge abused, or manifestly abused, his or her discretion.

Because the rules set out above are general, you must research the standard of review. Sometimes this research will be easy. In one of its opinions, the court will state the standard that is to be applied. At other times, the research is much more difficult. Although the court decides the issue, it does not explicitly state what standard it is applying. In such cases, read between the lines. Although the court does not state that it is reviewing the issue *de novo,* is that in fact what the court has done?

Because very few issues are pure questions of law or pure questions of fact, you may be able to argue the standard of review. While as the appellant you will argue that the appellate court should review the question *de novo,* the respondent will argue that the appellate court should affirm unless the trial court's ruling was clearly erroneous or the trial court abused its discretion.

Having gone through these four steps, Ms. Elder is ready to select the issues on appeal. She decides that both of the constitutional arguments are viable. Thus, she decides to challenge the trial court's denial of her motion to suppress on the grounds that the seizure was unlawful under the Fourth Amendment or, in the alternative, under the Washington Constitution. In addition, because both issues raise questions of law, she can argue that the standard of review is *de novo,* a standard that favors her client.

§8.5.3   Preparing an Abstract of the Record

Before beginning the brief, Elder does one last thing: She prepares an abstract of the record, noting each piece of relevant testimony.

EXAMPLE

EXCERPT FROM ABSTRACT OF RECORD

Direct Examination of Officer Hanson

RP 3	Officer Hanson has 440 hours of training at academy and 18 hours of training in narcotics identification
RP 4	Officer Hanson makes at least three to five drug-related arrests a week
RP 4	Area in which Strong was arrested has a high incidence of drug arrests
RP 6	Officer Hanson noticed Strong standing on corner—he testifies that at that time "nothing struck me as being suspicious" (line 19)
RP 6	Officer Hanson describes his initial conversation with Strong. He asked Strong his name and Strong replied

* * *

Although preparing such an abstract is time-consuming, it forces Elder to go through the record carefully, identifying each piece of relevant testimony. It also makes brief writing and preparation for oral argument easier. Instead of having to search through the entire record for the testimony she needs, Elder can refer to her abstract.

§8.5.4   Preparing the Record on Appeal

After having determined which issues she will raise on appeal, Ms. Elder goes back through the trial record, identifying those parts that she wants included as the record on appeal. She selects as clerk's papers the information, the motion to suppress, the finding of fact and conclusions of law and order denying the motion to suppress, the jury's verdict form, the judgment and sentence, and the notice of appeal. In addition, she includes the transcript of the evidentiary hearing on the motion to suppress. Because she was not assigning error to anything that happened during the trial, she did not have the trial record transcribed or transmitted. In addition, because there were no relevant exhibits, she did not have any of them designated as part of the record on appeal.

§8.6   RESEARCHING THE ISSUES ON APPEAL

How an individual researches an issue depends, in large part, on that individual's familiarity with the area of law. In this case, Ms. Elder is an experienced criminal defense lawyer who has handled hundreds of motions to suppress and who, as a result, knows the law relating to searches and seizures very well. As a consequence, she is able to start her research with a case, *California v. Hodari D.,* a 1991 decision in which the United States Supreme Court set out a two-part test for determining when a seizure occurs. Ms. Elder re-reads this case and then cite checks it.

Question

Would Ms. Elder find different information if she cite checked the case using the print version of *Shepard's* rather than LEXIS or Westlaw? Would she find different information if she cite checks the case using the S.Ct. or L.Ed. cite rather than the U.S. cite? What would Ms. Elder need to do to get even more current information?

———

Although Ms. Elder was able to start her research with a case, an individual who was less familiar with criminal law would have to take a different approach.

Somebody unfamiliar with search and seizure should begin with a secondary source. Such a resource would give an overview of the law and point to the governing authority (constitutions and cases rather than statutes). If there was a Washington state practice book on criminal procedure, that would be a good source. If not, there might be a law review article from one of the state's law schools that surveyed the law of search and seizure. In the alternative, an individual unfamiliar with search and seizure law might look for secondary sources that are not tailored to the specific state. A legal encyclopedia, nutshell, or hornbook would give an introduction to the topic. An ALR annotation on what constitutes a search would be useful in further research. Although Wayne LaFave's five-volume treatise on search and seizure may ultimately be useful in focusing in on the specific issue, it is probably too detailed for one unfamiliar with the topic at the outset of the research project. While learning about the law of search and seizure, the individual can begin to look for cases to cite as primary authority.

§8.7   PLANNING THE BRIEF

Having spent about four hours researching the issues, Ms. Elder is ready to begin working on the brief. She does not, however, begin by putting fingers to the keyboard. Instead, she spends another two or three hours analyzing the facts and the law, developing a theory of the case, and selecting an organizational scheme.

§8.7.1   Analyzing the Facts and the Law

To write an effective brief, Ms. Elder must master both the facts of the case and the law. Specifically, she needs to know what every witness said, and did not say, at the evidentiary hearing and every finding of fact and conclusion of law that the court entered. In addition, she needs to read carefully all of the relevant cases, thinking both about how she might be able to use them to support her argument and about how the State might use them in its arguments.

Ms. Elder also needs to think about what relief she wants and the various ways in which she might persuade the court to grant that relief. Here, ends-means reasoning often works well. She starts with the conclusion that she wants the court to reach and then works backwards through the steps in the analysis.

- **Relief wanted:** Charges dismissed
- **How to get charges dismissed:** Have appellate court reverse trial court
- **How to get appellate court to reverse trial court:** Show that the seizure was illegal
- **How to show that seizure was illegal:** Show that under Fourth Amendment there was a show of authority and that Strong submitted to that show of authority
- **How to show that there was a show of authority:** Show that spotlight was a show of authority or that the spotlight combined with the officer's other actions was a show of authority
- **How to show that spotlight was a show of authority:** Analogize spotlight to emergency light cases and headlight cases using

Stroud and *Vandover* as authority or argue that a reasonable person in same circumstances would not feel free to leave
- **How to show that spotlight combined with officer's other actions was a show of authority:** Use *Soto-Garcia* to argue that there was a progressive intrusion

In contrast, the State's ends-means analysis would look like this.

- **Relief wanted:** Jury verdict affirmed
- **How to get jury verdict affirmed:** Show that the trial court did not err when it denied Strong's motion to suppress
- **How to show that trial court did not err:** Show that the seizure was proper under the Fourth Amendment
- **How to show that the seizure was proper under the Fourth Amendment:** Show that there was no show of authority or, if there was a show of authority, that Strong did not submit to it
- **How to show that there was no show of authority:** Establish that there is no case law in Washington that says that a spotlight is a show of authority. In addition, distinguish spotlights from flashing emergency lights. In the alternative, establish that spotlight plus other actions were not a progressive intrusion. Distinguish *Soto-Garcia*
- **How to show that appellant did not submit:** Use record to establish that after spotlight was turned on Strong continued walking quickly away from the officer

§8.7.2   Developing a Theory of the Case

Having thoroughly mastered both the facts and the law, Ms. Elder is ready to develop her theory of the case. At its simplest, a theory of the case is the legal theory that the attorney relies on in arguing the case to the court. A good theory of the case, however, goes beyond a legal theory or legal argument. It become the lens through which the attorney and, if the attorney is effective, the court views the case.

In *State v. Strong,* Ms. Elder can argue several different legal theories. She can argue that the seizure was illegal under the Fourth Amendment, permissible under the Fourth Amendment but illegal under the Washington Constitution, or illegal under both the Fourth Amendment and the Washington Constitution. In contrast, the State has fewer options. To win, it must establish that the seizure was legal under both the Fourth Amendment and the Washington Constitution.

In addition, Ms. Elder can choose from among several different lenses. She can keep a narrow focus, emphasizing that Mr. Strong's rights were violated when the officer questioned him, ran a criminal history check on him, and then drove toward him, shining a spotlight on him, or she can choose a wider focus, arguing that this case is not just about Mr. Strong but about police officers who step over the line, by their own actions creating situations that allow them to stop citizens like you and me. She can choose an even wider focus, attacking the United States. Supreme Court. Will Washington follow the lead of the United States Supreme Court and adopt the *Hodari* test, a test that has been criticized by numerous commentators, or will it follow the lead of other states and, under an independent state analysis, reject *Hodari*?

The State has similar options. It can choose a narrow lens, emphasizing that Mr. Strong is a convicted felon who was in a high crime area late at night with crack cocaine, or it can choose a wider lens, emphasizing the need to give police officers the tools that they need to fight the war on drugs. Do we, as a society, want to make Officer Hanson wait until Mr. Strong commits a crime before we allow him to investigate? Isn't an ounce of prevention worth a pound of cure? Or the State can choose an even wider lens, arguing that the *Hodari* test is good law that helps protect us as citizens by discouraging suspects from fleeing.

In choosing her theory of the case for *State v. Strong,* Ms. Elder keeps in mind that the ones that tend to work best are those that appeal to both the head and the heart. In deciding a case, judges want to make sure both that the law that they are announcing and applying is sound and that the result is just. Judges are unlikely to adopt a rule if it produces, in the context of the case before them, an unjust result or to reach a particular conclusion, no matter how just, if the only way to do so is to adopt a rule that is unsound.

Question

In the *Strong* case, what theory of the case is likely to work best for Mr. Strong? For the State? Why?

§8.7.3 Selecting an Organizational Scheme

Because there needs to be a one-to-one correspondence between the questions presented and main headings (see sections 8.12 and 8.15) the last thing that Ms. Elder does before she begins writing is to select an organizational scheme. Should she have one question presented and therefore one main heading, two questions presented and therefore two main headings, or three or more questions and headings? In addition, she needs to decide the order in which she wants to present the questions and arguments. Should she start with the federal constitutional analysis or the state constitutional analysis?

a.   Deciding on the Number of Questions and Headings

In almost every case there is more than one way to organize the argument. You can choose to state the issue broadly, having one question presented and one main heading, or you can choose to state the issues more narrowly, having several questions presented and several main headings. For example, in the *Strong* case, Ms. Elder has the following options.

Option 1

One question presented:

Did the trial court err in denying Mr. Strong's motion to suppress?

One main heading with three subheadings:

I. THE TRIAL COURT ERRED IN DENYING MR. STRONG'S MOTION TO SUPPRESS
   A. There was a seizure under the Fourth Amendment.
   B. There was a seizure under the Washington Constitution.
   C. At the time of the seizure, Officer Hanson did not have an articulable suspicion that Mr. Strong was engaging in or about to be engaged in criminal conduct.

Option 2

Three questions presented:

1. Under the Fourth Amendment, did a seizure occur when Officer Hanson drove toward Mr. Strong, focusing his spotlight on him, and Mr. Strong, after walking out of the street and a few feet towards an apartment complex, dropped something behind a tree, turned, and stopped?

2. Did the trial court err when it ruled that Article I, section 7 of the Washington Constitution docs not provide more protection than the Fourth Amendment?

3. Did Officer Hanson have an articulable suspicion that Mr. Strong was engaging in or about to be engaged in criminal conduct at the time he focused his spotlight on him when the only facts before him were that Mr. Strong was in a high crime area, Mr. Strong had a criminal history, and Mr. Strong walked to the middle of the road and watched the police car?

Three main headings:

  I. THERE WAS A SEIZURE UNDER THE FOURTH AMENDMENT.
 II. EVEN IF THERE WAS NOT A SEIZURE UNDER THE FOURTH AMENDMENT, THERE WAS A SEIZURE UNDER THE WASHINGTON CONSTITUTION.
III. AT THE TIME OF THE SEIZURE, OFFICER HANSON DID NOT HAVE AN ARTICULABLE SUSPICION THAT STRONG WAS ENGAGING IN OR ABOUT TO BE ENGAGED IN CRIMINAL CONDUCT.

Option 3

Two questions presented:

1. Under the Fourth Amendment, did a seizure occur when Officer Hanson drove toward Mr. Strong, focusing his spotlight on him, and Mr. Strong, after walking out of the street and a few feet towards an apartment complex, dropped something behind a tree, turned, and stopped?

2. Did the trial court err when it ruled that Article I, section 7 of the Washington Constitution does not provide more protection than the Fourth Amendment?

Two main headings, each with two subheadings:

I. UNDER THE FOURTH AMENDMENT, STRONG WAS UNLAWFULLY SEIZED.
   A. A seizure occurred because Mr. Strong submitted to a show of authority.
   B. At the time of the seizure, Officer Hanson did not have an articulable suspicion that Strong was engaging in or about to be engaged in criminal conduct.

II. UNDER THE WASHINGTON CONSTITUTION, STRONG WAS UNLAWFULLY SEIZED.
   A. The Washington Constitution provides more protection than the Fourth Amendment.
   B. At the time of seizure, Officer Hanson did not have an articulable suspicion that Strong was engaging in or about to be engaged in criminal conduct.

Because we are still in the planning stage, the questions presented and argumentative headings are not in their final form. See section 8.12 for more on drafting the questions presented and section 8.15 for more on drafting the argumentative headings.

In selecting one option over others, first consider your theory of the case. Does one option allow you to present your theory better than the others? Second, determine how closely related the issues are. The more closely related they are, the more likely that you will want to treat them as one issue; the less closely related they are, the more likely it is that you should treat them as separate issues. For example, if all of your issues relate, as they do in the *Strong* case, to a single motion to suppress, you will probably want to treat them as one issue. If, however, they are unrelated, for example, one relates to a motion to suppress, another to a jury instruction, and the third to the sentence that was imposed, you will usually want to treat them as separate issues. Third, consider which option will allow you to divide your arguments into the most manageable chunks. You don't want to have one 50-page argument or 50 one-page arguments. Finally, consider which option will allow you to present your arguments most concisely, with the least repetition.

Although in the *Strong* case any of the three options would work, Ms. Elder chooses the second option. Although the issues are closely related, she wants to emphasize that Mr. Strong is entitled to relief on either of two grounds: the Fourth Amendment or the Washington Constitution. The second option emphasizes this fact without unnecessarily repeating the articulable suspicion argument.

b.   Ordering the Issues and Arguments

In many cases, logic dictates the order of your issues and arguments. Threshold questions — for example, issues relating to subject matter jurisdiction, service of process, and the statute of limitations — must be discussed before questions relating to the merits of the case. Similarly, the parts of a test should usually be discussed in order and, when one argument builds on another, the foundation argument must be put first.

When logic does not dictate the order of your issues and arguments, you will usually want to start with your strongest argument first. By doing so, you ensure that the judges will read your strongest argument and that your strongest argument is in a position of emphasis. You can then go through the rest of your issues and arguments in the order of their strength, or you can begin and end with strong issues and arguments, burying your weaker arguments in the middle.

In the *Strong* case, logic does not dictate the ordering of the issues or the arguments. Given the law, the appellant can present either the Fourth Amendment or the Article 1, section 7, argument first.

Having thoroughly analyzed the facts and the law, developed a theory of the case, and selected an organizational scheme, Ms. Elder is now ready to begin preparing the brief. Although Ms. Elder did not draft the sections in order — she started with the summary of the argument, the argumentative headings, and the argument and then drafted the assignments of error and the issues relating to the assignments of error, the statement of the case, the prayer for relief, and the tables — for the purpose of this chapter, we discuss the sections in the order that they appear in the brief.

§8.8   PREPARING THE COVER

The first page of your brief is the title page, or cover. As in most other jurisdictions, in Washington the cover is governed by court rules, which specify the color of paper that should be used, the information that should be included, and the format. (See Form 5 of the Washington Rules on Appeal.) The briefs at the end of the chapter show the correct format for briefs submitted to the Washington courts.

§8.9   Preparing the Table of Contents

The second page of your brief should be the table of contents. Once again, the rules specify the information that should be included and the format that should be used. (See Form 6 of the Washington Rules on Appeal and the sample briefs at the end of this chapter.)

§8.10   Preparing the Table of Authorities

Immediately following the table of contents is the table of authorities. In this section, you list each of the cases, constitutional provisions, statutes, rules, and other authorities cited in the brief. As a general rule cases are listed first, in alphabetical order, followed by constitutional provisions, statutes, court rules, and secondary authorities. See Form 6 of the Washington Rules on Appeal and the sample briefs at the end of this chapter.

In listing the authorities, use the citation form prescribed by your court rules (your jurisdiction may or may not have adopted the *Bluebook*) and include references to each page in the brief where the authority appears. Both LEXIS and Westlaw have programs that you can use to check your citations and prepare the table of authorities.

§8.11   Drafting the Assignments of Error

In some states, including Washington, the rules on appeal require the appellant to set out assignments of error.

RAP 10.3

(a) Brief of Appellant or Petitioner. The brief of the appellant or petitioner should contain . . .

(3) *Assignments of Error.* A separate concise statement of each error a party contends was made by the trial court.

RAP 10.3

(g) Special Provision for Assignments of Error. A separate assignment of error for each instruction which a party contends was improperly given or refused must be included with reference to each instruction or proposed instruction by number. A separate assignment of error for each finding of fact a party contends was improperly made or refused must be included with reference to the finding or proposed finding by number. The appellate court will only review a claimed error which is included in an assignment of error or clearly disclosed in the associated issue pertaining thereto.

The Washington courts have held that such assignments of error are jurisdictional. This means that if an assignment of error is not included, the court need not consider the issue, even if the issue is argued in the brief.

The format of such assignments of error is simple. Each begins with the assertion "The trial court erred when . . ." and then identifies the procedural act that the appellant claims was error.

EXAMPLE

The trial court erred when it denied Defendant's Motion to Suppress.

There need not be the same number of assignments of error as there are issues. One assignment of error could raise a number of issues, or a number of assignments of error could give rise to a single issue. Unless the respondent is counter-appealing, the respondent should not include assignments of error in its brief.

§8.12   THE ISSUES PERTAINING TO ASSIGNMENTS OF ERROR (QUESTIONS PRESENTED)

While the assignments of error are neutral statements of the errors that the appellant claims occurred at trial, the issues pertaining to the assignments of error, or questions presented, are not. Both the appellant and the respondent want to use the issues pertaining to the assignments of error section of the brief to present their theories of the case to the court.

Look, for example, at the following issue statements from *Hishon v. King & Spaulding*, a 1982 case in which the United States Supreme Court was asked to decide whether law firms were subject to federal civil rights laws prohibiting discrimination in employment on the basis of sex, race, religion, or national origin.

EXAMPLE

PETITIONER'S STATEMENT OF THE ISSUE

Whether King and Spaulding and other large institutional law firms that are organized as partnerships are, for that reason alone, exempt from Title VII of the Civil Rights Act of 1964, and are free (a) to discriminate in the promotion of associate lawyers to partnership on the basis of sex, race or religion; and (b) to discharge those associates whom they do not admit to partnership based on reasons of sex, race or religion under an established "up-or-out" policy.

RESPONDENT'S STATEMENT OF THE ISSUES

Whether law partners organized for advocacy are entitled to constitutionally protected freedom of association.

Whether Congress intended through Title VII of the Civil Rights Act of 1964 to give the Equal Employment Opportunity Commission, a politically appointed advocacy agency engaged in litigation, jurisdiction over invitations to join law firm partnerships.

The petitioner's issue statement sets out its theory of the case: that in this case the issue is whether law firms are free to discriminate on the basis of sex, race, religion, or national origin. Similarly, the respondent's issue statements set out its theory. To the respondent, this is not a case about discrimination. Instead, it is a case about whether the partners in a law firm are entitled to their constitutionally protected right of freedom of association and about whether members of a politically appointed advocacy agency have the right to determine who is invited to join a law firm.

§8.12.1   Selecting a Format

Most courts give you considerable latitude in selecting a format for your issue statements. You can state the question using the under-does-when format, the whether format, or a multi-sentence format.

EXAMPLES

"UNDER-DOES-WHEN" FORMAT

Under the Fourth Amendment, did a seizure occur when Officer Hanson drove toward Mr. Strong, focusing his spotlight on him, and Mr. Strong, after walking out of the street and a few feet towards an apartment complex, dropped something behind a tree, turned, and stopped?

"WHETHER" FORMAT

Whether a seizure occurred under the Fourth Amendment when Officer Hanson drove toward Mr. Strong, focusing his spotlight on him, and Mr. Strong, after walking out of the street and a

few feet towards an apartment complex, dropped something behind a tree, turned, and stopped.

MULTI-SENTENCE FORMAT

On the evening of May 17, 1997, William Strong was standing on a corner talking with an acquaintance when Officer Hanson
approached him and began questioning him. After receiving answers to his questions, Officer Hanson returned to his marked police car, drove a short distance, and then stopped and ran a
criminal history check. After completing this check, Hanson looked
in his rearview mirror and saw Mr. Strong standing in the road,
looking in his direction. Hanson immediately turned his car around
and, accelerating, drove towards Mr. Strong, focusing his spotlight
on him. Mr. Strong walked quickly out of the road, a few steps
toward an apartment complex and then, after dropping something
behind a tree, turned and stopped. Under these circumstances,
was Strong seized at the time Officer Hanson spotlighted him?

Although you may use any format, once you select one, use it for
each of your issues. Do not write one issue using the under-does-when
format and another using the whether format. Also remember that you
are not bound by your opponent's choices. You do not need to use the
format that he or she used, and you do not need to have the same number
of issues. Do not let your opponent dictate your strategy.

Question

What are the advantages and disadvantages of each format?

§8.12.2   Making the Issue Statement Subtly Persuasive

The best issue statements are those that are subtly persuasive. After
reading them, the judges are inclined to rule in favor of the party who
prepared the statement.

There are a number of techniques that can be used to make an issue
statement subtly persuasive: (1) you can state the question so that it suggests the conclusion you want the court to reach; (2) you can present the
facts in the light most favorable to your client, and (3) you can emphasize
or (de-emphasize) the standard of review.

a. State the Question So That It Suggests the Conclusion You Want the Court to Reach

The issue statement should be framed so that the question itself suggests the conclusion you want the court to reach. For example, in writing the first issue statement for *State v. Strong,* Ms. Elder frames the question so that it suggests that a seizure occurred under the Fourth Amendment while the prosecutor frames it so that it suggests that the trial court acted properly when it denied the Mr. Strong's motion to suppress.

Appellant's Statement of the Legal Question

Under the Fourth Amendment, did a seizure occur when. . . .

Respondent's Statement of the Legal Question

Was the trial court's denial of Defendant's motion to suppress proper when. . . .

b. Present the Facts in the Light Most Favorable to Your Client

In addition to stating the question so that it suggests a favorable conclusion, you also want to present the legally significant facts in the light most favorable to your client. For example, in writing her first issue statement, Ms. Elder emphasizes the favorable facts and de-emphasizes the unfavorable ones through her choice of words.

EXAMPLE

Under the Fourth Amendment, did a seizure occur when Officer Hanson drove toward Mr. Strong, accelerating and focusing his spotlight on him, and Mr. Strong, after moving out of the street and a few feet towards an apartment complex, dropped something behind a tree, turned, and stopped?

Note first that Ms. Elder included the legally significant facts, whether or not they were favorable. Thus, she included the fact that Mr. Strong dropped something behind the tree even though that fact does not favor her client. She did, however, de-emphasize the fact by burying it in the middle of the question and using a general rather than a specific term to describe what was dropped. In addition, she chose her words carefully. She referred to her client by name, and, in discussing facts that favor her client she used words that create a vivid image: "Officer Hanson drove towards Mr. Strong, accelerating and focusing his spotlight on him."

Question

In the following example, what techniques did the prosecutor use in framing his first issue statement?

RESPONDENT'S STATEMENT OF THE ISSUE:

Did the trial court properly deny defendant's motion to suppress when, after noting that the defendant was standing in the middle of the road staring at his car, Officer Hanson turned around and drove north on Chicago, only illuminating the area with his spotlight after the defendant walked quickly out of the road toward a dark wooded area.

c. *Emphasize or De-emphasize the Standard of Review*

Another way to make your issue statement subtly persuasive is to use the standard of review to your advantage. As a general rule, if the standard of review favors your client, include a reference to it in your issue statement; if it doesn't, don't mention it.

EXAMPLE 1   STANDARD OF REVIEW EMPHASIZED

Did the trial court act within its discretion when it ruled that Officer Hanson had an articulable suspicion that the defendant was engaging in or was about to be engaged in criminal conduct when . . . .

EXAMPLE 2   STANDARD OF REVIEW NOT EMPHASIZED

Did the trial court err when it ruled that Officer Hanson had an articulable suspicion that Mr. Strong was engaging or was about to be engaged in criminal conduct when . . . .

Question

How would you frame the issue statement so that you emphasized that the standard of review was *de novo?*

§8.12.3 Make Sure That the Issue Statement Is Readable

An issue statement that is not readable is not persuasive. Thus, during the revising process check your issue statement to make sure that a judge could understand it after reading it once. First, look at the length of your issue statement. If your issue statement is more than four or five lines long, try to shorten it. The longer the statement, the more difficult it becomes to read. Second, make sure that you have presented the information in manageable "chunks." One way to make a long issue statement easier to read is to use the three slots in a sentence:

_____ , _____   _____ .

introductory phrase   main clause   modifier
or clause

Finally, make sure that your statement of the issue does not contain any grammatical errors. In particular, make sure that your subject and verb agree and that in listing the facts, the items are parallel. See sections 26.4.1 and 26.7.

Checklist for Critiquing the Question Presented

I. Format

- There are the same number of issue statements as there are main argumentative headings.
- The attorney has used one of the conventional formats: under-does-when, whether, or multi-sentence.
- The same format has been used for each question presented.

II. Content

- The issue statement states the legal question and includes references to the legally significant facts. In addition, when appropriate, it also includes a reference to the rule of law.
- The legal questions have been framed so that they support the writer's theory of the case.

III. Persuasiveness

- The legal question has been framed so that it suggests an answer favorable to the client.

- Favorable facts have been emphasized and unfavorable ones de-emphasized.
- Words have been selected both for their denotation and their connotation.

IV. Writing

- The judge can understand the question presented after reading it through once.
- Punctuation has been used to divide the question presented into manageable units of meaning.
- When appropriate, parallel constructions have been used.
- In both the main and subordinate clauses, the subject and verb are close together.
- The question presented is grammatically correct and correctly punctuated.

§8.13   STATEMENT OF THE CASE

Over and over again, judges emphasize the importance of the facts. At both the trial and appellate court levels, judges want to know what the facts are and how the law should be applied to them.

Because the facts are so important, good advocates spend considerable time crafting their statement of the case. They think carefully about which facts they want to include, how those facts should be organized, and how the facts can be presented in the light most favorable to their client.

§8.13.1   Checking the Rules

Just as there are rules governing the cover, tables, and statement of issues, there is also a rule governing the statement of the case. RAP 10.3(a)(4) sets out the rule for the appellant's brief, and RAP 10.3(b) sets out the rule for the respondent's brief.

RAP 10.3(a) BRIEF OF APPELLANT OR PETITIONER

(4) *Statement of the Case.* A fair statement of the facts and procedure relevant to the issues presented for review, without argument. Reference to the record must be included for each factual statement.

RAP 10.3(b) BRIEF OF RESPONDENT

The brief of respondent should conform to section (a) and answer the brief of appellant or petitioner. A statement of the issues and a statement of the case need not be made if respondent is satisfied with the statement in the brief of appellant or petitioner.

Thus, in *State v. Strong,* Ms. Elder needs to include both a procedural history and a statement of the facts in her statement of the case. While the rules do not require the respondent to include a statement of the case, most prosecutors would include one. While the statement of the case cannot include argument, if Mr. Strong's attorney does a good job, she will present the facts in the light most favorable to her client.

§8.13.2   Drafting the Procedural History

Almost always, attorneys set out the procedural history first, using it to set the stage for the statement of facts and establishing that the case is properly before the appellate court. As a general rule, you will want to include the following facts in your procedural history: (1) a statement describing the nature of the action, (2) a description of any relevant motions and their disposition, (3) a statement telling the court whether the case was heard by a judge or a jury, (4) the date that final judgment was entered, and (5) the date the notice of appeal or the petition for review was filed. For example, in *State v. Strong,* the procedural history would look something like this.

**EXAMPLE   PROCEDURAL HISTORY FROM
             APPELLANT'S BRIEF**

William Strong was charged with one count of Possession of a Controlled Substance under Wash. Rev. Code § 69.50.401(d) (1996), one count of Unlawful Possession of a Firearm under Wash. Rev. Code § 9.41.040(1) (1996), and one count of Possession of Stolen Property in the Second Degree under Wash. Rev. Code § 9A.56.160 (1996). CP 1. After an evidentiary hearing, the trial court denied Mr. Strong's Motion to Suppress.

The case went to trial, RP 8, and on September 8, 1997, a jury found Mr. Strong guilty on all three counts. CP 5. Judgment and sentence were entered on September 24, 1997. RP 15. Mr. Strong filed his notice of appeal on October 16, 1997. CP 15.

Notice that each statement is supported by a reference to the rule. CP stands for Clerk's Paper, i.e., a document filed with the trial court; RP stands for report of proceedings, i.e., the transcript from a hearing or trial; and Ex for exhibit.

§8.13.3　Drafting the Statement of Facts

a.　Selecting the Facts

Like the statement of facts in an objective memo, the statement of facts contains three types of facts: legally significant facts, emotionally significant facts, and background facts.

Legally Significant Facts

Because the court rules require that the statement of the case be "fair," in writing the statement of facts you must include all of the legally significant facts, both favorable and unfavorable. Thus, in the *Strong* case, the parties must include all of the facts that will be relevant in determining whether there was a seizure. Ms. Elder must include the fact that Mr. Strong walked away from the officer, that he walked quickly, and that he dropped some type of "package" behind a tree. Similarly, the prosecutor must include the fact that the officer accelerated as he drove toward Mr. Strong, that he shone his spotlight on Mr. Strong, and that Mr. Strong stopped before being ordered to do so by the officer.

Emotionally Significant Facts

While you must include all of the legally significant facts, you do not need to include all of the facts that are emotionally significant. Although as a defensive move you may sometimes include an emotionally significant fact that is unfavorable, recharacterizing it or minimizing its significance, most of the time you will not. It is more common to include only those emotionally significant facts that favor your client.

The harder question is how to handle emotionally significant facts that are unfavorable to the other side. Should you sling mud, or should you take a higher road, omitting any reference to those facts? The answer is that it depends: It depends on the fact, on the case, and on the attorney. If the case is strong and the fact's connection to the case is tenuous, most attorneys would not include the fact. If, however, the case is weak and the fact's connection is closer, many attorneys would include it, some using it as a sword, others much more subtly.

Background Facts

Background facts play a different role in persuasive writing than they do in objective writing. In an objective statement of facts, the writer includes only those facts that are needed for the story to make sense. In a persuasive statement of facts, you want to do more. You want to use background facts to create a favorable context.

b. Selecting an Organizational Scheme

After selecting the facts, the next step is to select an organizational scheme. Should the facts be presented chronologically, topically, or in an organizational scheme that combines the two?

Unlike an objective statement of facts, in which the only selection criterion was logic, in writing a persuasive statement of facts there are two criteria: You want to select a scheme (1) that is logical and (2) that allows you to present the facts in an order most favorable to the client.

In *Strong,* the scheme that works best is chronological. Because the sequence of events is important, logic dictates that the facts be presented chronologically. A chronological scheme also allows both defense counsel and the respondent to present the facts in a favorable context. By starting with the initial encounter, defense counsel can start with something favorable: When approached by Officer Hanson, Mr. Strong was standing on a corner with a woman watching an encounter between Officer Hanson and another individual. Similarly, the State can start with something favorable: At the time he approached Mr. Strong, Officer Hanson had just finished responding to a call in a high crime area.

c. Presenting the Facts in the Light Most Favorable to the Client

Although the rules require that the statement of facts be fair, they do not require that it be objective. As an advocate, you want to present the facts in the light most favorable to your client.

There are a number of techniques that you can use to do this. You can present the facts in a favorable context, you can tell the story from your client's point of view, you can emphasize favorable facts and de-emphasize unfavorable ones, and you can pick words both for the meaning and for the images that they create.

Create a Favorable Context

A court will view a fact differently depending on the context in which it is presented. Consider, for example, the following sentence:

> He pulled out his gun and, at point-blank range, shot the woman in the head.

After reading this sentence, what is your reaction? Who is the "bad guy"? Who is the victim? For most, it is the gunman who is the bad guy. Having shot a woman at point-blank range, he is a cold-blooded killer who should be found guilty of murder.

Now read the following sentence.

> Pushing his young son out of harm's way, he pulled out his gun and, at point-blank range, shot the woman in the head.

Although he has shot a woman, our gunman is no longer a cold-blooded killer; he is a father shooting to save his son. The context has changed, and our father is no longer the bad guy; he and his son are the victims.

Consider one final sentence.

Having stalked his victim for days, the gunman pushed his young son behind him, pulled out his gun and, at point-blank range, shot the woman in the head.

Do we still have a father shooting to save his son? The answer is no. Now we have a gunman who is worse than the cold-blooded killer in the first example: We have a man who shoots a woman in front of his own son. Another context, a different verdict.

A favorable context can be created in a number of different ways. As the above example illustrates, one way is to start the story where it favors your client. In the following examples from *State v. Patterson,* defense counsel started the story where it started for his client: with his activities on the afternoon of August 13. In contrast, the respondent started the story where it started for the victim.

EXAMPLE   FROM THE APPELLANT'S BRIEF IN *STATE V. PATTERSON*

On Monday morning, August 13, 1995, twenty-two-year-old Dean Patterson returned home from working the graveyard shift as a security guard at Seymour University, where he is also a student. He went to bed and slept until about one o'clock that afternoon. At about 2:30, his wife received a phone call asking her to come to work at the local hospital where she is employed as a nurse. She got ready, and Mr. Patterson dropped her off at the hospital at about 3:10.

At about 3:30, Mr. Patterson called his wife to find out how long she would have to work; they had plans to go to a movie with a friend that evening, and he wanted to find out if he would have to change them. At about 3:40, Patterson called the friend, telling the friend that his wife would have to work that evening. After talking for about ten minutes, Mr. Patterson and his friend decided that they would go to the movie by themselves.

At about 3:50, Mr. Patterson took a load of wash to the apartment complex laundry room. When he returned to the apartment, he watched part of an old movie. At about 4:20, Mr. Patterson went again to the laundry room, putting the laundry in the dryer. On his way back, he went outside to check the gas in his car. In doing so, he noticed a parking spot much closer to his apartment and, after checking his gas, moved his car to that spot. After parking his car, he got out of the car and, because his driver's side door does not lock from the outside, walked to the passenger side to lock the doors. As he did so, he nodded to a parking enforcement officer who passed by.

By this time, it was 4:30, and Mr. Patterson decided to phone his wife again. They arranged to meet at 5:15 for her dinner break. Patterson cleaned up and left his apartment a little after five to walk to the hospital to meet his wife. He never made it.

EXAMPLE   **THE FIRST PARAGRAPH OF THE RESPONDENT'S STATEMENT OF THE CASE**

On Monday, August 13, 1995, seventeen-year-old Beatrice Martinez was assaulted with a deadly weapon. At a show-up thirty to forty minutes after the attack, Ms. Martinez positively identified the appellant, Dean E. Patterson, as her assailant. Four days after the assault, Ms. Martinez again positively identified Patterson as her assailant at a line-up conducted by the police.

Although the differences are more subtle, context is equally important in *State v. Strong.* Was Officer Hanson simply doing his job, introducing himself to the people in the area that he patrols, or did he go over the line, by his own conduct provoking the suspicious actions that the respondent argues established an articulable suspicion that Strong was engaging in or was about to be engaged in criminal conduct? Similarly, was Strong simply a bystander, looking on with others as Officer Hanson responded to a call, or was he a criminal in a high crime area? Although both stories start in the same place, defense counsel creates a favorable context by telling the story from Mr. Strong's point of view while the respondent creates a favorable context by telling the story from Officer Hanson's point of view.

EXAMPLE 1   **FIRST PARAGRAPH OF APPELLANT'S STATEMENT OF FACTS**

On the evening of May 17, 1997, William Strong was standing on the corner of Lincoln and Chicago in Tacoma talking to a friend when Officer Hanson approached him and began questioning him. RP 18. Standing only a foot or two from Strong, Officer Hanson asked Strong to identify himself and to explain what he was doing in the area. RP 18. Mr. Strong willingly answered Officer Hanson's questions, telling him that his name was William Strong. RP 19.

EXAMPLE 2   **FIRST PARAGRAPH OF THE RESPONDENT'S STATEMENT OF FACTS**

At approximately 11:00 p.m. on May 17, 1997, Officer Hanson noticed the appellant, an individual he did not recognize, in the McChord Gate area, an area noted for its high incidence of drug trafficking. RP 17. Because he makes a point to meet the people in his patrol area, Officer Hanson initiated a social contact. RP 18.

Note the last sentence in the second example. Even within the paragraph, the prosecutor is using context to his advantage. He uses the clause, "Because he makes a point to meet the people in his patrol area" to create a favorable context for the fact that Officer Hanson initiated a contact with Strong. The inference he wants the reader to draw is that Hanson is a conscientious police officer.

Tell the Story from the Client's Point of View

One of the most powerful persuasive devices is point of view. As a general rule, you will want to present the facts from your client's point of view. You can do this by telling the story as your client would tell it and by using your client as the actor in most sentences. Look again at the following examples. In the first example, the first paragraph from Mr. Strong's brief, the story is told how Mr. Strong would tell it, and he is the actor in both the first and third sentences. In contrast, in the second example, the first paragraph of the respondent's brief, the story is told as Officer Hanson would tell it, and Officer Hanson is the actor in both sentences. In each sentence, the subject of the sentence is in boldface type.

EXAMPLE 1   **FIRST PARAGRAPH OF APPELLANT'S STATEMENT OF FACTS**

On the evening of May 17, 1997, **William Strong** was standing on the corner of Lincoln and Chicago in Tacoma talking to a friend when Officer Hanson approached him and began questioning him. RP 18. Standing only a foot or two from Strong, **Officer Hanson** asked Strong to identify himself and to explain what he was doing in the area. RP 18. **Mr. Strong** willingly answered Officer Hanson's questions, telling him that his name was William Strong. RP 19.

EXAMPLE 2 FIRST PARAGRAPH OF THE RESPONDENT'S STATEMENT OF FACTS

At approximately 11:00 p.m. on May 17, 1997, **Officer Hanson** noticed the appellant, an individual he did not recognize, in the McChord Gate area, an area noted for its high incidence of drug trafficking. RP 17. Because he makes a point to meet the people in his patrol area, **Officer Hanson** initiated a social contact. RP 18.

Emphasize Those Facts That Support Your Theory of the Case and De-emphasize Those That Don't

In addition to presenting the facts from the client's point of view, good advocates emphasize those facts that support their theory of the case and de-emphasize those that don't. They do this by using one or more of the following techniques.

1. Airtime

Just as listeners remember best the songs that get the most airtime, readers remember best the facts that get the most words. Consequently, favorable facts should be given considerable "airtime" while unfavorable ones should be given little or no "play." For example, in the *Strong* case, Mr. Strong's attorney would want to give the initial encounter considerable airtime while the State would want to give it little play. Look again at the following paragraphs.

EXAMPLE 1 FIRST PARAGRAPH OF APPELLANT'S STATEMENT OF FACTS

On the evening of May 17, 1997, William Strong was standing on the corner of Lincoln and Chicago in Tacoma talking to a friend when Officer Hanson approached him and began questioning him. RP 18. Standing only a foot or two from Strong, Officer Hanson asked Strong to identify himself and to explain what he was doing in the area. RP 18. Mr. Strong willingly answered Officer Hanson's questions, telling him that his name was William Strong. RP 19.

| EXAMPLE 2 | FIRST PARAGRAPH OF THE RESPONDENT'S STATEMENT OF FACTS |

At approximately 11:00 p.m. on the evening of May 17, 1997, Officer Hanson noticed the appellant, an individual he did not recognize, in the McChord Gate area, an area noted for its high incidence of drug trafficking. RP 17. Because he makes a point to meet the people in his patrol area, Officer Hanson initiated a social contact. RP 18.

---

2. Detail

Just as readers tend to remember best those facts that get the most words, they also tend to remember best those things that are described in detail. The more detail, the more vivid the picture, the more vivid the picture, the more likely it is that the reader will remember the particular facts. Thus, airtime and detail work hand in hand. In contrast, to deemphasize unfavorable facts, good advocates describe them in only general terms, limiting the amount of airtime that they give to those facts. Compare the way in which the attorneys describe what happened after the initial contact between Officer Hanson and Mr. Strong.

| EXAMPLE 1 | FROM APPELLANT'S BRIEF |

After questioning Mr. Strong, Officer Hanson returned to his patrol car, got in the car, and drove about a block and a half down a hill. RP 6. He then ran a criminal history check, which showed that Mr. Strong had prior arrests but that there were no outstanding warrants. RP 7. Officer Hanson then looked in his rearview mirror and saw that Mr. Strong had walked to the middle of the street and was looking in his direction. RP 8. Officer Hanson immediately turned his car around and began driving toward Mr. Strong. RP 8. As Mr. Strong began moving toward the side of the street, Officer Hanson accelerated, turned on his spotlight, and focused the spotlight on Strong. RP 9-10.

| EXAMPLE 2 | FROM RESPONDENT'S BRIEF |

Officer Hanson then got in his car and began to leave the area. RP 6. After driving about one and a half blocks, Hanson stopped and ran a criminal history check on the defendant. RP 7. The check showed that the defendant had a long criminal history, including numerous arrests for drug-related crimes. RP 7.

After he completed the criminal history check, Officer Hanson once again began to drive away. RP 8. As he did so, he glanced in his rearview mirror and saw that the defendant had walked into the center of the street and was staring, for what seemed an unusually long period of time, at the police car. RP 8. Because the defendant's behavior seemed suspicious, Officer Hanson turned his car around and began driving back toward the defendant. RP 8. The defendant immediately moved from the middle of the street toward a dark wooded area. RP 9-10. So that he could see better, Officer Hanson turned on his spotlight, illuminating the area. Instead of stopping, the defendant continued to walk quickly away from Officer Hanson toward the wooded area. RP 10.

Note first the way in which the attorneys deal with the criminal history check. Ms. Elder uses few words and generic language. "Mr. Strong had prior arrests." In contrast, the prosecutor gives the fact considerably more airtime (the phrase criminal history check appears three times) and describes the history in as much detail as the record allowed. Similarly, the parties handle the spotlight differently. Although both sides give the fact about the same amount of airtime, Ms. Elder's description is more vivid than the prosecutor's.

3.   Positions of Emphasis

Another technique that can be used to emphasize favorable facts is to place those facts in positions of emphasis. Because readers remember better those things that they read first and last, favorable facts should be placed at the beginning and end of the statement of the case, at the beginning and end of paragraphs, and at the beginning and end of sentences. Unfavorable facts should be "buried" in the middle: in the middle of the statement of facts, in the middle of a paragraph, in the middle of a sentence. See section 23.6.3.

Look again at following excerpt from the appellant's brief. In the first paragraph, Ms. Elder has placed a favorable fact, that Officer Hanson questioned Mr. Strong, in a position of emphasis at the beginning of the paragraph and buried the unfavorable fact, that Mr. Strong has a criminal history, in the middle of the paragraph. In the second paragraph, she has placed favorable facts, that Officer Hanson turned his car around and began driving toward Mr. Strong and that Officer Hanson focused his spotlight on Strong at the beginning and end of the paragraph and the unfavorable fact, that Strong moved away from Officer Hanson, in the middle.

EXAMPLE   FROM APPELLANT'S BRIEF

After questioning Mr. Strong, Officer Hanson returned to his patrol car, got in the car, and drove about a block and a half down a hill. RP 6. He then ran a criminal history check, which showed that Mr. Strong had prior arrests but that there were no outstanding warrants. RP 7. Officer Hanson then looked in his rearview mirror and saw that Mr. Strong had walked to the middle of the street and was looking in his direction. RP 8. Officer Hanson immediately turned his car around and began driving toward Mr. Strong. RP 8. As Mr. Strong began moving toward the side of the street, Officer Hanson accelerated, turned on his spotlight, and focused the spotlight on Strong. RP 9-10.

The prosecutor has also taken advantage of the positions of emphasis, in the first paragraph putting the fact that Hanson began to leave the area at the beginning of the paragraph and that Strong had numerous arrests for drug-related crimes at the end. Examine the second paragraph. Did the prosecutor make good use of the positions of emphasis?

EXAMPLE   FROM RESPONDENT'S BRIEF

Officer Hanson then got in his car and began to leave the area. RP 6. After driving about one and a half blocks, Hanson stopped and ran a criminal history check on the defendant. RP 7. The check showed that the defendant had a long criminal history, including numerous arrests for drug-related crimes. RP 7.

After he completed the criminal history check, Officer Hanson once again began to drive away. RP 8. As he did so, he glanced in his rearview mirror and saw that the defendant had walked into the center of the street and was staring, for what seemed an unusually long period of time, at the police car. RP 8. Because the defendant's behavior seemed suspicious, Officer Hanson turned his car around and began driving back toward the defendant. RP 8. The defendant immediately moved from the middle of the street toward a dark wooded area. RP 9-10. So that he could see better, Officer Hanson turned on his spotlight, illuminating the area. Instead of stopping, the defendant continued to walk quickly away from Officer Hanson toward the wooded area. RP 10.

---

4.   Sentence Length

Just as airtime and detail work together, so do positions of emphasis and sentence length. Because readers tend to remember information placed in shorter sentences better than information placed in longer sentences, good advocates place favorable facts in short sentences in a position of emphasis. For instance, in the following example, defense counsel has buried the unfavorable fact, that Strong dropped a "package," in a long sentence in the middle of the paragraph and put the favorable fact, that Strong stopped, in a short sentence at the end of the paragraph. See section 23.5.

EXAMPLE   FROM APPELLANT'S BRIEF

As the patrol car came toward him, Strong walked quickly out of the road. RP 11, 12. He then walked two or three steps toward an apartment complex, dropped what appeared to Officer Hanson to be a package behind a tree, and then turned and walked two or three steps back toward Officer Hanson. RP 11, 12. He then stopped. RP 12.

---

5.   Sentence Construction

If you want to emphasize a fact, place it in the main clause in a relatively short sentence. If you want to de-emphasize a fact, place it in a dependent or subordinate clause in a relatively long sentence. In the following example, Ms. Elder has placed the facts that she wants to emphasize (that Officer Hanson turned his car around and began driving toward Mr. Strong, and that Officer Hanson accelerated, turned on his spotlight and focused the spotlight on Strong) in main clauses and the fact that she wants to de-emphasize (that Strong began to move to the side of the road) in a subordinate clause at the beginning of a relatively long sentence.

EXAMPLE   FROM APPELLANT'S BRIEF

Officer Hanson immediately turned his car around and began driving toward Mr. Strong. As Mr. Strong began moving toward the side of the street, Officer Hanson accelerated, turned on his spotlight, and focused the spotlight on Strong.

---

6. Active and Passive Voice

Good advocates use the active voice when they want to emphasize what the actor did and the passive voice when they want to draw the reader's attention away from his or her actions. Consider the following examples from the *Patterson* case.

EXAMPLE 1

Active Voice

Patterson assaulted Martinez.

EXAMPLE 2

Passive Voice

Martinez was assaulted by Patterson.

EXAMPLE 3

Passive Voice

Martinez was assaulted.

Because he wants to emphasize that it was Patterson who assaulted Martinez, the prosecutor should use the language in Example 1. In contrast, because she wants to draw the reader's attention away from what Patterson did, defense counsel should use the language in Example 3. See section 23.1 for more on the active and passive voice.

Question

Should Ms. Elder use the active or passive voice in describing Officer Hanson's actions in driving toward Mr. Strong? Why?

Choose Your Words Carefully

Words are powerful. Not only do they convey information, but they also create images. Consider for example, the labels that might be used to describe Mr. Strong.

EXAMPLE 1

Mr. Strong

William Strong

Strong

William

Willie

the appellant

the accused

While Ms. Elder would probably want to use "Mr. Strong," or "William Strong," or "Strong" in referring to her client, the prosecutor would want to use "appellant," "the suspect," or "the accused." By using his proper name, Ms. Elder makes her client a real person. The title "Mr. Strong" makes Strong seem less like a convicted felon and more like an average citizen. In contrast, by using the labels "appellant" or "the accused," the State de-humanizes Mr. Strong and suggests that he is guilty.

Question

Which side might want to refer to Mr. Strong as William or Willie? Why?

Also consider the words that can be used to describe what Mr. Strong and Officer Hanson said. Although all of the following words convey essentially the same information, their connotations are very different.

EXAMPLE 2

Says	Makes a statement
Alleges	Makes a controversial charge or statement without presentation of proof

Asserts	States or expresses positively
Affirms	States or expresses positively but with less force than asserts
Declares	Carries the approximate force of asserts but suggests a more formal statement
Claims	Maintains a position in the face of an argument
Maintains	Declares to be true
Avers	Declares in a positive or dogmatic manner
Argues	Implies intent to persuade an adversary through debate

While Ms. Elder would want to use words like "stated," "asserts," or "affirms" in describing Mr. Strong's statements, she would want to use words like "says," "claims," or "maintains" when talking about what Officer Hanson said. Conversely, the prosecutor would want to use words like "alleges," "claims," "maintains," or "argues" in describing Mr. Strong's statements and words like "says," "asserts," or "affirms" in describing Officer Hanson's statements.

In addition, in writing her statement of facts, Ms. Elder chooses words that create images consistent with her theory of the case. Look at the words and phrases that are in boldface type in the following example.

EXAMPLE

Officer Hanson immediately turned his car around and began driving toward Mr. Strong. **As Mr. Strong began moving toward the side of the street,** Officer Hanson **accelerated,** turned on his **spotlight,** and **focused** the **spotlight** on Strong.

Because she wants to establish that Officer Hanson's actions were a show of authority, Ms. Elder uses the phrase, "Officer Hanson immediately turned his car around and began driving toward Mr. Strong" rather than "Officer Hanson turned and began driving north on Chicago," the word "accelerated" rather than the phrase "increased his speed," the word "spotlight" rather than just "light" and the word "focused" instead of "turned." In addition, because she wants to establish that Mr. Strong submitted to Officer Hanson's show of authority, she chooses to say that "Mr. Strong began moving toward the side of the street" rather than "Mr. Strong began walking quickly away from Officer Hanson."

Question

What words and phrases would the prosecutor want to use in describing the same events?

Be Subtly Persuasive

Most beginning attorneys make one of two mistakes. They either present the facts objectively or, in an attempt to be persuasive, they go over the line, including argument in their statement of facts, setting out facts that are not supported by the record, or using purple prose.

EXAMPLE

Officer Hanson's action constitutes a show of authority. While Mr. Strong was standing in front of his apartment complex talking to a friend, Officer Hanson approached him and began interrogating him, demanding his name and questioning him about what he was doing. RP 4. Although Mr. Strong cooperated fully, Officer Hanson would not give up. RP 5. Hoping to find that there was a warrant for Strong's arrest, he went back to his car, drove a short distance away, and then stopped and ran a criminal history check. RP 7. Although the check did not reveal any outstanding warrants, Officer Hanson turned his car around, and, increasing his speed, drove directly toward Strong, capturing him in the blinding glare of his high-powered spotlight. RP 10, 11.

Most judges would not find this version of the statement of the facts persuasive. Instead of setting out facts, in the first sentence the author sets out a legal conclusion. Although a sentence like this one belongs in the arguments section of the brief, it does not belong in the statement of facts. In addition, the second and fourth sentences contain facts that are not in the record. Nothing in the record indicates that Mr. Strong was standing in front of his own apartment house or that Officer Hanson ran the criminal history check because he hoped to find that there was an outstanding warrant for Mr. Strong's arrest. Finally, the author has gone too far in trying to present the facts in a light favorable to Mr. Strong. Instead of creating a favorable context, words like "interrogating," "capturing," "blinding glare," and "high-powered spotlight" make the judge wary. For more on purple prose, see section 25.1.

Checklist for Critiquing the Statement of the Case

I. Organization

- The facts have been presented in a logical order (chronologically or topically).
- When possible, the facts have been presented in an order that favors the client.

II. Content

- The writer has included both the relevant procedural facts (procedural history) and the facts on which the case is based (statement of facts).
- All of the legally significant facts have been included.
- The emotionally significant facts that favor the client have been included.
- An appropriate number of background facts have been included.

III. Persuasiveness

- The writer has presented the facts so that they support the writer's theory of the case.
- The writer has presented the facts in a favorable context.
- The writer has presented the facts from the point of view that favors the client. (In telling the client's story, the writer has often used the client as the subject of most sentences.)
- The writer has emphasized favorable facts and de-emphasized unfavorable ones.
  - Favorable facts have been given more airtime than unfavorable facts.
  - Favorable facts have been described in detail; unfavorable facts have been described more generally.
  - The positions of emphasis have been used effectively. When possible, favorable facts have been placed at the beginning and end of the statement of the case, at the beginning and end of a paragraph, and at the beginning and end of a sentence.
  - Short sentences and short paragraphs have been used to emphasize favorable facts; unfavorable facts have been placed in longer sentences in longer paragraphs.
  - Active and passive voice has been used effectively.
  - Favorable information has been emphasized by placing it in the main, or independent, clause; unfavorable facts have been placed in dependent, or subordinate, clauses.
  - Words have been selected not only for their denotation but also for their connotation.

§8.14   Summary of the Argument

The summary of the argument is just what the title implies: a summary of the advocate's argument. Although some courts do not require one (the Washington rules state that the "argument *may* be preceded by a summary"), a summary can be a useful tool. For those judges who read the entire brief, it provides an overview of the arguments and authorities that support those arguments; for those judges who do not read everything, it sets out the key points.

You may want to write your summary of the argument twice. By writing a draft before you write the argument section, you will force yourself to focus. If you understand your arguments, you should be able to set out each of them in a paragraph or two. If you can't, more thinking and outlining are needed.

Preparing a second draft after you have written the argument section is equally useful. When strung together, the opening sentences of your paragraphs or paragraph blocks should provide the judges with a summary of the argument. If they don't, it is the argument section itself, and not the summary, that needs work.

The most common problem that attorneys have with the summary of the argument is length. They write too much. The summary of the argument should be no more than one or two pages long with one or two paragraphs for each argument. Citations to authority should also be kept to a minimum. Although you may want to refer to key cases and statutes, the focus should be on the arguments and not the citation. Another common problem is that the attorneys do not make clear the connections between their arguments. Use transitions to make clear when one argument is a continuation of another argument and when an argument is an alternative argument.

§8.15   Drafting the Argumentative Headings

Argumentative headings serve two functions in an appellate brief. They provide the court with an outline of the argument and they help persuade.

§8.15.1   Use the Argumentative Headings to Provide the Court with an Outline of the Argument

Just as posts and beams define the form of a building, argumentative headings define the form of the argument. When properly drafted, they provide the court with an outline of the argument. By quickly reading the headings set out in the table of contents, a judge can see a party's assertions, its support for those assertions, and the relationships among the arguments.

In addition to providing the court with an outline of your argument, argumentative headings serve several other purposes. They help the judge by dividing the argument into manageable sections and by acting as locators, allowing him or her to quickly locate a particular part of the argument. In addition, they help the attorney. Because attorneys like Ms. Elder seldom have large blocks of time available for writing, the brief must usually be written in sections. By drafting the headings first, an attorney can write one section or subsection at a time, putting the pieces together at the end.

§8.15.2　Use the Argumentative Headings to Persuade

Argumentative headings, however, do more than define the structure of your argument. If properly crafted, they can also persuade.

a.　*Write Your Headings as Positive Assertions*

If a heading is to be persuasive, it needs to be in the form of a positive assertion. For example, to persuade the appellate court that the trial court erred, Ms. Elder would make an assertion like the following one.

EXAMPLE

THE TRIAL COURT ERRED WHEN IT DENIED MR. STRONG'S MOTION TO SUPPRESS.

In contrast, to persuade the appellate court that the trial court acted properly when it denied Appellant's motion to suppress, the prosecutor would make the following assertion.

EXAMPLE

THE TRIAL COURT PROPERLY DENIED THE APPELLANT'S MOTION TO SUPPRESS.

---

b. Provide Support for Your Assertions

By itself, though, an assertion is not particularly persuasive. Thus, as a general rule, you will also want to support your assertions. For example, instead of just asserting that the trial court erred when it denied Mr. Strong's motion to suppress, Ms. Elder would want write a heading like the following one.

EXAMPLE

THE TRIAL COURT ERRED WHEN IT DENIED MR. STRONG'S MOTION TO SUPPRESS BECAUSE THE SPOTLIGHT WAS A SHOW OF AUTHORITY AND MR. STRONG SUBMITTED.

Similarly, instead of saying that the trial court acted properly when it denied Mr. Strong's motion to suppress, the prosecutor would write the following.

EXAMPLE

THE TRIAL COURT ACTED PROPERLY WHEN IT DENIED THE DEFENDANT'S MOTION TO SUPPRESS BECAUSE THE SPOT-LIGHT WAS NOT A SHOW OF AUTHORITY AND, EVEN IF IT WAS, THE DEFENDANT DID NOT SUBMIT.

As the above examples illustrate, one of the most common patterns for an argumentative heading is the following.

Assertion   +   because/when   +   support for assertion.

How general or specific your support is will depend on how you have organized your argument. If you have a main heading without any subheadings, your support should be as specific as possible. If, however, you have a main heading with subheadings and sub-subheadings, your main heading can be quite general. The sub-subheadings will provide the more specific support.

Exercise

Consider the following examples. Which does a better job of providing an outline of the argument? Which is most persuasive?

**EXAMPLE 1   MAIN HEADING BUT NO SUBHEADINGS;
SUPPORT SET OUT IN THE FORM OF KEY FACTS**

I. UNDER THE FOURTH AMENDMENT, A SEIZURE OC-
CURRED WHEN OFFICER HANSON DROVE TOWARD MR.
STRONG, ACCELERATING AND TURNING HIS SPOTLIGHT
ON HIM, AND MR. STRONG TOOK A FEW STEPS AND
STOPPED.

**EXAMPLE 2   MAIN HEADING BUT NO SUBHEADINGS;
SUPPORT SET OUT IN THE FORM OF LEGAL
CONCLUSIONS**

I. UNDER THE FOURTH AMENDMENT, THE TRIAL COURT
ERRED WHEN IT DENIED MR. STRONG'S MOTION TO SUP-
PRESS BECAUSE THE SPOTLIGHT WAS A SHOW OF AU-
THORITY AND MR. STRONG SUBMITTED.

EXAMPLE 3   MAIN HEADING AND SUBHEADINGS

I. THE TRIAL COURT ERRED WHEN IT DENIED MR.
STRONG'S MOTION TO SUPPRESS BECAUSE THE SPOT-
LIGHT WAS A SHOW OF AUTHORITY AND MR. STRONG
SUBMITTED TO THE SHOW OF AUTHORITY.
   A. The spotlight was a show of authority because a reasonable
      person would not have felt free to leave.
   B. Mr. Strong submitted to the show of authority when he did
      not leave the area lighted by the spotlight and stopped before
      being ordered to do so by the officer.

---

c.   Make the Headings as Specific as Possible

As a general rule, make your headings case specific. Instead of making statements that are so broad that they could apply to a number of
different cases, make statements that talk specifically about the parties
and facts in your case.

Compare the following examples.

EXAMPLES

Too general

The trial court erred when it denied defendant's motion to suppress.

The trial court erred when it denied defendant's motion to suppress because there was a show of authority and the defendant submitted.

The seizure was proper.

The seizure was proper because the officer had an articulable suspicion.

More specific

The trial court erred when it denied Mr. Strong's motion to suppress because the spotlight was a show of authority and Mr. Strong submitted when, after taking a few steps, he turned and stopped.

The seizure was proper because, after seeing the defendant drop a package behind the tree, Officer Hanson had an articulable suspicion that the defendant was engaged in or was about to be engaged in criminal conduct.

---

d. Make Your Headings Readable

A heading that is not read is not persuasive. For example, even though the following heading is in the proper form, it is not persuasive because very few judges would read it.

EXAMPLE

THE TRIAL COURT ERRED IN DENYING MR. STRONG'S MOTION TO SUPPRESS BECAUSE, UNDER THE TOTALITY OF THE CIRCUMSTANCES, A SEIZURE OCCURRED WHEN OFFICER HANSON, AFTER QUESTIONING MR. STRONG, DROVE AWAY, RAN A CRIMINAL HISTORY CHECK, AND THEN, AFTER SEEING MR. STRONG STANDING IN THE MIDDLE OF THE ROAD, DROVE BACK TOWARD MR. STRONG, SPOTLIGHTING HIM, AND, MR. STRONG, AFTER WALKING TOWARDS AN APARTMENT COMPLEX AND DROPPING AN ITEM BEHIND A TREE, TURNED AND STOPPED BEFORE BEING TOLD TO DO SO BY THE OFFICER.

In addition to keeping your headings short, usually no more than two or three lines long, use sentence constructions that make the headings easier to read. Use parallel constructions (see section 25.2.5) and, when appropriate, repeat the words that highlight the parallel structure (for example, "that" or "because"). Finally, when appropriate, use commas, semicolons, and colons to divide the sentence into more manageable units of meaning.

§8.15.3   Use the Conventional Formats for Headings

Although seldom set out in rules, in most jurisdictions there are conventions governing the number, type, and typeface for argumentative headings. For example, as we noted in section 8.12, convention dictates that you should have a main heading for each of your issue statements. Thus, if you have one issue you should have one main heading, if you have two issues, two main headings, and so on. The issue sets out the question, and the heading gives your answer to that question.

In addition to main headings, you can also use subheadings and sub-subheadings and, rarely, sub-sub-subheadings. There are, however, some things to keep in mind if you use additional headings. First, if you include one subheading, you need to have at least two at that same level. As a consequence, if you find that you have only one subheading in a section, either delete that heading or add at least one additional heading. Second, while you are not required to put text between the main heading and the first subheading, it is usually a good idea to do so. As a general rule, use this "space" to set out the general rule and a roadmap for that section of your brief. Finally, keep in mind the typefaces that attorneys use for the various levels of headings. The formats provide the judges with cues about where they are in the argument.

The following example shows one way of using headings. Note that following convention, all capitals have been used for the main headings and underlining for the subheadings.

Argument

I. FIRST MAIN HEADING [corresponds to first question presented]
    [general rule, roadmap]
    A. <u>First subheading</u>
        [specific rule, roadmap]
        1. First sub-subheading
            [Text of argument]
        2. Second sub-subheading
            [Text of argument]
    B. <u>Second subheading</u>
        [Text of argument]
    C. <u>Third subheading</u>
        [Text of argument]

II.   SECOND MAIN HEADING [corresponds to second question presented]
[general rule, roadmap]
A.   Rule <u>First subheading</u>
[Text of argument]
B.   <u>Second subheading</u>
[specific rule, roadmap]
1.   First sub-subheading
[Text of argument]
2.   Second sub-subheading
[Text of argument]

Checklist for Critiquing Argumentative Headings

I.   Content

- When read together, the headings provide the judge with an outline of the argument.

II.   Persuasiveness

- Each heading is in the form of a positive assertion.
- Each assertion is supported, either in the main heading or through the use of subheadings.
- The headings are case specific; that is, they include references to the parties and the facts of the case.
- Favorable facts are emphasized and unfavorable facts are de-emphasized or omitted if not legally significant.
- Favorable facts have been placed in the positions of emphasis.
- Favorable facts have been described vividly and in detail.
- Words have been selected both for their denotation and their connotation.

III.   Conventions

- The writer has used the conventional typefaces for main headings, subheadings, and sub-subheadings.
- There is never just one subheading or sub-subheading in a section.

IV.   Writing

- The judge can understand the heading after reading it through once. (Headings are not more than two or three lines long.)
- Punctuation has been used to divide the heading into manageable units of meaning.
- When appropriate, parallel constructions have been used.
- In both the main and subordinate clauses, the subject and verb are close together.
- The headings are grammatically correct and correctly punctuated.

§8.16　DRAFTING THE ARGUMENTS

A brief is only as good as its argument section. An argument section that is well written persuades; one that is not, does not.

§8.16.1　Knowing What You Need, and Want, To Argue

If your arguments are to be focused, you must know what you need, and want, to argue. You can't just throw out a number of assertions, rules, and cases and hope that the court will make sense of them for you.

Thus, before you begin to write, you need to determine what type of argument you are making. Are you asking the court to adopt a new rule? To apply an existing rule? To determine whether the trial court abused its discretion or whether there is sufficient evidence to support a jury's verdict? The following decision tree can help decide what type of argument you need to make.

Are you asking the appellate court to apply an existing rule or test or adopt a new rule or test?

If you are asking the appellate court to apply an existing rule or test, is the standard of review de novo or something more deferential?

If the standard of review is de novo, you need to set out the rule or test and then walk the court through it, showing why each part is or is not met.

If the standard of review is more deferential, for example, abuse of discretion, you need to show the appellate court why the trial court did or did not abuse its discretion.

If you are asking the appellate court to adopt a new rule or test, you need to establish (1) that the appellate court is not bound by mandatory authority, (2) that the rule that you are advocating is a better rule than the rule your opponent is advocating, and (3) that under your rule, you win. In addition, in the alternative, you may want to argue that you are entitled to relief under the rule that your opponent is advocating.

§8.16.2   Selecting an Organizational Scheme

Once you have determined what type of argument you want to make, you then need to select the organizational scheme that will work best for that argument.

If you are asking the court to adopt a new rule or test, you will usually use a version of Plan C set out in Chapter 6. You will start by establishing that there is no existing rule or test, then persuade the court that the rule or test that you are proposing is "better" than the rule or test being proposed by your opponent, and end by applying your proposed rule or test to the facts of your case. In addition, sometimes you will argue in the alternative: even if the court adopts the rule or test being advocated by opposing counsel, you still win under that test.

Plan C
Organizational Scheme for Issues of First Impression

    I. Introduction establishing that the issue is one of first impression.
   II. Assertion setting out proposed rule
  III. Arguments relating to why the court should adopt your proposed rule rather than the rule being proposed by your opponent
  IV. Application of your proposed rule to the facts of your case
   V. If appropriate, alternative argument asserting that even under the rule being proposed by your opponent you win

If you are asking the court to apply an existing rule or test, you have more options. You can use Plan A, setting out the rule or test first, the descriptions of analogous cases second, your arguments third, and your conclusion last; you can use the traditional format but integrate your discussion of the analogous cases into your arguments; or you can break with tradition and begin with the facts. You can also vary each of these organizational schemes by adding an assertion or a set of assertions at the beginning or, when the rule or test requires you to analyze a series of elements or factors, by dividing your argument into subsections, each with its own rules, descriptions of analogous cases, and arguments.

Organizational Schemes for Argument Involving
the Application of an Existing Rule or Test

Option 1:   <u>Traditional format</u>
                 Argumentative heading
                 Favorable statement of the rule
                 Descriptions of analogous cases

Your argument, including your response to your opponent's arguments
Conclusion

Option 2: Traditional argument but descriptions of cases inte-
grated into argument
Argumentative heading
Favorable statement of the rule
Your argument including cases and facts that support
your position and your response to your opponent's
arguments
Conclusion

Option 3: Nontraditional format: facts presented first
Argumentative heading
Legally and emotionally significant facts
Comparison of facts in client's case to facts in analogous
cases
Conclusion

Option 4: Traditional format with assertion at the beginning
Argumentative heading
Assertion
Favorable statement of the rule
Descriptions of analogous cases
Your argument, including your response to your oppo-
nent's arguments
Conclusion

Option 5: Nontraditional format with assertion at the beginning
Argumentative heading
Assertion
Legally and emotionally significant facts
Comparison of facts in client's case to facts in analogous
cases
Conclusion

Option 6: Traditional format with each element or factor discussed
in separate subsection and descriptions of analogous
cases integrated into arguments
Argumentative heading
Favorable statement of the general rule
First Element
Favorable statement of specific rule
Your argument including description of analogous
cases and facts that support your position and
your response to your opponent's arguments
Mini-conclusion
Second Element
Favorable statement of specific rule

> Your argument including description of analogous
> cases and facts that support your position and
> your response to your opponent's arguments
> Mini-conclusion
> Third Element
> Favorable statement of specific rule
> Your argument including description of analogous
> cases and facts that support your position and
> your response to your opponent's arguments
> Mini-conclusion
> General Conclusion

Question

What do each of the above options have in common? How are they different?

Although there is always a temptation to use the organizational scheme with which you are most comfortable, as an advocate this is a temptation you need to resist. If you are to persuade the court, you need to pick the scheme that allows you to emphasize the strongest parts of your argument. For example, if the rule strongly favors your client, you will usually want to select one of the more traditional organizational schemes that allows you to put the rule at the beginning, in the position of emphasis. Conversely, if the facts are very favorable, you will usually want to use a nontraditional organizational scheme that allows you to put them at the beginning. At other times, when there are a number of steps to the analysis, it works best to select an organizational scheme that allows you to begin your argument with your assertions, set out in the order that you discuss them.

Exercise

Set out below are three versions of an argument from Mr. Strong's appellate brief. Which example is most effective? Why?

EXAMPLE 1

Argumentative
Heading
(a subheading)

C. When Officer Hanson spotlighted Mr. Strong, he did not have an articulable suspicion that Mr. Strong was engaged in or was about to be engaged in criminal behavior.

A seizure is unlawful if an officer cannot point to specific and articulable facts giving rise to a reasonable suspicion that the person seized was engaged in or was about to be engaged in criminal activity. *Terry v. Ohio,* 392 U.S. 1, 21-22 (1968); *State v. Pressley,* 64 Wash. App. 591, 595, 825 P.2d 749,*** (1992). Although the courts look at the totality of the circumstances in determining whether the facts were sufficient to support a finding that the officer had an articulable suspicion, the courts have repeatedly held that the fact that the person was in a high crime area or an area known for drug trafficking is not sufficient to establish articulable suspicion. *State v. Gleason,* 70 Wash. App. 13, 851 P.2d 731 (1993); *State v. Soto Garcia,* 68 Wash. App. 20, 841 P.2d 1271 (1992); *State v. Pressley,* 64 Wash. App. 591, 825 P.2d 749 (1992). For example, in *Gleason,* the court found that an officer did not have an articulable suspicion that the defendant was engaged in or about to be engaged in criminal activity when the officer saw the defendant leave an apartment complex where narcotics were known to be sold. Similarly, in *Soto-Garcia,* the court held that the officer did not have an articulable suspicion that the defendant was engaged in or about to be engaged in criminal activity when the defendant was seen walking late in the evening in an area known for cocaine trafficking. In contrast, in *Pressley,* the court held that the officer did have an articulable suspicion when the defendants were in a high crime area, had their hands chest high, one of the defendants was pointing to an object in her hand and the other was staring at it, and, when the officer approached, the woman with the object in her hand said, "Oh shit" and closed her hand.

As in *Gleason* and *Soto-Garcia,* in this case the only fact before the officer was that Mr. Strong was in an area known for drug trafficking. Unlike the defendants in *Pressley,* Mr. Strong was not huddled with another individual pointing at his hand and when he was approached by the officer he did not close his hands or say, "Oh shit." Rather, when he was approached by the officer he answered all of the officer's questions. Walking into the middle of the street,

Favorable statement of the rule

Description of analogous cases

Appellant's arguments

Appellant's
response to the
Respondent's
argument

looking at a police car, and walking out of the street are not acts that are illegal or that indicate that an individual is about to engage in criminal conduct.

Conclusion

Because Officer Hanson did not have an articulable suspicion that Mr. Strong was engaging in or was about to be engaged in criminal conduct at the time he spotlighted Mr. Strong, the seizure was illegal, and the evidence must be suppressed.

EXAMPLE 2

Argumentative
Heading
(subheading)

C. The seizure was illegal because Officer Hanson did not have an articulable suspicion that Mr. Strong was engaged in or was about to be engaged in criminal conduct.

Assertion

At the time Officer Hanson spotlighted Mr. Strong, he did not have an articulable suspicion that Mr. Strong was engaged in or was about to be engaged in criminal conduct.

Favorable
statement of
the rule

A seizure is unlawful if an officer cannot point to specific and articulable facts giving rise to a reasonable suspicion that the person seized was engaged in or was about to be engaged in criminal activity. *Terry v. Ohio,* 392 U.S. 1, 21-22 (1968); *State v. Pressley,* 64 Wash. App. 591, 595, 825 P.2d 749, 751 (1992). Although the courts look at the totality of the circumstances in determining whether the facts were sufficient to support a finding that the officer had an articulable suspicion, the counts have repeatedly held that the fact that the person was in a high crime area or an area known for drug trafficking is not sufficient to establish articulable suspicion. *State v. Gleason,* 70 Wash. App. 13, 851 P.2d 731 (1993); *State v. Soto-Garcia,* 68 Wash. App. 20, 841 P.2d 1271 (1992); *State v. Pressley,* 64 Wash. App. 591, 825 P.2d 749 (1992).

In this case, the only facts before Officer Hanson at the time he spotlighted Mr. Strong were that Strong was in a high crime area; that Strong had cooperated with Officer Hanson, giving him his name and answering his questions; that after Officer Hanson left, Strong walked to the middle of the road; and that when Officer Hanson began driving toward Strong, Strong began walking out of the road toward an apartment complex.

In factually similar cases, the courts have held that such facts are not sufficient to support a finding of articulable suspicion. For example, in *Gleason,* the court held that an officer did not have an articulable suspicion that the defendant was engaged in or about to be engaged in criminal activity when the officer saw the defendant leave an apartment complex where narcotics were known to be sold. *Id.* at 18, 851 P.2d at 734. Similarly, in *Soto-Garcia,* the court held that the officer did not have an articulable suspicion that the defendant was engaged in or about to be engaged in criminal activity when the defendant was seen walking late in the evening in an area known for cocaine trafficking. *Id.* at 26, 841 P.2d at 1274.

An articulable suspicion exists only when the defendant is engaged in activities that strongly suggest criminal conduct. Thus, in *Pressley,* the court based its decision that the officer had an articulable suspicion on the fact that not only were the two women in a high crime area but that they had their hands chest high, one of the women was pointing to an object in her hand and the other was staring at it, and, when the officer approached, the woman with the object in her hand said, "Oh shit" and closed her hand. Because similar facts are not present in this case, Officer Hanson did not have an articulable suspicion, and the evidence should be suppressed. *Id.* at 597, 825 P.2d at 752.

Appellant's argument including facts and cases that support appellant's position

Appellant's Response to Respondent's Argument

EXAMPLE 3

Argumentative
Heading
(subheading)

C. The seizure was illegal because Officer Hanson did not have an articulable suspicion that Mr. Strong was engaged in or was about to be engaged in criminal conduct.

Legally
Significant
Facts

At the time he spotlighted Mr. Strong, the only facts before Officer Hanson were that Strong was in a high crime area; that Strong had cooperated with Officer Hanson, giving him his name and answering his questions; that after Officer Hanson left, Strong walked to the middle of the road; and that when Officer Hanson began driving toward Strong, Strong began walking out of the road toward an apartment complex.

Assertion

In similar cases, the courts have held that these types of facts are not sufficient to support a finding that at the time of the seizure the officer had an articulable suspicion that the defendant was or was about to engaged in criminal conduct. For example, in

Description of
Analogous
Cases

State v. Gleason, the court held that an officer did not have an articulable suspicion that the defendant was engaged in or about to be engaged in criminal activity when the officer saw the defendant leave an apartment complex where narcotics were known

Argument

to be sold. *Id.* at 18, 851 P.2d at 734. Similarly, in *State v. Soto-Garcia,* the court held that the officer did not have an articulable suspicion that the defendant was engaged in or about to be engaged in criminal activity when the defendant was seen walking late in the evening in an area known for cocaine trafficking and answered the officer's questions about why he was in the area. *Id.* at 26, 841 P.2d at 1274.

Response to
State's
Argument

Thus, for the court to find that the officer had an articulable suspicion, the State must show more than that the defendant was in a high crime area. It must be able to point to specific facts that indicate that the defendant is engaging or is about to engage in criminal conduct. Unlike *State v. Pressley,* in which the women were not only in a high crime area but one of them had something in her hand and the other was pointing to it and said, "Oh, shit" when the officer approached, *id.* at 597, 825 P.2d at 752, in this case there are no facts indicating that the defendant was about to engage in criminal activity. Walking to the middle of the street, watching a police car, and walking out of the street are not illegal and do not provide evidence that the defendant was about to engage in criminal activity.

Because the State has not been able to meet its burden, the seizure was illegal, and the evidence must be suppressed.

Conclusion

§8.16.3　Presenting the Rules, Descriptions of Analogous Cases, and Arguments in the Light Most Favorable to Your Client

Although the organizational schemes for an argument in a brief are similar to the organizational schemes for the discussion of an issue in an objective memorandum, the method of presentation is different. While in an objective memorandum you present the rules, cases, and arguments as objectively as possible, in a brief you want to present them in the light most favorable to your client.

a.　*Present the Rule in the Light Most Favorable to Your Client*

Good advocacy begins with a favorable statement of the rule. Although you do not want to misstate a rule, quote a rule out of context, or mislead a court, you do want to present the rule in such a way that it favors your client. There are a number of ways in which you can do this. You can present the rule in a favorable context, you can state the rule broadly or narrowly, you can state the rule so that it suggests the conclusion that you want the court to reach, and you can emphasize who has the burden of proof.

EXAMPLE 1　OBJECTIVE STATEMENT OF THE RULE

In determining whether a stop was justified, the courts examine the totality of the circumstances to determine whether there were specific and articulable facts that, taken together with reasonable inferences from those facts, suggest that the defendant was engaged in or about to be engaged in criminal activity. *State v. Glover,* 116 Wash. 2d 509, 513, 806 P.2d 760, 762 (1991) (*citing Terry v. Ohio,* 392 U.S. 1, 21-22 (1968)).

EXAMPLE 2   APPELLANT'S STATEMENT OF THE RULE

A seizure is unlawful if the State cannot prove that the officer had specific and articulable facts giving rise to a reasonable suspicion that the person seized was engaged in or about to be engaged in criminal activity. *Terry v. Ohio,* 392 U.S. 1, 21-22 (1968); *State v. Glover,* 116 Wash. 2d 509, 513, 806 P.2d 760, 762 (1991). Although the courts look at the totality of the circumstances in determining whether the facts were sufficient to support a finding that the officer had an articulable suspicion, the courts have repeatedly held that the fact that the person was in a high crime area or an area known for drug trafficking is not sufficient to establish articulable suspicion. *State v. Gleason,* 70 Wash. App. 13, 851 P.2d 731 (1993); *State v. Soto-Garcia,* 68 Wash. App. 20, 841 P.2d 1271 (1992); *State v. Pressley,* 64 Wash. App. 591, 825 P.2d 749 (1992).

EXAMPLE 3   RESPONDENT'S STATEMENT OF THE RULE

Because officers need to be able to question individuals suspected of committing a crime, a *Terry* stop is permitted whenever an officer has a reasonable and articulable suspicion that an individual is or is about to be engaged in criminal activity. *See Terry v. Ohio,* 392 U.S. 1, 21-22 (1968); *State v. Glover,* 116 Wash.2d 509, 513, 806 P.2d 760, 762 (1991). In making these stops, the officer does not need to have the level of information necessary to justify an arrest; he or she need only have the ability to reasonably surmise from the information at hand that a crime is in progress or has occurred. *State v. Kennedy,* 107 Wash. 2d 1, 6, 726 P.2d 445, 448 (1986).

In the first example, the rule is stated "objectively." In contrast, in the second example, Ms. Elder has presented the rule so that it suggests the conclusion that she wants the court to reach, that the seizure was unlawful. In addition, she has used several other persuasive techniques. She has emphasized that it is the State that has the burden of proof; she has selected her words carefully, using the word "seizure" instead of the word "stop" and the phrase "repeatedly held" instead of just "held"; and she has de-emphasized an unfavorable portion of the rule by placing it in a dependent clause in the middle of a long paragraph ("Although . . . suspicion").

Similarly, in Example 3, the prosecutor has used a number of persuasive techniques. He has placed the rule in a favorable context by emphasizing that officers need to be able to stop and question individuals suspected of committing crimes, he has stated the rule so that it supports the conclusion it wants the court to reach (a *Terry* stop is permitted), he has selected his words carefully ("reasonably surmise"), and he has emphasized a favorable portion of the rule by placing it at the end of the paragraph.

Exercise

Compare the following examples taken from briefs written by students representing the Respondent in *State v. Strong*. Which is more persuasive? Why?

EXAMPLE 1

The United States Supreme Court applies a two-prong test to determine what constitutes a seizure of a citizen by a police officer. *California v. Hodari D.,* 499 U.S. 621 (1991). Under this test, a seizure occurs only when an officer applies physical force or the citizen submits to a show of authority by the police officer. *Id.* at 624.

EXAMPLE 2

Recognizing that not all contacts between police officers and citizens are seizures, the Court has held that a seizure occurs only when a suspect is restrained by means of physical force or a show of authority. *California v. Hodari D.,* 499 U.S. 621 (1991).

EXAMPLE 3

    Because of society's need for effective law enforcement to combat the high incidence of crime, especially drug-related crime, the United States Supreme Court has held that a defendant is not seized under the Fourth Amendment unless he has been restrained by means of physical force or a show of authority. *California v. Hodari D.* 499 U.S. 621 (1991).

---

b. Presenting the Cases in the Light Most Favorable to Your Client

Just as you want to present the rules in a light favorable to your client, you also want to present the cases in a favorable light. The first step in this process is to determine whether you need to include descriptions of analogous cases. If you do, the second step is to determine how much you need to say about each case, and the final step is to determine how you can present each case in a light favorable to your client.

Step 1: Decide Whether You Need to Include Descriptions of Analogous Cases

Do not include descriptions of analogous cases just to include descriptions of analogous cases. Include them because (a) they provide support for your assertion, (b) you need to distinguish cases your opponent has used to support his or her assertion, or (c) even though the case does not support your assertion and has not been cited by your opponent, as an officer of the court you are obligated to bring the case to the court's attention. Remember, you can use a case as authority for a rule without setting out its facts, holdings, and rationale.

Step 2: Decide How Much You Need to Say About an Analogous Case

How much you say about a case depends on how you want to use that case. If the case is the centerpiece of your argument, you will usually describe the case in detail, setting out the facts, the court's holding, and the court's reasoning. You will then build your argument around this case, comparing the facts in your case to the facts in the analogous case and arguing for the same result. In contrast, if the case illustrates only one important but relatively minor point, you will usually say far less about the case, maybe only setting out the holding and one or two facts. In these situations, you can either set out the court's holding and the key facts in text or in a parenthetical following the citation to the case. See example 2 below.

EXAMPLE 1   CASE IS "CENTERPIECE" OF ARGUMENT

The facts in our case are significantly different from the facts in *California v. Hodari D.* In *Hodari D.,* two officers were on routine patrol when, rounding a corner in an unmarked car, they saw four or five youths huddled around a small red car parked at the curb. When the youths saw the police car, they panicked and began to run. Hodari and one companion ran west through an alley; the others ran south. Seeing the youths run, the officers became suspicious and gave chase. While one of the officers remained in the car, the other ran north along 63rd, then west on Foothill Boulevard, and then south on 62nd, getting ahead of Hodari. Because Hodari was looking over his shoulder and not where he was going, he did not see the officer until the officer was almost upon him. When he did see him, Hodari tossed what appeared to be a small rock. A moment later, the officer tackled Hodari.

Unlike Hodari, who ran several blocks, Mr. Strong only walked from the center of the road to the side of the road and then a few steps toward an apartment complex. As Officer Hanson testified, Strong "walked maybe ten or twelve feet." RP 43. In addition, unlike Hodari, who did not stop until he was tackled by the police officer, Mr. Strong stopped before being told to do so by Officer Hanson.

EXAMPLE 2   CASE USED TO ILLUSTRATE ONE IMPORTANT, BUT MINOR, POINT

The courts have consistently held that a seizure does not occur when an officer uses a device to see what he or she could see unaided in other circumstances. For example, in *State v. Rose,* the court held that a seizure did not occur when an officer used a flashlight to look through an unobstructed window. *Id.* at 397, 909 P.2d at 285. *Accord, State v. Young,* 28 Wash. App. 412, 416-17, 624 P.2d 725, 728-29 (1981) (holding that a search did not occur when an officer used a flashlight to look through a car's windows).

Step 3: Present the Case in the Light Most Favorable to Your Client

Just as there are a number of techniques that you can use to present a rule in the light most favorable to your client, there are a number of techniques that you can use to present a case in a favorable light. You can describe the facts of the case using general or specific terms, you can state the court's holding broadly or narrowly, and you can emphasize or de-emphasize particular material through your use of the positions of emphasis, sentence length and sentence construction, and your choice of words.

In the following example, Ms. Elder describes two favorable cases. Because she wants the court to find that her case is like these two cases, she describes the facts using general rather than specific terms, and she states the holding broadly rather than narrowly.

EXAMPLE

In factually similar cases, the courts have held that such facts are not sufficient to support a finding of articulable suspicion. For example, in *Gleason,* the court held that an officer did not have an articulable suspicion that the defendant was engaged in or about to be engaged in criminal activity when the officer saw the defendant leave an apartment complex where narcotics were known to be sold. *Id.* at 18, 851 P.2d at 734.

Similarly, in *Soto-Garcia,* the court held that the officer did not have an articulable suspicion that the defendant was engaged in or about to be engaged in criminal activity when the defendant was seen walking late in the evening in an area known for drug trafficking. *Id.* at 26, 841 P.2d at 1274.

In contrast, in the next paragraph, Ms. Elder wants to distinguish the case. As a consequence she describes the facts in more detail and states the holding more narrowly.

EXAMPLE

An articulable suspicion exists only when the defendant is engaged in activities that strongly suggest criminal conduct. Thus, in *Pressley,* the court based its decision that the officer had an articulable suspicion not only on the fact that the two women were in a high crime area but also on evidence establishing that they had their hands chest high, one of the women was pointing to an object in her hand and the other was staring at it, and, when the officer approached, the woman with the object in her hand said, "Oh shit" and closed her hand. *Id.* at 597, 825 P.2d at 752.

There are also several things that you do not want to do in presenting analogous cases. First, and probably most important, do not organize your arguments around individual cases. For example, do not use the following organizational scheme.

    Argumentative heading
    Favorable statement of rule

    Description of Case A
    Comparison of the facts in our case to the facts in Case A

    Description of Case B
    Comparison of the facts in our case to the facts in Case B

    Description of Case C
    Comparison of the facts in our case to the facts in Case C

    Conclusion

Instead, organize your arguments around assertions or legal principles, using the cases only as support for those assertions or as illustrations of those legal principles.

    Argumentative heading
    Favorable statement of rule

    Assertion 1
      Description of Case A
      Description of Case B
      Argument using Case A and Case B

    Assertion 2
      Description of Case C
      Argument using Case C

    Conclusion

Second, avoid starting a paragraph with a citation to a case. Because you are using the cases to illustrate an assertion or a principle, you will usually want to start the paragraph with a statement of that assertion or principle or with a transition indicating that you are presenting an example or illustration.

EXAMPLE 1   POOR OPENING

In *State v. Gleason,* the court held that a seizure occurred when the officer walked toward the defendant, asked him whether he could talk to him, asked him why he was there, and then demanded his identification. Although a reasonable person might have felt free to leave after the initial request, a reasonable person would not have felt free to ignore the officer's demand for identification. *Id.* at 18, 851 P.2d at 374. Similarly, in *State v. Soto-Garcia,* the court held that a seizure occurred when an officer approached the defendant on the street, asked him some questions, checked his identification, and then asked him if he had cocaine and if he could search him. *Id.* at 25, 841 P.2d at 1273.

EXAMPLE 2   BETTER OPENING

Courts look at the officers' conduct in determining whether a reasonable person would feel free to leave. *State v. Gleason,* 70 Wash. App. 13, 851 P.2d 731 (1993); *State v. Soto-Garcia,* 68 Wash. App. 20, 841 P.2d 1271 (1992). In *Gleason,* the court found that a seizure occurred when the officer walked toward the defendant, asked him whether he could talk to him, asked the defendant why he was there, and then demanded his identification. Although a reasonable person might have felt free to leave after the initial request, a reasonable person would not feel free to ignore the officer's demand for identification. *Id.* at 18, 851 P.2d at 734. Similarly, in *Soto-Garcia,* the court held that a seizure occurred when an officer approached the defendant on the street, asked him some questions, checked his identification, and then asked him if he had cocaine and if he could search him. Under these circumstances, a reasonable person would not feel free to leave. *Id.* at 25, 841 P.2d at 1273.

Third, avoid the temptation to include case description after case description. As a general rule, it is better to include one or two carefully selected cases than four, five, or six cases. Your brief will be shorter, something that will please almost every judge, and your preparation for oral argument will be easier. (Remember, for every case you cite, you need to know that case, inside and out, for oral argument.) When it is important to cite more than one or two cases, set out the best case or cases in text and then reference the other cases using parentheticals.

Finally, remember that if you describe a case you need to use that case in your argument. Don't leave cases hanging, hoping the judge will figure out why you included the case in your brief.

c.　Presenting the Arguments Effectively

It is not enough, however, to present the rules and cases in a light favorable to your client. If you are to persuade a judge, you must also use those rules and cases effectively.

Make Clear How the Rules and Cases Apply to Your Case

One of the most common mistakes that attorneys make in writing a brief is that they do not make explicit connections between the parts of their argument. They set out an assertion, but do not connect it to the rule, they set out the rule but do not connect it to the descriptions of analogous cases, and they set out descriptions of analogous cases but do not connect the facts and holdings in those cases to their case. Look, for instance, at the following example. Although all of the pieces are there, those pieces have not been connected. In particular, the writer has not used the language of the rule, that is "a show of authority occurs when a reasonable person would not feel free to leave" in describing the analogous cases, and he has not explicitly compared the facts in the analogous cases to the facts in *Strong*.

EXAMPLE 1　　**INEFFECTIVE ARGUMENT**

A show of authority occurs when a reasonable person would not feel free to leave. *California v. Hodari D.,* 499 U.S. 621 (1991). In *State v. Vandover,* 63 Wash. App. 754, 757, 822 P.2d 784, 785 (1992), the court held that a seizure occurred when an officer followed a car and then turned on his emergency lights. In *State v. DeArman,* 54 Wash. App. 621, 624, 774 P.2d 1247, 1248 (1989), the court held that a seizure occurred when an officer pulled up behind a parked vehicle and turned on his emergency lights. In our case, a seizure occurred when Officer Hanson approached Mr. Strong and turned on his light.

The following version is better.

EXAMPLE 2   **BETTER ARGUMENT**

A show of authority occurs when a reasonable person would not feel free to leave. *California v. Hodari D.,* 499 U.S. 621 (1991). For example, in *State v. Vandover,* 63 Wash. App. 754, 756, 822 P.2d 784 (1992), the court held that there was a show of authority when an officer began following the defendant's car and turned on his emergency lights because, under these circumstances, a reasonable person would not feel free to leave. *Id.* at 757, 822 P.2d at 785. Similarly, in *State v. DeArman,* 54 Wash. App. 621, 774 P.2d 1247 (1989), the court held that there was a show of authority when an officer pulled up behind a parked vehicle and turned on his emergency lights. As the court stated, "under these circumstances a reasonable person would not feel free to terminate the encounter." *Id.* at 624, 774 P.2d at 1248. Just as the officers in *Vandover* and *DeArman* approached the defendants and turned on their lights, Officer Hanson approached Mr. Strong and turned on his light. Thus, there was a show of authority because, under the circumstances, a reasonable person would not have felt free to leave.

---

d.   Don't Ignore the "Weaknesses" That Are Inherent in Your Argument

Another error that attorneys commonly make is that they don't deal with the "weaknesses" in their argument. Although sometimes this strategy works, more often it doesn't. Even if the opposing party doesn't notice the problems, the court will.

For example, in the example set out above, the writer doesn't deal with the fact that in the two analogous cases the lights were the officers' emergency lights while in *Strong* the light was a spotlight. By not dealing with this distinction in his own argument, the writer opens the door to an argument like the following one.

EXAMPLE   **EXCERPT FROM RESPONDENT'S BRIEF**

Neither of the cases that defendant relies on is on point. While in *Vandover* and *DeArman,* the officers turned on their flashing emergency lights, in our case Officer Hanson turned on his spotlight. . . .

Instead of ignoring problems, the better strategy is to deal with the problem "up front."

| **EXAMPLE** | **REWRITE OF APPELLANT'S ARGUMENT** |

A show of authority occurs when a reasonable person would not feel free to leave. *California v. Hodari D.,* 499 U.S. 621 (1991). For example, in *State v. Vandover,* 63 Wash. App. 754, 822 P.2d 784 (1992), the court held that there was a show of authority when an officer began following the Defendant's car and turned on his emergency lights because, under these circumstances, a reasonable person would not feel free to leave. *Id.* at 757, 822 P.2d at 785. Similarly, in *State v. DeArman,* 54 Wash. App. 621, 774 P.2d 1247 (1989), the court held that there was a show of authority when an officer pulled up behind a parked vehicle and turned on his emergency lights. As the court stated, "under these circumstances a reasonable person would not feel free to terminate the encounter." *Id.* at 624, 774 P.2d at 1248. Although both *Vandover* and *DeArman* involved emergency lights and not spotlights, the courts' reasoning applies here. Just as a reasonable person would not feel free to leave when an officer pulls up behind him and turns on emergency lights, a person would not feel free to leave when an officer turns his car around and, driving toward that person, focuses his spotlight on that person. Thus, just as there was a show of authority in *Vandover* and *DeArman,* there was also a show of authority in this case.

Questions

In the example set out above, did the author use the positions of emphasis effectively? How about sentence construction? Paragraph and sentence length?

Don't Overlook Good Arguments

Finally, sometimes attorneys miss their strongest argument. For example, in *Strong,* the defendant's strongest argument is that the show of authority resulted from a combination of events: the initial contact, the driving towards the defendant, and the spotlight. Compare the following example to the earlier examples.

EXAMPLE

     The first prong of the test, show of authority, is met whenever an officer's actions would indicate to a reasonable person that he or she is not free to leave or terminate the encounter. *California v. Hodari D.,* 499 U.S. 621 (1991). In deciding whether this prong is met, the courts do not look at a single action. Instead, they look at the totality of the circumstances to see whether the officer focused his attention on a particular individual or whether there has been a progressive intrusion into an individual's privacy. *See e.g., State v. Soto-Garcia,* 68 Wash. App. 20, 841 P.2d 1271 (1992); *State v. Vandover,* 63 Wash. App. 754, 756, 822 P.2d 784 (1992).

     In this case, Officer Hanson focused his attention on Mr. Strong. He stopped and questioned Mr. Strong, ran a criminal history check on Mr. Strong, and then turned his car around and drove toward Mr. Strong, accelerating and focusing his spotlight on him. Under similar circumstances, the courts have found that such actions are a show of authority. For example, in both *Vandover* and *State v. DeArman,* 54 Wash. App. 621, 624, 774 P.2d 1247, 1248 (1989), the court held that a seizure occurred when an officer pulled up behind a vehicle and turned on his emergency lights. Although these two cases involved emergency lights and not spotlights, in each instance the officers focused their attention on a particular individual, indicating to that individual that he was not free to leave or terminate the encounter.

     In addition, Officer Hanson progressively intruded into Mr. Strong's privacy. Although a reasonable person might have felt free to terminate the initial encounter, he would not feel free to leave when Officer Hanson drove toward him and turned his spotlight on him. As the court found in *Soto-Garcia,* while an individual may feel free to terminate an initial encounter, he may not feel free to leave if an officer continues questioning him. "Considering all of the circumstances . . . , the atmosphere created by Tote's progressive intrusion into Soto-Garcia's privacy was of such a nature that a reasonable person would not believe that he or she was free to end the encounter." *Id.* at 25, 841 P.2d at 1273.

     Thus, there was a show of authority under either rule. There was a show of authority because Officer Hanson focused his attention on Mr. Strong or, in the alternative, because Officer Hanson progressively intruded into Mr. Strong's privacy.

    Although adding the additional arguments makes the brief longer, in this instance doing so is a good choice. Because both her "focused attention" and "progressive intrusion" arguments are legally sound, Ms. Elder substantially increases her chances of getting a reversal by arguing in the alternative.

e. *Respond to Your Opponent's Arguments but Do Not Emphasize Them*

As the respondent, you need to address your opponent's arguments without emphasizing them. There are several ways in which you can do this. First, avoid starting an argument by repeating your opponent's argument. Instead, begin by setting out the rule in a light favorable to your client or by making your own positive assertion. Second, present your own argument as forcefully as you can, using the rules, cases, and facts to your advantage. Finally, try to de-emphasize the rules, cases, and facts that favor your opponent by giving them little air time, by using general rather than specific language, and using the positions of emphasis and sentence length and sentence construction to your advantage.

EXAMPLE　　　**APPELLANT'S ARGUMENT**

C. When Officer Hanson spotlighted Mr. Strong, he did not have an articulable suspicion that Mr. Strong was engaged in or was about to be engaged in criminal conduct.

A seizure is unlawful if an officer cannot point to specific and articulable facts giving rise to a reasonable suspicion that the person seized was engaged in or about to be engaged in criminal activity. *Terry v. Ohio,* 392 U.S. 1, 21-22 (1968); *State v. Pressley,* 64 Wash. App. 591, 595, 825 P.2d 749, 752 (1992). Although the courts look at the totality of the circumstances in determining whether the facts were sufficient to support a finding that the officer had an articulable suspicion, the courts have repeatedly held that the fact that the person was in a high crime area or an area known for drug trafficking is not sufficient to establish articulable suspicion. *State v. Gleason,* 70 Wash. App. 13, 851 P.2d 731 (1993); *State v. Soto-Garcia,* 68 Wash. App. 20, 841 P.2d 1271 (1992); *State v. Pressley,* 64 Wash. App. 591, 825 P.2d 749 (1992).

For example, in *Gleason,* the court held that an officer did not have an articulable suspicion that the defendant was engaged or about to be engaged in criminal activity when the officer saw the defendant leave an apartment complex where narcotics were known to be sold. *Id.* at 18, 851 P.2d at 734. Similarly, in *Soto-Garcia,* the court held that the officer did not have an articulable suspicion that the defendant was engaged in or about to be engaged in criminal activity when the defendant was seen walking late in the evening in an area known for cocaine trafficking. *Id.* at 26, 841 P.2d at 1274. In contrast, in *Pressley,* the court held that the officer did have an articulable suspicion when the defendants were in a high crime area, had their hands chest high, one of the defendants was pointing to an object in her hand and the other was staring at it, and, when the officer approached, the woman with the object in her hand said, "Oh shit" and closed her hand. *Id.* at 597, 825 P.2d at 752.

As in *Gleason* and *Soto-Garcia,* in this case the only fact before the officer was that Mr. Strong was in an area known for drug trafficking. Unlike the defendants in *Pressley,* Mr. Strong was not huddled with another individual pointing at his hand and when he was approached by the officer, he did not close his hands or say, "Oh shit." Rather, when he was approached by the officer, he answered all of the officer's questions. Walking into the middle of the street, looking at a police car, and walking out of the street are not acts that are illegal or that indicate that an individual is or is about to be engaged in criminal conduct.

Because Officer Hanson did not have an articulable suspicion that Mr. Strong was engaged in or about to be engaged in criminal conduct at the time he spotlighted Mr. Strong, the seizure was illegal, and the evidence must be suppressed.

EXAMPLE   **POOR RESPONSE BY RESPONDENT**

C. The search was legal because at the time he turned on his spotlight, Officer Hanson had an articulable suspicion that the defendant was engaged in or about to be engaged in criminal conduct.

Defendant argues that when Officer Hanson turned on his spotlight he did not have an articulable suspicion that Mr. Strong was engaged in or about to be engaged in criminal conduct. In particular, defendant argues that this case is more like *State v. Gleason,* 70 Wash. App. 13, 851 P.2d 731 (1993) and *State v. Soto-Garcia,* 68 Wash. App. 20, 841 P.2d 1271 (1992) than it is like *State v. Pressley,* 64 Wash. App. 591, 825 P.2d 749 (1992).

Although Officer Hanson did testify that one of the facts that he considered was the fact that the defendant was in a high crime area late at night, there were other facts. Thus, this case is unlike *Gleason* and *Soto-Garcia* and more like *Pressley.* Although Mr. Strong did not say "Oh shit" when Officer Hanson approached, he did walk to the middle of the road and then back toward a wooded area.

EXAMPLE **BETTER RESPONSE BY RESPONDENT**

C. <u>The seizure was legal because at the time he turned on his spotlight, Officer Hanson had an articulable suspicion that the defendant was engaged in or about to be engaged in criminal conduct.</u>

A stop is lawful if, at the time of the stop, the officer can point to specific and articulable facts giving rise to a reasonable suspicion that the person seized was engaged in or about to be engaged in criminal activity. *Terry v. Ohio,* 392 U.S. 1, 21-22 (1968); *State v. Pressley,* 64 Wash. App. 591, 595, 825 P.2d 749, 752 (1992).

In this case, Officer Hanson was able to point to specific and articulable facts. Unlike *Gleason* and *Soto-Garcia,* in which the only facts before the officers were that the defendants were in high crime areas, in this case there are a number of other facts indicating that the defendant was engaged in or about to be engaged in criminal conduct. For example, after Officer Hanson drove away, the defendant walked to the center of the road and stood there, apparently watching Officer Hanson, for what Officer Hanson described as an unusually long time. Then, after Officer Hanson turned his car around, the defendant began walking quickly toward a wooded area, bending down and dropping something behind a tree. Thus, this case is more like *Pressley.* Just as the defendant in *Pressley* engaged in conduct that appeared suspicious to an experienced police officer, so too did the defendant in this case.

---

§8.17 THE CONCLUSION OR PRAYER FOR RELIEF

The final section of the brief is the conclusion or the prayer for relief. In most jurisdictions this section is short. Unlike the conclusion in an objective memorandum, you do not summarize the arguments. Instead, you simply set out the relief that you are requesting. For example, as the appellant, you will usually be asking the court to reverse or remand, and if you are the respondent you will usually be asking the court to affirm or remand. Sometimes you will ask for a single type of relief; at other times you will ask for different types of relief for different errors or for alternative forms of relief. To determine what type of relief you can request, read cases that have decided the same or similar issues, looking to see what type of relief the parties requested and what type of relief the court granted.

In our example case, Ms. Elder asks the court to reverse or in the alternative to reverse and remand. While it is possible that the court would reverse, holding that evidence should have been suppressed and without that evidence there was insufficient evidence to convict, the court could also remand the case, leaving the decision as to whether the case is retried without the suppressed evidence to the State. In contrast, the State asks the appellate court to affirm the trial court's decision.

§8.18 SIGNATURE

Before submitting your brief to the court, you must sign it, listing your name and, in most jurisdictions, your bar number. The format that is typically used is as follows.

Date   Respectfully submitted,

_____

                                  Name of attorney
                                  Attorney for [Appellant or Respondent]

§8.19 APPENDIX

Most jurisdictions allow the parties to attach one or more appendices to their brief. Such appendices should be used, not to avoid the page limits, but to set out information that a judge would find useful but which might not be readily available. For example, if one of your issues requires the court to interpret the language of a particular statute or set of statutes, you can set out the text of the statute or statutes in an appendix. Similarly, if an issue requires the court to look carefully at the language of a case, particularly an out-of-state case or a recent case, or the parts of the record on appeal, you can set out a copy of the case or the relevant portions of the record in an appendix.

§8.20 REVISING, EDITING, AND PROOFREADING

It is impossible to state strongly enough the importance of revising, editing, and proofreading your brief. In both criminal and civil cases, your client is depending on you to make his or her case to the court.

Unfortunately, many of the briefs that are submitted to the courts are not well written. As judge after judge has complained, many briefs are too long. Instead of setting out their two or three best arguments, many attorneys make two or three times that many arguments. In addition, in many briefs, the attorneys don't clearly state either their position or the relief that they are requesting. In fact, in many instances, it appears that the attorneys don't understand either the law or their own arguments. Finally, some briefs are so poorly written that even the most easygoing judges become distracted by the long, hard-to-read sentences, dangling modifiers, comma splices, and misuses of the possessive.

Because she wants to do the best that she can for her clients, Ms. Elder spends almost as much time revising, editing, and proofreading her brief as she does researching the issues and preparing the first draft. For example, after completing the first draft, she sets it aside for a day or two while she works on other projects. When she comes back to the brief, she looks first at the arguments that she has made, asking herself the following questions. Has she identified all of the issues? For each issue, has she made clear her position and what relief she is requesting? Has she provided the best support for each of her assertions? Has she included issues, arguments, or support that is not necessary?

When she is happy with the content, Ms. Elder then re-reads her brief, trying to read it as a judge would read it. Is the material presented in a logical order? Has she made clear the connections between arguments and parts of arguments? Is each argument, paragraph block, paragraph, and sentence easy to read and understand? At this stage, Ms. Elder also works more on writing persuasively. She checks to make sure that she has presented the rules, cases, and facts in a light favorable to her client and that she has used persuasive devices effectively.

Ms. Elder then tries to put the brief down for at least a short period of time so that she can, once again, come back to it with "fresh eyes." This time, she works primarily on two things. She begins by looking at her writing style. Are there places where she could make her writing more eloquent? See Chapter 25. She then goes back through the brief, revising for conciseness and preciseness, and making sure that her writing is correct. In particular, she looks for the types of mistakes that she knows that she has a tendency to make. Finally, she goes back through her brief, checking her cites and adding the page numbers to her table of contents and table of authorities.

While this process is time-consuming, and thus expensive, Ms. Elder finds that the process pays off in a number of ways. First, and most importantly, she does a good job of representing her client. Because her briefs are well written, her clients get a fair hearing from the court. Second, because she has worked at it, through the years she has become both a better and a faster writer. Finally, she has protected and enhanced the only thing that an attorney has to sell: her reputation. Because her briefs are well written, judges tend to take them and her more seriously.

Note: In the following examples, the brief writers have cited according to the rules set out in the *Bluebook*. When writing your own brief, be sure to consult your own state's rules.

No. 97-1-00468-1

COURT OF APPEALS,
DIVISION II
OF THE STATE OF WASHINGTON

_____

State of Washington, Respondent,

v.

William Dennis Strong, Appellant.

_____

BRIEF OF APPELLANT

_____

Susan Elder
Attorney for Appellant
Office of Assigned Counsel
100 Main Street
Tacoma, Washington 98402

Table of Contents

A. Assignments of Error 1

Assignments of Error

     No. 1 1

     No. 2 1

     No. 3 1

     No. 4 1

     No. 5 1

     No. 6 1

Issues Pertaining to Assignments of Error

     No. 1 1

     No. 2 2

     No. 3 2

B. Statement of the Case 2

C. Summary of Argument 4

D. Argument

     I.   UNDER THE FOURTH AMENDMENT, A SEIZURE OCCURRED
         WHEN OFFICER HANSON DROVE TOWARD MR. STRONG,
         ACCELERATING AND FOCUSING HIS SPOTLIGHT ON HIM 5

         A.   A show of authority occurred when, after
               questioning Mr. Strong, Officer Hanson turned
               his car around and, accelerating, drove toward
               Mr. Strong, focusing his spotlight on him 6

B.   Mr. Strong submitted to the show of authority when he did not leave the area illuminated by the spotlight and stopped before being ordered to do so.......................... 8

II.   UNDER ARTICLE I, SECTION 7, THE PROPER TEST IS THE TEST SET OUT IN *UNITED STATES V. MENDENHALL* 9

    A.   Under *State v. Gunwall,* an independent state analysis is warranted because all six *Gunwall* factors are satisfied..10

    B.   An independent state analysis indicates that Article I, section 7, provides more protection than the Fourth Amendment 11

    C.   Under Article I, section 7, the correct test is an objective test : whether a reasonable person would feel free to leave or terminate the encounter 13

III.   UNDER BOTH THE FOURTH AMENDMENT AND ARTICLE I, SECTION 7, THE SEIZURE WAS ILLEGAL BECAUSE OFFICER HANSON DID NOT HAVE AN ARTICULABLE SUSPICION THAT MR. STRONG WAS ENGAGING OR ABOUT TO BE ENGAGED IN CRIMINAL CONDUCT 14

E.   Conclusion..15

Table of Authorities

A.   Table of Cases

Washington Cases

Seattle v. Mesianai, 110 Wash. 2d 454, 755 P.2d 775 (1988)......................12

State v. Boland, 115 Wash. 2d 571,

  800 P.2d 1112 (1990) 10, 11, 12

State v. DeArman, 54 Wash. App. 621,

  774 P.2d 1247 (1989) 7, 8

State v. Elwood, 52 Wash. App. 70, 757 P.2d 547 (1988) 11

State v. Gleason, 70 Wash. App. 13,

  851 P.2d 731 (1993)...14

State v. Gunwall, 106 Wash. 2d 54,

  720 P.2d 808 (1986)...9, 10, 11

State v. Johnson, 128 Wash. 2d 431,

  909 P.2d 293 (1996)... 10, 12

State v. Mennegar, 116 Wash. 2d 304, 787 P.2d 1247 (1990)................ 11, 13

State v. Pressley, 64 Wash. App. 591,

  528 P.2d 749 (1992)...15

State v. Soto-Garcia, 68 Wash. App. 20,

  841 P.2d 1271 (1992) 6, 7, 8, 11, 14

State v. Stroud, 30 Wash. App. 392, 634 P.2d 316 (1981),

  review denied, 96 Wash. 2d 1025 (1982) 7

State v. Stroud, 106 Wash. 2d 144, 720 P.2d 436 (1986).............................11

State v. Thorn, 129 Wash. 2d 347,

    917 P.2d 108 (1996)..5, 6, 11, 12, 13, 14

State v. Vandover, 63 Wash. App. 754,

    822 P.2d 784 (1992)...6, 7

State v. Young, 123 Wash. 2d 173, 867 P.2d 593 (1994)............................12

Other Cases

Brower v. Inyo County, 489 U.S. 593, 596 (1989)......................................8, 9

California v. Hodari D., 499 U.S. 621 (1991).........................6, 8, 9, 10, 11, 13

Florida v. Bostick, 501 U.S. 429 (1991)...5

United States v. Mendenhall, 446 U.S. 544 (1980).....................5, 6, 7, 13, 14

United States v. Wilson, 953 F.2d 116 (4th Cir. 1991)....................................8

B.   Constitutional Provisions

U.S. Const. amend IV.. *passim*

Wash. Const. art I, § 7 .... *passim*

C.   Statutes

Wash. Rev. Code § 9.41.040(1) (1996)...2

Wash. Rev. Code § 9A.56.160 (1996)...2

Wash. Rev. Code § 69.50.401(d) (1996) 2

D.   Other Authorities

3 Wayne LaFave, *Search and Seizure* § 9.3 (3d ed. 1996)......................6, 13

A. Assignments of Error

Assignments of Error

1. The trial court erred in denying Mr. Strong's Motion to Suppress. CP 5.

2. The trial court erred in entering Conclusion of Law No. 2: "Under the Fourth Amendment, no seizure occurred until the deputy asked the defendant to stop." CP 5.

3. The trial court erred in entering Conclusion of Law No. 3: "Article I, section 7, of the Washington Constitution provides no greater protection than the Fourth Amendment." CP 6.

4. The trial court erred in entering Conclusion of Law No. 4: "At the time the officer told the defendant to stop, the deputy had an articulable suspicion that the defendant was engaging or about to be engaged in criminal conduct." CP 6.

5. The trial court erred in entering Conclusion of Law No. 4: "Following the retrieval of the charred soda can, the officer had probable cause to arrest the defendant." CP 6.

6. The trial court erred in entering judgment and sentence. CP 18-19.

Issues Pertaining to Assignments of Error

1. Under the Fourth Amendment, did a seizure occur when Officer Hanson drove toward Mr. Strong, focusing his spotlight on him, and Mr. Strong, after moving out of the street and a few feet towards an apartment complex, dropped something behind a tree, turned, and stopped? (Assignments of Error 1, 2, 5, and 6.)

1

2. Did the trial court err when it ruled that Article I, section 7, of the Washington Constitution does not provide more protection than the Fourth Amendment? (Assignments of Error 1, 3, 5, and 6.)

3. Did Officer Hanson lack an articulable suspicion that Mr. Strong was engaged in or about to be engaged in criminal conduct when, at the time Officer Hanson focused the spotlight on Mr. Strong, the only facts before Officer Hanson were that Mr. Strong was in a high crime area, that Mr. Strong had a criminal history, and that Mr. Strong walked to the middle of the road and watched the police car? (Assignments of Error 1, 4, 5, and 6.)

B. Statement of the Case

Procedural History

William Strong was charged with one count of Possession of a Controlled Substance under Wash. Rev. Code § 269.50.401(d) (1996), one count of Unlawful Possession of a Firearm under Wash. Rev. Code § 9.41.040(1) (1996), and one count of Possession of Stolen Property in the Second Degree under Wash. Rev. Code § 9A.56.160 (1996). CP 1. After an evidentiary hearing, the trial court denied Mr. Strong's motion to Suppress. RP 4.

The case went to trial, RP 8, and a jury found Mr. Strong guilty on all three counts. CP 10. Judgment and sentence were entered on September 24, 1997. CP 18-19. Mr. Strong filed his notice of appeal on October 16, 1997. CP 20.

2

Statement of Facts

On the evening of May 17, 1997, William Strong was standing on the corner of Lincoln and Chicago in Tacoma, Washington, talking to a friend when Officer Hanson approached him and began questioning him. RP 4. Standing only a foot or two from Mr. Strong, Officer Hanson asked Mr. Strong to identify himself and to explain what he was doing in the area. RP 5. Mr. Strong willingly answered Officer Hanson's questions, telling him his name. RP 5.

After questioning Mr. Strong, Officer Hanson returned to his patrol car, got in the car, and drove about a block and a half down a hill. RP 6. He then ran a criminal history check, which showed that Mr. Strong had prior arrests but that there were no outstanding warrants. RP 7. Officer Hanson then looked in his rearview mirror and saw that Mr. Strong had walked to the middle of the street and was looking in his direction. RP 8. Officer Hanson immediately turned his car around and began driving toward Mr. Strong. RP 8. As Mr. Strong began moving toward the side of the street, Officer Hanson accelerated, turned on his spotlight, and focused the spotlight on Mr. Strong. RP 9-10.

As the patrol car came towards him, Mr. Strong walked quickly out of the road. RP 11, 12. He then walked two or three steps toward an apartment complex, dropped what appeared to Officer Hanson to be a package behind a tree, and then turned and walked two or three steps back toward Officer Hanson. RP 11, 12. He then stopped. RP 12.

At that point, Officer Hanson told Mr. Strong, who was already stopped, to stop, got out of his police car, walked to the tree, and picked up a soda can with a charred bottom. RP 13. Believing that the material inside the can was a controlled substance, Officer Hanson arrested Mr. Strong. RP 13-15. Mr. Strong did not resist arrest. RP 17.

C. Summary of Argument

Mr. Strong was illegally seized when Officer Hanson drove toward Strong, focusing his spotlight on him.

A seizure occurred under the Fourth Amendment because there was a show of authority to which Mr. Strong submitted. Officer Hanson focused his attention on Mr. Strong when he approached him and questioned him. He then progressively intruded into Mr. Strong's affairs when he ran a criminal history check on Mr. Strong and, after turning his car around, accelerated and drove toward Mr. Strong, shining his spotlight on him. Although Mr. Strong walked quickly to the side of the road, he did not flee. Instead, he stayed within the area illuminated by the spotlight and stopped before being ordered to do so.

In the alternative, a seizure occurred under Article I, section 7, of the Washington Constitution. In this case, only one of the six *Gunwall* factors is in dispute, and that factor, preexisting state law, is met because the Washington courts have consistently applied an objective rather than a subjective test in determining when a seizure occurs. In addition, an independent state analysis establishes that in cases like this one the courts have found that Article I, section 7, of the

Washington Constitution provides more protection than the Fourth Amendment: Washington citizens have an expectation that police officers will not progressively intrude into their personal affairs. Finally, under the *Mendenhall* test, a seizure occurred because a reasonable person would not have felt free to leave or terminate the encounter.

Whether the court applies the Fourth Amendment or Article I, section 7, the seizure was unreasonable because, at the time Officer Hanson focused his spotlight on Mr. Strong, he did not have an articulable suspicion that Mr. Strong was engaging or about to be engaged in criminal conduct. At that point, the only facts before Officer Hanson were that Mr. Strong was in a high crime area, had a criminal history, and was standing in the middle of the street watching the police car.

D. Argument

I. UNDER THE FOURTH AMENDMENT, A SEIZURE OCCURRED WHEN OFFICER HANSON DROVE TOWARD MR. STRONG, ACCELERATING AND FOCUSING HIS SPOTLIGHT ON HIM.

Because this case involves only issues of law, the standard of review is de novo. *See State v. Thorn,* 129 Wash. 2d 347, 351, 917 P.2d 108, 111 (1996).

Before 1991, the Supreme Court applied an objective test in determining whether a seizure occurred: A seizure occurred when a reasonable person would not feel free to leave or terminate an encounter. *See, e.g., Florida v. Bostick,* 501 U.S. 429 (1991); *United States v. Mendenhall,* 446 U.S. 544 (1980).

5

In 1991, the Supreme Court modified this test, adding a subjective component. *California v. Hodari D.,* 499 U.S. 621, 628 (1991). *See also* 3 Wayne LaFave, *Search and Seizure* § 9.3 (3d 1996) (criticizing *Hodari D.* and its policy implications). Under the test set out in *Hodari D.,* a seizure occurs either when the police use physical force or when a citizen actually submits to a show of authority. *Id.* at 628. Although Officer Hanson did not use physical force, he did make a show of authority to which Mr. Strong submitted.

A.   <u>A show of authority occurred when, after questioning Mr. Strong, Officer Hanson turned his car around and, accelerating, drove toward Mr. Strong, focusing his spotlight on him.</u>

A show of authority occurs whenever an officer's actions would indicate to a reasonable person that he or she is not free to leave or terminate an encounter. *California* v. *Hodari D.,* 499 U.S. 621, 628 (1991). In deciding whether this test is met, the courts do not look at a single action. Instead, they look at the totality of the circumstances to see whether the officer focused his attention on a particular individual or whether there was a progressive intrusion into an individual's privacy. *See, e.g., State v. Soto-Garcia,* 68 Wash. App. 20, 24, 841 P.2d 1271, 1274 (1992); *State v. Vandover,* 63 Wash. App. 754, 756, 822 P.2d 784, 785 (1992).

In the case before the court, Officer Hanson focused his attention on Mr. Strong. Officer Hanson stopped and questioned Mr. Strong, RP 4-5, ran a criminal history check on him, RP 7, and then turned his car around and drove toward Mr. Strong, accelerating and shining his spotlight on him, RP 9-10. Under similar

6

circumstances, the courts have found that such actions are a show of authority. *See, e.g., State v. Stroud,* 30 Wash. App. 392, 395, 634 P.2d 316, 318 (1981); *State v. Vandover,* 63 Wash. App. 754, 756, 822 P.2d 784, 785 (1992); *State v. DeArman,* 54 Wash. App. 621, 624, 774 P.2d 1247, 1248 (1989). For example, in *Stroud,* the court held that the use of emergency lights and high beam headlights constituted a show of authority. Similarly, in both *Vandover and DeArman,* the court held that a seizure occurred when an officer pulled up behind a vehicle and turned on his emergency lights. Although both of these cases involved emergency lights and not spotlights, in each instance the officers focused their attention on a particular individual, indicating to that individual that he was not free to leave or terminate the encounter.

In addition, Officer Hanson progressively intruded into Mr. Strong's privacy. Although a reasonable person might have felt free to terminate the initial encounter, he would not have felt free to leave once Officer Hanson drove toward him, focusing the spotlight on him. As the court found in *Soto-Garcia,* a case in which a police officer confronted an individual, questioned him, ran an identification check, and then asked him if he had cocaine, an individual may not feel free to leave if an officer continues questioning him. "Considering all of the circumstances . . . , the atmosphere created by [the officer's] progressive intrusion into Soto-Garcia's privacy was of such a nature that a reasonable person would not believe that he or she was free to end the encounter." *Id.* at 25, 841 P.2d at 1273.

Thus, there was a show of authority under either rule. There was a show of authority because Officer Hanson focused his attention on Mr. Strong or, in the alternative, because Officer Hanson progressively intruded into Mr. Strong's privacy.

B. Mr. Strong submitted to the show of authority when he did not leave the area lighted by the spotlight and stopped before being ordered to do so.

An individual submits to a show of authority when he or she stops or stays within the area controlled by a police officer. *See United States v. Wilson,* 953 F.2d 116 (4th Cir. 1991). For example, in a case in which an officer drove up behind the defendant's vehicle and turned on his emergency lights, the court held that the defendant had been seized at the time the police officer turned on his lights even though the defendant, who had been stopped at a stoplight, drove through the intersection and did not stop until a short time later. *State v. De-Arman,* 54 Wash. App. 621, 624, 774 P.2d 1247, 1248 (1989). Similarly, in *Wilson,* the court held that the defendant had submitted even though he continued walking towards his destination. *Id.* at 126.

Like the defendants in *DeArman* and *Wilson,* Mr. Strong stayed within the area controlled by the police officer. Although he took several steps after Officer Hanson turned on his spotlight, he never left the area being spotlighted by Officer Hanson, and he stopped before being told to do so. Thus, the facts in this case are very different from the facts in *Hodari D.* and *Brower v. Inyo County,* 489 U.S. 593, 596 (1989). Unlike Hodari, who ran several blocks, and Brower, who led

8

the police on a twenty-mile car chase, Mr. Strong took only a few steps. While both *Hodari D.* and *Brower* involved fleeing suspects, this case does not.

Because Mr. Strong did not flee, he should not be denied the protections granted to him under the Fourth Amendment. While he did not immediately stop, he submitted to the officer's authority by stopping shortly after walking to the side of the road and by staying within the area being spotlighted.

II. UNDER ARTICLE I, SECTION 7, THE PROPER TEST IS THE TEST SET OUT IN *UNITED STATES V. MENDENHALL.*

Even if the court determines that no seizure occurred under the Fourth Amendment, a seizure occurred under Article I, section 7, of the Washington Constitution.

In determining whether the Washington Constitution provides more protection than the United States Constitution, Washington courts do a three-part analysis. First, they analyze the factors set out in *State v. Gunwall,* 106 Wash. 2d 54, 720 P.2d 808 (1986), to determine whether an independent state analysis is warranted. Second, if the *Gunwall* factors indicate that an independent state analysis is warranted, the courts do an independent analysis, determining whether the Washington Constitution provides more protection than the United States Constitution. Finally, if the courts find that the Washington Constitution provides more protection, the courts determine what test is appropriate under the Washington Constitution and then apply that test.

9

A. Under *State v. Gunwall,* an independent state analysis is warranted because all six *Gunwall* factors are satisfied.

In determing whether an independent state analysis is warranted, the courts consider six nonexclusive factors: (1) the textual language of the Washington Constitution, (2) significant differences between the texts of parallel provisions in the Washington and United States Constitutions, (3) state constitutional and common-law history, (4) preexisting state law, (5) differences in structure between the Washington and United States Constitutions, and (6) whether the issue relates to matters of particular state interest or local concern. *State v. Gunwall,* 106 Wash. 2d 54, 61-62, 720 P.2d 808, 812-813 (1986). The Washington Supreme Court has previously held that factors one, two, three, five, and six are met in cases involving the interpretation of Article I, section 7. *See State v. Boland,* 115 Wash. 2d 571, 576-577, 800 P.2d 1112, 1115 (1990) (holding that factors one, two, three, and five are met) and *State v. Johnson,* 128 Wash. 2d 431, 446, 909 P.2d 293, 302 (1996) (holding that factor six is met). In addition, in the context of this case, factor four, preexisting state law, is also met.

In the other cases, the courts have found that factor four is met when Washington's preexisting law differs from federal law. For example, in *Gunwall,* the court held that factor four was met when there were preexisting state statutes protecting telephonic and electronic communications. *Id.* at 65, 720 P.2d at 815. Similarly, in *Boland* the court held that factor four was met when there was a preexisting local ordinance governing the placement of garbage cans. *Id.* at 576, 800 P.2d at 1115.

10

In this case, the preexisting state law also differs from the standard set out in *Hodari D.* While in *Hodari D.* the Supreme Court set out a subjective standard, looking to see whether the defendant did in fact submit, the Washington courts apply an objective standard, looking to see whether a reasonable person would have felt free to leave. *See e.g., State v. Thorn,* 129 Wash. 2d 347, 917 P.2d 108 (1996); *State v. Mennegar,* 116 Wash. 2d 304, 787 P.2d 1247 (1990); *State v. Soto-Garcia,* 68 Wash. App. 20, 841 P.2d 1271 (1992); *State v. Elwood,* 52 Wash. App. 70, 757 P.2d 547 (1988). Because the tests applied by the federal and state courts are different, the fourth factor is met, and an independent state analysis is warranted.

B. <u>An independent state analysis indicates that Article I, section 7, provides more protection than the Fourth Amendment.</u>

The Washington courts have consistently held that Article I, section 7, provides more protection than the Fourth Amendment.

In one line of cases, the Washington courts have held that this protection extends to an individual's property. For example, while the Fourth Amendment does not protect garbage placed in a can on the curb outside an individual's home, Article I, section 7, does. *State v. Boland,* 115 Wash. 2d 571, 800 P.2d 1112 (1990). Likewise, while the Fourth Amendment does not protect an individual's property stored in a jail lock box or in a locked container in a car, such property is protected under Article I, section 7. *State v. Stroud,* 106 Wash. 2d. 144, 720 P.2d 436 (1986).

11

In addition, in a second line of cases, the Washington courts have held that this additional protection extends to an individual's person. Under Article I, section 7, police cannot use thermal detection devices in the course of warrantless surveillance of an individual, *State v. Young,* 123 Wash. 2d 173, 186, 867 P.2d 593, 599 (1994), or stop all vehicles at mandatory check points without warrants justifying the stops or without individualized suspicion of criminal activity, *Seattle v. Mesianai,* 110 Wash. 2d 454, 457, 755 P.2d 775, 777 (1988).

More importantly, though, the Washington courts have always applied an objective test in determining whether a seizure occurred. To protect the rights of all citizens, the courts have looked at whether a reasonable person would have felt free to leave and not whether a particular individual did or did not submit. *See, e.g., State v. Thorn,* 129 Wash. 2d 347, 917 P.2d 108 (1996).

Because the Washington courts have consistently held that Article I, section 7, provides more protection than the Fourth Amendment and because the Washington courts have consistently applied an objective rather than a subjective test in determining whether a seizure occurred, the court should hold that Article I, section 7, provides more protection in this case. As the Washington Supreme Court states in *State v. Johnson,* the Washington Constitution protects "those privacy interests which the citizens of this state have held, and should be entitled to hold, safe from governmental trespass. . . ." *Id.* at 446, 909 P.2d at 302 (citing *State v. Boland,* 115 Wash. 2d 573, 800 P.2d 1112 (1990)).

12

C.　Under Article I, section 7, the correct test is an objective test: whether a reasonable person would feel free to leave or terminate the encounter.

The Washington courts should continue to apply the objective test set out in *United States v. Mendenhall,* 446 U.S. 544 (1980): A seizure occurs if a reasonable person would not have felt free to leave or terminate the encounter. This is the test that was applied by the Washington courts before the Supreme Court's decision in *Hodari D., see, e.g., State v. Mennegar,* 116 Wash. 2d 304, 787 P.2d 1247 (1990), and the test that the Washington courts have continued to apply after *Hodari D., see, e.g., State v. Thorn,* 129 Wash. 2d 347, 917 P.2d 108 (1996). In addition, this test is more consistent with public policy. As Professor LaFave has noted, the test set out in *Hodari D.* encourages police officers to "turn a hunch into a reasonable suspicion by inducing conduct justifying the suspicion." 3 Wayne LaFave, *Search and Seizure* 130 (1996).

As noted in Subsection IA, in this case an individual would not have felt free to leave or terminate the encounter. Officer Hanson both focused his attention on Mr. Strong and progressively intruded into his affairs when, after questioning Mr. Strong, he ran a criminal history check on Mr. Strong and then turned his car around and drove directly toward Mr. Strong, shining his spotlight on him.

13

III. UNDER BOTH THE FOURTH AMENDMENT AND ARTICLE I, SECTION 7, OF THE WASHINGTON CONSTITUTION, THE SEIZURE WAS ILLEGAL BECAUSE OFFICER HANSON DID NOT HAVE AN ARTICULABLE SUSPICION THAT MR. STRONG WAS ENGAGING OR ABOUT TO BE ENGAGED IN CRIMINAL CONDUCT.

At the time he spotlighted Mr. Strong, the only facts before Officer Hanson were that Strong was in a high crime area, RP 4; that Strong stood in the middle of the road apparently looking at Officer Hanson, RP 8; and that when Officer Hanson began driving toward Strong, Strong began walking from the middle of the road to the side of the road, RP 9-10.

In similar cases, the courts have held that these types of facts are not sufficient to support a finding that at the time of the seizure the officer had an articulable suspicion that the defendant was engaging or about to engage in criminal conduct. *State v. Gleason,* 70 Wash. App. 13, 851 P.2d 731 (1993); *State v. Soto-Garcia,* 68 Wash. App. 20, 841 P.2d 1271 (1992). In *Gleason,* the court held that an officer did not have an articulable suspicion that the defendant was engaging or about to be engaged in criminal activity when the officer saw the defendant leave an apartment complex where narcotics were known to be sold. *Id.* at 17, 851 P.2d at 734. Similarly, in *Soto-Garcia,* the court held that the officer did not have an articulable suspicion that the defendant was engaging or about to be engaged in criminal activity when the defendant was seen walking late in the evening in an area known for cocaine trafficking and answered the officer's questions about why he was in the area. *Id.* at 26, 841 P.2d at 1274.

14

Thus, for the court to find that the officer had an articulable suspicion, the State must show more than that the defendant was in a high crime area. It must be able to point to specific facts that indicate that the defendant is engaging or about to engage in criminal conduct. Unlike *State v. Pressley,* 64 Wash. App. 591, 597, 528 P.2d 749, 752 (1992), in which the women were not only in a high crime area but one of them had something in her hand and the other was pointing to it and said, "Oh, shit" when the officer approached, in this case there are no facts indicating that Mr. Strong was about to engage in criminal activity. Walking to the middle of the street, watching a police car, and walking out of the street are not illegal and do not provide evidence that Strong was about to engage in criminal activity.

Because the State has not been able to meet its burden, the seizure was illegal and the evidence must be suppressed.

E. Conclusion

For the reasons set out above, Mr. Strong respectfully requests that the Court of Appeals find that the trial court erred in denying his motion to dismiss and remand the case to the trial court for further proceedings.

Respectfully submitted this 22nd day of January, 1998.

_____

Susan Elder
WSBA No. 0000
Attorney for Appellant

15

No. 97-1-00468-1

COURT OF APPEALS,
DIVISION II
OF THE STATE OF WASHINGTON

State of Washington, Respondent,

v.

William Dennis Strong, Appellant.

BRIEF OF RESPONDENT

Samuel Lion
Attorney for Respondent
Pierce County Prosecutor's Office
900 Tacoma Avenue
Tacoma, Washington 98402

Table of Contents

A.   Issue Pertaining to Appellant's Assignments of Error.............................. 1

B.   Statement of the Case 1

C.   Argument

    I.   THE TRIAL COURT PROPERLY DENIED THE DEFENDANT'S

        MOTION TO SUPPRESS THE COCAINE AND STOLEN

        ROLEX WATCH.. 3

       A.   The trial court correctly concluded that a seizure did

           not occur until Officer Hanson asked the defendant

           to stop and the defendant stopped 4

       B.   The trial court correctly concluded that the

           Washington Constitution does not provide more

           protection than the Fourth Amendment................................... 7

          1.   The fourth *Gunwall* factor is not met in this case................. 7

          2.   In the alternative, even if an independent

             state analysis is warranted, Article I,

             section 7, does not grant more protection

             than the Fourth Amendment 8

          3.   No seizure occurred under the *Mendenhall* test

             because, like the defendant, a reasonable

             person would have felt free to leave or

             terminate the encounter...9

C. At the time that he told the defendant to stop, Officer Hanson had an articulable suspicion that the defendant was engaging or about to be engaged in criminal conduct.....................................10

D. Conclusion...11

Table of Authorities

A. Table of Cases

Washington Cases

Seattle v. Mesianai, 110 Wash. 2d 454, 755 P.2d 775 (1988).........................8

State v. Berber, 48 Wash. App. 583, 740 P.2d 863 (1987) 9

State v. Boland, 115 Wash. 2d 571, 800 P.2d 1112 (1990) 7, 8

State v. Glover, 116 Wash. 2d 509, 806 P.2d 760 (1991)............................10

State v. Gunwall, 106 Wash. 2d 54, 720 P.2d 808 (1986) 7

State v. Kennedy, 107 Wash. 2d 1, 726 P.2d 445 (1986) 9, 10

State v. Nettles, 70 Wash. App. 706, 855 P.2d 699 (1993),

     review denied, 123 Wash. 2d 1010 (1994) 5, 8

State v. Rose, 128 Wash. 2d 388, 909 P.2d 280 (1996)................................5

State v. Seagull, 95 Wash. 2d 898, 632 P.2d 44 (1981)................................9

State v. Soto-Garcia, 68 Wash. App. 20, 841 P.2d 1271 (1992) 5

State v. Stroud, 30 Wash. App. 392, 634 P.2d 316 (1981),

     review denied, 96 Wash. 2d 1025 (1982) 5, 7

State v. Stroud, 106 Wash. 2d 144, 720 P.2d 436 (1986)..............................8

State v. Thorn, 129 Wash. 2d 347, 917 P.2d 108 (1996)...............................8

State v. Young, 123 Wash. 2d 173, 867 P.2d 593 (1994) 8

Other Cases

California v. Hodari D., 499 U.S. 621 (1991) 4

Florida v. Bostick, 501 U.S. 429 (1991) 8

State v. Deptuch, 767 P.2d 471 (Or. Ct. App. 1989) 4

Terry v. Ohio, 392 U.S. 1 (1868) 4, 10

United States v. Mendenhall, 446 U.S. 544 (1980).......................................4

B.   Constitutional Provisions

U.S. Const. amend IV...1, 4, 7, 8, 9

Wash. Const. Art. I, § 7 .... 1, 8, 9

C.   Statutes

Wash. Rev. Code § 9.41.040(1) (1996) 1

Wash. Rev. Code § 9A.56.160 (1996)...1

Wash. Rev. Code § 69.50.401(d) (1996) 1

A. Statement of the Issue

Whether the trial court properly denied the defendant's motion to suppress, concluding (a) that no seizure occurred under the Fourth Amendment until Officer Hanson asked the defendant to stop, (b) that, under the circumstances of this case, Article I, section 7, of the Washington Constitution does not provide more protection than the Fourth Amendment, and (c) that at the time he asked the defendant to stop, Officer Hanson had an articulable suspicion that the defendant was engaged or about to be engaged in criminal conduct. (Appellant's Assignments of Error 1-6)

B. Statement of the Case

Procedural History

The defendant, William D. Strong, was charged under Wash. Rev. Code § 69.40.401(d) (1996) with possession of cocaine, under Wash. Rev. Code § 9A.56.160 (1996) with unlawful possession of stolen property in the second degree, and under Wash. Rev. Code § 9.41.040(1) (1996) with Unlawful Possession of a Firearm. CP 1. The defendant filed a motion asking the court to suppress both the cocaine and the Rolex watch. CP 3. After an evidentiary hearing, Judge Johnson denied the motion. CP 13-16.

The case went to trial, RPII 3, and on September 18, 1997, the jury entered a verdict of guilty, CP 18. Judgment and Sentence was entered on September 22, 1997. CP 18-19. Defendant's Notice of Appeal was timely filed on October 13, 1997. CP 20.

1

Statement of Facts

At about 11:00 p.m. on May 17, 1997, Officer Hanson was on patrol in the McChord Gate area of Tacoma, an area known for its unusually high level of drug activity and drug arrests. RP 4. After responding to a call at the corner of Lincoln and Chicago Avenues, Officer Hanson saw the defendant standing on the corner. RP 4. Because he did not recognize him, Officer Hanson followed his usual procedure and approached him, initiating a social contact. RP 5.

After talking with the defendant for one or two minutes, Officer Hanson returned to his car and drove one or two blocks down a hill. RP 6. He then ran a criminal history check on the defendant, using the name that the defendant had given him. RP 7. While the check did not indicate that there were any outstanding warrants, it did show that the defendant had an extensive criminal history, including arrests for selling controlled substances. RP 7.

After he completed his check, Officer Hanson began to drive away. RP 8. As he did so, he looked in his rearview mirror and noticed the defendant standing in the middle of the road, staring at him. RP 8. When the defendant continued to stand in the road, Officer Hanson turned his car around and began driving back up the hill. RP 9. As he did so, the defendant began to walk quickly out of the road toward a dark, wooded area. RP 9, 11.

2

Because it was difficult to see, Officer Hanson turned on his spotlight, illuminating the general area. RP 9-11. The defendant ignored the spotlight and continued walking. RP 11. As Officer Hanson watched, the defendant walked behind a tree and dropped what appeared to be a package. RP 11. He then turned and continued walking a few steps before stopping. RP 12.

As the defendant stopped, Officer Hanson stopped his vehicle and asked the defendant to stop. RP 12. Officer Hanson then walked behind the tree and picked up half a soda can that was charred on the bottom. RP 13. After inspecting the substance inside the can, Officer Hanson determined that the substance was cocaine. RP 14-15.

After reading the defendant his rights, Officer Hanson placed him under arrest. During a search incident to the arrest, Officer Hanson found a Rolex watch in the defendant's pocket. RP 16. A subsequent investigation established that the watch was stolen. RP 17.

Officer Hanson has had more than ten years of experience, has made numerous drug arrests, and has had extensive training in the identification of controlled substances. RP 2-3.

C. Argument

I. THE TRIAL COURT PROPERLY DENIED THE DEFENDANT'S MO-
    TION TO SUPPRESS THE COCAINE AND STOLEN ROLEX WATCH.

3

A.   The trial court correctly concluded that a seizure did not occur until Officer Hanson asked the defendant to stop and the defendant stopped.

Under the Fourth Amendment, a seizure does not occur until an officer uses physical force or the suspect submits to an officer's show of authority. *California v. Hodari D.* 499 U.S. 621, 629 (1991). In this case, Officer Hanson did not use any physical force. RP 17. In addition, he did not exercise his authority until, after seeing the defendant drop something behind a tree, he ordered the defendant to stop.

The courts have repeatedly held that officers have the right to approach individuals and ask them questions. *United States v. Mendenhall,* 446 U.S. 544, 553 (1980); *Terry v. Ohio,* 392 U.S. 1, 9 (1968). Thus, there was no show of authority when Officer Hanson approached the defendant and asked him his name.

In addition, there was no show of authority when Officer Hanson turned his car around and drove back up the hill or when he turned on his spotlight. While there are no Washington courts that have specifically dealt with this issue, the Oregon courts have held that the use of a spotlight does not constitute a show of authority. For example, in *State v. Deptuch,* 767 P.2d 471 (Or. Ct. App. 1989), the court held that there was no show of authority when an officer drove up next to the defendant's vehicle and shone a spotlight into the vehicle.

4

A show of authority has only been found in those circumstances where officers use a siren, emergency lights, or a gun. *Compare State v. Nettles,* 70 Wash. App. 706, 711, 855 P.2d 699, 702 (1993), *review denied,* 123 Wash. 2d 1010 (1994) *with State v. Stroud,* 30 Wash. App. 392, 396, 334 P.2d 316, 318 (1981), *review denied,* 96 Wash. 2d 1025 (1982). In *Nettles,* the court concluded that there was no show of authority when, after driving by the defendant twice, the officer pulled her car over and parked and told the defendant and his companion that she would like to speak to them and asked them to come to her car. *Id.* at 711, 855 P.2d at 702. In contrast, in *Stroud* the court concluded that there was a show of authority when two officers pulled up behind a legally parked car and turned on both their flashing light and their high beam headlights. *Id.* at 396, 334 P.2d at 318.

In this case, Officer Hanson did not turn on his siren or his emergency lights or pull his gun. RP 10. He simply turned his car around and drove back up the hill. RP 8. He used his spotlight, not to signal to the defendant to stop, but to illuminate the area. RP 10. As the Washington Supreme Court has stated, an officer can use light to illuminate what he or she could see if it were daylight. *State v. Rose,* 128 Wash. 2d 388, 396, 909 P.2d 280, 189 (1996).

In addition, Officer Hanson did not focus his attention on the defendant or progressively intrude into his affairs. Unlike *State v. Soto-Garcia,* 68 Wash. App. 20, 841 P.2d 1271 (1992), a case in which the officer questioned the defendant

5

for an extended period of time, taking the defendant's identification back to his patrol car and asking the defendant whether he had any cocaine on his person, in this case, Officer Hanson asked the defendant only one or two questions. Officer Hanson then left the area, driving a block to a block and a half away. RP 6. Although the defendant could also have left the area, he chose not to. Instead, he followed Officer Hanson: After Officer Hanson left, the defendant walked to the middle of the street and stood there, watching Officer Hanson. RP 8. Had the defendant not followed Officer Hanson and stood in the middle of road for an unusually long period of time, Officer Hanson would have driven away after completing the criminal history check. RP 15.

In the alternative, even if the spotlight was a show of authority, the defendant did not submit to it. After Officer Hanson turned on the spotlight, the defendant continued walking quickly toward the dark wooded area. RP 10. As Officer Hanson testified, "When he saw me turn around and come back up the street, he also turned and started heading toward the wooded area at a fast pace." RP 11.

Although the defendant did not run, he did flee. It was not until after the defendant dropped the cocaine behind the tree that he turned back towards the officer and began to stop. RP 11. Up until that time, he was not under Officer Hanson's control and could have, at any time, run into the wooded area.

B.   <u>The trial court correctly found that the Washington Constitution does not provide more protection than the Fourth Amendment.</u>

An independent state analysis is not warranted in this case because the fourth *Gunwall* factor, preexisting state law, is not met. *See State v. Gunwall,* 106 Wash. 2d 54, 720 P.2d 808 (1986). In the alternative, even if the fourth *Gunwall* factor is met, the Washington Constitution does not provide more protection than the Fourth Amendment and there was no seizure under the test suggested by the defendant.

   1.   The fourth *Gunwall* factor is not met in this case.

For the fourth *Gunwall* factor to be met, there must be preexisting state law that differs from the federal law. *See, e.g., State v. Boland,* 115 Wash. 2d 571, 576-577, 800 P.2d 1112, 1115 (1990) (concluding that there was a preexisting local ordinance governing the collection of garbage); *State v. Gunwall,* 106 Wash. 2d 54, 65, 720 P.2d 808, 815 (1986) (concluding that there were preexisting state statutes protecting telephonic and electronic communications.) In this case, there is no preexisting local ordinance or state statute. Instead, the Washington courts have always followed the lead of the federal courts. When the United States Supreme Court announced the *Mendenhall* test, the Washington courts adopted it, *see, e.g., State v. Stroud,* 30 Wash. App. 392, 396, 634 P.2d 316, 318 (1981), *review denied,* 96 Wash. 2d 1025 (1982). Similarly, when the United States Supreme Court modified the *Mendenhall* test in

Florida v. Bostick, 501 U.S. 429 (1991), the Washington courts followed the Supreme Court's lead, also adopting the *Bostick* test. *See, e.g., State v. Thorn,* 129 Wash. 2d 347, 352, 917 P.2d 108, 111 (1996); *State v. Nettles,* 70 Wash. 2d 706, 708, 855 P.2d 699, 700 (1993), *review denied,* 123 Wash. 2d 1010 (1994).

Because there is no preexisting municipal ordinance or state law and because the Washington courts have always followed the lead of the federal courts, the fourth *Gunwall* factor is not met, and an independent state analysis is not warranted.

> 2. In the alternative, even if an independent state analysis is warranted, Article I, section 7, does not grant more protection than the Fourth Amendment.

While the Washington courts have held that Article I, section 7, provides more protection than the Fourth Amendment in a limited number of circumstances, all of those cases involved either a defendant's property or a defendant in his home or car. *See e.g., State v. Young,* 123 Wash. 2d 173, 186, 867 P.2d 593, 599 (1994) (Officers used a thermal detection device to perform warrantless surveillance of the defendant's home.); *State v. Boland,* 115 Wash. 2d 571, 576, 800 P.2d 1112, 1115 (1990) (Officers removed garbage from the defendant's trash can and took it to police headquarters.); *Seattle v. Mesianai,* 110 Wash. 2d 454, 457, 755 P.2d 775, 777 (1988) (Officers stopped all motorists as part of sobriety checkpoint program.); *State v. Stroud,* 106 Wash. 2d 144, 152, 720 P.2d

436, 441 (1986) (Officers searched unlocked glove compartment and several unlocked containers.). There are no cases in which the Washington courts have held that Article I, section 7, provides more protection than the Fourth Amendment for activities conducted within public view.

In fact, the Washington courts have repeatedly held that an individual does not have an expectation of privacy in objects in public view or for activities done within public view. *See, e.g., State v. Kennedy,* 107 Wash. 2d 1, 726 P.2d 445 (1986); *State v. Seagull,* 95 Wash. 2d 898, 632 P.2d 44 (1981). In *Kennedy,* the court held that an individual has no expectation of privacy in a weapon clearly visible inside a parked car, and in *Seagull,* the court held that no reasonable expectation of privacy exists when an object is in plain view of someone standing in a public area. Similarly, the court has held that a defendant does not have an expectation of privacy in a public bathroom in which the toilets are exposed. *State v. Berber,* 48 Wash. App. 583, 589, 740 P.2d 863, 867 (1987).

In this case, the defendant chose to act, not within the privacy of his home, but on a public street. Under such circumstances, Article I, section 7, does not provide more protection than the Fourth Amendment.

3. No seizure occurred under the *Mendenhall* test because like the defendant, a reasonable person would have felt free to leave or terminate the encounter.

Even if the court adopts the *Mendenhall* test, no seizure occurred in this case. As discussed in section IA, there was no show of authority until Officer

Hanson told the defendant to stop. A spotlight is not a show of authority, and Officer Hanson did not turn on his siren or emergency lights or pull his gun. In addition, the defendant's own conduct indicates that under the circumstances a reasonable person would feel free to leave. After Officer Hanson turned on his spotlight, the defendant continued walking away from Officer Hanson toward a wooded area. RP 11-12.

     C.   <u>At the time that he told the defendant to stop, Officer Hanson had an articulable suspicion that the defendant was engaging or about to be engaged in criminal conduct.</u>

Because officers need to be able to question individuals suspected of committing a crime, a *Terry* stop is permitted whenever an officer has a reasonable and articulable suspicion that an individual is engaging or about to be engaged in criminal activity. *See Terry v. Ohio,* 392 U.S. 1, 21-22 (1968); *State v. Glover,* 116 Wash. 2d 509, 513, 806 P.2d 760, 762 (1991). In making these stops, the officer does not need to have the level of information necessary to justify an arrest; he or she need only have the ability to reasonably surmise from the information at hand that a crime is in progress or has occurred. *State v. Kennedy,* 107 Wash. 2d 1, 6, 726 P.2d 445, 448 (1986).

At the time that he told the defendant to stop, Officer Hanson had an articulable suspicion that the defendant was engaging or about to be engaged in criminal conduct. After Officer Hanson drove away, the defendant walked to the center of the road and stood there, staring at Officer Hanson's car for an un-

10

usually long period of time. RP 8. Then, when Officer Hanson turned his car around and began driving back up the hill, the defendant walked quickly to the side of the road toward a dark wooded area, walked behind a tree, and dropped something behind the tree. RP 11-12. Thus, Officer Hanson did not base his decision to stop the defendant merely on the fact that the defendant was in a high crime area or on the fact that he had a criminal history. Instead, Officer Hanson based his decision on conduct, which in light of his experience and training, indicated that the defendant was attempting to dispose of contraband.

D. Conclusion

For the reasons set out above, the State respectfully requests that the Court affirm the trial court's judgment.

Submitted this 17th day of March, 1998.

_____

Attorney for the State
Bar No. 999999

11

Chapter 9

Oral Advocacy

Oral argument. For some, it is the part of practice that they most enjoy; for others, it is the part they most dread.

Whichever group you fall into, oral argument is probably not what you expect. It is not a speech, a debate, or a performance. Instead, when done right, it is a dialogue between the attorneys, who explain the issues, law, and facts, and the judges, who ask questions, not because they want to badger the attorney or because they want to see how much he or she knows, but because they want to make the right decision.

§9.1 AUDIENCE

In making an oral argument, who is your audience? At the trial court level, the audience is the trial judge who is hearing the motion; at the appellate level, it is the panel of judges hearing the appeal. In both instances, the audience is extremely sophisticated. Although an eloquent oral argument is more persuasive than one that isn't, form seldom wins out over substance. If you don't have anything to say, it doesn't matter how well you say it.

At oral argument, the court can be either "hot" or "cold." The court is hot when the judges come to the oral argument prepared. The judges have studied the briefs and, at least in some appellate courts, have met in a pre-oral argument conference to discuss the case. In contrast, a cold court is not as prepared. The judge or judges are not familiar with the case and if they have read the briefs, they have done so only quickly.

As a general rule, hot courts are more active than cold ones. Because they have studied the briefs, they often have their own agenda. They want to know more about point A, or they are concerned about how the rule being advocated might be applied in other cases. As a consequence, they often take more control over the argument, directing counsel to discuss certain issues and asking a number of questions. A cold court is usually comparatively passive. Because the judges are not as familiar with the case, most of their questions are informational. They want counsel to clarify the issue, supply a fact, or explain in more detail how the law should be applied.

§9.2   PURPOSE

In making your oral argument, you have two goals: to educate and to persuade. You want to explain the law and the facts in such a way that the court rules in your client's favor.

§9.3   PREPARING FOR ORAL ARGUMENT

The key to a good oral argument is preparation. You must know what you must argue to win, you must know your case, and you must have practiced both the text of your argument and your responses to the questions the court can reasonably be expected to ask.

§9.3.1   Deciding What to Argue

In making your argument, you will have only a limited amount of time. Depending on the case and the court, you will be granted ten, fifteen, or thirty minutes to make your points, answer the judge or judges' questions and, if you are the appellant, to make your rebuttal. Because time is so limited, you will not be able to make every argument that you made in your brief. You must be selective.

In selecting the issues and arguments that you will make, choose those that are essential to your case. Don't spend your time on the easy argument if, to get the relief you want, you must win on the hard one. Make the arguments that you must make to win.

Also anticipate the arguments that the other side is likely to make. Although you don't want to make the other side's arguments, try to integrate your responses into your argument. Similarly, anticipate the court's concerns and decide how they can best be handled.

§9.3.2   Preparing an Outline

Do not write out your argument. If you do, you will either read it, or perhaps worse yet, memorize and recite it. Neither is appropriate. A dialogue does not have a predetermined text. Instead, prepare either a list of the points that you want to cover or an outline.

Because it is difficult to predict how much of the time will be spent answering the court's questions, most advocates prepare two lists or outlines: a short version, in which they list only those points that they must make, and a long version, in which they list the points that they would like to make if they have time. If the court is hot and asks a number of questions, they argue from the short list or outline; if the court is cold, they use the long one.

§9.3.3   Practicing the Argument

The next step is to practice, both by yourself and with colleagues. Working alone, practice your opening, your closing, your statements of the law, and the arguments themselves. Think carefully about the language that you will use and about how you will move from one issue to the next and, within an issue, from argument to argument. Also list every question that a judge could be reasonably expected to ask, and decide (1) how you will respond and (2) how you can move from the answer to another point in your argument.

Then, with colleagues, practice delivering the argument. Ask your colleagues to play the role of the judge(s), sometimes asking almost no questions and at other times asking many. As you deliver the argument, concentrate on "reading" the court, adjusting your argument to meet its concerns; on responding to questions; and on the transitions between issues and arguments. Before a major argument, you will want to go through your argument five to ten times, practicing in front of as many different people as you can.

§9.3.4   Reviewing the Facts and Law

You will also want to review the facts of the case, the law, and both your brief and your opponent's brief. When you walk into the courtroom, you should know everything that there is to know about your case.

In practice, months or years may pass between the writing of the brief and the oral argument. When this is the case, it is essential that you update your research, and, when appropriate, file a supplemental brief with the court.

§9.3.5   Organizing Your Materials

Part of the preparation is getting your materials organized. You do not want to be flipping through your notes or searching the record during oral argument.

a.   Notes or Outline

To avoid the "flipping pages syndrome," limit yourself to two pages of notes: a one-page short list or outline and a one-page long list or outline. These pages can then be laid side-by-side in front of you on the podium. (So that they don't blow off, many advocates staple the pages to the inside of a manila folder.) Colored markers can be used to highlight the key portions of the argument.

b.   The Briefs

You will want to take a copy of your brief and your opponent's brief with you to the podium, placing them on the inside shelf. Make sure that you know both what is in the briefs and where that information is located.

c.   The Record

In arguing an appeal, you will usually want to have the relevant portions of the record in the courtroom, either on the podium shelf or on counsel table. You should also be fully familiar with the record, as with the briefs, knowing both what is in the record and where particular information can be found. To assist them in quickly locating information, many attorneys tab the record or prepare a quick index.

d.   The Law

Although you do not need to have copies of all of the statutes and cases with you, you should be familiar with both the statutes and cases that you cited in your brief and those on which your opponent's case is based. If you do bring cases with you, have them indexed and highlighted for quick reference.

§9.4   COURTROOM PROCEDURES AND ETIQUETTE

Like much of law, oral argument has its own set of conventions and procedures.

§9.4.1   Seating

In most jurisdictions, the moving party sits on the left (when facing the court) and the responding party sits on the right.

§9.4.2   Before the Case Is Called

If court is not in session, sit at counsel table, reviewing your notes or quietly conversing with co-counsel. If court is in session, sit in the audience until the prior case is completed. When your case is called, rise and move to counsel table.

§9.4.3   Courtroom Etiquette

Stand each time you are instructed to do so by the bailiff. For example, stand when the bailiff calls court into session and announces the judge or judges, and stand when court is recessed or adjourned. In the first instance, remain standing until the judges are seated, and in the latter instance, remain standing until the judges have left the courtroom.

Also stand each time you address the court, whether it be to tell the court that you are ready to proceed, to make your argument, or to respond to a question.

In addressing the court, you will want to use the phrases "Your Honor," "Your Honors," "this Court," "the Court," or, occasionally, the judge's name: "Judge Brown" or "Justice Smith." Never use a judge's or justice's first name.

Finally, never speak directly to opposing counsel. While court is in session, all your comments must be addressed to the court. Also remember that you are always "on." While opposing counsel is arguing, sit attentively at counsel table, listening and, if appropriate, taking notes.

§9.4.4   Appropriate Dress

As a sign of respect, both for the court and the client, most attorneys dress for oral argument. Men wear conservative suits and ties, and women wear conservative dresses or suits. The key is to look professional but not severe. During oral argument, the judge's attention should be focused on your argument and not your attire.

§9.5   MAKING THE ARGUMENT

Like the brief, the oral argument has a prescribed format.

§9.5.1   Introductions

Begin your oral argument by introducing yourself and your client. At the trial court level, the language is relatively informal. Most attorneys say "Good morning, Your Honor," and then introduce themselves and the client. At the appellate level, the language is more formal. By convention, most attorneys begin by saying, "May it please the Court, my name is _____ , and I represent the [appellant] [respondent], _____ ."

In many courts, the introduction is also used to reserve rebuttal time. The attorney for the moving party reserves rebuttal either before introducing himself or herself or immediately afterwards. "Your Honor, at this time, I would like to reserve _____ minutes for rebuttal."

§9.5.2   Opening

The first minute of your argument should be memorable. The opening sentences should catch the judge's attention, making the case's importance clear, establishing the theme, and creating the appropriate context for the argument that follows.

§9.5.3   Statement of the Issues

a.   *The Moving Party*

If you are the moving party, you need to set out the issues. Sometimes this is best done as part of the opening. From the issue statement alone, the case's importance is clear: "In this case, the appellant asks the Court to overrule *Roe v. Wade.*" At other times, such a strategy is not effective. For example, few trial judges would find the following opening memorable: "In this case, the defendant asks the court to suppress identification testimony." In such cases, the opening and the statement of the issues should not be combined.

As a general rule, the statement of the issues should precede the summary of the facts. Before hearing the facts, the court needs a context. There are times, however, when it is more effective to set out the issues after the summary of the facts.

Wherever they are presented, the issue statements must be tailored to oral argument. What is effective in writing may not be effective when spoken. For example, although the under-does-when format works well in a brief, it does not work well orally. In oral argument, the issue needs to be presented more simply. "In this case, the court is asked to decide whether . . ." or "This case presents two issues: first, whether . . . and second, whether . . . ."

Even though they are streamlined, the issues should be presented in the light most favorable to the client. The questions should be framed as they were in the brief, and the significant and emotionally favorable facts should be included. See section 8.12.2.

b.   *The Responding Party*

As a general rule, the responding party does not restate the issue or issues. Instead, it states its position, either as part of its opening or as a lead-in to its arguments: "The cocaine and Rolex watch should be suppressed. At the time he told the defendant to stop, Officer Hanson had an articulable suspicion. . . ."

§9.5.4   Summary of Facts

a.   *The Moving Party*

When arguing to a cold court, you will want to include a summary of the facts, in one to three minutes telling the court what the case is about. You may also want to include a summary of the facts when arguing to a hot court. If the facts are particularly important, you will want to summarize them, refreshing the court's memory and presenting the facts in the light most favorable to the client. There will, however, be times when a separate summary of the facts is not the best use of limited time. In these cases, instead of presenting the facts in a separate summary at the beginning, integrate them into the argument.

b.   The Responding Party

As the responding party, you do not want to use your time repeating what opposing counsel just said. Consequently, for you a summary of the facts is optional, even if the court is cold. If opposing counsel set out the facts accurately, the summary can be omitted. Just integrate the significant facts into the argument. You will, however, want to include a summary if opposing counsel misstated key facts or omitted facts that are important to your argument or if you need to present the facts from your client's point of view.

c.   References to the Record

In presenting the facts, you will not, as a matter of course, include references to the record. You must, however, be able to provide such references if asked to do so by the court or if you are correcting a misstatement made by opposing counsel.

§9.5.5   The Argument

Unless the issues and arguments build on each other, start with your strongest issue and in discussing that issue, your strongest argument. This allows you to take advantage of the positions of emphasis and ensures that you will have the opportunity to make your best, or most crucial, arguments. In addition, it usually results in better continuity. Because the moving party's strongest issue is usually the responding party's weakest, the moving party's final issue will be the responding party's first, providing the responding party with an easy opening for his or her argument.

Moving Party	*Responding Party*
Issue 1 → Issue 2	Issue 2 → Issue 1

In presenting the arguments, do what you did in your brief, but in abbreviated form. When the law is not in dispute, begin by presenting the rule of law, presenting that law in the light most favorable to your client (see section 8.16.3). Then argue that law, explaining why the court should reach the result that you advocate (see section 8.16.3). When it is the law itself that is in dispute, argue your interpretation.

In both instances, you must support your position, presenting arguments based on the plain language of the statute or rule, legislative intent, policy, the facts of the case, or analogous cases. When appropriate, cite to the relevant portions of a statute or to a common law rule and, in using analogous cases, be specific, explaining the rule that the court applied, the significant facts, and the court's reasoning. Although you should have the full case citations available, you do not need to include them in your argument.

Although you want to cite to the relevant authorities, you do not, as a general rule, want to quote them or your brief. Reading more than a line is seldom effective. If it is important that the court have specific language before it, refer the judge or judges to the appropriate page in the brief or, better yet, prepare a visual aid.

There are several other things that you need to keep in mind in making your argument. First, it is usually more difficult to follow an oral argument than a written one. As a result, it is important to include sufficient roadmaps, signposts, and transitions. Make both the structure of your argument and the connections between ideas explicit.

Second, you need to manage your time. Do not spend so much time on one issue or argument that you do not have time for the other issue or issues or other arguments. Because it is difficult to predict how many questions the court will ask, practice a short and a long version of each argument.

§9.5.6   Answering Questions

You should welcome the court's questions. They tell you what the court is thinking about your case, what the judges understand, and what they still question. If you're not getting questions, it is usually a bad sign. The judges have either already made up their minds or are not listening.

Questions from the bench fall into several categories. Some are mere requests for information. The judge wants to clarify a fact or your position on an issue or wants to know more about the rule or how you think it should be applied.

Other questions are designed to elicit a particular response from you: Judge A agrees with your position and wants you to pursue a particular line of argument for the benefit of Judge B, who is not yet persuaded. Still other questions are designed to test the merits of your argument. These questions can have as their focus your case or, at the appellate level, future cases. If the court applies rule A, what does that mean for cases X, Y, and Z?

Whatever the type of question, when the judge begins to speak, you must stop. Although judges can interrupt you, you should not interrupt them. As the judge speaks, listen, not only to the question that is being asked but also for clues about how the judge is perceiving the case.

The hardest part comes next. Before answering the judge, think through your answer. Although the second or two of silence may make you uncomfortable, the penalty for answering too quickly can be severe. Although few cases are won at oral argument, some are lost, usually because in answering a question the attorney conceded or asserted too much. The second or two of silence is by far better than an unfavorable ruling.

When you know what you want to say, answer. In most instances, you will want to begin by giving the judge a one-, two-, or three-word answer. "Yes." "No." "Yes, but . . . ." "No, but . . . ." "In some cases, ..." Then explain or support your answer, integrating the points that you want to make into your answer when possible. Instead of thinking of questions as interruptions, think of them as another vehicle for making your argument.

There are a number of things that you should not do in responding to a question. First, do not tell the judge that you will answer the question later. It is you and not the judge who must be flexible.

Second, do not argue with the judge. Answer all questions calmly and thoughtfully. Do not raise your voice, and even if you are frustrated, don't let it show. If one line of argument isn't working and the point is essential to your case, try another, and if that line doesn't work, try still another. When the point is not important or you have given all the answers that you have, answer, and then without pausing move as smoothly as you can into the next part of your argument.

Third, after answering the question, don't stop and wait for the judge's approval or permission to continue. Answer the question, and then, unless asked another question, move to the next part of your argument.

Finally, don't answer by asking the judge a question. In oral argument, it is inappropriate to question a judge.

§9.5.7   Closing

The closing is as important as the opening. Because it is a position of emphasis, you want to end on a favorable point.

One way of doing this is to end with a summary of your arguments, reminding the court of your strongest points and requesting the appropriate relief. Although this is often effective, it can also be ineffective. Many judges stop listening when they hear the phrase "In conclusion" or "In summary." Consequently, when using a summary, avoid stock openers. Catch the court's attention by repeating a key phrase, weaving the pieces together, or returning to the points made in your opening.

Another way is to end on a strong point. If you are running out of time, it may be better to stop at the end of an argument or after answering a question than to rush through a prepared closing. Like a good comedian, a good advocate knows when to sit down.

§9.5.8   Rebuttal

Perhaps the hardest part of the oral argument is rebuttal. In one or two minutes you must identify the crucial issues and make your strongest argument or response.

As a general rule, do not try to make more than one or two points during rebuttal. The points should be selected because of their importance to your case: Do not merely repeat what you said in the main portion of your argument or respond to trivial points made by opposing counsel. Instead, make your rebuttal a true rebuttal, responding to significant points made by opposing counsel or questions or concerns raised by the court during opposing counsel's argument.

Because time is so limited, most advocates begin their rebuttal by telling the court how many points they plan to make: "I would like to make two points." This introduction tells the court what to expect. The advocate then makes his or her first point and supports it and, unless interrupted by a question, moves to the second point. Most advocates close by quickly repeating their request for relief.

§9.6   DELIVERING THE ARGUMENT

Every advocate has his or her own style. While some are soft-spoken, others are dynamic; while some are plain-speaking, others strive for eloquence. As an advocate, you will need to develop your own style, building on your strengths and minimizing your weaknesses.

Whatever your style, there are certain "rules" that you should follow.

§9.6.1   Do Not Read Your Argument

The first, and perhaps most important, rule is not to read your argument. Similarly, do not try to deliver a memorized speech. Know what you want to say and then talk to the court. You are a teacher, sharing information and answering the court's questions.

§9.6.2   Maintain Eye Contact

If you don't read, you will be able to maintain eye contact with the court. This is important for several reasons. First, it helps you keep the court's attention. It is very difficult not to listen to a person who is looking you in the eye. Second, it helps you "read" the court. By studying the judges, you can often determine (1) whether they already agree with you on a point and you can move to the next part of your argument; (2) whether they are confused; or (3) whether you have not yet persuaded them. Finally, eye contact is important because of what it says about you and your argument. An advocate who looks the judges in the eye is perceived as being more confident and more competent than one who doesn't.

When you are arguing to an appellate court, maintain eye contact with all of the judges. Even when answering a specific judge's question, maintain eye contact with all of the judges.

§9.6.3   Do Not Slouch, Rock, or Put Your Hands in Your Pockets

In delivering an oral argument to the court, stand erect, but not stiffly, behind the podium. Do not rock from foot to foot, and do not put your hands in your pockets.

Although it may be appropriate to move around the courtroom when arguing to a jury, you should not do so when arguing to the court.

§9.6.4   Limit Your Gestures and Avoid Distracting Mannerisms

Gestures are appropriate in an oral argument. They should, however, be natural and relatively constrained. If you talk with your hands, mentally put yourself inside a small telephone booth.

You also want to avoid distracting mannerisms. Do not play with a pen, the edge of your notes, or the keys in your pocket. In addition, do not repeatedly push hair out of your eyes or glasses back up on your nose.

§9.6.5   Speak So That You Can Be Easily Understood

In delivering your oral argument, speak loudly and clearly enough that you can be easily heard by the judges.

Also try to modulate your voice, varying both the pace and how loudly you speak. If you want to emphasize a point, speak more slowly and either more softly or more loudly.

§9.7   Making Your Argument Persuasive

In delivering your oral argument, you will want to use many of the same techniques that you used in writing your brief. In stating the issue, frame the question so that it suggests the answer favorable to your client and, in presenting the facts, emphasize the favorable facts by placing them in positions of emphasis and by using detail and sentence structure to your advantage. See section 8.13.3. Also present the law in the light most favorable to your client. State favorable rules broadly, use cases to your advantage, and emphasize the policies that support your client's position. See section 8.16.3.

You should also pick your words carefully. Select words both for their denotation and their connotation and avoid words and phrases that undermine the persuasiveness of your argument. If you are the plaintiff, don't say, "It is the plaintiff's position that the line-up was suggestive." Say "The line-up was suggestive." Similarly, don't say, "We feel that the prosecutor acted improperly when she referred to the defendant's post-arrest silence." Say instead, "The prosecutor acted improperly when she referred to the defendant's post-arrest silence."

§9.8   HANDLING THE PROBLEMS

Because an oral argument isn't scripted, you need to prepare for the unexpected, deciding in advance how you will handle the problems that might arise.

§9.8.1   Counsel Has Misstated Facts or Law

If opposing counsel misstates an important fact or the governing law, you will usually want to bring the error to the attention of the court. This should, however, be done carefully.

First, make sure that you are right. If there is time, double-check the record, the statute, or the case. Second, make sure that you are correcting a misstatement of fact or law and not opposing party's interpretation of a fact, statute, or case. Third, correct the mistake and not opposing counsel. Instead of criticizing or attacking opposing counsel, simply provide the court with the correct information and, if possible, the citation to the record or the language of the statute or case.

EXAMPLE

"Ms. Martinez did not see the assailant three times. She testified that she saw him twice: once when he drove by slowly and then when he pulled in front of her."

Finally, correct only those errors that are significant.

§9.8.2   You Make a Mistake

If you make a significant mistake, correct it as soon as you can.

§9.8.3   Not Enough Time

Despite the best of planning, you will sometimes run out of time. You may have gotten more questions than you expected, leaving you little or no remaining time for your last issue or your final points. When this happens, you have two options. You can either quickly summarize the points that you would have made, or you can tell the court that, because you are out of time, you will rely on your brief for the issues and arguments that you didn't cover.

What you don't want to do is exceed the time that you have allotted. Unless the court gives you permission to continue, you must stop when your time is up.

§9.8.4   Too Much Time

This is not a problem. You do not need to use all of your allotted time. When you have said what you need to say, thank the court and sit down.

§9.8.5   You Don't Know the Answer
to a Question

Occasionally you will be asked a question that you can't answer. If it is a question about the facts of your case or about the law, don't try to bluff. Instead, do one of the following: (1) if you can do so in a few seconds, look up the answer; (2) tell the judge that at this point you can't answer the question but that you will be glad to provide the information after oral argument, or (3) give the best answer that you can.

EXAMPLE

"So that I may answer correctly, let me quickly check the record."

"I'm not sure what the actual words were. I will check and provide you with that information after oral argument."

"As I recall, the police officer testified that he asked the question twice."

If the question raises an issue you hadn't considered, the options are slightly different. You can either trust yourself and, on the spot, give your best answer or tell the court that you need to give the question some thought.

§9.8.6   You Didn't Understand the Question

If you don't understand a question, tell the judge and either ask him or her to repeat the question or repeat the question in your own words, asking the judge whether you understood correctly. "I'm sorry, I'm not sure that I understand your question. Could you please rephrase it?" "If I am correct, you are asking whether . . . ."

§9.8.7   You Become Flustered or Draw a Blank

It happens, at some time or another, to almost everyone. You become flustered or draw a blank. When this happens, "buy" a few seconds by either taking a drink of water or taking a deep breath and looking down at your notes. If you still can't continue with the point that you were making, move to another one.

§9.8.8   You're Asked to Concede a Point

Concessions can work both to your advantage and to your disadvantage. You will win points by conceding points that you can't win or that are not important to your argument. You can, however, lose your case if you concede too much. You must, therefore, know your case, conceding when appropriate and otherwise politely, but firmly, standing your ground.

§9.9   A FINAL NOTE

No matter how much they dread it, initially most individuals end up enjoying oral argument for what it is, a stimulating dialogue among intelligent people.

Checklist for Critiquing the Oral Argument

I. Preparation

- The advocate knows the law and the facts of the case.
- The advocate has anticipated and prepared rebuttals for the arguments that the other side is likely to make.
- The advocate has anticipated and prepared responses to the questions that the court is likely to ask.
- The advocate has determined what arguments he or she needs to make to win.
- The advocate has prepared two outlines: a long outline, which can be used if the court asks only a few questions, and a short outline, which can be used in case the court asks more questions.

II. Content and Organization

A. Introduction

- The advocate identifies himself or herself and the client.
- When appropriate, the advocate requests rebuttal time.

B. *Opening and Statement of Issues or Position*

- The advocate begins the argument with a sentence or phrase that catches the attention of the court and establishes the client's theory of the case.
- The advocate then presents the question or states his or her position.
- The question or statement of position is framed so that it supports the advocate's theory of the case and suggests an answer favorable to the client.
- The question or statement of position is presented using language that is easily understood.

C. *Summary of Facts*

- When appropriate, the advocate includes a short summary of the facts in which he or she explains the case and establishes an appropriate context. When a separate summary of the facts is not appropriate, the advocate weaves the facts into the argument.
- The facts are presented accurately but in the light most favorable to the client. The positions of emphasis and detail are used effectively, and words have been selected for both their denotation and connotation.

D. *Argument*

- The advocate discusses the issues and makes the arguments needed to win.
- The argument is structured in such a way that it is easy to follow: (1) issues and arguments are discussed in a logical order and (2) sufficient roadmaps, signposts, and transitions are used.
- The arguments are supported. The advocate uses the law, analogous cases, policy, and the facts to support each of his or her assertions.
- The law, analogous cases, policies, and facts are presented accurately.
- The law, analogous cases, policies, and facts are presented in the light most favorable to the client.

E. *Questions from the Bench*

- When a judge asks a question, the advocate immediately stops talking and listens to the question.
- The advocate thinks before answering.
- As a general rule, the advocate begins his or her answer with a short response (Yes, No, In this case) and then supports that answer.
- After answering the question, the advocate moves back into his or her argument without pausing or waiting for the judge to give permission to continue.

- The advocate sees questions not as an interruption but as another opportunity to get his or her argument before the court.
- As he or she listens to the questions, the advocate adjusts the argument to match the concerns and interests of the court.

F. Closing

- The advocate ends the argument by summarizing the main points or on a strong point.
- When appropriate, the advocate includes a request for relief.

G. Rebuttal

- The advocate uses rebuttal to respond to the one or two most important points raised by opposing counsel or the court.

III. Delivery

- The advocate treats the argument as a dialogue; he or she does not read or recite the argument.
- The advocate maintains eye contact with all of the judges.
- The advocate has good posture, uses gestures effectively, and speaks so that he or she can be easily understood.
- The advocate is composed and treats the court and opposing counsel with respect.
- The advocate does not use phrases like "I think," "We maintain," or "It is our position that."

Section II

Resources in Legal Research, Style, and Grammar

Part III

A Guide to Legal Research

Most legal researchers remember their first trip to the law library. Problem in hand, they stood among the stacks, staring at row after row of books. What filled those thousands of volumes? Where to begin?

Although you may learn to do research through trial and error, that method is time-consuming and unreliable. You will become a better researcher faster if you go into the library knowing what types of material are there and the weight that should be given to each.

This part of the book gives you much of that information. The first chapters in Part III describe the various types of primary authority. Chapter 11 discusses constitutions and charters, and Chapters 12 through 14 discuss primary authorities from the three branches of government. The final four chapters discuss the most frequently used secondary sources, *Shepard's* citators, computer-assisted research, and research strategies.

Although these chapters can be used alone, they work best when read in conjunction with Chapters 5 and 6 which show how these tools are used to research a legal problem.

Chapter 10

Introduction to Legal Research

§10.1 WHAT LAWYERS RESEARCH

There are literally millions of laws in the United States (even excluding the Internal Revenue Code). What's worse, these laws are constantly changing. Obviously, then, a lawyer cannot practice law from memory alone. The lawyer must be able to find the law and to do so efficiently. That is the purpose of legal research.

Legal research encompasses many types of projects. One usually thinks that lawyers research to determine whether a particular activity is permissible or what steps to follow to legally perform an activity. To be sure, lawyers do research for such purposes. In addition, lawyers research to find support for an argument that one interpretation of the law should prevail over another. Lawyers research to find acceptable language for legal documents. They research to find out if a name is protected by trademark. They research to find out what the monetary value of pain and suffering is. Because there are so many tasks a lawyer does and each requires a slightly different technique, you should realize that there is no single method for performing legal research. Even given the same problem, there is no "best" method of researching it because each researcher has different knowledge and preferences based on previous experience.

That being said, there are still certain resources and strategies that have proven effective over the years. The purpose of the following chapters is to describe those resources and strategies to allow you to determine what works best for you.

The critical starting point in learning about legal research is understanding the legal system:

- Who makes the law?
- How is the law made?
- How are laws disseminated?

In the following chapters, you will discover (or be reminded) that there are numerous entities that make laws. For example, Congress makes laws, judges make law, and administrative agencies make law. Each of these entities makes law differently from the others. These laws are also disseminated to the public in different formats. The following chapters will discuss how these entities make and disseminate their laws. The focus will then shift to the user's viewpoint and discuss how to find such laws. Finally, after all the various forms of finding law are covered, the discussion will turn to choosing between these forms for finding the law and the strategies that you can use when doing legal research.

§10.2   LEGAL RESEARCH AS PART OF A PROCESS

As you learn the tools for legal research and how to use them, keep in mind that lawyers use these tools for a reason: problem solving.

Problem solving requires flexibility. As a lawyer uncovers the law governing one issue, he or she may begin to focus differently on the factual context. The lawyer may decide that the legal issue is different from what he or she originally thought. In such cases, the lawyer might begin researching anew on a different issue. In the alternative, he or she might seek to elicit more facts before researching any further. Similarly, the factual context may change during the process of legal research. For example, the lawyer might learn about additional facts that change the legal question being researched. The interplay of the factual context and the law together determine the end result of what the lawyer does.

§10.3   OUTLINE OF THE LEGAL SYSTEM OF
THE UNITED STATES

Our legal system has been discussed in detail in Chapters 1 and 2. However, since the following research chapters are presented hierarchically based on that system, here is a brief review.

Although they often seem forgotten as authority figures in the United States legal system, the "people" are the source of all governmental power. The United States Constitution itself begins "We the people" and only moves forward from that starting point. Although a lawyer rarely researches to find out the thoughts of the people, no lawyer should ever forget the ultimate source of the law: the consent of the governed.

The people create a government, grant it power, and enumerate those powers in the Constitution. The Constitution separates governmental power into three branches: legislative, judicial, and executive. The power of these branches, however, remains subordinate to the Constitution (the Supreme Law of the land). Whatever actions these branches take must be authorized by the Constitution. Through the process of "judicial review," the courts interpret the constitutionality of particular actions. Each of the three branches also delegates some of its authority to administrative agencies. The power of these agencies is subordinate not only to the Constitution but also to the power of the branch from which it derives its powers.

The following chapters elaborate on the above overview of structure and principles. As we discuss the creation and dissemination of the law in those chapters, keep the overall scheme in mind.

Chapter 11

Constitutions and Charters

§11.1 THE UNITED STATES CONSTITUTION

We begin with most primary of the primary sources: the United States Constitution.

The United States Constitution is the supreme law of the land. The principles that it announces bind the federal government as well as the states, local governments, and private individuals. The Constitution, however, does more than establish the basic principles of law: it establishes the framework within which our government and our systems of law operate. By dividing the power of the government between a federal government and states and among the legislative, executive, and judicial branches, the Constitution created our multilayered legal system. It is because of our Constitution that we have both federal and state statutes, federal and state regulations, and federal and state court decisions.

The text of the United States Constitution can be found in numerous places. Copies can be found in both general and legal encyclopedias, in the various versions of the United States Code, at the front of most state codes, in separately published pamphlets and, at least at one time, on the tray liners at McDonald's. Copies of the Constitution can also be found on the Internet, on CD-ROM products, and on LEXIS and Westlaw. These latter versions often offer the enhanced value of being full-text searchable. That is, you can search the Constitution for particular words or phrases to see where they appear.

Commentary, although plentiful, is not as generally available. The most readily available sources are the annotated United States Codes. In addition to setting out the text of the Constitution, both the United States Code Annotated (U.S.C.A.) and United States Code Service (U.S.C.S.) go through the Constitution clause by clause, for each clause listing cases that have interpreted or applied that particular clause. See Exhibit 11.1.

REPRESENTATIVES—QUALIFICATIONS   Art I, § 2, cl 2, n 2

seq.) was not illegal on ground that minors were unable to vote for Congress, which passed Act. George v United States (1952, CA9 Cal) 196 F2d 445, cert den 344 US 843, 97 L Ed 656, 73 S Ct 58 (disagreed with United States v Seeger (CA2 NY) 326 F2d 846, affd 380 US 163, 13 L Ed 2d 733, 85 S Ct 850 (ovrld Welsh v United States, 398 US 333, 26 L Ed 2d 308, 90 S Ct 1792) as stated in United States ex rel. Foster v Schlesinger (CA2 NY) 520 F2d 751).

Where candidate for office of Representative in United States Congress was registered as affiliated with the Republican Party, but not as Democrat, and received nomination of both parties, his certification as candidate of Democratic Party did not deprive any voters of right to vote for candidates for that office at general election, and it did not deprive them of any other rights; thus, political party can lawfully nominate, as its candidate for Representative in Congress, person not registered as affiliated with that party, but registered as affiliated with another political party, as such nominations are not contrary to federal Constitution or of any law of United States. Shaffer v Jordan (1954, CA9 Cal) 213 F2d 393.

> Text of the Constitution

Sec. 2, Cl. 2. Qualifications of Representatives.

No person shall be a Representative who shall not have attained to the Age of twenty five Years, and been seven Years a Citizen of the United States, and who shall not, when elected, be an Inhabitant of that State in which he shall be chosen.

CROSS REFERENCES

Power of each House to judge qualifications of its own members, USCS Constitution, Art. I, § 5, cl. 1.

RESEARCH GUIDE

> Annotations

Federal Procedure L Ed:
Government Officers and Employee, Fed Proc, L Ed, § 40:579.

INTERPRETIVE NOTES AND DECISIONS

1. Generally
2. Validity of qualifications or requirements established by state law
3. —Residency
4. —Candidate's moral qualifications
5. —Prohibiting office holder from running for Congress

> Annotations

1. Generally

Word "State" is used in Art. 1, § 2, cl. 2, of Constitution in its geographical sense. Texas v White (1869) 74 US 700, 19 L Ed 227, cause dismd 77 US 68, 19 L Ed 839 and (ovrld on other grounds Morgan v United States, 113 US 476, 28 L Ed 1044, 5 S Ct 588).

Representative, duly elected and meeting all constitutional requirements for service as such, could not legally be excluded by House of Representatives, and because he had properly alleged claim for back wages, fact that new Congress had convened in which he had been seated did not render his case moot. Powell v McCormack (1969) 395 US 486, 23 L Ed 2d 491, 89 S Ct 1944.

Portions of plea agreement entered by member of Congress who pled guilty to several federal crimes, pertaining to resignation from Congress and withdrawal as candidate for re-election are void since they represent unconstitutional interference by executive with legislative branch of government and with rights of defendant's constituents. United States v Richmond (1982, ED NY) 550 F Supp 605.

Since Congressman must be resident of state from which he is chosen, it is presumed that Congressman from Arkansas is resident thereof when elected and as such is subject to state income taxes. Cravens v Cook (1947) 212 Ark 71, 204 SW2d 909.

2. Validity of qualifications or requirements established by state law

As applied to persons seeking ballot positions as independent candidates for United States Congress, state election statute requiring that independent candidate, to obtain ballot status, must file nomination papers signed by specified percentage of vote cast in preceding general elec-

A more comprehensive source, at least for commentary, is *The Constitution of the United States of America: Analysis and Interpretation,* which is published by the Government Printing Office. This volume goes through the Constitution clause by clause, providing the researcher not only with the text of the Constitution and citations to significant cases but also with commentary. See Exhibit 11.2. It is periodically supplemented.

EXHIBIT 11.2　　**Sample Page from *The Constitution of the United States of America: Analysis and Interpretation* (U.S. Government Printing Office)**

ART. I—LEGISLATIVE DEPARTMENT　　　107

Sec. 2—House of Representatives　　　　　　　　　　　　　Cl. 2—Qualifications

Notwithstanding the vesting of discretion to prescribe voting qualifications in the States, conceptually the right to vote for United States Representatives is derived from the Federal Constitution [13] and Congress has had the power under Article I, § 4, to legislate to protect that right against both official [14] and private denial. [15]

Text of Constitution

Clause 2. No person shall be a Representative who shall not have attained to the Age of twenty-five Years, and been seven Years a Citizen of the United States, and who shall not, when elected, be an inhabitant of the State in which he shall be chosen.

QUALIFICATIONS OF MEMBERS OF CONGRESS

When the Qualifications Must Be Possessed

Commentary

A question much disputed but now seemingly settled is whether a condition of eligibility must exist at the time of the election or whether it is sufficient that eligibility exist when the Member-elect presents himself to take the oath of office. While the language of the clause expressly makes residency in the State a condition at the time of election, it now appears established in congressional practice that the age and citizenship qualifications need only be met when the Member-elect is to be sworn. [1] Thus, persons elected to either the House of Representatives or the Senate before attaining the required age or term of citizenship have been admitted as soon as they became qualified. [2]

Exclusivity of Constitutional Qualifications

Congressional Additions.—Writing in *The Federalist* with reference to the election of Members of Congress, Hamilton firmly stated that "[t]he qualifications of the persons who may . . . be

---

[13] "The right to vote for members of the Congress of the United States is not derived merely from the constitution and laws of the state in which they are chosen, but has its foundation in the Constitution of the United States." *Ex parte Yarbrough,* 110 U.S. 651, 663 (1884). *See also Wiley* v. *Sinkler,* 179 U.S. 58, 62 (1900); *Swafford* v. *Templeton,* 185 U.S. 487, 492 (1902); *United States* v. *Classic,* 313 U.S. 299, 315, 321 (1941).

[14] *United States* v. *Mosley,* 238 U.S. 383 (1915).

[15] *United States* v. *Classic,* 313 U.S. 299, 315 (1941).

[1] *See* S. Rept. No. 904, 74th Congress, 1st sess. (1935), reprinted in 79 *Cong. Rec.* 9651–9653 (1935).

[2] 1 A. Hinds' *Precedents of the House of Representatives* (Washington: 1907), § 418; 79 *Cong. Rec.* 9841–9842 (1935); cf. Hinds' *Precedents, supra,* § 429.

§11.2   STATE CONSTITUTIONS

Like the United States Constitution, state constitutions are primary authority. Within the state, they are the supreme law of the land, binding both the government and the people of the state and creating the state's system of government.

Although state constitutions cannot limit the rights granted by the United States Constitution, they can grant additional rights. For example, in some states, the state's Due Process Clause grants criminal defendants more rights than they have under the Due Process Clause of the United States Constitution.

The easiest place to find a copy of a particular state's constitution is in the state code for that state. If the code is unannotated, you will find only the text of the constitution; if the code is annotated, you will find both the text and annotations to cases that have interpreted it.

When you want to compare the text of the constitutions of the various states, the best source is *Constitutions of the United States, National and State,* which is published by Oceana. Although unannotated, this book collects in one place the constitutions of all fifty states.

§11.3   CHARTERS

Although not usually thought of as constitutions, charters serve the same function, granting and limiting power, but at the county or municipal level. Copies of city and county charters are not usually widely distributed; they are usually published as part of the county or city code.

Chapter 12

The Legislative Branch

While the Constitution provides the overriding principles of our legal system, statutes created by the legislative branch provide the basic framework of our laws. Much of case law, for example, is concerned with interpreting statutory provisions. In addition, it is primarily from statutory authority that administrative regulations are promulgated. Because statutes are so fundamental to our laws, you should always look for statutory authority even if you have found other relevant authority. You should also always verify that the text you are using is the correct (usually this means the most current) version of the statute.

With the proliferation of statutes, more and more legislation is done through the amendment or repeal of existing statutes. Because of this, you should understand the difference between looking for a statute as it was enacted or as it has been codified into existing law. A discussion of that follows.

If constitutional, the statutes enacted by the legislative branch are primary authority, binding both the judicial and executive branches. The judiciary interprets the statutes enacted by the legislature, and the executive branch enforces them. See Exhibit 12.1.

§12.1 LOCATING STATUTES

Most statutes can be found in more than one source: in the session laws, in an unannotated code, and in an annotated code.

§12.1.1 Session Laws

Session laws are the statutes published in chronological order. At the end of a legislative session, the statutes enacted during that session are collected and arranged, not by topic, but by date.

Exhibit 12.2 is taken from the *Statutes at Large,* the session laws of the United States Congress. Note that the statutes are arranged by their

EXHIBIT 12.1   **The Branches of Government**

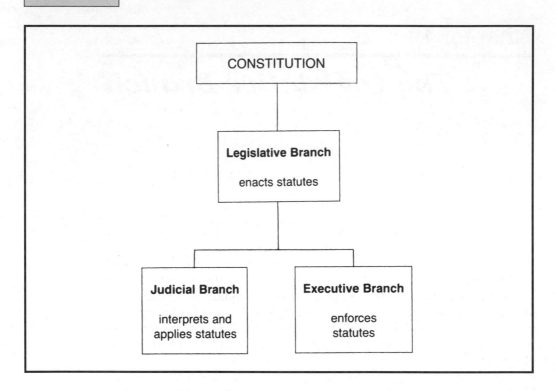

Public Law Number, a number that is assigned at the time the law is enacted. The first of the two numbers identifies the Congress, the second the particular statute. Thus, in the following example, the statute was the 508th statute enacted during the 99th Congress.

Public Law   99-508

Congress   Statute Number

Similar numbering systems are used for state statutes.

The text of newly enacted federal statutes can be found in the slip laws for the *Statutes at Large,* the advance sheets for U.S.C.A. and U.S.C.S., and the advance sheets for *United States Code Congressional and Administrative News* (USCCAN).

Although session laws are the "first" place that a statute appears, they are not usually the source of first choice. Because the statutes are arranged by date and not by topic, you will usually need to check several volumes to find the current version of the statute. The original version of the statute will be found in one volume and amendments in later ones. Consequently, session laws should be used only when (1) you are pre-

---

EXHIBIT 12.2	Sample Page from United States Statutes at Large

---

100 STAT. 1848   PUBLIC LAW 99–508—OCT. 21, 1986

Public Law 99–508
99th Congress

An Act

Oct. 21, 1986
[H.R. 4952]

To amend title 18, United States Code, with respect to the interception of certain communications, other forms of surveillance, and for other purposes.

Electronic
Communications
Privacy Act of
1986.
18 USC 2510
note.

Be it enacted by the Senate and House of Representatives of the United States of America in Congress assembled,

SECTION 1. SHORT TITLE.

This Act may be cited as the "Electronic Communications Privacy Act of 1986".

TITLE I—INTERCEPTION OF COMMUNICATIONS AND RELATED MATTERS

SEC. 101. FEDERAL PENALTIES FOR THE INTERCEPTION OF COMMUNICA-
TIONS.

(a) DEFINITIONS.—(1) Section 2510(1) of title 18, United States Code, is amended—

(A) by striking out "any communication" and inserting "any aural transfer" in lieu thereof;

(B) by inserting "(including the use of such connection in a switching station)" after "reception".

(C) by striking out "as a common carrier" and

(D) by inserting before the semicolon at the end the following: "or communications affecting interstate or foreign commerce and such term includes any electronic storage of such communication, but such term does not include the radio portion of a cordless telephone communication that is transmitted between the cordless telephone handset and the base unit".

(2) Section 2510(2) of title 18, United States Code, is amended by inserting before the semicolon at the end the following: ", but such term does not include any electronic communication".

(3) Section 2510(4) of title 18, United States Code, is amended—

(A) by inserting "or other" after "aural"; and

(B) by inserting ", electronic," after "wire".

(4) Section 2510(5) of title 18, United States Code, is amended in clause (a)(i) by inserting before the semicolon the following: "or furnished by such subscriber or user for connection to the facilities of such service and used in the ordinary course of its business".

(5) Section 2510(8) of title 18, United States Code, is amended by striking out "identity of the parties to such communication or the existence,".

(6) Section 2510 of title 18, United States Code, is amended—

(A) by striking out "and" at the end of paragraph (10);

(B) by striking out the period at the end of paragraph (11) and inserting a semicolon in lieu thereof; and

(C) by adding at the end the following:

"(12) 'electronic communication' means any transfer of signs, signals, writing, images, sounds, data, or intelligence of any paring a legislative history, (2) you are looking for a copy of a statute that is no longer in effect, or (3) you are looking for a copy of a statute that has just been enacted.

§12.1.2   Codes

When you want the text of a current statute, the best source is a code. Unlike session laws, codes are organized by topic and not by date. All statutes on the same topic that are currently in effect are placed together, with amending language inserted where appropriate and repealed language deleted.

The numbering system used in codes reflects the difference in organization. Instead of using numbers that indicate the order in which the statutes were enacted, codes use a numbering system based on subject matter.

The United States Code, for example, uses a two-part numbering system. The first number identifies the title or topic, and the second identifies the particular section. For example, in the citation 18 U.S.C. § 2510, the first number, 18, identifies the title. Title 18 of the United States Code deals with Crimes and Criminal Procedure. Section 2510 is the Definitions section for the chapter on "Wire and Electronic Communications Interception and Interception of Oral Communications."

Some states have numbering systems similar to the United States Code. Others include chapters or articles to further break down their titles. For example, in Washington, Title 9 concerns crimes and punishments; Chapter 73 concerns violations of privacy rights; section 030 concerns intercepting private communications. Thus, the citation to the Revised Code of Washington for requiring consent to intercept or record private communications is Wash. Rev. Code § 9.73.030 (title, chapter, section).

Finally, some states do not use titles at all. Instead, they break down the state code into smaller codes denominated by name. California, for example, calls its crime and punishment provisions its Penal Code. The citation to California's code concerning eavesdropping on or recording of confidential communications, then, is Cal. Penal Code § 632.

a.   Official versus Unofficial Codes

In those jurisdictions with more than one version of the code, one will be designated as the official code and the other or others as unofficial. For example, in the federal system, Congress has designated the *United States Code,* which is published by the Government Printing Office, as the official code and *United States Code Annotated* (U.S.C.A.) and *United States Code Service* (U.S.C.S.) as unofficial. Although you can do your research in any of these three codes (the text of the statutes should be identical), the citation should be to the official code.

b. Annotated versus Unannotated Codes

When you are interested in only the text of an act, the best source is an unannotated code. Because there are no annotations, the relationship among individual sections is more easily seen. See Exhibit 12.3.

The format used in the Revised Code of Washington is similar to that used in other unannotated codes. The section number and title are set out first; the text of the statute second; and the history of the statute (the information in brackets) last.

The bracketed material following 9.73.030 tells you that section 9.73.030 was enacted during the 1967 extraordinary session; that its session law number was chapter 93, section 1; and that it has been amended three times: in 1977, 1985, and 1986.

When you need not only the text of the statute but also citations to cases interpreting and applying it, the best source is an annotated code. Like an unannotated code, an annotated code sets out the text of the statute. In addition, most annotated codes provide you with cross-references to other potentially applicable statutory sections; a list of law review articles discussing the section; references to other materials produced by the same publisher that may provide useful information; and, in the Notes of Decision section, one-paragraph annotations for cases that have interpreted or applied the statute. See Exhibit 12.4.

c. Updating Annotated and Unannotated Codes

Codes are updated in one of two ways: through the use of pocket parts and supplements or, if the code is published in a loose-leaf binder, by replacing pages. To find the most recent version of a statute, check the pocket parts and supplements through the date the legislative body last met. For example, the definition of "electronic communication" under 18 U.S.C. § 2510 needs to be amended constantly to cover changes in technology. Even in a bound volume that is less than four years old, the pocket part contains at least two amendments to that definition. Failure to check the supplementation may result in an inaccurate analysis or an inaccurate interpretation of the communications interception provisions.

d. Research Strategies

A particular statutory section can be located in a number of different ways, through the use of (1) the subject index, (2) the popular name table, or (3) codification tables. If you already know the statute's title and section number, look up that title and section number in the main volumes.

1. Subject Index

The most common way of locating a particular statutory section is through the subject index, which, depending on the code, either pre-

EXHIBIT 12.3	**Sample Page from an Unannotated Code (Revised Code of Washington)**

9.72.090   Title 9 RCW: Crimes and Punishments

produced before him or her or direct it to be delivered to the prosecuting attorney. [1987 c 202 § 141; 1909 c 249 § 107; RRS § 2359.]

> Intent—1987 c 202: See note following RCW 2.04.190.

Chapter 9.73
PRIVACY, VIOLATING RIGHT OF

Sections
9.73.010   Divulging telegram.
9.73.020   Opening sealed letter.
9.73.030   Intercepting, recording or divulging private communica-
            tion—Consent required—Exceptions.
9.73.040   Intercepting private communication—Court order permitting
            interception—Grounds for issuance—Duration—
            Renewal.
9.73.050   Admissibility of intercepted communication in evidence.
9.73.060   Violating right of privacy—Civil action—Liability for dam-
            ages.
9.73.070   Persons and activities excepted from chapter.
9.73.080   Intercepting, recording, or divulging private communica-
            tion—Penalty.
9.73.090   Certain emergency response personnel exempted from RCW
            9.73.030 through 9.73.080—Standards—Court authoriza-
            tions—Admissibility.
9.73.095   Intercepting, recording, or divulging inmate conversations—
            Conditions—Notice.
9.73.100   Recordings available to defense counsel.
9.73.110   Intercepting, recording, or disclosing private communica-
            tions—Not unlawful for building owner—Conditions.
9.73.120   Reports—Required, when, contents.
9.73.130   Recording private communications—Authorization—
            Application for, contents.
9.73.140   Recording private communications—Authorization of or
            application for—Inventory, contents, service—
            Availability of recording, applications, and orders.
9.73.200   Intercepting, transmitting, or recording conversations con-
            cerning controlled substances—Findings.
9.73.210   Intercepting, transmitting, or recording conversations con-
            cerning controlled substances—Authorization—Monthly
            report—Admissibility—Destruction of information.
9.73.220   Judicial authorizations—Availability of judge required.
9.73.230   Intercepting, transmitting, or recording conversations con-
            cerning controlled substances—Conditions—Written
            reports required—Judicial review—Notice—
            Admissibility—Penalties.
9.73.240   Intercepting, transmitting, or recording conversations con-
            cerning controlled substances—Concurrent power of
            attorney general to investigate and prosecute.

9.73.010   Divulging telegram. Every person who shall wrongfully obtain or attempt to obtain, any knowledge of a telegraphic message, by connivance with the clerk, operator, messenger or other employee of a telegraph company, and every clerk, operator, messenger or other employee of such company who shall wilfully divulge to any but the person for whom it was intended, any telegraphic message or dispatch intrusted to him for transmission or delivery, or the nature or contents thereof, or shall wilfully refuse, neglect or delay duly to transmit or deliver the same, shall be guilty of a misdemeanor. [1909 c 249 § 410; Code 1881 § 2342; RRS § 2662.]

> *Intercepting, delaying telegram:* RCW 9A.48.070, 9A.48.080.

9.73.020   Opening sealed letter. Every person who shall wilfully open or read, or cause to be opened or read, any sealed message, letter or telegram intended for another person, or publish the whole or any portion of such a

message, letter or telegram, knowing it to have been opened or read without authority, shall be guilty of a misdemeanor. [1909 c 249 § 411; RRS § 2663.]

9.73.030   Intercepting, recording or divulging private communication—Consent required—Exceptions. (1) Except as otherwise provided in this chapter, it shall be unlawful for any individual, partnership, corporation, association, or the state of Washington, its agencies, and political subdivisions to intercept, or record any:

(a) Private communication transmitted by telephone, telegraph, radio, or other device between two or more individuals between points within or without the state by any device electronic or otherwise designed to record and/or transmit said communication regardless how such device is powered or actuated, without first obtaining the consent of all the participants in the communication;

(b) Private conversation, by any device electronic or otherwise designed to record or transmit such conversation regardless how the device is powered or actuated without first obtaining the consent of all the persons engaged in the conversation.

(2) Notwithstanding subsection (1) of this section, wire communications or conversations (a) of an emergency nature, such as the reporting of a fire, medical emergency, crime, or disaster, or (b) which convey threats of extortion, blackmail, bodily harm, or other unlawful requests or demands, or (c) which occur anonymously or repeatedly or at an extremely inconvenient hour, or (d) which relate to communications by a hostage holder or barricaded person as defined in RCW 70.85.100, whether or not conversation ensues, may be recorded with the consent of one party to the conversation.

(3) Where consent by all parties is needed pursuant to this chapter, consent shall be considered obtained whenever one party has announced to all other parties engaged in the communication or conversation, in any reasonably effective manner, that such communication or conversation is about to be recorded or transmitted: PROVIDED, That if the conversation is to be recorded that said announcement shall also be recorded.

(4) An employee of any regularly published newspaper, magazine, wire service, radio station, or television station acting in the course of bona fide news gathering duties on a full time or contractual or part time basis, shall be deemed to have consent to record and divulge communications or conversations otherwise prohibited by this chapter if the consent is expressly given or if the recording or transmitting device is readily apparent or obvious to the speakers. Withdrawal of the consent after the communication has been made shall not prohibit any such employee of a newspaper, magazine, wire service, or radio or television station from divulging the communication or conversation. [1986 c 38 § 1; 1985 c 260 § 2; 1977 ex.s. c 363 § 1; 1967 ex.s. c 93 § 1.]

> **Reviser's note:** This section was amended by 1985 c 260 § 2 and by 1986 c 38 § 1, each without reference to the other. Both amendments are incorporated in the publication of this section under RCW 1.12.025(2). For rule of construction, see RCW 1.12.025(1).
>
> **Severability—1967 ex.s. c 93:** "If any provision of this act, or its application to any person or circumstance is held invalid, the remainder of

EXHIBIT 12.4 | **Sample Pages from *Annotated Revised Code of Washington****

§ 9.73.010   CRIMES AND PUNISHMENTS   128

Sec.
    stances — Conditions — Written reports
    required — Judicial review — Notice —
    Admissibility — Penalties.
9.73.240. Intercepting, transmitting, or recording

conversations concerning controlled substances — Concurrent power of attorney
general to investigate and prosecute.

§ 9.73.010. Divulging telegram.

Every person who shall wrongfully obtain or attempt to obtain, any knowledge of a telegraphic message, by connivance with the clerk, operator, messenger or other employee of a telegraph company, and every clerk, operator, messenger or other employee of such company who shall wilfully divulge to any but the person for whom it was intended, any telegraphic message or dispatch intrusted to him for transmission or delivery, or the nature or contents thereof, or shall wilfully refuse, neglect or delay duly to transmit or deliver the same, shall be guilty of a misdemeanor. [1909 c 249 § 410; Code 1881 § 2342; RRS § 2662.]

Cross References.
  Intercepting, delaying telegram: RCW 9A.48.070,
9A.48.080.

JUDICIAL DECISIONS

Emergency phone call.
  An emergency phone call to a police station may be a private conversation within the meaning of this statute. State v. Wanrow, 14 Wash. App. 115, 538 P.2d 849 (1975), aff'd, 88 Wash. 2d 221, 559 P.2d 548 (1977).

§ 9.73.020. Opening sealed letter.

Every person who shall wilfully open or read, or cause to be opened or read, any sealed message, letter or telegram intended for another person, or publish the whole or any portion of such a message, letter or telegram, knowing it to have been opened or read without authority, shall be guilty of a misdemeanor. [1909 c 249 § 411; RRS § 2663.]

§ 9.73.030. Intercepting, recording or divulging private communication — Consent required — Exceptions.

(1) Except as otherwise provided in this chapter, it shall be unlawful for any individual, partnership, corporation, association, or the state of Washington, its agencies, and political subdivisions to intercept, or record any:

(a) Private communication transmitted by telephone, telegraph, radio, or other device between two or more individuals between points within or without the state by any device electronic or otherwise designed to record and/or transmit said communication regardless how such device is powered or actuated, without first obtaining the consent of all the participants in the communication;

(b) Private conversation, by any device electronic or otherwise designed to record or transmit such conversation regardless how the device is powered or actuated without first obtaining the consent of all the persons engaged in the conversation.

(2) Notwithstanding subsection (1) of this section, wire communications or conversations (a) of an emergency nature, such as the reporting of a fire, medical emergency, crime, or disaster, or (b) which convey threats of extortion, blackmail, bodily harm, or other unlawful requests or demands, or (c) which occur anonymously or repeatedly or at an extremely inconvenient hour, or (d) which relate to communications by a hostage holder or barricaded person as defined in RCW 70.85.100, whether or not conversation ensues, may be recorded with the consent of one party to the conversation.

(3) Where consent by all parties is needed pursuant to this chapter, consent shall be considered obtained whenever one party has announced to all other parties engaged in the communication or conversation, in any reasonably effective manner, that such communication or conversation is about to be recorded or transmitted: PROVIDED, That if the conversation is to be recorded that said announcement shall also be recorded.

(4) An employee of any regularly published newspaper, magazine, wire service, radio station, or television station acting in the course of bona fide news gathering duties on a full time or contractual or part time basis, shall be deemed to have consent to record and divulge communications or conversations otherwise prohibited by this chapter if the consent is expressly given or if

EXHIBIT 12.4   *(continued)*

---

129   PRIVACY, VIOLATING RIGHT OF   § 9.73.030

the recording or transmitting device is readily apparent or obvious to the speakers. Withdrawal of the consent after the communication has been made shall not prohibit any such employee of a newspaper, magazine, wire service, or radio or television station from divulging the communication or conversation. [1986 c 38 § 1; 1985 c 260 § 2; 1977 ex.s. c 363 § 1; 1967 ex.s. c 93 § 1.]

Reviser's note: This section was amended by 1985 c 260 § 2 and by 1986 c 38 § 1, each without reference to the other. Both amendments are incorporated in the publication of this section pursuant to RCW 1 12.025(2). For rule of construction, see RCW 1 12.025(1).

Severability — 1967 ex.s. c 93: "If any provision of this act, or its application to any person or circumstance is held invalid, the remainder of the act, or the application of the provision to other persons or circumstances is not affected." [1967 ex.s. c 93 § 7.]

JUDICIAL DECISIONS

ANALYSIS

Constitutionality
Applicability
Compliance with section
Consent
Emergency phone calls
Evidence
—Admissibility
—Authentication
—Inadmissible
Illegal recordings
Preemption
Privacy interest
Private communications
Recorded conversations
Recording or transmitting devices
Standing
Videotape recording
—Testimony

Constitutionality.

Policemen, who listened but did not record phone conversation between defendant and informant as the informant tipped the phone receiver in their direction, did not violate the Washington privacy act or the Washington constitution. State v. Corliss, 67 Wash. App. 708, 838 P.2d 1149 (1992).

The admission of a tape recording does not violate a criminal defendant's right to confront witnesses against him, even though the recording is crucial to the state's case, when its authenticity is firmly established and the declarant's unavailability is certain. State v. Smith, 85 Wash. 2d 840, 540 P.2d 424 (1975).

Applicability.

The Washington privacy act applies to evidence gathered by federal agents which is to be used in a state criminal proceeding. State v. Williams, 94 Wash. 2d 531, 617 P.2d 1012 (1980).

This provision is not applicable to sounds of an event which do not constitute a private conversation as that term is ordinarily used. State v. Smith, 85 Wash. 2d 840, 540 P.2d 424 (1975).

Compliance with section.

Where all that was learned from the pager was the telephone number of one party, the party dialing, and where discovery of the number did not affect other persons, involve multiple invasions of privacy, or record the exchange of information such as dialing from one telephone number to another, this section was not violated. State v. Wojtyna, 70 Wash. App. 689, 855 P.2d 315 (1993).

Consent.

Consent to taped conversation need not appear on the tape so long as the announcement that the conversation is being taped is on the tape. State v. Rupe, 101 Wash. 2d 664, 683 P.2d 571 (1984).

Admission into evidence of tape recording of a conversation with defendant was error where the tape did not contain a statement that the conversation was being recorded, but the error was not prejudicial. State v. Rupe, 101 Wash. 2d 664, 683 P.2d 571 (1984).

Where four tape recorded conversations of private conversations made without a warrant concerning a conspiracy to commit murder were consented to by one party to the conversation but not by the defendant, all four recordings were admissible although only the first recording contained defendant's request to commit murder since the later recordings pertained to implementation of the murder. State v. Caliguri, 99 Wash. 2d 501, 664 P.2d 466 (1983).

Recorded statements from persons under custodial arrest are inadmissible unless waiver by consent is capable of proof by the recording itself. State v. Cunningham, 93 Wash. 2d 823, 613 P.2d 1139 (1980).

There was no interception, for the purposes of this section, when police officers overheard defendant's confession on a extension telephone with consent of police dispatcher telephoned by defendant. State v. Bonilla, 23 Wash. App. 869, 598 P.2d 783 (1979).

Emergency phone calls.

1977 amendments to this section indicate the legislature's intention that emergency calls to police and fire stations be exempt from the wiretapping laws. State v. Bonilla, 23 Wash. App. 869, 598 P.2d 783 (1979).

Evidence.

—Admissibility.

When an officer knowingly transmits a private conversation, without court authorization or without the consent of all the parties, any evidence obtained, including simultaneous visual observation and assertive gestures, is inadmissible in a criminal trial. State v. Fjermestad, 114 Wash. 2d 828, 791 P.2d 897 (1990).

RCW 9.73.090, which excepts certain emergency telephone calls from the prohibition against nonconsensual recordings of private conversations, does not except such calls from the provision of RCW 9.73.050 declaring all such recordings to be inadmissible in evidence. State v. Wanrow, 14 Wash. App. 115, 538 P.2d 849 (1975), aff'd, 88 Wash. 2d 221, 559 P.2d 548 (1977).

Wiretap evidence obtained in violation of neither

cedes or follows the main volumes. Subject indices are arranged alphabetically by topic and for each topic include references to the appropriate
title and section number. The subject index may itself be periodically
updated through the use of pocket parts or supplements.

For example, if you look up "Wire tapping" in a U.S.C. index, you
are referred to "Interception of Wire, Oral or Electronic Communications." That topic has several entries. One of them, "Electronic communication, defined," refers you to 18 U.S.C. § 2510. See Exhibit 12.5.

2.   Popular Name Table

When an act has a popular name (Social Security Act, Civil Rights
Act, Electronic Communications Privacy Act, Superfund Act), the easiest
way of finding the act is to use the Popular Name Table, which is found
in the index volumes of most codes. This table lists acts by their popular
name, for each act listing the title(s) and section number(s) where the
act, or parts of it, can be found. See Exhibit 12.6. This table is important
because popular names are not usually listed in the subject index. For
example, although "Superfund" is listed in the Popular Name Table, it is
not listed in the subject index.

3.   Codification Tables

If you know the public law number, the title and section numbers
can be located using the codification tables accompanying the code.

For example, if you knew the public law number for the Electronic
Communications Privacy Act was Pub. L. 99-508, you could look in the
codification tables and find that it is codified, among other places, at 18
U.S.C. § 2511. See Exhibit 12.7.

§12.1.3   Statutes Available on Computer Databases

Statutes can also be located using LEXIS, Westlaw, CD-ROM products, and the Internet. Although using some of these services can be more
expensive than looking up the statute in printed form, they are useful
when you want to find the text of a statute from another jurisdiction and
you do not have access to that jurisdiction's printed code. If the online
version is full-text searchable (as it is on LEXIS and Westlaw and most CD-
ROM products), you can use an online version to find all the places in
the code in which a particular word or phrase appears. In addition, because LEXIS and Westlaw are updated frequently, they can be used to find
the most recent version of a statute.

For researching laws by subject, a current print copy of the code is
usually preferable if it is available because the statutes in a code have
been put in a particular order to simplify their use. Definition sections
are often found at the beginning of code titles and chapters. These can
affect how other sections within those titles and chapters are interpreted.

EXHIBIT 12.5   Index to United States Code Annotated*

INTERCEPTION OF WIRE, ORAL, OR ELECTRONIC COMMUNICATIONS
—Cont'd

Department of Justice Telecommunications Carrier Compliance Fund, establishment, deposits, etc., 47 § 1021

Devices. Electronic, mechanical, or other device, generally, post, this heading

Digital and other communications. See specific index lines under this heading

Disclosure,
  Authorization, 18 § 2517
  Certain instances, 18 § 2511
  Information,
    Liability for civil damages, 18 § 2511
    Providers of wire or electronic service, no cause of action against, 18 § 2511
  Prohibited, 18 § 2511; 47 § 605

Disposition of confiscated devices, laws applicable, 18 § 2513

Distribution,
  Intercepting devices,
    Offense, sentencing guidelines, 18 USSG § 2H3.2
    Prohibition, 18 § 2512
  Possession and advertising of intercepting devices, prohibitions, 18 § 2512

Documentary evidence, application for order authorizing, 18 § 2518

Duration of order authorizing, 18 § 2518

Electronic, mechanical, or other device,
  Confiscation, 18 § 2513
  Defined, 18 § 2510
  Interception by prohibited, 18 § 2511
  Manufacture, distribution, etc., prohibited, 18 § 2512

Electronic communication, defined, 18 § 2510

Electronic communications system, defined, 18 § 2510

Electronic messaging services, defined, digital and other communications, 47 § 1001

Electronic storage, defined, 18 § 2510

Electronic surveillance,
  Assistance for law enforcement, by telecommunications carrier [Fut. Eff.], 47 § 1002
  Foreign intelligence purposes. Surveillance, generally, this index

Emergencies, conspiratorial activities characteristic of organized crime, orders, time limitations, 18 § 2518

Emergency interception,
  Application for order after, 18 § 2518
  Assistance for law enforcement, requirements [Fut. Eff.], 47 § 1002

Employee benefit plan, influencing operations, offenses, application for order, 18 § 2516

Employees and officers of Government, Federal officials, etc., authorization, 18 § 2516

Encryption, decryption by telecommunications carrier, assistance for law enforcement [Fut. Eff.], 47 § 1002

Energy facilities, authorization, 18 § 2516

Enforcement, civil action, by AG, penalties, considerations, definitions, 18 § 2522

INTERCEPTION OF WIRE, ORAL, OR ELECTRONIC COMMUNICATIONS
—Cont'd

Enforcement orders,
  Civil action, by AG, penalties, considerations, definitions, 18 § 2522
  Issuance, compliance, limitations, assistance for law enforcement, 47 § 1007

Enumeration of offenses for which authorization may be granted, 18 § 2516

Equipment manufacturers,
  Cooperation with telecommunications carriers, consultations, etc., assistance for law enforcement, 47 § 1005
  Technical requirements, standards, compliance, deadlines, petitions to FCC, assistance for law enforcement, 47 § 1006

Equitable, declaratory relief, civil actions, 18 § 2520

Escape from custody, authorization, 18 § 2516

Espionage, offenses, application for order, 18 § 2516

Evidence,
  Derived from intercepted communication, authorization for disclosure, 18 § 2517
  Documentary evidence supporting application for order authorizing, 18 § 2518
  Furnishing parties with application and order as prerequisite to receipt, 18 § 2518
  Litigation concerning sources of,
    Congressional Statement of Findings, 18 § 3504 nt
    Evidence, 18 § 3504
  Suppression of contents, motion, 18 § 2518
  Unlawful act, defined, litigation concerning sources of evidence, 18 § 3504

Ex parte order authorizing, 18 § 2518

Exceptions, interceptions, not for commercial gain, etc., provisions, 18 § 2511

Exclusivity of remedies, 18 § 2518

Exigent circumstances, assistance for law enforcement, requirements [Fut. Eff.], 47 § 1002

Explosives, offenses, unlawful use of explosives, authorization for, 18 § 2516

Exports, regulation and control of, reexports, authority for, national security controls, 50 Ap § 2404

Extension of order authorizing, application, 18 § 2518

Extortionate credit transactions, offenses, application for order, 18 § 2516

False identification documentation, authority, 18 § 2516

Federal agency, authorization by Federal judge, 18 § 2516

Federal attorney, authorization, interception by investigative or law enforcement agencies, felonies, 18 § 2516

Federal Bureau of Investigation, authorization by Federal judge, 18 § 2516

Federal Communications Commission,
  Exception, 18 § 2511

Electric and Hybrid Vehicle Research, Development, and Demonstration Act of 1976
Pub.L. 94–413, Sept. 17, 1976, 90 Stat. 1260 (15 §§ 2501 to 2514; 42 §§ 2451, 2473)
Pub.L. 95–238, Title VI, §§ 601 to 603, Feb. 25, 1978, 92 Stat. 91 to 93 (15 §§ 2506, 2507, 2509)
Pub.L. 96–470, Title I, § 105, Oct. 19, 1980, 94 Stat. 2238 (15 § 2506)
Pub.L. 97–375, Title I, § 106(b), Dec. 21, 1982, 96 Stat. 1820 (15 § 2506)
Pub.L. 103–437, § 5(d), Nov. 2, 1994, 108 Stat. 4582 (15 §§ 2506, 2509)
Pub.L. 104–66, Title I, Subtitle E, § 1051(*o*), Dec. 21, 1995, 109 Stat. 717 (15 § 2513)

Electric Consumers Protection Act of 1986 (ECPA)
Pub.L. 99–495, Oct. 16, 1986, 100 Stat. 1243 (16 §§ 791a note, 797, 797 notes, 797b, 800, 802, 803, 803 note, 807, 808, 817, 823a, 823a note, 823b, 824a–3, 824a–3 note, 824j, 825h)

Electric Home and Farm Authority Act
Mar. 31, 1936, ch. 163, 49 Stat. 1186

Electric Utility Companies Act
June 10, 1920, ch. 285, pts. II, III, as added, Aug. 26, 1935, ch. 687, § 213, 49 Stat. 847 (16 §§ 791a, 824 to 825r)

Electronic Communications Privacy Act of 1986
Pub.L. 99–508, Oct. 21, 1986, 100 Stat. 1848 (18 §§ 1367, 2232, 2510, 2510 notes, 2511 to 2521, 2701, 2701 note, 2702 to 2711, 3117, 3121, 3121 note, 3122 to 3127)

Electronic Freedom of Information Act Amendments of 1996
Pub.L. 104–231, Oct. 2, 1996, 110 Stat. 3048 (5 § 552, 552 notes)

Electronic Fund Transfer Act (EFTA)
Pub.L. 95–630, Title XX, Nov. 10, 1978, 92 Stat. 3728 (15 §§ 1601 note, 1693 to 1693r)
Pub.L. 97–375, Title II, § 209(a), Dec. 21, 1982, 96 Stat. 1825 (15 § 1693p)
Pub.L. 101–73, Title VII, § 744(*o*), Aug. 9, 1989, 103 Stat. 440 (15 § 1693*o*)
Pub.L. 102–242, Title II, Subtitle A, § 212(f), Dec. 19, 1991, 105 Stat. 2301 (15 § 1693*o*)
Pub.L. 104–193, Title VIII, Subtitle C, § 891, Title IX, § 907, Aug. 22, 1996, 110 Stat. 2346, 2350 (15 § 1693b)

Elementary and Secondary Education Act of 1965
Pub.L. 89–10, Apr. 11, 1965, 79 Stat. 27 (20 §§ 236 to 244, 331 to 332b, 821 to 827, 841 to 848, 861 to 870, 881 to 885, 2701, 2711, 2712, 2721 to 2731, 2741 to 2749, 2761 to 2765, 2765a, 2765b, 2766, 2767, 2767a, 2768, 2781 to 2783, 2791 to 2796, 2801 to 2804, 2811, 2812, 2821 to 2826, 2831 to 2839, 2851 to 2854, 2861 to 2864, 2881 to 2883, 2891, 2901, 2911, 2912, 2921, 2922, 2931, 2932, 2941 to 2943, 2951, 2952, 2961 to 2966, 2971 to 2976, 2981 to 2992, 2994, 2994a to 2994g, 2996, 3001 to 3006, 3011, 3012, 3021 to 3032, 3041 to 3047, 3061 to 3068, 3081, 3091, 3092, 3101, 3102, 3111, 3112, 3121 to 3130, 3141, 3142, 3151 to 3156, 3156–1, 3156a, 3156b, 3157, 3161, 3161a to 3161g, 3171 to 3173, 3181, 3182, 3191 to 3197, 3201 to 3203, 3211 to 3217, 3221 to 3224, 3224a, 3224b, 3227, 3231 to 3233, 3241 to 3248, 3261 to 3266, 3271, 3272, 3281 to 3283, 3291, 3292, 3301 to 3307, 3321 to 3325, 3331, 3332, 3341, 3381 to 3384, 3386)
Pub.L. 89–750, Title I, §§ 111(f), 121 to 123, 131 to 134, 151 to 154, 161, 171, 181, Nov. 3, 1966, 80 Stat. 1196, 1199 to 1209 (20 §§ 821 to 823, 841 to 844, 861 to 864, 867, 871 to 886)
Pub.L. 90–247, Title I, §§ 101 to 104(a), (b), 105 to 110, 114, 121, 131, 141 to 145(a), (b), 146, 151 to 154, 156, 171, Title II, §§ 201 to 208, 217, 218, Title III, § 301, Title IV, §§ 401 to 405, Title VII, §§ 702, 703, Jan. 2, 1968, 81 Stat. 783 to 820 (20 §§ 237 to 239, 241 note, 241–1, 241a to 241m, 244, 618, 633, 635, 640 note, 644 to 646, 821, 822, 841 to 845, 847 to 848, 861 to 863, 865, 871 to 874, 876, 877a to 880, 880b to 880b–6, 881 to 888, 1221 to 1225)
Pub.L. 90–567, Title III, § 307, Oct. 16, 1968, 82 Stat. 1097 (20 § 241c)
Pub.L. 91–230, Title I, Apr. 13, 1970, 84 Stat. 121 to 154 (20 §§ 241a to 241d–2, 241d–11 to 241m, 331a, 821, 822, 824, 841 to 845, 847, 847a, 861 to 864, 866 to 869b, 880b–1, 880b–3a to 880b–6, 881, 883, 887 to 887b)
Pub.L. 91–260, May 21, 1970, 84 Stat. 254 (20 § 635)
Pub.L. 92–318, Title IV, §§ 411(b)(1), (2), 421(a), (b)(1)(A), (B), Title V, §§ 504(a), 507(a), (b), 508, 509(a), June 23, 1972, 86 Stat. 338 to 341, 346–348, 352 (20 §§ 241c, 241e, 822, 823, 842, 843, 863, 887c, 900 to 900a–5)
Pub.L. 93–380, Title I, Title IV, §§ 401, 402(c)(2)(i), (iii), 407(a), Title VI, §§ 631(a), 632(a), Title VIII, §§ 843(a), 845(a) to (c), Aug. 21, 1974, 88 Stat. 488, 535, 546, 553, 585, 586, 611, 612, (20 §§ 241a note, 241b to 241d, 241d–11, 241e to 241h, 241j to 241*l*, 241n, 241*o*, 821, 822, 841, 842, 844a, 845, 847a, 861, 862, 866, 866a, 867, 880b, 880b–1, 880b–7 to 880b–13, 884, 887, 887a, 887c, 887d, 887e, 900a–1, 900a–5, 1801 to 1806, 1821, 1831, 1832)

1986   **99–509**

	§ 1001(b)(8)	100 Stat 1842	29 § 740	Elim.
	§ 1001(d)(1)	100 Stat 1842	29 § 772	
	§ 1001(c)	100 Stat 1843	29 § 761a	
	§ 1001(d)(2)	100 Stat 1843	29 § 773	
	§ 1001(e)	100 Stat 1843	29 § 780	
	§ 1001(f)(1)	100 Stat 1843	29 § 791	
	§ 1001(f)(2), (3)	100 Stat 1843	29 § 793	
	§ 1001(f)(4)	100 Stat 1843	29 § 794c	
	§ 1001(g)(1)	100 Stat 1843	29 § 796a	Rep.
	§ 1001(g)(2)	100 Stat 1843	29 § 796b	Rep.
	§ 1001(g)(3)	100 Stat 1843	29 § 796d	Rep.
	§ 1001(g)(4)	100 Stat 1843	29 § 796f	Rep.
	§ 1002(a)	100 Stat 1844	29 § 706	
	§ 1002(b)(1)	100 Stat 1844	29 § 750	
	§ 1002(b)(2)(A)	100 Stat 1844	29 § 751	Rep.
	§ 1002(c)	100 Stat 1844	29 § 761a	
	§ 1002(d)(1)	100 Stat 1844	29 § 771	Rep.
	§ 1002(d)(2)	100 Stat 1844	29 § 771a	
	§ 1002(d)(3)	100 Stat 1844	29 § 775	
	§ 1002(d)(4)	100 Stat 1844	29 § 776	
	§ 1002(e)(1), (2)(A)	100 Stat 1844	29 § 791	
	§ 1002(e)(2)(B) to (D)	100 Stat 1844	29 § 792	
	§ 1002(e)(3)	100 Stat 1844	29 § 793	
	§ 1002(e)(4)	100 Stat 1844	29 § 794	
	§ 1002(f)	100 Stat 1844	29 § 795	
	§ 1002(h)	100 Stat 1844	29 § 796a	Rep.
	§ 1003	100 Stat 1845	42 § 2000d–7	
	§ 1005	100 Stat 1845	20 § 1414 nt	Elim.
	§ 1006	100 Stat 1846	29 § 701 nt	
99–507	§ 1	100 Stat 1847	30 § 1401 nt	
	§ 2	100 Stat 1847	30 § 1470	
99–508	§ 1	100 Stat 1848	18 § 2510 nt	
	§ 101(a)	100 Stat 1848	18 § 2510	
	§ 101(b)	100 Stat 1849	18 § 2511	
	§ 101(c)(1)(A)	100 Stat 1851	18 § 2510 to 2513	
	§ 101(c)(1)(A)	100 Stat 1851	18 § 2516 to 2519	
	§ 101(c)(1)(B)	100 Stat 1851	18 § 2511	
	§ 101(c)(2)	100 Stat 1851	18 § prec. 2510	
	§ 101(c)(3)	100 Stat 1851	18 § prec. 1	
	§ 101(c)(4)	100 Stat 1851	18 § 2510	
	§ 101(c)(5)	100 Stat 1851	18 § 2511	
	§ 101(c)(6)	100 Stat 1851	18 § 2511	
	§ 101(c)(7)	100 Stat 1851	18 § 2512	
	§ 101(c)(8)	100 Stat 1852	18 § 2518	
	§ 101(d)	100 Stat 1852	18 § 2511	
	§ 101(e)	100 Stat 1853	18 § 2518	
	§ 101(f)(1)	100 Stat 1853	18 § 2511	
	§ 101(f)(2)	100 Stat 1853	18 § 2512	
	§ 102	100 Stat 1853	18 § 2511	
	§ 103	100 Stat 1854	18 § 2520	
	§ 104	100 Stat 1855	18 § 2516	
	§ 105	100 Stat 1855	18 § 2516	
	§ 106(a) to (d)(3)	100 Stat 1856, 1857	18 § 2518	
	§ 106(d)(4)	100 Stat 1857	18 § 2519	
	§ 107	100 Stat 1858	18 § 2510 nt	
	§ 108(a)	100 Stat 1858	18 § 3117	
	§ 108(b)	100 Stat 1858	18 § prec. 3101	
	§ 109	100 Stat 1858	18 § 2232	
	§ 110(a)	100 Stat 1859	18 § 2521	
	§ 110(b)	100 Stat 1859	18 § prec. 2510	
	§ 111	100 Stat 1859	18 § 2510 nt	
	§ 201(a)	100 Stat 1860 to 1868	18 § prec. 2701	
	§ 201(a)	100 Stat 1860 to 1868	18 § 2701 to 2709	
	§ 201(a)	100 Stat 1868	18 § 2711	
	§ 201(b)	100 Stat 1868	18 § prec. 1	
	§ 202	100 Stat 1868	18 § 2701 nt	
	§ 301(a)	100 Stat 1868 to 1870	18 § prec. 3121	
	§ 301(a)	100 Stat 1868 to 1870	18 § 3121 to 3124	
	§ 301(a)	100 Stat 1868 to 1870	18 § 3126	
	§ 301(a)	100 Stat 1868 to 1870	18 § 3127	
	§ 301(b)	100 Stat 1872	18 § prec. 3001	
	§ 302	100 Stat 1872	18 § 3121 nt	
	§ 303(a)	100 Stat 1872	18 § 1367	
	§ 303(b)	100 Stat 1873	18 § prec. 1361	
99–509	§ 1001	100 Stat 1874	7 § 1929a nt	
	§ 1001(b)	100 Stat 1874	7 § 1929a	
	§ 1002	100 Stat 1875	7 § 1929 nt	
	§ 1011(a)	100 Stat 1875, 1876	7 § 936a, 936b	
	§ 1011(b)	100 Stat 1876	7 § 936 nt	Rep.
	§ 1011(c)	100 Stat 1876	7 § 936a nt	
	§ 1021	100 Stat 1877	7 § 1445j nt	
	§ 1031	100 Stat 1877	12 § 2001 nt	
	§ 1032	100 Stat 1877	12 § 2001	

Print versions usually make a code's organizational structure more apparent and useful. Eventually, hypertext links may make online statutes easier to browse. However, that is not the current state of online texts.

§12.2　Compiling a Legislative History

Legislative histories. The thought of doing one makes the blood pressure of even the most experienced researchers rise. For most interns, being sent to do a legislative history is the most severe of punishments.

Although compiling a legislative history can be time-consuming and frustrating, such histories are often essential. The court needs to know what the legislature intended when it enacted the statute.

§12.2.1　The Legislative Process

a.　*Introduction of a Bill*

The first step in the legislative process is the drafting of a bill. This may be done by a private individual; a special interest group; a legislator; or at the request of a legislator, a legislative staff member, or the code reviser's office.

The second step is the introduction of the bill. Although the drafting of a bill can be done by anyone, bills can only be introduced by a member of the legislative body. At the time the bill is introduced, it is given a number. At the federal level, bills introduced into the House are designated with "H.R." and bills introduced into the Senate are designated "S.": H.R. 21, S. 129. Note that although the number identifies the chamber into which the bill was introduced, it does not identify the Congress.

The third step, assigning the bill to the appropriate standing or ad hoc committee, occurs after a bill has been introduced.

b.　*Consideration by a Committee*

Much of the work on a bill is done at the committee level. Members of the committee's staff may research the bill; the committee may hold hearings; and in some cases, the committee may issue a report in which it (a) discusses the need or lack of need for such legislation, (b) explains the bill and its individual provisions, and (c) recommends passage or nonpassage. Two things can happen as a result of the committee's work. The committee can allow the bill to "die," or the committee can refer it back to the originating house.

c.　*Floor Debates*

When a bill is referred back to the originating house, the presiding officer reads the bill into the record and opens the floor for debate. At the federal level, these debates are published in the *Congressional Record,* which appears in two forms. The daily version is published at the end of each day that Congress is in session, and the multivolume edition is published at the end of the session. The pagination in the two versions is different, and there is no cross-referencing system.

You should realize that the material that appears in the *Congressional Record* may not accurately reflect what was said on the floor. Members of Congress are permitted to edit their remarks and to add additional information or statements. Consequently, the *Congressional Record* is often not given great weight in determining what Congress actually intended in enacting a particular statute.

d.　Consideration by the Other House

If a bill passes one house, it is then referred to the next, where it is "read" for the first time and then referred to committee. The second committee has the same options as the first: the bill may be researched by the committee's staff, hearings may be held, and a report may be issued.

At this point, one of four things can happen: (1) the bill can die in the second committee, (2) the bill can be forwarded to the floor of the second house where, after debate, it fails to pass, (3) the bill passes the second house and is forwarded to the President (or the governor, at the state level) for signature,or (4) the bill is passed in a different form.

In the latter case, the bill is returned to the originating house for consideration. If the originating house passes it in its amended form, the bill is forwarded for signature; if it is not passed, it is sent to a conference committee made up of members from both houses.

e.　Approval or Veto by the President or the Governor

After a bill has been passed by both houses, it is sent to the executive branch: at the federal level to the President or, at the state level, to the governor. The President may (1) sign the bill, in which case the bill becomes law; (2) veto the bill (or parts of it), in which case the bill (or vetoed parts) dies unless the Congress overrides the veto by a two-thirds majority vote; or (3) take no action. If the President takes no action within ten days, the bill becomes law without the President's signature.

There is one exception to the ten-day rule. If Congress adjourns within the ten-day period, the bill dies. This is known as the pocket veto.

The documents produced at any one of these stages can be used in compiling a legislative history. The sponsor's intent can be drawn from the initial language of the bill, the committee's intent from its report, and the house's intent from its debate or from the amendments it rejected or accepted.

§12.2.2　Compiled Legislative Histories

Whenever possible, use a compiled legislative history. Don't do work that others have done for you.

The best source of compiled legislative histories is *Sources of Compiled Legislative Histories* by Nancy Johnson. This looseleaf publication includes, in chart form, a list of all public laws in which a legislative history has been compiled, telling the researcher where the history was published.

Another source is CCH's *Public Laws — Legislative Histories on Microfiche.* This source, which covers laws beginning with the 96th Congress, provides the researcher with the text of the House or Senate bill as introduced; the reported House or Senate bill; committee reports and conference reports, if any; and relevant legislative debate as reported in the *Congressional Record.*

§12.2.3　Sources for Federal Legislative Histories

At the federal level, the most comprehensive source is the Congressional Information Service (CIS). The bound volumes contain references to congressional documents; the documents themselves are available on microfiche. Unfortunately, CIS includes only documents published since 1970.

Another source is *United States Code Congressional and Administrative News* (USCCAN). Begun in 1941, it provides a history of bills, providing references to committee reports and to the dates a particular bill was considered in Congress. In addition, it selectively publishes some committee reports.

A very few legislative histories are available online. In addition, services like LEXIS and Westlaw contain documents such as reports, hearings, and the *Congressional Record* for recent sessions of Congress. Some of these documents are also available on the Internet.

Partial legislative histories and references to legislative documents can sometimes be found in cases and law review articles. If so, you may be able to use these resources for determining what legislative documents contain the most relevant information.

For additional sources and legislative history before 1941, consult your law librarian.

§12.2.4　Sources for State Legislative Histories

Compiling a legislative history for a state statute is even more difficult than compiling one for a federal statute. Traditionally, many states had few or no published legislative histories, and what was available was often stored in the state archives, accessible only to the state archivists.

Increasingly, state government information is being made available on the Internet. Unfortunately, the information is sometimes removed after the legislative session ends.

Consequently, if you need to do a legislative history for a state statute, start with your law librarian. A law librarian can tell you what sources are available and how they can be accessed.

Chapter 13

The Executive Branch and Administrative Agencies

Article II of the United States Constitution grants the President all executive powers including the power to execute, or enforce, all laws. Although the Constitution grants the President only the power to execute laws, in practice the President also creates law. The President issues executive orders and proclamations. In addition, administrative agencies, which act under the power granted to them by the executive and legislative branches, routinely promulgate regulations, which are similar in form and content to statutes.

§13.1 · PRESIDENTIAL DOCUMENTS

Presidents issue a variety of documents. Some, like speeches and formal statements, are not law. At best, they are persuasive authority, indicating general policy or the executive branch's opinion about how a particular statute should be interpreted. Others, like executive orders and proclamations, have the effect of law and, as such, are primary authority.

The best source of presidential documents is the *Weekly Compilation of Presidential Documents,* published by the United States Government Printing Office. Published weekly as the name suggests, it includes the text of all presidential documents issued during the prior week.

Executive orders and proclamations are also published in the *Federal Register* and, subsequently, under Title 3 in the *Code of Federal Regulations.* Title 3 is not, however, cumulative. Unlike other titles, which include the text of all regulations currently in effect, Title 3 contains only the executive orders and proclamations issued during the previous year.

A particular presidential document can be located using one of sev-

413

eral sources: (1) the *CIS Index to Presidential Executive Orders and Proclamations;* (2) *Codification of Presidential Proclamations and Executive Orders,* which is published by the Office of the Federal Register; (3) a carefully worded search on either LEXIS or Westlaw; or (4) the Internet (the President's website, for example, is at: ⟨www.whitehouse.gov⟩).

§13.2   ADMINISTRATIVE AGENCIES

The *Federal Register* and *Code of Federal Regulations* are also the published sources for administrative regulations. Although not mentioned in the Constitution, administrative agencies have become an integral part of our governing system.

§13.2.1   Delegation of Power

Over the course of history, the laws of Congress have grown to encompass more and more areas. Fields such as telecommunications, environmental protection, and nuclear regulation did not even exist when the first Congress began enacting legislation. Other areas, such as taxation, have grown increasingly more complex. As this context developed, it became apparent that Congress alone could not effectively regulate all the areas that needed federal oversight. Congressional response was to delegate some of its authority to agencies whose charge was to create and administer laws covering distinct subject matters. Employees of these administrative agencies were chosen because of their familiarity and expertise with the area of law.

There are now hundreds of administrative agencies within the federal government. They are not limited to the legislative branch. Both the executive branch and, to a lesser extent, the judicial branch have created administrative agencies as well. State governments also delegate power to their own administrative agencies.

When power is delegated to an administrative agency, the agency not only enacts laws (called "regulations" or "rules"), but also enforces them (like the executive branch) and adjudicates controversies relating to the subject matter (like the judicial branch). Thus, there may be different kinds of laws issuing from an administrative agency.

One limitation on this type of law is that an administrative agency may only act to the extent of the power delegated to it. For this reason, agency regulations are often challenged for exceeding the scope of delegation. If you want to determine the scope of delegation for a particular agency, remember that the scope of delegation must be found in the laws of the delegating authority. For example, if an agency's power was delegated by Congress, look in the laws of Congress (the United States Code) for the scope of the delegation. Do not look in the regulations of the agency itself (although sometimes those do give a reference to the authority for an action).

Because administrative agencies occupy so much of today's legal landscape, it is critical that you understand how to find their regulations and decisions, which is the topic in the following sections.

§13.2.2　Federal Regulations

When acting pursuant to the power granted them by the legislative or executive branch, administrative agencies have the power to promulgate regulations that, when specified procedures have been followed, have the effect of law and are, therefore, primary authority.

For most agencies, the procedures for promulgating regulations are set out in the Administrative Procedure Act. This Act, which is codified at 5 U.S.C. §551 *et seq.,* requires (1) that notice of a proposed rule be published in the *Federal Register,* (2) that there be time for comment and hearings, and (3) that the enacted version of the regulation be published initially in the *Federal Register* and permanently in the *Code of Federal Regulations.*

§13.2.3　The Federal Register

The *Federal Register,* which is published every working day, contains both notices of proposed rules and the text of those that have been enacted. As in the *Statutes at Large,* the material is organized chronologically. See Exhibit 13.1.

Copies of the *Federal Register* are available at Government Depository Libraries, at many law libraries, and online on LEXIS, Westlaw, CD-ROM products, and the Internet. Although the Government Printing Office publishes an index to the *Federal Register,* many researchers prefer the more detailed *CIS Federal Register Index,* which is published by Congressional Information Service.

§13.2.4　The Code of Federal Regulations

Permanent regulations are published in the *Code of Federal Regulations* (C.F.R.), which is published by the United States Government Printing Office. Like the *United States Code,* it is organized by topic, each regulation being codified under one of fifty titles.

	Statutes	*Regulations*
Organized Chronologically	*Statutes at Large*	*Federal Register*
Organized Topically	*United States Code*	*Code of Federal Regulations*

There is not an annotated version of the *Code of Federal Regulations.* To find a case interpreting or applying a particular regulation, use

EXHIBIT 13.1 | **Sample Page from the *Federal Register***

Federal Register / Vol. 62, No. 90 / Friday, May 9, 1997 / Rules and Regulations **25469**

Number (ECCN) and the item description, in the designated spaces of a SED covering an export under a license issued by BXA (the space for the item description on the SED form may be headed "commodity description"). If you intend to include other items on the SED that may be exported under a License Exception, or under the "No License Required" (NLR) provisions of the EAR (as described in § 758.1(a) of this part) you must show the License Exception or NLR symbol, along with the specific description (quantity, Schedule B number or "other number acceptable to the Foreign Trade Division, Bureau of the Census", value) of the item(s) to which the authorization applies in the designated spaces on the SED continuation sheet.

*   *   *   *   *

(m) * * *
(3) * * *
(ii) * * *
(C) For intransit shipments of items of U.S.-origin eligible for the *intransit* provisions of License Exception TMP (see § 740.9(b) of the EAR), enter the following statement:

*   *   *   *   *

(iii) The items must be described in terms of Schedule B, including the appropriate Schedule B number or "other number acceptable to the Foreign Trade Division, Bureau of the Census".

*   *   *   *   *

(o) * * *
(2) *Applicability.* Approved parties may file monthly SEDs with the Bureau of the Census for export to destinations in Country Groups B and D (see Supplement No. 1 to part 740 of the EAR).

*   *   *   *   *

86. Section 758.7(b)(6) is amended by revising the phrase "both customs officials" to read "both Customs officials" in the third sentence.

PART 762—[AMENDED]

87. Section 762.3(a)(7) is amended by revising the phrase "Parking material" to read "Packing material".

PART 764—[AMENDED]

88. Section 764.2 is amended by revising paragraph (f) to read as follows:

§ 764.2 Violations.

*   *   *   *   *

(f) *Possession with intent to export illegally.* No person may possess any item controlled for national security or foreign policy reasons under sections 5 or 6 of the EAA:
(1) With intent to export or reexport such item in violation of the EAA, the

EAR, or any order, license or authorization issued thereunder; or
(2) With knowledge or reason to believe that the item would be so exported or reexported.

*   *   *   *   *

90. Section 764.3 is amended:
a. By revising paragraph (b)(1);
b. By revising paragraph (b)(2)(i);
c. By revising paragraph (b)(2)(ii); and
d. By revising paragraph (b)(2)(iii), as follows:

§ 764.3 Sanctions.

*   *   *   *   *

(b) * * *
(1) *General.* Except as provided in paragraph (b)(2) of this section, whoever knowingly violates or conspires to or attempts to violate the EAA, EAR, or any order or license issued thereunder, shall be fined not more than five times the value of the exports or reexports involved or $50,000, whichever is greater, or imprisoned not more than five years, or both.
(2) *Willful violations.* (i) Whoever willfully violates or conspires to or attempts to violate any provision of the EAA, the EAR, or any order or license issued thereunder, with knowledge that the exports involved will be used for the benefit of, or that the destination or intended destination of items involved is, any controlled country or any country to which exports or reexports are controlled for foreign policy purposes, except in the case of an individual, shall be fined not more than five times the value of the export or reexport involved or $1,000,000, whichever is greater; and, in the case of an individual, shall be fined not more than $250,000, or imprisoned not more than 10 years, or both.
(ii) Any person who is issued a license under the EAA or the EAR for the export or reexport of any items to a controlled country and who, with knowledge that such export or reexport is being used by such controlled country for military or intelligence gathering purposes contrary to the conditions under which the license was issued, willfully fails to report such use to the Secretary of Defense, except in the case of an individual, shall be fined not more than five times the value of the exports or reexports involved or $1,000,000, whichever is greater; and in the case of an individual, shall be fined not more than $250,000, or imprisoned not more than five years or both.
(iii) Any person who possesses any item with the intent to export or reexport such item in violation of an export control imposed under sections 5 or 6 of the EAA, the EAR, or any order or license issued thereunder, or

knowing or having reason to believe that the item would be so exported or reexported, shall, in the case of a violation of an export control imposed under section 5 of the EAA (or the EAR, or any order or license issued thereunder with respect to such control), be subject to the penalties set forth in paragraph (b)(2)(i) of this section and shall in the case of a violation of an export control imposed under section 6 of the EAA (or the EAR, or any order or license issued thereunder with respect to such control), be subject to the penalties set forth in paragraph (b)(1) of this section.

*   *   *   *   *

91. Section 764.5 is amended:
a. By revising paragraph (c)(4)(ii);
b. By amending paragraph (c)(7), as follows:
i. By revising the phrase "Facsimile: (617) 835–6039" to read "Facsimile: (617) 565–6039" under the paragraph for "Boston Field Office";
ii. By revising the phrase "Facsimile: (214) 729–9299" to read "Facsimile: (214) 767–9299" under the paragraph for "Dallas Field Office";
iii. By revising the phrase "Facsimile: (714) 791–9103" to read "Facsimile: (714) 251–9103" under the paragraph for "Los Angeles Field Office"; and
iv. By revising the phrase "Facsimile: (718) 370–8226" to read "Facsimile: (718) 370–0826" under the paragraph for "New York Field Office".

§ 764.5 Voluntary self-disclosure.

*   *   *   *   *

(c) * * *
(4) * * *
(ii) Any relevant documents not attached to the narrative account must be retained by the person making the disclosure until OEE requests them, or until a final decision on the disclosed information has been made. After a final decision, the documents should be maintained in accordance with the recordkeeping rules in part 762 of the EAR.

*   *   *   *   *

PART 768—[AMENDED]

92. Section 768.1(d) is amended by revising the phrase "Kyrgystan" to read "Kyrgyzstan" under the definition for "Controlled countries".

PART 770—[AMENDED]

93. Section 770.2 is amended:
a. By revising the phrase "their original identify" to read "their original identity" in paragraph (g)(3);
b. By revising the phrase "Slovak Republic" to read "Slovakia" in the introductory text of paragraph (k); and

Shepard's Citator to the Code of Federal Regulations or LEXIS or Westlaw.

a.   Search Tools

Regulations can be found using either of two methods. When the question is whether there is a regulation implementing a particular federal statute, the best source is the *Index and Finding Aids to the Code of Federal Regulations* volume of the *United States Code Service* (U.S.C.S.). See Exhibit 13.2. By using the tables in this volume, you can move from the *United States Code* section to the C.F.R. section or from the C.F.R. section to the *United States Code* section.

Regulations can also be found using either the C.F.R. subject index, which is published annually by the United States Government Printing Office, or one of the more detailed indices published by Congressional Information Service.

b.   Updating the C.F.R.

Because regulations are promulgated almost daily, updating the C.F.R. is a complicated and sometimes tiresome process.

Instead of publishing a new set once a year, the Government Printing Office updates the C.F.R. in stages, revising one-quarter of the volumes every three months. Thus, although each volume is revised once a year, at any given time some volumes will be three months old, others six months old, and still others nine or twelve months old. Because of this, the updating process begins with the date on the front of the C.F.R. volume. Once you know that date, you know how much updating is necessary.

To determine whether new regulations have been proposed or promulgated since the date the C.F.R. volume was revised, use the *List of Sections Affected* volumes, which are published monthly and which are usually shelved at the end of the C.F.R. See Exhibit 13.3. If a new regulation has been proposed or promulgated, there will be a page reference to the *Federal Register.*

Depending on when the C.F.R. volume was revised, it may be necessary to consult more than one *List of Sections Affected* volume. It will also be necessary to consult the "C.F.R. Parts Affected During the Month" table that is published at the back of each *Federal Register* issue. You will need to look at the most recent issue of the *Federal Register* to update through the current month. It may also be necessary to use the last issue of the preceding month to update for that month.

The C.F.R. can also be updated using LEXIS and Westlaw. Once a regulation is on the screen, you can update it using a single update command.

TABLE I—AUTHORITIES

USCS	CFR	USCS	CFR
18 USCS—Cont'd		18 USCS—Cont'd	
201 note	20 Part 360	847	27 Parts 55, 178
202	14 Part 300	921—928	27 Part 178
	29 Part 100	921	27 Part 72
203	7 Part 1	926	27 Part 200
	28 Part 45	951	28 Part 73
	31 Part 8	981	39 Part 233
205	7 Part 1	1001	7 Part 1443
	14 Part 300		32 Part 525
	28 Part 45	1001ff	38 Part 21
	31 Part 8	1114	28 Part 64
207	5 Parts 1304, 2641	1116	22 Part 2
	7 Parts 0, 1	1261	27 Part 72
	11 Part 7	1324A	28 Part 0
	12 Parts 400,	1382	32 Parts 527, 552, 770
	932, 933, 2434, 2637	1512	28 Part 551
	14 Parts 300, 1207	1693—1699	39 Parts 310, 320
	15 Part 0	1752	31 Part 408
	16 Part 1030	1791—1792	28 Part 511
	17 Part 140	1791	28 Parts 6, 540
	19 Part 200	1793	28 Part 511
	22 Parts 18, 223, 525, 710	1851—1861	43 Part 9260
	24 Part 0	1851—1858	43 Part 9230
	28 Part 45	1905	21 Part 20
	29 Parts 0, 2604		45 Part 5
	31 Part 15	1956—1957	39 Part 233
	32 Part !690	2071	49 Part 801
	36 Part 905	2152	32 Part 761
	39 Parts 10, 447, 956	2254	39 Part 233
	41 Part 105-735	2257	28 Part 75
	45 Parts 73b, 500	2341—2346	27 Part 296
	46 Parts 500, 502	2386	28 Part 10
	49 Parts 98, 1000	2510 et seq.	15 Parts 768,
208—209	28 Part 45		770-779, 785, 786, 789-791,
208	12 Part 264a		799
	15 Part 0	3001 note	28 Part 42
	16 Part 5	3013	28 Part 545
	18 Part 1301	3050	28 Part 511
	22 Part 606	3056	31 Part 409
	31 Part 0	3059	28 Part 7
	34 Part 73	3061	39 Parts 232, 233
	46 Part 500	3401—3402	32 Part 1290
210—212	24 Part 0	3401	28 Part 52
437	25 Part 140		32 Part 516
474	31 Parts 402, 405	3481 et seq	28 Part 524
492	31 Parts 101, 402, 403	3496	22 Part 92
513	32 Part 516	3500	32 Part 518
515	32 Part 516	3521—3528	28 Part 524
543	32 Part 516	3521	28 Part 0
545	19 Parts 11, 145, 161	3551—3586	36 Part 242
546	19 Part 162		50 Part 100
550	19 Part 191	3559	10 Part 860
641	43 Part 8200	3565	28 Parts 527, 571
	49 Part 801	3568—3569	28 Part 571
701	32 Part 507	3568	28 Part 523
	50 Part 80	3569	28 Part 527
702	32 Part 507	3571	10 Parts 860, 1048
707	7 Part 8		28 Part 545
711	36 Part 271	3621—3622	28 Parts 500,
751—752	28 Part 511		511, 513, 522, 523, 540, 541-545,
751	28 Part 570		549, 550, 551, 552, 570, 571
798	32 Parts 322, 518	3624	28 Parts 500,
799	14 Parts 1203a, 1214		511, 513, 522, 523, 540, 541-545,
831—835	49 Parts 392, 396, 398		549, 550, 551, 552, 570, 571
831—833	49 Part 397	3663	28 Part 545
834	49 Part 178	4001—4002	28 Part 26
835	49 Part 397	4001	28 Parts 500,
841 et seq	27 Part 55		501, 503, 504, 511, 512, 522-524,

EXHIBIT 13.3   Sample Page from C.F.R. *List of Sections Affected*

---

44   LSA—LIST OF CFR SECTIONS AFFECTED

CHANGES JANUARY 2, 1997 THROUGH MAY 30, 1997

TITLE 15 Chapter VII—Con.

762.3 (a)(7) amended 25469
764.2 (f) revised 25469
764.3 (b)(1), (2)(i), (ii) and (iii) revised 25469
764.5 (c)(4)(ii) revised; (c)(7) amended 25469
768.1 (d) amended 25469
770.2 (k) amended 6686
   (g)(3) and (k) introductory text amended 25469
   (k)(26) amended 25470
770.3 (c)(1) and (2) amended; (d)(1)(i)(B), (ii) and (2)(ii) revised 25470
772 Amended 6686, 25470
774 Supplement No. 1, Category 1 amended (ECCN 1C350)..............6686
   Supplement No. 1, Category 1 amended (ECCN 1C995)..............6688

Chapter VIII—Bureau of Economic Analysis, Department of Commerce (Parts 800—899)

801.10 Revised 1667

Chapter IX—National Oceanic and Atmospheric Administration, Department of Commerce (Parts 900—999)

902.1 (b) table amended (OMB numbers) 1831, 13299, 13986, 27182
   (b) table amended (OMB numbers); interim..................15385, 19043
921.1 (f) amended.............................12540
921.20 Amended 12540
921.31 Amended 12540
921.32 (c) amended...........................12541
921.50 (b) amended 12541
921.60 (b) amended 12541
921.70 (b) amended 12541
922 Nomenclature change 3789
922.1 Revised (effective date pending) 4607, 14815
922.3 Amended (effective date pending)......................................4607
922.40 Revised (effective date pending) 4607, 14815
922.41 Revised (effective date pending) 4607, 14815
922.42 Revised (effective date pending) 4607, 14815
922.43 Revised (effective date pending) 4607, 14815
922.44 Revised (effective date pending) 4607, 14815

922.45 (a) revised (effective date pending)....................................4607
922.47 (b) revised (effective date pending)....................................4607
922.48 (a) and (b) revised (effective date pending).....................4607
922.49 Revised (effective date pending)....................................4608
922.50 (a)(1) introductory text and (iii) amended (effective date pending)...........................4608
922.160—922.167 (Subpart P) Added (effective date pending) 4608
922.180—922.187 (Subpart Q) Added (effective date pending)......................................14815
923 Authority citation revised........12541
923.121 (a) amended; (g) revised
  12541
923.122 (b)(9) added 12541
929 Removed....................................4622
930 Authority citation revised........12541
930.130 (b) removed; (c) and (d) redesignated as (b) and (c)........12541
937 Removed....................................4622
950 Appendix A added 24813

Proposed Rules:

3...27556
304..14049
403..14050

TITLE 16—COMMERCIAL PRACTICES

Chapter I—Federal Trade Commission (Parts 0—999)

23.7 Revised 16675
303.7 (v) added...............................28344
305.9 (a) revised 5318
305 Appendix F revised 26384
423.2 (b) revised; interim 5731
   (b) revised...................................29008
423.8 (g) added; interim 5731
   (g) revised...................................29008

Chapter II—Consumer Product Safety Commission (Parts 1000—1799)

1507.3 Regulation at 61 FR 67200 eff. 2–3–97 4910
1700.14 (a)(26) added 28801

§13.3   STATE REGULATIONS

Like their federal counterparts, many state agencies promulgate regulations. As in the federal system, these regulations are usually published first in the state register and then in the state administrative code. The name of each state's register and administrative code is set out in the Tables section of the *Bluebook.*

§13.4   ADMINISTRATIVE DECISIONS

In addition to their legislative role, many state and federal administrative agencies serve a judicial function, deciding disputes that arise under the statutes that they are responsible for implementing or the regulations that they have themselves promulgated.

Although copies of these decisions are on file in the agency, the agency offices are usually not the best source for these decisions. For the federal agencies, better sources are decisions disseminated by the Government Printing Office, looseleaf services published by commercial publishing companies (see section 15.2.2), and LEXIS, Westlaw, CD-ROM products, and at an agency's website on the Internet.

A list of federal administrative agencies and where their decisions are available can be found in the appendix of West's hornbook, *How to Find the Law.*

Chapter 14

The Judicial Branch

Article III of the United States Constitution created the Supreme Court and gave Congress the power to create such inferior courts as it might "from time to time ordain and establish," giving those courts the power to hear all cases arising under the Constitution and the laws of the United States and between citizens of different states. Similarly, through its constitution each state created its own judiciary, giving its highest court and inferior courts the power to hear cases arising within the state's jurisdiction.

The reason that court decisions are particularly important in our legal system is the doctrine of "*stare decisis*." That Latin maxim means to abide by decided cases. Under the doctrine of *stare decisis,* courts must interpret the law in accordance with the holdings of previously decided cases by higher courts. Thus, if a state's highest court holds that a particular motor vehicle statute applies to snowmobiles, all the trial courts and intermediate appellate courts of that state are bound by that determination.

Because appellate court cases are mandatory authority, attorneys usually must look at case law for precise interpretations of the law. Like constitutions, statutes, and administrative regulations, cases are primary authority. Each time a court decides a case, it creates law.

§14.1　Court Decisions

Just as statutes and regulations are published at different times in different forms, so are cases. Cases are initially published as slip opinions. Reported cases are then collected and published in advance sheets and then in bound reporters.

§14.1.1　Slip Opinions

A "slip opinion" is the opinion in the form in which it is released by the court. Each opinion is issued individually and, as a general rule, the opinions are typed rather than printed. Because the opinions have not yet been "processed," there is no syllabus, no headnotes, and no citation.

Although the slip opinions of the United States Supreme Court are widely distributed, the slip opinions of the other federal and most state courts are not. As a general rule, slip opinions are sent only to the parties, to the reporter, to other courts and, when special arrangements have been made, to local or law school libraries. However, many slip opinions are posted at various sites on the Internet.

§14.1.2   Advance Sheets

Bimonthly or monthly, the slip opinions for reported cases are collected and published in softbound pamphlets known as "advance sheets." These advance sheets are part of a particular reporter: Opinions from the federal district courts are published in the advance sheets for the *Federal Supplement*, opinions from the Virginia Supreme Court in the *South Eastern Reporter*.

Unlike slip opinions, the opinions that appear in the advance sheets have been processed. A citation has been assigned, and a syllabus and headnotes have often been added.

Most advance sheets are widely distributed. In law firms, advance sheets are circulated among the attorneys, each attorney reading those cases that relate to his or her area of practice; in law libraries, they are filed at the end of the bound reporters.

§14.1.3   Bound Reporters

When a sufficient number of decisions have been issued, the advance sheets are replaced by a bound volume, which then becomes a permanent part of that reporter.

Although the bulk of each volume is taken up by opinions, other information is included. In a typical reporter, you will find the following information:

1. a list of the courts whose opinions appear in that reporter;
2. a list of the judges or justices sitting at the time the opinions were issued;
3. a table listing, in alphabetical order, the cases appearing in that volume;
4. in many state reporters, the names of the attorneys just admitted to the bar;
5. amendments to existing court rules or new or proposed court rules; and
6. a subject index for the cases in that volume.

§14.1.4 The National Reporter System

In most law libraries, reporters fill row after row in stack after stack. There are reporters for federal cases, reporters for state cases, regional reporters, and specialized reporters. A particular opinion may appear in only one of these reporters or in several different ones.

Although some reporters are published by the courts themselves, most are published by West Publishing Company. Its network of reporters, which is known as the National Reporter System, includes the following.

Regional Reporters:

Atlantic Reporter (begun in 1886)
    Connecticut
    Delaware
    District of Columbia
    Maine
    Maryland
    New Hampshire
    New Jersey
    Pennsylvania
    Rhode Island
    Vermont

California Reporter (begun in 1960)

New York Supplement (begun in 1888)

North Eastern Reporter (begun in 1885)
    Illinois
    Indiana
    Massachusetts
    New York (only Court of Appeals after 1888)
    Ohio

North Western Reporter (begun in 1885)
    Iowa
    Michigan
    Minnesota
    Nebraska
    North Dakota
    South Dakota
    Wisconsin

Pacific Reporter (begun in 1884)
    Alaska
    Arizona
    California (after 1960, Supreme Court only)
    Colorado
    Hawaii

Idaho
Kansas
Montana
Nevada
New Mexico
Oklahoma
Oregon
Utah
Washington
Wyoming

South Eastern Reporter (begun in 1887)
Georgia
North Carolina
South Carolina
Virginia
West Virginia

South Western Reporter (begun in 1887)
Arkansas
Kentucky
Missouri
Tennessee
Texas

Southern Reporter (begun in 1887)
Alabama
Florida
Louisiana
Mississippi

Federal Reporters:

Supreme Court Reporter (S. Ct.): decisions of the United States
Supreme Court

Federal Reporter, Federal Reporter, Second Series, and *Federal Reporter, Third Series* (F., F.2d, and F.3d): decisions of the United States Court of Appeals

Federal Supplement (F. Supp.): decisions of the United States District Court

Bankruptcy Reporter (begun in 1980): decisions of the United States Bankruptcy Courts and other decisions involving bankruptcy issues

Claims Reporter (begun in 1992): decisions of the Court of Federal Claims (formerly Claims Court and Court of Claims)

Federal Rules Decisions (begun in 1940): decisions from the United States district courts on issues related to the federal rules of criminal and civil procedure

West Key Number System

Each of these reporters uses the West Key Number System, a system that allows West to categorize each rule of law set out in a case.

The system works as follows. When West receives a case, the case is assigned to an editor. The editor identifies each rule of law set out in the court opinion and then categorizes each rule, assigning both a topic and, within that topic, a key number. This information is then used in two ways: (1) the rules, with their topic and key numbers, become the headnotes that appear at the beginning of each West opinion and (2) the headnotes are collected and printed in digests, the subject indices for cases. Exhibit 14.1 illustrates West Key Numbers as they appear at the beginning of a case; Exhibit 14.2 illustrates West Key Numbers as they appear in a digest.

For example, the West editor who was assigned the case of *Williams v. Poulos* identified the first rule of law in that case as

"Trial court's findings of fact will not be set aside unless they are demonstrated to be clearly erroneous; where there are two permissible views of evidence, interpretation assigned by trial court must be adopted."

The editor then determined that the rule of law should be assigned the topic "Federal Courts" in the key number system. Within the "Federal Courts" topic, the editor assigned the key numbers 850 and 851. By looking in a West digest, you would find that these fit within the outline classification as follows:

Topic: Federal Courts
   VIII. Courts of appeals (key numbers 521-970)
     (K) Scope, Standards, and Extent (key numbers 751-920)
       5. Questions of Fact, Verdicts and Findings (key numbers 841-890)
         850. Clearly erroneous findings or court of jury in general.
         851. Conflicting evidence; undisputed evidence.

By using the West Key Number System, a researcher can quickly locate that portion of the opinion in which the court sets out a particular rule and, having identified the relevant topic and key number, can use a digest to locate other cases in which the court has applied or discussed the same rule of law. Given the usefulness of West's Key Number System, it is not surprising that many researchers still follow Horace Greeley's advice and "go West." A list of the topics that West uses appears at the front of most West digest volumes.

§14.1.5 Other Reporters

Two annotated reporters, the *Supreme Court Reporter, Lawyer's Edition* and *American Law Reports,* provide an alternative to the West National Reporter System. The *Supreme Court Reporter, Lawyer's Edition* (L. Ed. or L. Ed. 2d) contains the text of all United States Supreme Court decisions plus, at the end of the volume, annotations discussing issues raised in selected opinions appearing in that volume. *American*

EXHIBIT 14.1   **Key Numbers in a Case***

WILLIAMS v. POULOS   **271**
Cite as 11 F.3d 271 (1st Cir. 1993)

construction. In such a case the statute declares itself. *Vezina v. Bodreau*, 86 R.I. 87, 133 A.2d 753; *Long v. Langlois*, 93 R.I. 23, 170 A.2d 618. We may not where no ambiguity exists search beyond the statute for a different meaning. *Hathaway v. Hathaway*, 52 R.I. 39, 156 A. 800. Even hardship does not justify a court in reading into a statute something contrary to its unequivocal language. *Clark v. Orabona*, 1st Cir., 59 F.2d 187. Only when the legislature sounds an uncertain trumpet may the court move in to clarify the call. But when the call is clear and certain as it is here we may not consider whether the statute as written comports with our ideas of justice, expediency or sound public policy. In such circumstances that is not the court's business. *Blais v. Franklin*, 31 R.I. 95, 77 A. 172.

Kastal v. Hickory House, Inc., 95 R.I. 366, 187 A.2d 262, 264–65 (R.I.1963).

Out of an abundance of caution we have examined similar statutes in other jurisdictions because we think the Rhode Island Supreme Court might possibly have done so. Of the more than thirty states surveyed, many have prejudgment interest statutes accompanied by rejected-settlement-offer provisions, or separate statutes that are invoked in tandem to expedite claims settlement. *See, e.g.,* Cal.Civ.Code § 3291 (West Supp. 1993); Conn.Gen.Stat. § 52–192a(b); Minn. Stat.Ann. § 549.09, subd. 1(b) (West Supp. 1993); Mo.Ann.Stat. § 408.040.2 (Vernon 1990); Ohio Rev.Code Ann. § 1343.03(C) (Anderson Supp.1993). Our survey has not disclosed a single instance where prejudgment interest has been held not to apply to a rejected-settlement-offer statute. Given the rejected-settlement-offer statute's plain language and the Rhode Island courts' long history of applying the prejudgment interest statute in tort cases, we think the Rhode Island Supreme Court would apply its prejudgment interest statute to the rejected-settlement-offer statute.

Affirmed. Costs on appeal awarded to appellee.

George C. WILLIAMS, et al.,
Plaintiffs, Appellants,

v.

Richard E. POULOS, et al.,
Defendants, Appellees.

George C. WILLIAMS, et al.,
Plaintiffs, Appellees,

v.

Richard E. POULOS, et al.,
Defendants, Appellees,

Ralph A. Dyer, Intervenor, Appellant.

George C. WILLIAMS, et al.,
Plaintiffs, Appellees,

v.

Richard E. POULOS, et al.,
Defendants, Appellees,

Rodney P. Rodrigue, Defendants,
Appellants.

George C. WILLIAMS, et al.,
Plaintiffs, Appellees,

v.

Richard E. POULOS, et al.,
Defendants, Appellants.

Nos. 93–1366 – 93–1368, 93–1680.

United States Court of Appeals,
First Circuit.

Heard Aug. 4, 1993.

Decided Dec. 14, 1993.

RICO defendants brought action against plaintiffs alleging violations of federal and state wiretapping laws. The United States District Court for the District of Maine, Morton A. Brody, J., 801 F.Supp. 867, granted injunctive relief, and cross appeals were taken. The Court of Appeals, Stahl, Circuit Judge, held that: (1) neither "business exten-

EXHIBIT 14.1 *(continued)*

sion" nor "consent" exceptions to federal wiretap law were applicable; (2) exclusion of expert testimony was not abuse of discretion; (3) evidence supported finding that plaintiffs' counsel violated wiretap statutes; (4) scope of injunction was not abuse of discretion; and (5) defendants' claim for statutory damages was waived.

Affirmed.

1. Federal Courts ⟅850, 851

Trial court's findings of fact will not be set aside unless they are demonstrated to be clearly erroneous; where there are two permissible views of evidence, interpretation assigned by trial court must be adopted. Fed. Rules Civ.Proc.Rule 52(a), 28 U.S.C.A.

2. Federal Courts ⟅754

Although clearly erroneous standard applies to review of trial court's resolution of mixed questions of law and fact, standard does not apply if trial court based its findings upon mistaken impression of applicable legal principles. Fed.Rules Civ.Proc.Rule 52(a), 28 U.S.C.A.

3. Federal Courts ⟅814

Nature and extent of injunctive relief are reviewed only for abuse of discretion; nonetheless, appellate court will reverse if trial court committed clear error of law.

4. Telecommunications ⟅495

Employer's interceptions of employee telephone calls did not come within business extension exception to federal wiretapping law; custom-made monitoring device was not "telephone or telegraph instrument, equipment or facility, or * * * component thereof," within meaning of exception. 18 U.S.C.A. §§ 2510(4, 5), 2511(1)(a).

5. Federal Courts ⟅921

Although it is ordinarily not province of appellate court to make findings of fact or to resolve, in first instance, mixed questions of law and fact, when only one resolution of predominantly fact bound question would, on full record, be sustainable, Court of Appeals can, and often should, decline to remand where there has been legal error committed.

6. Telecommunications ⟅495

Employer's interception of employee telephone calls did not come within consent exception to federal and Maine wiretapping laws; although intercepted corporate officer was told that employee calls would be monitored, officer was not told of manner in which monitoring was conducted or that he himself would be monitored. 18 U.S.C.A. § 2511(1)(a), (2)(d); 15 M.R.S.A. §§ 709, subd. 4, par. C, 710, subd. 1.

7. Evidence ⟅546

Exclusion of wiretapping defendants' expert witness was not abuse of discretion; court had excluded experts for both sides, based on its determination that it could understand evidence and determine facts in issue without assistance of experts. Fed. Rules Evid.Rule 702, 28 U.S.C.A.

8. Federal Courts ⟅13

Claims against wiretapping defendants' counsel were not rendered moot by plaintiffs dropping of claims for monetary damages; though injunctive relief still sought against defendants would have been binding on counsel without their being named defendants, plaintiffs also sought declaration that counsel themselves had violated wiretapping laws irrespective of their relationship with defendants, and were seeking to recover attorney fees.

9. Telecommunications ⟅498

In civil action for violation of federal wiretapping law, plaintiff must demonstrate that information used or disclosed came from intercepted communication, and sufficient facts concerning circumstances of interception such that defendant could, with presumed knowledge of law, determine that interception was prohibited in light of law; this demonstration includes showing that any statutory exceptions asserted by defendant do not, in fact, apply. 18 U.S.C.A. § 2511(1)(a).

10. Attorney and Client ⟅26

Evidence supported finding that counsel knew or had reason to know that client's interceptions of employee telephone calls violated federal wiretapping statute, thereby rendering counsel liable for disclosure and

EXHIBIT 14.1 *(continued)*

WILLIAMS v. POULOS

Cite as 11 F.3d 271 (1st Cir. 1993)

273

use of contents of intercepted communications; good faith defense did not apply where any belief on counsel's part that statutory exceptions applied was premised only upon mistakes of law. 18 U.S.C.A. §§ 2511(1)(a), 2520(d).

11. Federal Courts ⬤714

Perfunctory argument in appellate brief will not be addressed.

12. Injunction ⬤138.78

Preliminary injunction against plaintiffs' further use or disclosure of information allegedly obtained in violation of federal wiretapping laws properly permitted use of information for limited purposes of aiding court in making admissibility determinations in underlying suit, but not for purposes of impeachment in suit. 18 U.S.C.A. §§ 2511(1)(a), 2515.

13. Injunction ⬤26(3)

Racketeer Influenced and Corrupt Organizations Act (RICO) action would not be enjoined, despite court's determination that plaintiffs had violated federal and state wiretapping laws, given determination that evidence unrelated to illegally obtained information could support lawsuit. 18 U.S.C.A. §§ 1961–1968, 2511(1)(a); 15 M.R.S.A. § 710, subd. 1.

14. Federal Civil Procedure ⬤2646
Federal Courts ⬤829

Decision to grant or deny motion to alter or amend judgment is committed to wide discretion of district court and must be respected absent abuse. Fed.Rules Civ.Proc. Rule 59, 28 U.S.C.A.

15. Federal Civil Procedure ⬤2652

Denial of motion to alter or amend judgment was not abuse of discretion where motion sought relief not requested in complaint. Fed.Rules Civ.Proc.Rule 59, 28 U.S.C.A.

16. Telecommunications ⬤498

Fourth Amendment doctrines like independent source rule do not apply in private civil actions implicating federal wiretapping law. U.S.C.A. Const.Amend. 4; 18 U.S.C.A. § 2511(1)(a).

17. Telecommunications ⬤494.1

Federal wiretapping law prohibits more than just initial wrongful invasion; disclosure and/or use of information obtained through wrongful invasion amounts to separate injury prohibited by statute, and makes person subjected to such disclosure and/or use victim once again of federal crime. 18 U.S.C.A. § 2511(1)(a).

18. Federal Courts ⬤617

Plaintiffs alleging violation of federal and state wiretapping laws, who abandoned claim for statutory damages so as to avoid jury trial, could not claim failure to award statutory damages as error on appeal. 18 U.S.C.A. § 2511(1)(a); 15 M.R.S.A. § 710, subd. 1.

Allen S. Rugg, with whom Ronald R. Massumi, Kutak, Rock & Campbell, Washington, DC, John S. Whitman, Richardson & Troubh, Portland, ME, were on brief, for plaintiffs-appellants George C. Williams, Allied Capital Corp., Allied Inv. Corp., Allied Venture Partnership, Allied Capital Corp. II, David P. Parker, David Gladstone, Brooks H. Browne, Frederick L. Russell, Jr., and Thomas R. Salley, E. Stephen Murray, with whom Murray, Plumb & Murray, Portland, ME, were on brief, for intervenor-appellant Ralph A. Dyer.

John A. McArdle, III, with whom Daniel G. Lilley and Daniel G. Lilley Law Offices, P.A., Portland, ME, were on brief, for defendants/appellees/cross-appellants Rodney P. Rodrique, Wayne E. Bowers, Sr. and John Robichaud.

Peter J. DeTroy, III, with whom Norman, Hanson & DeTroy, Portland, ME, were on brief, for defendants/appellees/cross-appellants Richard E. Poulos, John S. Campbell and Poulos & Campbell, P.A.

Before SELYA and STAHL, Circuit Judges, and FUSTE,* District Judge.

STAHL, Circuit Judge.

Following a six-day civil bench trial, the district court ruled that the former principal

---

* Of the District of Puerto Rico, sitting by designation.

EXHIBIT 14.2 | **Key Numbers in a Digest***

55 F P D 4th—515

FEDERAL COURTS ⚷851

C.A.9 (Wash.) 1992. Court of Appeals will reverse factual findings of district court only if they are clearly erroneous.—Folden v. Washington State Dept. of Social and Health Services, 981 F.2d 1054.

C.A.9 (Wash.) 1991. Court of Appeals reviews de novo district court's interpretations of state law in actions under Federal Tort Claims Act and applies clearly erroneous standard to findings of fact. 28 U.S.C.A. § 2674.—Daly v. U.S., 946 F.2d 1467.

C.A.9 (Wash.) 1990. Factual determinations made by the district court are reviewed for clear error and conclusions of law are reviewed de novo. —Sheet Metal Workers Intern. Ass'n, Local Union No. 150 v. Air Systems Engineering, Inc., 948 F.2d 1089, as amended.

C.A.9 (Wash.) 1990. U.S. v. City of Spokane, 918 F.2d 84, certiorari denied 111 S.Ct. 2888, 501 U.S. 1250, 115 L.Ed.2d 1053.

C.A.7 (Wis.) 1995. On appeal from bench trial, Court of Appeals accepts district court's findings of fact unless they are clearly erroneous.—Patterson v. Caterpillar, Inc., 70 F.3d 503, rehearing denied.

C.A.7 (Wis.) 1995. Court of Appeals reviews court's findings of fact for clear error and decisions of law de novo.—American Suzuki Motor Corp. v. Bill Kummer, Inc., 65 F.3d 1381, rehearing denied.

C.A.7 (Wis.) 1994. On appeal, district court's interpretation of regulation is reviewed de novo and its findings of fact are reviewed for clear error. —U.S. v. Wisconsin Power and Light Co., 38 F.3d 329.

On appeal, district court's application of law to particular set of facts is reviewed under clearly erroneous standard.—Id.

C.A.7 (Wis.) 1994. District court's findings of fact are reviewed under clearly erroneous standard.—Badger Meter, Inc. v. Grinnell Corp., 13 F.3d 1145.

C.A.7 (Wis.) 1992. When reviewing trial court's evidentiary decision, Court of Appeals accords great deference to its determinations, and will not overturn them in absence of clear abuse of discretion.—Rodriguez v. Anderson, 973 F.2d 550.

C.A.10 (Wyo.) 1994. Court of Appeals reviews findings of fact for clear error. Fed.Rules Civ. Proc.Rule 52(a), 28 U.S.C.A.—Unicover World Trade Corp. v. Tri-State Mint, Inc., 24 F.3d 1219.

M.D.Ala. 1995. On motion for judgment on partial findings, court set forth findings of fact and conclusions of law, subject to reversal only if clearly erroneous. Fed.Rules Civ.Proc.Rule 52(c), 28 U.S.C.A.—Grant v. Bullock County Bd. of Educ., 895 F.Supp. 1506.

S.D.Fla. 1995. Findings of fact are subject to review on clearly erroneous standard.—Cohen v. U.S., 191 B.R. 482.

N.D.Ill. 1995. Under clearly erroneous standard, court must give great deference to trier of fact's findings.—Matter of Garofalo's Finer Foods, Inc., 186 B.R. 414.

W.D.Mich. 1991. Whether to issue preliminary injunction is within district court's discretion, and court's decision is reviewed for abuse of that discretion; district court's findings of fact will be upheld unless clearly erroneous.—Lapeer County Medical Care Facility v. State of Mich. Through Dept. of Social Services, 765 F.Supp. 1291.

E.D.N.Y. 1995. On appeal, trial court's findings of fact may be disturbed only if they are found to be clearly erroneous, while trial court's conclusions of law are subject to de novo review.—Allied Semi-Conductors Intern., Ltd. v. Pulsar Components Intern., Inc., 907 F.Supp. 618.

S.D.N.Y. 1993. Factual evaluations of evidence at trial level involving application of legal standard should be respected unless clearly erroneous.—In re Barral, 153 B.R. 15, affirmed 17 F.3d 1426.

E.D.Pa. 1996. Clearly erroneous standard does not permit court to reverse findings simply because reviewing court would have decided differently.— In re Sugarhouse Realty, Inc., 192 B.R. 355.

9th Cir.BAP (Cal.) 1996. Trial court's findings of fact are reviewed under clearly erroneous standard.—In re Casa Blanca Project Lenders, L.P., 196 B.R. 140.

⚷**851. —— Conflicting evidence; undisputed evidence.**

C.A.2 1993. Trial court's finding is not "clearly erroneous" when it is based on court's choice between two permissible inferences or views of evidence.—Bailey v. C.I.R., 993 F.2d 288.

C.A.Fed. (Mass.) 1995. Court of Appeals does not review de novo proceedings of district court; party seeking reversal of district court decision bears burden of showing reversible legal error or clear factual errors in light of trial record, and, where record viewed in its entirety renders district court's account of evidence plausible or discloses two permissible readings of evidence, fact-finder has committed no clear error.—King Instruments Corp. v. Perego, 65 F.3d 941, rehearing denied, in banc suggestion declined 72 F.3d 855, certiorari denied 116 S.Ct. 1675, 134 L.Ed.2d 778.

C.A.Fed. (Pa.) 1993. "Clearly erroneous" standard does not entitle Court of Appeals to reverse district court's findings simply because it would have decided case differently; where fact finder's account of evidence is plausible in light of entire record or where it chooses one of two permissible views of evidence, it has committed no clear error. Fed.Rules Civ.Proc.Rule 52(a), 28 U.S.C.A.—Miles Laboratories, Inc. v. Shandon Inc., 997 F.2d 870, rehearing denied, in banc suggestion declined, certiorari denied 114 S.Ct. 943, 127 L.Ed.2d 232.

C.A.8 (Ark.) 1995. If there is more than one permissible view of the evidence, Court of Appeals may not hold that choice made by trier of fact was clearly erroneous, and even greater deference is required where factual findings call for assessment of witness credibility and no documents or objective evidence contradict testimony.—In re Central Arkansas Broadcasting Co., 68 F.3d 213.

C.A.9 (Cal.) 1996. Under "clearly erroneous" standard of review, reviewing court may not reverse district court's findings simply because it is convinced that it would have decided case differently; where there are two permissible views of evidence, fact finder's choice between them cannot be clearly erroneous.—Granite State Ins. Co. v. Smart Modular Technologies, Inc., 76 F.3d 1023.

C.A.9 (Cal.) 1994. Grant or denial of preliminary injunction will be reversed only where district court abused its discretion or based its decision on erroneous legal standard or on clearly erroneous findings of fact.—Miller for and on Behalf of N.L.R.B. v. California Pacific Medical Center, 19 F.3d 449.

C.A.10 (Colo.) 1993. If there are two permissible views of evidence, fact finder's choice between them cannot be clearly erroneous.—Sorensen v. City of Aurora, 984 F.2d 349.

C.A.2 (Conn.) 1994. Matters of motive and causation are questions of fact, and findings on such issues by the court as fact finder after trial may not properly be overturned unless they are clearly erroneous; finding cannot be termed "clearly erroneous" if it rests on a choice between two permissible inferences.—Sedor v. Frank, 42 F.3d 741, certiorari denied 115 S.Ct. 2279, 132 L.Ed.2d 283.

C.A.11 (Ga.) 1996. When there are two permissible views of evidence, fact finder's choice between them cannot be clearly erroneous.—Caban-Wheeler v. Elsea, 71 F.3d 837.

C.A.7 (Ill.) 1995. Trial court's choice between two permissible views of evidence cannot be clearly

---

EXHIBIT 14.2 *(continued)*

erroneous. Fed.Rules Civ.Proc.Rule 52(a), 28 U.S.C.A.—Thornton v. Brown, 47 F.3d 194.

C.A.7 (Ill.) 1994. District court does not abuse its discretion in denying leave to amend if proposed repleading would be futile, and futile repleadings include restating same facts using different language, reasserting claims previously determined, failing to state valid theory of liability, and inability to survive a motion to dismiss. —Garcia v. City of Chicago, Ill., 24 F.3d 966, rehearing and suggestion for rehearing denied, certiorari denied 115 S.Ct. 1313, 131 L.Ed.2d 194.

C.A.7 (Ill.) 1993. Where there are two permissible views of evidence, fact finder's choice between them cannot be clearly erroneous.—Mendiola v. U.S., 994 F.2d 409.

C.A.7 (Ill.) 1993. District court's factual findings are "clearly erroneous" only when reviewing court is left with definite and firm conviction that mistake has been committed; if district court chooses between two permissible views of evidence, its decision between the two views cannot be clearly erroneous. Fed.Rules Civ.Proc.Rule 52(a), 28 U.S.C.A.—U.S. v. Board of Educ. of Consol. High School Dist. 230, Palos Hills, Ill., 983 F.2d 790.

C.A.7 (Ill.) 1992. Factual finding which is based on district court's decision to credit the testimony of particular witness, who has told a coherent and facially plausible story that is not contradicted by extrinsic evidence, can virtually never be clear error, if finding is not internally inconsistent.—Ambrosino v. Rodman & Renshaw, Inc., 972 F.2d 776.

C.A.7 (Ind.) 1993. If there are two permissible views on evidence, district court's choice between them cannot be clearly erroneous. Fed.Rules Civ. Proc.Rules 34, 52(a), 28 U.S.C.A.—Rennie v. Dalton, 3 F.3d 1100, certiorari denied 114 S.Ct. 1054, 127 L.Ed.2d 375.

C.A.7 (Ind.) 1992. Where two permissible conclusions may be drawn from evidence, fact finder's choice between them is not clearly erroneous, even though Court of Appeals might be convinced that it would have weighed evidence differently.—Bennett v. Local Union No. 66, Glass, Molders, Pottery, Plastics and Allied Workers Intern. Union, AFL-CIO, CLC, 958 F.2d 1429.

C.A.10 (Kan.) 1991. Where trial is to court, resolution of facts lies solely with finding should clearly erroneo Bank of Kansas

C.A.6 (Ky.) 1 based on phys viewing court i novo, and revie court's findings two permissibl Scheirich Co., 982 F.2d 945.

C.A.5 (La.) 1994. Where two permissible views of evidence exist, fact finder's choice between them cannot be clearly erroneous, even if reviewing court would have weighed evidence differently.— Sockwell v. Phelps, 20 F.3d 187.

C.A.5 (La.) 1993. Clearly erroneous standard does not apply to decisions made by district court judges when they apply legal principles to essentially undisputed facts.—Walker v. Braus, 995 F.2d 77, on remand 861 F.Supp. 527.

C.A.1 (Me.) 1993. Trial court's findings of fact will not be set aside unless they are demonstrated to be clearly erroneous; where there are two permissible views of evidence, interpretation assigned by trial court must be adopted. Fed.Rules Civ.Proc.Rule 52(a), 28 U.S.C.A.—Williams v. Poulos, 11 F.3d 271.

C.A.1 (Mass.) 1995. For purposes of reviewing federal district court's findings of fact made in conjunction with bench trial, if there are two permissible views of the evidence, interpretation assigned by trial court will be adopted.—Windsor Mount Joy Mut. Ins. Co. v. Giragosian, 57 F.3d 50.

C.A.6 (Mich.) 1995. Where there are two permissible views of the evidence, the factfinder's choice between them cannot be "clearly erroneous."—In re Cleveland Tankers, Inc., 67 F.3d 1200, rehearing denied, certiorari denied American S.S. Co. v. Cleveland Tankers, Inc., 116 S.Ct. 1848, 134 L.Ed.2d 949.

C.A.6 (Mich.) 1992. If two views of evidence in case are permissible, choice between those views made by fact finder is not clearly erroneous.—State of Mich. v. City of Allen Park, 954 F.2d 1201.

C.A.8 (Mo.) 1994. Where two permissible views of the evidence exist, district court's choice between them cannot be clearly erroneous.—Favors v. Fisher, 13 F.3d 1235.

C.A.8 (Mo.) 1979. Merrill Lynch, Pierce, Fenner & Smith, Inc. v. Goldman, 593 F.2d 129, on subsequent appeal U. S. ex rel. Goldman v. Meredith, 596 F.2d 1353, certiorari denied 100 S.Ct. 76, 444 U.S. 838, 62 L.Ed.2d 50.

C.A.1 (N.H.) 1996. When there are two permissible views of the evidence, fact finder's choice between them cannot be clearly erroneous.—Smith v. F.W. Morse & Co., Inc., 76 F.3d 413.

C.A.1 (N.H.) 1995. When there are two permissible views of evidence, factfinder's choice between them cannot be clearly erroneous.—Johnson v. Watts Regulator Co., 63 F.3d 1129.

C.A.2 (N.Y.) 1996. When there are two permissible views of evidence, fact finder's choice between them cannot be clearly erroneous and is not to be overturned on appeal. Fed.Rules Civ.Proc. Rule 52(a), 28 U.S.C.A.—S.E.C. v. Lorin, 76 F.3d 458.

C.A.2 (N.Y.) 1995. When trial judge's finding is based on decision to credit testimony of one of two or more witnesses, each of whom has told coherent and facially plausible story that is not contradicted by extrinsic evidence, that finding, if not internally inconsistent, can virtually never be clear error.— U.S. v. Milbrand, 58 F.3d 841, certiorari denied 116 S.Ct. 1284, 134 L.Ed.2d 228.

C.A.2 (N.Y.) 1994. Where evidence is contradic... e views, trial t be clearly 5. whose testi- peting infer- of fact, and e overturned r Oil, S.A. v. en evidence ted contrary es drawn by court were clearly erroneous.—Id.

C.A.2 (N.Y.) 1991. When trial court's view of evidence is plausible in light of entire record, or if it makes choice between two permissible views of evidence, Court of Appeals will not substitute its judgment for trial court's even if Court of Appeals would have weighed evidence differently had it been sitting as trier of fact. Fed.Rules Civ.Proc. Rule 52(a), 28 U.S.C.A.—ABKCO Music, Inc. v. Harrisongs Music, Ltd., 944 F.2d 971.

C.A.6 (Ohio) 1995. Court of Appeals reviews federal district court's findings of fact for clear error and under this standard of review, where there are two permissible views of the evidence, fact finder's choice between them cannot be clearly erroneous.—Brunet v. City of Columbus, Ohio, 58 F.3d 251, rehearing and suggestion for rehearing denied.

C.A.1 (Me.) 1993. Trial court's findings of fact will not be set aside unless they are demonstrated to be clearly erroneous; where there are two permissible views of evidence, interpretation assigned by trial court must be adopted. Fed.Rules Civ.Proc.Rule 52(a), 28 U.S.C.A.—Williams v. Poulos, 11 F.3d 271.

Law Reports (A.L.R., A.L.R.2d, A.L.R.3d, A.L.R.4th, A.L.R.5th, and A.L.R. Fed.) selects noteworthy decisions from both the federal and state courts. For each of these decisions, it publishes a summary of the attorneys' arguments, the text of the court's opinion, and an annotation collecting and summarizing other cases discussing the same issue. (For more on A.L.R., see section 15.2.1.)

§14.1.6   Online Court Decisions

All of the above decisions are available online as well as in print format. LEXIS and Westlaw are comprehensive sources for court decisions. Several CD-ROM products contain decisions from particular courts. Court decisions are also available at numerous Internet sites. The coverage and searching capabilities of these varies by site.

Online decisions that are full-text searchable provide a powerful alternative to the published digests and indices (discussed below). The advantage is that (with limited exceptions) every word in the text of an opinion is searchable. Consequently, you can search more narrowly for specific facts (for example, searching for a company or product name). You can also search for novel legal issues that do not fit neatly into the digest and other case indexing systems. Furthermore, many of the search engines used to find online cases allow you to restrict your search to particular portions of an opinion (such as the case name or the authoring judge). These capabilities may make using online versions the preferred method of retrieving cases in many instances. Full-text searching is discussed more fully in Chapter 17.

§14.2   COURT RULES

The judicial branch does more than just decide cases. It also promulgates the procedural rules that govern the cases that come before it. The United States Supreme Court promulgates the rules that govern federal cases, and the highest courts in each state promulgate the rules that govern cases in their state systems. Lower courts and, even within a court, particular judges, may promulgate their own local rules.

Court rules can be found in a number of different places. The Federal Rules of Civil Procedure are published as an appendix to Title 28 in both the *United States Code* and the *United States Code Annotated* and as separate volumes in the *United States Code Service.* The rules also appear in commercial publications, including supplements to Civil Procedure case books and *Federal Civil Judicial Procedure and Rules* by West. Finally, there are numerous online versions of the rules on LEXIS, Westlaw, various CD-ROM products, and the Internet.

Annotated court rules are like annotated codes. They contain the text of the court rule followed by references that aid in interpreting its language. Usually, the official comments of the rule's drafters are included, along with citations to law review articles, case digests, and other references.

Other good sources for researching court rules are treatises. *Federal Practice and Procedure* (also known as Wright and Miller) and *Moore's Federal Practice* are multivolume sets containing not only the text of the rules but also commentary and references to cases that have interpreted or applied the rules. Cases can also be found in West's *Federal Rules Decisions* (locate cases using the *Federal Practice Digest*) and in Callaghan's *Federal Rules Service.*

State rules are occasionally published at the beginning of the state's code and in separate publications. The publisher may be the court itself or a commercial publisher. As is true with the federal rules, most state rules are available in numerous online versions. Local rules are available from either the court or the judge or, for the larger courts, from the local entity or a commercial publisher. Annotated court rules and treatises on state rules are also published for many states.

§14.3   DIGESTS

Cases can be found in a variety of ways: (1) by using the annotations that follow the text of the statute or court rule in an annotated code; (2) by looking up the citations found in a legal encyclopedia, hornbook, treatise, or other secondary source; (3) by using LEXIS or Westlaw; or (4) by using a digest.

Digests are the subject indices for case reporters. Abstracts of cases are arranged by topic and, within each topic, by subtopic. See Exhibits 14.3, 14.4 and 14.5.

Just as there are numerous reporters, there are also numerous digests. The most comprehensive (and the most time-consuming to use) is the *Decennial Digest,* which lists cases from both the federal courts and all of the state courts. Smaller in scope but easier to use are the federal digests, the regional digests, and the state digests.

Federal Digests:

> *Federal Digest.* Through 1940.
> *Modern Federal Practice Digest.* 1940-1960.
> *Federal Practice Digest 2d.* 1961-November 1975.
> *Federal Practice Digest 3d.* 1975-(no specific cutoff date).
> *Federal Practice Digest 4th.* Supplements *Federal Practice Digest 3d.*

Regional Digests: The digests that are available vary from region to region.

State Digests: Some states have their own digest; others do not.

TELECOMMUNICATIONS

References are to Digest Topics and Key Numbers

TEACHERS—Cont'd
SERVICE academies, basic and special pay. Armed S 13.1(6)
SERVICE credit, pensions and benefits. Schools 146(6)
SICK leave—
 Reduction of accumulation. Schools 144(1)
 Due process. Const Law 278.5(4)
SUPERINTENDENT of schools, recommendation by. Schools 133.3
SUPPLY teachers, permanent tenure. Schools 133.12
SUSPENSION. Removal or suspension, generally, ante
TENURE. Permanent tenure, generally, ante
TERM of employment in general. Schools 133.5–133.13
TRANSFER. Schools 141
VALIDITY of contracts. Schools 135(3–5)
WARNINGS—
 Necessity for adverse action. Schools 147.26

TEAMS
EXEMPTION from process. Exemp 44
LICENSES or tax on. Licens 14
LIVERY stable keepers, see this index **Livery Stable Keepers**

TECHNICAL ERRORS
INDICTMENT or information, ground for arrest of judgment. Crim Law 970(9)
PLEADING—
 Aider by verdict. Plead 433(4)
 General demurrer.
 Waiver of objectio
REVIEW. App & E
 Administrative age   udicial errors. Admin Law 765
 Criminal prosecutions. Crim Law 1165(2), 1186.4

Reference to topic and key number

TECHNICAL EVIDENCE
ADMINISTRATIVE agencies, etc., judicial review. Admin Law 792

TECHNICAL QUESTIONS
ADMINISTRATIVE agencies, etc., judicial review of discretion. Admin Law 759

TECHNICAL TERMS
CONTRACTS, construction of technical terms as jury question. Contracts 176(4)
INDICTMENT or information. Ind & Inf 76
 Rape prosecution. Rape 25
INSTRUCTIONS, definition or explanation. Crim Law 800(3)
PLEADING. Plead 27
WILLS. Wills 102, 457, 591

TELECOMMUNICATIONS
ACTIONS—
 Administrative proceedings. Tel 11–15
 Interception or disclosure of communications. Tel 498
ADMINISTRATIVE procedure. Officers, commissions and agencies, generally, post
ADMISSIONS. Evid 205(3)
ADVERTISING. Tel 462
ALARM systems. Tel 463
"BEEPERS," see this index **Tracking Devices**
BILL of particulars. Ind & Inf 121.2(9)
BOARDS. Officers, commissions and agencies, generally, post
CANVASSING and soliciting. Tel 462
CENSORSHIP. Tel 429–437
COIN-OPERATED machines, music and entertainment. Tel 470, 471
COMMON carrier status. Tel 2, 3
COMMUNICATIONS Commission. Officers, commissions and agencies, generally, post
COMPETENCY as evidence. Evid 148
CONSPIRACY, wire fraud, evidence. Consp 47(5)

TELECOMMUNICATIONS—Cont'd
CONSTITUTIONAL and statutory provisions. Tel 4
 Interception or disclosure of communications. Tel 492
CONTRACTS—
 Cellular communications. Tel 461.5
COURTS, authorization of interception or disclosure of communications. Tel 496
DECISIONS of officers, commissions and agencies. Tel 7
DELIVERY service. Tel 466
ELECTRONIC surveillance, see Interception or disclosure of communications, post
EMERGENCIES—
 Electronic surveillance. Tel 511
 Federal control. Tel 17
EQUAL time. Tel 384
 First Amendment. Const Law 90.1(9)
EXHAUSTING administrative remedies, judicial remedies and review. Tel 12
FEDERAL Communications Commission. Officers, commissions and agencies, generally, post
FEDERAL preemption—
 State laws or regulations. States 18.81
FRAUD. Tel 361–363
GOVERNMENT or public operation, see this index **Government or Public Operation of Telecommunications**
INJUNCTIONS, administrative proceedings. Tel 15
INTERCEPTION or disclosure of communications. Tel 491–530
 Acts constituting. Tel 494, 495
 Civil liability. Tel 498
 Consent. Tel 495
 Constitutional provisions. Tel 492
 Courts, authorization by. Tel 496, 510–530
 Drug searches of carriers. Drugs & N 182(6)
 Evidence wrongfully obtained. Crim Law 394.3
 Federal preemption—
  State laws or regulations. States 18.81
 Foreign intelligence. Armed S 47(7)
 Military cases. Mil Jus 1080
 Minimization requirement. Tel 520
 Persons concerned. Tel 495
 Prosecution. Tel 497
 Public officers, authorization by. Tel 496, 512
 Transcripts—
  Expungement. Tel 527
 Warrants. Tel 518
JUDICIAL remedies—
 Actions, generally, ante
 Administrative proceedings. Tel 11–15
LEASED wires. Tel 464, 465
MESSENGER service. Tel 466
MONEY, transmission by, see this index **Money**
MUSIC and entertainment, transmission of, generally. Tel 470, 471
NEWS and information. Tel 472, 473
OFFICERS, commissions and agencies. Tel 5–17
 Administrative procedure. Tel 8–15
  Determination and disposition of judicial remedies and review. Tel 15
  Exhausting administrative remedies. Tel 12
  Findings. Tel 10
  Injunction. Tel 15
  Investigation. Tel 9, 412
  Judicial remedies and review. Tel 11–15
  Orders. Tel 10
  Parties to judicial remedies and review. Tel 13
  Reports. Tel 9
  Scope of inquiry and powers of court. Tel 14
  Stay orders. Tel 15
  Time for judicial remedies and review. Tel 12
 Decisions, effect. Tel 7
 Interception or disclosure of communications, authorization. Tel 496

TELECOMMUNICATIONS — Topic

SUBJECTS INCLUDED

The transmission of communications or entertainment at a distance, otherwise than by mail

More particularly, telegraphs, telephones, television, radio and special services or activities

Companies and associations engaged in this industry and their rights and liabilities peculiar to it

Government ownership, operation and regulation of such activities

SUBJECTS EXCLUDED AND COVERED BY OTHER TOPICS

Commerce, regulation of, see COMMERCE

Corporations, matters applicable to in general, see CORPORATIONS

Defamation, liability for, see LIBEL AND SLANDER

Electricity used in telecommunications, injuries caused by, see ELECTRICITY

Eminent domain, see EMINENT DOMAIN

Gambling, offense of using telecommunications for, see GAMING — Cross-references

Mail, communication by, see POST OFFICE

Municipalities' powers in general, see MUNICIPAL CORPORATIONS

Property rights in communications, see COPYRIGHTS AND INTELLECTUAL PROPERTY

Taxation of telecommunication facilities generally, see TAXATION

For detailed references to other topics, see Descriptive-Word Index

---

Analysis

I. IN GENERAL, ☞1–30.

II. TELEGRAPHS AND TELEPHONES, ☞31–380.

    (A) IN GENERAL, ☞31–70.

    (B) OPERATION FRANCHISES OR LICENSES AND RIGHTS OF WAY, ☞71–100.

    (C) CONSTRUCTION, EQUIPMENT AND MAINTENANCE, ☞101–140.

    (D) TELEGRAPH SERVICE, ☞141–260.

    (E) TELEPHONE SERVICE, ☞261–300.

    (F) CHARGES AND RATES, ☞301–360.

    (G) OFFENSES AND PENALTIES, ☞361–380.

III. TELEVISION AND RADIO, ☞381–460.

IV. SPECIAL SERVICES OR ACTIVITIES, ☞461–490.

Topic analysis (subject outline)

*Reprinted from West's *Federal Practice Digest 4th*, © 1992 (West's National Reporter System), with permission of West Group.

EXHIBIT 14.4 *(continued)*

90 F P D 4th—383　　　　　　　　　　**TELECOMMUNICATIONS**

V. INTERCEPTION OR DISCLOSURE OF COMMUNICATIONS; ELECTRONIC SURVEILANCE, ☞491–541.

    (A) IN GENERAL, ☞491–509.

    (B) AUTHORIZATION BY COURTS OR PUBLIC OFFICERS, ☞510–539.

    (C) TRACKING DEVICES, ☞540–541.

I. IN GENERAL.

    ☞1. Communications and regulation thereof in general.

    2. Common carrier or public utility, status in general.

    3. —— Television, radio and special services.

    4. Constitutional and statutory provisions.

    5. Officers, commissions and agencies.

    6. —— Powers in general.

    7. —— Rules and regulations; effect of decisions.

    8. Administrative procedure.

    9. —— Investigations and reports.

    10. —— Findings and orders.

    11. Judicial remedies and review.

    12. —— Time for proceedings; exhausting administrative remedies.

    13. —— Parties and procedure.

    14. —— Scope of inquiry and powers of court.

    15. —— Determination and disposition; injunctions and stay orders.

    16. Government or public operation and ownership.

    17. —— Federal emergency control.

> Topic analysis
> (subject outline)

II. TELEGRAPHS AND TELEPHONES.

  (A) IN GENERAL.

    ☞31. Nature, status and regulation in general.

    32. —— Companies and persons subject.

    33. —— Judicial remedies and review.

    34. Constitutional and statutory provisions.

    35. Corporations and enterprises for profit.

    36. —— Powers in general; corporate franchise.

    37. —— Finances and accounting; mortgages.

    38. —— Actions in general.

    39. —— Jurisdiction, venue and process.

    40. —— Loss of corporate franchise or dissolution; insolvency and reorganization.

    41. —— Foreign corporations.

    42. Cooperatives and mutual or nonprofit organizations.

    43. —— Supervision by officers and commissions in general.

    44. Relations between companies in general; transfers of assets.

    45. Affiliation, consolidation and merger.

    46. Interconnection and mutual service; operating agreements.

    47. —— Legality and approval of agreements.

    48. —— Duty to connect with other lines or furnish service thereto.

    49. —— Compelling connection or mutual service; procedure.

    50. Leases between companies.

    51. Railroads operating lines or dealing with companies.

90 F P D 4th—549   **TELECOMMUNICATIONS** ☞495

For references to other topics, see Descriptive-Word Index

forcement officer in ordinary course of duties. 18 U.S.C.A. § 2510(5)(a)(ii).

U.S. v. Noriega, 764 F.Supp. 1480.

C.D.Ill. 1992. In light of criminal penalties provided for unauthorized descrambling of satellite programming, descrambling was not intended to be included in wiretap laws; satellite transmission interception by home viewers was mentioned in legislative history of wiretap laws only in context of excepting unscrambled satellite transmissions. 18 U.S.C.A. § 2511.

U.S. v. Shriver, 782 F.Supp. 408.

Use of term "surreptitious" in wiretap laws referred to design of interception device and not its use, and, thus, modified satellite television descramblers were not within spectrum of devices prohibited by wiretap laws, despite their illegitimate use. 18 U.S.C.A. §§ 2511, 2512; Communications Act of 1934, § 705, as amended, 47 U.S.C.A. § 605.

U.S. v. Shriver, 782 F.Supp. 408.

Because section of wiretap laws providing criminal penalties for those who manufacture or distribute unauthorized satellite television descramblers was clearly intended to have exclusive control of private viewing of cable programming, defendants who allegedly conspired to manufacture and sell modified television descramblers could not be charged with violations under section of wiretap laws prohibiting surreptitious interception of electronic communications. 18 U.S.C.A. §§

[Key number]

Communications Act of 1934, § 70 ~~ ed, 47 U.S.C.A. § 605.

U.S. v. Shriver, 782 F.Supp. 408.

N.D.Ill. 1989. Undercover agent did not "intercept" conv~~~~ of trader in foreign currency pit of [Squib (abstract)] hrough use of recording ~~ cquired trader's utterances by means of his naked ear, and device simply preserved what agent was hearing independently thereof. 18 U.S.C.A. § 2510(4).

Matter of John Doe Trader No. One, 722 F.Supp. 419, on subsequent appeal 894 F.2d 240.

M.D.La. 1986. Edwards v. Bardwell, 632 F.Supp. 584, affirmed 808 F.2d 54.

S.D.N.Y. 19~~88~~ Receipt of computerized financial inform~~ [Citation] ch per~~ mitted subscribe~~ ~~vice to copy provider's data base, would be unauthorized within meaning of Telecommunications Act inasmuch as service provider's agreement with subscribers provided that they could not interface any foreign equipment or move provider's equipment. Communications Act of 1934, § 705, as amended, 47 U.S.C.A. § 605.

Telerate Systems, Inc. v. Caro, 689 F.Supp. 221.

If subscribers of computerized financial information service were to view service provider's database by means of unauthorized copying, such act would constitute prohibited "publication" within meaning of Telecommunications Act. Communications Act of 1934, § 705, as amended, 47 U.S.C.A. § 605.

Telerate Systems, Inc. v. Caro, 689 F.Supp. 221.

N.D.Ohio 1990. Defendant broadcasting company's interview of plaintiff took place on public street, and thus, did not violate statute making it illegal to violate any regulation issued by Federal Communications Commission, specifically, regulation stating that no person shall use device required to be licensed for purpose of overhearing or recording private conversations of others. Communications Act of 1934, § 502, 47 U.S.C.A. § 502.

Brooks v. American Broadcasting Companies, Inc., 737 F.Supp. 431, affirmed in part, vacated in part 932 F.2d 495.

S.D.Ohio 1991. Officers executing search warrant did not improperly "intercept" any "wire, oral, or electronic communication" when they overheard answering machine during their search of premises; officer simply overheard clearly audible transmissions while they were lawfully in same room with answering machine. U.S.C.A. Const.Amend. 4; 18 U.S.C.A. § 2511(1); Ohio R.C. § 2933.51 et seq.

U.S. v. Upton, 763 F.Supp. 232.

W.D.Okl. 1988. Federal wiretapping statute applies to interspousal surveillance within marital home. 18 U.S.C.A. §§ 2510 et seq., 2520.

Heggy v. Heggy, 699 F.Supp. 1514.

☞**495. —— Persons concerned; consent.**

C.A.D.C. 1991. Nonresident aliens who entered the United States on the basis of student or visitor visas did not qualify as "United States persons" for purposes of provision of the Foreign Intelligence Surveillance Act (FISA) prohibiting a United States person from being considered a foreign power or agent solely on the basis of First Amendment activities. Foreign Intelligence Surveillance Act of 1978, § 105(a)(3)(A), 50 U.S.C.A. § 1805(a)(3)(A); U.S.C.A. Const.Amend. 1.

ACLU Foundation of Southern California v. Barr, 952 F.2d 457, rehearing denied.

Provision of the Foreign Intelligence Surveillance Act (FISA) prohibiting a United States person from becoming a target of surveillance solely on the basis of First Amendment activity cannot be violated by the mere overhearing of someone who is not a target and did not apply to attorneys who were overheard during authorized surveillance directed at their clients. Foreign Intelligence Surveil-

For cited U.S.C.A. sections and legislative history, see United States Code Annotated

Specialized Digests (representative examples):

> *Bankruptcy Digest*
> *Education Law Digest*

Most digests have the same format. They are almost always multi-volume sets containing descriptive word index volumes, volumes containing the case abstracts, and volumes containing other finding tools (for example, tables of cases, defendant-plaintiff tables, and a words and phrases volume). With the exception of the *Decennial* and *General Digests,* all digests are kept current through the use of pocket parts, which are usually published yearly, and supplemental pamphlets, which may be published monthly or quarterly.

The best way to use a digest depends on what you already know and what you are looking for.

1. Location of a specific case. If you know the name of a case but not the citation, the best source is the Table of Cases or the Defendant-Plaintiff table. By looking up either the case name or the plaintiff's or defendant's name, you can find the case citation.

2. Other cases discussing the same point of law. If you have found one case that is on point, you can find others discussing the same point by looking up the topic and key number in the main volumes of the digests. For example, if you want to find other cases discussing the point of law set out in headnote 6 in *Williams v. Poulos,* you would locate the digest volume containing the topic "Telecommunications." You would then locate that topic and, within that topic, key number 495.

3. Cases discussing a particular point of law. If you have not yet found a case discussing a particular point of law, you can use a digest to find the first case. The best way of doing this is through the digest's descriptive word index. Look up your search terms in the index, for each term noting the topic and key number references. Then look up the topic and key numbers that appear to be most on point in the main volumes of the digest. See Exhibit 14.3.

4. Cases defining a particular word or phrase. If you are looking for a definition, the best source is the words and phrases volume. If the word or phrase has been defined, the word or phrase and the citation to the case or cases in which it has been defined will be listed.

Chapter 15

Secondary Sources

Unlike primary sources, secondary sources do not contain the law itself. Instead, they summarize, explain, or comment on the law.

As a researcher, you will use secondary sources in a variety of ways. When you are unfamiliar with a particular area of law, you can use secondary sources to obtain an overview of the area of law. See section 15.1. Secondary sources can, however, be used in other ways: to locate the key cases in your, or other, jurisdictions and, at times, as authority. When there is no mandatory authority, or the mandatory authority does not support the position you are advocating, secondary sources can be cited as persuasive authority.

Although any given source can be used for more than one purpose, some are better for one purpose than they are for another. For example, although a legal encyclopedia may be a good source for background reading, you would not want to cite it as persuasive authority.

To help you determine which sources are best for particular purposes, this chapter groups and discusses secondary sources according to their primary purpose: Secondary sources that can be used for background reading are discussed first, secondary sources that are effective finding tools are discussed second, and secondary sources that can be used as persuasive authority are discussed third.

The number of secondary sources available online is growing. To determine online availability, you can look in the contents publications from LEXIS and Westlaw. You can also use library catalogs, directories, and other resources for searching the Internet. Nevertheless, you will probably find print versions of most secondary sources easier to use because of their organizational structure.

§15.1   Sources for Background Reading

Probably the best sources for background reading are legal encyclopedias, hornbooks, and practice books. Depending on the problem, useful back-

439

ground information can also be found in a legal dictionary, in *American Law Reports* (A.L.R.), or in a law review or book.

§15.1.1   Legal Encyclopedias

Like ordinary encyclopedias, legal encyclopedias are sources of generalized information. They provide the researcher with a summary of the law on a wide range of topics. The two major legal encyclopedias, *Corpus Juris Secundum* (C.J.S.) and *American Jurisprudence* (now Am. Jur. 2d), are very similar. See Exhibits 15.1 and 15.2. Both have subject indices, both are organized topically by subject, both have textual material supported by footnotes, and both are kept current through annual pocket parts. The major difference is in the cross-references. While C.J.S. provides cross-references to other West publications (West digests, West practice books), Am. Jur. 2d provides cross-references to *American Law Reports* and other publications in the American Jurisprudence series such as *Am. Jur. Proof of Facts* and *Am. Jur. Legal Forms.* Even though West publishes C.J.S., the topic and section numbers in C.J.S. are not part of West's Key Number System. The key numbers are set out in the "Library References" section that follows some sections.

As Exhibits 15.1 and 15.2 illustrate, legal encyclopedias do not provide the researcher with a state-by-state or circuit-by-circuit summary of the law. Instead, they set out general rules. Because of this general approach, you should not use an encyclopedia as the source, or authority, for a particular rule of law. Although the rules set out in the encyclopedia may be the rules followed in most jurisdictions, they may not be the law in yours. Use a legal encyclopedia only as a source of background information and not as a source of law.

§15.1.2   Hornbooks

Like legal encyclopedias, hornbooks are also a source of background information. In one volume, they provide the researcher with an overview of a particular area of law.

Because the primary market for hornbooks is law students, there are hornbooks for most of the subjects taught in law school, for example, basic property, tort, and contract law and the uniform commercial and tax codes.

Most of these books are written by well-known experts in the area, and most use the same format: textual material at the top of the page and footnotes citing to representative cases at the bottom. See Exhibit 15.3. Information can be found using either the table of contents at the beginning of the volume or the subject index at the back.

Although hornbooks are not usually cited as authority, they are a better source than a legal encyclopedia. An up-to-date hornbook can be cited as authority when describing the history of particular rule or doc-

---

EXHIBIT 15.1　　**Sample Page from *Corpus Juris Secundum* (West), a Legal Encyclopedia***

---

§§ 286–289　TEL. & TEL., RADIO & TELEVISION　　　86 C.J.S.

doing so is a question for the jury[11] where the facts are disputed or the evidence is conflicting,[12] but not when the facts are not disputed,[13] or are not conflicting,[14] or are conclusively proved.[15]

§ 286.　Acts of Third Persons

The failure of a person in whose care a tele-

gram is addressed to communicate it to the sendee, as affecting the telegraph company's liability for delay in delivery, is discussed supra § 149.

Examine Pocket Parts for later cases.

XVIII.　WIRE TAPPING AND OPENING MESSAGES ADDRESSED TO ANOTHER

§ 287.　Wire Tapping

One who taps another's telephone wire is liable to the latter in tort.

Under the general rule, discussed in Right of Privacy § 7, that an unwarranted invasion of the right of privacy will sustain an action in tort, a person who taps the telephone wire used by another is liable to such other person in an action in tort.[16] The Federal Communications Act § 605, 47 U.S.C.A. § 605, prohibiting the unauthorized interception, publication, or use of an interstate communication imposes a civil liability, although not expressly, on one who without authorization publishes a telephoned message.[17] In an action, under the act, for damages for intercepting and publishing telephone conversations between plaintiff and defendant's employees, whether the plaintiff had consented

to such publication, and, if so, the scope of such consent, are questions for the jury.[18]

§ 288.　Opening Message

Under a statute so providing, one who opens a telegram addressed to another will be compelled to pay appropriate damages.

In a jurisdiction in which statutes authorize recovery of treble damages from one who willfully and unlawfully opens a sealed telegram addressed to another, one who thus opens a telegraph message addressed to another in order to obtain information permitting him to exchange land with the addressee and resell to the sender of the telegram must pay the difference between the value of the land given the addressee and that of the land received.[19]

XIX.　WIRELESS TELEGRAPHS AND TELEPHONES

§ 289.　In General

A contract to install wireless equipment is not within a statute requiring wireless companies to file rates for transmitting messages.　Contracts for hiring wireless outfits have been construed according to the general principles of contracts, including the measure of damages for breach.

A contract by a wireless company to install wireless equipment and maintain operators therefor is not within the provisions of a statute requiring wireless companies to print and file a schedule of rates for the transmission of messages,[20] nor is such contract made illegal by the statutory provi-

---

Fla.—W. U. Tel. Co. v. Thomas, 190 So. 878, 139 Fla. 474.
Okl.—W. U. Tel. Co. v. Martin, 95 P.2d 849, 186 Okl. 24.

(2) To prove the contrary.
U.S.—Dismang v. W. U. Tel. Co., D.C.Okl., 24 F.Supp. 782.
D.C.—Tipton v. Western Union Tel. Co., D.C., 68 F.Supp. 854.
Mo.—Green v. Western Union Tel. Co., App., 58 S.W.2d 772.
Va.—Western Union Tel. Co. v. Phelps, 169 S.E. 574, 160 Va. 674.

11. U.S.—Western Union Telegraph Co. v. Kirby, C.C.A.Pa., 37 F.2d 480 —White v. Pacific Telephone & Telegraph Co., D.C.Or., 24 F.Supp. 871.
Fla.—W. U. Tel. Co. v. Thomas, 190 So. 878, 139 Fla. 474.
S.C.—Matheson v. American Telephone & Telegraph Co., 135 S.E. 306, 137 S.C. 227.

12. Va.—Western Union Tel. Co. v. Phelps, 169 S.E. 574, 160 Va. 674.

13. Va.—Western Union Tel. Co. v. Phelps, supra.

14. U.S.—Dismang v. W. U. Tel. Co., D.C.Okl., 24 F.Supp. 782.

15. Va.—Western Union Tel. Co. v. Phelps, 169 S.E. 574, 160 Va. 674.

16. Ky.—Rhodes v. Graham, 37 S.W. 2d 46, 238 Ky. 225.
Wire tapping as criminal offense see supra § 122.

17. U.S.—Reitmeister v. Reitmeister, C.C.A.N.Y., 162 F.2d 691.
Intra-state messages over interstate wires
The act forbids interception of intra-state messages if sent over interstate wires, and civil rights for violation of statute are coextensive with the criminal liability.—Reitmeister v. Reitmeister, supra.

Acts constituting interception
Where defendant had a telephone extension in his own separate office leading from main wire, and attached recording machine to receiver at extension and recorded conversations between plaintiff and defendant's employees, defendant, in recording the conversations, intercepted messages within prohibition of act.—Reitmeister v. Reitmeister, supra.

Playing records of telephone conversations in court was held not basis of claim under act.—Reitmeister v. Reitmeister, supra.

18. U.S.—Reitmeister v. Reitmeister, supra.

19. Wash.—Deighton v. Hover, 107 P. 853, 58 Wash. 12, 137 Am.S.R. 1035, 21 Ann.Cas. 860.

20. Cal.—Marconi Wireless Telegraph Co. of America v. Northern Pacific S. S. Co., 173 P. 103, 36 Cal.App. 653.

Reprinted from Corpus Juris Secundum, © 1943, with permission of West Publishing Company.

transmitter is located, since all radio communications are interstate where the transmissions in fact extend beyond the borders of the state.[90]

The fact that a complaint alleged that the defendant unlawfully used "certain apparatus" for the transmission of communications and signals, for which apparatus no license had been granted by the Commission, instead of alleging unlawful use of a "station," has been held not to have rendered insufficient a warrant based upon the complaint, since the two terms quoted might be considered to be interchangeable, within the meaning of the statute.[91] An indictment charging the defendant with unlawfully operating certain apparatus for the transmission of radio signals without first having obtained an operator's license required by the federal statute has been held not insufficient, even though it did not in terms charge that the defendant operated the apparatus for the purpose of transmitting signals or intelligence beyond the borders of the state.[92]

Unlicensed operation of radio apparatus is not established by evidence that the defendant was seen bending over the apparatus, handling wires that came into the building and adjusting some screws.[93]

XIII. INTERCEPTION AND DIVULGENCE OF COMMUNICATIONS: WIRETAPPING

§ 209. Generally.[93.1]

Under acts of Congress[94] and state legislation, it is unlawful to intercept, reveal the existence of, and disclose or divulge the contents of, wire or oral communications, unless the interceptor has previously obtained an order of a court permitting a wiretap or other interception of the communication,[95] or one party has consented to the interception.[96] A violation of such statutes is a criminal offense,[97] the communication may not be received in evidence,[98] and a

90. United States v Betteridge (DC Ohio) 43 F Supp 53.

91. United States v Splane (DC NY) 2 F Supp 685.

Annotation: 104 ALR 872, 880, s. 124 ALR 982, 171 ALR 765.

92. United States v Molyneaux (CA2 NY) 55 F2d 912.

Annotation: 82 ALR 1106, 1111, s. 89 ALR 420, 104 ALR 872, 124 ALR 982, 171 ALR 765.

93. United States v Molyneaux (CA2 NY) 55 F2d 912.

Annotation: 82 ALR 1106, 1107, s. 89 ALR 420, 104 ALR 872, 124 ALR 982, 171 ALR 765.

93.1. *Practice Aids.*—29 Am Jur Proof of Facts 591, Wiretapping §§ 1 et seq.

94. See 18 USCS § 2511, and 47 USCS § 605.

The original federal statute prohibiting the interception and divulgence of wire or oral communications was 47 USC § 605. In 1968 the legislative pattern was changed, with the adoption of the omnibus crime bill, so that § 605 now relates primarily to the divulgence of interstate or foreign communications by wire or radio by persons, such as telephone company employees, who aid in receiving the communications, and to the unauthorized reception, interception, and publication or divulgence of radio communications or the use of such communications for the benefit of the interceptor or for the benefit of another not entitled to use it. On the other hand, the general subject of the interception of wire and oral communications, including judicial orders and other regulations and restrictions on such interception, is included in 18 USCS §§ 2510–2520.

95. §§ 212, 213, infra.

96. § 217, infra.

97. § 215, infra.

98. The admissibility of evidence obtained by wiretapping, or by mechanical or electronic eavesdropping, is discussed at 29 Am Jur 2d, Evidence §§ 428–433.

EXHIBIT 15.3	**Sample Page from LaFave & Israel, *Criminal Procedure, Second Edition* (Hornbook)***

"are not governed by Title III." The Court reasoned:

> Pen registers do not "intercept" because they do not acquire the "contents" of communications, as that term is defined by 18 U.S.C. § 2510(8). Indeed, a law enforcement official could not even determine from the use of a pen register whether a communication existed. These devices do not hear sound [and thus] do not accomplish the "aural acquisition" of anything. They decode outgoing numbers by responding to changes in electrical voltage caused by the turning of the telephone dial (or the pressing of buttons on push button telephones) and present the information in a form to be interpreted by sight rather than by hearing.[12]

By like reasoning, it may be concluded that it is not an interception within the meaning of Title III to use a diode device to determine the origin of an incoming call, to examine telephone company toll records, or to trace a signal given out by a transmitting device ("beeper") concealed in a vehicle or object to facilitate surveillance of it. Such results may be more readily reached under the 1986 amendment to the statute which deleted from the definition of "contents" reference to information concerning "the identity of the parties to such communication or [its] existence."

(b) Phone Company Activities. By virtue of the limitations upon the meaning of "interception" in the context of Title III, discussed above, it is clear that certain activities engaged in by telephone companies are not at all proscribed by the Act. This includes the making and keeping of toll records, the use of pen registers or other call-tracing devices to see if a particular person is making harassing phone calls or is otherwise misusing the telephone service, and the use of a diode trap whereby annoying phone calls can be traced by preventing disconnection when a call is made to a phone to which the device is attached. But sometimes investigations conducted by telephone companies go beyond this. Especially when the company is investigating the fraudulent use of company lines by the use of a "blue box" or other equipment which permits the bypassing of long distance automatic billing mechanisms, investigators will actually monitor and record calls to determine the speakers' identities and the extent of illegal use.

Because such activity *does* fall within the statutory definition of what constitutes an interception, it must be assessed under a special provision which declares that it is not unlawful "for an operator of a switchboard, or an officer, employee, or agent of a provider of wire or electronic communication services, whose facilities are used in the transmission of a wire communication, to intercept, disclose, or use that communication in the normal course of his employment while engaged in any activity which is a necessary incident to the rendition of his service or to the protection of the rights or property of the carrier of such communication."[13] (This statute goes on to say that these providers may "not utilize service observing or random monitoring except for mechanical or service quality control checks.") Monitoring by the company to obtain evidence for a wire fraud prosecution falls within the "protection of the rights or property" part of the statute. Such monitoring has been upheld where it continued for several weeks, where it continued after the identity of one perpetrator was learned but it was known unidentified others were involved, and even where entire conversations were recorded. As for the "rendition of his service" part of the statute, it has been held to permit, for example, a long distance operator to remain on the line to verify that the call has been connected.

(c) Consent. An important exception to the usual Title III requirement that an interception occur only pursuant to a court order has to do with interceptions made by prior consent. The Act specifically provides that it "shall not be unlawful under this chapter for

---

12. Later, in Smith v. Maryland, 442 U.S. 735, 99 S.Ct. 2577, 61 L.Ed.2d 220 (1979), the Court held that use of a pen register is not governed by the Fourth Amendment. See § 3.2(j).

13. 18 U.S.C.A. § 2511(2)(a)(i).

EXHIBIT 15.3   *(continued)*

---

143   TITLE III: SURVEILLANCE COVERED   259

a person acting under color of law to intercept a wire, oral or electronic communication, where such person is a party to the communication or one of the parties to the communication has given prior consent to such interception."[14] A similar provision covers persons not acting under color of law.[15] The legislative history indicates that the consent exception was intended to reflect existing law in such cases as *Lopez v. United States*[16] and *On Lee v. United States,*[17] which has since been followed by the Court in *United States v. White.*[18] It is thus clear that law enforcement authorities are free to make consensual interceptions in a variety of ways: (1) by having the consenting party wear or carry a tape recorder with which he records his face-to-face conversations with another; (2) by having the consenting party wear a transmitter which broadcasts his conversations to agents equipped with a receiver; or (3) by having the consenting party to a telephone conversation record it or permit another to listen in on an extension.

The legislative history sheds some light upon the scope of this consent exception. For one thing, the "prior consent" language of the statute means that retroactive authorization would not be possible. Secondly, the requisite consent may be express or implied. Surveillance devices in banks or apartment houses for institutional or personal protection would be impliedly consented to. And finally, "party" would mean the person actually participating in the communication, so that interception by impersonation is permissible under the consent provision. For example, if police officers executing a search warrant for gambling paraphernalia answer the phone while there, impersonate the gambler and record the ensuing conversation, this is lawful under Title III.

(d) National Security Surveillance. When Title III was enacted, there was included in it an express declaration that nothing therein "shall limit the constitutional power of the President to take such measures as he deems necessary to protect the Nation against actual or potential attack or other hostile acts of a foreign power, to obtain foreign intelligence information deemed essential to the security of the United States, or to protect national security information against foreign intelligence activities," or "to protect the United States against the overthrow of the Government by force or other unlawful means, or against any other clear and present danger to the structure or existence of the Government."[19] Since at least 1940, there had been presidential sanction for warrantless electronic surveillance in furtherance of national security, and the apparent purpose of the above language was not to disturb whatever powers in this regard the President actually has under the Constitution.

The scope of those powers was at issue in *United States v. United States District Court,*[20] where the government claimed that its warrantless surveillance of a purely domestic radical group engaged in a conspiracy to destroy federal government property was authorized under that statutory provision. But the Court without dissent concluded "that the Government's concerns do not justify departure in this case from the customary Fourth Amendment requirement of judicial approval prior to initiation of a search or surveillance." That conclusion was rested upon the following four considerations: (1) Though in a case such as this the investigative duty of the executive may be stronger, it is equally true that "Fourth Amendment protections become the more necessary when the targets of official

14. 18 U.S.C.A. § 2511(2)(c).

15. 18 U.S.C.A. § 2511(2)(d), which is however qualified so as to not cover the situation in which "such communication is intercepted for the purpose of committing any criminal or tortious act in violation of the Constitution or laws of the United States or of any State or for the purpose of committing any other injurious act."

16. 373 U.S. 427, 83 S.Ct. 1381, 10 L.Ed.2d 462 (1963) (bribe offer recorded by use of concealed recorder).

17. 343 U.S. 747, 72 S.Ct. 967, 96 L.Ed. 1270 (1952) (incriminating remarks made to undercover agent wired for sound).

18. 401 U.S. 745, 91 S.Ct. 1122, 28 L.Ed.2d 453 (1971).

19. Former 18 U.S.C.A. § 2511(3), repealed upon enactment of the Foreign Intelligence Surveillance Act of 1978, discussed herein.

20. 407 U.S. 297, 92 S.Ct. 2125, 32 L.Ed.2d 752 (1972).

trine, for the policies underlying a common law rule, or for the general rule in other jurisdictions.

§15.1.3　Practice Books

Practice books are books that are written for practitioners. Although they take many different forms, the types that are most useful for background reading are deskbooks and practice manuals.

Unlike legal encyclopedias and hornbooks, most practice books are jurisdiction-specific. They are usually written by local practitioners and explain what the law is in that practitioner's state. For example, many state bar associations publish deskbooks summarizing their state's criminal, property, commercial, and family law. In addition, in many states, West publishes a set of practice books that summarize both the state's substantive law and its criminal and civil procedural rules. See Exhibit 15.4.

As a general rule, practice books should not be cited as authority. Use them to obtain an overview of the law and to locate sources of primary authority.

§15.2　Sources That Can Be Used
　　　　as Finding Tools

Legal encyclopedias, hornbooks, and practice books can, however, be used for more than background reading. They are also finding tools. Legal encyclopedias and hornbooks cite to landmark or representative cases from a variety of jurisdictions; practice books cite to the key cases within the jurisdiction. Several other secondary sources can also be used as finding tools.

§15.2.1　American Law Reports

American Law Reports (A.L.R.) was first published in 1919 to compete against West's National Reporter System. Instead of publishing every state and federal appellate opinion, A.L.R. is selective, publishing only "significant" cases.

Today, most researchers do not use A.L.R. as a source for the text of an opinion. Instead, they use it for the annotations. These annotations, which are researched and written by attorneys, explain and discuss the issue raised in the selected case and provide summaries and lists of cases from other jurisdictions dealing with the same issue. See Exhibit 15.5.

§ 187. Communications Covertly Recorded or Intercepted

1. Scope and Purpose of Statute

West's RCWA 9.73 prohibits, with some exceptions, the interception or recording of a private communication or conversation without the consent of all participants. Information obtained in violation of the statutory prohibition is generally inadmissible in any proceeding in any state court.[1] The statute was substantially

ment appearing in 98 Wn.2d xix (January 7, 1983 Advance Sheet) explained the provision as follows:

Section (f). This would be a new section. In 1978, the Supreme Court upheld the search of a newsroom by police searching for evidence of a crime. Zurcher v. Stanford Daily, 436 U.S. 547, 98 S.Ct. 1970, 56 L.Ed.2d 525 (1978). In response to *Stanford Daily*, Congress and the Legislature each enacted provisions to give news media protection against certain kinds of searches. Pub.L. No. 96–440, 42 U.S.C. §§ 2000aa et seq.; Laws of 1980, ch. 52, § 1; RCW 10.79.015(3). The two enactments are not equivalent. The federal statute is much more detailed and makes distinctions based on the type of material sought. The federal statute also applies to a broader range of media than does the state statute.

One element that the two enactments do have in common is the recognition of the subpoena duces tecum as the preferred method of obtaining the desired material. The criminal rules currently contain no provisions for issuance of a subpoena duces tecum. In addition, the normal procedure for subpoenas provides that a party may issue the subpoena. In cases involving a search for evidence, there may frequently be no action yet filed and, therefore, no parties.

The proposed new section has been drafted to avoid an interpretation of when the statutes apply and how

they relate to one another. Any time a search warrant of a person who may be protected by the statutes is sought, a judge will need to determine whether either of the statutes controls. The section also recognizes that there are circumstances in which the statutes permit issuance of search warrants instead of the subpoena duces tecum. The rule does not repeat the statutory provisions.

§ 187

1. Statutes

The general rules are set forth in West's RCWA 9.73.030 and West's RCWA 9.73.050. The statutes provide:

"9.73.030 **Intercepting, recording or divulging private communication—Consent required—Exceptions.** (1) Except as otherwise provided in this chapter, it shall be unlawful for any individual, partnership, corporation, association, or the state of Washington, its agencies, and political subdivisions to intercept, or record any:

(a) Private communication transmitted by telephone, telegraph, radio, or other device between two or more individuals between points within or without the state by any device electronic or otherwise designed to record and/or transmit said communication regardless how such device is powered or actuated, without first obtaining the consent of all the

*Reprinted from Karl B. Tegland, 5A Washington Practice—Evidence, 3d ed., © 1989, with permission of West Publishing Company.

| EXHIBIT 15.5 | Sample Pages from *American Law Reports* (Lawyers Co-operative)* |

ANNOTATION

INTERCEPTION OF TELECOMMUNICATION BY OR WITH CONSENT OF PARTY AS EXCEPTION, UNDER 18 USCS § 2511(2)(c) and (d), TO FEDERAL PROSCRIPTION OF SUCH INTERCEPTIONS

by

Glenn A. Guarino, J.D.

_____

I. PREFATORY MATTERS

§ 1. Introduction:
  [a] Scope

TOTAL CLIENT-SERVICE LIBRARY® REFERENCES

74 Am Jur 2d, Telecommunications § 217

Annotations: See the related matters listed in the annotation, infra.

12 Federal Procedure, L Ed, Evidence § 33:399

23 Am Jur Pl & Pr Forms (Rev), Telecommunications, Forms 151–153

29 Am Jur Proof of Facts 591, Wiretapping

1 Am Jur Trials 481, Investigating the Criminal Case §§ 55–62

18 USCS § 251·1

4 US L Ed Digest, Communications § 9

L Ed Index to Annos, Consent; Informer; Telegraphs and Telephones; Wiretapping

ALR Quick Index, Consent; Eavesdropping; Exceptions or Exclusions; Informers; Privacy; Telecommunications; Wiretapping

Federal Quick Index, Consent; Exemptions; Informers; Interception of Communications; Privacy; Telecommunications; Telephones and Telegraphs

Auto-Cite®: Any case citation herein can be checked for form, parallel references, later history, and annotation references through the Auto-Cite computer research system.

Consult POCKET PART in this volume for later cases and statutory changes

EXHIBIT 15.5   *(continued)*

TELECOMMUNICATION INTERCEPTION   67 ALR Fed
67 ALR Fed 429

[b] Related matters
[c] Text of relevant statutory provisions
§ 2. Summary and comment:
[a] Generally
[b] Practice pointers

II. INTERCEPTION ON BEHALF OF GOVERNMENT, BY OR WITH
CONSENT OF PARTY TO COMMUNICATION, UNDER 18 USCS
§ 2511(2)(c)

§ 3. View that interception is not violative of nonconsenting party's constitutional rights
§ 4. Who may be considered "party" to communication
§ 5. Interception as having been made "under color of law":
[a] "Color of law" held established
[b] "Color of law" held not established
§ 6. Validity of informant's consent:
[a] Valid consent held established
[b] Valid consent held not established

III. INTERCEPTION BY OR WITH CONSENT OF PRIVATE PARTY
UNDER 18 USCS § 2511(2)(d)

§ 7. Validity of consent to interception:
[a] Valid consent held established
[b] Valid consent held not established
§ 8. Wrongful intent rendering exception inapplicable:
[a] Held established
[b] Held not established

INDEX

Accomplice, police impersonating, § 4
Affidavits of consent, § 6[a]
Antitrust suit, § 8[b]
Attorney's expectation of privacy, §§ 3, 6[a]
Barter association's civil rights action, § 3
Blackmail, § 8
Bookie's telephone answered by police, § 4
Bribery, §§ 7[a], 8[b]
Campaign bribes, §§ 7[a], 8[b]
Civil rights action, § 3
"Color of law," interception under, § 5
Comment and summary, § 2
Congressional investigatory team posing as prospective insurance purchasers, § 5[b]
Conspiracy, §§ 7[a], 8[b]
Constitutional rights, generally, § 3
Convicts, § 6[b]
Domestic matters, § 8[a]

Drug offenses, §§ 3, 5[a], 6[a], 8[b]
Due process, § 3
Eavesdropping on multiple conversations, § 3
Election campaign bribes, §§ 7[a], 8[b]
Embarrassment of wife by husband, § 8[a]
Employee of client, attorney's conversation with, §§ 3, 6[a]
Employer's monitoring of personal calls, § 7[b]
Extortion, § 8
Forms of consent, § 6[a]
Gambling offenses, § 4
Government agents, §§ 3-6[a], 7[a]
Husband-wife matters, § 8[a]
Immunity from prosecution in return for informant's consent, § 6[a]
Informants, §§ 3-6[a]
Inmates, § 6[b]
Insurance investigations, §§ 5[b], 8[b]
Intent, wrongful, § 8

EXHIBIT 15.5   *(continued)*

---

67 ALR Fed   TELECOMMUNICATION INTERCEPTION   § 1[b]
67 ALR Fed 429

Introduction, § 1

Leniency in return for informant's consent, § 6[a]

Marital affairs, § 8[a]

Miranda distinguished, § 3

Monitoring policy, knowledge of, §§ 6[b], 7[b]

"Moral issues," informant's consent in respect to, § 6[a]

Multiple conversations, eavesdropping on, § 3

Narcotics offenses, §§ 3, 5[a], 6[a], 8[b]

Nixon tapes, § 7[a]

"Party," construed, § 4

Perjury prosecution, § 8[b]

Plea bargaining agreement with informant, § 6[a]

Practice pointers, § 2[b]

Presidential tapes, § 7[a]

Prison inmates, § 6[b]

Privacy violation, generally, § 3

Real estate broker's conversation, § 5[a]

Related matters, § 1[b]

Relative's testimony upon unavailability of consenting party, § 7[a]

Sales representative's personal call, § 7[b]

Scope of annotation, § 1[a]

Sheriff's acceptance of campaign bribes, §§ 7[a], 8[b]

Summary and comment, § 2

Television tape of insurance presentation, § 5[b]

Text of statute, § 1[c]

Unavailability of consenting party, §§ 7[a], 8[b]

Undercover agents, §§ 3-6[a], 7[a]

Underworld figure as unavailable consenting party, §§ 7[a], 8[b]

Validity of consent, §§ 6, 7

Watergate tapes, § 7[a]

Workmen's compensation investigation, § 8[b]

Wrongful intent, § 8

TABLE OF COURTS AND CIRCUITS

Consult POCKET PART in this volume for later cases and statutory changes

Sup Ct: §§ 2[a]

First Cir: §§ 2[b], 6[b]

Second Cir: §§ 3, 6[a, b]

Third Cir: §§ 2[b], 6[a]

Fourth Cir: §§ 5[b], 6[a]

Fifth Cir: §§ 2[a, b], 4, 5[a], 6[a], 8[a, b]

Sixth Cir: §§ 2[a], 3, 6[a], 7[a], 8[a, b]

Seventh Cir: §§ 3, 5[a], 6[a], 8[b]

Eighth Cir: §§ 2[a], 6[a], 8[b]

Ninth Cir: §§ 2[b], 3, 6[a], 8[b]

Tenth Cir: §§ 2[b], 3, 6[a], 7[b]

Eleventh Cir: §§ 5[a], 6[a], 7[b]

Dist Col Cir: §§ 3, 7[a]

I. Prefatory matters

§ 1. Introduction

[a] Scope

This annotation collects and analyzes the federal cases in which the courts have considered the interception of telecommunications by or with the consent of a party as an exception, under 18 USCS § 2511(2)(c) and (d), to the federal proscription of such interceptions.

[b] Related matters

Propriety of monitoring of telephone calls to or from prison inmates under Title III of Omnibus Crime Control and Safe Streets Act (18 USCS §§ 2510 et seq.) prohibiting judicially unauthorized interception of wire or oral communication. 61 ALR Fed 825.

Who may authorize application for order to intercept wire or oral communications under Title III of Omnibus Crime Control and Safe Streets Act of 1968 (18 USCS §§ 2510 et seq.). 64 ALR Fed 115.

Like other reporters, A.L.R. is organized chronologically. The oldest cases and annotations are printed in A.L.R. and the most recent in A.L.R.5th or A.L.R. Fed.

A.L.R.	1919-1948
A.L.R.2d	1948-1965
A.L.R.3d	1965-1980
A.L.R.4th	1980-1991
A.L.R.5th	1992-current
A.L.R. Fed.	1969-current

Annotations can be located in a number of different ways. The easiest is through the subject indices that accompany the various sets. Recent annotations can be found using the Index to Annotations, which includes references to annotations published in A.L.R.2d, A.L.R.3d, A.L.R.4th, A.L.R.5th, and A.L.R. Fed. Older annotations can be found using the Quick Index for the individual set.

Annotations can also be found using one of the tables contained in the index volume. Annotations discussing a particular section of the United States Code or the Code of Federal Regulations or a particular court rule, uniform act, or restatement section can be located using the Table of Laws, Rules, and Regulations; in the older sets, annotations discussing a particular case can be found using the Table of Cases.

Finally, annotations can be found using a computer. ALR annotations are available on LEXIS, Westlaw, and CD-ROM. Because the full text of each annotation is online, use standard search procedures to find annotations. (See Chapter 17.)

Updating an A.L.R. annotation may vary depending on the series. Through the years, different methods have been used to keep the annotations up to date. In some instances, older annotations have been superseded by newer annotations in later volumes. (To determine whether an annotation has been superseded, use the Annotation History Table, which is located in the Index to Annotations.) In other instances, the annotations have been supplemented. Below is a series list followed by the manner of supplementation.

A.L.R.	Supplemented through use of *A.L.R. Blue Book of Supplemental Decisions.* (Note: These supplements are not cumulative.)
A.L.R.2d	Supplemented using A.L.R.2d Later Case Service. A.L.R.2d Later Case Service is kept current through the use of cumulative pocket parts.
A.L.R.3d, A.L.R.4th, A.L.R.5th, A.L.R. Fed., L. Ed., and L. Ed. 2d	Updated through the use of pocket parts at the back of each volume. There is also a toll-free number (listed on the front of the pocket part) for cases decided since the pocket part was published.

Quick Index   The index is kept current through the use of
   for A.L.R.3d,   pocket parts at the end of each index volume.
   A.L.R.4th,
   A.L.R.5th, and
   A.L.R. Fed.

Although A.L.R.'s primary use is as a finding tool, the annotations
are sometimes cited as persuasive authority. For example, an author may
cite an annotation as authority for what the majority and minority rules
are or as support a statement about current trends. You should not, however, cite A.L.R. as the source of a rule. Instead, cite the primary authority,
that is, the statutes, regulations, and cases discussed in the annotation.

Although the A.L.R. annotations are usually well researched and well
written, do not cite a source discussed in the annotation without reading
the source itself. Never cite a statute, regulation, or case that you have
not read in its primary form.

§15.2.2 Looseleaf Services

Looseleaf services can be used both as a finding tool and as a source
of primary authority. They provide a researcher with up-to-date information on a particular area of law.

There are almost as many looseleaf services as there are areas of law.
There are looseleaf services for most areas of administrative law and for
many specialized areas of practice (for example, BNA's *Environment Reporter* and CCH's *Standard Federal Tax Reporter*). See Exhibit 15.6. In
addition, some looseleaf services have as their primary purpose providing
up-to-date information about court decisions (see, for example, *United
States Law Week*). To determine whether there is a looseleaf service covering the topic that you are researching, check *Legal Looseleafs in Print*
or your library's catalog, or ask a person who practices in that area.

Although each service is unique, they share some common characteristics. First, most are difficult to use, at least initially. Many have
multiple parts and the index or indices may be difficult to use. Consequently, before attempting to use a particular service, either read the
"How to Use This Service" section that is at the beginning of most services
or ask an experienced researcher or librarian to walk you through the
service, explaining how the material is organized and indexed.

Second, most looseleaf services are published in notebook form, the
subscriber being sent additional or replacement pages regularly. Although
this format causes some of the indexing problems noted above, it allows
the publisher to keep the set up to date.

Finally, most looseleaf services contain several types of information;
any given service may have within it the text of court and administrative
decisions, current and proposed statutes, regulations and rules, information about court judgments or the settlement of particular cases, and
commentary.

No. 134   IERM 509:701

Privacy

Search And Surveillance

INTRODUCTION

Searches of employees or their possessions and surveillance of their activities on the job may be regarded by the employees as an invasion of privacy, and by employers as a necessary evil to prevent theft and to control their operations. This chapter discusses legislative actions and judicial decisions concerning workplace monitoring.

BODY SEARCHES

Courts that have reviewed this issue generally balance the intrusiveness of the search against the need to conduct it. Of all types of searches, body searches are the most intrusive and must be counterbalanced by a strong need. After the threshold problem of establishing the need for the search, courts consider the methods by which the search was conducted and whether less intrusive means were available.

Body searches, including pat-downs and strip searches, have been relatively rare in the employment context. Strip searches are an extremely intrusive search, and even law-enforcement authorities need a reasonable basis to strip search suspected criminals.

Testing for drugs and AIDS, and genetic testing, are types of body searches. Drug testing is discussed at IERM 509:101. For information on AIDS testing, see BNA's *Personnel Management.* Only a few states prohibit or regulate genetic testing. Copies of those statutes may be found in BNA's *Fair Employment Practices Manual.*

Fourth Amendment

Body searches of the following employees were held to be reasonable under the given circumstances:

• a corrections officer who an anonymous caller claimed would be reporting to work at the jail with an ounce of cocaine, where supervisors had prior suspicions of the employee's involvement in drug trafficking at the jail, and the caller provided the employee's name, place of employment, work shift, and the quantity of drugs she would be carrying. *Profitt v. District of Columbia,* 790 F.Supp. 304, 6 IER Cases 1318 (DC DC 1991) (strip and alleged visual body-cavity search).

• officers at correctional institutions, if the search was based on reasonable suspicion, in light of the legitimate governmental interest in maintaining security at correctional institutions. But asking employees to strip before giving a urine specimen was not justified, since less intrusive measures could be taken to insure the validity of the specimen. *McDonnell v. Hunter,* 809 F.2d 1302, 1 IER Cases 1297 (CA 8 1987) (strip searches).

However, a New York Department of Corrections' random-search policy for strip searches and body-cavity searches was unreasonable, since a reasonable suspicion directed to a specific person was required. *Sec. & Law Enforcement Emp., Dist. C. 82 v. Carey,* 737 F.2d 187 (CA 2 1984).

§15.3   SOURCES THAT CAN BE CITED AS PERSUASIVE AUTHORITY

Some of the most frequently cited secondary sources are treatises and other books, law reviews, and the comments accompanying uniform acts and the restatements.

§15.3.1   Treatises and Other Books

Most treatises are multivolume works on a single topic. Written by recognized experts in the area, treatises provide the researcher with an in-depth explanation of even narrow issues, citations to supporting cases and statutes, and, at least in some treatises, the author's comments or other commentary. Books are what the name implies. They are single volumes written by scholars, practitioners, or nonlawyers.

Treatises and books can be located through the library's catalog using the author, title, or subject index. (To determine which sources are considered best, ask the law librarian or consult with someone who is familiar with the area of law.) To find the relevant sections within a treatise or book, use the index.

Although treatises and books are not primary authority, they can be used as persuasive authority. The weight that will be given to a particular treatise or book depends on its author. The more respected the author, the more persuasive the source.

§15.3.2   Law Reviews and Other Legal Periodicals

Like treatises and books, law reviews are a source of in-depth information, citations to supporting authority, and commentary. The difference is in their scope. While treatises and books cover broad topics (such as the Federal Rules of Evidence), law reviews focus on much narrower issues (such as the application of a particular rule in a particular circumstance).

Most law reviews are published by law schools. Some of these journals are general in nature, publishing articles on a wide range of topics. Others deal with a specific subject area, for example, international or environmental law.

In most law reviews, there are four types of "articles": (1) lead articles, which are written by professors, judges, or practitioners; (2) comments, which are written by students and which focus on a particular legal topic; (3) notes, which are written by students about a particular case or statute; and (4) book reviews, which are usually written by professors, judges, or practitioners. The students who are on law reviews decide which articles are published.

Like treatises, law review articles have two parts: text and footnotes.

In the text, the author usually defines the issue or problem, summarizes and comments on the existing law, and proposes a solution to the issue or problem. The footnotes provide supporting documentation and, for the researcher, additional research sources.

Law review articles can be located using a number of different indices.

Index to Legal Periodicals (I.L.P.). Prior to 1980, the *Index to Legal Periodicals* was the only index. In book form, it provides access to most law review articles through author, title, subject, case name, and statute indices. The *Index to Legal Periodicals* is also available on CD-ROM. It is also available on Westlaw.

Current Law Index (C.L.I.). In 1980, Information Access Company began publishing the *Current Law Index.* Like the *Index to Legal Periodicals,* this index is available in both book and CD-ROM form (the latter is called LegalTrac). In addition, it is available on LEXIS and Westlaw. Unlike the *Index to Legal Periodicals,* which uses its own index system, the *Current Law Index* uses the Library of Congress subject headings. As a consequence, its headings are usually more specific, making it easier to locate relevant articles. (Note: C.L.I. indexes only articles published after 1980.)

LEXIS and Westlaw. In addition to the availability of the indices mentioned above, LEXIS and Westlaw now have the full text of a number of law reviews online. This feature allows a researcher to locate information contained in the text or footnotes that might not be identifiable through the other indices.

Current Index to Legal Periodicals (C.I.L.P.). This index, which is published by the University of Washington Law Library, is a weekly publication listing just-published law review articles. C.I.L.P. is available in paper, on disk, and online via Westlaw or the Internet.

Index to Foreign Legal Periodicals. This index can be used to locate articles relating to foreign, comparative, or international law published in the major legal periodicals of foreign countries. Some of the articles have English translations; many do not.

Index to Periodical Articles Related to Law. This publication lists articles that are published in nonlaw publications that relate to law or have an impact on law.

In addition to law reviews, there are a number of other legal periodicals published by national, state, and local bar associations, special interest groups, and commercial publishers. These publications usually contain information of a more practical nature and may include articles on law office management, courtroom tips, or the handling of particular types of cases. Two of the most popular legal periodicals are the *American Bar Association Journal,* which is published by the American Bar Association, and *Trial,* which is published by the Association of Trial Lawyers of America.

§15.3.3   Uniform Laws and Model Acts

Another frequently cited secondary source is the official comments accompanying uniform laws. If a state has enacted the uniform law, these comments can be used as evidence of "legislative intent."

Uniform laws are drafted by the Commission on Uniform Laws, which was established in 1912 to "promote uniformity in the law among the several states on subjects where uniformity is desirable and practicable."

Once a year, commissioners from each of the fifty states and the District of Columbia meet to consider drafts of proposed uniform laws. If the commissioners approve a draft, they then take the draft to their own state legislatures, urging their legislatures to enact it. As of this date, the commissioners have approved more than 200 uniform laws. A proposed uniform law does not become law until it has been enacted by the legislature.

If your state has adopted a uniform act, the commissioners' comments can usually be found in your state's annotated code following the text of the statute. They can also be found in *Uniform Laws Annotated* (U.L.A.), a multivolume set that contains the text of the uniform laws, the commissioners' official comments, a list of the states that have enacted the uniform law in whole or in part, and annotations, or notes of decisions, for cases and law review articles interpreting or applying the uniform law. The set also contains, in pamphlet form, a Directory of Uniform Acts and a Table of Adopting Jurisdictions.

Model acts are similar to uniform laws: They propose legislation. Some model acts are put forward by the Commission on Uniform Laws; others, by sections of the American Bar Association or by special interest groups.

Most model acts adopted by the Uniform Commission on State Laws are published in *Uniform Laws Annotated*; other model acts are separately published. To find a copy, use your library's catalog.

§15.3.4   Restatements

While uniform laws are prospective, restatements are retrospective. Drafted by the American Law Institute, a consortium of legal scholars, the restatements describe existing common law on a wide range of topics.

Because the drafters of the restatements are so well respected, the restatements and the reporter's notes and illustrations that accompany them are given more weight than a typical treatise. A restatement is usually the most persuasive of persuasive authority.

Each of the restatements is published separately. The main volumes of the restatements contain the restatement sections themselves and the reporter's comments. Annotated volumes contain citations to cases, cross-references to West's Key Number System and *American Law Reports* (A.L.R.), and an index. To find a particular restatement, use your library's catalog. Restatement sections can be shepardized using *Shepard's Restatement of the Law Citations.*

§15.4   OTHER SECONDARY SOURCES

§15.4.1   Legal Dictionaries

Just as ordinary encyclopedias have their legal counterparts, so do ordinary dictionaries. As a student, you will use legal dictionaries to learn the "language of the law"; as a practitioner, you will use them to translate the Latin maxims that continue to haunt judicial opinions.

Although there are numerous legal dictionaries, the two major ones are *Black's Law Dictionary* and *Ballentine's Law Dictionary*. Both include definitions, guides to pronunciation, and, for many of the definitions, citations to authority. Another dictionary worth noting is *Bouvier's Law Dictionary & Concise Encyclopedia*. Although last published near the turn of the century, it is well respected and useful for looking up terms that are no longer widely used.

Dictionaries are frequently cited as persuasive authority.

§15.4.2   Words and Phrases

Another source of definitions is a set called *Words and Phrases*. In addition to including definitions for legal terms, *Words and Phrases* defines words that may be important in a legal dispute. For example, it defines "assemble," "movable," "acquiesce," and even "electronic communications." Like a legal dictionary, it also includes citations to cases and can, therefore, be used both as persuasive authority and as a finding tool.

West also includes a words and phrases section in its digests. Usually located at the end of the Descriptive Word Index volumes, these sections include pinpoint citations to cases that have judicially defined particular words and phrases.

§15.4.3   Form Books

Form books are—surprise, surprise—books of forms. They also contain clauses that can be inserted into forms. A number of form books are on the market. Some, such as Bender's *Federal Practice Forms,* include forms for a specific jurisdiction. Others, such as *Fletcher Corporation Forms Annotated* (Callaghan) have forms for a particular area of law. Still others, such as *West's Legal Forms* and *Am. Jur. Legal Forms,* include a wide range of forms that can be adapted to a number of different jurisdictions. The forms contained in form books should be used only as a guide. The language that you use will be determined by the facts in your case and your jurisdiction's law.

A particular form can be located using the form book's index or using cross-references contained in other publications. A limited but growing number of legal forms are available online. Because of their capabilities for downloading, editing and then printing or transmitting, online versions of forms may become the preferred format.

Chapter 16

Citators

One of the most embarrassing things that can happen to an attorney is to learn, while standing in front of the court, that the case that he or she has relied on has been overruled. The conversation usually goes something like this.

Attorney: We have based our position on *State v. Smith,* a 1991 decision by the Court of Appeals. In that case, the State —

Judge: (interrupting the attorney) Counsel, are you aware that that decision was overruled by the Supreme Court earlier this month?

Attorney: *(long pause)* No, your Honor. I was not.

To make sure that you don't find yourself in this position, cite check every statute and every case that you cite in your brief. In addition, cite check every statute and case cited by your opponent. One of the easiest ways to win a case is to show that the case that the other side has relied on is no longer good law.

Because the cite checking process is discussed in detail in section 5.3 and section 17.2.12, this chapter sets out only some general information about *Shepard's.*

§16.1   HOW CITATORS WORK

Citators serve two purposes: They tell you whether the original source is still good law, and they provide you with a list of authorities that have cited that source. For example, a case citator (1) tells you whether the case that you are relying on was reversed on appeal or overruled in a later case and (2) provides you with a list of cases, law review articles, and A.L.R. annotations that have cited the case.

Citators do this by listing the sources that have cited the original source. This list is then annotated. For example, in a case citator, the abbreviations before the history entries tell you whether the citation is to the same or a connected case, whether certiorari was granted or denied, and whether the higher court affirmed or reversed. The abbreviations before the treatment citations tell you whether the cite is to a case in which the court questioned or explained the decision in the cited case or followed or overruled the cited case's holding. (See Exhibit 16.1.)

§16.2   *SHEPARD'S* CITATORS

Shepard's publishes a wide variety of citators. There are *Shepard's* citators for state and federal statutes, state and federal cases, and a variety of secondary sources (for example, law reviews, restatements, uniform laws). The following is a partial list of the *Shepard's* citators.

> *Shepard's Banking Law Citations*
> *Shepard's Bankruptcy Citations*
> *Shepard's Code of Federal Regulations Citations*
> *Shepard's Corporation Law Citations*
> *Shepard's Federal Occupational Safety and Health Citations*
> *Shepard's Federal Rules Citations*
> *Shepard's Federal Tax Citations*
> *Shepard's Hawaii Citations*
> *Shepard's Law Review Citations*
> *Shepard's Military Justice Citations*
> *Shepard's Professional and Judicial Conduct Citations*
> *Shepard's Restatement of the Law Citations*
> *Shepard's Southern Reporter Citations*
> *Shepard's Uniform Commercial Code Citations*
> *Shepard's United States Citations* (cases)
> *Shepard's United States Citations* (statutes, court rules)
> *Shepard's United States Patents and Trademarks Citations*
> *Shepard's Wyoming Citations*

§16.3   COVERAGE OF DIFFERENT CITATORS

Not all *Shepard's* citators have the same coverage. Consequently, what you get when you shepardize depends, at least in part, on which citator you use.

§16.3.1   Differences in Coverage of State and Regional Reporters

State cases can be shepardized in either the citator for that state or the appropriate regional citator.

When a state's decisions are published in both an official (state) reporter and regional reporter, the case can be shepardized under either citation. If you shepardize the case in the state citator using the citation to the state reporter, you obtain the following information.

- a parallel citation to the regional reporter
- citations to other decisions from the same state
- citations to federal cases
- citations to law review articles, A.L.R. annotations, annotations in L. Ed. 2d, and selected treatises

If you shepardize the same case in the same citator but under the regional reporter citation, you find the following.

- a parallel citation to the state reporter
- citations to other decisions from the same state
- citations to federal cases

You get still different entries if you shepardize the case in the regional citator using the citation to the regional reporter. You will find the following:

- a parallel citation to the state reporter
- citations to other decisions from the same state
- citations to decisions from other states
- citations to federal cases
- citations to A.L.R., L. Ed. 2d, and selected treatises

Exhibits 16.1 to 16.4 show the information that you would find if you shepardized the same case in both the state and regional citators and online.

§16.3.2   Differences in Coverage for Various Supreme Court Citators and Reporters

United States Supreme Court decisions can also be shepardized under more than one citation. The most comprehensive list of sources can be found under the official (U.S.) citation:

- parallel citations to S. Ct. and L. Ed.
- citations to other federal cases
- citations to state cases
- citations to administrative decisions, articles in the ABA journal, and selected treatises

The following information is obtained when the same case is shepardized using the S. Ct. or L. Ed. citation.

EXHIBIT 16.1   Sample Page from *Shepard's Washington Citations**

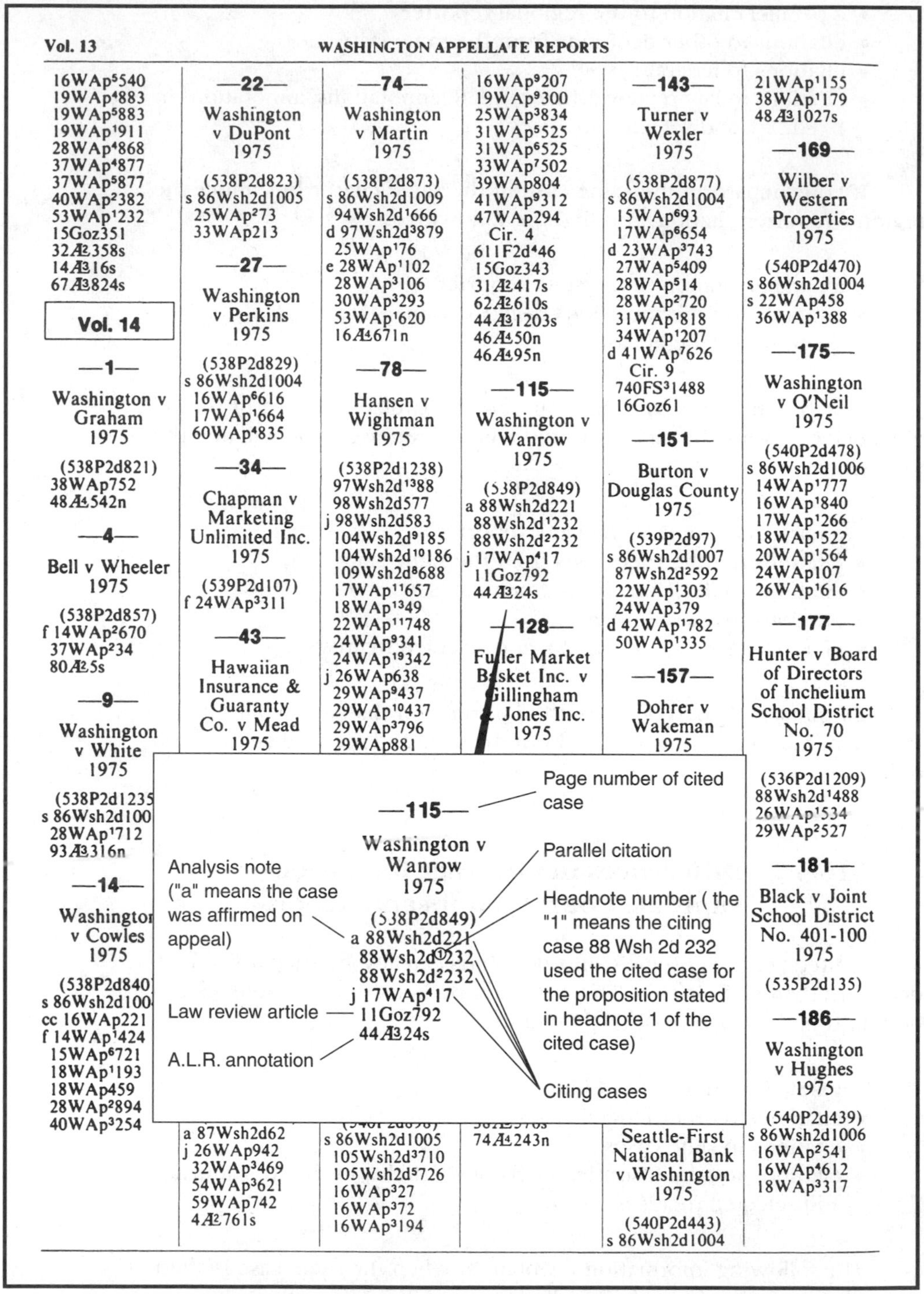

Vol. 13   **WASHINGTON APPELLATE REPORTS**

16WAp⁵540	**—22—**	**—74—**	16WAp⁹207	**—143—**	21WAp¹155

$16WAp^5540$
$19WAp^4883$
$19WAp^5883$
$19WAp^1911$
$28WAp^4868$
$37WAp^4877$
$37WAp^5877$
$40WAp^2382$
$53WAp^1232$
$15Goz351$
$32 \mathcal{A}2358s$
$14 \mathcal{A}316s$
$67 \mathcal{A}3824s$

Vol. 14

—1—

Washington v
Graham
1975

$(538P2d821)$
$38WAp752$
$48 \mathcal{A}4542n$

—4—

Bell v Wheeler
1975

$(538P2d857)$
$f 14WAp^2670$
$37WAp^234$
$80 \mathcal{A}2.5s$

—9—

Washington
v White
1975

$(538P2d1235)$
$s 86Wsh2d100$
$28WAp^1712$
$93 \mathcal{A}3316n$

—14—

Washington
v Cowles
1975

$(538P2d840)$
$s 86Wsh2d100$
$cc 16WAp221$
$f 14WAp^1424$
$15WAp^6721$
$18WAp^1193$
$18WAp459$
$28WAp^2894$
$40WAp^3254$

—22—

Washington
v DuPont
1975

$(538P2d823)$
$s 86Wsh2d1005$
$25WAp^273$
$33WAp213$

—27—

Washington
v Perkins
1975

$(538P2d829)$
$s 86Wsh2d1004$
$16WAp^6616$
$17WAp^1664$
$60WAp^4835$

—34—

Chapman v
Marketing
Unlimited Inc.
1975

$(539P2d107)$
$f 24WAp^3311$

—43—

Hawaiian
Insurance &
Guaranty
Co. v Mead
1975

—74—

Washington
v Martin
1975

$(538P2d873)$
$s 86Wsh2d1009$
$94Wsh2d^1666$
$d 97Wsh2d^3879$
$25WAp^176$
$e 28WAp^1102$
$28WAp^3106$
$30WAp^3293$
$53WAp^1620$
$16 \mathcal{A}4671n$

—78—

Hansen v
Wightman
1975

$(538P2d1238)$
$97Wsh2d^1388$
$98Wsh2d577$
$j 98Wsh2d583$
$104Wsh2d^9185$
$104Wsh2d^{10}186$
$109Wsh2d^8688$
$17WAp^{11}657$
$18WAp^1349$
$22WAp^{11}748$
$24WAp^9341$
$24WAp^{19}342$
$j 26WAp638$
$29WAp^9437$
$29WAp^{10}437$
$29WAp^3796$
$29WAp881$

—115—

Washington v
Wanrow
1975

$(538P2d849)$
$a 88Wsh2d221$
$88Wsh2d^1232$
$88Wsh2d^2232$
$j 17WAp^417$
$11Goz792$
$44 \mathcal{A}324s$

—128—

Fuller Market
Basket Inc. v
Gillingham
& Jones Inc.
1975

16WAp⁹207
$19WAp^9300$
$25WAp^3834$
$31WAp^5525$
$31WAp^6525$
$33WAp^7502$
$39WAp804$
$41WAp^9312$
$47WAp294$
Cir. 4
$611F2d^446$
$15Goz343$
$31 \mathcal{A}2417s$
$62 \mathcal{A}2610s$
$44 \mathcal{A}31203s$
$46 \mathcal{A}450n$
$46 \mathcal{A}495n$

—143—

Turner v
Wexler
1975

$(538P2d877)$
$s 86Wsh2d1004$
$15WAp693$
$17WAp^6654$
$d 23WAp^3743$
$27WAp^5409$
$28WAp^514$
$28WAp^2720$
$31WAp^1818$
$34WAp^1207$
$d 41WAp^7626$
Cir. 9
$740FS^31488$
$16Goz61$

—151—

Burton v
Douglas County
1975

$(539P2d97)$
$s 86Wsh2d1007$
$87Wsh2d^2592$
$22WAp^1303$
$24WAp379$
$d 42WAp^1782$
$50WAp^1335$

—157—

Dohrer v
Wakeman
1975

—143— *(column continues)*

$21WAp^1155$
$38WAp^1179$
$48 \mathcal{A}31027s$

—169—

Wilber v
Western
Properties
1975

$(540P2d470)$
$s 86Wsh2d1004$
$s 22WAp458$
$36WAp^1388$

—175—

Washington
v O'Neil
1975

$(540P2d478)$
$s 86Wsh2d1006$
$14WAp^1777$
$16WAp^1840$
$17WAp^1266$
$18WAp^1522$
$20WAp^1564$
$24WAp107$
$26WAp^1616$

—177—

Hunter v Board
of Directors
of Inchelium
School District
No. 70
1975

$(536P2d1209)$
$88Wsh2d^1488$
$26WAp^1534$
$29WAp^2527$

—181—

Black v Joint
School District
No. 401-100
1975

$(535P2d135)$

—186—

Washington
v Hughes
1975

$(540P2d439)$
$s 86Wsh2d1006$
$16WAp^2541$
$16WAp^4612$
$18WAp^3317$

(inset explanatory diagram)

—115—

Washington v
Wanrow
1975

$(538P2d849)$
$a 88Wsh2d221$
$88Wsh2d^9232$
$88Wsh2d^2232$
$j 17WAp^417$
$11Goz792$
$44 \mathcal{A}324s$

Page number of cited case

Parallel citation

Headnote number (the "1" means the citing case 88 Wsh 2d 232 used the cited case for the proposition stated in headnote 1 of the cited case)

Analysis note ("a" means the case was affirmed on appeal)

Law review article

A.L.R. annotation

Citing cases

(bottom of columns)

$a 87Wsh2d62$
$j 26WAp942$
$32WAp^3469$
$54WAp^3621$
$59WAp742$
$4 \mathcal{A}2761s$

(540P2d898)
$s 86Wsh2d1005$
$105Wsh2d^3710$
$105Wsh2d^5726$
$16WAp^327$
$16WAp^372$
$16WAp^3194$

$561 \mathcal{A}570s$
$74 \mathcal{A}4243n$

Seattle-First
National Bank
v Washington
1975

$(540P2d443)$
$s 86Wsh2d1004$

---

*Reproduced from *Shepard's Washington Citations*, 7th ed. © 1994, by permission of Shepard's. Further reproduction is strictly prohibited.

EXHIBIT 16.2	Sample Page from *Shepard's Pacific Reporter Citations**

Vol. 538   **PACIFIC REPORTER, 2d SERIES (Washington Cases)**

f 541P2d[13]1019
551P2d[10]1381
553P2d[1]134
554P2d[13]1087
557P2d[10]366
570P2d1210
578P2d[8]84
578P2d[10]84
578P2d[1]86
626P2d[8]550
684P2d[3]730
684P2d[8]731
699P2d[3]228
699P2d[5]228
766P2d[1]501

—538—

Washington
v Lee
1975

(13WAp900)
542P2d[3]130
567P2d654
598P2d[6]787
630P2d[10]1390
666P2d[10]383
676P2d524
746P2d[5]318
754P2d[5]1023

—544—

Singer Credit
Corp. v
Mercer Island
Masonry Inc.
1975

(13WAp877)
585P2d[7]815
612P2d[3]373
612P2d[4]373
617P2d[11]713
639P2d[4]829
639P2d[11]829
667P2d[11]1122
713P2d[11]119
776P2d[11]726
816P2d[11]92
Cir. 9
681F2d[11]1232

—551—

Maynard v
England
1975

(13WAp961)
565P2d[3]1239
573P2d[6]1319
822P2d[8]816

—559—

Burgess
v Towne
1975

(13WAp954)
635P2d[7]701
635P2d[8]701
684P2d[4]772
717P2d[3]276
758P2d[3]502
758P2d[4]502
773P2d87
816P2d77
822P2d[2]247
826P2d[2]223

—563—

General
Insurance
Company of
America
v Gauger
1975

(13WAp928)
544P2d[3]765
590P2d[2]377
608P2d[3]259
724P2d[1]422
Cir. DC
520FS[2]289
Cir. 2
f 704F2d[1]84
704F2d[1]85
Cir. 8
576FS[1]806
ICCD§ 5.19

—567—

Washington
v Pearson
1975

(13WAp870)
553P2d[5]1094

—849—

Washington v
Wanrow
1975

(14WAp115)
a 559P2d548
559P2d[3]554
j 560P2d[4]718

Romaine
1975

(14WAp58)
a 549P2d491
j 614P2d698

648P2d[3]895
774P2d1255
801P2d262
831P2d1127

—821—

Washington v
Graham
1975

(14WAp1)
689P2d[2]419

—823—

Washington
v DuPont
1975

(14WAp22)
604P2d[3]1021
604P2d[4]1021
653P2d646

—826—

Wickert v
Board of
Prison Terms
and Paroles
1975

(13WAp917)
595P2d66
f 627P2d[5]544
d 827P2d[4]350

—829—

Washington
v Perkins
1975

(14WAp27)
559P2d[8]10
564P2d[11]186
810P2d[5]3

—834—

569P2d[3]1181
594P2d[9]938
604P2d[1]1333

639P2d[11]870
648P2d[11]490
790P2d[11]625

—840—

Washington
v Cowles
1975

(14WAp14)
cc 556P2d247
f 542P2d[1]128
552P2d[9]1063
567P2d[1]251
569P2d[3]77
626P2d[2]1023
698P2d[3]1062

—845—

In the Matter
of Waggener
1975

(13WAp911)
d 542P2d[1]466
f 588P2d[1]740
654P2d[1]222
d 704P2d[2]1229
705P2d[1]279

—849—

Washington v
Wanrow
1975

(14WAp115)
a 559P2d548
559P2d[3]554
j 560P2d[4]718

—857—

Bell v Wheeler
1975

(14WAp4)
545P2d[4]30
545P2d[5]30

842P2d[1]518

—861—

Washington
v Compton
1975

(13WAp863)
f 603P2d[1]379
612P2d[1]393
j 612P2d398
616P2d[1]687
637P2d[1]1015
746P2d[1]346
826P2d[1]701
827P2d[1]285
4MJ672

—862—

Washington
v Cuzick
1975

(13WAp896)
545P2d[2]574
557P2d[1]16
557P2d[1]1314

—865—

Hawaiian
Insurance &
Guaranty
Co. v Mead
1975

(14WAp43)
567P2d[3]1154
f 578P2d[5]892
586P2d[2]529
645P2d[5]1137
665P2d[6]1386
707P2d[1]1325

—873—

Washington
v Martin
1975

(14WAp74)

Wexler
1975

(14WAp143)
546P2d[12]1252
564P2d[12]838

d 598P2d[6]419
618P2d[5]1026
621P2d[4]1302
626P2d[4]50
644P2d[3]1217
660P2d[2]324
d 705P2d[13]297
Cir. 9
740FS[6]1488

—1209—

Washington
v Sam
1975

(85Wsh2d713)
544P2d[2]779
553P2d[1]134
558P2d[1]810
626P2d43
698P2d1059

—1212—

In the Matter
of Harbert
1975

(85Wsh2d719)
548P2d343
557P2d[4]1304
559P2d[14]577
564P2d331
569P2d1159
j 569P2d1160
570P2d[1]135
572P2d[1]1098
580P2d[3]642
580P2d[4]642
580P2d[5]642
581P2d[2]1368
588P2d[14]1163
592P2d[1]662
611P2d[14]1347
613P2d[14]560
616P2d[1]683
618P2d[6]125
618P2d[9]125
618P2d[14]532
f 619P2d703
625P2d[1]705
j 627P2d950
635P2d[12]147
635P2d[13]147
635P2d[6]150
655P2d[4]1196
656P2d[2]1061
656P2d[2]1105
665P2d[1]911
690P2d1178
834P2d[14]1091

> Note that there are no law review citations, no A.L.R. annotations, and no citations to decisions from states outside of Washington.

EXHIBIT 16.3   **Sample Page from *Shepard's Washington Citations* (Pacific Reporter Citation)***

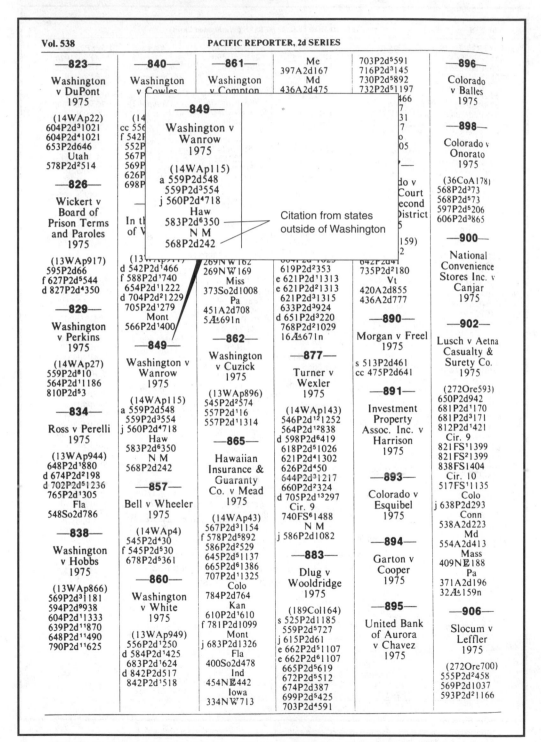

Vol. 538		PACIFIC REPORTER, 2d SERIES			
—823— Washington v DuPont 1975 (14WAp22) 604P2d³1021 604P2d⁴1021 653P2d646 Utah 578P2d²514 **—826—** Wickert v Board of Prison Terms and Paroles 1975 (13WAp917) 595P2d66 f 627P2d⁵544 d 827P2d⁴350 **—829—** Washington v Perkins 1975 (14WAp27) 559P2d⁸10 564P2d¹1186 810P2d⁵3 **—834—** Ross v Perelli 1975 (13WAp944) 648P2d¹880 d 674P2d²198 d 702P2d⁵1236 765P2d¹305 Fla 548So2d786 **—838—** Washington v Hobbs 1975 (13WAp866) 569P2d³1181 594P2d⁹938 604P2d¹1333 639P2d¹¹870 648P2d¹¹490 790P2d¹¹625	**—840—** Washington v Cowles cc 556 f 542F 552P 567P 569P 626P 698P In th of V (13 d 542P2d¹466 f 588P2d¹740 654P2d¹1222 d 704P2d²1229 705P2d¹279 Mont 566P2d¹400 **—849—** Washington v Wanrow 1975 (14WAp115) a 559P2d548 559P2d³554 j 560P2d⁴718 Haw 583P2d⁶350 N M 568P2d242 **—857—** Bell v Wheeler 1975 (14WAp4) 545P2d⁴30 f 545P2d⁵30 678P2d⁵361 **—860—** Washington v White 1975 (13WAp949) 556P2d¹250 d 584P2d¹425 683P2d¹624 d 842P2d517 842P2d¹518	**—861—** Washington v Compton **—849—** Washington v Wanrow 1975 (14WAp115) a 559P2d548 559P2d³554 j 560P2d⁴718 Haw 583P2d⁶350 N M 568P2d242 269NW162 269NW169 Miss 373So2d1008 Pa 451A2d708 5A2d691n **—862—** Washington v Cuzick 1975 (13WAp896) 545P2d²574 557P2d¹16 557P2d¹1314 **—865—** Hawaiian Insurance & Guaranty Co. v Mead 1975 (14WAp43) 567P2d³1154 f 578P2d⁵892 586P2d²529 645P2d⁵1137 665P2d⁶1386 707P2d¹1325 Colo 784P2d764 Kan 610P2d¹610 f 781P2d1099 Mont j 683P2d1326 Fla 400So2d478 Ind 454NE442 Iowa 334NW713	Me 397A2d167 Md 436A2d475 641P2d1625 619P2d²353 e 621P2d¹1313 e 621P2d²1313 621P2d³1315 633P2d³924 d 651P2d³220 768P2d²1029 16A2d671n **—877—** Turner v Wexler 1975 (14WAp143) 546P2d¹²1252 564P2d¹²838 d 598P2d⁶419 618P2d⁵1026 621P2d⁴1302 626P2d⁴50 644P2d³1217 660P2d²324 d 705P2d¹³297 Cir. 9 740FS⁶1488 N M j 586P2d1082 **—883—** Dlug v Wooldridge 1975 (189Col164) s 525P2d1185 559P2d⁵727 j 615P2d61 e 662P2d⁵1107 e 662P2d⁶1107 665P2d⁵619 672P2d⁵512 674P2d387 699P2d⁵425 703P2d⁴591	703P2d⁵591 716P2d³145 730P2d⁵892 732P2d⁵1197 466 7 31 7 o 05 — do v Court econd District 5 159) 2 642P2d4 735P2d²180 Vt 420A2d855 436A2d777 **—890—** Morgan v Freel 1975 s 513P2d461 cc 475P2d641 **—891—** Investment Property Assoc. Inc. v Harrison 1975 **—893—** Colorado v Esquibel 1975 **—894—** Garton v Cooper 1975 **—895—** United Bank of Aurora v Chavez 1975	**—896—** Colorado v Balles 1975 **—898—** Colorado v Onorato 1975 (36CoA178) 568P2d³73 568P2d⁵73 597P2d⁵206 606P2d³865 **—900—** National Convenience Stores Inc. v Canjar 1975 **—902—** Lusch v Aetna Casualty & Surety Co. 1975 (272Ore593) 650P2d942 681P2d¹170 681P2d³171 812P2d¹421 Cir. 9 821FS¹1399 821FS²1399 838FS1404 Cir. 10 517FS¹1135 Colo j 638P2d293 Conn 538A2d223 Md 554A2d413 Mass 409NE188 Pa 371A2d196 32A2d159n **—906—** Slocum v Leffler 1975 (272Ore700) 555P2d²458 569P2d1037 593P2d²1166

Citation from states outside of Washington

| EXHIBIT 16.4 | Online *Shepard's* Citations* |

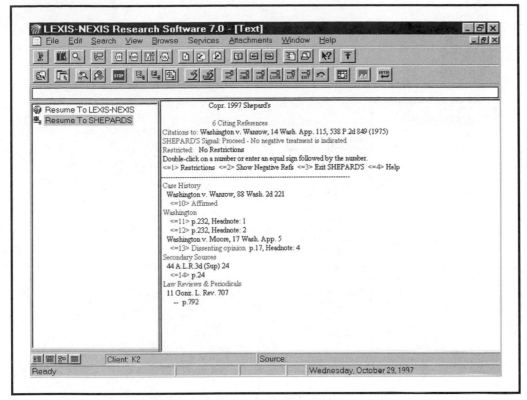

- parallel citation to U.S.
- citations to other federal cases
- citations to state cases after 1984
- citations to A.L.R.

Citations to law reviews can be found using *Shepard's Federal Law Citations in Selected Law Reviews.*

§16.4 TIPS ON USING *SHEPARD'S*

In using *Shepard's* citators, keep the following in mind.

1. *Shepard's* citators are not cumulative. Depending on how old the case is, you may need to look in a number of different volumes (hardbound volume, hardbound supplement, and one or more paper supplements). To determine what volumes you need, check the coverage notes printed on the cover of the most recent supplement.

| EXHIBIT 16.4 | *(continued)* |

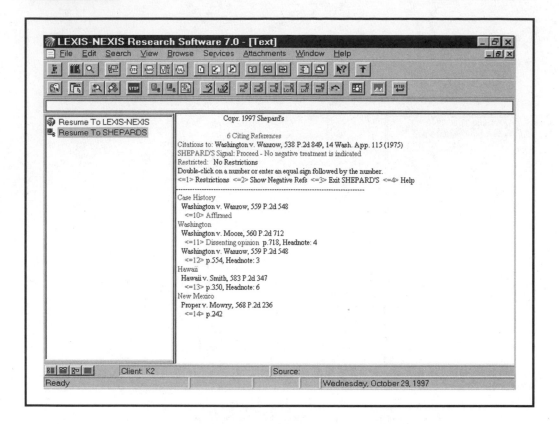

2. You may obtain different information depending on which citator and citation you use.

3. If you are citing a case using its official (state reporter) citation, use the headnote numbers that appear in the official reporter; if you are using the regional reporter citation, use the headnote numbers that appear in the regional reporter.

4. You don't need to read every case cited in *Shepard's*. If the list of cites is long, check those cases whose citation is preceded by an "o" (overruled), an "r" (reversed), an "m" (modified), a "q" (questioned), or a "c" (criticized). If the list of citations is short, you may want to check each case listed.

§16.5   *SHEPARD'S* ONLINE

Online versions of *Shepard's* are treated more fully in Section 17.2.12. It merits mentioning that absent availability and cost considerations, online cite checking is probably preferred. Not only does the online version cumulate the various volumes, it allows you to focus narrowly on particular types of treatment or analysis by later courts, or on specific headnotes.

§16.6   KEYCITE

In 1997, a new cite checking service, KeyCite, was introduced to the legal profession. Lawyers can access KeyCite either through Westlaw or the Internet (⟨www.keycite.com⟩).

KeyCite is only available for cite checking cases (statutes and secondary sources are not linked with KeyCite). In Westlaw, you can access KeyCite either by typing "kc" or by clicking on the KeyCite icon. Like *Shepard's*, KeyCite gives the prior and later history of the case. Also like *Shepard's*, KeyCite lists cases that have cited the case you are cite checking.

An important component to KeyCite is its flagging system. Cases either have a red flag, a yellow flag, or no flag at all (the "flags" may appear as the words "red flag" or "yellow flag" on some versions of KeyCite). A red flag indicates that the case is no longer good law for at least one of the propositions stated in it. A yellow flag indicates that the case has some negative history. Additionally, a "History" flag indicates that the case has some history available. By accessing KeyCite from a flagged case, you can determine with more certainty which issue is questionable and how it was treated in subsequent cases.

In addition to the above references, KeyCite has a "depth of treatment" classification system. This system is desiged to tell you whether the cited case is analyzed in detail in the citing case or is merely contained as part of a string cite. Four stars (****) is the top rating (called "examined"). Four stars means the citing case contains an extended discussion of the cited case. One star (*) is the lowest rating (called "mentioned"). It means that the citing case contains a brief reference to the cited case, usually in a string citation. KeyCite also indicates (by quotation marks: ") if the cited case is quoted in the citing case.

One of the KeyCite's most powerful features is its ability to limit the types of cases retrieved when you cite check. By clicking on particular boxes, you can limit the citing cases by such factors as:

- West headnote (*e.g.*, only cases cited for the proposition in headnote 1)
- jurisdiction (*e.g.*, only Texas cases)
- date
- negative treatment
- depth of treatment

These and other limitations can be used independently or in conjunction with other limitations. An example of KeyCite can be seen in Exhibit 16.5.

EXHIBIT 16.5	KeyCite*

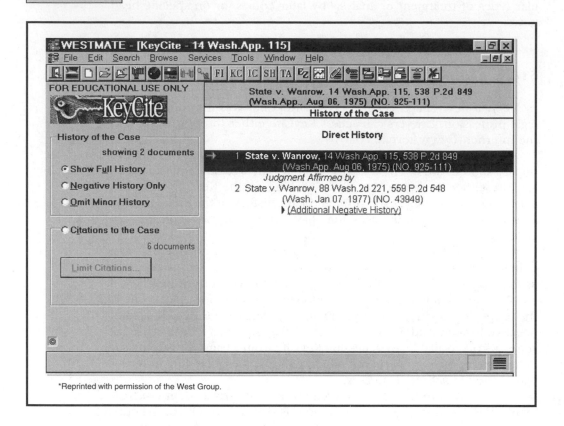

*Reprinted with permission of the West Group.

One caution about using KeyCite is in order. Because KeyCite uses red and yellow flags to warn you about potential problems with using a case as authority, you might be inclined to think that a case without a flag is good law. It might be. However, you should verify this with additional research. If, for example, the legislature enacted a statute after the case that superseded the case, that would probably not be "flagged" by KeyCite.

Chapter 17

Computer-Assisted Legal Research

Few people have a neutral attitude about computers. Either they are high-tech demons that have depersonalized and dehumanized modern life, making it more alien, more Orwellian; or they are the panacea for all problems, the scientific solution for the information explosion.

The same is true for people's attitudes about computer-assisted research. It is seen by some as an overrated, overpriced, glitzy shortcut that can lead to shoddy work and by others as an efficient, effective, modern approach to accessing information. In short, book researchers often consider computers anathema; computers researchers often consider books anachronistic. And never the twain shall meet.

Or will they? Effective researchers have always known when to use what. Long before the age of LEXIS and Westlaw, astute researchers knew the benefits and limitations of an annotated versus an unannotated code and when to and when not to use other finding tools such as the looseleaf services. Computer-assisted research is no different. It is a tool, and in this case, the tool includes a system, usually LEXIS, Westlaw, CD-ROM products, and the Internet.

Many of the resources discussed in the preceding six chapters are available via computer as well as in their original print form. The computer is merely an alternative means for accessing these resources. The question then is, when should one use the books and when should one use the machine?

This chapter will discuss not only how to use computers to do legal research but also when to use them. Much of the "when" information is integrated in the discussion that follows, but as a general rule, you may find the following advice helpful: Use computers when you cannot easily find the same information in a book.

It really is that simple.

§17.1   INDICES AND FULL-TEXT SEARCHING

The unique power of computer-assisted research is its ability to search documents "full-text." The ability to do full-text searching means that, with limited exceptions, every word in a document can be used as an access point. The practical benefit of full-text searching is that you no longer need to rely on an index as the sole means for obtaining references to authority.

For example, suppose you are looking for cases concerning a police officer stopping and frisking a person. If you had to rely on an index, you might look under "stop" or "frisk" or even "arrest" and find nothing. Suppose that in this particular index cases of this type are listed under "warrantless searches." If you are unfamiliar with this terminology or even if you know the term but have temporarily forgotten it, the index will be worthless to you in this instance. In fact, it could even be detrimental because you might assume there are no such cases because you were unable to locate them in the index.

Full-text searching allows you to bypass indices. If you want to look for cases using the word "frisk," the computer will retrieve all cases in which that word is used anywhere in the case.

Another problem with indices is that they require generalization. For example, cases concerning cars, regardless of model, will probably be indexed under either "car" or "automobile." But what if you want to find cases about a certain kind of car, such as a Pinto? An index will refer you to cases about cars, but then you have to locate those concerning Pintos by browsing through all the cases. Full-text searching, by contrast, allows you to search for cases with the word "Pinto."

Full-text searching ability, then, is one reason why computer-assisted research can be the more efficient way to do legal research. Used judiciously, it can overcome the what-is-the-right-search-term problem as well as focus the research in ways that are not possible when researching in books. Throughout this discussion, search terms and commands (that is, material you would actually type into the computer) appear in italic type.

§17.2   LEXIS AND WESTLAW

§17.2.1   Similarities and Differences in the Two Systems

When lawyers talk about computer-assisted research, they usually mean LEXIS and Westlaw, two separate services for accessing legal materials via computer. LEXIS and Westlaw are similar in that both have the same types of information available. Both services have the text of state and federal cases. Both have the United States Code, Code of Federal Regulations, Federal Register, decisions of many administrative agencies, and many law review articles. Both have the statutes (codes) of all fifty states. Their dates of coverage differ for some materials (such as state court decisions), but both continue to add retrospectively.

LEXIS and Westlaw also have some important differences. LEXIS is part of LEXIS/NEXIS, a computer-assisted research service that comes with a LEXIS subscription and that includes national newspapers, financial information, medical informaton and other nonlegal information.

Westlaw, by contrast, allows access to DIALOG, which is mostly nonlegal, scientific, technical, or business-related material. Much of the material on DIALOG is in indexed or digest form rather than full-text. An even more important Westlaw feature, however, is that within Westlaw you can use the West Key Number System and other West-created enhancements for searching in its databases. This feature allows you to search the West synopses and headnotes. Furthermore, you can run a key number search online, either using the key number alone as a search term or using it in combination with keyword searching.

LEXIS and Westlaw also differ in many coverage dates and in their pricing. The two systems also use different terminology to describe similar entities. Despite what may seem like a litany of differences, though, the two systems are still far more alike than they are different. Consequently, it makes sense to learn about them together, noting the differences as they occur.

§17.2.2 Composition of LEXIS and Westlaw Services

The structure and mechanics of LEXIS and Westlaw, like much else in the systems, are similar. It is the terminology that each uses to describe its system that varies.

In LEXIS, you first choose a "library". A "library" in this sense is a broad collection of documents. The GENFED library, for instance, contains federal documents such as the *United States Code,* the *Code of Federal Regulations,* and federal cases.

Once you select a LEXIS library by typing in its name and transmitting it to the computer, you then must select a LEXIS "file."

A file is a subcategory of a library. Files vary in size. In the GENFED library, for instance, the DIST file contains all published cases (and some unpublished cases) from federal district courts. The COURTS file, by contrast, contains cases from all federal courts. The libraries and files are entered into through the "Look in Sources" box. See Exhibit 17.1. If you do not know the name of the library and file, you can click on the "More Sources" button. By following the trail in the topical source list (see Exhibit 17.2), you can ultimately find the appropriate library and file and click on them.

In Westlaw, you select a "database" from the screen's menu before running a search. Unlike LEXIS, there is no subcategory. Databases, like libraries and files, vary in size. The ALLFEDS database, for example, contains published cases from all federal courts after 1944. The DCT database contains only cases from the federal district courts. See Exhibits 17.3, 17.4, and 17.5.

| EXHIBIT 17.1 | **LEXIS-NEXIS Searcher Screen*** |

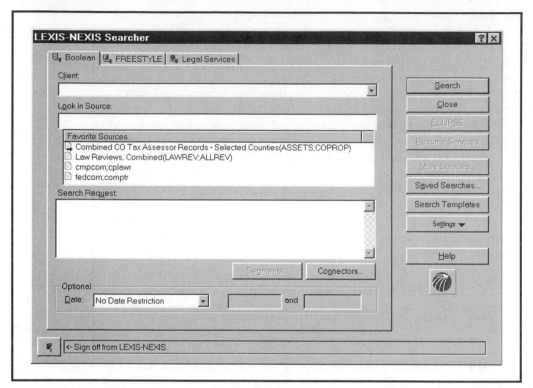

The documentation for the services contains a complete list of the available files and databases. Many users prefer to bypass these, however, because the systems are menu-driven. Once you have entered a valid password and identified the research (for billing purposes), the initial screen that appears is a menu screen.

From the first menu screen, you can select other menu screens to locate the appropriate library and file, or database, to be searched. After entering the name of the library and file, or database, you enter the search. If you know the identifier (for the library and file or for the database), you can enter it at the initial menu screen, thereby bypassing the other menu screens and saving time.

§17.2.3   Search Words

Because computers can search for nearly every word in a document, the basic search component in computer-assisted research is "the word." A "word" for these purposes is defined as any string of characters with a

EXHIBIT 17.2	LEXIS-NEXIS Sources Screen*

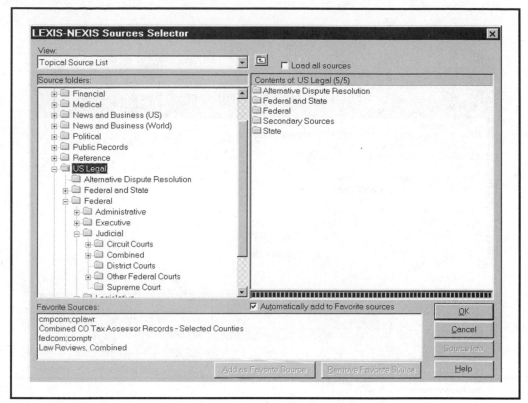

*Reprinted with the permission of Reed Elsevier, Inc., provider of the LEXIS®/NEXIS® services.
© 1997 Reed Elsevier, Inc.

space on either side. Consequently, words in computer-assisted research include not only standard words such as *contract* or *tort* but also "words" like *WD-40* and *26.04.010.*

In fact, because unique words are more useful as search words than common words, numbers like *26.04.010* are some of the best search words. Strings of numbers in a legal document, like *26.04.010,* usually refer to a citation, and a citation is often the perfect search word for finding specific documents, such as cases or statutes.

In contrast, common words such as *will* and *service* are poor search words because they have many meanings other than as references to legal concepts. Unfortunately, because these words often appear in legal materials with these alternative meanings, using such words as search words can retrieve irrelevant cases. Therefore, unique words, when they exist, are generally the best ones for full-text searching.

EXHIBIT 17.3	Westlaw Directory Menu*

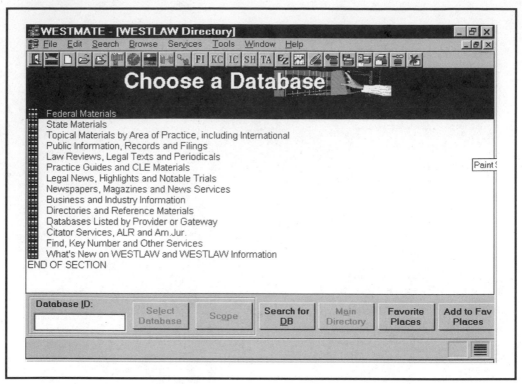

*Reprinted with permission of West Group.

§17.2.4   Truncation and Root Expansion

One problem with language is that there are many ways to describe the same concept. More precisely, a root word may have many endings. For example, the concept of contributing negligence may be referred to in the following ways:

> contributory negligence
> contributorily negligent
> negligent contributorily
> contributed to the negligence
> contribution on the plaintiff's part

This list of choices does not even take into account the fact that some jurisdictions may refer to this concept as *comparative negligence* rather than *contributory negligence.*

Because it would be burdensome to enter all the alternative forms into the computer, both computer services allow truncation and root

EXHIBIT 17.4	Westlaw Federal Materials Directory*

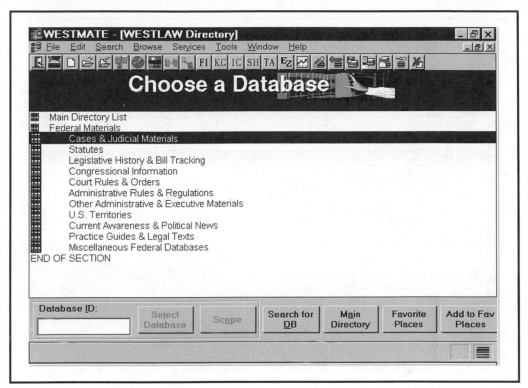

*Reprinted with permission of West Group.

expansion. All you need to do is type the root word and use the truncation symbol at the end.

There are two symbols that can be used to truncate: the asterisk (*) and the exclamation point (!). The * is a universal character. It occupies one space and only one space. Thus, *contribut** would obtain documents with *contribute* but not *contributor* or *contribution*.

More than one * may be used to truncate. Adding additional asterisks will expand the root up to and including the number of asterisks. For example, *contribut**** would obtain *contribute, contributory,* and *contribution*. It would not obtain *contributorily*.

Usually, root expansion is best done with the !. A single ! gets all suffixes to the root regardless of the number of letters. Thus, *contribut!* would obtain *contribute, contribution, contributory,* and *contributorily*.

Why then would a researcher ever use an asterisk rather than an exclamation point for truncation? An example of a rare occasion when the * might be preferable in truncating would be *execut**** to obtain *executor, executive,* and *executrix* but eliminate *executioner*.

The * does, however, have a use that the ! does not. It can be used in the middle of a word. Thus, *dr*nk* would obtain *drink, drank,* and *drunk*.

EXHIBIT 17.5	Westlaw Federal Materials, Cases & Judicial Materials Directory*

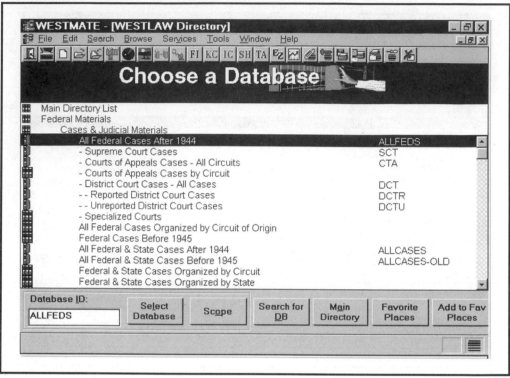

*Reprinted with permission of West Group.

Note too, though, that if the * is used in the middle of a word, some character must be in the * location for it to be retrieved. Thus, *judg*ment* does *not* obtain both forms of the word (*judgement* and *judgment*). It obtains only *judgement.*

Finally, neither the * nor the ! can be used at the beginning of a word. Thus, **regulation* will obtain nothing.

§17.2.5   Hyphenation

Another feature in our language that complicates computer-assisted research is the hyphen. Unfortunately, LEXIS and Westlaw differ in their treatment of hyphens.

LEXIS treats hyphens as spaces. Thus, in LEXIS *pre-judgment* would obtain *pre judgment* and *pre-judgment* but not *prejudgment.*

Westlaw, by contrast, "normalizes" hyphenated words. "Normalizing" means a hyphenated query will retrieve the hyphenated word, the phrase as two words and the word as a single word. Thus, in Westlaw *pre-judgment* would obtain *pre-judgment, pre judgment* and *prejudg-*

ment. Note, however, that the hyphenation must be in the typed query for the normalization to occur. Thus, *prejudgment* will not obtain *pre-judgment* in either Westlaw or LEXIS.

Retrieval

Search Word	LEXIS	Westlaw
prejudgment	prejudgment	prejudgment
pre-judgment	pre-judgment	pre-judgment
	pre judgment	prejudgment
	but not	*but not*
	prejudgment	pre judgment

LEXIS: hyphen = space
Westlaw: hyphen = word with or without hyphen

§17.2.6   Plurals and Capitalization

Both systems are programmed to retrieve the plural form of a word if the singular is searched. This feature can be turned off on Westlaw by typing the pound sign (#) in front of the word. In LEXIS, you can do the same by typing the word "singular" in front of the word in parentheses:

singular (security)

In LEXIS, a search of a plural form retrieves the singular form as well. The feature can be turned off by typing the word "plural" in front of the word in parentheses:

plural (goods)

In Westlaw, a search of the plural form only retrieves that form.

§17.2.7   Noise Words (Stop Words)

Neither system will search for certain words known as "noise words" or "stop words." These are words that are so commonly used in the language that searching for them would be of little value and would significantly burden the computer's abilities. Examples are words like *of, the*, and *very*.

There are approximately 100 noise or stop words. A complete list of each system's noise or stop words can be found in their respective documentation.

§17.2.8   Connectors

Although it is true that unique words are the best search terms, rarely does a single word or phrase retrieve relevant documents without also retrieving a large number of irrelevant documents.

A good search usually requires a combination of several words. The relationship between the words is expressed to LEXIS and Westlaw by the use of connectors. Four connectors are used in computer-assisted legal research: *or, and*, the proximity connector */#,* and *not.*

a.   OR

The connector *or* is used for synonymous terms. It means that either the word to the left of the *or* or the word to the right of the *or* must appear in the document for it to be retrieved. In LEXIS, the convention used for the *or* connector is merely typing *or* between the two words. Thus, in LEXIS, *car or automobile* retrieves all documents with either *car* or *automobile* anywhere in the document.

The same convention (adding *or*) also works in Westlaw. However, the preferred method of searching using the *or* connector in Westlaw is to leave a space between the words. In other words, in Westlaw, a space is treated as an *or* connector. Therefore, in Westlaw, *car automobile* will retrieve all documents with either *car* or *automobile* anywhere in the document.

To reiterate, typing the word *or* will work in both LEXIS and Westlaw. In addition, Westlaw treats a space as the connector *or.*

This difference is probably the single most important distinction in search logic between the two systems. Where it becomes problematic is in phrase searching. If, for example, you want to search for cases dealing with the writ of habeas corpus, the search is done on LEXIS as *habeas corpus.*

If the same string of characters is typed into Westlaw, however, that service will read it *habeas or corpus.* Thus, the lawyer would retrieve not only cases with *habeas corpus* in them, but also all cases with *corpus juris* or *corpus delicti.* Many an unwary or infrequent Westlaw user has fallen into this trap.

The way to do a phrase search in Westlaw is to put the phrase in quotation marks (" "). Thus, in Westlaw, *"habeas corpus"* would retrieve all cases with the phrase *habeas corpus* in them.

To review, then, the connector *or* is used for synonymous terms. It means that either the word on its left or the word on its right must appear in the document for it to be retrieved. The convention for entering this connector in a search is to type *or.* However, in Westlaw, a space is also treated as an *or.* Finally, to search for a phrase in Westlaw, quotation marks must surround the phrase. Quotation marks are not necessary for a phrase search in LEXIS.

b.   AND

The second connector is *and.* It is narrower than *or* but still fairly broad. The *and* connector requires that both the word to the left of *and* and the word to the right of *and* appear in the same document. One can be the first word in the document, the other the last word, but as long as they both appear somewhere in the document, the document will be retrieved.

In both LEXIS and Westlaw, the convention for entering this connector is merely typing the word *and.* In Westlaw, the ampersand (&) may also be used. Thus, in both services, *slip and fall and snow* would retrieve all documents that have all three words—*slip, fall,* and *snow*— somewhere in the document.

And is used when the words that a lawyer wants to find may not be located close to each other. An example might be when a lawyer wants to find cases on the statute of limitations for negligent manufacture resulting in the explosion of a motor vehicle's gas tank. The words relating to the vehicle, the gas tank, and the explosion will probably be located near one another. They would likely be in the court's recitation of the facts. For these words, proximity connectors (discussed in the next section) would be better than *and.* However, it might be several pages before the court's analysis turned to issues of negligent manufacture or the statute of limitations. Therefore, the words used to search for those concepts should probably be connected to the exploding gas tank concept with *and.*

c. Proximity Connectors

There are two types of proximity connectors. The first is the numerical connector. The second is the grammatical connector.

Numerical Connectors

Numerical connectors specify that only a certain number of words can intervene between the connected words. The convention used in numerical connectors is /# (# representing any number from 1 to 255). For numbers larger than 255, an *and* connector is appropriate. You may also see the *w/#* convention used in documentaton (or by other research services). In both LEXIS and Westlaw, *w/#* works the same as /#.

Earlier, we discussed the different ways of referring to the concept of contributory negligence. Below is an example of a search for this concept that works in both systems.

contribut! /4 negligen!

Recall that the ! is used to expand the roots of both words. The /4 requires that, at the most, four words can intervene between *contribut!* and *negligen!.* Therefore, the search would retrieve all of the following:

> *contributory negligence,*
> *contributorily negligent,*
> *negligent contributorily,* and
> *contributed to the negligence*

It will not retrieve *contribution on the plaintiff's part* because the search requires that the word *negligen!* be used within four words of *contribut!*, and it does not in this phrase.

Notice that /# does not specify order. That is, it does not matter which word occurs first in the text. Order can be specified by using the connector *pre/#* in LEXIS and +# in Westlaw (although each service often upgrades its system so that it can read the other's searching conventions). The following are examples of these connectors:

> LEXIS: *John pre/1 Kennedy*
> Westlaw: *John + 1 Kennedy*

The *pre/#* and +# are useful in searching for citations. In a case citation, the name of the case always precedes the volume number and the volume number always precedes the page number. When looking for cases *citing University Nat. Co. v. Gray's Harbor County,* 12 Wash. 2d 549, 122 P.2d 501, the following searches might be used:

> LEXIS: *University pre/10 12 pre/2 549*
> Westlaw: *University + 10 12 + 2 549*

This example raises two issues. The first issue is, why not specify *12 Wash. 2d 549* itself? The answer is that the reporter abbreviation may be a problem. The *Bluebook* says *Washington Reports, Second Series* is abbreviated Wash. 2d. The *Washington Style Sheet* (used by that state) says the correct abbreviation is Wn.2d.

In addition, problems often occur in reporter abbreviations because of punctuation (here, the period) and spacing. All the following can be found as abbreviations for Washington Reports, Second Series, in both LEXIS and Westlaw.

Wash.2d	Wn.2d
Wash. 2d	Wn. 2d
Wash2d	Wn2d
Wash 2d	Wn 2d

The point is that the volume and page numbers are the most important part of a citation. If they alone are not enough to limit the search to only those documents citing the case, then the name can be added. Using *pre/#* or +# eliminates the pitfalls that reporter abbreviations can create.

The second issue raised by the example is, why would anyone search for a case citation when the case can be updated with a citation service? The answer is that many of the materials available online are available long before they appear in print. United States Supreme Court cases, for example, are available within hours of their release. Unfortunately, it may be a matter of weeks before a case that cites another is available in *Shepard's.*

Consequently, because *Shepard's* is not useful for finding cases that are very recent, using the computer as a citator (using the citation as a search) is an effective way of updating *Shepard's.* KeyCite also takes some time to process cases.

To recap, /# allows you to specify the proximity of search words to each other. This connector is narrower than the *and* connector. The /# does not specify sequence. However, sequence can be specified with the *pre/#* and +#. When these connectors are used, the word to the left of the connector must occur in the text before the word to the right of the connector.

Finally, one difference between the two services is in what is considered a "word" for the purpose of counting intervening words. LEXIS does not count noise or stop words (see section 17.2.7) as intervening words; Westlaw does. The result is that /25 in LEXIS is different from /25 in Westlaw. The /25 of LEXIS is probably closer to /40 in Westlaw. The following sentence may be illustrative:

> Common law copyright is that right that an author has in his or her unpublished literary creations.

Suppose a researcher did the following searches in both LEXIS and Westlaw:

copyright /5 unpublished

LEXIS would retrieve a document with the illustrative sentence because it would not count the noise words: *is, that, that, an, has, his, or, her.* Thus, only three words intervene in the LEXIS search. Westlaw would count all intervening words, including stop words. Because eleven words intervene, the document would not be retrieved in Westlaw. This fact is important to remember when deciding what number to use in searches using a proximity connector.

Grammatical Connectors

In addition to the numerical proximity connector, LEXIS and Westlaw also have grammatical connectors. The connectors are /s for words in the same sentence and /p for words in the same paragraph. Sequence can be specified by using *pre/s* and *pre/p* (in LEXIS) or +s and +p (in Westlaw) for preceding words in the same sentence and preceding words in the same paragraph, respectively. With these connectors, the number of intervening words is irrelevant. As long as the connected words occur within the same grammatical component, the document will be retrieved.

This type of connector is useful because the English language is based on grammar rather than on word proximity. The latter can roughly estimate grammar, but the real thing is usually better. The following are examples of grammatical connectors:

> *copyright /s unpublished*
> *libel! slander! defam! /p "public figure"*

d. NOT

The final connector is the *not* connector. LEXIS calls it "and not"; Westlaw calls it "but not." The *not* connector excludes terms to the right of the connector. Terms to the left are treated as they normally would be in a search request. The convention used in LEXIS is to type *and not*. Westlaw's convention is the percent sign (%). The following are examples of the *not* connector:

> LEXIS: *breach! w/5 warranty and not contract*
> Westlaw: *breach! /s warranty % contract*

The above searches might be used if a researcher is looking for breach of warranty as a cause of action in tort. This leads to a caution. Always remember that the computer itself is literal; it is not intelligent. In the above example, it is possible that a judge might write an opinion that says: "Breach of warranty is usually an issue in contract law. Here, however, we explore its effect in tort law." This is exactly the type of case that the researcher wants to find. It would not be retrieved, though, because the word *contract* appeared. The *not* connector may have utility (especially with the field searches, discussed shortly), but it should be used with some caution.

§17.2.9   Search Order of Connectors

Both LEXIS and Westlaw are programmed so that they search certain connectors first. The search order is as follows:

1. *or*
2. proximity connectors from smallest to largest (for example, */5* before */25*)
3. grammatical connectors (*/s* before */p*)
4. *and*
5. *not*

The computer's search order may seem like a small, technical point, but it is important practical knowledge for the legal researcher. You may have used the right words and connectors, but the computer may still not be running the search you think it is.

For example, if you want cases dealing with worker's compensation the following searches might be used:

> LEXIS: *industrial insurance or work! /2 compensation*
> Westlaw: *"industrial insurance" work! /2 compensation*

The above searches will not retrieve the desired documents. The reason is the searching order of connectors. Because the computer is programmed to search *or* first, it will initially come up with the subset of documents with either the phrase *industrial insurance* or words with the root *work*. It will then take this subset and combine it with *compensation* (requiring that *industrial insurance or work!* precede *compensation* with two or fewer intervening words). The result is that the search retrieves all occurrences of *worker's compensation* or *workmen's compensation;* however, it gets only documents with the phrase *industrial insurance* if that phrase precedes *compensation* by two or fewer words (which is unlikely). Thus, the search will fail to retrieve most occurrences of *industrial insurance.*

Any search that doesn't do what you think it will is obviously a problem. The solution is to override the programmed search order. The convention used to override the programmed search order is to place the words that are to be searched together in parentheses. In the above example, the correct search would be the following:

> LEXIS: *industrial insurance or (work! w/2 compensation)*
> Westlaw: *"industrial insurance" (work! /2 compensation)*

You can use as many sets of parentheses as are necessary in a search. Indeed, because you may not recall the order of searching, the safest way of searching is to use parentheses.

§17.2.10   Segment/Field Searching

The computer's ability to do full-text searching is enhanced even further by the ability to limit the word search to certain portions of the document. These portions are called "segments" by LEXIS or "fields" by Westlaw.

As each document is entered into the computer, certain identifiable parts are labeled to allow for segment and field searching. Unfortunately, the two services use different labeling for these parts. For example, the following labels are for some of the parts of a case that can be searched:

LEXIS case segments	*Westlaw case fields*
name	title
counsel	attorney
opinionby	judge
headnote[1]	digest
date	date

The segments and fields available differ with the type of document. Those available in each file or database can be found in the documentation for each service or by entering the appropriate command while online. With rare exceptions, the convention for running a segment or field

---

1. In LEXIS, the headnote includes only non-West produced headnotes. If the official state reporter has headnotes, they are searchable in LEXIS. Because the *Federal Reporter* and *Federal Supplement* (among other reporters) are published by West Publishing Company and the headnotes are created and copyrighted by it, there is no searchable headnote segment in LEXIS for cases reported in them. Westlaw, by contrast, has the headnotes from the regional reporter in its database.

search is to type the name of the segment or field followed by the words to be found within it in parentheses.

The following are some uses of segment and field searches with cases. If the parties to a case are known, these searches could identify the case:

> LEXIS: *name (planned parenthood and casey)*
> Westlaw: *title ("planned parenthood" and casey) OR*
> *ti("planned parenthood and casey)*

In this search, *and* is used as a connector instead of looking for *planned parenthood v. casey* because the case caption may actually read: *Planned Parenthood of Southeastern Pennsylvania, et al. v. Robert P. Casey.* Remember, the computer looks for exact strings of characters and because these strings do not match, the case would not be retrieved.

In both LEXIS and Westlaw, you may use upper or lower case; they are both read the same. In addition, when using Westlaw, you may abbreviate field names, as was done in the last example above.

A proximity connector is not used in the above example because Planned Parenthood may be the first name in a class action that includes hundreds of plaintiffs. In other words, the phrase *planned parenthood* may not be close to *casey.* Because the search is limited only to words in the name or title of the case, you need not worry about using the normally broad connector *and.*

As you undoubtedly remember, similar research can be done using conventional resources. Case names can be found using the Table of Cases or Defendant-Plaintiff Table in a digest. The computer, however, allows you to go a step further. On the computer, a title or name search can be combined with other search terms. Thus, if you are preparing for litigation against Sears on a discrimination claim, the following searches could prove useful:

> LEXIS: *name (sears) and employ! w/5 discriminat!*
> Westlaw: *ti(sears) and employ! /s discriminat!*

Citing another suit against the same defendant as authority in current litigation can be quite persuasive. This type of research cannot easily be done using conventional resources.

Another example of a segment/field search that cannot be easily done by conventional means is looking for opinions by a certain judge. With computers, the search is as follows:

> LEXIS: *OPINIONBY (aldisert) OR*
> *writtenby (aldisert)*
> Westlaw: *JU(aldisert)*

In LEXIS, *opinionby* retrieves cases for which the judge wrote the opinion of the court; *writtenby* retrieves all of the judge's opinions (including concurrences and dissents).

Again, the search can also be tailored to allow searching for opinions on certain topics:

> LEXIS: *opinionby (aldisert) and antitrust*
> Westlaw: *ju(aldisert) and antitrust*

Sometimes students find it useful when preparing for job interviews to look at cases argued by potential employers. This search can be done with the *counsel* segment (LEXIS) or the *attorney* (or its abbreviation, *at*) field (Westlaw). Finally, sometimes a researcher wants cases only before or after a certain date—perhaps because of legislation changing the law. This can be done with the *date* segment or field.

All of the above are merely examples of what segments and fields are available and how they might be useful. To get more information on what is searchable in LEXIS and Westlaw, consult the documentation provided by the services.

§17.2.11   Natural Language Searching

An alternative search technique to the Boolean (terms and connectors) approach discussed in the previous sections is natural language searching. Natural language searching allows you to enter a search without truncating words, using connectors and parentheses, or any of the other protocols of Boolean searching. You merely type in a query as though you were writing a question to the computer. The computer then retrieves cases or other documents based on statistical probabilities. The computer retrieves a preset number of documents (the default number is 25) that you can review just as you would Boolean results. One useful feature of the natural search engines is that you may list retrieved documents in order of relevance (based on the computer's algorithm). Each system's algorithm for determining relevance is slightly different from the other's so a similar search will probably obtain different results depending on which service you use.

Natural language searching is easier for a searcher to use. However, you should not forego learning Boolean search techniques. Knowledge of terms and connectors and how a computer searches will make you a much better researcher regardless of how you access LEXIS, Westlaw and other databases. Furthermore, most other computer research systems (such as CD-ROM products discussed in section 17.3) do not offer natural language searching so, ultimately, you need to understand Boolean search techniques anyway.

§17.2.12   Cite-Checking Online

a.   *Shepard's Online*

In addition to the full-text searching capacity of documents and parts of documents, both LEXIS and Westlaw have citation services available. By merely typing the appropriate command, you can find in one place all of *Shepard's* entries for a particular case. This display has the advantage over the print version of *Shepard's* of including all the necessary *Shepard's* volumes. Unlike *Shepard's* in print form, *Shepard's* online is cumulative.

Another advantage of *Shepard's* online is that the notations in the margins (concerning analysis and treatment) are spelled out in full, making it unnecessary to consult the prefatory material in the book to interpret the abbreviations.

A third advantage of *Shepard's* online is that a copy of a display can be made by merely entering the print command. Finally, from the online *Shepard's* display, you can look at any of the citing cases in the citation list by merely typing the number assigned to that case. The computer will then go to the place in the citing case where the shepardized case is cited. From this screen, you can continue with further research or return to the original *Shepard's* display by entering the appropriate command.

Both LEXIS and Westlaw make cite-checking online more current than using print versions. LEXIS updates its *Shepard's* online every day. That does not mean it is current within one day, only that new citatons are added each day. It still takes time to receive new cases, find citations in them, and determine treatment and analysis codes. The updated citations in LEXIS are accessed by merely shepardizing in the usual way. Westlaw also has a more current update to *Shepard's*. It is called *Shepard's Preview* and can be accessed by typing *sp* on a displayed case or followed by a citation.

b.   KeyCite

As stated previously, Westlaw has a unique citator for cases called KeyCite. There is no print counterpart to KeyCite. It is discussed in more detail in section 16.6.

c.   AutoCite and InstaCite

Both LEXIS and Westlaw contain a citation verification service for cases that is more current than the citators. LEXIS calls its service AutoCite; Westlaw calls its service InstaCite. They are similar to each other, but slightly different from *Shepard's* and KeyCite.

Instead of giving cites to every case that has mentioned the case being researched, AutoCite and InstaCite give citations to only those cases that may affect the validity of the holding in the case being cite-checked. If a later case uses the earlier one as authority for a certain proposition, or if it follows the holding of the earlier decision, it will not appear in the AutoCite or InstaCite display. In other words, the only cases that appear are those that criticize, disagree with, or otherwise change the holding.

The AutoCite or InstaCite display also contains any additional published court proceedings in the same case whether they alter the holding or not. Thus, the services include lower court opinions and related subsequent actions concerning the parties to the suit.

The purpose of AutoCite and InstaCite is strictly citation verification. They exist to answer the question: "Is this case still good law?" Although *Shepard's* and KeyCite can also be used for citation verification, AutoCite and InstaCite have the advantage of being more current than these citators. *Shepard's* and KeyCite, on the other hand, have their own advantage: Besides supplying information on whether an authority is still good, they give other cases that may provide additional, more recent, or better authority.

Many recently released cases have not been processed into the AutoCite, InstaCite, *Shepard's*, or KeyCite services. However, these cases can still be full-text searched using the techniques previously learned. By using some combination of the case name and cite as search terms, recent cases citing a known case can be found. If the case is a heavily cited authority, a date restriction can be added to limit the number of cases retrieved. For instance, to find recent cases citing the landmark libel case of *New York Times v. Sullivan,* 376 U.S. 254 (1964), the following searches might be used:

LEXIS: *sullivan pre/5 376 pre/5 254 and date aft 1997*
Westlaw: *sullivan +s 376 +s 254 and date(after 1997)*

Using LEXIS or Westlaw as a citator does not provide the additional analysis available in the cite-checking services. However, it is the way to find most current cases citing a given authority.

§17.2.13   Costs of Computer-Assisted Legal Research

The single greatest drawback to computer-assisted legal research is its cost, or rather its costs. The computer, printer, and other equipment cost money. A subscription to LEXIS or Westlaw costs money. The searching itself costs money. Depending on how it is done, printing may also cost money. Finally, long-distance phone charges may apply.

The following discussion addresses only those costs charged by LEXIS and Westlaw and not costs such as the purchase of equipment or long-distance charges.

The costs of the LEXIS and Westlaw services are always changing; furthermore, the services sometimes offer special deals and packages for different types of lawyers. The following, however, are the basic costs.

a.   Subscription

A full subscription to either LEXIS or Westlaw is approximately $125-$150 per month. The price may be reduced if the user guarantees a certain amount of online use each month. The subscription allows access to the services. Limited subscriptions (for instance, access to a single state's resources) may be available at a reduced rate.

b.   Search Costs

Once online, you incur additional charges. Typically, both LEXIS and Westlaw bill for the amount of time spent online. The rate is approximately $180 per hour, or $3 per minute. Certain larger files or databases (such as those covering all state cases) cost substantially more (approximately 1.75 times the normal rate). All of these prices may be reduced for higher volumes of use.

LEXIS has an alternative method of billing. This second method has two components. The first component is the online charge (like that discussed above). The user is charged a flat rate from sign-on to sign-off. The rate, however, is much lower than that for the other billing method (about 55 cents per minute). The second component of this billing method is a search charge. Each time you send a search request to the computer (including cite checks), you are charged a fee for the search. The price of a search depends on the size of the file. The typical state file costs about $30 per search. The largest files cost over $100 per search. Cite-checking is less expensive; in 1992, it cost approximately $2.50 per citation checked.

Both services also offer special limited packages. For example, attorneys may obtain unlimited access to their state materials for as low as $65 per month. Use of other materials like *Shepard's* and federal or other state cases attach additional costs.

All of the above prices are approximations. Both services commonly negotiate individual accounts.

c.   Printing

There are no printing costs while you are online. However, if you choose to send material to the printer or download material in large portions after sign-off, costs attach. The reason is that if a user prints while online, the services make money through the online charges. If, however, a user signs off while the material is printed or downloaded, that money would be lost. To make up for this loss, both LEXIS and Westlaw charge either: 1) per line of text (about 2 cents per line), or 2) per document ($2 for the average document) for offline printing and downloading.

As you can see, the use of computers for legal research can be expensive. However, computer-assisted legal research can also save you time, which in turn may save money.

Furthermore, there are some research tasks that can be done on computers that cannot be done using conventional resources. All of these factors — cost, time, research capability — should be considered in choosing any approach to researching a legal problem.

§17.3   OTHER COMPUTERIZED RESEARCH SERVICES

Apart from LEXIS and Westlaw, other vendors offer computer-assisted research products. A growing number of legal publishers are publishing their materials in CD-ROM format. The information available through these services is obtained from the compact disc rather than from a mainframe computer via phone lines. It is not as current, then, as services such as LEXIS and Westlaw, but no phone charges are incurred.

CD-ROM services may include bibliographic citations and indexing or indexing only (for example, WILSONDISC's *Index to Legal Periodicals* or Infotrac's *LegalTrac*). They may include abstracts as well as bibliographic records (for example, Congressional Information Service's *CIS Abstracts*). They may also be full-text (for example, Hyperlaw publishes CD-ROM products with federal cases).

CD-ROM products can be expensive. The format, however, is ideal for printed matter that takes up large amounts of space or is difficult to access even with an index. The value of the ability to look for any terms in a document is hard to overestimate, especially in obscure subjects. Furthermore, it may be less expensive to spend a large amount of money once to purchase a CD-ROM product than to spend a smaller amount of money time and again over the years for a subscription or for search costs.

Each of these CD-ROM products and other available computerized resources uses different search conventions. Documentation or instruction is usually available from the vendors.

Some vendors are also creating legal research databases that are available through the Internet. Although they are not as comprehensive or sophisticated as LEXIS and Westlaw, they offer attorneys a less expensive alternative to many legal materials. Law Office Information Systems (LOIS) and Lawyers' Legal Research also known as Versuslaw are two prominent Internet legal publishers. The Internet is discussed more fully below at section 17.4.

In addition to the legal research services, several online research services offer access to materials that are primarily nonlegal and that concern all aspects of life. They contain material such as scientific and technical publications, statistics, and current awareness information. Some of this information might be useful to you in a particular case. Probably the most prominent of these services is called DIALOG. Although DIALOG is now available through Westlaw, it is also available independent of Westlaw.

§17.4   RESEARCH ON THE INTERNET

§17.4.1   Overview of the Internet

Increasingly, attorneys and others doing research are turning to the Internet for their information needs. Basically, the Internet is a global network of computers. Each computer on the Internet is connected to every other computer on the Internet. Because of this, a computer user can access information located (or published) on computers all around the world. The World Wide Web is one component of the Internet. It allows a user to access graphical images (pictures) and sounds as well as text. The Web is the component of the Internet that most persons use to do research.

Many of the computers on the Internet contain publicly accessible documents (note that a "document" may be a picture, sound, or other means of communication as well as printed text). For example, a computer at General Motors contains a posted copy of its annual report. By connecting to that computer, a person anywhere in the world can look at that annual report. In addition to containing actual documents, many sites (also known as Web pages or sites) contain links to documents at other sites. An investment company, for instance, might have a list of recommended stocks listed at its site. The text of its listing might say: "For more information on the stock, click on its name." When a user of the site pointed to and clicked on "General Motors," the user would end up at the General Motors site mentioned above (and no longer be at the site of the investment company). Documents like this that allow you to jump from place to place are known as "hypertext" documents.

The way the Internet works is essentially as follows. Every computer connected to the Internet has a unique identification number. Many of these numbers, however, have been converted to more easily remembered names such as: "cocacola.com" or "naacp.org." These names are called "domain names." Domains can be further broken down and usually documents that are published on the Internet can be found in subdomains or pages within the primary domain. Thus, the mission statement for Coca Cola can be found at:

http://www.cocacola.com/co/mission.html

The preceding string of characters is called the Uniform Resource Locator (URL), or oftentimes, the web address or Internet address. The key to finding a document on the Internet is discovering and linking to its URL.

As with businesses, schools, and other components of society, more and more goverment entities are creating web pages. Additionally, more information is constantly being added to existing pages. Many of the legal publications mentioned in the preceding chapters are now available on the Internet, including LEXIS and Westlaw.

§17.4.2   Finding Information on the Internet

Users of the World Wide Web access the information on it by using browser software. The two most prominent browsers are Netscape's Navigator and Microsoft Explorer. They both work in a similar manner.

There are three primary methods for navigating the Internet: (1) entering the address of a known site, (2) using a search engine to find

EXHIBIT 17.6	Yahoo! Search Engine and Directory as Displayed on Netscape Browser*

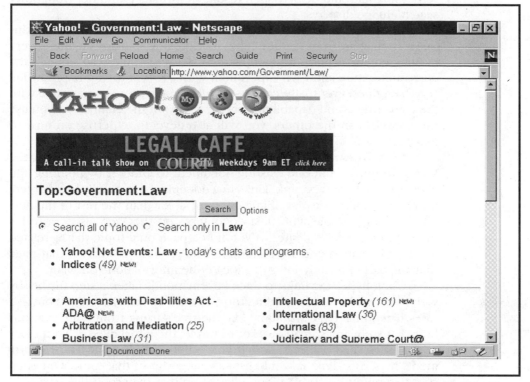

relevant sites and then linking to them, and (3) using a site that contains links to other sites.

Entering the address of a known site: More and more, the government and business organizations are announcing their Internet addresses in other media. A television or radio advertisement often refers to the company's web page. Newspaper articles also make reference to information on the Internet. To retrieve the information if you already have the address to the information, you merely click on the command (in Netscape, "Open") that allows you to enter a URL and type in that address.

If you do not already have the URL for the information you want, there are two main methods to locate it.

Using search engines: One of the ways to locate the Internet address for particular information is to use a search engine. There are several search engines available. Browser software usually has a command such as "Search the Net" that you can point at and click that will bring up search engine options. See Exhibit 17.6.

Search engines essentially scan pages on the Internet for words or phrases that the user asks the search engine to find. Each search engine works differently from the others. Some engines search entire documents, some search headings or links, some search discussion lists and other Internet documents as well as web pages. The engines may also rank retrieval results and display such results in formats that differ from other search engine displays.

Comparing Internet search engines is beyond the scope of this book. Even apart from the difficulty of discussing so many engines, every existing engine is periodically upgraded. A user should read some of the current literature and then experiment with a few of the more promising search engines. Eventually, each user will become more comfortable with the conventions and capabilities of one or two of the engines. As you use these more than the others, you will also develop expertise on how to use them more effectively.

Directories and using hypertext links: The final way to navigate the Web is to move from one existing document to another by pointing and clicking on a hypertext link. Links in a document are usually highlighted, underlined and/or displayed in a different color than the rest of the document. Many people who post documents on the Web also create hypertext links to related sites. If you find a page on a topic that is related to the information you are looking for, there may be links on that page that you can ultimately follow to locate the information you want.

Using hypertext links to trace information is taken a step further by web sites that have created directories. These directories branch out like trees. The initial page would be like the tree's trunk from which various branches stem and spread out. For example, the initial page of a directory might list several major topics. If you point and click on the "Government" hypertext link, it would list subcategories of that topic. One such subtopic might be "Law." If you clicked on that hypertext link, it would lead you to subtopics within law such as "International Law." See Exhibit 17.6. Ultimately, you might be able to find a particular treaty you are looking for by following the narrowing links.

Probably the best known of the Internet directories is Yahoo. As is the case with search engines, there are numerous directories available for a researcher to use. Some of these directories focus specifically on legal research. The Legal Research Institute (created and maintained by Cornell Law School) and Thomas (created and maintained by the United States House of Representatives and named for Thomas Jefferson) are two of the most prominent legal research sites. Many Internet legal researchers will begin their research from sites like these and follow the site's links to locate the information they need. They place a "bookmark" at these sites to give them easy access to the URL (browser software has a bookmarking function that allows you to jump immediately to a site you have previously found and bookmarked).

§17.4.3   Internet Research Benefits and Problems

One reason to use the Internet for research is that the information you seek may be most readily available there. For example, tax attorneys can download tax forms from the Internet instead of having to order them from the Internal Revenue Service. In fact, sometimes the information you seek may be exclusively available on the Internet.

Another important reason to use the Internet is cost. Much of the information on the Internet is available at a relatively low cost. A user usually pays a predetermined fee to a service provider for access to the Internet. Access to the information from most of the sites is free of additional charges. There are, however, a growing number of sites that charge for access to their information. Some of these are in the legal publishing business (such as LOIS and Versuslaw mentioned previously). Although they charge users to access their sites, they may still be less expensive alternatives to the larger and better known online research services (*e.g.,* LEXIS and Westlaw).

Before leaving the subject, it is important to note that there are several problems with finding materials on the Internet. First, even with the search engines and directories mentioned above, the Internet is somewhat chaotic. Services like LEXIS and Westlaw are highly organized. Because of this, those services are much easier to navigate. The Internet is probably more useful for finding a particular document or source of information than for finding general information about a topic. Government information and information that is not readily available locally (such as foreign publications) are examples of searches that may be more efficiently performed on the Internet. A second drawback with Internet research is that most information is not on the Internet. If you are having trouble finding something on the Internet, it might be because the information is not available there (of course, it could also be that it is there and you just have not found it). Another problem with Internet information is determining that what you found is from a reliable source. There are millions of people "publishing" documents on the Internet. Documents may be biased or even fraudulent. In addition, online documents are much more subject to alteration or corruption than print resources. Finally, when information becomes outdated, it often remains on the Internet. Whenever you find information on the Internet, you should check not only to see if it is authentic, but also to see if it is the current version of the document.

§17.5   ONLINE SEARCH STRATEGIES

Now that we have touched on the various aspects of computer-assisted legal research, we can effectively discuss strategy. This discussion assumes you have decided to do an online search. (The next chapter will discuss how to choose which research tool is best for a particular issue.)

Step 1: Choose Your Resource

Even if you have determined that online research is in order, you must choose which online source to use. You should look at the various options (LEXIS, Westlaw, CD-ROM and Internet) to determine where you think the information is available. If the information is available from several services, cost and ease of use should determine which of those services is appropriate.

Step 2: Plan Your Search

The first rule in online searching is to think about the legal problem carefully before going online. Plan your search; know what you will do with the retrieved documents (for example, browse through them or print the cites). Also, have contingency plans in case the search doesn't retrieve what you thought it would. For example, one option is to print the screen that is retrieved and then sign off or enter a command (such as *db* in Westlaw) that stops the billing. You can then look at the printout to determine what went wrong without worrying about online costs accruing.

Step 3: Prepare Search Terms

In creating a computer search, focus on the words that would typically be used in a discussion of the issue. The words may refer to a thing (such as a weapon), an action (such as a slap), a place (such as a store), or a person (such as a child). If any of the words are unique, all the better. And remember, citations are considered words by the computer.

Next, determine any synonyms for those words. They will be combined with each other by an *or* connector. Also, any words that have alternative forms of their root should be truncated.

Step 4: Prepare Connectors and Analyze Their Order

The next step is to identify how the words will be related to each other in a document discussing the issue. How would a judge (or legislator, or author) say this? Based on knowledge of the language and of the law, choose connectors that approximate where you think the words would appear in a relevant document. The ability to approximate effectively is more of an art than a science; you will get better with time and practice.

It is a good idea to write a search out before going online. That way, you can analyze whether connectors will be searched in the proper order. Verify any questionable spellings and check documentation so that you can enter the correct identifier for the file or database without relying on menu screens. You should look for that file or database that contains the potentially relevant documents at the least cost. For example, looking for Arizona cases in the MEGA file of the STATES library on LEXIS, or the ALLSTATES database on Westlaw, rather than in the particular file or database for Arizona, is a costly mistake.

Step 5: Reviewing, Evaluating, and Recording Results

When the results of your search are displayed, you should look at some of the retrieved documents to make sure the search worked the way you thought it would. LEXIS and Westlaw both have display options that allow you to easily find where in the document your search terms are.

If the retrieved documents do not fit your needs, you can edit your search and reenter it with modifications that you think are likely to retrieve documents more in accord with your needs. As stated in Step 2, you should already have considered these contingencies.

In all instances, you should keep a record of your searches and their results. To help you remember at a later date, you should also note what was wrong with the search and the results.

Step 6: Updating

As in all forms of research, you should make sure your research is as current as possible. This often includes shepardizing and using other cite-checking services. Always make sure you understand how the online resources you use can be updated.

If you are having difficulty in online searching, remember that you can call others for help. Both LEXIS and Westlaw have 800 numbers to help you with searching strategy. Other vendors generally have some type of assistance as well. You can also enlist the aid of law librarians and students and attorneys who are more familiar with the online product.

Chapter 18

How to Approach a Legal Research Problem: Sample Research Plans

Although each client's case is unique, the process of researching each legal question is not. Just as there are standard plans for organizing an objective memorandum, opinion letter, and brief, there are also standard research plans.

One of those plans, the plan for doing statutory research, is set out in Chapter 5. Section 5.2 describes the planning process, and section 5.3 shows how an attorney would do the research itself.

This chapter builds on this material and the material set out in Chapters 10 through 17, providing you with research plans for the most common types of research problems. Although these plans may need to be modified to fit your particular problem, they provide the basic framework for researching each type of problem.

In using these plans, begin by determining the type of research. Is the issue governed by statute? common law? administrative rule or regulation? international law? If you are unsure, consult a secondary source covering the subject area. Then go through the steps outlined in section 5.2: (1) draft a preliminary issue statement, (2) determine what law governs, (3) decide what sources to use, and (4) prepare a list of search terms. Also remember the value of doing background reading. The time spent obtaining an overview of the area of law almost always makes the subsequent research, analysis, and writing more efficient and more sophisticated.

The following is a list of the research plans presented in this chapter.

Plan 1   Statutory Research: When the Governing Statute Is Known
Plan 2   Statutory Research: When the Governing Statute Is Not Known
Plan 3   Statutory Research: Federal Legislative Histories
Plan 4   Federal Administrative Law
Plan 5   Common Law Research: When the Name of the Case Setting Out the Common Law Rule Is Known
Plan 6   Common Law Research: When the Name of the Case Setting Out the Common Law Rule Is Not Known
Plan 7   Procedural Issues
Plan 8   International Law

Research Plan 1
Statutory Research: When the Governing Statute Is Known

Legal Question: Whether a particular statute applies or how a particular statute should be interpreted or applied

Jurisdiction: (Can be either federal or state)

Type of Law: Statutory

Search Terms:

Step 1:   Using the statute's section number, locate the text of the statute in the main volume of the annotated code. (If you know the name of the statute but not its number, use the Popular Name Table.)

Step 2:   Update the statute using the pocket part and other supplementation, *Shepard's,* and, if there is a possibility of recent legislative action, LEXIS or Westlaw.

Step 3:   Read and analyze the statute, applying the language of the statute to the facts of the client's case. Also locate and read (a) the official comments, if any, (b) any introductory sections (for example, sections setting out the purpose or effective date), and (c) any cross-references.

Step 4:   If it is clear that the elements are (or are not) met, stop. If it is not clear whether the elements are met, continue.

Step 5:   Locate cases interpreting and applying the statute using the Notes of Decision that follow the text of the statute in the annotated code. To locate recent cases, use the pocket part and citator services.

Step 6:   Analyze and cite check those cases that appear useful.

Step 7: If necessary, locate and analyze persuasive authority. Use LEXIS, Westlaw, the regional or decennial digests, *American Law Reports* (A.L.R.), or *Uniform Laws Annotated* (U.L.A.) to locate cases from other jurisdictions. Use the *Index to Legal Periodicals* (I.L.P.), *Current Law Index* (C.L.I.), *Current Index to Legal Periodicals* (C.I.L.P.), or LEXIS or Westlaw to locate law review articles.

Step 8: If necessary, check the legislative history. (See Research Plan No. 3.)

Research Plan 2
Statutory Research: When the Governing Statute Is Not Known

Legal Question: Whether a particular statute applies or how a particular statute should be interpreted or applied

Jurisdiction: (Can be either federal or state)

Type of Law: Statutory

Search Terms:

Step 1: Use the subject or topic index to locate the numbers of the potentially relevant statutory sections. (Use the search terms listed above; as a general rule, move gradually from the narrowest to the broadest search term.) Look up those sections in the main volumes of the annotated code.

Step 2: Update the relevant statutory sections using the pocket part and other supplementation, *Shepard's,* and, if there is a possibility of recent legislative action, LEXIS or Westlaw.

Step 3: Read and analyze the statute, applying the language of the statute to the facts of the client's case. Also locate and read (a) the official comments, if any, (b) any introductory sections (for example, sections setting out the purpose or effective date), and (c) any cross-references.

Step 4: If it is clear that the elements are (or are not) met, stop. If it is not clear whether the elements are met, continue.

Step 5: Locate potentially applicable cases using the Notes of Decision following the statute, the pocket part, and citators.

Step 6: Analyze and cite check those cases that appear useful.

Step 7: If necessary, locate and analyze persuasive authority. Use LEXIS, Westlaw, the regional or decennial digests, *American Law Reports* (A.L.R.), or *Uniform Laws Annotated*

(U.L.A.) to locate cases from other jurisdictions. Use the *Index to Legal Periodicals* (I.L.P.), *Current Law Index* (C.L.I.), *Current Index to Legal Periodicals* (C.I.L.P.), or LEXIS or Westlaw to locate law review articles.

Step 8:   If necessary, check the legislative history. (See Research Plan No. 3.)

Research Plan 3
Statutory Research: Federal Legislative Histories

Legal Question: Whether a particular statute applies or how a particular statute should be interpreted or applied

Jurisdiction: Federal

Type of Law: Statutory

Search Terms:

Step 1:   Using Nancy Johnson's *Compiled Sources of Legislative History,* determine whether there is a prepared legislative history. If there is, locate and use that history.

Step 2:   If there is no prepared legislative history, use the historical information following the text of the statute to determine the date on which the statute was enacted.

Step 3:   If the statute was enacted before 1941, use the Congressional Index Service (C.I.S.) indices (Serial Set Index, Committee Print Index, and Committee Hearing Index) to locate references to reports, hearings, prints, and other documents. The documents themselves are available on microfiche in most large or government depository libraries. Use the indices to the *Congressional Record* or *Congressional Globe* to locate references to the pages on which the floor debates appear.

If the statute was enacted between 1941 and 1969, use *United States Code, Congressional and Administrative News* (U.S.C.C.A.N.) to locate excerpts from House and Senate hearings and reports and the dates the act was considered in Congress. The dates of consideration can then be used to locate relevant material in the *Congressional Record.* The full text of House and Senate hearings and reports can often be found on microfiche in large libraries or in federal depositories.

If the statute was enacted after 1969, locate citations to House and Senate Hearings, House and Senate Reports, and the *Congressional Record* using the Abstracts (Volume 1) and Index (Volume 2) of Congressional Information Service (C.I.S.) for the year the statute was enacted. The full text of the hearings and reports can then be found on microfiche available in most large libraries or federal depositories. The relevant portions of the *Congressional Record* can be found using the dates of consideration.

Note: U.S.C.C.A.N. can also be used for statutes enacted after 1969. It is not, however, as comprehensive as C.I.S.

For more about the sources cited, see section 12.2.

Research Plan 4
Federal Administrative Law

Legal Question: Whether a particular federal regulation applies or how a particular federal regulation has been interpreted or applied

Jurisdiction: Federal

Type of Law: Enacted

Search Terms:

Step 1:   Determine whether there is a looseleaf or similar service that brings together the relevant statutes, regulations, administrative decisions, and commentary. If there is, read the "How to Use This Set" section at the beginning of the set to determine (a) what the set contains, (b) how the set is organized and indexed, and (c) when and how the material contained in the set is updated. Then use the set to research the question.

Step 2:   If there is no looseleaf or similar service or if the looseleaf service does not contain all of the necessary information, use Research Plan 2 to locate the citation to the relevant United States Code section.

Step 3:   Locate the citations to the relevant federal regulations using (a) the index to the *Code of Federal Regulations (C.F.R.)*, (b) the cross-reference tables in the "Index and Finding Aids to the Code of Federal Regulations" volume to the *United States Code Service* (U.S.C.S.), or (c) a key word search in LEXIS or Westlaw.

Step 4:   Using the citations, locate and read the relevant regulations in the main volumes of the C.F.R.

Step 5:   Update the C.F.R. using the "List of Sections Affected" volumes of the C.F.R. Further update using "C.F.R. Parts Affected During (Month)" tables located at the back of the most recent volumes of the *Federal Register* (check the volumes for the periods not covered by the "List of Sections Affected") or LEXIS or Westlaw.

Step 6:   Apply the regulation to the facts of the client's case. If the application is clear, stop. If the application is not clear, continue.

Step 7:   Use a citator to locate cases, law review articles, and other materials discussing the relevant regulations. Cases can also be found in looseleafs, online, or as separately published government publications. If you have difficulty locating cases, try calling the agency. For federal agencies, phone numbers can be located using the *United States Government Manual.*

Step 8:   Read and analyze the materials located. Remember to cite check cases to determine (a) whether they are still good law and (b) whether there are more recent cases on point.

Research Plan 5
Common Law Research: When the Name of the Case Setting Out the Common Law Rule Is Known

Legal Question: Whether a particular common law rule applies or how a particular common law rule has been interpreted or applied

Jurisdiction: (Can be either federal or state)

Type of Law: Common Law

Search Terms:

Step 1:   If appropriate, do background reading in a legal encyclopedia, hornbook, treatise, practice book, *American Law Reports* (A.L.R.), or law review to obtain an overview of the area of law.

Step 2:   If the citation to the case is known, locate the case in the official or regional reporter. (If possible, use a reporter published by West; this will allow you to use West's Key Number System to find additional cases.) If the citation is not known, locate the citation using the Table of Cases or Defendant-Plaintiff tables in the digest or *Shepard's.*

Step 3:   Read and analyze the case.

Step 4:   If the case is on point, cite check it.

Step 5:   If the case answers the question, stop. If it does not, locate additional cases from the same jurisdiction by looking up (a) the cases cited by the court in its opinion, (b) the applicable key numbers in the digest for that jurisdiction, or (c) the relevant citations from *Shepard's.*

Step 6:   Read, analyze, and cite check cases found as a result of Step 5 and follow up on any additional leads.

Step 7:   If necessary, locate and analyze persuasive authority. Use LEXIS, Westlaw, the regional or decennial digests, or A.L.R. to locate cases from other jurisdictions. Use the *Index to Legal Periodicals* (I.L.P.), *Current Law Index* (C.L.I.), *Current Index to Legal Periodicals* (C.I.L.P.), or LEXIS or Westlaw to locate law review articles.

Research Plan 6
Common Law Research: When the Name of the Case Setting Out the Common Law Rule Is Not Known

Legal Question: Whether a particular common law rule applies or how a particular common law rule has been interpreted or applied

Jurisdiction: (Usually state)

Type of Law: Common Law

Search Terms: _____

Step 1:   If appropriate, do background reading in a legal encyclopedia, hornbook, treatise, practice book, *American Law Reports* (A.L.R.), or a law review to obtain an overview of the area of law. If the name of a case is located, switch to Research Plan 5: When the Name of the Case Setting Out the Common Law Rule Is Known. If a case is not located, continue.

Step 2:   Locate cases using either the applicable digest or LEXIS or Westlaw. If you use a digest, use the subject or topic index to locate the potentially applicable topic headings and, if it is a West publication, key numbers. (As a general rule, begin with your narrowest search term and then move gradually to the broadest.) If you use LEXIS or Westlaw, select the appropriate library and file (or database) and search, using terms that are likely to have been used by the courts.

Step 3:   Look up the applicable topic headings and key numbers. Read through the Notes of Decisions, identifying the five or six cases that appear most useful.

Step 4:   Locate, read, and analyze the cases identified as part of Step 3. If the cases appear useful, cite check them (a) to determine whether they are still good law and (b) to locate additional cases.

Step 5:   If the cases answer the question, stop. If they do not, locate additional cases from the same jurisdiction by looking up (a) additional cases from the Notes of Decision, (b) cases cited by the courts in their opinions, or (c) cases located during cite checking.

Step 6:   Read, analyze, and cite check the cases found as a result of Step 5 and follow up on any additional leads.

Step 7:   If necessary, locate and analyze persuasive authority. Use LEXIS, Westlaw, the regional or decennial digests, or A.L.R. to locate cases from other jurisdictions. Use the *Index to Legal Periodicals* (I.L.P.), *Current Law Index* (C.L.I.), *Current Index to Legal Periodicals* (C.I.L.P.), or LEXIS or Westlaw to locate law review articles.

Research Plan 7
Procedural Issues

Legal Question: Whether a particular procedural rule applies or how a particular procedural rule has been interpreted or applied

Jurisdiction: (Can be state, federal, or local)

Type of Law: Procedural

Search Terms:

Step 1:   If necessary, do background reading to determine whether the issue is governed by a court rule or by statute or other authority. Practice books are usually the most helpful.

Step 2:   Once you have determined the type of authority (for example, court rule or statute), use the index in the appropriate set to locate the applicable rule or rules. Check the pocket part or other supplementation to make sure that you have the current version of the rule.

Step 3:   Read and analyze the rule and the official comments, if any. If the rule answers the question, stop. If it does not, continue.

Step 4:   Use the Notes of Decision following the rule or a citator to locate cases interpreting or applying the rule. Update these sources using a citator.

Step 5:   If necessary, locate secondary sources discussing the rule and its application. Treatises are often a good source. Note: Because many state rules are modeled on the federal rules, commentary on the federal rules may be relevant to state court interpretations.

Step 6:   For some procedural issues, it may be necessary to locate the appropriate form. Look for references to forms in annotated codes, practice books, and specialized form books.

Research Plan 8
International Law

Although international law and research are beyond the scope of this book, we have included this research plan to assist those students competing in Jessup, the international law moot court competition.

There are two branches of international law: public international law and private international law. Public international law focuses on the relationships among nations (usually referred to as states). In contrast, private international law focuses on the relationships among individuals or entities in different states. Most Jessup questions involve questions of public international law.

In public international law, the four most important sources of law are (1) international conventions (treaties and other international agreements), (2) international custom, (3) general principles of law recognized by civilized nations, and (4) judicial decisions and teachings of the most highly qualified publicists (expert commentators) of the various nation states. See Article 38(1) of the Statutes of the International Court of Justice.

Step 1:   Begin by doing background reading to familiarize yourself with the basic concepts and terminology. An excellent source is *An Introduction to International Law* by Mark W. Janis (Little, Brown, 2d ed. 1993).

Step 2:   Use the *Index to Legal Periodicals* and the *Index to Foreign Legal Periodicals* to locate law review articles discussing, in either general or specific terms, the type of international dispute in question.

Step 3:   Locate and read potentially applicable articles. Note the issues discussed and the authorities cited.

Step 4:   Identify and locate the relevant treaties. If the United States is a probable signatory, use *Treaties in Force* or *A Guide to Treaties in Force*. If the United States is not a signatory, use *Multilateral Treaties: Index and Current Status*.
The text of treaties to which the United States is a signatory can usually be found in *United States Treaties and*

Other International Agreements. To find the text of treaties to which the United States is not a signatory, check
the *Consolidated Treaty Series,* the *United Nations Treaty
Series,* and the *League of Nations Treaty Series.*

Step 5:   Determine if the states involved in the dispute are currently signatories and thus bound by the treaty. (Even if a
party is not a signatory, you may be able to use the treaty
as evidence of international custom.)

Step 6:   Analyze the text of the treaty.

Step 7:   Look for additional authority: for example, look for evidence of custom, general principles of law, judicial decisions, and teachings of publicists. Useful sources for this
research include the *Restatement of the Law, The Foreign
Relations Law of the United States 3d, The Encyclopedia
of Public International Law, Principles of Public International Law* by Ian Brownlie, and articles from law reviews and other legal periodicals.

Note: Because the International Court of Justice and
other international judicial tribunals decide so few cases,
it is unlikely that you will find a case "on point." You may,
however, be able to use the principles enunciated in those
cases. Decisions of the International Court of Justice are
published in its *Reports of Judgments, Advisory Opinions
and Orders.* Recent decisions are also available online on
LEXIS and Westlaw. The decisions of other tribunals (for
example, the Court of Justice of the European Community
or the European Court of Human Rights) can be located
in major law libraries and are increasingly available online.

Step 8:   Update the materials you have found. Although this updating is not easy, the following steps should be taken:
(a) shepardize treaties and international agreements to
which the United States is a signatory using *Shepard's
United States Citations;* (b) use LEXIS or Westlaw to find
recent law review articles and citations to pre-existing authorities; (c) use *International Legal Materials* to determine whether new documents have been published on
the subject.

Another way of double-checking your research is to
begin your research from a different starting point than
your original one. If you end up with the same result, you
are probably safe.

A reminder: International law is governed by different principles than the domestic law of the United States.
Understanding those principles is the key component in
doing effective research in international law.

Part IV

A Guide to Effective Writing

Although we attempt in this part of the book to give legal writers general recommendations and rules of thumb about what makes some legal writing effective, it is important to remember at least three points about the notion of "effective legal writing."

First, effectiveness in legal writing is a relative thing. The same level of effectiveness is not needed in every situation. The trick, of course, is to make the writing effective enough so that it accomplishes its goal without laboring over it to the point that it consumes all of the working day and night. In short, some balance is appropriate.

Second, effectiveness in legal writing, and in all writing for that matter, always depends on the context. What will please and even delight one reader may irritate or anger another. An organizational scheme that is effective in one instance may be dead wrong in another. Even precision and conciseness, those most sought-after characteristics of effective legal writing, can be ineffective in some instances in which vagueness and verbosity accomplish the desired objective. In other words, writing that most readers would consider competent, stylistically pleasing, and even eloquent in the abstract but that does not work in a given context is, in that context, ineffective.

Finally, effectiveness is a fairly subjective notion. Again, we can give you the standard advice and some insights of our own about what is and is not effective legal writing, but then you must filter all that through your own sense of whether you think something works. If, as you are writing a given piece, your instincts tell you it is working (or it is not working) and all the theory and advice tell you the opposite, we suggest that you look at it again. If your instincts and common sense still insist that the conventional wisdom about effective legal writing is not working here, then trust your instincts.

Chapter 19

Effective Writing—
The Whole Paper

§19.1 THE PSYCHOLOGY OF WRITING

Writing is not for the faint-hearted. It takes courage, perseverance, creativity, and flexibility, not to mention intelligence and a solid foundation of writing skills. A fair number of lawyers and judges profess to like writing and even say that they find the process satisfying. If you are in this fortunate group, this section is not addressed to you.

If you are among the less fortunate—those who have felt overwhelmed by the prospect of writing, who have struggled with writer's block, who have found writing to be a difficult, perhaps even painful process—there is hope. Writing, like most other skills, becomes more pleasurable with each successful experience. It also helps to know where the usual stumbling blocks are in the process and how to get past them.

Few legal writers have trouble getting started on the research phase of a writing project. Many encounter their first stumbling block when it is time to move from research to writing. A typical avoidance mechanism is to keep researching long past the point of need. Writers who have developed this pattern of approaching writing tasks usually postpone putting pen to paper or fingers to keyboard until the last possible moment. Then they write, almost out of desperation, and end up turning in as a final product something that is really a rough draft. By delaying the writing process, they make it virtually impossible to do any quality drafting, revising, editing, and proofreading. The result is yet another unsatisfying writing experience.

If this describes your typical writing process, you may be able to break out of this habit by developing a schedule for the completion of the entire document. In this schedule, allot a reasonable amount of time to complete the research but be firm about when you will begin writing.

Give yourself mini-deadlines for completing an outline, producing a first draft, revising, editing, and proofreading. Allow breathing room in this timetable for problems such as a printer malfunction or a flat tire. If at all possible, plan as though your deadline is sooner than the real deadline. To do this, you may find it easier to write the schedule backwards, starting with the final deadline and allowing time for proofreading, then editing, all the way back to research.

Sample Schedule for a Two-Week Writing Project

Week 1   research and organize research
Week 2   Day 1 brainstorm, create plan, outline
          Day 2 drafting
          Day 3 drafting
          Day 4 revising
          Day 5 editing, last-minute citation checks
          Day 6 proofreading
          Day 7 final product (ready a day early!)

For shorter time frames and quick turnarounds, a writing schedule is even more critical. In such cases, you will probably be working with half-day, quarter-day, or even hour units, but the principles are still the same. Figure out how much of the total time should be spent researching and how much should be spent writing. Create mini-deadlines for yourself. Start with your final deadline and work backwards as you plan.

Sample Schedule for a Two-Day Writing Project

Day 1   research and organize research
Day 2   by 10:00 a.m. brainstorm, plan outline
         by 2:00 p.m. drafting
         by 3:00 p.m. revising
         by 4:00 p.m. editing
         by 4:30 p.m. proofreading
         by 5:00 p.m. final product completed (and in the partner's
                      hands!)

With practice, you may find that you don't need as much time for research and that you can begin to allow a larger percentage of your time for writing.

Schedules are invaluable, but many writers need more than a schedule to get them started writing. It is an enormous help if your research notes are organized in a way that will facilitate the writing process. Instead of organizing your research around cases, organize it around the law or the points you want to make. Under each point, list the statutes, cases, or authorities on which you will rely and a quick summary of how they support that point. See section 5.4.

You can then color code any photocopies you made of those authorities. For instance, for the consent to intercept phone calls problem in Chapter 6, you might decide to use blue for anything related to "implied consent," red for anything about the "express consent," and so on.

Color coding helps during the drafting phase because it gives you a quick way to gather up all the information you have collected on a given point (grab all the red) and then physically order those sheets. The same sheets may have other colors on them, but while you are writing about the "red point"—express consent—you can stay focused on the part of the notes and photocopied cases that concern that point. When it comes time to do the "blue point," the same sheets get picked up and ordered into the information about "implied consent."

If color coding does not appeal to you, you may find that having separate file folders or a tabbed notebook does. The key is to develop files or sections of the notebook for the points you want to make in the whole document, not separate files or notebook sections for each analogous case. This means you may need two or more photocopies of the same page of a case so that it may be filed under each of the appropriate points.

§19.2   OUTLINES, WRITING PLANS, AND ORDERED LISTS

Unfortunately, student writers are taught to write outlines long before they ever need one. Sometime in junior high most of us were first exposed to outlines, but the outlines were for relatively short, uncomplicated papers whose organization we could keep in our heads. The task wasn't large enough or complex enough to warrant an outline. As a result, many student writers believe outlines or written writing plans are useless because they were useless for papers in the seventh grade.

For professional writers (and lawyers are professional writers) who must organize extensive and complex material, spending time creating an outline or writing plan or even just an ordered list almost always saves time in the end. Done properly, an outline or plan will keep you from backtracking, repeating yourself, missing a key point, or finally discovering what it is you want to say after you have written the whole thing the wrong way.

But creating order in extensive and complex material is not easy; it takes the writer's complete attention. Consequently, it deserves a distinct block of time for just that task. Don't fall into the trap of trying to create order at the same time you are drafting sentences and paragraphs. That approach forces you to keep track of several big tasks all at once. Writing under such conditions is needlessly stressful.

Writing a good outline or plan may also mean that you have to change some of your preconceived ideas about outlines. First of all, the outline or plan is for you, the writer, not for a teacher. Roman numerals and capital A's and B's are not important. Use them if they help; discard them if they hinder. If you discard the roman numerals, letters, and numbers, keep the indentations. They will help you distinguish among main points, subpoints, sub-subpoints, and supporting details.

As the writer, what you want and need from the outline is the big picture of how the pieces fit together. To make sure you can see everything at once, write your outline on one side of a page or pages. That way you can lay the whole outline out before you and get an overview of the entire structure.

There are as many ways to go about creating an outline or writing plan as there are writers. Below are some time-tested techniques that you may find helpful. Use whichever ones work for you and any others that have been successful for you in previous writing projects.

§19.2.1   Read It All; Mull It Over

Before beginning to write the outline or plan, read through all of your research. Let your mind mull it over while you do some mindless task such as mowing the lawn or taking a bath. While you are engaged in the mindless task, your mind will almost certainly begin organizing the ideas.

§19.2.2   Don't Overlook the Obvious

One obvious way of beginning to organize is to determine how the court will approach the problem. Are there any threshold questions the court will consider first? If so, place them first in your outline. What will the court look at and decide second, third, and so on? Your organizational scheme should mirror the process the court will follow.

Furthermore, in creating an organization for your document, do not assume that you always have to create a brand-new, never-before-seen organizational scheme. Most documents fit comfortably in one of the common organizational plans. Borrow freely from the bank of common knowledge about how to organize an elements analysis, a balancing test, or a discussion of the development of a trend, to name but a few. Many discussion sections follow an IRAC (issue, rule, analysis, conclusion) plan or use mini-IRACs in some of the sections. See Chapters 5 and 6.

§19.2.3   Find Order Using a
Three-Column Chart

The three-column chart can be an effective way to find order in a document, particularly when the document does not immediately appear to fall into any of the typical organizational patterns. In the first column, make one giant list of everything you think the final document should include. Be as comprehensive as possible. Dump everything you have in your brain about the problem into this list. Do not worry about the order of the items.

Below is an example of a brain dump used to find organization for a legal problem concerning whether some carpeting made for a customer fell within the UCC exception to specially manufactured goods. (See chapter 4, Example 1, for the sample memo written from the outline created by this three-column chart.)

COLUMN ONE: THE BRAIN DUMP

- Requirements for exception
  1. goods specially manufactured for buyer
  2. unsuitable for sale to others in ordinary course of seller's business
  3. manufacture commenced
- no written contract
- oral contracts should be the rule
- "specially manufactured" not defined
- "specially manufactured" refers to nature of goods
- manufacturer had to specially set looms
- *Flowers:* buyer's name/artwork on wrapping material
- wrapping material & carpet are personalized
- a family flower is not a name
- *Colorado Carpet:* carpeting available at outlets
- policy: goods themselves are evidence of contract
- seller of custom-made goods not exempt from Statute of Frauds
- if all goods custom, no written contract necessary seller of custom goods as likely to fabricate
- contract as seller of ready-made goods
- quote from *Wackenhut* court
- undue hardship for seller
- wholesaler easily sold rugs to a third party

Once the first column is complete, the writer then uses the second column to begin doing some preliminary ordering of the list in Column One. Column One will probably already contain some natural groupings of ideas. If so, the writer places them together in Column Two at roughly the point in the document where she guesses they will go.

For example, the writer of the specially manufactured goods memo knew that the rule section should come early in the memo, so she moved the requirements for the exception close to the top of Column Two. She then considered whether anything should precede or immediately follow the requirements. A quick glance down Column One yielded at least one other point about rules: There is no written contract. She added this point before a discussion of the exception and its requirements.

After the list of requirements, it seemed natural to move right to the first requirement and *Flowers,* the case that helps explain what constitutes "specially manufactured for the buyer." Because the writer knew she wanted to make an argument for BCC based on *Flowers,* that argument was placed next on the list.

The writer proceeded down the list from Column One and found roughly where each item fit in Column Two. By the end, she had some stray items: "goods themselves are evidence of the contract" and "undue hardship for seller." Stray items can be worked into the organization now or saved for Column Three.

COLUMN TWO: PRELIMINARY ORDERING OF IDEAS

- no written contract
- specially manufactured goods exception
- requirements for exception
  1. goods specially manufactured for buyer
  2. unsuitable for sale to others in ordinary course of seller's business
  3. manufacture commenced under circumstances . . . & prior to receipt of notice of repudiation
- First requirement: goods specially manufactured for buyer
- *Flowers:* buyer's name & artwork on wrapping material
- wrapping paper is personalized
- BCC's argument: like wrapping material, rugs are personalized
- Therefore, rugs specially manufactured for buyer . . .

Column Three is used to further refine the order of the list. This is the time to test out various places where the stray items may fit. In this case, because two of the items seemed to be policy reasons for the specially manufactured goods exception, they could fit right before or after the list of requirements. The other two items—" 'specially manufactured' not defined" and " 'specially manufactured' refers to nature of goods"—belong in the rule section of the first requirement.

While preparing Column Three, also check to see if anything was forgotten. Look for all the standard features of legal analysis (burden of proof, plain language arguments, policy arguments, and so on) and all the standard "moves" a lawyer makes (argument, counterargument, rebuttal, countervailing policy argument, and so on).

In the specially manufactured goods case, who has the burden of proof? Does the other side have an argument based on the first requirement? based on *Flowers?* based on policy? Where will these counterarguments and rebuttals fit? Given the rough plan from Column Two, it was relatively easy to add in those pieces as needed. The added pieces are in boldface type in the following chart.

COLUMN THREE: REFINED ORDER/CHECK FOR STANDARD FEATURES AND "MOVES"

- no written contract
- specially manufactured goods exception
- requirements for exception
- **party seeking exception has burden of proof**
  1. goods specially manufactured for buyer
  2. unsuitable for sale to others in ordinary course of seller's business
  3. manufacture commenced under circumstances . . . & prior to receipt of notice of repudiation
- **policy underlying exception**
  1. goods themselves are evidence of contract
  2. undue hardship for seller
- First requirement—goods specially manufactured for buyer
- **"specially manufactured" not defined**
- **"specially manufactured" refers to nature of goods**
- *Flowers:* buyer's name & artwork on wrapping material.

- wrapping paper is personalized
- **contrast with *Colorado Carpet*: carpeting available at outlets, so not specially manufactured**
- **BCC's plain language argument**
- BCC's argument: like wrapping material, rugs are personalized
- **distinguish rugs from carpet in *Colorado Carpet***
- Therefore, rugs specially manufactured for buyer

Working in this way, you will find that the secret to the three-column chart is that you focus on one main task with each column, and as you move through the columns, you get more and more control over the material. For example, when the writer of the specially manufactured goods memo moved from her Column Two to Column Three, she began to see that the material did fit into one of the standard organizational plans after all. By the time she had reached Column Three, voila! She had an outline.

§19.2.4   Talk to a Colleague

Whenever you are having trouble getting a large amount of material organized in your mind, try talking it over with a colleague. Use the approach that you are going to explain the issue(s) to your listener. As you are talking, notice how you naturally organize the material. Jot down key words and phrases that come to mind as you are speaking. Don't be afraid to talk through the parts with which you are having the most difficulty. It may free you to address these areas if you begin by saying something like "this is the part I'm having trouble with" or "this is the part that is still rough in my mind." Let your listener question you and provide his or her own insights.

If talking out the issue(s) seemed helpful, sit down immediately afterwards and write out the organization you discovered as you were speaking. If talking-before-writing becomes a valuable organizing technique for you, you may even want to tape record the talk-before-write sessions.

§19.2.5   Try a New Analogy or Format

If you have a phobia about outlines, relabel or redesign what it is you are doing when you develop the organization for a document. Some writers are more comfortable developing a "writing plan." Others like to think in terms of an "ordered list." You may need an entirely new analogy for what you are doing. Think instead of an architect creating a blueprint for a building or an engineer designing an aircraft.

Some people prefer horizontal flow charts to vertical outlines. There is nothing magical about organizing ideas from top to bottom in an outline. If working from left to right in a flow chart feels more comfortable to you, do it.

EXHIBIT 19.1	Basic Cluster for *Strong*

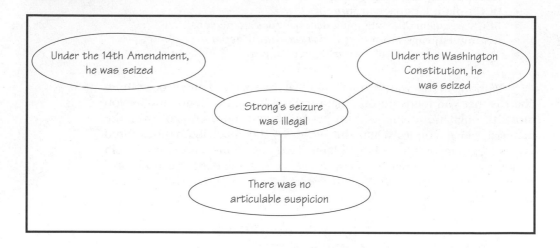

Others can find and better visualize an organizational scheme by using a technique called clustering. To use clustering, simply begin by putting one main idea in a circle and then attach related subpoints. Exhibit 19.1 is an example of a basic clustering for the *Strong* case in Defendant's brief in Chapter 8.

Once you have a basic cluster, begin a new circle for each main idea, each time attaching related subpoints. See Exhibit 19.2. for an expanded but not yet complete cluster for the *Strong* case. By continuing to expand the cluster diagram, you will end up with a map of how your mind is thinking about a legal problem.

Now look for clusters of ideas; these will usually become sections in the final document. You may even find that after doing the clustering diagram you can see that the material fits into one of the standard organizational plans. The final step is to translate the clustering diagram into a traditional outline.

Notice too that beginning with a clustering diagram has one advantage over beginning with a traditional outline. Traditional outlines develop a hierarchy that suggests that all the items have superordinate-subordinate relationships. Such a hierarchical framework may artificially limit your thinking. Clustering, on the other hand, lends itself to thinking about a variety of relationships, such as contrast, cause/effect, and possession.

§19.2.6   Consider Your Reader, Purpose, and How You View the Case

After spending hours doing research in the library — in the trenches, so to speak — it is a good idea to review the basics before composing a battle plan. For either a memo or a brief, ask yourself, for whom am I

EXHIBIT 19.2 Expanded Cluster for *Strong*

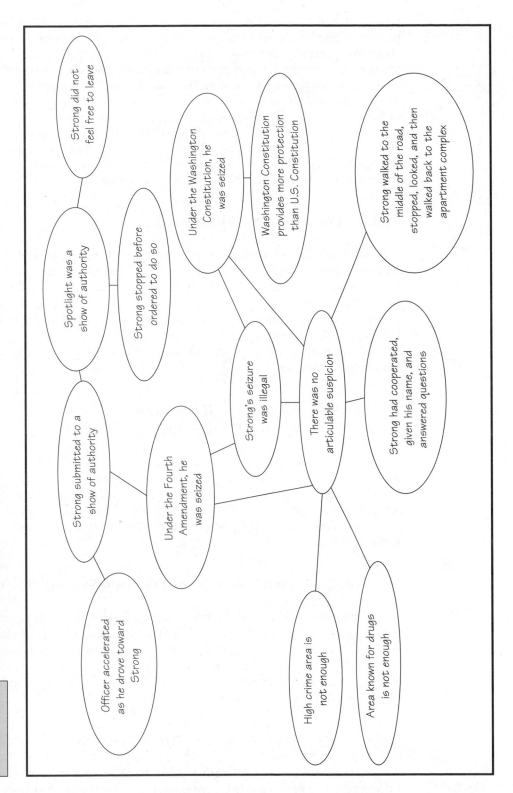

writing this document? What are that reader's purposes? What are my purposes? For briefs, ask yourself, what is my overall theme? Is this a case about mistaken identity, inappropriate police procedures, self-defense, or freedom to assemble? The theme, or what some lawyers call "the theory of the case" in persuasive writing (see section 8.7.2), should be evident in every section of the outline, from the statement of facts or statement of the case to the rule, discussion, or argument sections.

One final note before leaving the subject of outlines: Like the blueprint for a building or the design for an aircraft, outlines should be aids and not straitjackets for the writer. Don't be afraid to change an outline when it isn't working or when you get a better idea.

§19.3   DRAFTING THE DOCUMENT

If creating an outline is the first stumbling block for most writers, the second comes when it is time to start drafting. Some people call it "writer's block"; others call it "the white page syndrome." Whatever the name, the experience is essentially the same. Faced with what seems to be an overwhelming task, the writer freezes. Nothing seems like the perfect beginning, so nothing gets written.

If you tend to freeze when you must start writing, try some of the following techniques.

§19.3.1   Give Yourself Optimum Writing Conditions

Make writing as pleasant as possible. Start drafting at the time of day and in the place where you do your best thinking and writing. If you are a morning person, don't start drafting at 5 p.m. unless you absolutely must. If you prefer a legal pad to a computer, by all means use a legal pad. Treat yourself to a new fancy pen if that will make you feel better about writing.

§19.3.2   Trick Yourself into Getting Started

If you have written an outline or kept research notes in your own words, you have already started drafting. By expanding outline labels into phrases, then clauses, then sentences, you can gradually slip into creating the first draft. By fleshing out your research notes, you begin developing the language that will appear in your draft. For some writers, this gradual "drift" into drafting helps them avoid writer's block.

§19.3.3   Write What You Know Best First

For some reason, many writers seem to think that they must write a document in order—the first sentence first, then the second sentence, the first paragraph before the second paragraph, and so on. This notion about writing is not a problem as long as the writer knows how to begin.

However, when you are not quite sure how to begin, it's often a good idea to start writing a draft at the point in the material where you are the most confident. Get the writing rolling and let your subconscious work through how to begin the document.

The same is true when you are hopelessly stuck in the middle of a document. Try skipping over the problem area for a time and write another section. With a bit of luck, you may figure out what to do about the problem area without letting it bring the project to a halt.

One caution, though: If you start in the middle of a document or if you skip over a problem area for the time being, you will have to come back and make sure the sections are logically and stylistically connected.

§19.3.4 "Get the Juices Flowing"

Athletes who are preparing to perform do warm-up and stretching exercises. Some writers find that freewriting has similar benefits when done before drafting. Others find that they can "get the writing juices flowing" by reading similar documents or rereading other documents that they have written.

§19.3.5 Take It One Step at a Time

Many writers are overwhelmed by the prospect of drafting twenty pages or more. Writing a page or even just a paragraph, however, seems relatively easy. The trick then is to give yourself small parts of the whole document to do at a time.

Your goal for the next hour, for example, may be to write the rule section. Before lunch you may want to complete a paragraph about the plaintiff's policy argument on the last element. By breaking the large task into several smaller tasks, you allow yourself to focus on one part at a time and direct all your energy toward writing that part well.

§19.3.6 Reward Yourself

As you complete small parts of the larger writing task and as you see yourself meeting deadlines in your personal timetable, reward yourself. Rewards can be something as small as a coffee break or as large as an evening off for a movie. What matters is that writing becomes a pleasurable task at which you feel successful. If rewards along the way help promote those feelings, they are worth a try.

§19.4   REVISING

Revision, or re-vision, means "to see again." When you revise, you step back from the project and try to see it with fresh eyes. This is not an easy thing to do. Many writers have difficulty adopting a revisionist perspective. Most avoid rethinking the whole document and prefer the safety of tinkering with smaller editing issues such as sentence structure or word choice.

To help make the shift from drafter to reviser, you may find one of the following techniques helpful.

§19.4.1   Develop a Revision Checklist

A revision checklist should focus on the large issues in writing. Below is a sample revision checklist that can be used for most documents.

Revision Checklist

- Will this document meet the reader's needs?
- Is the tone right for this document and this reader?
- Is the document well organized?
- Are the ideas well developed?
- Is the analysis conclusory or superficial? What would make it more sophisticated?
- What else should be included?
  - A plain language argument?
  - An argument based on an analogous case?
  - A policy argument?
  - A countervailing policy argument?
  - A rebuttal to an argument?
- What can be omitted?
- Is the theme, or theory of the case, evident in all sections of the document?

On your own revision checklist, add any other habitual writing problems that have been pointed out to you by your legal writing professor, classmates, colleagues, or other readers.

§19.4.2   Write an After-the-Fact Outline

Of all the areas to rethink when you are revising, the most challenging is often the organization. One simple way to check the paper's organization is to create an after-the-fact outline. An after-the-fact outline is an outline of what you actually wrote, not a plan that precedes the writing.

To create an after-the-fact outline, read each of your paragraphs and try to sum up the point in that paragraph in a phrase, clause, or, at most, a sentence. (If you can't do this summarizing, that alone suggests that the paragraph needs revision.) Record the summarizing phrase, clause, or sentence on the outline, using indentations to show what are main points, subpoints, and sub-subpoints. Keep the outline on one side of a page or pages so that you can lay out the whole outline and see it all at once. (See section 5.13.3.)

Use after-the-fact outlines the way you would an aerial photograph of ground you just covered on a hike. Seen from this perspective, is the way you traveled through the material the most efficient one? Do you have any needless backtracking? Repetition? Did you miss anything along the way? If so, where can you easily add it?

Now that you have the "big picture" in mind, are there ways you can prepare your reader for the twists and turns your path will take? For example, are there insights you should add to your roadmap paragraph that will help your reader? What kinds of signposts will help the reader stay on track? (See section 20.2.)

§19.4.3   Do a Self-Critique

Revision can be the most satisfying of all the stages in writing because it is a bit like having a good debate with yourself. The draft is your own initial thinking and organization. (It is recorded so you don't have to worry about losing or forgetting something as you test it.) Now, leave the role of the writer and become a critical reader. Step back and examine the quality of the work. Play the devil's advocate. Where can you punch holes in this thing? Where are its weaknesses? Where are its strengths? Using what you find, you can return to the role of the writer and improve the draft.

§19.4.4   Check for Unity and Coherence

For a draft to be well written, the entire document, as well as each paragraph and section, must have unity and coherence. Unity at the document level means that every part of the document contributes to the overall thesis. In a memo, the thesis is essentially the same as your conclusion.

Many writers, though, do not have a clear idea of what their thesis is until they have completed a draft. While drafting, however, they discover what it is they are trying to say. This way of arriving at a thesis, or controlling idea, is perfectly fine. What it means, though, is that now that the writer has discovered the thesis he or she must go back through the draft with that thesis in mind, making sure that all parts are working toward that goal.

The same process may be true at the paragraph level. The writer may begin drafting the paragraph without a clear idea of what point he or she is trying to make. After drafting the paragraph, however, the writer discovers what the point is and how it contributes to the larger whole. At this point, then, the writer should first add or revise the topic sentence and then go back through the paragraph making sure all the parts contribute to the paragraph's point. See section 21.2.1 for more about unity.

Like unity, coherence is also important at both the document and the paragraph level. Consequently, a good revision strategy is to check at both the document and the paragraph level to see if you are using the common devices for creating coherence.

- logical organization
  - chronological, spatial, topical
  - general to specific, specific to general
  - IRAC: issues → rules → application → conclusion
- roadmap paragraphs
- topic sentences
- signposts, dovetailing, and transitions
- repetition of key terms
- parallelism
- pronouns

See section 21.2.2 for more about how these devices create coherence.

Two final points about revising: First, drafting and revising are not always distinct stages in the writing process; some revising occurs even as the first draft is being written. Second, if possible, do some revising on a hard copy. Seeing your writing on just a computer screen can be misleading. Because you can see only a small portion of a whole document at a time, you may overlook problems with some of the larger issues in writing.

§19.5   EDITING

Editing is an examination of the smaller issues in writing. As with revising, you must once again step out of the role of the drafter and look at the writing with a critical eye, but this time the critical eye is focused on smaller issues such as sentence structure and word choice.

When editing for sentence structure, writers should pay particular attention to the subjects and verbs of their sentences. If the subject-verb combination is effective, many other writing problems will clear up automatically. See section 5.14 and Chapter 23.

Legal writers should also make an extra effort to edit for precision and conciseness. See sections 24.1 and 24.2. Sloppy word choice and added verbiage may be overlooked in other types of writing, but they are unforgiveable in legal writing. In addition to editing for sentence structure and word choice, each writer should edit for his or her habitual problem areas.

If this seems like a lot to think about all at once, you are right. For this reason, many writers find it easier to edit for just one or two writing problems at a time. If, for example, you know that you have problems with spelling, do one reading in which you focus just on spelling every word correctly. If, on the other hand, your habitual problem is wordiness, do one reading with the single goal of editing out all unnecessary words.

Editing Tips

1. Don't let yourself fall in love with a particular phrase or sentence. No matter how well crafted it might be, if it doesn't work with the whole paragraph, indeed the whole document, it is not an effective phrase or sentence.

2. Be selective about whom you ask for editing advice. Although you can sometimes get excellent editing advice from others, there are far too many examples of the blind leading the mildly nearsighted. What often works better is to notice the parts of the paper that your reader/editor pointed out as problems and figure out with that reader what threw him or her off track. This procedure is much less risky than the unquestioning use of an inexperienced editor's rewrites.

3. Use creative ways to get the editing information that you need. For example, if you are wondering whether to add a transition at a given point in the paper, ask a reader to read up to that point and then, without reading what follows, to predict what will be discussed next. If the reader can easily predict where the writing is headed, a transition is probably unnecessary. If the reader is unsure or wrong about where the writing is headed, a transition will signal the shift in thought. Such techniques are more "editor-proof" than asking the same person if a transition is needed at that point.

4. Read your writing aloud or, better yet, have a colleague read it aloud to you while you follow along on another copy. Mark any part that the reader misreads or stumbles over or anything that just doesn't sound right. This technique will not tell you how to fix something, but it will give you a good idea of what needs to be fixed.

5. Spend the majority of your editing time on the section(s) of the document that you found hardest to write. No need to keep massaging the opening sentence long after you know it reads smoothly. Force yourself to focus your editing energy on the rockiest parts of the paper.

6. As with revising, if at all possible, do some of your editing on hard copy. The same language looks slightly different on a page than it does on a computer screen. For some reason, that small change from screen to page allows you to see the writing with different, fresh eyes.

§19.6   PROOFREADING

Whether you or your secretary types your writing, you will be the one who is responsible for the final product. Any missed words, format problems, or typos are ultimately your missed words, format problems, or typos. Consequently, every lawyer, no matter how competent his or her support staff, needs to know a few simple proofreading strategies.

First of all, proofreading is a distinct skill. It is not the same as normal reading or revising or editing. It is reading for errors. Consequently, to proofread properly, you need to remember a few important things.

Slow down. Speed reading and proofreading are mutually exclusive terms. Proofreading should be done at your slowest reading rate. One technique for slowing yourself down is to cover up all but the line you are proofreading with another sheet of paper. This technique also helps you to focus on the individual words on the page, so you will see transposed letters in the middle of words and notice missing words rather than read them in where they should be.

Consider proofreading the last third of your document first. Chances are there are more errors in the last sections simply because you and your typist were probably more tired and rushed when they were done. If that's true, then it makes sense to use the time when you are freshest on the part of the document that needs it most.

If at all possible, do your proofreading at a completely separate time—ideally, a day or more after you have completed drafting and revising. Even a small break in time allows you to see the document anew and bring fresh eyes to the pages.

Proofread all parts of the document, including headings, charts, appendices, captions, and page numbers.

Double check all dates and monetary figures and the spelling of every name.

§19.7   MYTHS ABOUT WRITING

No one seems to know exactly where they come from, but over the years a number of myths have developed about writing. Many of these myths have been repeated and even taught to several generations so that they now have an air of legitimacy. They seem to be part of the common knowledge about writing, although one never sees them repeated in reputable composition textbooks.

Grammar historians have uncovered the source of one or two of these myths, such as the so-called rule never to split an infinitive, but most of the myths seem to have developed from some short-cut methods used decades ago by elementary school teachers to prevent young children from writing sentence fragments. For example, if a child is taught "never to start a sentence with *because*," perhaps the child will stop treating dependent clauses that begin with "*because*" as sentences.

The most unfortunate consequence of these myths is the unnecessary constraints they place on sophisticated writers. In the office memorandum concerning the consent exception (Chapter 5), for example, the memo writer needed to use the split infinitive "to effectively monitor the type of service their employees are providing . . . ." All other options seem awkward or imprecise. Similarly, in the respondent's brief, the brief writer used the language for the rule on articulable suspicion that included a split infinitive (the officer "need only have the ability to reasonably surmise from the information at hand that a crime is in progress or has occurred"). Still, the myth hovers over the writer's head, creating uneasiness about using split infinitives.

What to do? Because at least some of the myths are treated as gospel by some readers, it is probably unwise to make split infinitives or any of the other myths a trademark of your writing style. When another, equally good construction is available, use it instead. But when the best thing to do is to start the sentence with "and" or "but" (as this sentence does) or to violate any of these other non-rules, do so—and do so without guilt.

Myth: Never Split an Infinitive

Grammar historians tell us that we acquired this non-rule at the time grammarians attempted to force the English language into the Latin grammar system. In Latin, infinitives are one word; hence, Latin infinitives are never split. Without regard to either the obvious fact that infinitives are two words in English (to see, to argue, to determine) or the obvious fact that speakers of English regularly split infinitives with a modifier, the non-rule was created so that English grammar could conform to Latin grammar.

This all seems terribly silly until you remember that at the time English was considered an inferior, upstart, unruly language, and Latin was considered a superior, well-designed, systematic language. Moreover, devising a grammar that actually described the way English was used was unheard of at the time. The purpose of grammar, it was thought, was to bring order to a language raging out of control.

What should a legal writer do then about split infinitives? Because the split infinitive myth is entrenched in many educated readers' minds, it is not worth the possible negative reaction to a given split infinitive if there are reasonably good ways to change it. In fact, many split infinitives are redundant ("to completely comprehend," "to finally finish") and need the modifier removed.

However, when the split infinitive is the best, indeed the most precise, way to express a point, stand your ground and use it. Note, however, that infinitives should not be split by the word "not." The correct way to write the negative form of an infinitive is to place the "not" before the infinitive.

EXAMPLE

The defendant explained that to not attend the meeting would have drawn undue attention to him.

Revised:

The defendant explained that not to attend the meeting would have drawn undue attention to him. *OR*

The defendant explained that not attending the meeting would have drawn undue attention to him.

Myth: Never Start a Sentence with "And," "But," or "Or"

Although there is no real rule that you cannot start a sentence with "and," "but," or "or," it is often a good idea to choose a more specific transition. If using one of these three words is a hasty or lazy choice, it is probably the wrong choice.

Occasionally, however, one of these three words is the perfect transition, especially because each is a one-syllable word that gets the next sentence started quickly. For this reason, it is usually not a good idea to start a sentence with "and," "but," or "or" and then follow the conjunction with a comma. When you do, you start the sentence up quickly only to immediately slow it down.

One final caveat about using "and," "but," or "or" at the beginnings of sentences: As transitions, these three words tend to sound informal.

Myth: Never Start a Sentence with "Because" or "However"

Legal writers often need to describe cause/effect relationships. In such cases, the best sentence structure is often "Because (fill in the cause), (fill in the effect)." This is an exceedingly useful sentence structure, and no rule prohibits its use. (Unfortunately, in erroneously trying to avoid beginning a sentence with "because," some writers use "since" to begin sentences depicting a cause/effect relationship. See "as," "because," and "since" in the Glossary of Usage for preferred usage for these three words.)

Similarly, no rule prohibits beginning a sentence with "however." Stylistically, however, it is often a better idea to move the transition "however" further into the sentence so that it immediately precedes the point of contrast, as is the case in this sentence.

Myth: Never End a Sentence with a Preposition

Winston Churchill did more than anyone else to debunk this writing myth. Churchill pointed out the idiocy of this non-rule when he wrote the following marginal comment on a state document: "This is the sort of English up with which I will not put."

Notwithstanding Churchill's remark, many readers claim to be offended by sentences that end with prepositions. For this reason, it is not a good practice to end sentences with prepositions when they can be easily revised.

EXAMPLE

Winfield may be able to get title to the entire triangle, not just the part which the bathhouse is built upon.

Revised:

Winfield may be able to get title to the entire triangle, not just the part upon which the bathhouse is built.

Notice that some sentences ending with a preposition are not easily revised using the technique above because the preposition works with the verb to create a meaning that is different from the meaning of the verb alone. For example, "to put up with" has a meaning far different from the meaning of "to put." Consequently, the best way to revise such verb + preposition combinations is to use a synonym ("to put up with" = "to tolerate").

Myth: Never Write a One-Sentence Paragraph

One-sentence paragraphs are not wrong per se, although they are often a sign of lack of development of the ideas in the writing. Numerous one-sentence paragraphs have the added drawback of making the writing seem unsophisticated.

For these reasons, use one-sentence paragraphs infrequently. Save them for occasions when the paragraph serves as a transition between two large sections of a document or when a shorter paragraph will give the reader a breather between two extremely long paragraphs. Notice too that a well-written one-sentence paragraph is usually made up of a fairly long sentence, although on rare occasions a one-sentence paragraph composed of a short sentence can be quite dramatic. See section 21.4 for more about paragraph length.

Chapter 20

Connections Between Paragraphs

§20.1 HEADINGS

Headings serve two purposes for the reader: They signal the overall organization, and they help the reader locate where he or she is in a document.

As indicators of organization, headings work a bit like a table of contents. They give the reader the framework within which to fit the ideas. They are reminders of what is a large concept, what is a subpoint, and what is a supporting detail in this document.

As locating devices, headings are invaluable to readers. A reader who does not have the time to read the whole document can use the headings to find the exact section he or she must read. For readers who have read the whole document and later need to refer to a point, headings are a quick way to locate that point.

Like all other headings, argumentative headings in briefs must be both indicators of overall organization and locating devices. In addition, they must persuade. See section 8.15 for more on writing argumentative headings.

Even though headings in objective memos are somewhat less important to the overall document than argumentative headings are to a brief, they still must be well written. The best headings in memos are fairly short, not more than one typed line and usually less than half a line, and they capture the content in a nutshell.

For headings to be helpful organizational indicators, they must be written in parallel form (see section 26.7) and in a consistent format. If the document has headings and subheadings, the reader will be able to identify the different levels of headings if they use compatible but different formats. For example, the main headings may use roman numerals and boldface and the subheadings may use capital letters and underlining. See section 28.2.2 for capitalization in headings.

EXAMPLE

   I. **Main Heading**
       A.   Subheading
       B.   Subheading

   II. **Main Heading**
       A.   Subheading
       B.   Subheading

When creating headings, remember the time-honored advice that "You can't have a 1 without a 2, and you can't have an A without a B." In other words, do not create a heading or a subheading unless there is at least one more heading or subheading at that same level.

Developing a good format for headings is simple. The bigger challenge is composing their content. To be useful finding devices, headings must capture the essence of the following section with enough specificity to be meaningful and enough generality to encompass the entire section.

Often the law itself will suggest the content of various sections of the document and hence the headings. An elements analysis or a list of factors, for example, lends itself to a document with the elements or factors as the headings.

But don't automatically assume that each element or factor deserves its own heading. Because undisputed elements will probably require minimal discussion, the document will appear chopped up if the writer uses a separate heading for each one. More importantly, the reader is not likely to need a heading for each undisputed element. In such cases, it usually works better to group all the undisputed elements under one heading and the disputed elements under a second heading with separate subheadings for each disputed element.

EXAMPLE

   I. **Undisputed Elements**
   II. **Disputed Elements**
       A.   Open and Notorious
       B.   Hostile

To compose good headings, find the key words and phrases that sum up the following section. Sometimes the easiest way to write a heading is to reread the section and ask yourself, "In a nutshell, what is this section about?" The answer should be close to what would make a good heading. For example, if the answer is "the court's lack of jurisdiction in this matter," then omit what can be easily inferred and the heading becomes "Lack of Jurisdiction."

Another way to arrive at the right heading is to assume you are discussing the document with a colleague and need to refer to a given section. What would you call that section? If "the history of the statute" is the first thing that comes to mind, then that may very well be the best heading.

But suppose you were writing an office memo for a case and the first thing that came to mind for a particular section was something like "whether or not the court will admit the eyewitnesses' line-up identifications"? Although this clause may accurately sum up the section, consider how it will look as a heading:

EXAMPLE   **WEAK HEADING**

Whether or not the Court Will Admit the Eyewitnesses'
Line-up Identifications

The example heading exceeds the one-line limit and includes some information that the reader can easily infer. Now consider these four substitute headings for the same section:

EXAMPLE   **SUBSTITUTE HEADINGS**

1. The Line-up
2. Line-up Identifications
3. Admissibility of Line-up Identifications
4. Admissibility of Eyewitnesses' Line-up Identifications

Option 1 is probably too general. It is unlikely the following section will include everything about the line-up. The reader will need more specific direction. Option 2 is better. Even so, if the focus of the following section is on the *admissibility* of the identifications, that key word in the heading will be helpful to the reader. Option 4 is also acceptable, but the word "eyewitnesses" can probably be inferred. Option 3 is the best. It sums up the section; it includes the key words and phrases; and it is short enough to be read at a glance.

One last thought about headings: Headings are for the reader, not the writer. The most common mistake legal writers make regarding headings is to use them as crutches for the writer rather than as aids for the reader. Headings should not be used as artificial bridges between two sections of the document. The connection between the sections should be made without the heading. If the headings in a document were removed, the sections should still naturally flow from one to the next.

§20.2   ROADMAPS AND SIGNPOSTS

§20.2.1   Roadmaps

Roadmaps are introductory paragraphs that give readers an overview of the entire document. They give readers the "big picture" perspective so that readers will be able to understand how numerous discrete bits of information fit together in the larger whole.

Like real roadmaps, roadmap paragraphs orient readers in several ways: They establish the parameters and overall structure of the discussion; they suggest what will be important and hence what deserves the readers' particular attention; and they create expectations for how the discussion will unfold and conclude. See section 5.13.4.

Although not every objective memo needs a roadmap paragraph, those with several steps in the analysis are easier to read if the writer uses a roadmap to set the stage for what follows. For example, the attorney writing the EMF memo used the following roadmap to show the two steps in the court's analysis.

EXAMPLE

In deciding whether New Mexico will allow a cause of action in nuisance, the New Mexico courts are likely to look first at whether EMFs constitute a public nuisance and then at whether they constitute a private nuisance.

If the attorney requesting the Beaver Custom Carpet memo in Chapter 5 had asked a broader question, such as whether the contract was enforceable under the UCC Statute of Frauds, the memo would have required several more steps in the analysis. Consequently, a roadmap paragraph like the one that follows would have provided a helpful overview.

EXAMPLE

The McKibbins claim that because there was no written contract, the oral contract is unenforceable under this state's version of the UCC Statute of Frauds. The first thing the court will have to determine, then, is whether the UCC applies at all. If the court finds that the UCC does govern the contract, the court will then have to decide whether the Statute of Frauds bars BCC's claim. Because BCC did not comply with the formal requirements of the Statute of Frauds, the court will find that the contract is unenforceable unless one of the exceptions included in the Statute applies. The only exception likely to apply is the specially manufactured goods exception.

A good roadmap paragraph also tells readers where to focus their attention. For example, if the applicable law includes several elements or factors, the reader will find it helpful to be told in the roadmap paragraph which elements or factors are critical to a case.

EXAMPLE

To claim a prescriptive easement, the Oregon Wilderness Watchers will have to satisfy four elements by clear and convincing evidence: 1) that its use was open and notorious; 2) that its use was continuous and uninterrupted; 3) that its use was adverse to the right of the owner; and 4) that its use of the property met each of the other requirements for over ten years. *See Thompson v. Scott,* 528 P.2d 509, 510 (Or. 1974). Although OWW should have no difficulty satisfying the first and fourth elements, the second element and especially the third element will be difficult to satisfy.

Roadmap paragraphs that use the "first, we will look at _____; then we will look at _____; and finally we will look at _____" approach tend to sound unsophisticated. Substituting "I" or "this memorandum" is no better. A better approach is to use the court as the actor. "First, the court must determine _____; if the court finds _____, it must then consider _____."

Compare the following roadmap paragraphs. Notice how much more sophisticated Examples 2 and 3 sound. Example 2 uses the two parties as actors to get away from the "you-and-me, dear reader" approach and to set up a logical progression of sub-issues. Notice that "we" in Example 2 refers to the client and attorney, not to the writer and reader. Example 3 uses the court as the actor, so it is now clear to the reader that the memorandum is tracking the court's decisionmaking process.

EXAMPLE 1   **UNSOPHISTICATED ROADMAP PARAGRAPH**

In this memorandum, we will examine three issues. First, we will look at whether the statute applies. If we find that it does not, then we will look at whether the Oregon Wilderness Watchers had an easement. If we find that an easement was created, then we will examine the scope of the easement.

EXAMPLE 2   **BETTER ROADMAP**

Our client would like to prevent or limit the use of a path across his property by the Oregon Wilderness Watchers (OWW). An Oregon statute exists that provides for public recreational use, while protecting the owner's interest in his land, and we will argue that it applies to this case. OWW will contend that the statute does not apply and that a prescriptive easement exists. If a prescriptive easement does exist, our client wants to limit the scope of its use.

EXAMPLE 3   **BETTER ROADMAP**

In deciding this case, a court will consider three issues. First, a court will determine whether the statute applies. If it does not, the court will then determine whether the Oregon Wilderness Watchers had an easement. If the court determines that an easement had been created, the court will then decide the scope of the easement.

---

§20.2.2   Signposts

Signposts are those words and phrases that keep readers oriented as they progress through a piece of writing. They can be used as a connecting thread throughout a whole document or through a smaller section.

To be the most effective, a series of signposts needs to be signaled in advance. For example, a writer may signal a series of signposts when he or she opens a section by saying, "There are four exceptions to the

Statute of Frauds." In the subsequent discussion, the writer can then use the words "first," "second," "third," "fourth" (or "final" or "last"), and "exception" to signal shifts to each new exception.

The following example is an excerpt from a memo about whether a contract is enforceable under the UCC Statute of Frauds. The set-up for the signpost series and the signposts are in boldface type.

EXAMPLE

There are four exceptions to the Statute of Frauds, but three of them are not applicable. The first of these inapplicable exceptions, § 4-2-201(2), applies only to transactions "between merchants." In an earlier section, § 4-2-201(1), a merchant is defined as "a person who deals in goods of the kind or otherwise holds himself out as having knowledge or skill peculiar to the practices or goods involved in the transaction or to whom such knowledge or skill may be attributed by his employment of an agent or broker or other intermediary who by his occupation holds himself out as having such knowledge or skill." Because the McKibbins presumably had little or no experience in the carpeting business and because they hired no intermediary to negotiate the transaction for them, the court will probably not find that they are merchants. This exception, then, does not apply.

The second inapplicable exception, § 4-2-201(3)(b), provides that a contract that does not satisfy the requirements of subsection (1) is still enforceable if the party against whom enforcement is sought admits in his pleading, testimony, or otherwise in court that a contract for sale was made. Because we are not at the litigation stage of this case yet, this exception does not apply.

The third inapplicable exception, § 4-2-201(3)(c), provides that a contract is enforceable with respect to goods for which payment has been made and accepted or which have been received and accepted. The McKibbins made no payment for the rugs, and they never received the rugs, so this exception also does not apply.

The exception that may be applicable is the exception for specially manufactured goods . . . .

Notice that most signpost series use the ordinal numbers (first, second, third, and so on) before a noun such as "element," "exception," "factor," "issue," "part," "prong," "reason," "requirement," "question," or "section."

EXAMPLES

three issues
the first issue, the second issue, the third issue

a two-part test
the first part of the test, the second part of the test

three questions to consider
the first question, the second question, the final question

Once a signpost series is set up, do not change terminology. If there were "three questions" in the introduction to the series, it may confuse readers if the second question is suddenly re-labeled "the second issue." See section 24.1.4.

Do not worry that legal readers will find such consistency boring. Legal readers are reading for information, not entertainment. Consistent terminology in signposts adds to the document's clarity.

Chapter 21

Effective Paragraphs

§21.1 THE FUNCTION OF A PARAGRAPH

Paragraphs exist for many reasons. First, they help writers organize what they are writing. Second, they help readers see and understand that organization. Third, they give readers a psychological, as well as a logical, break.

Writers need paragraphs to help them stay in control of what they are writing. Paragraphs are like tidy boxes in which to sort information. They make writing a manageable task.

Readers need paragraphs so that they can absorb information in manageable bits. If the typical legal reader must comprehend twenty hours' worth of research in the roughly twenty minutes it takes to study an eight-page memo, he or she will need some way to see significant groupings of ideas. That way is the paragraph.

But paragraphing is more than a matter of logic and organization. It is also a matter of reader comfort and aesthetics. After all, those "boxes" into which the writer is fitting ideas can be huge containers that are too heavy to lift or small cartons with barely enough room for half an idea.

When paragraphs are too long, readers tend to become bewildered, even lost, or worse, lulled into inattention. Paragraphs that are too short, on the other hand, make the writing and the thinking seem skimpy and inconsequential. Readers need paragraphs that are the right size to comfortably follow what the writer is saying.

Paragraphs also change the look of a page. They create more white space, which can be a welcome relief. Anyone who has opened a book to see a solid mass of type on page one knows how intimidating overly long paragraphs can be. In contrast, the visual break at the beginning of a paragraph signals a brief mental breather.

As the first significant grouping of sentences, a paragraph becomes a kind of mini-composition all its own. It has a beginning, a middle, and an end.

The following paragraph, which is taken from the middle of an argument section of a brief in opposition to a motion to disclose the identity of a state informant, illustrates how a paragraph is a mini-composition.

EXAMPLE

Beginning

The fact that the informer is present at the alleged drug transaction is not determinative of whether the testimony of that informant is relevant or necessary. *Lewandowski v. State,* 389 N.E.2d 706 (Ind. 1979). In *Lewandowski,* the Indiana Supreme Court held that "[m]ere presence of the informer when marijuana was sold to a police officer

Middle

has been held to be insufficient to overcome the privilege of nondisclosure." *Id.* at 710. The court made the same ruling on nearly identical facts (informant introduced officer to defendant and was present during purchase of illegal drugs) in *Craig v. State,* 404 N.E.2d 580 (Ind. 1980). In the instant case,

Ending

the state's informant served mainly as a line of introduction and as such her testimony does not automatically become relevant or necessary to the defendant's case simply because she was present at the scene.

Paragraphs, then, function as mini-compositions within the larger composition, or document. They divide up the information and present it in neat little packages.

§21.2   Unity and Coherence in Paragraphs

§21.2.1   Paragraph Unity

To be a mini-composition, a paragraph must have its own topic, that is, its own point to make, and all elements in the paragraph must work together to make that point. When they do, the paragraph has unity.

Look again at the paragraph about the state informant.

EXAMPLE

> The fact that the informer is present at the alleged drug trans-
> action is not determinative of whether the testimony of that infor-
> mant is relevant or necessary. *Lewandowski v. State,* 389 N.E.2d
> 706 (Ind. 1979). In *Lewandowski,* the Indiana Supreme Court held
> that "[m]ere presence of the informer when marijuana was sold to
> a police officer has been held to be insufficient to overcome the
> privilege of nondisclosure." *Id.* at 710. The court made the same
> ruling on nearly identical facts (informant introduced officer to de-
> fendant and was present during purchase of illegal drugs) in *Craig
> v. State,* 404 N.E. 2d 580 (Ind. 1980). In the instant case, the
> state's informant served mainly as a line of introduction and as
> such her testimony does not automatically become relevant or
> necessary to the defendant's case simply because she was pres-
> ent at the scene.

All of the information is about one topic: the informant's testimony
is not necessarily relevant or necessary simply because the informant was
present at the drug transaction. This topic is introduced at the beginning
of the paragraph by a topic sentence, developed and supported by two
sentences in the middle of the paragraph, and then concluded by the last
sentence.

What the paragraph does not do is stray from this topic. Even though
the writer will need to refer to both *Lewandowski* and *Craig* later in the
memo to support other points, he or she did not get sidetracked and try
to do it here. The paragraph stays on course and makes its point. It has
a clear focus; it has unity.

§21.2.2   Paragraph Coherence

When a paragraph is coherent, the various elements of the paragraph are connected in such a way that the reader can easily follow the
writer's development of ideas. Coherence can be achieved in a number
of ways: by using familiar organizational patterns, particularly those that
are established patterns for legal writing; by establishing and then using
key terms; and by using sentence structure and other coherence devices
to reinforce the connections between ideas.

a.   Using Familiar Organizational Patterns

The most important way of achieving coherence is to arrange the
ideas in a predictable, familiar pattern. All readers expect certain patterns—cause/effect, problem/solution, chronological order—and when
writers meet those expectations, the ideas are easy to follow. Legal read-

ers have some additional patterns that they expect in legal writing. For example, once a rule, standard, or definition has been laid out, legal readers expect it to be applied. They expect a court's holding to be followed by its rationale. In office memos, arguments are almost always followed by counterarguments. In both office memos and briefs, the IRAC pattern (issue, rule, analysis/application, and conclusion) and all its variations are commonplace and expected.

Notice how the following paragraph uses the IRAC pattern to achieve coherence.

EXAMPLE

Issue	The second element, continuous, is in dispute. To satisfy this element, OWW does not need to establish that its use was con-
Rule	stant. *See Kondor v. Prose,* 622 P.2d 741 (Or. Ct. App. 1981). It need show only that its use of the path was consistent with its
Application	needs. *Id.* OWW will argue that its use was consistent with its needs. To do its research, OWW needed to use the path only two or three times per month, and it did so from 1967 to 1977. Although the plaintiff could argue that use of the path two or three times per month is sporadic, this argument is not persuasive because of the rural quality of
Conclusion	the land. Therefore, the court will probably find that OWW satisfies this element.

Writers can also achieve coherence in paragraphs by creating reader expectations and then fulfilling them. For example, when a writer sets up a list of factors, elements, reasons, or issues, the reader expects the writing to follow up on that list. In the following paragraph, the writer uses this technique to create a coherent discussion of how the statutory term "ways of this state" will be construed in a case in which an intoxicated driver was on the shoulder of the road.

EXAMPLE

A narrow construction of the term "ways" is unlikely. In fact, there are two strong indications that Montana will favor a broad construction: 1) an extension stated in the statutory definition of "highway"; and 2) an interpretation of "ways" given in a Montana

Supreme Court decision. By statutory definition, "[h]ighway means the entire width between the boundary lines of every publicly maintained way when any part thereof is open to the use of the public for purposes of vehicular travel, *except that for the purpose of chapter 8 the term also includes ways which have been or shall be dedicated to public use*" (emphasis added). Mont. Code Ann. § 61.1.201 (1983). Chapter 8 includes offenses committed while under the influence of alcohol. Because the legislature expanded the statutory definition for alcohol-related offenses, it follows that the legislature intended to broaden, not narrow, the term. Following the legislature's lead, the Montana Supreme Court stipulated that "ways" encompasses state and county right-of-ways, including borrow pits, which road maintenance crews use as sources of dirt and gravel. *State v. Taylor,* 661 P.2d 33, 35 (Mont. 1983). It is highly unlikely that the court would include borrow pits but exempt shoulders from the term "ways." Therefore, the court will probably conclude that Mr. Renko's truck was on the ways of the state open to the public.

b.   Using Key Terms

Of the various methods writers have for creating coherence, repetition of key terms is the easiest and one of the most important. In the following paragraph about the state informant, key terms—informant, **present** or **presence**, testimony, and RELEVANT OR NECESSARY—appear, in a different typeface, in every sentence. Together they are part of a network of connecting threads that create a coherent theme for the paragraph.

EXAMPLE   **WITH KEY TERMS HIGHLIGHTED**

The fact that the informer is **present** at the alleged drug transaction is not determinative of whether the testimony of that informant is RELEVANT OR NECESSARY. *Lewandowski v. State,* 389 N.E.2d 706 (Ind. 1979). In *Lewandowski,* the Indiana Supreme Court held that "[m]ere **presence** of the informer when marijuana was sold to a police officer has been held to be insufficient to overcome the privilege of nondisclosure." *Id.* at 710. The court made the same ruling on nearly identical facts (informant introduced officer to defendant and was **present** during purchase of illegal drugs) in *Craig v. State,* 404 N.E.2d 580 (Ind. 1980). In the instant case, the state's informant served mainly as a line of introduction and as such her <u>testimony</u> does not automatically become RELEVANT OR NECESSARY to the defendant's case simply because she was **present** at the scene.

The following paragraph from the memo concerning the intoxicated driver on the shoulder of the road also demonstrates the repetition of key terms. Notice how the writer makes logical connections between the key terms to show that **ways of the state open to the public** may not be construed to include SHOULDERS of the road.

EXAMPLE   **WITH KEY TERMS HIGHLIGHTED**

Although the primary issue of the case focuses upon resolving questions pertaining to actual physical control, the issue of whether Mr. Renko's truck was on the **ways of the state open to the public** deserves brief analysis. The traffic code states that "'**ways of the state open to the public**' means any highway, road, alley, lane, parking area, or other public or private place <u>adapted and fitted for public travel</u> that is in common use by the public." Mont. Code Ann. § 61.8.101 (1) (1983). The language specifically states <u>"adapted and fitted for public travel."</u> Because Mr. Renko's truck was found on the SHOULDER, the court would have to determine whether the SHOULDER of a highway is <u>adapted and fitted for public travel.</u> In defining other statutory language, the Montana Supreme Court resorted to dictionary definitions. Webster defines SHOULDER as "either edge of a roadway: specifically: the part of the roadway *outside the <u>traveled</u>* way" (emphasis added). It is possible, then, that the court could interpret the statutory language narrowly and conclude that the term **"ways"** does not encompass SHOULDERS.

In short, this paragraph is itself an analysis of the key terms.

ways of the state open to the public = *adapted and fitted for public travel*

SHOULDER = *outside the traveled way*; therefore,
SHOULDER may not = **ways of the state open to the public**

c.   *Using Sentence Structure and Other Coherence Devices*

In addition to using familiar organizational patterns and repeating key terms, writers can create coherence through sentence structure and through a number of other common coherence devices. Dovetails (beginning a sentence with a reference to the preceding sentence) and other transitions create connections by establishing links between sentences. See section 22.3. Parallelism within a sentence or between sentences shows the reader which ideas should be considered together and which should be compared and contrasted. See section 26.7. Even pronouns in their own small way provide subtle links within the writing because they are a connection to the noun they replace.

EXAMPLE

The fact that the informer is present at the alleged drug transaction is not determinative of whether the testimony of that informant is relevant or necessary. LEWANDOWSKI V. STATE, 389 N.E.2d 706 (Ind. 1979). IN LEWANDOWSKI, the Indiana Supreme Court held that "[m]ere presence of the informer when marijuana was sold to a police officer has been held to be insufficient to overcome the privilege of nondisclosure." *Id.* at 710. The court made the same ruling on nearly identical facts (informant introduced officer to defendant and was present during purchase of illegal drugs) in *Craig v. State*, 404 N.E.2d 580 (Ind. 1980). In the instant case, **the state's informant** mainly as a line of introduction and as such **her** testimony does not automatically become relevant or necessary to the defendant's case simply because **she** was present at the scene.

DOVETAILING

Parallelism

Parallelism

Pronouns

For the following paragraph, notice how the parallel phrases "on the defendant's ability to operate the vehicle" and "on the vehicle's condition" in the opening topic sentence set up the organizational pattern. The writer then signals the beginning of each half of the discussion by using the parallel sentence openers "in focusing on the defendant's condition" and "in focusing on the vehicle's condition." Note too the dovetailing between sentences 2 and 3 ("he would have been able to operate the vehicle" → "not only is it possible that he could have operated the truck") and between sentences 4 and 5 ("defined" → "by that definition"). Once again, pronouns also subtly provide coherence ("defendant" → "he," "truck" → "it," "court" → "it").

EXAMPLE

> If some form of operability is required, then the court must decide whether to focus on the defendant's ability to operate the vehicle or on the vehicle's condition. *See State v. Smelter,* 674 P.2d 690, 693 (Wash. App. 1983). In focusing on the defendant's condition, the court could find that because the defendant had the key and was in the cab of the truck, he would have been able to operate the vehicle had he been awakened. Not only is it possible that he could have operated the truck, it is evident that he did drive the truck from the tavern to the freeway before parking it on the shoulder. In focusing on the vehicle's condition, the Washington court used the trial court's "reasonably operable" standard and defined that term as any malfunction short of a cracked block or a similar problem that would render the vehicle totally inoperable. *Id.* at 693. By that definition, Mr. Renko's truck was reasonably operable regardless of whether it would start. Therefore, if the Montana court considers operability an issue, it would probably find that Mr. Renko was capable of operating the vehicle and that the vehicle was in reasonably operable condition.

To sum up, then, if a paragraph has unity, it has all the right pieces. If a paragraph is both unified and coherent, then all the right pieces are arranged and connected in such a way that the reader can easily follow them.

§21.3 PARAGRAPH PATTERNS

Every paragraph needs a focus, a topic, a point to make. In addition, every paragraph needs a shape, a way of moving through sentences to make that point. The earlier example paragraph about the relevance of the informant's testimony has one of the most common shapes or patterns: that of a fat hourglass.

An hourglass paragraph begins with a general statement about the topic. This statement may take up one or more sentences. The paragraph then narrows to the specific support or elaboration or explanation the writer has for that general statement. The paragraph concludes with a more general sentence or two about the topic.

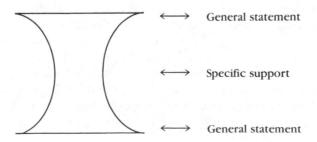

←→ General statement

←→ Specific support

←→ General statement

A variation of this pattern is the V-shaped paragraph, which is the most common structure for rule paragraphs. Like the hourglass paragraph, the V-shaped paragraph begins with a general discussion of the topic and then narrows to the specific support. The V-shaped paragraph ends with the specific support; it does not return to a general statement.

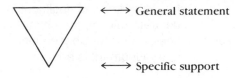

←——→ General statement

←——→ Specific support

EXAMPLE   **V-SHAPED PARAGRAPH**

Kraft Savings, one of three savings and loans represented on Kraft Island, does a significant amount of the banking business on Kraft Island. As of 1986, Kraft Savings had 2.2 million dollars in deposits, 9.6 million dollars in outstanding loans, and a large volume of business with the Kraft City Council. In 1986, Kraft Savings handled 40 million dollars in transactions for almost 1900 customers in about 2400 accounts.

General statement

Specific support

Both the hourglass and the V-shaped paragraph patterns work well in legal writing. Both use the opening sentence or sentences as an overview of what is to come and then proceed to support that generalization with specifics. In some senses, both patterns, but particularly the hourglass pattern, resemble deductive reasoning.

EXAMPLE   **PARAGRAPH USING DEDUCTIVE REASONING**

The purpose of summary judgment is to eliminate useless trials on formal issues that cannot be factually supported or, if factually supported, cannot as a matter of law lead to a result favorable to the non-moving party. *Buris v. General Ins. Co.,* 553 P.2d 125 (Wash. 1976). A summary judgment motion permits the court to pierce formal allegations of fact in pleadings and grant relief to a plaintiff when it appears from uncontroverted

Major premise

Minor premise   facts that no genuine issue exists. *Preston v. Duncan,* 349 P.2d 605 (Wash. 1960). Here the facts regarding the accident are undisputed. Ms. Hawkins readily admits that her car collided with Eli Reisman's car. CP 27. Officer Sanchez's testimony establishes that Ms. Hawkins was negligent in failing to concentrate fully on the hazardous road condi-

Conclusion   tions. RP 59. Consequently, partial summary judgment is appropriate.

Less common, but also useful, is the inverted V paragraph. Here, the writer begins with the specifics and then concludes with a general statement. This pattern resembles inductive reasoning, and, like inductive reasoning, has some risks. Readers may feel disoriented without an overview statement, or they may miss the relevance of some supporting evidence because they do not know where the writer is heading. Even so, the inverted V pattern can be effective, particularly in persuasive writing, if the writer is able to lay out the specific support in such a way that readers reach the desired conclusion even before it is stated. This technique has the effect of making readers feel like they arrived at the conclusion independently, not after being told what to think.

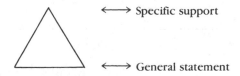

⟵⟶ Specific support

⟵⟶ General statement

§21.4   PARAGRAPH LENGTH

First, the truth. Not all paragraphs are three to five sentences long. Most are, but not all. In fact, quite a few well-written paragraphs are as short as two sentences and, yes, some well-written paragraphs contain only one sentence. One-sentence paragraphs are neither a goal to strive for nor a taboo to be feared. Writers simply need to know when they have finished what they set out to do in the paragraph.

Similarly, good paragraphs may run many sentences longer than five. It is not outrageous for a paragraph in legal writing to include seven or even eight sentences, as long as the writer needed that many to make the point. However, writers should keep in mind the reader's comfort and avoid seven- and eight-sentence paragraphs about complicated discussions of law. Remember too that an eight-sentence paragraph is likely to create a solid page of type, which has a negative psychological impact on readers. See section 21.4.

The following five-paragraph example is from a section in an appellate brief. Notice the number of sentences in and the length of each paragraph. Citation sentences are not counted as substantive sentences.

EXAMPLE

I. The Trial Court Erred in Holding That the Plaintiff Is a Public Figure as a Matter of Law

The states have a legitimate interest in compensating plaintiffs for damage to reputation inflicted through defamatory publications. *Gertz v. Robert Welch, Inc.,* 418 U.S. 323, 341 (1974). While recognizing that "[s]ome tension necessarily exists between the need for a vigorous and uninhibited press and the legitimate interest in redressing wrongful injury," the U.S. Supreme Court has stressed that the plaintiff's right to the protection of his reputation must not be sacrificed when the court balances these two competing interests. *Id.*

Two-sentence paragraph

In an attempt to balance the interests of the media against the interests of plaintiffs injured by defamatory statements, the Court developed three classes of plaintiffs: public officials, public figures, and private figures. *Gertz,* 418 U.S. at 343; *Curtis Publishing Co. v. Butts,* 388 U.S. 130 (1966); *New York Times v. Sullivan,* 376 U.S. 254, 279 (1964). Because public figure plaintiffs are held to a higher standard of paragraph proof in defamation suits, the Court has made it clear that the public figure standard is to be construed narrowly. *Gertz,* 418 U.S. at 341, 352. The Court will not lightly find a plaintiff to be a public figure. *Id.*

Three-sentence paragraph

The first class of public figure defined by the Court in *Gertz* is the limited purpose public figure. To become a limited purpose public figure, a plaintiff must voluntarily inject himself into a particular public controversy and attempt to influence its outcome. *Id.* at 351, 352. By doing so, the plaintiff invites public attention and comment on a limited range of issues relating to his involvement in the controversy. *Id.* at 351.

Three-sentence paragraph

One-sentence
paragraph

The Court described the second class of public figure, the all-purpose public figure, as having "assumed roles of especial prominence in the affairs of society," or as occupying "positions of such persuasive power and influence," or as "achieving such pervasive fame or notoriety that he becomes a public figure for all purposes and in all contexts." *Id.* at 345, 351.

Six-sentence
paragraph

Under these narrow definitions laid down by the U.S. Supreme Court, Vashon Savings and Loan is neither a limited purpose public figure nor an all-purpose public figure. Therefore, the trial court erred in granting defendants' motion for partial summary judgment on the public figure issue. Furthermore, this error was prejudicial because it resulted in the plaintiff's being held to a higher standard of proof at trial. But because the standard of review is *de novo* when a partial summary judgment order is appealed, this court is not bound by the erroneous trial court decision below. *Herron v. Tribune Publishing Co.,* 108 Wash. 2d 162, 169, 736 P.2d 249, 255 (1987); *Noel v. King County,* 48 Wash. App. 227, 231, 738 P.2d 692, 695 (1987). Rather, the court should apply the *Gertz* public figure standard to the facts of this case and reach its own independent determination. Correct application of the standard will result in a holding that Vashon Savings and Loan is a private figure for purposes of this defamation suit.

First, a few comments about the preceding example. Notice that the length of each paragraph is primarily determined by content. The writer wrote as few or as many sentences as she needed to make each point. The length of each paragraph is further determined by reader comfort and interest. Some variety in paragraph length helps keep the writing interesting. Short, one- or two-sentence paragraphs tend to work in places where the reader needs a bit of a break before or after an unusually long paragraph. Too many short paragraphs, though, and the writing begins to seem choppy and undeveloped.

An occasional long paragraph allows the writer to go into depth on a point. Too many long paragraphs, though, and the writing slows down to a plod and seems heavy and ponderous.

Short paragraphs can also be effective when the writer is making a major shift, change, or connection between ideas. Consequently, short paragraphs frequently serve as transitions between major sections and as introductions or conclusions to major sections.

In the following example, the writer had just concluded his discussion of the first requirement of the statutory exception in the preceding paragraph. The one-sentence paragraph that follows introduced several paragraphs that dealt with the second requirement.

EXAMPLE   **EXAMPLE OF AN INTRODUCTION TO A SECTION**

The second requirement of the statutory exception — that the goods be unsuitable for sale in the ordinary course of the manufacturer's business — will probably be met.

Occasionally, extremely short paragraphs can be effective attention grabbers, particularly in persuasive writing. This technique will work only if the writer uses short paragraphs infrequently. Long paragraphs work best in situations where the writer has been careful to lay out an organizational plan for the paragraph and then uses signposts (see section 20.2.2) to keep the reader oriented.

In short, there is no magic or perfect length for a paragraph. When Abraham Lincoln was asked how tall a man should be, he said, tall enough so that his legs reach the ground. How long should a paragraph be? Long enough to make the writer's point. See Exercises 21.A and 21.B in the *Practice Book.*

§21.5   TOPIC AND CONCLUDING SENTENCES

Again, the truth. Not all paragraphs have topic and concluding sentences. In fact, many well-written paragraphs have neither.

However, and this is a big "however," most well-written paragraphs do have topic sentences, and those that don't, have an implied topic sentence that governs the paragraph as firmly as any written topic sentence. The same is true for concluding sentences. Well-written paragraphs that do not have an explicit concluding sentence have an implied concluding sentence. The writer may have chosen not to write out the concluding sentence because it is painfully obvious; nevertheless, even without an explicit concluding sentence, the reader knows what the paragraph's conclusion is.

The point then is to know what topic and concluding sentences do for a paragraph. Once you know how they work, then you can decide whether a stated or an implied topic or concluding sentence works in a given situation. When in doubt, state your topic sentence. If you don't, your reader may also be in doubt.

§21.5.1   Stated Topic Sentences

The following examples demonstrate how the standard topic sentence works. Notice that the topic sentence has two functions: It introduces or names the topic and it asserts something about the topic.

EXAMPLE 1

In determining whether service was proper under Fed. R. Civ. P. 4(d) (1), courts have considered several other factors. First, the courts recognize that "each decision proceeds on its own facts." *Karlsson*, 318 F.2d at 668. Second, the courts consider whether the defendant will return to the place where service was left. *Id.* Third, the courts look at whether service was reasonably calculated to provide actual notice to the defendant. *Minnesota Mining & Mfg. Co. v. Kirkevold*, 87 F.R.D. 317, 323 (D. Minn. 1980).

EXAMPLE 2

Defendants have successfully used the following articulated reasons to rebut a plaintiff's prima facie case. In *Kelly*, the defendant testified that the plaintiff was terminated because he was the least effective salesman. *Kelly*, 640 F.2d at 977. Similarly, in *Sakellar*, the defendant alleged that the plaintiff lacked the skills and experience for the position. *Sakellar*, 765 F.2d at 1456. And in *Sutton*, the defendant discharged the plaintiff for "intemperate and impolitic actions." *Sutton*, 646 F.2d at 410.

One common weakness of some novice legal writers is to write topic sentences that merely name the topic. These "topic sentences" fall under the category of "The next thing I'm going to talk about is . . . ."

Compare the following two topic sentences. Which will a reader find more helpful?

EXAMPLE 1

Another case that discussed actual malice is *Rosenbloom v. Metromedia, Inc.,* 403 U.S. 29 (1971).

EXAMPLE 2

The court extended these protections in *Rosenbloom*, holding that plaintiffs in a defamation action would have to prove actual malice if the published statements were of public or general interest. *Rosenbloom v. Metromedia,* 403 U.S. 29 (1971).

The topic sentence in Example 1 does little more than name a case. The topic sentence in Example 2 is far superior. It introduces the point the paragraph will make—that plaintiffs in a defamation action would have to prove actual malice if the statements published were of public or general interest.

In addition, the topic sentence in Example 2 demonstrates an excellent method for writing topic sentences that introduce a new case: It begins with a transition that relates the point from the new case to the previous discussion and then follows with a paraphrase of the holding. The following example shows how the writer completed the paragraph.

EXAMPLE 3

The court extended these protections in *Rosenbloom*, holding that plaintiffs in a defamation action would have to prove actual malice if the published statements were of public or general interest. *Rosenbloom v. Metromedia,* 403 U.S. 29 (1971). The Court wrote, "If a matter is a subject of public or general interest, it cannot suddenly become less so merely because a private individual is involved, or because in some sense the individual did not 'voluntarily' choose to become involved." *Rosenbloom,* 403 U.S. at 43.

The next two examples also show how to use a court's holding for the topic sentence. In Example 1, the writer develops the topic sentence by setting out the facts in the analogous case and then distinguishing them from the client's case. In Example 2, the writer develops the topic sentence by setting out the facts of the case and then returns to the holding.

EXAMPLE 1

In *Messenger*, **the court found that the trespassory slashing of trees was a permanent form of property damage.** *Messenger v. Frye*, 28 P.2d 1023 (Wash. 1934). However, the tree slashing in that case was extensive. It was the extent of the injury, not the type of injury, which made the damage irreparable and therefore permanent. Unlike the slashed trees, the damage to the rosebushes in our case should not be considered extensive because only four out of twenty rosebushes were destroyed. The rosebushes can probably be replaced, thus restoring the Archers' property to its original condition. Therefore, the damage to the rosebushes and buds is temporary, and the Archers will recover only for the restoration cost of the rosebuds and bushes, as well as the diminished use value of their property.

EXAMPLE 2

In an analogous Arizona case, *State v. Thomas*, **the court held that the trial court committed an error of constitutional magnitude when it allowed the prosecution to do exactly as the prosecution did in the instant case.** *Thomas*, 636 P.2d at 1219. In *Thomas*, the only pertinent evidence was the testimony of the defendant, who stood accused of rape, and the testimony of the prosecuting witness. During the trial, the prosecution questioned the witness about her religious beliefs and church-related activities, eliciting from her that she was a religious person. *Id.* at 1217. In closing argument, the prosecution told the jury that the ultimate issue was the credibility of the witnesses, and that before the jury could believe the defendant, it had to believe that the prosecuting witness, an "uprighteous, religious, moralistic type," was a liar. *Id.* The appellate court held that admission of the religious references was an error of constitutional magnitude. *Id.* at 1219.

As we have seen, the first sentence of a paragraph is usually the topic sentence. Topic sentences may, however, appear later in a paragraph, particularly if the opening sentence or sentences are used to provide a transition to or background for the topic.

The following example is taken from the beginning of the second argument in the same memorandum in opposition to the defendants' motion for partial summary judgment. Notice how sentence 1 serves as a transition between the two arguments and sentence 2 provides background for sentence 3, the topic sentence.

EXAMPLE

Sullivan and *Gertz* dealt with individual citizens who had been libeled and who had sought redress in the courts. The case before the court today is different; the plaintiff is a state chartered savings and loan, a business entity. The significance of the different status of a business entity and its reputation, as compared to a private individual, has been recognized in several federal courts. In *Martin Marietta v. Evening Star Newspaper,* 417 F. Supp. 947, 955 (D.D.C. 1976), the court stated that "[t]he law of libel has long reflected the distinction between corporate and human plaintiffs" and that "a corporate libel action is not a basic [sic] of our constitutional system, and need not force the first amendment to yield as far as it would be in a private libel action." *Martin Marietta,* 417 F. Supp. at 955 (citations omitted). The *Marietta* court continued, "Corporations, which do not possess private lives to begin with, must similarly [to public figures] be denied full protection from libel." *Id.*	Transition Background Topic sentence

---

See Exercise 21.C in the *Practice Book.*

§21.5.2 Implied Topic Sentences

Many paragraphs with implied topic sentences occur in statements of fact. Although some statements of fact have paragraphs that are thematically organized and use traditional topic sentences, most have a chronological organization with implied topic sentences. Many use a mix of the two.

Practically all paragraphs in statements of fact depend on their narrative, or storytelling, quality to keep the writing organized. The organizing principle, or topic, of such paragraphs may be what happened in a given time period, what happened to a given person, or what facts make up a given part of the situation.

The following paragraph appeared in the statement of facts from a case about whether service of process was valid when it was left at a spouse's home. The preceding paragraph explained that the defendant, Ms. Clay-Poole, has a job and residence in New York and that her husband has a job and residence in California. In this paragraph, no topic sentence is stated, but one is certainly implied.

EXAMPLE

Ms. Clay-Poole and Mr. Poole usually see each other about once a month for three or four days. They split the traveling about equally, although Ms. Clay-Poole travels to San Diego somewhat more frequently than Mr. Poole travels to Albany. They are happy with this arrangement; consequently, they do not intend to move in together permanently.

The implied topic sentence of this paragraph is that Ms. Clay-Poole and Mr. Poole have a commuter marriage. The writer could have stated the topic sentence, but in this case it was sufficiently obvious to leave it implied.

§21.5.3   Concluding Sentences

To be worthwhile, concluding sentences need to do more than just restate the topic sentence. If they don't, then the paragraph will not have advanced the line of reasoning in the memo or brief. Look again at the paragraph about whether a drug informant's testimony is relevant. Notice how the topic and concluding sentences are not simply artful clones of each other.

EXAMPLE

Topic sentence	The fact that the informer is present at the alleged drug transaction is not determinative of whether the testimony of that informant is relevant or necessary. *Lewandowski v. State,* 389 N.E.2d 706 (Ind. 1979). In
Supporting sentences	*Lewandowski,* the Indiana Supreme Court held that "[m]ere presence of the informer when marijuana was sold to a police officer has been held to be insufficient to overcome the privilege of nondisclosure." *Id.* at 710.

The court made the same ruling on nearly identical facts (informant introduced officer to defendant and was present during purchase of illegal drugs) in *Craig v. State*, 404 N.E.2d 580 (Ind. 1980). The state's informant in the instant case served mainly as a line of introduction and does not as such automatically become relevant or necessary to the defendant's case simply because she was present at the scene.	Supporting sentences Conclusion

The topic sentence introduces the topic and serves as a general statement of that point. The concluding sentence advances the line of reasoning by taking that topic, or that point, and applying it to the instant case. It rather neatly argues that the rationale in *Craig v. State* is applicable in the instant case because in both cases the informant "served mainly as a line of introduction." This concluding sentence is not just extra baggage, the obligatory "Now I'm going to tell you again what I told you before." It is a working sentence, a significant sentence, perhaps the most significant sentence in the paragraph.

In the following example, the writer of another memo uses the concluding sentence of a paragraph to extend the point made in the topic sentence. The topic sentence makes the point that the plaintiff has certain interests and rights; the concluding sentence furthers the discussion by saying that the plaintiff has been deprived of those rights.

EXAMPLE

The plaintiff will probably compare the facts of the instant case to the facts of *Moore* to show the court's recognition of an individual's proprietary interests in the tissue of her body. There as here, the defendant used tissue from the plaintiff's body to develop a commercially valuable product. There as here, the "owner" did not consent to the use of his tissue for the development of this product. Therefore, the defendant's action in *Moore* violated the plaintiff's rights under *Bouvia* to determine what should have been done with his body. Likewise, the women in our case had no knowledge of the use of fetal tissue for research. Therefore, the University's actions deprived the women of their right to determine what should have been done with the fetal tissue taken from their bodies.

The subsequent paragraph in the same memorandum demonstrates a slightly different and effective way to use topic and concluding sentences. In the following example, notice how the topic sentence introduces an argument and the concluding sentence extends the point by drawing the logical conclusion if that argument is accepted.

EXAMPLE

Conversely, the University will argue that fetal tissue does not meet the broad definition of property. The fetal tissue had no exchangeable value at the time of the abortion, or the plaintiff would not have had the abortion in the first place. The lack of value is demonstrated by the plaintiff's signing away of her rights to the fetal tissue before the abortion procedure. In fact, the fetal tissue by itself has no exchangeable value; it is the cell line developed from the tissue that carries value. If the fetal tissue has no exchangeable value, then the University cannot invade plaintiff's property rights by actionable wrong. No actionable wrong exists if no value is recognized in the fetal tissue.

Earlier we saw how a paraphrase of the holding often makes an excellent topic sentence. Paraphrasing the holding can also be an effective way to conclude a paragraph about an analogous case.

EXAMPLE

Recently, the Georgia appellate court addressed the issue of consent in relation to the disposal of a stillborn child. *See McCoy v. Georgia Baptist Hospital,* 306 S.E.2d 746 (Ga. Ct. App. 1983). In that case, the mother delivered a stillborn child in the defendant hospital. Both parents had signed a consent form authorizing the hospital to dispose of the body "in any manner they deem advisable." *Id.* at 747. Thereafter, the mother discovered that the body had been placed in a freezer and left there for approximately one month. The court held that the parents released their quasi-property interests in the child's body to the defendant hospital when they signed the consent form.

Another effective technique for writing concluding sentences is to use a particularly apt quotation. This technique allows the writer to introduce the point in the topic sentence with language of his or her own making and then finish with a memorable quotation from the court or another authority.

EXAMPLE

The California Court of Appeals recently decided that an individual is entitled to full property rights in his organs and other bodily tissue. In *Moore v. Regents of UCLA*, 249 Cal. Rptr. 494 (Cal. Ct. App. 1988), the appellant's diseased spleen was removed by the appellee research hospital. Appellee subsequently discovered that Moore's spleen and other bodily tissue had unique characteristics that could be used to develop substances with potential commercial value. Moore was never told of appellee's discovery and continued to allow appellee to extract bodily tissue from him under the auspices of continuing treatment. The appellate court held that Moore had certain rights in his bodily tissue that should be recognized and protected. The court went on to say that "[t]he rights of dominion over one's own body, and the interests one has therein . . . are so akin to property interests that it would be a subterfuge to call them something else." *Id.* at 505.

One word of caution, though: Many legal writers overuse quotations. For the technique of concluding with a quotation to be effective, it should be used only occasionally and only when the quotation is unusually well stated.

Remember, too, that every paragraph does not have to have a stated concluding sentence. As with implied topic sentences, implied concluding sentences are permissible as long as the reader can easily surmise what the paragraph's conclusion is.

As a writer, you must decide when a concluding sentence will help your reader and when it will seem like overkill. When in doubt, include a concluding sentence. What may seem obvious to you as the writer may not be so obvious to the reader.

Another rule of thumb for deciding when a concluding sentence can be left implied is to note when the concluding sentence simply restates the topic sentence and does not extend the line of reasoning being developed. Read the following paragraph, first with the concluding sentence and then without it.

EXAMPLE

Topic sentence	In our case, the plaintiff will argue that fetal tissue is recognized as property under the general definition set forth in *Washington Fruit* and *Labberton* because it has exchangeable value and because it is the subject of ownership.
Supporting sentences	The exchangeable value of fetal tissue is evidenced by the agreement between the abortion clinics and the University to exchange the use of the tissue in research for the rendering of pathological services. The University must believe that the fetal tissue has value, or it would not be willing to provide medical services in exchange for the use of the fetal tissue. Additionally, fetal tissue is the subject of ownership because it was once part of the plaintiff's body, and an individual has certain property interests in the tissue of her body.
Concluding sentence	Thus, the plaintiff will argue that because the fetal tissue has exchangeable value and because it is the subject of ownership, fetal tissue is property.

When revising, the writer decided that such a concluding sentence would be overkill. We agree. Rather than restate the obvious, he decided to open the next paragraph with a sentence that assumed the implied conclusion of the preceding paragraph.

EXAMPLE   NEXT PARAGRAPH

The plaintiff will further argue that the clinics recognize these property interests by obtaining a signed consent form relinquishing possession of the aborted fetus to the clinic for disposal.

Notice that the phrases "further argue" and "these property interests" signal to the reader that he or she should assume an implied conclusion to the preceding paragraph. See Exercise 21.D in the *Practice Book*.

§21.6   PARAGRAPH BLOCKS

One reason why many paragraphs may not have topic sentences or concluding sentences yet function well in a piece of writing is that the paragraphs are part of a larger organizational element: a paragraph block. Like paragraphs, paragraph blocks are mini-compositions, only this time the beginning is likely to be a paragraph or two, the middle is usually several paragraphs, and the end is also a paragraph or more.

The beginning paragraph or paragraphs work like a topic sentence. They are general statements that introduce the topic of the paragraph block and assert something about that topic. Usually, beginning paragraphs will include a transition from the previous discussion.

The middle paragraphs contain the subpoints—the explanation, elaboration, or specifics that support the topic paragraph. Ideally, each of the middle paragraphs will be organized like a mini-composition with its own topic sentence, supporting sentences, and concluding sentences.

The concluding paragraph or paragraphs work in the block the same way a concluding sentence works in a paragraph. They bring the discussion back to the broad general topic, but in a way that advances the line of reasoning. Frequently this is done by pointing out the ultimate outcome of the discussion in the paragraph block or by applying the discussion in the paragraph block to the instant case.

The following example demonstrates how a typical paragraph block works.

EXAMPLE	PARAGRAPH BLOCK

There is only one recent case in which a court has found a financial institution to be an all-purpose public figure. That case, *Coronado Credit Union v. KOAT Television, Inc.,* 656 P.2d 896 (N.M. Ct. App. 1982), was decided incorrectly. In holding that a credit union was an all-purpose public figure, the New Mexico Court of Appeals extended and broadened the *Gertz* standard in a way the Supreme Court never intended.	Topic paragraph
By ignoring the Court's mandate to construe the all-purpose public figure standard narrowly, the *Coronado* court extended this standard to include all financial institutions. The court considered the following factors to reach this *per se* rule: 1) Financial institutions as corporations are chartered by the state; 2) Financial institutions are regulated by the state through statutes; and 3) Financial institutions deal in areas of general public concern. *Id.* at 904.	Supporting paragraph

Supporting
paragraph

The fatal flaw in the court's analysis is best illustrated by applying these three factors to the fact pattern in *Gertz*. In *Gertz*, the Supreme Court held that the plaintiff attorney was not an all-purpose public figure. 418 U.S. at 352. But if the *Coronado* analysis is used, the opposite result would have been reached: 1) Attorneys must be licensed by the state to practice law and must meet certain state requirements to obtain that license; 2) Attorneys are subject to regulation by the state through Professional Codes of Conduct; and 3) Attorneys deal in areas of general public concern and interest. In fact, lawyers are officers of the court, and as such, must seek the public good in the administration of justice.

Concluding
paragraph

Thus, under the *Coronado* analysis, Mr. Gertz and indeed all attorneys would be classified as all-purpose public figures. Such a result is in direct opposition to the Court's holding in *Gertz.* Consequently, the rule applied in *Coronado* is far too broad and could not withstand constitutional scrutiny.

The following excerpt from a memo shows how two paragraph blocks work together to complete a section under the heading of "negligence." An elements of the law analysis lends itself nicely to paragraph block writing. In the example, notice how the paragraph that concludes one paragraph block also serves as the topic paragraph for the second block.

EXAMPLE

Negligence

Topic
paragraph

If Dennis's negligence created the emergency, then he cannot use the emergency doctrine. Negligence is defined as failing to act as a reasonable person. This general principle is best explained by way of illustration, and the courts provide numerous examples.

Speed excessive to conditions can be negligent. For example, when a defendant's logging truck rounded a curve and was unable to stop within three hundred seventy-five feet, his speed was found to be negligent. *Sandberg v. Spoelstra,* 285 P.2d 564 (Wash. 1955). When early morning visibility was restricted to seventy-five feet by a heavy rainfall, the court held that a speed of fifty miles per hour could be negligent. *Pidduck v. Henson,* 467 P.2d 322 (Wash. Ct. App. 1970). Finally, when daylight visibility exceeding one hundred feet was restricted to about three car lengths at night because of the glare of a street light, the court held that a speed under the twenty-five miles per hour posted limit could be negligent. *Sonnenberg v. Remsing,* 398 P.2d 728 (Wash. 1965).

> Topic sentence
>
> **Supporting paragraph**

Failure to heed road hazard warnings can also be negligent. Thus, when a driver confronted a multiple car accident on the freeway, where patrol cars were present with flashing lights and other cars were parked along the shoulder and median, the driver was negligent for not slowing down. *Schlect v. Sorenson,* 533 P.2d 1404 (Wash. Ct. App. 1975). Likewise, when a driver is warned of a fog hazard, drives into a deteriorating fog bank, and collides with a stopped vehicle, the driver is negligent. *Hinkel v. Weyerhaeuser Co.,* 494 P.2d 1008 (Wash. Ct. App. 1972).

> Topic sentence
>
> **Supporting paragraph**

Finally, violations of the rules of the road can be negligent per se. When the driver of a semi-trailer observed a car stalled in the road ahead of it, slowed, switched lanes, and passed to the rear of the automobile where it struck one of the occupants on the highway, the driver was negligent. The driver was negligent as a matter of law for failing to obey several rules of the road: 1) reducing speed when confronted with hazards, 2) sounding horn to warn pedestrians of danger, 3) changing lanes only when safe to do so, and 4) signaling a lane change for one hundred feet before turning. *Nesmith v. Bowden,* 563 P.2d 1322 (Wash. Ct. App. 1977).

> Topic sentence
>
> **Supporting paragraph**

Concluding paragraph/ topic paragraph

Plaintiff is likely to employ all the above arguments. She will argue that Dennis was negligent because his speed was excessive, because he failed to heed road hazards, and because he violated the rules of the road.

Topic sentence

Supporting paragraph

Dennis's speed was not excessive for the conditions he faced. Although plaintiff may cite *Sandberg, Pidduck*, and *Sonnenberg*, Dennis can distinguish the conditions in *Pidduck* and *Sonnenberg* from the conditions that Dennis faced. In both cases, visibility was restricted by unusual circumstances. Dennis faced no unusual circumstances. He was rounding a gradual curve under the speed limit, and there is no indication that the curve was so sharp that it required a reduced speed limit. Nor is there any indication that there was a lower speed limit for night driving as opposed to day driving. In *Sandberg*, the driver had three hundred seventy feet in which to stop, and there was no obstruction in his lane when the driver collided with a vehicle in the other lane. Although the exact distance is unknown in Dennis's case, apparently Dennis had much less space in which to stop. Also, he faced an obstruction in his own lane.

Topic sentence

Supporting paragraph

Concluding sentence

Dennis's situation is analogous to the situation in *Ryan v. Westgard*, 530 P.2d 687 (Wash. Ct. App. 1975), where the driver was found to be not negligent. There, the driver was following approximately one hundred feet behind another car. This car swerved into another lane, and the following driver confronted yet another car going extremely slowly. He attempted to stop, but collided with the slower vehicle. The court reasoned that the plaintiff was following the car in front of him at a proper speed until the moment that vehicle swerved out into the adjoining lane. Like the driver in *Ryan*, Dennis too was travelling at a proper speed until the moment his vehicle encountered the stalled bus. Therefore, Dennis's speed was not excessive.

Pair of topic sentences

Plaintiff will also argue that Dennis was negligent for failing to slow when confronted with a road hazard. Again, Dennis can distinguish the warning that he had from the warnings given in *Schlect* and *Hinkel*. Dennis was not warned several miles in advance of the obstruction as was the driver in *Hinkel*. Nor did he confront a multiple car accident with flashing patrol car lights and cars parked along the highway as did the driver in *Schlect*.

Supporting paragraph

Dennis rounded a curve and confronted a bus with flashers on that was stopped in the left lane of the freeway at 11:30 p.m. His situation is more analogous to the cases in which drivers faced sudden and unexpected obstacles after little warning. *Haynes v. Moore*, 545 P.2d 28 (Wash. Ct. App. 1975); *Leach v. Weiss*, 467 P.2d 894 (Wash. Ct. App. 1970). In *Haynes*, the driver confronted a car, which he first saw when fifty feet away, stopped on a bridge. He braked, but collided with the car. He was found to be not negligent. Likewise, in *Leach*, the driver confronted a car stopped on a bridge, braked, crossed the center line, and collided with another vehicle. The driver was not negligent. Neither is Dennis negligent.

Topic sentence

Supporting paragraph

Concluding sentence

Finally, plaintiff will argue that our client was negligent for violating the rules of the road. Dennis was driving in the left hand lane and was not passing or turning. This conduct violates Wash. Rev. Code §46.61.100, which requires that a driver stay in the rightmost lane except when passing or turning. Under *Nesmith*, 563 P.2d at 1326, this violation creates a prima facie case of negligence. However, Dennis can argue that this conduct was not negligence because it did not endanger the class of persons that this rule was designed to protect. The purpose of Wash. Rev. Code §46.61.100 is to protect vehicles traveling in the same direction by promoting safe passing. *Sadler v. Wagner*, 486 P.2d 330 (Wash. Ct. App. 1971). Edith was not passing Dennis, and Dennis was not passing Edith. Thus, Edith does not fall within the class of persons this rule was designed to protect, and Dennis was not negligent.

Topic sentence

Supporting paragraph

Concluding sentence

Dennis was not negligent because of excessive speed, he was not negligent for failing to heed road hazard warnings, and he

Concluding **paragraph**	was not negligent for failing to obey the rules of the road. His conduct did not create the emergency. He can submit substantial evidence in support of this second element, even though he can expect opposing counsel to make this a difficult issue.

Lest we leave you with the impression that all paragraph blocks exactly follow the models we have shown, let's look at a variation on the theme before leaving the subject of paragraph blocks.

Notice in the next example that one sentence at the beginning of the first paragraph in the block serves as the topic "paragraph" for the three-paragraph block. Each paragraph then has its own individual topic sentence and conclusion. The paragraph block, however, has no stated conclusion. The writer chose to use an implied conclusion to avoid conclusion overkill.

EXAMPLE

Topic "paragraph" Topic sentence	In addition, the University can distinguish this case from *Moore* on several grounds. First, in *Moore* the appellee and the appellant had a direct relationship with each other. The appellant entrusted his physical well-being and continuing medical treatment to the appellee, hoping to be cured of his disease. Therefore, the appellee had a higher duty of care to Moore while administering continuing treatment. In our case, the only connection between the University and the plaintiff is that the University conducts pathological tests on the fetal tissue to determine if there are any diseases or genetic disorders present. The clinical patients do not entrust the University with their care, nor do they depend on the University directly for treatment or medical advice.
Concluding sentence	Therefore, the University's duty of care is limited to the proper administration of pathological testing and the timely relaying of the test results to the clinic.

Second, the tissue taken from Moore had unique qualities that allowed the appellee to develop products it could not have developed with another individual's tissue; therefore, the uniqueness of Moore's tissue made it very valuable. In our case, the University can derive the same cell line from approximately one percent of the fetal cells it uses. Consequently, the fetal cells used for this product are not unique, nor can the traits of one fetal cell be distinguished from the traits of another. Thus, the substantial value of fetal tissue is questionable.

Topic sentence

Concluding sentence

Finally, the decision in *Moore* was based largely on punitive measures rather than on the use of the appellant's tissue. The appellees in *Moore* continued to extract bodily tissue and fluids from appellant for many years after his splenectomy. Moore repeatedly travelled from Washington State to California at the request of the appellee with the impression that these trips were for continued care relating to Moore's disease. Instead, the sole purpose of the appellee's actions were to further its research. Here, the University makes no representations of continued care or treatment to the plaintiffs, nor does it repeatedly extract tissue from the plaintiffs for the purpose of furthering its research. Unlike the defendant in *Moore*, the University does not deliberately deceive plaintiffs to obtain additional tissue; rather, the University obtains fetal tissue that would have normally been disposed of by the clinics.

Topic sentence

Concluding sentence

See Exercises 21.E, 21.F, and 21.G in the *Practice Book.*

Chapter 22

Connections Between Sentences

Transitions are the primary connectors between sentences. Used properly, transitions express the relationship between the ideas in the sentences they serve to connect and signal how the ideas are moving in a line of reasoning.

Three types of transitions connect sentences:

1. generic transitions,
2. orienting transitions, and
3. substantive transitions.

Still other transitions, headings and signposts, are used to make connections between paragraphs and over a longer piece of writing. See Chapter 20.

§22.1 GENERIC TRANSITIONS

Generic transitions include those words and phrases that are used in every kind of writing. Exhibit 22.1 lists the most common generic transitions grouped by function.

§22.1.1 Using Generic Transitions

The first question writers have about generic transitions is when to use them. In theory, that seems simple. Because generic transitions signal those shifts or changes inherent in human thought, it would seem that all writers should have to do is insert an appropriate transition to signal each time they make such a shift in their writing.

EXHIBIT 22.1 | Generic Transitions

For Contrast

however	nevertheless*	but
on the other hand	conversely	still yet
by (in) contrast	notwithstanding	instead
on the contrary	nonetheless*	though
contrary to _____	alternatively	although
unlike _____	even so*	even though
despite _____	rather	

For Comparison

similarly	analogously	in like manner
likewise	in the same way	
	for the same reason	

For Cause and Effect

therefore*	accordingly	hence
consequently*	thus*	since
as a result	because	so
		for

For Addition

also	moreover	besides
further	too	and
in addition	additionally	
furthermore		

For Examples

for example	to illustrate	specifically
for instance	namely	that is*

For Emphasis

in fact	certainly	still*
above all	indeed	clearly

For Evaluation

more important	surprisingly	unquestionably
unfortunately	allegedly	
fortunately	arguably	

*Generic transition that falls under more than one category.

EXHIBIT 22.1 *(continued)*

For Restatement

in other words	more simply	to put it differently
that is*	simply put	

For Concession

granted	of course	to be sure

For Resumption After a Concession

still*	nonetheless*	all the same
nevertheless*	even so*	

For Time

subsequently	later	earlier
recently	eventually	afterwards
meanwhile	shortly thereafter	until now
initially	simultaneously	since
formerly	at the time	by the time

For Place

adjacent to	here	nearby
next to	beyond	opposite to

For Sequence

first, second, third	next	then
former, latter	final	later
in the first place	finally*	primary, secondary

For Conclusion

in summary	in brief	thus*
in sum	in short	therefore*
to sum up	to conclude	consequently*
finally*	in conclusion	to (in) review

*Generic transition that falls under more than one category.

In practice, it is not so simple. For one thing, there are no hard and fast rules for when a transition is required. In fact, experienced writers do not always agree about when a transition is appropriate and when it is cumbersome. For beginning law students and new associates in a firm, such differences in opinion can be confusing; one reader wants more transitions added, the next reader edits them out.

The truth is that, to some extent, the number and placement of generic transitions is a matter of personal style and preference. That being said, there is still a general consensus about when to use generic transitions. You can find that consensus and develop your own sense about when to use generic transitions in one or more of the following ways. First, observe how other writers, particularly professional writers, use generic transitions. For example, notice how they rarely omit transitions that signal contrast and ones that show movement up or down the ladder of abstraction. Observe the ways skilled legal writers use generic transitions to keep their readers on track.

Second, read your own writing aloud. Let your ear tell you when a new sentence starts with a jolt rather than a smooth connection.

Third, listen to someone else read your writing aloud. Try stopping that reader at several points along the way (particularly when there is no transition) and asking if he or she can guess what the next sentence will discuss. If the connections between the ideas are so obvious that the reader can anticipate where the writing is headed, probably no transition is needed. Conversely, if your reader needs more guidance through your points, add the appropriate generic transitions as needed.

Fourth, and most important, when writing, constantly ask yourself what will help your reader. Keeping the reader's perspective and needs in mind will help you decide when a generic transition is a helpful guide and when it is extra baggage.

§22.1.2   Problems with Generic Transitions

Some legal writers have a tendency to write as though others can read their minds. *They* know where they are headed in their writing, so they blithely assume their readers do too. These writers omit transitions because the connections between the ideas are obvious to them. They forget to consider whether these connections are obvious to the reader. For example, notice in the first pair of sentences that follow how jarring the second sentence seems without the transition for contrast, and then notice how in the revised second sentence the reader easily adjusts once the generic transition for contrast is added.

EXAMPLE

Mr. Wry, the owner of the Fitness Club, may claim that although Hillary's restaurant has lost several customers, the majority of the customers will return. Mr. Hillary may argue that the loss of several customers is significant to his business.

Revised:

Mr. Wry, the owner of the Fitness Club, may claim that although Hillary's restaurant has lost several customers, the majority of the customers will return. Mr. Hillary, *on the other hand*, may argue that the loss of several customers is significant to his business.

Other writers omit transitions in hopes of being more concise, forgetting that being concise, although important, is a relative luxury compared to being clear.

Legal writers should also take great care to select the precise transition that best describes the relationship between the two ideas or sentences. Selecting the wrong transition can be even more misleading than using no transition at all. In the following example, the writer mistakenly selected a transition for comparison rather than one for addition.

EXAMPLE

Because some overt physical activity and noise are normally generated by fitness and aerobics classes, the Fitness Club's classes are not unreasonably noisy or offensive. *Similarly*, bathing suits are not unusual or unanticipated sights in a waterfront area.

Revised:

Furthermore, bathing suits are not unusual or unanticipated sights in a waterfront area.

The need for precision in transitions also means that it is not enough simply to select the right category of generic transition. Generic transitions within the same category often have distinct meanings and connotations. For example, two transitions for conclusion—"to sum up" and "finally"—have entirely different meanings. "To sum up" should signal a brief overview or general statement about the entire piece of writing; "finally" should signal that the last point is about to be made.

In some instances, generic transitions are similar in meaning but quite different in tone. For example, two transitions for cause and effect—"therefore" and "hence"—mean almost the same thing, but "therefore" creates a matter-of-fact tone while "hence" carries with it a feeling of heavy solemnity and old wisdom.

A word of warning then: Use the list of generic transitions in Exhibit 22.1 with care. Do not automatically assume that transitions grouped in the same category are synonymous.

Of course, you will find that some generic transitions in the same category are virtually synonymous. In such instances, you may find that the list offers some variety that may free you from using the same generic transition ad nauseam.

Some final advice about transitional expressions: First, because transitions show the connection between two ideas, it is best to place the transition right at the point of connection. In the following example, the transition showing the cause/effect relationship comes too late to help the reader very much.

EXAMPLE

Hillary was made insecure in the use of his property when patrons threatened not to return. The Fitness Club and its activities constitute a nuisance as a result.

Revised:

As a result, the Fitness Club and its activities constitute a nuisance.

Second, the break between paragraphs can also serve as a kind of transition. The white space is a strong signal that the writing is moving to a new point. See Exercise 22.A in the *Practice Book.*

§22.2 Orienting Transitions

Orienting transitions provide a context for the information that follows. They serve to locate for the reader—physically, logically, or chronologically—the ideas or points in the rest of the sentence.

Two of the most common orienting transitions in legal writing are (1) those that include times and dates and (2) those that refer to cases.

EXAMPLES

On October 26, 1997, Leonard Thomas was admitted to Mountain View Rest Home and Retirement Village.

At 2:00 a.m. on January 1, 1998, David Wilson was arrested and charged with reckless driving and driving while intoxicated.

In *Bugger*, the court found that the position of the driver was insignificant.

In the instant case, the son was not the executor of the will.

In the case at hand, there is no indication that the defendant intended to deceive the plaintiff about her rights under the contract.

Note that one commonly used orienting transition, the word "here," can be ambiguous when the previous sentence ends with a citation. Some readers may interpret "here" to refer to the previously cited case; others may interpret "here" to refer to the case at hand.

EXAMPLE

If some form of operability is required, then the court must decide whether to focus on the defendant's ability to operate the vehicle or on the vehicle's condition. *State v. Smelter*, 674 P.2d 690 (Wash. Ct. App. 1984). Here, the defendant had the key and was in the cab of the truck.

Revised:

In the case at bar, the defendant had the key and was in the cab of the truck. *OR*

In *Smelter*, the defendant had the key and was in the cab of the truck.

Other orienting transitions create a context by directing the reader to adopt a certain point of view, by supplying the source of the information that follows, or by locating the information historically or chronologically.

EXAMPLE

From the bank's perspective, granting a second loan would be ill-advised and risky.

According to Dallas Police Department Officer James Richardson's report, Officers Richardson and Loe entered the warehouse at 12:30 a.m.

Over the last twenty years, courts have realized that some exceptions to the general principle were necessary.

Orienting transitions frequently occur at the beginning of a section.
In such positions, orienting transitions are not so much connections between points within the writing as they are connections between the
writing and the mind of a reader first coming to the material.

Orienting transitions also occur at the beginning of paragraphs.
From this position, they help readers adjust or "shift gears" as they mentally move along a line of reasoning within a larger idea. Of course, orienting transitions can occur within a paragraph, and when they do, they
work like all other transitions to bridge the gap between sentences and
between ideas.

Here are several more examples of orienting transitions. Note the
variety of ways orienting transitions provide a context for what follows.

To give a historical perspective:

EXAMPLES

In the 1970s, the court narrowed the scope of the "discretionary"
category by emphasizing that the State must show that "a policy
decision, consciously balancing the risks and advantages, took
place . . . ."

In a recent decision, the court upheld a conviction when the driver
was asleep or passed out and remained in a position to regulate
the vehicle's movement.

To suggest a case's importance:

EXAMPLE

In an often cited case, the court overturned a conviction for "actual
physical control" when the motorist's vehicle was parked on the
shoulder of the highway.

To give a chronology:

EXAMPLE

In March of 1985, the Wilsons were advised that their fence encroached approximately 30 feet on the Anders' property. In response, the Wilsons claimed previous and current exclusive right, as well as title and interest to the disputed property.

To announce a shift in topic:

EXAMPLES

As for damages, the court will probably enjoin those activities that constitute a private nuisance.

In regard to the prosecution's allegation that Mr. Hayes's original attorney thwarted the discovery process, Mr. Hayes will point out that he was unaware that his original attorney shredded the requested documents.

Some legal writers avoid the orienting transitions beginning with "as for," "as to," "in regard to," and "regarding" in sentences like the preceding examples on the grounds that these transitions are an abrupt, an ineffective, or a lazy way to make a significant shift in topic. These writers prefer that significant shifts in topics be introduced by full sentences.

EXAMPLES

Revised:

The question of damages will be more difficult to predict. The court will probably enjoin those activities that constitute a private nuisance, but awarding damages for Hillary's lost profits is less likely.

Revised:

The prosecution's second allegation, that Mr. Hayes's original attorney thwarted the discovery process, should be directed at Mr. Hayes' original attorney, not at Mr. Hayes. Mr. Hayes was unaware that his original attorney shredded the requested document. He cannot be held responsible for the unsanctioned actions of his lawyer.

As with generic transitions, the biggest problem writers have with orienting transitions is the question of when to use them. The answer is the same for all types of transitions: Use them when the reader needs them.

§22.3   SUBSTANTIVE TRANSITIONS

Thus far, we have looked at generic transitions, which are like glue between sentences, and at orienting transitions, which are backdrops for information or sometimes windows through which information can be seen.

The third type of transition, substantive transitions, can best be compared to the interlocking links of a chain. Like the links of a chain, substantive transitions serve two functions: they make a connection and they provide content. In short, they live up to their name—they are both substantive and transitional. The following two sentences include an example of a substantive transition.

EXAMPLE

Bugger and *Zavala* are the only cases in which a conviction was overturned when the motorist's vehicle was totally off the road. While these holdings could be helpful to Mr. Renko, the Montana court will still probably interpret the statute to include the shoulder of the highway.

Here, the substantive transition is "while these holdings could be helpful to Mr. Renko." It serves as a transition connecting the two sentences for two reasons: first, it is placed at or near the beginning of the following sentence, where it can help bridge the gap between the ideas; and second, it uses the phrase "these holdings" to refer back to the information in the previous sentence. In short, the transition looks both forward and back.

But, as we said before, a substantive transition does not serve merely as a transition; it also provides new content. It points out that "these holdings" "could be helpful to Mr. Renko" before going on to the main point of the sentence, that the court still is likely to interpret the statute as including the shoulder of the highway.

§22.3.1   The Structure of Substantive Transitions

Substantive transitions often employ a technique called dovetailing as the basis for their structure.

Dovetailing

A carpenter who wants a strong joint between two pieces of wood is likely to use the dovetail, a special joint characterized by the tight fit of interlocking pieces of wood. Similarly, a writer who wants a strong joint between two sentences uses a dovetail of words to connect the ideas. Through the dovetail, he or she interlocks ideas by creating an overlap of language. The overlap of language may be as simple as the repetition of terms from one sentence to the next or use of pronouns to refer back to an earlier noun.

Here is an example of a dovetail that uses repetition of terms.

EXAMPLE

In *Esser*, four people agreed to share costs and build a road. After the road was built, each person used the road under a claim of right.

Sentence 1	Sentence 2
. . . four people . . . build a road.	After the road was built, each person used the road . . .

Note that words may be repeated in their exact form or in a similar or related form.

A slightly more complicated dovetail than the one in the previous example requires the writer to find a word or phrase to use in the second sentence that sums up the idea of the previous sentence. Here is an example of a dovetail that uses a summarizing phrase.

EXAMPLE

Search and seizures are governed by the Fourth Amendment to the U.S. Constitution and Article I, Section 7 of the Washington Constitution. Both of these provisions have been interpreted as requiring that search warrants be valid and that searches and seizures be reasonable.

Sentence 1	Sentence 2
Fourth Amendment . . . and Article I	Both of these provisions . . .

Note that in both cases the words in the dovetail tend to be toward the end of the first sentence and toward the beginning of the second.

Often the summarizing noun or phrase will be preceded by a hook word such as "this," "that," "these," "those," or "such."

The following example includes a dovetail using a hook word and a summarizing noun phrase.

EXAMPLE

Realizing that she would not be able to stop in time to avoid hitting the bus, Mrs. Long swerved her vehicle around the bus and into the parallel lane of traffic. This evasive action resulted in her side-swiping another vehicle in the oncoming lane.

Connecting idea	*Connecting idea*
swerved . . . into . . . traffic	This evasive action
	hook *summarizing*
	word *noun phrase*

To form an effective dovetail, then, a legal writer can use one or more of the following techniques:

1. move the connecting idea to the end of the first sentence and to the beginning of the second sentence;
2. repeat key words from the first sentence in the second sentence;
3. use pronouns in the second sentence to refer back to nouns in the first sentence;
4. state the connecting idea in a specific form in the first sentence and then restate it in a summarizing noun or phrase in the second sentence;
5. use hook words such as "this," "that," "these," "those," and "such" before a repeated key word or summarizing noun or phrase.

Another way to think about dovetailing is to remember that most sentences are made up of two parts: old information and new information. The old information is what has already been named or discussed. It usually appears near the beginning of a sentence. The new information is the point the writer wants to add. It usually appears near the end of a sentence.

Sentence	
old information	new information

A dovetail takes the new information from the end of one sentence and restates it as the now old information at the beginning of the subsequent sentence.

Sentence 1		Sentence 2	
A	B →	B	C
old	new	old	new
information	information	information	information

Obviously, though, it is unrealistic to assume that all sentences should follow a strict A + B, B + C, C + D pattern. In reality and in good legal writing, the pattern is not followed rigidly. Quite often, for example, sentence three will start with old information B.

Sentence 1		Sentence 2		Sentence 3	
A	B	B	C	B	D
old	new	old	new	old	new

EXAMPLE

In 1983, the Montana legislature adopted new and stricter laws to deal with drunk drivers. This legislation extended law enforcement jurisdiction and generally provided for faster and stiffer penalties. Brendon J. Rohan, *Montana's Legislative Attempt to Deal with the Drinking Driver: The 1983 DUI Statutes*, 46 Mont. L. Rev. 309, 310 (1985). This legislation also demonstrates a definite trend in Montana towards greater liability for the individual and a preference toward upholding drunk driving convictions regardless of mitigating circumstances.

Another useful variation of the pattern is to begin a sentence with a combination of two earlier pieces of old information.

Sentence 1		Sentence 2		Sentence 3	
A	B	B	C	B + C	D
old	new	old	new	old + old	new

EXAMPLE

When the defendant entered his hotel room, he was surprised to find two men rummaging through his suitcase. One of the men turned toward him, drew his gun, and aimed it at the defendant.

Under these circumstances, the defendant had every reason to believe that he was being robbed and that his life was in danger.

This pattern works well when the writer wants to point out the similarity in two or more cases just cited.

EXAMPLES

Courts in both Arizona and Utah did not uphold convictions when the vehicle's motor was off. *State v. Zavalo*, 666 P.2d 456 (Ariz. 1983); *State v. Bugger*, 483 P.2d 442 (Utah 1971). These cases are significant because in both instances the engine was off and the vehicle was completely off the highway.

In *Rogers*, the city was held responsible when a building inspector erroneously told a builder that certain property was zoned for apartments. *Id.* at 1098. In a similar case, the court held that common sense would dictate that reliance on a building permit was justified; otherwise there would be no purpose in requiring a permit. *J & B Dev. Co. v. King County*, 669 P.2d at 472. These building permit cases may be distinguished from the present situation because the purpose of providing some measure of increased safety would be served whether or not the parents relied on the report.

Some writers unconsciously reverse the old → new pattern. They begin a sentence with new information and tack on the old, connecting information at the end. The result is a halting, disjointed style. If you examine your own writing, you may find that you can quickly improve the flow simply by revising with the old → new pattern in mind.

EXAMPLE

The defendant need not insure the plaintiff's safety; he need exercise only reasonable care. *Potter v. Madison Tavern*, 446 P.2d at 322. He has breached his duty to the plaintiff if he has not exercised reasonable care.

Revised:

If he has not exercised reasonable care, he has breached his duty to the plaintiff.

Occasionally, however, it is awkward, if not impossible, to move the old information to the very beginning of a sentence and the new information to the very end. In such cases, remember that the old → new pattern is a general principle, not an absolute rule. In the following sentence, for example, it would be awkward to move the first half of the dovetail—whether the secretary's actions were capricious and arbitrary—to the end of the first sentence.

EXAMPLE

The issue is whether the Secretary's actions were capricious and arbitrary when he failed to hire the required number of inspectors. If his actions were of such a nature, then the court would find the State liable.

Two final bits of advice about dovetailing:

1. Avoid using hook words without repeating a key term or using a summarizing noun or phrase. See section 26.5.2 on broad pronoun reference.

EXAMPLE

At common law, a duty is established when the defendant stands in a special relationship to the plaintiff. This can exist between a specific plaintiff and a specific defendant.

Revised:

This special relationship can exist . . . .

---

2. Consider using dovetailing to break up overly long sentences.

EXAMPLE

This holding by the *Knoll* court is considered the "ratified intent" approach to analyzing searches, which suggests that when evidence is taken to aid the government and when the government uses the evidence, the taint of the illegal action is transferred to the government, which makes the use unlawful.

Revised:

This holding by the *Knoll* court is considered the "ratified intent" approach to analyzing searches. This approach suggests that when evidence is taken to aid the government and when the government uses the evidence, the taint of the illegal action is transferred to the government. The transfer of the taint of the illegal action makes the use unlawful.

The following example shows how dovetailing (→) works in a longer piece of writing, a fact section for an opinion letter. Note that generic transitions (GT), orienting transitions (OT), and substantive transitions (ST) work together to create flow.

EXAMPLE

Your husband Don had been suffering from lung cancer for the past six months and was placed on the respirator machine. During that time, he spoke frequently about committing suicide in order to end the pain. To understand the pain your husband was going through, you attended several Euthanasia Society meetings.

"past six months" → "during that time"

"to end the pain" → "to understand the pain" (ST)

On July 15, 1990, you were with your husband in the hospital all day. Again, your husband told you about his pain and thoughts of committing suicide. Afterwards he fell asleep. Later, on the same day, you watched your husband awake from his sleep and attempt unsuccessfully to flip the switch on the respirator machine. After his unsuccessful attempts, you helped your husband flip the switch off and then walked out of the room. When you realized that your husband might die because of your assistance in flipping off the switch, you ran back to the room and flipped the switch back on. By that time, your husband was dead.

OT: "On July 15, 1990 . . . all day" → "again"

GT: "afterwards"
GT: "later"
"On the same day" dovetails back to "July 15, 1990"

"Attempt unsuccessfully" → summarizing noun phrase "his unsuccessful attempts"
ST: "When you realized . . . your assistance"; note summarizing noun phrase "your assistance"
GT: "by that time"

See Exercises 22.B, 22.C, 22.D, and 22.E in the *Practice Book.*

§22.3.2   The Content of Substantive Transitions

The content in substantive transitions can be compared to half steps in a line of reasoning. Sometimes these half steps are articulated inferences that one can reasonably draw from the previous sentence or idea.

EXAMPLE

The owners of the factory could agree to release the fumes only after certain hours at night or only under certain weather conditions. While these steps may ameliorate the situation, the question remains whether any emission of toxic fumes is reasonable.

In the preceding example, a thoughtful reader would surely be able to infer the content of the substantive transition — "while these steps may ameliorate the situation" — after reading the first sentence. Consequently, some may argue that it would be better to replace the substantive transition with a more concise generic transition like "even so" or "still." Obviously, writers must exercise judgment and weigh the relative merit of completeness versus conciseness.

In the following two examples, notice how the generic transition, although more concise, is less persuasive for the Bells than the substantive transition.

EXAMPLE

Generic Transition:

The Bells' doctor, Peter Williams, advised them that future pregnancies had a seventy-five percent chance of ending in a stillbirth. Consequently, the Bells decided that Mr. Bell would have a vasectomy.

Substantive Transition:

The Bells' doctor, Peter Williams, advised them that future pregnancies had a seventy-five percent chance of ending in a stillbirth. Relying on Dr. Williams's advice, the Bells decided that Mr. Bell would have a vasectomy.

Notice how the generic transition "consequently" seems fairly neutral. It suggests that the Bells' decision to have Mr. Bell undergo a vasectomy was the expected consequence of an unfavorable statistical probability. The substantive transition "relying on Dr. Williams's advice," on the other hand, stresses the Bells' dependence on their doctor's professional opinion. Mentioning the doctor again by name not only reminds the reader that the doctor was the source of the information but also emphasizes the role he played in the Bells' decision.

Although it would be impossible to enumerate the many ways substantive transitions are used in legal writing, there are a few common situations in which they are particularly effective.

a.   Bridging the Gap Between Law and Application

Perhaps the most common use of substantive transitions in legal writing occurs at junctures between law and application. Again, because it is a given in legal writing that the law will be applied, some may argue that substantive transitions at those points merely state the obvious. Most readers, however, seem to prefer a smooth "shifting of gears" to leaping into the application "cold."

Compare the following two examples and note how the substantive transition "under the rule announced in *Parnell*" draws the rule and its application together better than a generic transition can.

EXAMPLE

Generic Transition:

When a juror could have been excused for cause, reversible error occurs when the accused is forced to exercise all his peremptory challenges before the jury is finally selected. *State v. Parnell*, 463 P.2d 134 (Wash. 1969). *See also State v. Gilchrist*, 590 P.2d 809 (Wash. 1979). In the case at hand, Chapman accepted the jury with one peremptory challenge unexercised. Thus, he was not forced to use all his peremptory challenges before the final selection of the jury. Therefore, the Court of Appeals' decision in finding harmless error is sustainable.

Substantive Transition:

When a juror could have been excused for cause, reversible error occurs when the accused is forced to exercise all his peremptory challenges before the jury is finally selected. *State v. Parnell*, 463 P.2d 134 (Wash. 1969). *See also State v. Gilchrist*, 590 P.2d 809 (Wash. 1979). In the case at hand, Chapman accepted the jury with one peremptory challenge unexercised. Thus, he was not forced to use all his peremptory challenges before the final selection of the jury. Under the rule announced in *Parnell*, the Court of Appeals' decision in finding harmless error is sustainable.

Frequently the factors or elements in the law are mentioned well before the point where they are applied. When there is intervening information, the substantive transition becomes even more important in helping the reader follow the discussion.

In the following example, the five factors that the Tenth Circuit listed for determining an expert's status were first named on page four of a memo. The first opportunity the writer had for showing how the court would apply these factors occurred two pages later. In such a situation, the substantive transition is critical.

EXAMPLE

Applying the factors listed in *Ager*, 622 F.2d at 501, the court will first find that the consultation was initiated as custom dictated.

---

b.   *Applying Another Court's Rationale*

Similarly, substantive transitions are often used when the reasoning of one court has been laid out in detail and this reasoning will now be applied to the case at hand. Note that in the following example, as in the previous example, the substantive transition begins with that important signal word "applying."

EXAMPLE

Recent Washington court decisions have developed a more liberal definition of inadvertent. *State v. Henry*, 676 P.2d 521 (Wash. Ct. App. 1984). In *Henry*, officers had learned from an informant that the defendant was heavily armed, and one officer testified during the trial that he was looking for guns as well as cocaine, which was specified in the warrant; yet, the court held that the guns were found inadvertently. *Id.* at 533. In doing so, the court relied on the definition of "inadvertent" provided in *State v. Callahan*, 644 P.2d 735, 736 (Wash. Ct. App. 1982): "[T]he term 'inadvertent' in the context of the plain view doctrine, simply means that the officer discovered the evidence while in a position that does not infringe upon any reasonable expectation of privacy, and did not take any further unreasonable steps to find the evidence from that position." The *Henry* court concluded that the officers were looking in places that were likely to contain drugs, that a person can harbor no reasonable expectation of privacy concerning a place that is likely to contain drugs, and that the officers took no further, unreasonable steps to find the guns. Therefore, the discovery was inadvertent by the Washington definition. *Henry*, 676 P.2d at 523. The court added that there was no evidence that the drug search was a pretext for a gun search. *Id.*

The state's position in the instant case is stronger. At the time the officers received the search warrant for marijuana, they neither had knowledge nor expected that they might find incriminating photographic evidence of another crime. When he looked in the envelope, Morrison had no reason to believe that the photographs would be evidence of any crime.

Thus, applying the *Henry* rationale to *Ehrlich*, the court would probably find that Morrison was looking in a place that was likely to conceal drugs (the envelope might have contained drugs as well as photographs), so Ehrlich had no reasonable expectation of privacy. After looking in the envelope, Morrison took no further unreasonable steps to find the photographs. Therefore, the discovery was inadvertent.

---

c.   Gathering Together Several Facts

Another juncture where substantive transitions can be used effectively occurs between a list of numerous individual facts and a statement about their collective significance.

In the following example, the substantive transition "based on these admissions" is essential. It is the one place where the point is made that three facts taken together were the basis for the court's action.

EXAMPLE

In his deposition, Edwards acknowledged that the railroad tie had appeared wet and slippery before he stepped on it. He also stated that he had regularly delivered mail to the Bates's residence for two years and that he was familiar with the premises, including the railroad tie. Finally, Edwards acknowledged that he attended weekly postal safety meetings and knew about the hazards posed by wet surfaces. Based on these admissions, the trial court granted summary judgment in favor of Bates and dismissed Edwards's negligence action.

In the next example, the substantive transition "when faced with all these facts" is not so much essential as it is persuasive.

EXAMPLE

Ms. Jones admits that the weather on the morning of the accident was cold and overcast. Ms. Jones further admits that there was still snow on the ground and that she had considered putting chains on her tires before leaving for work. The other two drivers, Mr. Smith and Ms. Block, both state that the traffic was traveling more slowly than usual because of hazardous icy conditions. The police officer who arrived on the scene shortly after the accident also reports that the weather was cold and the roads were icy. When faced with all these facts, Ms. Jones had to know of the danger of ice on the road that morning.

---

d.   Gathering Together Several Ideas

Substantive transitions can also be used to pull together two or more large ideas that have been developed over several paragraphs or even several sections of a memo or brief.

The following example appeared toward the end of an appellate court opinion that affirmed the trial court's decision to grant the petition for modification of child support. Earlier in the opinion, the appellate court reviewed the trial court's findings (1) that the child support modification would not inflict a financial hardship on the supporting parent and (2) that the factual circumstances (the child's age and propensity for higher education) had changed substantially, thereby allowing the court to modify the support order. The Court of Appeals added a third point, a policy consideration. The court observed that because children of parents who are still married often continue to receive support after majority for higher education, it would be a special disadvantage of children of divorced parents if one of their parents were not expected to provide advanced education. Each of these three points was fully developed in one or more paragraphs.

Now notice how the substantive transition brings all three points together as the basis for the court's decision and how it allows the writer to move smoothly to the last section of the memo.

> **EXAMPLE**
>
> Absent any financial hardship to the father and given the change in circumstances, the father should, as a matter of policy, be required to contribute to his daughter's higher education.

e.   *Bridging the Gap Between Sections of a Document*

Substantive transitions are more effective than generic transitions at junctures between large sections of a paper. Even when headings are used for larger sections, substantive transitions are still needed to show the similarities or differences between the sections.

In the following example, the writer has just completed a long section on the Ninth Circuit's comments on the inappropriateness of bonuses for services rendered to a bankrupt estate. The following sentence begins the section under the heading Contingency Fees. The substantive transition — "unlike a bonus fee arrangement" — shows the connection between the sections.

> **EXAMPLE**
>
> **Contingency Fees**
>
> Unlike a bonus fee arrangement, there is nothing that prevents a contingency fee agreement from being enforced in bankruptcy. *In re Yermahov*, 718 F.2d 1465, 1470 (9th Cir. 1983).

To sum up then, substantive transitions are those special points in writing where the writer pulls two or more thoughts together and, in doing so, creates a powerful bond between ideas. By overlapping the language and merging the ideas, the writer does more than just connect the points; he or she weaves them together.

Some final thoughts about transitions: Although the artificial division of transitions into separate categories makes it easier to understand their separate functions, it also masks the ways in which generic, orienting, and substantive transitions are similar. One can argue, for example, that all transitions, including generic transitions, provide some content or that all transitions orient the reader. Consequently, how you categorize a particular transition is not really important; what is important is that you be able to use all three categories of transitions to create connections in your own writing.

Chapter 23

Effective Sentences

Effective sentence writing begins with the subject-verb unit. Those two key sentence positions should contain the crux of the sentence's message. If these two parts of the sentence are written well, then many of the other parts of the sentence will fall into place.

Consequently, our discussion of effective sentence writing begins with four points about the subject-verb unit: the use of active and passive voice, the use of concrete subjects, the use of action verbs, and the distance between subjects and verbs. The remainder of the chapter addresses points that concern the whole sentence: sentence length and emphasis.

§23.1 ACTIVE AND PASSIVE VOICE

The term "voice," when it is applied to the subject-verb unit, refers to the relationship of the subject to the action expressed in the verb. This rather vague concept is easier to understand in terms of the difference between active and passive voice.

§23.1.1 Identifying Active and Passive Voice

In the active voice, the subject of the sentence is doing the action described by the verb.

The judge overruled the objection.
   (subject)   *(verb)*   *(direct object)*

In the sentence above, the subject "judge" is doing the verb "overruled." Another way to look at it is to remember that in the active voice the subject is "active," or acting.

In the passive voice, the subject of the sentence is having the action of the verb done to it.

The objection was overruled by the judge.
  (subject)   *(verb)*

In this sentence, the subject "objection" is not doing the overruling; rather, the verb "was overruled" is being done to the subject. Another way to look at it is to remember that in the passive voice the subject is "passive." It is not acting; it is acted upon.

Notice that in the passive voice the person or thing doing the verb is either mentioned in a prepositional phrase ("by the judge," as in previous example) or omitted, as in the example below.

The objection was overruled.
  (subject)   *(verb)*

Note that passive voice is different from past tense. Even though both concern the verb, past tense refers to the time of an action and passive voice refers to the relationship of an action to the subject of the sentence. See Exercise 23.A in the *Practice Book*.

§23.1.2   Effective Use of Active Voice

Generally, the active voice is preferred over the passive voice for several reasons:

1. It is more concise.

EXAMPLES

The marshal left the summons.

(active voice — 5 words)

The summons was left by the marshal.

(passive voice — 7 words)

---

2. It uses a more vigorous verb.

EXAMPLES

The plaintiffs filed a complaint in the Superior Court of Chavez County, New Mexico.

(active voice — verb "filed" is crisp and vigorous)

A complaint was filed by the plaintiffs in the Superior Court of Chavez County, New Mexico.

(passive voice—verb "was filed" loses much of its vigor; the auxillary verb "was" and the preposition "by" dilute the energy of "filed")

---

3. It allows information to be processed more readily.

EXAMPLE

The defendant's attorney must offer the deposition into evidence.

This active voice sentence is easy to process mentally. The reader can visualize the subject "defendant's attorney" doing the verb "must offer" to the object "deposition" as quickly as the words are read. The sentence suggests a mini-drama that readers can visualize in their minds.

EXAMPLE

The deposition must be offered into evidence by the defendant's attorney.

Although the information in this passive voice sentence is not difficult to process, readers must read the entire sentence before they will be able to visualize the sentence in their minds. By the midpoint in the sentence, "The deposition must be introduced into evidence," the action has begun, but it is being done by unseen hands. The "actor" in the mini-drama does not come in until the end of the sentence.

In both objective and persuasive legal writing, active voice is usually preferred when you want to make a point that someone or something performed a particular action. Active voice emphasizes who or what is responsible for committing an act. See Exercise 23.B in the *Practice Book*.

EXAMPLES

The defendant embezzled over $1,000,000.

(active voice—emphasizes that the defendant is responsible for the act)

Over $1,000,000 was embezzled by the defendant.

(passive voice — it is still clear that the defendant performed the act, but now the emphasis is on the amount of money)

Over $1,000,000 was embezzled.

(passive voice — doer of the action is either unknown or left unsaid; emphasis is on the amount of money)

---

§23.1.3   Effective Use of Passive Voice

Although it is true that active voice is generally preferable over passive voice, there are several situations in which passive voice is more effective.

1. Use passive voice when the person or thing performing the action is unknown or relatively unimportant.

EXAMPLES

A portion of the tape was erased.

The safe's hinges must be examined before the manufacturer's liability can be determined.

---

2. Use passive voice when it is undesirable to disclose the identity of the person or thing performing the action.

EXAMPLES

The plaintiff's retirement benefits were discontinued.

Toxic fumes were ventilated out of the plant between 2:00 and 3:00 a.m.

---

3. Use passive voice when the deed, rather than the doer, should be emphasized.

EXAMPLES

A cure for Alzheimer's disease has been found.

All four defendants were convicted of first degree murder.

---

4. Use passive voice when the passive voice allows the writer to keep the focus of the writing where it belongs, as in the following example from a paragraph about a mistake in a contract.

EXAMPLE

A mistake can also be attributed to Lakeland Elementary School for believing the price of the playground equipment included installation.

---

5. Use passive voice when it provides a stronger link between preceding and subsequent sentences or clauses. See section 22.3 on dovetailing. This link is enhanced by moving the connecting ideas to the end of the first sentence (or clause) and then picking up on that point at the beginning of the second sentence (or clause).

Sentence 1	*Sentence 2*
connecting idea	connecting idea

EXAMPLE

Under the Revised Code of Washington, Title 62A, contracts for the sale of goods are regulated by the Uniform Commercial Code. The UCC outlines the requirements for a valid contract for the sale of goods and the various steps necessary to the contract's performance.

The first sentence uses passive voice so that "Uniform Commercial Code" will be at the end of the sentence. The second sentence begins with "The UCC" to provide a strong link between the sentences.

Sentence 1	*Sentence 2*
by the Uniform Commercial Code	The UCC

EXAMPLE

Big Yard Toys, Inc. bid on the manufacture of the playground equipment, and the bid was accepted by Lakeland Elementary School.

The second main clause uses passive voice. It begins with "the bid" as a strong link to the preceding main clause.

Clause 1	*Clause 2*
bid on the manufacture	and the bid was accepted

Avoid mixing active and passive verbs when writing a compound verb. (Reminder: Both parts of a compound verb have the same subject.)

EXAMPLES

Draft: Ms. Meyers left her motel room and was followed
             (subject)   (active)   (passive)
             by the defendant.

Revised: After leaving her motel room, Ms. Meyers was followed by the defendant.

Draft: Roger Harrison sent in his 1991 tax form and was
             (subject)   (active)
             later audited by the I.R.S.
                   (passive)

Revised: Roger Harrison sent in his 1991 tax form, which was later audited by the I.R.S.

For legal writing, you will need passive voice for both objective and persuasive writing. In objective writing, you will often have instances when the person or thing performing the action is unknown; when the deed, rather than the doer of the deed, should be emphasized; when the passive voice allows the writer to keep the focus of the writing where it belongs; and when the passive voice provides a stronger link between preceding and subsequent sentences or clauses.

In persuasive writing, you will find that the passive voice allows you to downplay who performed certain actions. For example, counsel for the defense may want to use the passive voice when admitting wrong-doing by the defendant.

EXAMPLE

A purse was taken from the plaintiff by the defendant.
(passive voice used to downplay defendant's action)

Counsel for the plaintiff will use active voice to emphasize that it was the defendant who took the purse.

EXAMPLE

The defendant took the plaintiff's purse.

See Exercise 23.C in the *Practice Book*.

§23.2   CONCRETE SUBJECTS

Effective subjects of sentences are concrete rather than abstract. They are real people and real things that readers can mentally visualize.

Unfortunately, in legal writing we are often forced to use abstractions as subjects of our sentences. The law and its application often require that we focus on ideas and concepts; consequently, we often end up placing these ideas and concepts in the subject position. Even so, legal readers appreciate having as many concrete subjects as possible to help bring the writing back down to earth.

To find the most effective concrete subject of a sentence, ask yourself, "Who (or what) is doing something in this sentence?" Then place that real person (or thing) in the subject position of the sentence.

EXAMPLE

Draft: A <u>decision</u> <u>was made</u> by the district manager to elim-
                  (subject)   *(verb)*
              inate all level four positions.

Revised: The <u>district manager</u> <u>decided</u> to eliminate all level four
                 (subject)   *(verb)*
              positions.

Note that the preceding example illustrates a common problem in legal writing known as nominalization. Nominalization is the process of converting verbs into nouns (for example, "decide" ⟶ "decision"). The effect in the sentence is twofold: (1) the real action of the sentence is buried in a noun, making the sentence more ponderous and turgid, and (2) the verb becomes either a passive voice substitute or a "*to be*" verb substitute, making the sentence less energetic.

In many sentences, the real person or thing acting in the sentence has been buried in an abstraction or omitted altogether.

EXAMPLES

Draft: The <u>awarding</u> of damages <u>will be left</u> to judicial dis-
                (subject)   *(verb)*
             cretion.

Revised: The <u>judge</u> <u>will decide</u> whether to award damages.
                (subject)   *(verb)*

Draft: Determination of legislative intent requires reading
             legislative history.

Revised: An attorney must read legislative history to determine
             legislative intent.

Often the subject position in the sentence is taken up by an almost meaningless abstraction such as "nature of," "kind of," "type of," "aspect of," "factor of," or "area of." Notice how the sentence improves when these meaningless abstractions are omitted and real people and real things are placed in the subject position.

EXAMPLE

Draft: The <u>nature</u> of the defendant's argument <u>was</u> that he
                (subject)   *(verb)*
             was "temporarily insane."

> ***Revised:***   The <u>defendant</u> <u>argued</u> that he was "temporarily in-
>   *(subject)*   *(verb)*
>   sane."

Both the subject position and verb position are often taken up by the many weak subject-verb combinations that use the "it is _____ that" pattern.

> It is important to note that
> It is likely (unlikely) that
> It is obvious (clear) that
> It is essential that

To revise sentences with this weakness, look after the "that" for the real subject and verb. See Exercise 23.D in the *Practice Book.*

EXAMPLE

> ***Draft:***   <u>It is</u> obvious that the defendant was not read his rights.
>   *(subject/verb)*

> ***Revised:***   The <u>defendant</u> <u>was</u> not <u>read</u> his rights.
>   *(subject)*   *(verb)*

> ***Draft:***   <u>It is</u> unlikely that the defendant will plead guilty.
>   *(subject/verb)*

> ***Revised:***   The <u>defendant</u> probably <u>will</u> not <u>plead</u> guilty.
>   *(subject)*   *(verb)*

---

§23.3   ACTION VERBS

Effective verbs show real action rather than vague action or state of being. To find the most effective verb for a sentence, ask yourself, "What is someone (or something) actually doing in the sentence?" Then place that action in the verb position.

Common Pitfalls to Avoid When Selecting a Verb

1. Avoid overusing forms of the verb "to be" ("am," "are," "is," "was," "were") as a main verb. Use forms of the verb "to be" only as the main verb when the point of the sentence is that something exists.

EXAMPLE

Draft: The <u>owner</u> of the land <u>is</u> East Coast Properties, Inc.
              (subject)   *(verb)*

Revised: <u>East Coast Properties, Inc.</u> <u>owns</u> the land.
              (subject)   *(verb)*

Draft: There <u>are</u> four <u>elements</u> that must be proved to re-
              (verb)   *(subject)*
              cover damages under the family car or purpose doc-
              trine.

Revised: Four <u>elements</u> <u>must be proved</u> to recover damages
              (subject)   *(verb)*
              under the family car or purpose doctrine.

Notice that the sentence openers "There is" or "There are" or "There was" or "There were" are weak unless the point of the sentence is that something exists. With these four sentence openers, the subject comes after the verb.

2. Avoid using vague verbs. Verbs such as "concerns," "involves," "deals (with)," and "reveals" tell the reader little about the real action in the sentence.

EXAMPLES

Draft: <u>*Swanson*</u> <u>dealt</u> with a sales contract that contained
              (subject)   *(verb)*
              an open item and that was signed by a homebuilder
              and a couple who were prospective buyers of a home.

Revised: In *Swanson,* a <u>homebuilder</u> and a <u>couple</u> who were
                              (subject)   *(subject)*
              prospective buyers of a home <u>signed</u> a contract that
                                           (verb)
              contained an open item.

---

3. Avoid nominalization, that is, burying the real action in a noun, and avoid burying the action in an adjective. See Exercise 23.E in the *Practice Book.*

EXAMPLES

Draft: The <u>corporate officers</u> <u>had</u> an informal meeting at an
                  (subject)   *(verb)*
              undisclosed location.

Revised: The <u>corporate officers</u> <u>met</u> informally at an undis-
                  (subject)   *(verb)*
              closed location.

Draft: Rhode Island <u>courts</u> <u>have</u> not yet <u>made</u> a decision
                    (subject)   *(verb)*
              about whether public schools can refuse admission to
              a student with acquired immune deficiency syndrome
              (AIDS).

Revised: Rhode Island <u>courts</u> <u>have</u> not yet <u>decided</u> whether
                    (subject)   *(verb)*
              public schools can refuse admission to a student with
              acquired immune deficiency syndrome (AIDS).

Draft: The <u>policy</u> underlying the doctrine of adverse posses-
                  (subject)
               sion <u>is</u> favorable to the Morgans.
              (verb)

Revised: The <u>policy</u> underlying the doctrine of adverse posses-
                  (subject)
               sion <u>favors</u> the Morgans.
               (verb)

---

§23.4   DISTANCE BETWEEN SUBJECTS AND VERBS

An effective sentence has its subject and verb close together. When they are close together, the reader can identify the subject-verb unit quickly and comprehend the entire sentence more easily. When they are far apart and separated by many intervening words, the reader will find it much more difficult to understand the sentence.

EXAMPLES

Draft: <u>Information</u> about Mutual Trust Bank's standard op-
            (subject)
            erating procedures and about how the contractor drew
            up his loan application <u>will be required</u> by the court.
                                          (verb)

Revised: The <u>court</u> <u>will require</u> information about Mutual Trust
            (subject)   *(verb)*
            Bank's standard operating procedures and about how
            the contractor drew up his loan application.

In some cases, the writer will have to rewrite one sentence as two sentences to keep the subjects and verbs close together.

EXAMPLES

Draft: A <u>case</u> in which a section 11-902 charge was dropped
            (subject)
            because the driver was found lying in the highway
            near his truck <u>shows</u> that a driver's presence in the
                                 (verb)
            vehicle is a prerequisite for finding him guilty.

Revised: In one case, the <u>court</u> <u>dismissed</u> a section 11-902
                              (subject) (verb)
            charge because the driver was found lying in the high-
            way near his truck. The <u>court</u> <u>reasoned</u> that a driver's
                                     (subject) (verb)
            presence in a vehicle is a prerequisite to finding the
            defendant guilty.

Another reason for keeping subjects and verbs close together is to reduce the chance that they will not agree in number. See section 26.4. In the following example, the writer has mistakenly made the verb agree with the singular noun "script" when the plural subject "quality and mutilation" requires the plural verb "are."

EXAMPLE   **SUBJECT AND VERB DO NOT AGREE**

Inferior <u>quality and mutilation</u> of the musical play *Not Enough*
       (subject)
Lovin' as a result of Skylark Productions' revisions of the script <u>is</u>
hard to establish.   *(verb)*

Occasionally a writer must separate the subject and verb with quite a bit of information. In such cases, if the intervening information can be set off by punctuation, the reader will still be able to identify the subject-verb unit fairly easily.

EXAMPLE

The <u>Lanham Trademark Act</u>, a law primarily designed to prevent
       (subject)
deceptive packaging of goods in interstate commerce, <u>has been</u>
                                           (verb)
<u>interpreted</u> to include false attribution and distortion of literary and
artistic works.

Remember too that keeping subjects and verbs close together is desirable but not absolutely required. There will be times in legal writing when it is all but impossible to keep subjects and verbs close together. See Exercises 23.F and 23.G in the *Practice Book*.

§23.5   SENTENCE LENGTH

Whenever a legal writer asks "how long should my sentences be?" the only possible answer is "it depends." Obviously sentence length is primarily governed by what you are trying to say. Some ideas take more words to convey than others. Even given that constraint, though, a writer still has quite a bit of flexibility regarding the length of each sentence. Decisions on sentence length, then, should also be made based on two other factors: the reader and the context.

§23.5.1   The Reader

Effective sentence length is that which the reader can handle comfortably. Educated readers — judges, attorneys, some clients — can comfortably read somewhat longer sentences than the general public. Consequently, legal writers can usually write sentences for their readers that average about twenty-two words per sentence with only a rare sentence exceeding a thirty-five word limit. For readers with less education, shorter sentences are usually more effective.

Notice how the overly long sentence in the following example creates a feeling in the reader of a mental overload. Several overly long sentences written one after another only compound this feeling.

EXAMPLE

The post-trial motion was supported by an affidavit by a juror that stated that a fellow juror discussed the case with a professional truck driver who was familiar with the accident scene and who told the juror that the accident could not have occurred as the plaintiff stated. (48 words)

There are several ways to revise overly long sentences such as the one in the example above so that they become more readable. The first way is to break up an overly long sentence into two or more separate sentences.

EXAMPLE

Revised:

The post-trial motion was supported by an affidavit by a juror. In his affidavit, the juror stated that a fellow juror discussed the case with a professional truck driver who was familiar with the accident scene. The truck driver told the juror that the accident could not have occurred as the plaintiff stated.

The second way to revise an overly long sentence is to create manageable units of meaning within the sentence. A writer can do this by identifying structural components within the sentence, especially phrases and clauses, and setting them off with appropriate punctuation.

Obviously, the writer must still comply with the rules of punctuation and not assume he or she can punctuate randomly. One rule of punctuation that can be used in such situations is comma rule 2 for setting off introductory phrases and clauses. See section 27.1. Notice how much more readable the following example becomes when, in Revision 1, the "if" clause is moved to the front of the sentence where it can be set off from the rest of the sentence by a comma.

EXAMPLE

The Reynoldses will be responsible for both the attacks on the Halversons' chickens and Mr. Halverson's medical bills resulting from the dog bite if the plaintiff can show that the Reynoldses should have known of their dog's viciousness. (38 words)

Revision 1:

If the plaintiff can show that the Reynoldses should have known of their dog's viciousness, (15 words) then they will be responsible for both the attacks on the Halversons' chickens and Mr. Halverson's medical bills resulting from the dog bite. (23 words)

Other punctuation marks, such as the colon, can sometimes be added to create a break within a sentence.

EXAMPLE

Revision 2:

If the plaintiff can show that the Reynoldses should have known of their dog's viciousness, (15 words) then they will be responsible for the following: (8 words) the attacks on the Halversons' chickens and Mr. Halverson's medical bills resulting from the dog bite. (16 words)

This technique of arranging phrases and clauses so that they can be set off by punctuation is particularly helpful when writing issue statements, or questions presented. In the following example, the reader is expected to absorb the information in fifty-six words straight without a punctuation break.

EXAMPLE

Under New Hampshire law did the trial court commit prejudicial error by refusing plaintiffs' motion for a new trial because of jury misconduct when the motion was supported by a juror affidavit stating that another juror discussed the case with an alleged expert outside the trial context and then related the information to the entire jury?

In Revision 1, the writer has broken up this same information into more readable units by using a comma to set off the introductory phrase and a conjunction between two main clauses. See section 27.1, Rules 1 and 2.

EXAMPLE

Revision 1:

Under New Hampshire law, did the trial court commit prejudicial error by refusing plaintiffs' motion for a new trial because of jury misconduct when the motion was supported by a juror affidavit, (32 words) and that affidavit stated that another juror discussed the case with an alleged expert outside the trial context and then related the information to the entire jury? (27 words)

In Revision 2, the writer has used commas between a series of parallel clauses (here, "when" clauses) to help break up the information into manageable units. See section 26.7. Even though the revised sentence is longer than the original, it is more readable because the reader gets the information in smaller, more manageable units.

EXAMPLE

Revision 2:

Under New Hampshire law, did the trial court commit prejudicial error when it refused plaintiffs' motion for a new trial because of jury misconduct, (24 words) when the motion was supported by a juror affidavit, (9 words) and when that affidavit stated that another juror discussed the case with an alleged expert outside the trial context and then related information to the entire jury? (27 words)

The third way to solve sentence length problems is to eliminate wordiness. See section 24.2.

EXAMPLE

Proceeding on the assumption that all lawyers have a basic understanding of the more traditional torts, the speaker outlined and presented the following synopsis and review of what are considered to be the most prominent contemporary types of legal actions for which a general business attorney should prepare and in which he or she should reasonably expect to participate at some point in his or her career. (67 words)

Revised:

Assuming lawyers understand traditional torts, the speaker described the main types of tort cases that a business attorney should be prepared to handle. (23 words)

See Exercises 23.H and 23.I in the *Practice Book*.

§23.5.2　The Context

Earlier we said that decisions about sentence length should be based on both the reader and the context. Readers rarely see a sentence in isolation. Most sentences occur in a context; they are preceded by other sentences and followed by other sentences. Consequently, how readers respond to the length of any given sentence depends, in part, on the sentences that surround it.

For example, a forty-word sentence that is unwieldy in one context may work in another. A short, snappy sentence that drives a point home in one paragraph may seem trite and unsophisticated in another. Even a steady diet of medium-length sentences is unappetizing. Such writing tends to be monotonous and bland.

When it comes to sentence length, then, consistency is not a virtue. Effective sentences, that is, sentences that convey the desired information and keep the reader interested, vary in length.

The following example from a statement of facts shows how lack of variety in sentence length makes the writing less interesting to read. In the eleven sentences that follow, the range in sentence length is only from nine words in the shortest sentence to nineteen words in the longest sentence.

EXAMPLE

On December 15, 1996, Officers Jack Morrison and Wayne Fiscis of the Phoenix Police Department searched Victor Ehrlich's apartment. (17 words) They had in their possession a valid search warrant for marijuana. (11 words) Marijuana was found in both the living room and the kitchen. (11 words) While searching the bedroom, Officer Morrison found a large manila envelope in one of the dresser drawers. (17 words) Photographs were protruding from the top of the envelope. (9 words) Morrison looked inside and found photographs of Ehrlich with three young girls sitting on his lap. (16 words) Ehrlich was wearing only boxer shorts, and the girls were nude from the waist up. (15 words) Considering the photographs to be perverse, Morrison showed them to Fiscis, who agreed that they looked suspicious. (17 words) They seized the photographs as well as the marijuana. (9 words) The defendant, Victor Ehrlich, has now contested this seizure. (9 words) He has made a motion to suppress the photographic evidence as the result of an unconstitutional seizure. (17 words)

The following revised version is more interesting to read because sentence length now ranges from six words in the shortest sentence to twenty-nine words in the longest.

EXAMPLE

Revised:

On December 15, 1996, Officers Jack Morrison and Wayne Fiscis of the Phoenix Police Department searched Victor Ehrlich's apartment. (17 words) They had in their possession a valid search warrant for marijuana. (11 words) After finding marijuana in both the living room and the kitchen, they searched the bedroom, where Officer Morrison found a large manila envelope in one of the dresser drawers. (29 words) Seeing photographs protruding from the top of the envelope, Morrison looked inside and found photographs of Ehrlich with three young girls sitting on his lap. (25 words) Ehrlich was wearing only boxer shorts. (6 words) The girls were nude from the waist up. (8 words) Considering the photographs to be perverse, Morrison showed them to Fiscis, who agreed that they looked suspicious. (17 words) They seized the photographs as well as the marijuana. (9 words) The defendant, Victor Ehrlich, has now contested this seizure and has made a motion to suppress the photographic evidence as the result of an unconstitutional seizure. (26 words)

Part of what makes the revised version effective is its use of short sentences. The four short sentences were all used to highlight particularly significant facts. In the next section we will discuss how to use short sentences to best effect.

§23.5.3   The Power of the Short Sentence

Used sparingly, short sentences can energize writing. Not only can they provide relief to readers who have just labored through several long sentences, they also tend to highlight the information they contain.

Note how in the following example the short sentence serves both as a welcome break after two fairly long sentences and as a way to emphasize the significant point that individuals in both cases were possibly motivated by a reward.

EXAMPLE

In two older decisions, *United States v. Snowadzki*, 723 F.2d 1427 (9th Cir. 1984), and *United States v. Black*, 767 F.2d 1334 (9th Cir. 1985), individuals conducting unlawful searches were considered to have acted as private parties, not as government agents. In both cases, the individuals obtained the documents unlawfully and then turned them over to the government, which later submitted them as evidence at trial. In each instance, a reward was offered.

In the following example, the writer has remembered how readers welcome a short sentence after several long sentences, but has forgotten that a short sentence also highlights the information it contains.

EXAMPLE

At about 2:00 a.m. on Saturday, February 22, 1993, our client, Mr. David Lendl, left a local restaurant where he had been drinking and began driving south on Interstate 10 to his sister's home in El Paso, Texas. After driving for approximately ten minutes, Mr. Lendl realized that he was becoming sleepy and somewhat nauseous, so he decided to change destinations and head back to his own apartment in Las Cruces. Feeling increasingly tired and ill, he pulled off the freeway and onto the shoulder of an exit ramp where he stopped and got out of the car. There he threw up. He then attempted to restart the car's engine but was unable to do so because the carburetor was flooded.

Unless the writer believes that the client's act of throwing up is particularly significant, it does not deserve the emphasis that comes with a short sentence. See Exercises 23.J and 23.K in the *Practice Book*.

§23.6 EMPHASIS

Creating emphasis is important in both objective and persuasive legal writing. In objective writing, the writer needs to let the reader know where to focus his or her attention. By using emphasis properly, the writer signals to the reader the main point or thrust of an objective discussion or explanation.

In persuasive writing, emphasis becomes one of the advocate's most effective tools. Emphasis allows the advocate to spotlight those points that favor the client and downplay those that hurt the client. It also allows the advocate to hammer home his or her theory of the case so that the reader begins to see the case as the writer does.

Emphasis, then, is a natural part of all writing. In fact, you will probably find that you are already using some of the strategies for emphasis that will be discussed in this section. In the previous section, for example, we saw how short sentences can be used to emphasize key points. Notice again how the revision of the following sentence demonstrates the startling effect a short sentence can have.

EXAMPLE

Original:

The defendant lied when she testified that she was in St. Paul, Minnesota, at the time of the robbery.

Revised:

The defendant testified that she was in St. Paul, Minnesota, at the time of the robbery. She lied.

Besides short sentences, emphasis can be achieved in several other ways:

    A. telling the reader what is important
    B. underlining (or italics or boldface)
    C. using positions of emphasis
    D. using punctuation to highlight a point
    E. using single-word emphasizers
    F. changing the normal order in a sentence
    G. repeating key words
    H. setting up a pattern (and sometimes breaking it)

Of all these strategies, the most common and least sophisticated are the first two: (A) simply telling the reader what is important and (B) underlining. Some writers consider these first two strategies too obvious and overused to be effective. Others feel that they can be effective if used selectively. Regardless of which point of view you agree with, be sure not to overuse these two strategies or, for that matter, any of the eight strategies, because overuse dilutes the impact they have on readers.

§23.6.1 Telling the Reader What Is Important

Sentence openers such as "it is important to note that," "it is noteworthy that," "most important," or "above all" serve only one purpose — to alert the reader to the importance of the point that follows. Used rarely, these sentence openers can help the reader identify which points deserve heightened emphasis. Used frequently, these same sentence openers bog down the writing and make it wordy. The following examples from persuasive and objective writing show how these sentence openers may be used.

EXAMPLES

Above all, the court should consider the defendant's past record as a good husband, model father, and leader in the community.

It is important to note that the check was postdated.

Notice that the last example may be even more emphatic when revised into a short sentence: The check was postdated.

You may also tell the reader what is important in mid-sentence. Expressions such as "especially," "particularly," and "most important" can be used in this way when they are inserted right before the point to be emphasized.

EXAMPLES

The court should consider the defendant's past record as a good husband, model father, and, most important, leader in the community.

Lying, particularly lying in court, is not the mark of an innocent man.

---

§23.6.2   Underlining

Underlining is undoubtedly the simplest and least sophisticated strategy for emphasis. It requires no restructuring of the sentence and little, if any, planning. The writer simply underlines the word or words to signal emphasis. If you do decide to use underlining for emphasis, be extremely selective. The following examples show how underlining may be used for emphasis.

EXAMPLES

The contract <u>permits</u> but does not <u>require</u> the tenant to add landscaping and similar outdoor improvements.

Lionel Porter's uncle promised to pay for his college education <u>if</u> he majored in business.

It is sometimes tempting to assume that readers will not detect subtle emphasis and must be told which words are crucial. Many writers would consider the underlining in the previous two examples unnecessary and possibly even condescending. The remaining strategies for emphasis are significantly more subtle and therefore more suitable for sophisticated readers.

§23.6.3   Using Positions of Emphasis

When it comes to emphasis, all parts of the sentence are not created equal. That is, the beginning, middle, and end of a sentence are not equally emphatic.

In most sentences, writers place new information at the end of a sentence. Also, the end of the sentence is the point of climax. Everything in the sentence builds toward the words at the end. Consequently, in most sentences, the most emphatic position is at the end.

The next most emphatic position is usually at the beginning. Here the writer typically sets the stage for the rest of the sentence. The reader expects the beginning of the sentence to demonstrate how the new information in this sentence is connected with what has already been discussed.

The middle of the sentence is usually the least emphatic. Skillful advocates know that in this part of the sentence they can place unfavorable information and points they do not wish to highlight.

The following grid illustrates the positions in a sentence and their degree of emphasis.

SENTENCE

beginning	middle	end
somewhat emphatic	least emphatic	most emphatic

Examine the following two examples, either of which could appear in an objective memo. Example 1 places "are not attractive nuisances" in the end position, so this version should occur in a memo that emphasizes the point that natural streams are usually not attractive nuisances.

EXAMPLE

Unless they are concealing some dangerous condition, natural streams that flow through the hatchery are not attractive nuisances.

Example 2 places "unless they are concealing some dangerous condition" in the end position, so this version is likely to occur in a memo that emphasizes that a concealed dangerous condition made a natural stream an attractive nuisance.

EXAMPLE

Natural streams that flow through the hatchery are not attractive nuisances, unless they are concealing some dangerous condition.

Now in the following example from a persuasive brief, note how the end position emphasizes that the error was harmless.

EXAMPLE

Even if the trial court mischaracterized the property, the entire division was fair; thus, the error was harmless.

To emphasize that the entire division of property was fair, the same sentence can be revised.

EXAMPLE

Even if the trial court mischaracterized the property, the error was harmless because the entire division was fair.

The following example shows how the beginning position, as well as the end position, can be used to highlight points.

EXAMPLE

Despite his earlier attempts at plea bargaining, the defendant now claims not only that he is innocent but also that he has been framed.

As ethical members of the legal profession, legal writers must often include information that is unfavorable to their client. Rather than concede a point in a short sentence, which will highlight the unfavorable point, it is often better to include it with the favorable point and arrange the material so the reader ends with the point favorable to your client. Consequently, the middle or the beginning of the sentence is a better position for unfavorable information.

EXAMPLE

Although Mr. Brown admits that he raised his voice during the altercation with Mrs. Smith, he never threatened Mrs. Smith, as Mrs. Smith claims, but rather reminded her of his rights as a property owner.

Combining the End Position with Other Strategies for Emphasis

By using the emphatic end position in combination with another strategy for emphasis, legal writers can achieve even more emphasis.

Here the end position, combined with punctuation, is used for dramatic effect.

EXAMPLE

The courtroom fell silent in anticipation of the jury's verdict: guilty.

In the next example, the end position, combined with use of a phrase telling the reader what is important, is used to suggest a climax.

EXAMPLE

Before awarding custody, the court must consider the mental and physical health of all individuals involved, the child's adjustment to home and school, the relationship of the child with his parents and siblings, the wishes of the parents, and, most important, the wishes of the child.

In the next example, the end position, combined with the technique of setting up a pattern and breaking it, is used to startle the reader.

EXAMPLE

Daniel Klein was loyal to his parents, loyal to his wife, loyal to his friends, and disloyal to the company that had employed him for thirty years.

Two final points before leaving the topic of positions of emphasis: First, the positions of emphasis can also be applied at the paragraph and document levels; second, the characterization of most emphatic, somewhat emphatic, and least emphatic for the end, beginning, and middle of sentences is a general, not an absolute, principle. In the following subsections we will see how punctuation, single-word emphasizers, and changing normal word order can make the beginning and even the middle of sentences strong points of emphasis.

§23.6.4   Using Punctuation for Emphasis

Commas, colons, and dashes can all be used to set up a point in an appositive at the end of a sentence. An appositive is a restatement of an earlier word or group of words. It is often a more detailed substitute for the earlier word or group of words. In the following examples "expert witness" is an appositive for "one term," "bribe" is an appositive for "exchange of money," and "greed and more greed" is an appositive for "two things."

EXAMPLES

All of the prosecution's arguments depend on the definition of one term, "expert witness."

Throughout the United States, such an exchange of money is known by one name: bribe.

The defendant was motivated by only two things—greed and more greed.

Notice in the three following examples how all three marks of punctuation cast a slightly different light on the words that follow them. The comma, as a rather commonplace punctuation mark, suggests in the first of these examples that there is nothing too surprising about the silent partner being his brother.

EXAMPLE

The construction contract included a silent partner, his brother.

The colon requires a longer pause; consequently the phrase "his brother" receives more emphasis in the example that follows. Colons also have an aura of formality that somehow suggests the seriousness of what follows them.

EXAMPLE

The construction contract included a silent partner: his brother.

The longer pause from the dash gives even more emphasis to "his brother." Also, the dash suggests that it is rather surprising that the brother is the silent partner.

EXAMPLE

The construction contract included a silent partner—his brother.

One thing legal writers should consider before using dashes, however, is that some readers feel dashes also convey a sense of informality. Consequently, many legal writers avoid the dash in legal prose.

Pairs of commas or pairs of dashes can also be used to set off appositives and parenthetical expressions in the middle of sentences. Because pairs of commas are the standard punctuation in such cases, they give the enclosed information less emphasis than a pair of dashes. See Exercise 23.L in the *Practice Book*.

EXAMPLES

Defense counsel's final argument, that the accident was unavoidable, will fail because the defendant's earlier statement shows that she considered the possibility of an injury during a high wind storm.

Defense counsel's final argument—that the accident was unavoidable—will fail because the defendant's earlier statement
shows that she considered the possibility of an injury during a high
wind storm.

§23.6.5   Using Single-Word Emphasizers

Certain words in our language ("no," "not," "never," "only," "any,"
"still," "all," "every," "none") convey natural emphasis because they either
dramatically change or intensify the meaning of the words they modify.

EXAMPLE

A change made to the contract must be approved by both parties.

Revision 1:

Any change made to the contract must be approved by both
parties.

Revision 2:

A change may be made to the contract only if approved by both
parties.

Note that the most effective way to use "not" for emphasis is to
place a comma before it and use it as a contrasting element.

EXAMPLES

It is the taxpayer, not the tax preparer, who is responsible for the
accuracy of all information on the form.

Mrs. Field's express wish was for the jewelry to go to her niece,
not her daughter.

Three other single-word emphasizers ("clearly," "obviously," and
"very") are so overused by legal writers and, in the case of "very," by the
general public that they have lost much of their ability to emphasize.

Ironically, then, sentences that contain "clearly," "obviously," and "very" seem to have more impact when these words are omitted.

EXAMPLE

Weak:

Clearly, the defendant knew she was committing a crime.

Revised:

The defendant knew she was committing a crime.

Notice that in the example, "clearly" would be stressed. In the revision, "knew" gets the natural stress.

EXAMPLE

Weak:

Many residents complained about the very loud noise coming from the factory.

Revised:

Many residents complained about the loud noise coming from the factory.

"Very" is often an unnecessary prop for a word. Usually, a word such as "loud" conveys the right level of meaning by itself. If, however, "loud" is too weak a term for your purpose, it is better to choose a stronger term rather than to rely on "very" to bolster meaning. See Exercise 23.M in the *Practice Book*.

EXAMPLE

Revised:

Many residents complained about the ear-splitting noise coming from the factory.

---

§23.6.6   Changing the Normal Word Order

Readers expect the traditional subject-verb-object order in sentences. When a writer changes this expected order, the change draws attention to itself and emphasizes whatever words are out of the traditional order.

The most common change is from active voice to passive voice (see sections 23.1.1 to 23.1.3). Another fairly common change is to insert the words to be emphasized between either the subject and the verb or between the verb and its object.

EXAMPLES

Martin Fuller, blinded by grief, lost his grip on reality and opened fire on the parking lot.

(subject and verb separated by "blinded by grief")

He shot—apparently at close range—both of the parents of Tim O'Connell.

(verb and object separated by "apparently at close range")

Another, less frequent change is to delay the subject and verb and open the sentence with a part of the sentence that would normally come at the end.

EXAMPLE

Mrs. Taylor rewrote her will only one week before she died.

Revised:

Only one week before she died, Mrs. Taylor rewrote her will.

An even more radical change is to begin an active voice sentence with its object.

EXAMPLE

The jury did not believe her testimony.

Revised:

Her testimony the jury did not believe.

Notice that some of the preceding examples seem to contradict the earlier advice about keeping subjects and verbs close together and using the end position in sentences to achieve emphasis. None of the strategies for emphasis work as an absolute rule. The writer should use his or her judgment in selecting which strategy is effective in each instance.

As a strategy for emphasis, changing the normal word order should be used carefully and rarely. Frequent use, particularly of delaying the normal word order and beginning active voice sentences with the object, will make that writing sound awkward and contrived. See Exercise 23.N in the *Practice Book*.

§23.6.7   Repeating Key Words

Many writers mistakenly assume that repetition is a sign of incompetence. This assumption leads them to search desperately for synonyms of words that recur frequently in a given office memo or brief.

While it is true that needless repetition is ineffective, it is also true that deliberate repetition can be a powerful strategy for emphasis. Key terms and key points should reverberate throughout a piece of legal writing. Like the dominant color in a beautiful tapestry, key words and phrases should be woven throughout to create an overall impression that *this* is what the case is about.

Consider the following excerpt from the respondent's brief in a case where the appellant, a church, wants to operate a grade school without the special use permit required by the city's zoning ordinance for all schools in residential areas. Throughout the excerpt, three different words — "code," "use," and "school" — are deliberately repeated for emphasis. We have boldfaced these three words so you can see how frequently they appear.

EXAMPLE

ARGUMENT

I. THE TRIAL COURT PROPERLY CONSTRUED AND APPLIED BOTH THE ZONING AND BUILDING **CODES** BECAUSE THE

CHURCH HAS CHANGED THE **USE** OF ITS BUILDING BY OP-
ERATING A FULLTIME GRADE **SCHOOL.**

The church must comply with the requirements of the zoning
and building **codes** before it may legally operate its **school.** Each
of these **codes** makes accommodation for **uses** that legally existed prior to enactment of the **code.** However, the church never
operated a **school** prior to the **codes'** enactment, so full compliance with the **codes** is required for the new **use** involved in operating a **school.**

§23.6.8   Setting up a Pattern

The earlier strategy of repeating key words is closely tied to another
strategy for emphasis: setting up a pattern. In such cases a pattern is set
up and key words are repeated within that pattern. This kind of deliberate
repetition can be used effectively within one sentence or in a sequence
of sentences.

EXAMPLES

The prosecution's case depends on solid evidence, solid reasoning, and solid authority.

Lieutenant Harris has been described by his superiors as an "exemplary officer" —exemplary in his demeanor and professionalism, exemplary in his management of subordinates, exemplary in
his performance of duty, and exemplary in his loyalty to the service.

Both women were abducted in the same locale. Both women were
abducted at night. Both women were abducted while alone. Both
women were abducted by the same man: Edward Smith.

Note that to achieve a climactic effect, the writer usually used parallel structure (see section 26.7) to create the pattern and then arranged
the material in an order of increasing importance. Thus, emphasis was
achieved by the pattern, the repetition of key words, and the end position. Notice too that this strategy for emphasis is best suited for persuasive
writing.

§23.6.9   Variation: Deliberately Breaking a Pattern

A rather dramatic variation of the pattern strategy is to set up the pattern and then deliberately break it. This variation depends on the pattern and repetition of key words to create a certain expectation in the reader. The reader's surprise when the pattern is broken creates heightened emphasis. See Exercise 23.O in the *Practice Book*.

EXAMPLES

The defendant acted under a common scheme, for a common motive, but with uncommon results.

It is true that, in New York, many activities engaged in by a church are held to be an integral part of that church, *see, e.g., Unitarian Universalist Church of Central Nassau v. Shorten*, 63 Misc. 2d 978, 314 N.Y.S.2d 66 (1970). It is also true, however, that each case rests on its own facts. *Community Synagogue v. Bates*, 1 N.Y.2d 445, 453, 154 N.Y.S.2d 15, 22, 136 N.E.2d 488, 493 (1956).

---

§23.6.10   Strategies for Emphasis in Context

Up until now we have examined and practiced the strategies for emphasis in mostly isolated sentences or short sequences of sentences. To understand how these strategies are used in context, read the following excerpt from a respondent's brief. Note which strategies are used extensively and which are used less frequently. The boldface type indicates repetition of key words. Pattern sentences are underscored.

EXAMPLES

C. The trial court properly found that the church had to comply with the minimum safety standards set out in the building **code** because operation of the **school** is a changed **use** of the building rather than a prior, legal **use.**

The Sumner Church has changed the way it **uses** its building. It first **used** its building only for church services; now it **uses** the building for church services and as a **school.**	Short sentence "only" as emphasizer End position

"only" as
emphasizer /
Two short
sentences /
"Only" used twice
for emphasis /
Pattern
sentences

Before 1985, the church building was used for weekly church services and for occasional meetings. The only **"school"** was the one-hour Sunday **school** offered on Sunday mornings and the vacation bible school offered for two weeks each summer. Neither of these **"schools"** was a **school** in the traditional sense. The only instruction given was religious instruction. The only teachers were ministers and unpaid volunteers from the congregation.

End position /
Change in
normal order
in sentence

End sentence

"not" as
emphasizer /
End position

In contrast, the **school** that the Church is now operating in the building is a traditional **school.** Instead of operating for one hour a week or for two weeks each summer, the school operates all day long, five days a week, nine months a year. Furthermore, the curriculum is similar to that offered in public grade **schools.** Although the children receive some religious instruction, most of their time is spent on reading, spelling, arithmetic, social studies, and science. Their teachers are full-time, paid faculty members who are certified by the State, not ministers or volunteers. Consequently, despite any church involvement with the **school,** the First Christian Academy is an "educational **use**" of the building as defined by the **code.**

"even" as
emphasizer

End position

End position
End position

Setting up a
pattern

End position

The Michigan Court of Appeals has recognized that even **schools** operated as part of churches are subject to building codes applicable to **schools.** *Hough v. North Star Baptist Church*, 312 N.W.2d 158 (Mich. Ct. App. 1981). The church in *Hough* sought to operate a fulltime **school** without meeting the fire **code.** Even though the court recognized that the **school** was an integral part of the church program, the court held that it was also a **school** under the **code.** As a **school,** the building had to comply with fire regulations for **schools.**

Contrary to the Sumner Church's contention, the **school** does not qualify under the **code's** grandfather clause as a prior, legal **use** because it was opened after the building **code** was adopted. It is important to note that[1] Section 306 of the **code** specifies that if there is <u>any</u> change in the **use** of the building, Section 502 applies. Section 502 specifies that if the changed **use** of the building would fall within a category of occupancy different from that of the original **use,** a new certificate of occupancy is required. Furthermore, the grandfather clause indicates that the drafters intended to accommodate prior **uses,** not changes or extensions of a **use.** Clearly,[2] a fulltime grade **school** is not the same **use** as a two-week bible school.

    <u>Also contrary to the church's contention,</u> *Westbury* is not controlling in the present case on the issue of whether the Sumner Church has changed the **use** of its building. *Westbury Hebrew Congregation v. Downer*, 59 Misc. 2d 387, 302 N.Y.S.2d 923 (1971). *Westbury* is a zoning ordinance case. This is a building **code** case. In *Westbury,* the court held that it was unreasonable for the city to require a church to buy an additional 34½ acres of land merely because the church had opened a **school** in its building. The *Westbury* court also held that at the city had no important interest in requiring a church to occupy fifty acres of land if it wanted to operate a **school.** In fact, in a previous proceeding, the ordinance at issue had already been declared arbitrary and unreasonable. Furthermore, the ordinance at issue applied only to parochial **schools,** not public **schools.** Based on that discrimination, the statute was held to be unconstitutional on its face.

    In contrast to *Westbury,* <u>the City of Sumner Building **Code** does not discriminate</u> between church educational **uses** and public educational **uses.** The **code** requires that any building that is **used** for educational

Telling what is important
Underlining

"not" as emphasizer / "not" as emphasizer

Repeating earlier pattern

Short sentence
Short sentence

"no" as emphasizer

"only" as emphasizer / "not" as emphasizer
End position

Sets up a pattern

"any" as emphasizer

---

    1. Many legal writers would consider "it is important to note that" a wordy construction and simply begin the sentence with "Section 306."

    2. Many legal writers avoid "clearly" as an emphasizer because it is often overused.

Short sentence

"no" as
emphasizer

<u>Pattern
repeated</u>

End position
Punctuation /
"Nowhere" as
emphasizer /
Change in normal
word order /
<u>Sets up a pattern</u> /
"no" as
emphasizer /
<u>Pattern
repeated</u> /
End position

purposes for more than four hours per day or twelve hours per week meet Group C occupancy requirements. The Church's **use** subjects it to the **code's** requirement. Unlike *Westbury*, there is no unconstitutional discrimination against churches on the face of the law.

Furthermore, <u>the City of Sumner's Building</u> **Code** requirements are not arbitrary and unreasonable. In contrast to *Westbury*, the city has an important interest in assuring that fire regulations are met: public **safety.** Nowhere in *Westbury* does that court indicate that had a fire **safety** regulation been at issue, the church would be excused from compliance. <u>The zoning ordinance in *Westbury* was unreasonable because</u> no important state interest was shown in the case. <u>The building</u> **code's** <u>regulation is reasonable because</u> of a demonstrated importance to public **safety.**

See Exercises 23.P and 23.Q in the *Practice Book.*

Chapter 24

Effective Words

A powerful agent is the right word. Whenever we
come upon one of those intensely right words in a
book or a newspaper the resulting effect is physical
as well as spiritual, and electrically prompt.
—Mark Twain,
Essay on William Dean Howells

§24.1   DICTION AND PRECISION

Such a seemingly simple thing. Use the right word, Twain tells us, and
the effect is physical, spiritual, electric, prompt. But right is a relative
thing, isn't it? Some words are more right than others. Some words approach the desired meaning; others capture it, embody it, nail it to the
wall in a way that leaves both the writer and reader satisfied, almost
breathless.

Take the word "right," for example. Twain chose "right" to describe
the kind of word he meant, even though the thesaurus suggests that he
might have chosen any number of so-called synonyms. How about the
"noble" word, the "proper" word, the "suitable" word, the "exact" word,
the "accurate" word, the "correct" word, or even the "precise" word?

What is it about "right" that makes it the right choice?

First of all, denotation—that is, the word's definition. "Noble" is the
wrong choice because it has the wrong denotation. Webster tells us that
"noble" means "possessing outstanding qualities." The definition of "noble" also includes a tie to some kind of superiority. Something is "noble"
because it has a "superiority of mind or character or ideals or morals."
The kind of words Twain talks about do something different than possess
outstanding qualities or superiority.

"Proper" seems to have the right denotation. "Proper" is defined as
"marked by suitability, rightness, or appropriateness." Later in the definition we find "strictly accurate" and "correct." These meanings seem

closer to Twain's intention. But wait a minute. Further still in the definition we see "respectable," "strictly decorous," and "genteel." But do we have to include all of the possible definitions of a word when we use it? Obviously not, but in the case of "proper," these later definitions are clues about the connotations, or associations, that the word carries.

The word "proper" has close ties with the word "propriety," which means "the quality or state of being proper." "Propriety" also means "the standard of what is socially acceptable." If "the proper thing to do" has overtones of decorum and civility, then "the proper word" might also suggest a bit of politeness in its selection. It's doubtful that Twain meant that a "polite word" is a powerful agent.

"Suitable" has similar denotation and connotation problems. Part of the definition of "suitable" is "adapted to the use or purpose." If "suitable words" are those that are adapted to a certain use or purpose, then it is unlikely anything with such a chameleon-like quality can ever be physical, spiritual, electric, or prompt.

"Exact" has the virtue of meaning in "strict, particular, and complete accordance with fact" and the minor flaw of connoting a kind of mathematical or scientific measurement. Still, it is a far better choice than "noble," "proper," or "suitable."

In fact, "exact," "accurate," "correct," "precise," and "right" all have what dictionaries call "the shared meaning element." They all mean "conforming to fact, truth, or a standard."

What is it then about the word "right" that makes it preferable to the other four words, that makes it just right? It has the right denotation and the right connotation, and it has the right sound.

Go back to the quotation at the beginning of the chapter. Try reading the first sentence aloud as it is. Now, one at a time, substitute the words "exact," "accurate," "correct," and "precise" for "right." Read each of these versions aloud. Notice how much harder it is to get the desired emphasis with the three-syllable *accurate.* Even the two-syllable words dilute, albeit just a bit, the punch that we hear in the one syllable *right.* Furthermore, *right* has a kind of honesty and simplicity that captures the spirit of Twain's insight.

Now what does all of this mean for a writer of legal briefs and memos? The same thing it means for any good writer. Finding the right word to express one's meaning is critical to clear communication. With anything other than the right word, you have sacrificed precision; you have sacrificed exact meaning.

In cases like Twain's in which several words can express the intended meaning, the writer can then go beyond precision to eloquence to find the word with just the right sound. See Chapter 25: Eloquence. For now, though, we will focus just on diction and precision and the word choice problems that frequently occur in legal writing. (Three categories of word choice problems, legalese, gender-neutral language, and bias-free language, deserve special attention and are discussed in sections 24.3, 24.4, and 24.5 respectively.)

§24.1.1   Colloquial Language

Word choice, like every other choice in legal writing, is governed by the document's purpose, the reader's expectations, and the writer's role. Because legal writing is done for serious reasons and in a professional context, legal writers should select words that reflect seriousness and professionalism. Slang, colloquialisms, or informal expressions that are acceptable in everyday spoken language are usually out of place in legal writing.

EXAMPLES

Poor:

The defendant's sister is into stained glass windows.

Revised:

The defendant's sister makes stained glass windows as a hobby.

Poor:

The prosecutor noted that Mr. Webb is hung up about how clean his car is, what gas is used in it, and how it is driven.

Revised:

The prosecutor noted that Mr. Webb feels strongly about how clean his car is, what gas is used in it, and how it is driven.

There is only one exception to the general ban on using slang, colloquialisms, and informal language in legal writing—when the writer is quoting. While a writer of a trial brief would be ill-advised to call the defendant "a bad dude," he or she may effectively use that expression if it appeared in the record.

§24.1.2   Reader Expectations and Idioms

A writer's choice among synonyms should also be affected by the reader's expectations. Legal readers, for example, expect to hear about "analogous" cases or "similar" cases, not "comparable" cases or "matching" cases or "kindred" cases.

Read the following example and see if any word is jarring for legal readers.

EXAMPLE

Beaver Custom Carpets will probably argue that there are significant parallelisms between its case and *Flowers.*

Revised:

Beaver Custom Carpets will probably argue that there are significant similarities between its case and *Flowers.*

Similarly, some synonyms have the correct denotation and connotation, but their use is jarring because the reader expects certain idiomatic combinations.

Consider the following example. Which word doesn't seem quite right?

EXAMPLE

Corporations can elude liability by dissolution.

Although the thesaurus may list "elude" as a synonym for "avoid" and "escape," legal readers expect either the idiom "avoid liability" or the idiom "escape liability."

EXAMPLE

Revised:

Corporations can avoid liability by dissolution.

Numerous verbs have certain prepositions with which they commonly combine. In common usage, for example, one always "infers *from*" something. A client may "agree *to*" sign a contract, but she may not "agree *with*" the way you are handling her case. Although one can fear *for* one's life, one can live in fear *of* a lawsuit.

When in doubt about which idiom or preposition is appropriate, consult one of the better dictionaries or a usage guidebook. Another strategy to try is to read the sentence aloud. Native speakers of English can usually "hear" which preposition is correct. Try reading the following example aloud to determine which preposition needs to be changed.

EXAMPLE　　**WRONG PREPOSITION**

Publishers must be able to publish matters of public concern without fear for a lawsuit.

Revised:

Publishers must be able to publish matters of public concern without fear of a lawsuit.

---

§24.1.3　Not-Really-Synonymous Synonyms

Of the many types of imprecision, the most common is the simple substitution of a not-really-synonymous "synonym." In the following example, the writer knew that there were several things he had to prove under the doctrine of adverse possession, but he forgot what to call those "things."

EXAMPLE

The *condition* of hostility must also be proved.

"Condition" is not completely wrong; the reader can probably figure out what the writer intended. But "condition" is not precise. By using the precise term "element," the writer conveys the exact intended meaning, and he makes it clear that he is doing an elements analysis of the problem.

EXAMPLE

Revised:

The element of hostility must also be proved.

Notice that in the above example the term "element" is used when there are indeed "elements" that must be proved. Some legal writers mistakenly use the terms "element" and "factor" as if they were synonyms. The term "element" refers to a requirement—something that must be proved or met. "Factors," on the other hand, refers to what a court must consider. For example, courts must examine several factors to determine which parent gets custody of a child.

Another group of problematic terms that some legal writers use imprecisely includes the words, "part," "prong," and "step." If there is a

two-part test, then both parts must be satisfied. If there are two prongs
to a test, then the test can be satisfied in either of the two ways. If there
is a two-step test, both steps must be satisfied in sequence.

Unfortunately, however, you may occasionally find that courts themselves sometimes use the terms "factor," "element," "part," "prong," and
"step" imprecisely when describing a test. In such instances, you will
probably want to adopt the court's word choice if you are writing to that
same court. In writing for others, however, you will probably want to
adopt the precise term.

Yet another precision problem occurs when writers try to dress up
a simple idea in a fancy vocabulary word and end up instead with a word
choice that misses the mark.

EXAMPLE

The McKibbins may argue that rugs are totally diverse from closed
circuit television camera security systems because few consumers
have a need for such elaborate security systems.

Revised:

The McKibbins may argue that rugs differ from closed circuit television camera security systems because few consumers have a
need for such elaborate security systems.

The most serious type of "not-really-synonymous synonym" problem
occurs when writers attempt to use words they are not quite sure of.
Needless to say, it can be embarrassing to find that you have used a word
that only sounds like the word you intended.

EXAMPLE

Mrs. Harris's most saline point is that Mr. Harris intends to move
the children over 250 miles away.

Undoubtedly, the writer intended the point to be "salient," not salty.
See Exercise 24.A in the *Practice Book*.

§24.1.4   Same Term for the Same Idea

Another common precision problem in legal writing is the misuse
of elegant variation. In other words, legal writers sometimes try to use
synonyms for key terms in their writing in the mistaken belief that using
the same term over and over again bores their readers.

What they have forgotten, though, is that their legal readers have been carefully trained to read statutes and, according to the rules of statutory construction, a different term signals a different idea.

Many legal readers carry this rule over into their memo and brief reading. A change in a key term starts them wondering: "Does the writer mean the same thing as before, or is this really something new?" In short, in legal writing, using an elegant variation of a key term probably will not make the writing more interesting, but it may make the writing confusing.

Read the following example, and note how the writer uses the term "stability" and its variations consistently but floats back and forth among the terms "factor," "principle," and "element."

EXAMPLE

Under the applicable case law, the relevant **factors** used by the courts in deciding custody disputes are the stability of the parent and the role of the primary caregiver. *In re Maddox*, 641 P.2d 665 (Or. Ct. App. 1982). Stability seems to be the overriding **principle** that the Oregon courts use to decide custody disputes. It seems that if the court can determine that one parent is more stable than the other, custody is usually granted to the more stable parent. Another **element** appears, as in *Maddox*, where the father argued that he devoted a significant amount of time to the children, even though the mother was the primary caregiver during the marriage. *Id.* at 667. Both of these **factors** relate back to the first part of the statute, which deals with the emotional ties and interest and attitudes.

In cases like the example above, the reader does not know whether to accuse the writer of sloppy writing or to try to make some fine distinction between "factor," "principle," and "element." In many cases, there is a legal distinction between "factor" and "element" or between "factor" and "principle." In those cases, substituting the terms for each other would be more than confusing; it would be legally inaccurate.

In short, then, legal readers appreciate appropriate variety, but they do not appreciate variety at the expense of clarity.

Sometimes legal writers inadvertently use different terms for the same idea. This inadvertent use seems to occur most frequently when the writer was the one to label an idea. For example, after reading numerous cases on a given issue, the writer may realize that courts typically go through three steps in their analysis. The writer may then refer to a three-step analysis or a three-part analysis or a three-pronged analysis, depending on which best describes what courts have done.

Once a writer has decided which label to use, though, he or she must be consistent. A reader who was introduced to a "three-pronged" analysis will be confused if later in the writing the "second prong" is called the "second step" or the "third prong" is called the "third part" or, worse yet, the "third test." See Exercise 24.B in the *Practice Book*.

§24.1.5   Apples and Rutabagas

In the preceding sections, we saw how disconcerting it can be for readers when writers aren't careful about what they call something. Equally disconcerting for readers are situations in which writers are sloppy about the comparisons they make.

EXAMPLE

The facts of *Turner* are similar to our case.

Because a case includes more than just the facts, it is incongruous to compare just the facts of one case to another entire case.

EXAMPLE

Revised:

The facts of *Turner* are similar to the facts in our case.

See Exercise 24.C in the *Practice Book*.

§24.1.6   Subject-Verb-Object Mismatch

Not all problems of precision are a matter of just one poorly chosen word. All too frequently, the problem is a poorly chosen combination of words. Read the following example from a case about a custody dispute and see if the subject, verb, and object go together.

EXAMPLE

Dr. Davis's <u>occupation</u> as an obstetrician <u>has shown</u> a <u>diminished</u>
      (subject)   *(verb)*   *(object)*
<u>ability</u> to provide consistent care and guidance for her children.

Can an occupation show a diminished ability to do anything? Obviously not. What has happened to this writer is that she has gotten tangled in her own verbiage and written something nonsensical. What she wants to say is that Dr. Davis is an obstetrician and that people who are obstetricians often have demanding, irregular schedules and therefore less time and energy to give consistent care and guidance to their own children.

Consider the following possible revision.

EXAMPLE

Possible Revision:

As an obstetrician, Dr. Davis may be unable to provide consistent care and guidance for her children.

Of course, the revision's meaning is somewhat different from the meaning in the original sentence. Dr. Davis, rather than the profession of being an obstetrician, has become the subject. In the earlier sentence, she merely had a "diminished ability" to provide consistent care and guidance for her children; in the revision, she is "unable" to do these things.

Consider the following compromise revision.

EXAMPLE

Possible Revision:

Dr. Davis's occupation, obstetrician, may impair her ability to provide consistent care and guidance for her children.

To determine whether this or any other subject-verb-object combination is mismatched, lift those three parts out of the sentence and see if they make sense as a unit.

occupation	may impair	ability
(subject)	*(verb)*	*(object)*

Does "occupation may impair ability" make sense? Most readers would say that it does; some, however, would argue against the personification of "occupation" and suggest that occupations cannot "impair" anything. Precision, as we said earlier, is a relative thing.

One common personification used in law that many readers consider imprecise is the use of a case in the subject position when the writer actually means the court that presided over that case.

EXAMPLE

The case *In re Miller*, 670 P.2d 819 (Colo. Ct. App. 1983), reversed the trial court's decision because of the trial court's undue emphasis towards "motherly instincts."

Using the "lift-out" strategy, we get the following combination:

case	reversed	decision
(subject)	*(verb)*	*(object)*

To be more precise, place the real actor, the appellate court, in the subject position.

EXAMPLE

Revised:

In *In re Miller*, 670 P.2d 819 (Colo. Ct. App. 1983), the appellate court reversed the trial court because of the trial court's undue emphasis towards "motherly instincts."

---

appellate court	reversed	trial court
(subject)	*(verb)*	*(object)*

Occasionally, legal writers mistakenly end up with a combination that essentially means "X equals X"; that is, the subject or beginning of the sentence and object or end of the sentence are the same.

EXAMPLE

The purpose of the legislation is compensatory intent.

---

purpose   is   intent
(subject)   *(verb)*   *(predicate nominative)*[1]

There is virtually no difference between "the purpose of the legislation" and "the intent of the legislation." More than likely, the writer intended to say that the purpose of the legislation was to compensate someone.

EXAMPLE

Revised:

The purpose of the legislation is to compensate victims of such crimes.

Part of matching the right subject with the right verb is understanding how the legal system works. Knowing exactly what courts, juries, parties to litigation, legislatures, and agencies do and don't do makes it easier to select appropriate verbs.

For example, "the court finds" is the right combination for describing the action a court takes in a finding of fact. "The court held" is the right combination for describing the actions of a court in a particular case. "The court ruled" is the right combination for describing the actions a court takes on a particular issue, such as a motion or an objection, in a particular case. Courts can also "deny motions" or "grant injunctions"; they can "take something under advisement."

Courts can "apply the law," they can "apply a standard," and they can "apply a test"; they never "apply the facts." In other words, courts apply law to fact, not fact to law.

EXAMPLE

Incorrect:

Applying the facts of this case to the law, the court held that the defendant was negligent.

Correct:

Applying the law to the facts of this case, the court held that the defendant was negligent.

---

1. The term "predicate nominative" is used instead of "object" with linking verbs. See section 26.1.

In cases in which the court is both the decider of law and the trier of fact, courts perform an additional set of duties. When no jury is present, the court will "find" the criminal defendant guilty or innocent, and the court will "award" civil damages.

As both the decider of law and the trier of fact, the court may "make determinations" or simply "determine" something about the law or the facts. Even so, "determine" is more commonly used for findings of fact.

For cases up on appeal, appellate courts have a variety of actions they can perform. They can "affirm," "modify," "reverse," or "remand" a case; they can also "criticize," "distinguish," "explain," "follow," "limit," "overrule," or "question" the decisions in another case.

The court never takes on the role of one of the parties to litigation. Consequently, as a general rule, the court does not "claim," "allege," "assert," or "argue." The court is in a position to "say," not to "claim."

Even though it is technically incorrect to say "the court claimed," "the court asserted," or "the court argued," there are a few times when these combinations may be strategic word choices. In instances in which the writer is disagreeing with another court, for example, a writer may deliberately use "the court claimed" as a pejorative attack on another court's reasoning. The effect, of course, is the subtle undermining of the court's authority.

Another instance in which it is appropriate to use a combination like "the court argued" occurs when members of the same court differ. Consequently, a law professor or the author of a law review article may say "Justice X argued" to describe a position that justice took when trying to persuade the other members of the same court.

Juries, on the other hand, are charged with different tasks from judges. They "find" that a defendant is guilty or innocent, they "determine liability," and they "award damages," but they do not "rule" on the law. Consequently, "a jury found," "a jury determined," and "a jury awarded" are appropriate combinations. In a jury trial, the jury, not the judge, "renders a verdict," and the judge, not the jury, "enters a judgment" based on that verdict. In a bench trial, the judge "renders a verdict."

Defendants and plaintiffs perform certain acts as well. They "argue," "state," "ask," "claim," "contend," "allege," "assert," "respond," "rebut," and "counter," but they do not "apply" the law. That is for the court to do.

EXAMPLE

Incorrect:

Applying the majority rule, the defendant will argue that the benefit of having a healthy baby outweighs the burden.

Correct:

The defendant will argue that the court should apply the majority rule and hold that having a healthy baby outweighs the burden.

Either party to litigation can make a preliminary motion. Although you often hear, for example, that "the plaintiff made a motion for summary judgment," it is more concise to say "the plaintiff moved for summary judgment."

Legislatures, of course, perform entirely different functions from judges, juries, and litigants. The legislature may "enact a statute," it may "amend a statute," and it may "pass a law." It does not "hold" or "find." When it comes to policy, it is appropriate to say that the legislature "intended," "wanted to promote," "wanted to encourage," "wanted to prevent," or "wanted to protect."

Like judges, agencies "make determinations" (or just "determine"), and they "decide" things. Rarely does an agency "hold"; save "hold" for the few times when an agency issues an opinion. Even then, it is more likely to "rule." And of course, agencies perform many other functions such as "promulgate," "investigate," "propose," and "decide."

Perhaps the most glaring errors in word choice made by novice legal writers are those that stem from confusion over criminal and civil cases. Use "accused," "prosecuted," and "charged" for criminal cases. The defendant in a civil suit may be "sued" or "an action may be filed" against him or her; a civil suit defendant is not "accused," "prosecuted," or "charged."

Similarly, defendants in civil suits are not "found guilty or not guilty"; they are "found liable" or "not liable."

The outcome of a trial is a "judgment," not a "settlement." Use "settlement" for those agreements reached by parties through negotiation, not litigation. Parties may "settle out of court." See Exercise 24.D in the *Practice Book.*

Criminal Cases	*Civil Cases*
accused	sued
charged	action filed against
guilty	liable
not guilty	not liable

§24.1.7　Grammatical Ambiguities

Before leaving the topic of precision, we must consider those times when writing becomes ambiguous and imprecise because the writer has not paid close attention to the grammar of the sentence. Modifiers, in particular, can create unintended meanings because modifiers seem to be free-floating spirits that can find a home in many different spots in a sentence.

Consider, for example, that all-purpose and significant modifier "only." In the following nine-word sentence, "only" can find a home in no fewer than four places, but each time "only" moves, the meaning of the sentence changes.

EXAMPLE

The defendant talked to the plaintiff on July 1.

Only the defendant talked to the plaintiff on July 1. *(No one but the defendant talked to him.)*

The defendant **only** talked to the plaintiff on July 1. *(He did not write to him, threaten him, whatever; they only talked.)*

The defendant talked **only** to the plaintiff on July 1. *(The defendant did not talk to anyone else, just the plaintiff.)*

The defendant talked to the plaintiff **only** on July 1. *(The talk occurred only on one day, July 1.)*

"Only" is not the only modifier legal writers have to keep close tabs on; other single-word modifiers such as "almost," "even," "hardly," "just," "merely," "nearly," "scarcely," and "simply" can also float around in a sentence, radically changing meaning with each move.

The rule for "only" and other single-word modifiers is to place them immediately before the word(s) they modify. See section 26.6.1 for more on misplaced modifiers.

Other modifiers create ambiguity or uncertainty because they are "dangling"; that is, they don't have a noun in the sentence to modify.

EXAMPLE   DANGLING MODIFIER

By calling attention to the defendant's post-arrest silence, the jury was allowed to make prejudicial and false inferences.

Who, or for that matter what, called attention to the defendant's post-arrest silence? Grammatically, it appears that it was the jury because "jury" is the noun closest to that modifying phrase. Logically, though, we know that that meaning is unlikely. Who did it, then? The prosecutor? The defendant's counsel? The judge? We can only guess because the writer left that modifier dangling with no stated noun to modify. For a more detailed explanation of dangling modifiers, see section 26.6.2.

EXAMPLE

Possible Revision:

By calling attention to the defendant's post-arrest silence, the prosecutor allowed the jury to make prejudicial and false inferences.

Finally, a third type of modifier problem can also make legal writing ambiguous. Although known in grammar books as squinting modifiers, these modifiers are misnamed because they do not really squint; rather, they appear to be looking both forward and back. See section 26.6.3 for more on squinting modifiers.

EXAMPLE   **SQUINTING MODIFIER**

Taxpayers who file their returns promptly receive their refunds.

What does "promptly" modify? Does the filing occur promptly, or does the receipt of refunds occur promptly? It cannot be both because a modifier can modify only one grammatical element in a sentence.

EXAMPLE

Possible Revisions:

Taxpayers who promptly file their returns receive their refunds.

Taxpayers who file their returns receive their refunds promptly.

Taxpayers who promptly file their returns receive their refunds promptly.

In addition to modifiers, there are a few clauses that can sometimes be ambiguous. Be particularly careful with clauses that begin with "because." They can appear to be modifying either the main verb or a preceding clause.

EXAMPLE   AMBIGUOUS "BECAUSE" CLAUSE

Our client will not be able to assert that it is in his daughter's best interest to live with him because she is better adjusted to her home in Colorado.

Does the writer mean that the client won't be able to make this assertion because the daughter is better adjusted to the Colorado home, or does the writer mean that because she is better adjusted to the Colorado home, it is in her best interest to live with the client? See Exercise 24.E in the *Practice Book*.

EXAMPLE

Possible Revisions:

Because his daughter is better adjusted to her Colorado home, our client will not be able to assert that it is in her best interest to live with him.

Our client will not be able to assert that, because his daughter is better adjusted to her Colorado home, it is in her best interest to live with him.

---

§24.2   Conciseness

Imagine for a moment that you are at a great steak house, deciding what to order. It's a special occasion, so you order the best steak on the menu. When your meal arrives, however, you find that the steak is surrounded by an inch of fat. Appealing? Hardly. The meat itself may be tender and juicy, but you find it hard to appreciate its flavor with all that fat staring up off the plate at you. Why, you wonder, didn't the chef trim off the fat before your meal was served to you?

Wordy writing is like a steak surrounded by fat. It may have great analysis and brilliant arguments, but if you haven't trimmed the fat, the reader is still likely to find the writing unappealing.

The question for most legal writers is how to transform fatty writing into writing that is lean and appealing. The first and most important way to achieve this kind of strong efficiency is for the writer to keep the context of the writing uppermost in mind. Context here includes at least three considerations:

1.   who the reader is;
2.   what the reader wants to get out of the writing; and
3.   what the writer wants the reader to get out of the writing.

Remembering the context in which a piece of writing occurs will do more than anything else to keep the writing focused and therefore concise. Forgetting the context will lead to many wordiness problems, including the first three discussed in this chapter.

§24.2.1   Don't State the Obvious

Judges, lawyers, and most clients are well informed, busy people. They appreciate legal writers who recognize their intelligence and value their time. They don't want to spend time reading the legal equivalent of "the sky is blue" or "people breathe air," unless, of course, you have something new to say about what is obvious.

Wasting time with sentences in a memo or a brief like "Now I am going to discuss the cases that are relevant to this issue" or "The appellate court will not reconsider factual issues" annoys legal readers. It is a given that an office memo will discuss cases that are relevant to the issue; it is old news unworthy of both the writer's and reader's time to say that appellate courts don't retry a case on its facts.

Novice legal writers often state the obvious because it reminds them of the steps they must go through in legal analysis. For example, a writer who begins the discussion section of a memo with "To determine the answer to this question, we must first look at the rule that . . ." has not recognized that a legal reader would be shocked to find something other than the rule at this point in the memo.

Consider the following excerpt from a draft of a memo.

EXAMPLE

Our client bears the burden of establishing that the action meets the federal removal requirements. Some of these requirements are more important than others, but all are required before removal may occur. To understand these requirements, it is easiest to break down 28 U.S.C. § 1441(a) (1988) into its component parts and discuss each part separately.

Besides the wordiness that comes from the redundancy in the first two sentences — requirements are required — the last sentence is no more than an announcement that one should do the obvious: analyze the requirements. Such a statement to a legal reader is a bit like a restaurant adding to its menu that silverware will be provided. While such reminders to self are natural in an early draft, they should be edited out before the writing is submitted to the reader.

Novice and experienced legal writers often fall into the "stating the obvious" trap when they are trying to compose topic and transitional sentences within a discussion or argument section.

Suppose, for example, that a writer has just completed a paragraph about the holding, rationale, and facts of an analogous case. The writer now wants to compare the facts of the analogous case with those of the instant case. At first the writer may be tempted to begin with something like "*Moore* and our client's case are factually similar." This announcement should be quickly obvious, however, and unworthy of mention. What the writer needs to discuss in this topic sentence is the nature of these similarities or why those similarities suggest a certain outcome. A topic sentence more like "Similarly, in our case, the defendant also used tissue from the plaintiff's body to produce a commercially valuable product" not only moves the discussion along more quickly, it also helps the reader to see how the upcoming information should be used.

§24.2.2   Don't Start Too Far Back

Some novice legal writers fall prey to a cousin of the "stating the obvious" problem—starting too far back. They forget that there is common knowledge among legal readers and that these same readers don't need to be taken all the way back to the United States Constitution for every issue any more than they need to be reminded that we are a society governed by laws. In short, the writing problem often is one of determining where to begin and what not to say.

Consider the following example of starting too far back from a draft of a memo about a case in which criminal charges had been filed against the client who had photocopied a dollar bill and, after a friendly bet, had tried it in a change machine.

EXAMPLE

Counterfeiting has been classified as an offense affecting the administration of governmental functions because the power to coin money was expressly granted to Congress and denied to the states by the terms of the Constitution. Hence, counterfeiting is a federal crime and the penalty for passing counterfeit money is found in the United States Code. Congress has enacted statutes making counterfeiting a federal offense; the various counterfeiting crimes are defined by these statutes, and these statutes determine the essential elements of the respective crimes.

The background information in the preceding example is unnecessary. The writer of this excerpt seems to have forgotten who the reader is and what that reader is likely to know.

Writers who have a tendency to start too far back often fill their writing with background information that *they* needed in order to focus their ideas or to clarify a point. Even if they needed the information to analyze the problem, that does not automatically mean that their reader will need it too.

For example, because of a lack of experience, the writer may have had to do a fair amount of spade work to fill in a skimpy background in a given area of law. Unless the writer believes the reader needs the same kind of review or preliminary discussion, it should be omitted from the reader's version.

Furthermore, writers are obliged to save their readers from at least some of the blind alleys they explored. Legal writers who were successful writers as undergraduates often have a difficult time realizing this. In law there is no extra credit for arguments that don't work. Legal writing is not an account of all the work that the writer did; it is an account of what the reader needs to know.

Another way this tendency to write for oneself rather than for the reader manifests itself is in the narrative style some legal writers adopt. Rather than give the reader a carefully crafted explanation of the issue at hand, some writers tend to describe their own process of discovery. At worst, this narrative-of-their-discovery sounds like this: "First, I looked at _____; then I realized _____, which reminded me that _____, so I looked at _____ and found _____.

Happily, few legal writers err to that degree. More common, however, is an occasional intrusive phrase like "when researching our client's case, I proceeded under the assumption that . . . ," which can easily become "presumably."

Thus far, we have primarily discussed legal writing that starts too far back analytically. Occasionally legal writers start too far back historically. They give long, careful explanations of how a particular area of law has evolved when all the reader wants is a discussion of how the end result of that evolutionary process applies to the facts of a case at hand.

This is not to say that tracing the history of a statute or a judicial trend is never appropriate. The point is to consider your specific reader and that reader's purposes, and then ask yourself if it is appropriate in the document you are writing. Put another way, don't write a law review article when the senior partner has assigned you an office memo.

§24.2.3   Don't Overuse Quotations

When to quote and how much to quote—these are two questions that all legal writers wrestle with. Like many other issues in legal writing, there is a range of opinion about when quoting is appropriate, even required, and when the writer should merely paraphrase and cite to authority.

Most legal readers agree that relevant portions of statutes should be quoted. The trick, of course, is to pare the quotation down to that which is relevant.

In the following example, the writer has mistakenly quoted more of the statute than her reader needs. The case she is working on does not have anything to do with obstruction of a highway or the closing of a channel, but rather with whether a noisy aerobics club with patrons in skimpy attire is a private nuisance.

EXAMPLE   OVERQUOTING A STATUTE

In determining whether there is a cause of action for private nuisance, the court is guided by Washington Revised Code §7.48.010 (1996), which provides the following:

> The obstruction of any highway or closing the channel of any stream used for boating or rafting logs, lumber or timber, or whatever is injurious to health or indecent or offensive to the senses, or an obstruction to the free use of property, so as to essentially interfere with the comfortable enjoyment of the life and property, is a nuisance and the subject of an action for damages and other and further relief.

First, edit out all of the statute that is extraneous to the case:

> [t]he obstruction of any highway or closing the channel of any stream used for boating or rafting logs, lumber or timber, or whatever is injurious to health or indecent or offensive to the senses, or an obstruction to the free use of property, so as to essentially interfere with the comfortable enjoyment of the life and property, is a nuisance and the subject of an action for damages and other and further relief.

Appropriately pared down then, the quotation looks like this:

> [W]hatever is . . . indecent or offensive to the senses, or an obstruction to the free use of property, so as to essentially interfere with the comfortable enjoyment of the life and property, is a nuisance . . . .

Note the use of ellipses to indicate words omitted in the middle and at the end of the quotation. The brackets, which are used to show that the "w" was not capitalized in the original, also show that the original did not begin at the word "whatever." See section 27.5 for more on the use of ellipses and brackets in quotations.

Although there is a great deal of agreement about quoting relevant portions of statutes, there is some disagreement about whether common law should be set out verbatim. One rule of thumb is that if a specific phrase reappears in the cases, then that phrase has become the standard or familiar "rule" and should therefore be quoted.

Generally, it is best to paraphrase the holding and rationale and cite to authority. Occasionally, however, the particular language of the holding or court's reasoning is so apt or well stated that a quotation is effective. This tactic works best when used rarely.

Never quote facts of a case, although you may want to quote the exact words of a person in a fact statement when those words suggest the person's attitude, motive, or intention.

It may also be helpful to know what your reader prefers. Some readers like to see the original language; many would rather read a paraphrase that more directly addresses the issue at hand.

Remember, too, that many readers skim or even skip over quotations. If the only place a given point is made is in a quotation, then that point won't reach the quotation "skimmers" and "skippers."

When deciding how much to quote, consider as well what your purpose is. In persuasive writing, you will probably use fairly extensive quoting from the record to make points about errors and conflicting testimony. You might also use a few more quotations from analogous cases because they allow you to create emphasis and effective repetition. A well-written lead-in to a quotation, which makes your point, followed by a carefully selected quotation, which makes your point, allows you to make that point twice without being tedious. The same tactic used in objective writing, however, would be tedious.

The cardinal rule of quotations can be summed up as follows: *Quote only when the language itself is worth attention.* The language of statutes is always worth our attention; the specific language of common law is sometimes worth our attention; and, occasionally, the language of a court stating its holding or expressing its rationale is so memorable that it should not escape our attention. In all three instances, quote; otherwise, don't.

§24.2.4   Create a Strong Subject-Verb Unit

The quickest way to achieve an energetic yet lean style is to make sure that the subject-verb unit carries the core of meaning in the sentence. In other words, put the real action of the sentence in the verb; put the doer of that action in the subject.

All too frequently in ineffective legal writing, the real action of the sentence (what should be the verb) is buried in a noun. This practice of changing verbs to nouns, known as nominalization, tends to make sentences wordy and lifeless (see section 23.3). Because the real action in the sentence is somewhere other than the verb, the writer must find a substitute to fill the verb slot in the sentence, usually either a form of the verb "to be" or some other filler verb that expresses no real action. Such substitutes rob the sentence of its energy and crispness.

EXAMPLE

Our case <u>is</u> an illustration of this point.
    (verb)

Revised:

Our case <u>illustrates</u> this point.
       (verb)

The following examples are but a few of the many ways legal writers can make their writing more concise by finding the real action in the sentence. The trick is to ask yourself "what are the people really doing?" Are they "reaching" or are they "agreeing"? Is the court "making" something or "stating" something?

reached an agreement	→	agreed
made a statement	→	stated
perform a review	→	review
made a recommendation	→	recommended
supports an inference	→	infers
made the assumption	→	assumed

If the real doer of the action is somewhere other than in the subject, then the subject of the sentence is also inevitably wordy because the writer has had to manufacture some language to fill that slot in the sentence.

Sometimes writers fill the subject slot with wordy expletives like "there is," "there are," "there was," "there were," "it is," or "it was." Avoid these expletive constructions unless the point of the sentence is that something exists.

EXAMPLE

It was his intention to return to Maryland.

Revised:

He intended to return to Maryland.

When writers inadvertently slip into the passive voice (see section 23.1), they inevitably create a wordy sentence with a weak subject.

EXAMPLE

Authorization for the contract was given by the district manager.

Revised:

The district manager authorized the contract.

If the doer of the action is not in the sentence at all, then the sentence is not just wordy; it may be vague, imprecise, overly abstract, and wordy.

EXAMPLE

These are the facts that were used to make an assessment of your situation.

Revised:

I used these facts to assess your situation.

---

§24.2.5   Avoid Throat-Clearing Expressions

Frequently legal writers create wordy sentences because they fill both the subject and verb slots with throat-clearing expressions that add little, if any, meaning to the sentence. These expressions seem to have more to do with getting the writer warmed up to the task of articulating his or her point than with content.

EXAMPLE

It must be remembered that the statute requires that service be made at the dwelling house or usual place of abode.

Revised:

The statute requires that service be made at the dwelling house or usual place of abode.

Most but not all of these throat-clearing expressions fall into the pattern "It is _____ that":

It is expected that
It is generally recognized that
It is significant that
It is a known fact that
It is obvious that
It is believed that
It is felt that
It is essential that
It is crucial that
It is conceivable that

Some add a bit more content by using a verb other than "is," but waste the subject and verb slots on something other than the real actor and action.

EXAMPLE

<u>It would appear</u> that we can draw many parallels between *Walter*
(s)   (v)
and the instant case.

Revised:

Apparently, <u>we</u> <u>can draw</u> many parallels between *Walter* and the
       (s)   (v)
instant case.

The writer who revises out the throat-clearing "it would appear that" may then realize that even "apparently" is filler in this sentence.

EXAMPLE

Revised:

We can draw many parallels between *Walter* and the instant case.

Notice how the following throat-clearing expressions may be reduced to one word or completely edited out.

It seems more likely than not that	→ probably
It can be presumed that	→ presumably
It may be argued that	→ arguably *or* say who may argue

A fair number of the throat-clearing expressions spend time saying that someone should take note of something.

It should also be noted that
It is interesting to note that
It is worth noting that
It is crucial to note that
It is important to note that

If the writer can presume that the reader is already taking special note of all that is written, then such expressions are superfluous.

To sum up, then, a writer can create a strong, concise subject-verb unit in four ways:

1.　making the doer of the action the subject;
2.　making the real action the verb;
3.　avoiding expletive constructions; and
4.　avoiding throat-clearing expressions.

For an extended discussion on writing strong subject-verb units, see sections 23.2 and 23.3.

One common sense reminder: Do not edit out every conceivable bit of wordiness from your writing. If you do, your writing will become sparse and lifeless. The key is to develop judgment for when a given expression fleshes out a point and when it merely pads or weighs it down.

After attending to these first two considerations—focus and subject-verb units—legal writers should then look for other kinds of wordiness that can be revised and edited out. Note that the previous sentence said "revised and edited out." Being concerned about wordiness in the early stages of drafting is premature. First efforts and early drafts are, by nature, wordy and over-written.

In fact, at the beginning of the writing process, it may even be healthy for a writer to have an excess of words to work with. Thus, all the suggested strategies for conciseness in this section (with the important exception of considering the reader, the reader's goal, and the writer's goal) should be applied late in the drafting stage or in the revising or editing stages. See Exercise 24.F in the *Practice Book*.

§24.2.6　Don't Use Pompous Language

A traveling geological formation acquires little vegetative growth. Translation: A rolling stone gathers no moss.

If only that were true. All too often, legal writers who are really "rolling" through an analysis begin gathering all kinds of moss in the form of stilted, stuffy, overly formal words. Instead of valuing their ideas for their clarity and simplicity, legal writers sometimes feel that they have to "dress them up" so that they look lawyerly and sound erudite. They may have forgotten that their readers want to understand what they are saying, not be impressed by their vocabulary.

The following are but a few of the many words and expressions that legal writers use to dress up an otherwise simple point. Resist the temptation. Keep it simple. Your readers will love you for it.

allocate	→ give, divide
ascertain	→ make sure
cease	→ stop
commenced	→ began
constitute	→ make up
emulate	→ copy
endeavor	→ try
finalize	→ complete, finish, end
implement	→ carry out or put into effect
initiated	→ began
objective	→ goal, aim
originate	→ start
preclude	→ shut out, prevent
prior to	→ before
promulgate	→ issue, publish
pursuant	→ under
render	→ make, give
secure	→ get, take, obtain
subsequent	→ after
terminated	→ ended, finished
utilize	→ use
verification	→ proof

§24.2.7   Don't Repeat Yourself Needlessly

Language seems to be inherently redundant. Start trying to string a few words together and fairly soon some of those words will start making the same point. No matter how hard we try, words just keep coming out at a faster rate than the ideas, so naturally some words double up and say the same thing.

Some of this doubling up seems to come from a lack of faith in the words themselves. Somehow we don't quite trust them to mean what they say. For example, why does anyone ever say or write "close proximity"? Isn't proximity always close? How about "mutual cooperation"? When is cooperation not mutual?

What logic is there in the expression "sworn affidavit"? If an affidavit is a "sworn statement in writing," then is a "sworn affidavit" a "sworn sworn statement in writing"?

The following is a sampling of many common redundancies adapted from a list called "Dog Puppies" compiled by writer and editor Yvonne Lewis Day.[2] A few extra redundant phrases have been added by the authors. The word or words in parentheses should be omitted.

3 a.m. (in the morning)	(advance) warning
11 p.m. (at night)	alongside (of)
red (in color)	(and) moreover
(a distance of) twenty feet	appreciate (in value)
(a period of) six months	(as) for example
(absolute) guarantee	ascend (up)
(absolutely) clear	ask (a question)
(actual) experience	(as to) whether
(advance) planning	(at a) later (date)
at (the) present (time)	emergency (situation)
(basic) fundamentals	(empty) space
belief (system)	(end) result
(but) however	eradicate (completely)
(but) nevertheless	(essential) element
(close) scrutiny	(established) pattern
combine (together)	estimated (roughly) at
(complete) monopoly	(false) pretenses
(completely) destroyed	few (in number)
consensus (of opinion)	(foreign) imports
crisis (situation)	free (of charge)
(current) trend	(future) plans
daily (basis)	(general) public
depreciate (in value)	healing (process)
descend (down)	(important) essentials
(different) kinds	indicted (on a charge)
(direct) confrontation	(integral) part
during (the course of)	is (now) pending
during (the year of) 1957	join (together)
each (and every)	(local) residents
each (separate) incident	(major) breakthrough
(many) (different) ways	recur (again)
(mass) media	refer (back)
merged (together)	reflect (back)
my (own) opinion	reiterate (again)
my (personal) opinion	repeat (again)
never (at any time)	reported (to the effect) that
never (before)	revert (back)
off (of)	risk (factor)
(over) exaggerate	scrutinize (carefully)
(past) experience	(separate) entities
(past) history	shooting (incident)
(past) records	(specific) example

2. Adapted from "The Economics of Writing" by Yvonne Lewis Day, reprinted with permission from the August 1982 issue of *The Toastmaster*.

permeate (throughout)	(State's) prosecutor
(personal) friendship	(subtle) nuance
(plan) ahead	(sudden) outburst
postponed (until later)	(suddenly) exploded
(pre-) planned	(temporary) reprieve
probed (into)	(thorough) investigation
protest (against)	(underlying) (basic) assumption
(rate of) speed	(unexpected) surprise
	(usual) custom

Many redundancies and wordy expressions have an "of" in them. Some legal writers find that they can spot many wordy constructions simply by searching for "of"'s and editing out about half of them.

The preceding list of redundancies includes those expressions that are common to writers in all disciplines. The language of law is much worse; it has made redundancy an art. In fact, to the average reader, the lawyer's motto seems to be: "When in doubt, say it twice."

One source of these redundancies, according to David Mellinkoff,[3] has been the law's tendency to draw on more than one language at a time to describe a single idea. Consequently, we get tautologies such as "null and void" when either "null" or "void" alone would be sufficient.

buy (Old English) or purchase (French)
own (Old English) or possess (French)
minor (Latin) or child (Old English) or infant (French)
will (Old English) or testament (Latin)
property or chattels (French) or goods (Old English)
pardon (French) or forgive (Old English)
constable (French) or sheriff (Old English)
larceny (French) or theft or stealing (Old English)
attorney (French) or lawyer (Old English)

Mellinkoff adds that other redundancies such as "aid and abet," "part and parcel," and "safe and sound" come from law's early oral tradition when the rhythm and sound of the words made them not only more memorable but also more powerful in the minds of the people.[4]

The question for modern legal writers, then, is whether doubling phrases serve any purpose for their readers. Is there some important distinction between "perform" and "discharge"? Is "cease and desist" more memorable or more emphatic than just "cease" or "desist"?

If the answer to these questions is no, then what the writer has done by using doubling phrases is to double the words the reader must read. No new content, just more words—not exactly the way to win over a busy reader.

The last-ditch argument usually raised by the defenders of doubling phrases is that these phrases are "terms of art" and therefore precise,

---

3. David Mellinkoff, *The Language of the Law* 58 (1963).
4. David Mellinkoff, *supra,* 42-44.

untouchable descriptions of legal concepts. According to Mellinkoff, however, a legal term of art is "a technical word with a specific meaning."[5] He points out that most of the doubling phrases do not qualify as terms of art because they are either "not technical or have no specific meaning."[6]

If, in fact, a doubling phrase comes from an applicable statute or case law, then it may be a good idea for a legal writer to use it in the same form. It *may* be. The point is to choose words based on reasons, not on habit.

(Admittedly, some repetition in legal writing is done for effect. Used properly, repetition can be persuasive and even eloquent. Obviously, the discussion in this section refers to mindless, not deliberate, repetition.)

§24.2.8   Clean Out the Clutter

Some legal writers are word pack rats. They love words and collect them for their own sake. And like most pack rats, they are not particularly discriminating. They have extra words, often meaningless words, stashed in every nook and cranny of their writing.

Real pack rats have a right to the clutter they collect. After all, they are the only ones who live in it. Unfortunately, legal writers who are word pack rats force their readers to live in their clutter as well. Most readers would rather not.

Clutter in writing takes several forms. One of the most common is the extraneous prepositional phrase. Notice how easily prepositional phrases can begin to grow and multiply.

EXAMPLE

We are filing a motion for summary judgment.

Clutter:

We are in the process of filing a motion for summary judgment.

More Clutter:

At this point in time, we are in the process of filing a motion for summary judgment.

Still More Clutter:

At this point in time, we are in the process of filing a motion for summary judgment with the court.

---

5. David Mellinkoff, *Legal Writing: Sense & Nonsense* 7 (1981).
6. *Id.*

Eight words have quickly grown to twenty, with no real gain in content.

Again, as we saw in the earlier list of redundancies, the "of" preposition tends to be a frequent offender. Although we cannot write without any "of" phrases, in most people's writing about half of them can be eliminated or tidied up.

EXAMPLE

Persons with emphysema who voluntarily move to the city of Los Angeles have contributed to their own illness.

Revised:

Persons with emphysema who voluntarily move to Los Angeles have contributed to their own illness.

EXAMPLE

In the absence of any evidence of drugs on the premises, the police officers' actions can be given the interpretation of an invasion of privacy.

Revised:

Without evidence of drugs on the premises, the police officers' actions were an invasion of privacy.

Notice that the "of the" can be eliminated from some phrases and made into possessives in others.

all of the defendants	→ all defendants
some of the evidence	→ some evidence
none of the witnesses	→ no witness
the family of the victim	→ the victim's family
the position of the employees	→ the employees' position
the reasoning of the court	→ the court's reasoning

Before leaving the topic of extraneous "of" phrases, we should discuss their frequent companion: empty nouns. Nouns like "area," "aspect," "basis," "character," "circumstances," "field," "kind," "manner," "matter," "nature," "situation," and "type" rarely add any real content to writing. Most should be edited out.

the basis of your testimony	→	your testimony
the field of chemical engineering	→	chemical engineering
the nature of the defendant's argument	→	the defendant's argument

Other modifiers besides prepositional phrases like to clutter up sentences. Adverbs, in particular, like to creep in legal writing sentences, often in the disguise of precision. You can usually (there's one!) spot adverbs by their *-ly* ending, but look out for "quite," "rather," "somewhat," and "very," too.

EXAMPLE　　ADVERB CLUTTER

Basically, the witness seemed quite relaxed as she carefully outlined the rather long list of extremely technical calculations she had made.

Revised:

The witness seemed relaxed as she outlined the long list of technical calculations she had made.

Frequently, adverbs do add a shade of meaning that the writer intends. "The witness spoke softly" is not the same as "the witness spoke." The question for the careful legal writer, then, is (1) whether the adverb adds important content, and, (2) if so, whether the adverb is the best way to express that content. "Spoke softly" may be more precisely and more concisely written as "whispered," "murmured," or "mumbled."

One adverb that deserves special mention is "clearly." It is so overused in legal writing that one has to wonder if it has any meaning left. **Clearly,** it is time to think of a more sophisticated way to begin sentences. Legal writers **clearly** need to be more imaginative in their choice of modifiers for verbs. See Exercise 24.G in the *Practice Book*.

§24.2.9　Focus and Combine

Combining sentences and distilling ideas is an art. It does not come easily or quickly, but when it happens it is satisfying. If there is one magic formula for seeing what to cut and how to cut it, it is contained in the idea of focus, the first fundamental discussed in this section. Knowing exactly what your point is allows you to concentrate on that point and eliminate everything else.

Consider the following draft of a paragraph in a memo.

EXAMPLE

The fact that Acme is a lawful business will probably not be an issue in this case. Acme has satisfied all the necessary zoning and licensing requirements. Both parties will agree that Acme is a lawful business. **The probable issue, then, will be whether Acme's use of the property is reasonable.** Standard will argue that Acme's property use is unreasonable and therefore constitutes a nuisance; Acme will argue that the property use is reasonable and not a nuisance.

Once the writer realizes that the sentence in boldface is the focus of this paragraph, then he or she can begin combining and editing.

EXAMPLE

Revised:

Acme is a lawful business; it has satisfied all the necessary zoning and licensing requirements. The issue, then, will be whether Acme's use of the property is reasonable.

A clear focus will also help you decide which sentences can be combined and, when combining, which parts to keep as the main subject and verb and which parts to subordinate. For example, two sentences can often be combined into one by changing one of the sentences into a relative clause beginning with "which," "who," "whom," "whose," or "that."[7]

---

7. Use "who" for persons and the nominative case; use "whom" for the objective case; use "whose" when you need the possessive. Use "that" and "which" for things, but use "that" for restrictive clauses and "which" for nonrestrictive clauses.

EXAMPLE

Lewis appealed his sentence to Division II of the Court of Appeals. Division II of the Court of Appeals reversed and remanded for re-sentencing.

Combined:

Lewis appealed his sentence to Division II of the Court of Appeals, which reversed and remanded for resentencing.

EXAMPLE

The State's main witness was Arthur Hedges. Arthur Hedges agreed to testify after reaching a favorable plea bargain.

Combined:

The State's main witness was Arthur Hedges, who agreed to testify after reaching a favorable plea bargain.

In some cases, these same relative clauses can be reduced to phrases by deleting unnecessary who's, which's, and that's.

EXAMPLE

Her father, who is the president of the company, was indicted by a grand jury.

Revised:

Her father, the president of the company, was indicted by a grand jury.

Revised Again:

Her father, the company's president, was indicted by a grand jury.

EXAMPLE

The defendant lived in a room that was over the garage.

Revised:

The defendant lived in a room over the garage.

Frequently, two sentences can be combined when one of them defines or identifies part of the other.

EXAMPLE

For purposes of Georgia's wrongful death statute, a fetus is a child when the fetus is "quick." "Quick" is defined as having been perceived as moving in the mother's womb.

Combined:

For purposes of Georgia's wrongful death statute, a fetus is a child when the fetus is "quick," that is, having been perceived as moving in the mother's womb.

EXAMPLE

Upon entering the house, the police smelled phenyl-2-propanone. Phenyl-2-propanone is an organic chemical that is a necessary precursor ingredient of amphetamine.

Combined:

Upon entering the house, the police smelled phenyl-2-propanone, an organic chemical that is a necessary precursor ingredient of amphetamine.

A colon can sometimes be used to combine two sentences when the first sentence introduces a list or an explanation that will be given in full in the second sentence.

EXAMPLE

To assert the emergency doctrine, the defendant must be able to satisfy four elements. The four elements are (1) that he was suddenly confronted by an emergency; (2) that he did not cause the emergency by any negligence on his part; (3) that he was compelled to decide a course of action instantly; and (4) that he made such a choice as a reasonably careful person placed in such a position might have made.

Combined:

To assert the emergency doctrine, the defendant must satisfy the following four elements: (1) he was suddenly confronted by an emergency; (2) he did not cause the emergency by any negligence on his part; (3) he was compelled to decide a course of action instantly; and (4) he made such a choice as a reasonably careful person placed in such a position might have made.

EXAMPLE

Immediately after the assault, the plaintiff gave a description of his attacker to the police. He described his attacker as being a white female who was 5′10″, blonde, with blue eyes and a fair complexion.

Combined:

Immediately after the assault, the plaintiff gave the following description of his attacker to the police: a white female who was 5′10″, blonde, with blue eyes and a fair complexion.

Occasionally, two or more sentences that have the same subject can be combined by using compound verbs or by changing one set of verbs into participles.

EXAMPLE

The police officers discovered the laboratory used to make the amphetamine. The officers found a propane burner.

Combined (compound verbs):

The police officers discovered the laboratory used to make the amphetamine and found a propane burner.

> EXAMPLE

Deascon asks this court to review the lower court's decision. He argues that the reasons given by the trial court for imposing an exceptional sentence are not supported by the record.

Combined (participle):

Deascon asks this court to review the lower court's decision, arguing that the reasons given by the trial court for imposing an exceptional sentence are not supported by the record.

To reduce phrases to words, be on the lookout for wordy constructions like "the fact that," most phrases built around "regard," "of" prepositional phrases, and phrases that end in "that."

because of the fact that	→ because
despite the fact that	→ although, even though
due to the fact that	→ because
except for the fact that	→ except for
in spite of the fact that	→ although, even though
in view of the fact that	→ because, considering that
owing to the fact that	→ because
the fact that he asked	→ his question
in regard(s) to	→ about, concerning
with regard to	→ about, concerning
by means of	→ by
by virtue of	→ by, under
for the purpose of	→ to
has the option of	→ may
in compliance with your request of	→ as requested, as you requested
in favor of	→ for
in the absence of	→ without
in the neighborhood of	→ about, approximately
on the basis of	→ from
over the signature of	→ signed by
in the event that	→ if
for the reason that	→ because

Legal writers are divided over whether (or not) to omit the "or not" in the expression "whether or not." Notice, for example, that the "or not" can be deleted from the preceding sentence with no loss in meaning. In such cases, it is better to delete it. Sometimes, however, the sentence becomes nonsensical if the "or not" is omitted.

EXAMPLE

Mr. Smith intends to pay for his daughter's college education whether or not the court awards him full custody.

Usually, the "or not" can be omitted when the word "if" can substitute for "whether." Retain "or not" if the substitution of "if" for "whether" changes the meaning, as it does in the example above.

Some phrases are deadwood and can be omitted or replaced with one word. See Exercises 24.H, 24.I, and 24.J in the *Practice Book*.

at this point in time	→ omit or use "now"
at that point in time	→ omit or use "then"
in this day and age	→ omit or use "now," "nowadays"
in the case of	→ omit or use "in"
in reality	→ omit
in terms of	→ omit
in a very real sense	→ omit

§24.2.10   Avoid Excessive Conciseness

The question, of course, with the reducing and combining advocated in this section, is how much is too much? When does editing for conciseness improve the writing, and at what point does it hinder the readability of sentences?

Properly done, reducing and combining can make writing more focused and concise. Overdone, it can ruin writing by packing it too tightly and by creating overly long and overly complicated sentences.

One result of overdone combining is compound noun phrases, also known as noun strings. Like those Russian dolls that have a seemingly endless progression of smaller and smaller dolls inside each doll, compound noun phrases have modifier modifying modifier modifying modifier to the point that the reader forgets where the whole thing began. Such overpacking in a sentence strains even the most cooperative reader.

The prize for compound noun phrases goes to an insurance service that offers the following policy:

LIMITED PRACTICE LAWYERS PROFESSIONAL INDEMNITY INSURANCE
DISCIPLINARY PROCEEDINGS DEFENSE COVERAGE

One cannot help but wonder if the title is any indication of how readable the policy itself is.

Here is an example from a brief to the Supreme Court.

EXAMPLE

Alabama's silent prayer statute's failure to satisfy "the purpose" prong of the *Lemon* test renders it unconstitutional.

Revised:

Alabama's silent prayer statute fails to satisfy "the purpose" prong of the *Lemon* test; therefore, it is unconstitutional. *OR*

Alabama's statute on silent prayer fails . . . .

Notice that in the preceding example a nominalization, "failure," became the verb and the revision eliminated one of the possessives, "statute's." Because multiple possessives are always awkward, avoid them whenever possible.

Also remember that some nominalizations can be unpacked and improved by changing the noun into the participle, or adjective form, as is done with "exclusion" in the following example.

EXAMPLE

a broad prior conviction evidence exclusion rule

Revised:

a broad rule excluding evidence of prior convictions

Notice too from the preceding revision that not all "of" prepositional phrases should be eliminated.

Like all tricks of the trade, then, editing for conciseness must be used with discretion and an eye toward what the reader will find easier to read and understand.

§24.3   Plain English v. Legalese

> Early in law school there seems to be an almost irresistible urge to clothe everything in the diction and style of the most incomprehensible insurance policy.
>
> —Norman Brand and John O. White[8]

---

8. *Legal Writing: The Strategy of Persuasion* 107 (1988).

> To communicate upon matters of technicality and
> complexity . . . is impossible with (and for) the
> nontechnical and simple person; and to use the
> language of simplicity in addressing a learned
> profession is to insult that profession.

—Ray J. Aiken[9]
"Let's Not Oversimplify Legal Language"

Above are but samplings of the heated, ongoing debate over legalese. Proponents of the traditional style of legal writing argue that legalese is part of the specialized discourse of lawyers and that it serves worthwhile purposes for lawyers and their readers. Proponents of "plain English," on the other hand, argue that legalese is responsible for many of the ills that plague legal writing, not the least of which is that lay readers cannot readily comprehend what their attorneys are writing.

If you read the law journals, you may get the impression that the advocates for simplified, plain English are winning the debate. Article after article decries the use of such mainstays of legal writing as Latin phrases and legal argot. Perhaps a more significant indication that legalese is on the way out is that several state legislatures have passed legislation requiring "simple," "clear," "understandable" language that uses "words with common and everyday meanings" in consumer contracts and insurance policies.[10]

If you read the writing of most practicing attorneys, however, you might get the impression that the advocates for the traditional style of legal writing have won the day. Corporate lawyers rely heavily on boilerplate, and most practitioners seem to have absorbed the language of their law school casebooks. They may have heard that legalese is dead, but they don't write like they believe it.

And so the debate rages on, and although the plain English v. legalese issue has been before the collective "court" of legal professionals and their clients for some time now, we have yet to reach a verdict. The trend seems to be toward plain English, but the resistance is strong. In short, in the matter of Plain English v. Legalese, the jury is still out.

So what is a legal writer to do? While the profession continues to wrestle with this issue, we would like to offer a simple test for determining whether any given bit of legalese should be used or relegated to the dustbin.

The Test

Given the document's reader, writer, purpose, and surrounding circumstances, does the legalese increase or decrease communication between writer and reader?

---

9. *Let's Not Oversimplify Legal Language*, 32 Rocky Mtn. L. Rev. 364 (1960).

10. *See, for example*, Minn. Stat. § 325G.30.3, N.Y. Gen. Oblig. Law § 5-702, N.J. Rev. Stat. § 56:12-1, Conn. Gen. Stat. §§ 38-68s-x.

Under this test, if both reader and writer understand the phrase *res ipsa loquitur* and find it a concise way of expressing a concept, then the phrase is effective legal writing. If, on the other hand, the same phrase sends a client reader scurrying to a dictionary, then the virtue of its conciseness is outweighed by its lack of clarity for that reader. Thus, in the second context, the same phrase is ineffective legal writing.

With the test as a backdrop, let's examine legalese and its characteristics.

First of all, there is no agreed-upon definition of "legalese." One law review author has defined a legalism as "a word or phrase that a lawyer might use in drafting a contract or a pleading but would not use in conversation with his wife." George R. Smith, *A Primer of Opinion Writing, for Four New Judges*, 21 Ark. L. Rev. 197 (1967).

With a bit of editing, we can modify the definition to omit the sexism and to describe legalese: Legalese is language a lawyer might use in drafting a contract or a pleading but would not use in ordinary conversation. In short, legalese is distinct from human talk; it is law talk.

What then are the characteristics that distinguish law talk from ordinary human talk?

Group 1

- long sentences, especially those with excessive modification and qualification
- abstractions as subjects — the real "doers" or actors are often omitted or relegated to a prepositional phrase
- weak verbs — both passive voice and nominalizations sap the sentences of their natural energy

Group 2

- archaic word choice
- foreign phrases
- terms of art and argot
- use of "said" and "such" as articles
- omission of articles, especially "the"
- use of "same" as a noun
- avoidance of the first and second person (I, we, you)
- doubling phrases

The first group of characteristics primarily involve syntax, that is, the sentence structure. Traditionally, legal writing has been known for its overly long sentences (see section 23.5), with multiple intrusive phrases that added extensive modification and qualification. Frequently, readers had a hard time comprehending these sentences because either the subject or verb of these sentences was delayed by numerous details and exceptions. Furthermore, the subject and its verb were so far apart that the reader had difficulty finding the actor and action on which to hang all this modification and elaboration (see section 23.4).

Adding to the confusion were other characteristics, such as nominalizations (see sections 23.2 and 23.3) and passive voice (see section 23.1), that disguised the real actor and action in the sentence. Nominalizations (creating the noun form of a verb by adding a noun ending such as -tion) and passive voice teamed up to give the sentences a static quality: Nobody was home in traditional legal sentences, or if they were, they weren't doing anything.

The second group of characteristics occurs at the word level. They are more about vocabulary: Is it better to use a formal word, an unfamiliar word, a foreign word, or a simple word? When is a word or phrase an unnecessary legalism, and when is it a term of art? When is one word enough, and when should it be bolstered by one or more synonyms to cover every possible contingency?

These characteristics of legalese are the focus of this section.

§24.3.1 Archaic Word Choice

In his article *The End of Legalese: The Game Is Over*, Robert W. Benson described legalese as "the medieval armor of lawyers." Robert W. Benson, *The End of Legalese: The Game Is Over*, XIII Rev. of Law & Soc. Change 519, 522 (1984-85). His phrase is apt for a number of reasons, not the least of which is that the some of the language of law is straight out of the Middle Ages.

When, for example, have you heard a person on the street say "herein" or "witnesseth"? What is achieved then by retaining Old or Middle English words? A legal ring to the words? If so, at what cost? If clarity is the price the writer and reader pay, then the price is too high. If, on the other hand, the archaic language somehow gives the document the formality it needs without sacrificing clarity, then perhaps the language is suitable for the occasion.

Consider, for example, a story told by an attorney who was an advocate of plain English. Her client wanted her to draft a will. She drafted two versions: a plain English version and a traditional version. Although the attorney recommended the plain English version, the client selected the traditional version because it "sounded like a will." For this document and its purpose, the formality of "I hereby give, devise, and bequeath" was appropriate. It created the tone, the solemnity, and the timeless quality that the client wanted.

But what about client letters, office memoranda, and briefs to the court? Although these documents are formal in nature, do they require archaic language? Most authorities on legal language agree that they don't. In fact, research shows that appellate judges, who are the readers of the most formal of these documents, appellate briefs, strongly prefer plain English.[11]

---

11. Robert W. Benson & Joan B. Kessler, *Legalese v. Plain English: An Empirical Study of Persuasion and Credibility in Appellate Brief Writing*, 20 Loyola of Los Angeles L. Rev. 301–319 (1987).

The standard argument that "if I don't sound like a lawyer, I won't be believable" was strongly refuted in this research. In fact, the research showed that the judges were more likely to categorize writing in legalese as "poorly worded, unconvincing, vague, not concise, unpersuasive, uncreative, unscholarly, from a non-prestigious firm or an ineffective appellate advocate, unpowerful, incomprehensible and ambiguous."[12]

The legalese-ridden documents that the judges read included Old and Middle English words like "thereby" and "herein." Below is a fairly comprehensive list of other Old and Middle English words and phrases that should be avoided in client letters, office memoranda, and briefs. In some cases, a more appropriate substitute word or phrase follows in italics.

Compound words that begin with *here-*, *there-*, and *where-*

hereafter	thereabout	whereas[13]
herebefore	thereafter	whereat
hereby	therefrom	whereby
herein	therein	wherefore
hereinabove → *above*	thereof	wheresoever
hereinafter	thereon	wherein → *there*
hereinunder → *below*	thereto	whereof
hereof	thereunto	whereon
heretofore → *before,*	therewith	whereupon
up to		
this time		
hereunder		

herewith (enclosed herewith → *enclosed*)

aforementioned (omit or substitute *previously mentioned*)
aforesaid (omit or substitute *above*)
behoove → *to be necessary, to be proper*
comes now the plaintiff
foregoing (for the foregoing reasons) → *for these reasons*
forthwith → *immediately*
henceforth[14]
hitherto → *until this time, up to now*
pursuant to → *under or according to*[15]

---

12. *Id.* p. 315.

13. "Whereas" can often be eliminated or replaced with "because," "considering that," "while on the contrary," or "inasmuch as." At other times, it can be used but with care. Frequently, writers use it without seeming to know what it means. At times, "whereas" is the best choice; for example, using "whereas" is certainly better than the wordy "in view of the fact that."

14. Many would not object strenuously to "henceforth," but find it a bit dated. "From now on" is a satisfactory plain English substitute.

15. Sometimes "pursuant to" is a useful legalism that lawyers and judges find acceptable. Avoid, however, with nonlawyers.

thence → *from there, from that place, time or source, for that
　　reason*
thenceforth → *from that time on, after that*
thereafter → *from that time on*
to wit → *namely, that is to say*
whence → *from where*
whensoever → *whenever*

§24.3.2　Foreign Phrases

Many of the Latin phrases that appear in legal writing create a barrier
between writer and reader. Only a student on the way home from Latin
class (or possibly a lawyer specializing in property) will be comfortable
with a phrase like *Cujus est solum ejus est usque ad coelum et usque
ad infero*. The rest of us would do one of two things: use the context to
try to figure out what the writer meant or reach for the *Unabridged
Black's Law Dictionary*. In either case, the Latin has not aided communication. Even the conscientious consulter of the dictionary will understand the writer's meaning only by looking up the explanation the writer
should have given the reader in the first place.

More often, the Latin is not so much confusing as it is unnecessary.
Why say "*supra*" when "above" works just as well? Unnecessary Latin
phrases make the writing appear stuffy and pretentious. When a simple
English equivalent can be used without loss of meaning, use it.

Latin Words or Phrases to Avoid

arguendo → for the sake of argument
et al. → and others
infra → below
inter alia → among other things
per curiam → by the court
res gestae → use modern rules of evidence to characterize state-
　　　　　　 ments
seriatum → in turn, serially, one after another
sui generis → unique
supra → above
viz. (abbreviation for "videlicet") → namely or that is to say

Not all Latin should be replaced, however. Some Latin phrases
("gratis," "per diem") are sufficiently familiar to educated readers that
their use does not impair communication. In fact, these phrases are often
accepted as English.

Other Latin phrases ("amicus curiae," "per se") are equally familiar
to lawyers and judges and can be used for these readers without a second
thought. They are the "shop talk" of law. The same phrases, though, may
need substitutes or explanation for client readers.

A final group of Latin phrases are so useful that few are willing to discard them. "Respondeat superior," for example, sums up a whole doctrine in tort law; "res judicata" is a fundamental rule of Civil Procedure. While these phrases will probably need clarification for readers who are not lawyers, the average legal reader would find them not only familiar but indispensable.

Latin Words or Phrases to Keep for Readers Who Are Lawyers

ad hoc	mandamus
ad litem	modus operandi
amicus curiae	nexus
bona fide	nolo contendere
caveat emptor	non sequitur
certiorari	penumbra
consortium	per diem
corpus delecti	per se
de facto, de jure	post mortem
de novo	prima facie
dicta, dictum	pro bono
ex parte	quorum
ex post facto	quid pro quo
gratis	res ipsa loquitur
habeas corpus	res judicata
id. (abbreviation for *idem*)	respondeat superior
in limine	scintilla
in personam	stare decisis
ipso facto	supersedeas
mens rea	

Of course, Latin is not the only foreign language that appears frequently in legal writing. Thanks to the Norman Conquest and its subsequent effect on the language of England, French plays an important role in the language of law.

The vast majority of the words derived from French are common terms that are already fully incorporated into English and as such pose few if any problems for readers ("assault," "defendant," "heir," "larceny," "mortgage," "plaintiff," "pleadings," "tort," "reprieve," and "verdict," to name just a few).

More likely as troublemakers are those words and phrases that are Old French. For the following French terms, use the suggested plain English substitutes.

alien or *aliene* (used as a verb) → to convey or to transfer
cestui que trust → beneficiary
cy-pres → as near as possible
en ventre sa mere → in its mother's womb

en vie → alive
feme covert → married woman
feme sole → single woman
save → except
seisin → possession or ownership

As we saw with Latin, though, there are French words and phrases that are terms of art for which we have no satisfactory plain English substitute. Although they will almost certainly require explanation for readers who are not lawyers, they are indispensable vocabulary for a lawyer.

French Words and Phrases to Keep

estoppel   laches   voir dire

Unfortunately, not all authorities on legal language agree about what is and is not a legal term of art. *De son tort*, for example, from the phrases *executor de son tort* and *trustee de son tort*, is sometimes replaced by the English equivalent "of his own wrong" and at other times treated as an indispensable phrase.

§24.3.3   Use of Terms of Art and Argot

In the preceding discussion on foreign words and phrases, we suggested that some Latin and French terms simply muddied the water for legal readers while others were indispensable. The difference between the dispensable and indispensable Latin and French was whether there was a satisfactory plain English substitute.

Terms of art, by definition, do not have satisfactory substitutes. Even though one might be able to give a short explanation of a term of art's meaning, complete understanding would take an extensive explanation.

A term of art, according to David Mellinkoff, is "a technical word with a specific meaning."[16] In *The Dictionary of Modern Legal Usage*, "terms of art" are defined as "words having specific, precise significations in a given specialty."[17]

Given these requirements, it should not be surprising that there are relatively few terms of art in law. Still, many lawyers seem to think that just about any word or phrase frequently used by lawyers or written into cases is a term of art. This misperception leads to a far more serious misperception that all these false terms of art are somehow precise and therefore good legal writing.

---

16. David Mellinkoff, *The Language of the Law* 16 (1963) (quoting *Webster's New International Dictionary* (2nd ed. 1934).

17. Bryan A Garner, *The Dictionary of Modern Legal Usage* 872 (2d ed. 1995).

In fact, what we see here is mistaken cause/effect reasoning. If a term is specific and precise, then it may be a term of art, not the reverse: It sounds like a term of art; therefore, it must be specific and precise.

"Certiorari" is an excellent example of a true term of art. Perhaps a satisfactory short explanation is that it refers to the order written by a higher court to a lower court requiring the lower court to produce a certified record of a certain case.

For a full understanding of "certiorari," however, one would have to lay out a much larger context: how discretionary review and the appellate process work in general and specifically how the Supreme Court of the United States chooses cases it wishes to hear.

Argot, by contrast, is legal jargon, or lawyers' shop talk. It is the shorthand of law, the quick-and-easy term or phrase that lawyers use among themselves. For this reason, argot is inappropriate when communicating with nonlawyers. Used with discretion, it can be effective communication among lawyers.

"Case on all fours" is a classic example of argot. Other common examples include "adhesion contract," "attractive nuisance," "Blackacre," "case at bar," "case-in-chief," "clean hands," "cloud on title," "court below," "four corners of the document," "horse case," "instant case," "off the record," "pierce the corporate veil," "reasonable man," "res ipsa loquitur," "sidebar," and "Whiteacre."

In writing, avoid argot that has degenerated into slang. "Cert denied" or "resipsey case" sounds cute rather than professional.

§24.3.4   Use of "Said" and "Such" as Adjectives

If you were a stand-up comic trying to make fun of the way lawyers write, all you would have to do is put "said" or "such" before almost every noun.

EXAMPLE

It was snowing and icy on January 9, 1998, when Mr. Smith, the plaintiff, was driving home from work along a deserted highway in his 1995 Honda Accord with chains on said vehicle's tires. Suddenly said plaintiff felt said vehicle jerk violently, and then said plaintiff heard a loud clanging of metal. Such clanging continued until such time as said plaintiff was able to pull said vehicle over to the shoulder of said highway. Upon inspection of said vehicle, said plaintiff realized that such clanging was caused when said chains had broken and then wrapped around the axle of said plaintiff's said vehicle. "Oh, *!?/*!" said said plaintiff.

In client letters, office memos, and briefs, rigorously avoid all use of "said" as an adjective. Replace with "the," "that," "this," or an appropriate, unambiguous pronoun.

"Such" can be used as an adjective with categories of persons, things, or concepts. For example, "such instances of neglect," "such witnesses as these," and "such an example of compassion" is not legalese. These phrases are good writing.

Do not, however, use "such" with singular nouns that are not categories of persons, things, or concepts but rather specific references to the same, previously mentioned singular noun. For example, "such payment" should be revised to "this payment"; "such stock certificate" should be changed to "the stock certificate."

§24.3.5   Omission of the Article "The"

Occasionally, one sees legal writing that has the sound of a police report.

EXAMPLE

Defendant denies that she hit plaintiff.

This rather terse style is achieved by omitting the article "the." The reason for omitting "unnecessary" articles in police reports may be that information needs to be recorded on forms. Happily, lawyers do not have such requirements, so they do not have to sacrifice a fluid writing style.

EXAMPLE

Revised:

The defendant denies that she hit the plaintiff.

---

§24.3.6   Use of "Same" as a Pronoun

The phrase "acknowledging same" smacks of legalese. Replace "same" with "it," "them," or the noun "same" is replacing. These substitutes can be used whenever "same" is used as a pronoun.

EXAMPLE

The defendant first threatened Ms. Tyler with the tire wrench and then used same to smash her windshield.

Revised:

The defendant first threatened Ms. Tyler with the tire wrench and then used it to smash her windshield.

---

§24.3.7   Absence of First- and Second-Person Pronouns

By convention, legal writers use the pronouns "I," "me," "we," "us," "you" and "your" rarely. Occasionally, in a client letter, a lawyer might write "I recommend" or, more commonly, "in my opinion." Much less frequent would be the phrase "I think" or (horrors!) "I feel" (the common explanation for the horrified reaction being that lawyers are paid to think, not to feel) in an office memorandum. Pity the naive attorney, though, who writes in a brief "you should rule" or "you must determine."

To get around the I's and you's in legal writing, because after all it is I, the writer, who is recommending and thinking, and it is you, the judge and reader, who is ruling and determining, legal writers resort to all sorts of linguistic gymnastics. Before discussing which of these gymnastic moves work and which lead to new problems, let's examine why the first- and second-person pronouns are *persona non grata* in legal writing.

First of all, remember the long-standing tradition of avoiding first and second person in any formal writing. While the recommendations about this issue have relaxed considerably for undergraduate research papers and the like, the original rationale applies to most legal writing. The facts and the application of law to those facts are the focus of attention for both writer and reader. As such, they should occupy center stage.

Second, the use of "I" and "you" often creates an inappropriately informal tone. While a bit of informality and familiarity may be appropriate in some client letters and an occasional office memo, generally these documents should be formal and professional in tone. (Remember, though, formal does not mean stilted.)

Third, indiscreet use of "you" in client letters and especially in briefs may make the writer appear arrogant, pushy, and disrespectful. Readers rarely like to be ordered around. Not surprisingly, "you must" or "you should" language often backfires. Rather than encouraging the reader to act as the writer wants, such language sets the stage for resistance to the writer's recommendations and arguments.

In the following example, the inclusion of "my," "I," and "you" is both distracting and inappropriate. The first-person references incorrectly place the emphasis on the writer, and the second-person references may even anger the judge.

EXAMPLE

In my research, I found that you must apply Washington Rule of Evidence 609(a) to determine the admissibility of evidence of a criminal defendant's prior convictions.

Revised:

In Washington, the admissibility of evidence of a criminal defendant's prior convictions is governed by Washington Rule of Evidence 609(a). *OR*

Washington Rule of Evidence 609(a) governs the admissibility of evidence of a criminal defendant's prior convictions.

The first revision of the example illustrates one of the common gymnastic moves that legal writers use to avoid the first- and second-person pronouns: use of the passive voice. While the passive voice is a good choice in some instances (see section 23.1.3), it can easily lead to dull, lifeless writing. Use with care.

Some legal writers use the pronoun "one" to get around using "you." This tactic works reasonably well as long as the writer does not use "one" several times and then shift—incorrectly—from "one" to the third-person pronoun "he," "she," "him," "her," "it," "they," or "them."

EXAMPLE

Incorrect:

One should avoid first-person pronouns in his or her legal writing.

Revised:

One should avoid first-person pronouns in one's legal writing.

Better:

One should avoid first-person pronouns in legal writing.

In office memos, some writers slip into a *we-they* style as they describe the various arguments the two sides can make. While this practice is accepted in some firms, it can easily be avoided by simply naming the parties.

Thus, instead of "they will argue . . . and we will rebut this argument by showing . . . ," legal writers can easily say "Smith will argue . . . and Jones will rebut this argument."

Frequently, a writer of an office memo is tempted to use "we" in the following situation. The writer has just explained the law or just described an analogous case to the reader. Now the writer wants the reader to follow along as he or she applies that law or case.

The writer might begin by saying "If we apply the plain meaning of statute X to our facts, we can see that the photocopy is a similitude" or "If we compare the actions of the defendant in *Smith v. Jones* to the actions of Brown, we can see that Brown, unlike Jones, knew he was lying to the F.B.I." This is not a serious writing sin, of course, but it is one that can be easily avoided.

Unfortunately, some writers try to write around the "we" in such instances and end up with a dangling modifier. See section 26.6.2.

EXAMPLES

Incorrect:

Applying the plain meaning of statute X to our facts, the photocopy is a similitude.

Comparing the actions of the defendant in *Smith v. Jones* to the actions of Brown, Brown, unlike Jones, knew he was lying to the F.B.I.

There is a better way. The writer does want the reader to follow along as he or she makes the next logical connection, but the writer also wants to suggest that the court must see the same logical connection. Therefore, it makes good sense, both in terms of writing style and strategy, to say "If the court applies the plain meaning of statute X to our facts, it will find . . ." or "Applying the plain meaning of statute X to our facts, the court will find . . . ."

One final note about first- and second-person pronouns: Because these pronouns have gained acceptance in some other types of formal writing, they are likely to gain increasing acceptance in all but the most formal documents in legal writing. Watch the trend, and you will be able to adjust accordingly, especially if you keep in mind the test of always considering your reader, purpose, and the document's surrounding circumstances when making decisions about writing.

§24.3.8   Some Final Words About Legalese

In short, like most questions concerning law, the question "is legal-ese good or bad?" is best answered "it depends." It depends on the reader; it depends on the writer; it depends on the purpose of the document; it depends on the circumstances surrounding the document.

The thinking lawyer does not adopt the style of his or her prede-cessors without examining whether that style aids or hinders communi-cation. Nor does the thinking lawyer automatically edit out all legalese simply because a few law review articles suggest it is passé or worse.

Different situations may require different choices. All will require a deliberate choice. See Exercise 24.K in the *Practice Book*.

§24.4   Gender-Neutral Language

Contrary to what many legal writers believe, the jury is in on the issue of gender-neutral language. Authorities as different as *The New York Times Manual of Style and Usage*, the United States Department of La-bor's *Dictionary of Occupational Titles*, and the United Church of Christ agree that gender-neutral language is here to stay.

The language of law, while a bit slower to change than the language of journalism, government, and even religion, has also begun to move in the direction of gender-neutral word choices. Numerous states now re-quire gender-neutral language in their legislation. Increasingly, legislators, practitioners, and jurists are realizing that some language they previously considered to be inclusive has just the opposite effect: It excludes.

Exclusion stemming from sexist language is not a new issue. For years feminists have argued against the subtle conditioning and precon-ceptions sexist language promotes. For example, if the members of a hiring committee agree that they should get "the best man for the job," are they as likely to select a woman to fill the position? What if these same members of the hiring committee simply refer to the person they want to hire as "he"? "He must be willing to work long hours." "If his previous experience includes a judicial clerkship, he will know the courts." "Can he bring in his fair share of clients?" Many are arguing that such uses of the masculine pronouns to refer supposedly to both sexes subtly, or not so subtly, suggest that the new hire will be male.

And how about language closer to law? If "judge" is defined as "an officer so named in his commission, who presides in some court . . . ,"[18] does that definition encourage women to aspire to the bench? If the law itself refers to "a landowner" by the masculine pronoun "he," does this reference somehow suggest that women do not own land?

Sexist language in law hurts women. There is no doubt about that. But it hurts men too. If we unconsciously refer to perpetrators of aggres-sive acts with masculine nouns and pronouns, even when the gender of

---

18. *Black's Law Dictionary* 435 (6th ed. abridged 1990).

the attacker is unknown, we set ourselves up to assume that the attacker was male. If men are referred to by their last names and women are referred to by their first names, the reader is being encouraged to think of men objectively and women sympathetically.

Aside from the significant issues of fairness and prejudice, legal writers should also avoid sexist language because it is often ambiguous and imprecise. Does the sentence "Lieutenant Perkins is the woman pilot who was the first to challenge the Air Force's minimum height requirement for pilots" mean that Lieutenant Perkins was the first of all pilots to challenge this requirement, or does it mean that she was the first of that group of pilots who are women to challenge it? If a corporation's policy on sexual harassment reads, "Any man who sexually harasses a fellow employee will be fired immediately," does this policy mean that women employed by the corporation are free to harass "fellow employees"? Does it mean that men and women may harass employees that are not "fellows"?

Perhaps the most immediate and pressing reason for using gender-neutral language is the very real possibility that you may offend some readers if you don't.

In short, there are at least four good reasons for making the effort to use gender-neutral language: fairness, clarity, precision, and reader reaction. These reasons more than justify the effort it takes to master the five problem areas legal writers face when trying to use gender-neutral language.

§24.4.1 Generic Use of "Man"

Avoid using the term "man" to mean all people or all of humanity. Similarly, avoid using expressions and other derivatives built on this broad use of the term *man*.

Sexist Terms	*Gender-neutral Substitutes*
man (noun) or mankind	people, humanity, human race, human beings, human population, *homo sapiens*
man (verb) as in "man the office"	staff, operate, run, work
a man who . . .	an individual who . . . , a person who . . . , one who . . . , someone who . . .
the common man, the average man, the man in the street	the common individual, the average citizen, the person in the street, ordinary people
man-made	hand-crafted, handmade, manufactured, machine-made, fabricated, synthetic, created

Sexist Terms	*Gender-neutral Substitutes*
manpower	human energy, human resources, work force, personnel, staff
man-sized job	big job, enormous job
man-to-man	face-to-face, person-to-person

§24.4.2   Generic Use of "He"

It used to be standard practice for grammar and writing texts to advise writers to use masculine pronouns when the gender of the antecedent noun or pronoun could be either male or female. Now most grammar and writing texts advise writers to avoid the generic use of "he." Unfortunately, though, we have been unable to agree on a gender-neutral singular pronoun as a substitute. Until we do, we will need to use one or more of several approaches for avoiding the generic use of the masculine pronouns.

a.   Revise the Sentence So That the Antecedent and Its Pronoun Are Plural

EXAMPLE

The holding suggests that a defendant waives his constitutional rights only through an affirmative or overt act.

Revision:

The holding suggests that defendants waive their constitutional rights only through affirmative or overt acts.

b.   Revise the Sentence So That a Pronoun Is Not Needed

EXAMPLE

As a general rule, an employer is not liable for the work performed by his independent contractors.

Revision:

As a general rule, an employer is not liable for the work performed by independent contractors.

c.   *Replace the Masculine Noun and Pronoun with "One," "Your," or "He" or "She," as Appropriate*

EXAMPLE

Every man has a right to defend his home.

Revisions:

One has a right to defend one's home.

You have a right to defend your home.

Everyone has a right to defend his or her home.

---

d.   *Alternate Male and Female Examples and Expressions*

EXAMPLE

If a student enrolls at a university with the promise that he will receive an athletic scholarship and he later finds out that his scholarship has been revoked, he can sue the university for breach of contract. If, on the other hand, a student enrolls at a university with the promise that he will receive an athletic scholarship and he later refuses to play the sport, the university can sue him for breach of contract.

Revision:

If a student enrolls at a university with the promise that she will receive an athletic scholarship and she later finds out that her scholarship has been revoked, she can sue the university for breach of contract. If, on the other hand, a student enrolls at a university with the promise that he will receive an athletic scholarship and he later refuses to play the sport, the university can sue him for breach of contract.

---

e.   *Repeat the Noun Rather Than Use an Inappropriate Masculine Pronoun*

EXAMPLE

Joinder of counts should not be used to embarrass or prejudice a defendant or to deny him a substantial right.

Revised:

Joinder of counts should not be used to embarrass or prejudice a defendant or to deny a defendant a substantial right.

One approach that is occasionally recommended for avoiding the generic "he" is to use the plural pronouns "they" and "their" for singular nouns and indefinite pronouns, such as "everyone" or "anybody." While using this approach may arguably solve the sexism problem, it still leaves the writer with an error in pronoun agreement (see section 26.4.2) as well as with more than a few logical inconsistencies, for example, "Everyone is entitled to their opinion." Rather than trade one problem for another, use one of the other five strategies outlined above for avoiding the generic "he."

§24.4.3   Gender-Neutral Job Titles

Avoid job titles that suggest it is nonstandard for women to hold the position.

Sexist Terms	*Gender-neutral Substitutes*
businessman	business executive, manager
chairman	coordinator, presiding officer, head, chair
Congressman	Representative, member of Congress, congressional representative, Senator
councilman	council member
deliveryman	delivery clerk, courier
draftsman	drafter
doorman	doorkeeper
fireman	firefighter
foreman (as the head of a group of workers)	supervisor, hcad worker, section chief

Sexist Terms	*Gender-neutral Substitutes*
insuranceman	insurance agent
juryman	juror
landlord	owner, manager, lessor
mailman, postman	postal carrier, postal worker, mail carrier
middleman	negotiator, liaison, intermediary
newspaperman	reporter, editor
paperboy	newspaper carrier
policeman	police officer
salesman	sales associate, sales representative
spokesman	representative, spokesperson
steward, stewardess	flight attendant
watchman	guard

§24.4.4 Sexist Modifiers

Unconsciously, writers sometimes assign needless sexist modifiers to words. Avoid modifiers that suggest that it is unusual for either a woman or a man to occupy a certain position.

Sexist Modifier	*Revised*
female judge	judge
lady lawyer	lawyer
male nurse	nurse
woman attorney	attorney

§24.4.5 Other Sexist Language

Avoid feminizing a word with a suffix, for example, "actress," "executrix," "testatrix." Such endings suggest that it is nonstandard for women to fill certain roles.

Avoid terms with connotations of youth (girl), decorum (lady), or informality (gal) unless the comparable term for males (boy, gentleman, guy) is also appropriate.

When using titles (Miss, Mrs., Ms.) before women's names, follow the particular woman's preference, if known, or, if unknown, use no title. In professional contexts, professional titles take precedence over social titles for both women and men, for example, Justice Sandra Day O'Connor, not Mrs. O'Connor. In salutations in letters, avoid using the outdated "Dear Sir" or "Gentlemen" when the gender of the receiver is unknown. Acceptable substitutes include "Dear Sir or Madam," "Ladies and Gentlemen," or the title of the receiver(s), as in "Dear Members of the Board." Some writers omit the salutation and use a reference line such as "To the Director of Operations" or "Re: Credit Department."

Sexist Term	*Gender-neutral Substitutes*
coed	student
divorcee	divorced person
forefathers	ancestors, forerunners, forebears
girl or girls (when applied to adult females)	woman or women
lady or ladies	woman or women (unless the equivalent "gentleman" or "gentlemen" is also used for men)
househusband, housewife	homemaker
man and wife	man and woman, husband and wife
old wives' tale	superstitious belief or idea

See Exercises 24.L, 24.M, and 24.N in the *Practice Book.*

§24.5 Bias-free Language

In addition to the concern that legal writers use gender-neutral language in their documents, there are related concerns that the language of law be free of bias against other groups, such as racial, religious, and ethnic minorities, homosexuals, the elderly, the poor, and persons with disabilities.

Making bias-free language choices is not always easy, though, particularly when one realizes that the preferred terms are constantly changing and not all members of any given group have the same preferences. These challenges tempt some to ignore or just give up on the issue of bias-free language in law. The argument seems to go something like this: "Why should I bother when they can't even decide what they want to be called?"

The temptation to avoid the issue is easier to resist, however, when one considers the power of language and its ability to shape perception. How we label something affects how we see it. Thus, language can serve to perpetuate stereotypes, or it can bring new insight and perspective. Choices in language can suggest that members of a group are inherently inferior or that they are valued members of society.

In short, what we call ourselves or someone else matters. Naming, or labeling, is both an enormous power and an enormous responsibility.

The following five general recommendations outline some advice for legal writers concerning the issue of bias-free language. Many of the specific recommendations and examples for commonly encountered terms are taken from McGraw-Hill's "Guidelines for Bias-Free Publishing" and from the President's Committee on Employment of People with Disabilities.

§24.5.1   Stay Abreast of the Preferred Terminology

All language changes over time. Some parts of language tend to change more rapidly, however, because of rapid changes in sensibilities and society's collective thinking about certain issues.

Notice, for example, the changes in terminology for these groups of people.

Colored People → Negro → Black → Black-American → African-American or Afro-American

Indian → American Indian → Native American

Oriental → Asian-American

Mexican-American → Chicano/Chicana or Hispanic or Latino

Handicapped → Disabled → Physically Challenged or Persons of Differing Abilities or Persons with Exceptionalities or Exceptional Persons

Elderly → Senior Citizens

Notice too that several of these progressions end with two or more choices, indicating a lack of consensus among the members of the group about the current preferred term.

Indeed, the lack of consensus may extend beyond different preferences among current terms. It is not uncommon, for instance, for older members of a group to prefer earlier, more traditional terms. Younger members of the black community may prefer to be called African-Americans while their parents or grandparents may prefer to be called blacks.

Does this mean that legal writers are faced with the impossible task of choosing among competing terms, each of which will inevitably make someone unhappy? Possibly.

In making the choice, though, legal writers are not without direction. Indeed, at least five factors can serve as guides. First, which term is preferred by this group of people at this time? Second, do the specific individuals involved, especially the clients, have a preference? Third, does the reader of this document have a preference? Fourth, does the law itself use a term for this group of people? Fifth, does the writer have a preference?

In other words, as with so many other tough questions in writing, the astute legal writer will use the overall context of the document, including reader, writer, and purpose, when making choices that concern bias-free language.

Exercise

Assume that you are representing a gay male who has been the victim of a hate crime. He has expressed a preference for the term "gay," rather than "homosexual." You strongly suspect, however, that the judge in the case prefers the term "homosexual." What do you do? Which term do you use when writing to the court?

---

§24.5.2   Avoid Irrelevant Minority References

Perhaps the most subtle and possibly the most insidious forms of prejudice in some legal writing are unnecessary references to race, ethnic origin, or other minority categories. In a case in which the description of an individual is necessary to the analysis (such as a case in which the police apprehended an individual based on the individual matching a victim's description), including the race of the individual is obviously appropriate. Unless a crime was racially motivated, however, it is probably inappropriate to include the race of a victim.

The test, then, for whether to include a minority reference is the same test for all other facts surrounding a case: If the fact affects the analysis, include it; if the fact is irrelevant to the analysis, leave it out.

§24.5.3   Use Racial, Ethnic, and Religious Terms Precisely

Citizens from countries in both North and South America have from time to time expressed irritation and resentment over the use of the term "American" to refer to persons and things that are limited to the United States. America, they are quick to point out, includes more than just the United States of America. Indeed, it is imprecise to refer to the American economy or American law when one means the United States economy or United States law. Similarly, avoid the use of "we" or "our" to refer to the United States.

Notice too that the term "Jew" is not synonymous with the term "Israeli." Not all Israelis are Jews and not all Jews are Israelis. Similarly, the term "Arab" is not interchangeable with the term "Muslim." The term "Hebrew" refers to a language. Do not use it to refer to a person or a religion, except in references to ancient Israel.

§24.5.4   Choose the More Specific Term

Although there are exceptions, in most cases choose a more specific term over a more general term when using descriptive labels for groups of people.

For example, although "Asian" is acceptable, "Chinese," "Japanese," or other specific Asian nationalities are preferred when known. Names of specific tribes, such as Mohawk or Navaho, are preferred over the more general "Native American," but do not use the redundant "Navaho Indian."

A relatively new term, "people of color," has gained considerable acceptance within the United States as an encompassing term for African-Americans, Native Americans, Mexican-Americans, and Asian-Americans. Although the term is more general than specific (contrary to the advice above), the term is increasingly preferred when describing lack of diversity or discriminatory practices that affect all these groups.

§24.5.5   Choose Words That Emphasize the Person, Not the Disability

When you refer to a person with a disability, refer to the person first. For example, "people with disabilities" is preferred over "the disabled"; "person with epilepsy" rather than "epileptic"; and "person affected by cerebral palsy" rather than "cerebral palsy victim."

Avoid cliched verbs that over-emphasize the disability. For example, rather than say "person confined (or restricted) to a wheelchair," use "person who uses a wheelchair." Rather than "person who suffers a hearing loss," use "person who is deaf (or hearing impaired)". Rather than a "person stricken by muscular dystropy," use "person who has muscular dystrophy."

Chapter 25

Eloquence

Is it unrealistic for legal writing to be eloquent? After all, lawyers write under enormous time pressure. Who has the time to massage language to the point at which someone would call it "eloquent"?

Further, is it appropriate for legal writing to be eloquent? Should an office memo sound like it was written by Shakespeare? What client is willing to pay for a client letter that waxes poetic? Are judges more impressed by arguments or by the language they are wrapped in?

All these good questions really boil down to one question: Should a lawyer strive to write eloquently?

Yes, at least sometimes.

While it wouldn't hurt if every office memo and client letter were written eloquently, the one area in which eloquence undoubtedly pays off is briefs. An eloquent brief is a more persuasive brief. Of course the arguments must be sound and persuasive in and of themselves, but one cannot divorce the content of the argument from the form in which it is written. What one says and the way one says it are inextricably linked.

One striking bit of evidence that eloquent briefs are persuasive is the frequency with which well-articulated arguments from briefs reappear in judicial opinions. If imitation is the highest form of flattery, there can be nothing more flattering to a brief writer than to have a judge "lift" a phrase or more from the brief and incorporate it into the opinion.

But as we suggested before, eloquence is not something legal writers can add as a kind of finishing touch. Eloquence is not a tuxedo or an evening gown. A writer cannot "put on" eloquence any more than an artist can put on originality.

Eloquence in legal writing and originality in art are there throughout the creative process, often at the point of conception, again through the drafting and revising, and yet again in the final polishing.

§25.1   PURPLE PROSE

Like artists who try to force themselves to be original, legal writers who try to force themselves to be eloquent will probably end up creating something that is either absurd or monstrous.

The following excerpt is from the Statement of Facts in a case about whether racial slurs create a cause of action for tort of outrage.

> Our client, Mr. Silvino Gomez, is a twenty-year-old of Mexican-American descent. Mr. Gomez's prowess as a basketball player brought him to the delighted attention of enthusiastic recruiters from several private colleges. He ultimately accepted an athletic scholarship from the University of Newton, where he matriculated and began playing his chosen sport in September 1996. His maiden voyage into the waters of college life was off to a promising start: Barely out of the starting gate, he showed himself to be as talented in the classroom as on the court, and his grades reflected his academic acumen. His interests that fall also included the very beautiful Elizabeth Jaynes, former steady of the team's star guard, Michael Wilson.

Some call writing like the example above "purple prose." Like the color purple, it is just too much. Instead of focusing the reader's attention on the point being made, it calls attention to itself. What's worse, the effort shows. Here's more purple prose from the same office memorandum.

> Silvino's freshman year was not to be without troubles, however. Storm clouds gathered on the horizon as the season got underway. Gomez, playing well, sensed that Wilson considered him a threat, and tension between the two stirred the air as Wilson harassed Gomez on the court. Although there was no "name-calling" during October, the dust flew in November when Wilson thundered at Gomez, "You fucking spic!" At first, the insults were made only when the coaches were absent, but in late November Wilson hurled them like lightning bolts during several practices in the presence of the coaches. In December, even the fans at several games were listening as Wilson's insults fell like hailstones on Gomez.

How to prevent the "purple prose syndrome"? The best safeguard is the axiom "when in doubt, don't." If you think the writing may be "too much," it probably is. Err on the side of subtlety.

Or if you are fortunate enough to have a candid colleague, get a second opinion. If you fear that something you have written may be overdone, ask that colleague to read the writing and let you know if you have stepped over the invisible line and into the realm of purple prose.

You might also try watching out for some of the common features of purple prose, many of which appear in the example above.

- excessive use of adjectives and adverbs: *delighted* attention, *enthusiastic* recruiters, *the very beautiful* Elizabeth Jaynes
- cliche-ridden phrases and images: *the dust flew*, *hurled them like lightning bolts*

- mixed metaphors: *maiden voyage* mixed with *out of the starting gate*
- overdeveloped metaphors: the weather metaphor in the second half of the example
- pretentious vocabulary: academic *acumen*

Other common features of purple prose not demonstrated in the previous example include the following:

- too much of any one of the poetic devices (for example, excessive alliteration, or the Peter Piper effect)
- heavy-handed use of stylistic devices
- excessive use of underlining and italics for emphasis

§25.2 COMMON FEATURES OF ELOQUENT WRITING

Before writing can be considered eloquent, it must be clear, competent, and readable. Eloquent writing, however, goes a step beyond competence. The language is more than clear and energetic: It is memorable, striking, even poetic because the writer has paid attention to the sound, rhythm, and imagery of language.

Features of language that one may not have thought about since that last class in poetry—alliteration, assonance, cadence, stressed and unstressed syllables, onomatopoeia, simile, and metaphor—may be used, but they do not overwhelm eloquent legal writing. Rhetorical features that one may have noticed in aphorisms—parallelism, balance, antithesis—may also be used, particularly at key points.

Other features, such as electric verbs (see section 23.3), occasional short sentences (see section 23.5), variety in sentence length and sentence openers, and subtle devices for creating emphasis (see section 23.6), are fairly common.

Best of all, all this occurs naturally, apparently effortlessly, even though we know better. Like a pair of dancers who move as one body or a well-executed double play, eloquent writing is the perfect, harmonious matching of form and content. The reader feels satisfied, perhaps even uplifted, by the writing.

§25.2.1 Alliteration and Assonance

Eloquent writing begs to be read aloud. One wants to savor the language. Every word and phrase seems to be just the right choice. Quite simply, the writing sings.

Of the numerous features that affect the sound of a piece of writing, alliteration and assonance are probably the easiest to identify. Alliteration, or the repetition of consonant sounds, must be subtle or the writing will begin to sound like "Peter Piper picked a peck of pickled peppers." One way accomplished writers work in alliteration without overpowering the prose is to use it in the middle of words as well as at the beginning.

The following example demonstrates a subtle use of alliteration. The example is taken from the amicus brief for the United States in the landmark Supreme Court case *Wallace v. Jaffree,* which concerned the constitutionality of a state statute authorizing public school teachers to allow a moment of silence at the beginning of the school day for "prayer or meditation."

> Moment of silence statutes are libertarian in the precise spirit of the Bill of Rights: they accommodate those who believe that prayer should be an integral part of life's activities (including school), and do so in the most neutral and noncoercive spirit possible. The student may pray, but is equally free to meditate or daydream or doze. No one can even know what the other chooses to do: silence is precious because it creates the possibility of privacy within public occasions. To hold that the moment of silence is unconstitutional is to insist that any opportunity for religious practice, even in the unspoken thoughts of schoolchildren, be extirpated from the public sphere. It is to be censorial where the Religion Clauses are libertarian; it would make the very concept of religious accommodation constitutionally suspect.

The alliteration in this example is unobtrusive. In fact, most of us can read this passage and never consciously notice that it includes alliteration. Look again at these phrases:

> the most neutral and noncoercive spirit possible
> daydream or doze

The brief writer could have said "the most impartial and noncoercive spirit possible" or "the most objective and noncoercive spirit possible" or even "the most equitable and noncoercive spirit possible," but didn't. "Neutral," when coupled with "noncoercive," has both the right meaning and the right sound.

The same is true of "daydream and doze." Rather than select "doze," the writer could have easily said "nap," "rest," "sleep," or "snooze." All have similar meanings, but try substituting any one of the four in the original sentence to see what is gained by the alliterative "doze."

The brief writer saves the most subtle and arguably the most powerful alliteration for the clause "silence is precious because it creates the possibility of privacy within public occasions." This clause has two layers of alliteration. The more obvious is the repetition of the p sounds: "silence is precious because it creates the possibility of privacy within public occasions." The second layer is the repetition of s sounds, which is done by both the letters s and c: "silence is precious because it creates the possibility of privacy within public occasions."

The soft "s" and "sh" sounds work perfectly in this context. They underscore the writer's meaning by gently, almost imperceptibly reminding the reader of the kind of quiet the writer wants the schoolchildren to have.

Assonance, or the repetition of vowel sounds, is similar to alliteration. In the following example, the brief writer repeated the *a* sound.

EXAMPLE

The absurdity of this implicit assumption is apparent when applied to the motivations of those responsible for the First Amendment itself.

Is the assonance overdone in the example above? Read it aloud to determine if it works.

§25.2.2   Cadence

Cadence is the rhythmic flow of the writing, what musicians might call "the beat." Unlike music, though, writing has no apparent time signature and few overt signals for where to place the emphasis. Even so, good writers control the pace and emphasis in their sentences by artful use of sentence structure, sentence length, punctuation, and stressed and unstressed syllables. Like good musicians, they "hear" what they are creating. They have developed an ear for language.

Read aloud the following selection from Supreme Court Justice Louis Brandeis.

> In a government of laws, existence of the government will be imperiled if it fails to observe the law scrupulously. Our Government is the potent, the omnipresent teacher. For good or for ill, it teaches the whole people by its example. Crime is contagious. If the Government becomes a lawbreaker, it breeds contempt for law; it invites every man to become a law unto himself; it invites anarchy. To declare that in the administration of the criminal law the end justifies the means — to declare that the Government may commit crimes in order to secure the conviction of a private criminal — would bring terrible retribution. Against that pernicious doctrine this Court should resolutely set its face.

This excerpt is rich with the features of eloquent prose, but for now let's look just at the rhythm in the language. Consider, for example, the phrase "the potent, the omnipresent teacher." The more common way to write two adjectives before a noun is "the potent, omnipresent teacher," without the extra "the." Why the extra "the" in the Brandeis version? Try scanning the phrase as you would a piece of poetry.

   ⏑ / ⏑ / ⏑ / ⏑   /   ⏑
the po-tent, om-ni-pres-ent teach-er

The unvarying unstressed, stressed, unstressed, stressed syllable pattern is flat and lifeless, particularly when it comes in two-syllable, sing-song units. It does not give "omnipresent" enough emphasis. Add the extra "the," however, and the rhythm is more interesting and, more important, more compatible with the desired emphasis.

Now look at the last sentence of this selection.

> . . . this Court should resolutely set its face.

This clause is easy to read aloud. It is a grand, solemn conclusion. Why? Scan the last four words.

   / ⏑ / ⏑ / ⏑ /
res-o-lute-ly set its face

The three one-syllable words "set its face" break up any sing-song effect. Further, notice where the stress falls—on "set" and "face." Thus, by ending the selection on a stressed syllable, a strong note, Justice Brandeis creates the sound of finality and conviction. Had Brandeis arranged the last clause so that it ended on "resolutely" (as he had the earlier one, "to observe the law scrupulously"), the unstressed syllable at the end of "resolutely" would have fought against the decisive closure he wanted.

   / ⏑ / / ⏑ / ⏑
set its face res-o-lute-ly

Does this mean Justice Brandeis scanned his prose for stressed and unstressed syllables as he was writing it? That's highly unlikely. What is likely is that he *heard* the sound he was creating and, perhaps through trial and error, manipulated the words until he achieved the aural effect he wanted.

The preceding examples show that an extra syllable here or there or changing a stressed to an unstressed syllable or vice versa can make a difference in how writing sounds. Adding or deleting an extra word or syllable also makes a difference in the pace of the writing. Such a change in pace is particularly obvious when the word added or omitted is a conjunction in a series.

A typical series reads like "one, two, and three" or "red, white, and blue." Asyndeton, or the deliberate omissions of conjunctions in a series, quickens the pace. The same series without the conjunction—"red, white, blue"—sounds slightly rushed.

Polysyndeton, or the deliberate use of many conjunctions in a series, slows the pace and drags out the prose. Now the series takes more time: "red and white and blue."

Compare the following examples from a child custody case, in which the court looks at which of the parties was the child's primary caregiver. In an objective, neutral discussion of the father's care of the child, the following series may appear.

EXAMPLE

Mr. Lundquist had certain responsibilities regarding his daughter Anna's care: he drove her to school, checked her homework, and took her to medical appointments.

The attorney for Lundquist's former wife may use asyndeton to create the impression that Mr. Lundquist's care of his daughter was minimal.

EXAMPLE

Mr. Lundquist had few responsibilities regarding his daughter Anna's care: he drove her to school, checked her homework, took her to medical appointments.

Mr. Lundquist, on the other hand, will probably want to create the impression that he was an involved parent who spent a great deal of time with his daughter. Notice how the use of polysyndeton, in combination with other persuasive devices such as characterizing the facts and adding detail, creates the desired effect.

EXAMPLE

Mr. Lundquist had several significant responsibilities regarding his daughter Anna's care: he drove her to school each day and checked her homework every evening and took her to all regularly scheduled and emergency medical appointments.

To stretch out the series a bit further, the writer can even use both the conjunctions and the commas.

EXAMPLE

Mr. Lundquist had several significant responsibilities regarding his daughter Anna's care: he drove her to school each day, and checked her homework every evening, and took her to all regularly scheduled and emergency medical appointments.

Compare the following.

EXAMPLE   A TYPICAL SERIES

First-year law students take Contracts, Torts, Civil Procedure, Legal Writing, and Criminal Law.

Dropping the conjunction makes the writing sound clipped and a bit breezy.

EXAMPLE   ASYNDETON

First-year law students take Contracts, Torts, Civil Procedure, Legal Writing, Criminal Law.

Adding in all the conjunctions, on the other hand, suggests that the coursework for a first-year law student is overwhelming.

EXAMPLE   POLYSYNDETON

First-year law students take Contracts and Torts and Civil Procedure and Legal Writing and Criminal Law.

§25.2.3   Variety in Sentence Length

In section 23.5, we said that legal readers can comfortably read sentences that average around twenty-two words in length. We also suggested that long sentences, thirty-five words or more, are difficult to read unless they are broken into manageable units of meaning. Finally, we briefly touched on the power of the short sentence. All of these points apply to eloquent writing.

Let's look again at the earlier excerpt from Justice Brandeis.

> In a government of laws, existence of the government will be imperiled if it fails to observe the law scrupulously. Our Government is the potent, the omnipresent teacher. For good or for ill, it teaches the whole people by its example. Crime is contagious. If the Government becomes a lawbreaker, it breeds contempt for law; it invites every man to become a law unto himself; it invites anarchy. To declare that in the administration of the criminal law the end justifies the means—to declare that the Government may commit crimes in order to secure the conviction of a private criminal— would bring terrible retribution. Against that pernicious doctrine this Court should resolutely set its face.

A reader's sense of how long a sentence is depends partly on the number of words in the sentence but also on the number of syllables in the sentence. Here's how the sentences in the Brandeis excerpt break down, both in the number of words they contain and in the number of syllables.

sentence 1	20 words	32 syllables
sentence 2	8 words	15 syllables
sentence 3	13 words	17 syllables
sentence 4	3 words	5 syllables
sentence 5	24 words	38 syllables
sentence 6	37 words	62 syllables
sentence 7	11 words	18 syllables

The variety in sentence length in this selection is remarkable—from 3 words to 37 words. Having variety, though, is not an end in itself. Notice how Brandeis uses sentence length. The one extremely short sentence, "Crime is contagious," is startling in its brevity. It hits the reader like a slap in the face. Its terseness creates the emphasis this point deserves.

The longest sentence in the selection has to be longer just to get across its points, but it also needs more words to create the effect of building to a climax. This sentence needs time to gather momentum. And even though it is fairly long, 37 words or 62 syllables, this sentence is easy to read because it comes in manageable units of meaning: 15 words, 18 words, and 4 words.

Such variety in sentence length helps create an interesting and varied pace. Deliberately breaking the "rules" can be another effective way to create reader interest. In the following excerpt from *Edwards v. Aguillard,* Justice Scalia uses a marathon sentence to help make a point.

> But the difficulty of knowing what vitiating purpose one is looking for is as nothing compared with the difficulty of knowing how or where

to find it. For while it is possible to discern the objective "purpose" of a statute (*i.e.,* the public good at which its provisions appear to be directed), or even the formal motivation for a statute where that is explicitly set forth (as it was, to no avail, here), discerning the subjective motivation of those enacting the statute is, to be honest, almost always an impossible task. The number of possible motivations, to begin with, is not binary, or indeed even finite. In the present case, for example, a particular legislator need not have voted for the Act either because he wanted to foster religion or because he wanted to improve education. He may have thought the bill would provide jobs for his district, or may have wanted to make amends with a faction of his party he had alienated on another vote, or he may have been a close friend of the bill's sponsor, or he may have been repaying a favor he owed the Majority Leader, or he may have hoped the Governor would appreciate his vote and make a fundraising appearance for him, or he may have been pressured to vote for a bill he disliked by a wealthy contributor or by a flood of constituent mail, or he may have been seeking favorable publicity, or he may have been reluctant to hurt the feelings of a loyal staff member who worked on the bill, or he may have been settling an old score with a legislator who opposed the bill, or he may have been mad at his wife who opposed the bill, or he may have been intoxicated and utterly *un*motivated when the vote was called, or he may have accidentally voted "yes" instead of "no," or, of course, he may have had (and very likely did have) a combination of some of the above and many other motivations. To look for *the sole purpose* of even a single legislator is probably to look for something that does not exist.

Sentence 5 is a linguistic tour de force. At 202 words, it must set some kind of record for sentence length, yet the sentence is quite readable because it is broken up into manageable units that vary between 8 and 24 words.

But no one thinks Justice Scalia wrote this sentence to demonstrate that he can write a long sentence that is readable. Rather, in this rare instance, an extremely long sentence dramatically made his point that there is an extremely long list of reasons why any single legislator may vote for a bill.

The selection also demonstrates our earlier point about variety in sentence length. Here the range is from 15 words to 202 words.

sentence 1	27 words
sentence 2	64 words
sentence 3	15 words
sentence 4	30 words
sentence 5	202 words
sentence 6	22 words

Notice what points Justice Scalia makes in his two shorter sentences.

§25.2.4   Variety in Sentence Openers

It is risky to suggest that legal writers should occasionally vary the openings of their sentences. In the hands of the wrong writer, this advice can lead to some clumsy prose.

For the most part, writers should follow the more traditional advice and begin the majority of their sentences with the subject. Writers who use all sorts of sentence openers other than the subject tend to write prose that sounds jumpy and disjointed. But writers who oversubscribe to the idea of starting sentences with the subject write incredibly boring prose.

The question then is when should a writer use something other than the subject to begin a sentence? Even in garden-variety prose, subjects are frequently preceded by phrases or clauses that establish a context or pick up on a previously established theme. (See sections 22.2 and 22.3 on orienting transitions and dovetailing.)

What is far more unusual and, when done well, more striking, is the inverted word order of some sentences. Such an inversion, known in classical rhetoric as anastrophe, focuses particular attention on whatever words are out of their normal or expected order. The Brandeis excerpt ended with an example of inverted word order.

> Against that pernicious doctrine this Court should resolutely set its face.

As always, to understand the drama and power this arrangement creates, all one has to do is read the sentence in the normal, expected word order.

> This Court should resolutely set its face against that pernicious doctrine.

Here are some more excerpts from the briefs in *Wallace v. Jaffree*. From the brief of the appellees:

> With great difficulty the state attempts to argue that this case creates tension between the Establishment and Free Exercise clauses.

From the amicus brief from the American Jewish Congress:

> The public schools serve as vehicles for "inculcating fundamental values," including "social, moral, or political" ones. *Bd. of Educ. v. Pico*, 102 S. Ct. 2799, 2806 (1982). Pointedly absent from this list are religious values. Education in those values is not, under the Constitution, the responsibility of the public schools; it is that of family and church.

The expected word order of the second sentence in the second example is "Religious values are pointedly absent from this list." Notice that by inverting the order, the brief writer not only places emphasis on what is out of order, "pointedly absent," but also strengthens the emphasis on "religious values" by moving it to the end of the sentence.

§25.2.5   Parallelism

Parallelism, or the use of similar grammatical structures in a pair or series of related words, phrases, or clauses, is required in some contexts. See section 26.7. Accomplished writers, however, treat parallelism not just as a grammatical requirement but as a stylistic opportunity. They use parallelism and its related forms to create special effects, emphasis, and euphony.

Here's an excerpt from the appellants' brief in *Wallace v. Jaffree:*

> This development is a tribute not only to the good sense of the American people, but also to the genius of the Framers of the body of the Constitution.

> *not only*   *to the good sense of the American people,*
> *but also*   *to the genius of the Framers of the body of the*
> *Constitution*

Look again at the Scalia excerpt. Justice Scalia uses a specialized version of parallelism called isocolon when he matches both the structure and the length of the parallel elements in the following sentence.

> In the present case, for example, a particular legislator need not have voted for the Act either because he wanted to foster religion or because he wanted to improve education.

> *either*   *because he wanted to foster religion*
> *or*   *because he wanted to improve education*

Some examples of isocolon go beyond matching the number of words and even match the number of syllables.

The same excerpt from Justice Scalia includes examples of another specialized form of parallelism: balance. In the sentence below, notice how the first half of the sentence is balanced against the second half.

> To look for the sole purpose of even a single legislator is probably to look for something that does not exist.

> *To look for*   *is*   *to look for*
> *the sole purpose*   *probably*   *something that*
> *of even a*   *does not exist.*
> *single legislator*

The amicus brief of the United States in *Wallace v. Jaffree* also includes an excellent example of balance.

> To hold that the moment of silence is unconstitutional is to insist that any opportunity for religious practice, even in the unspoken

thoughts of school children, be extirpated from the public sphere.

> *To hold that . . .   is   to insist that . . . .*

Balance can also be created in a number of other ways. Here's an excerpt from Cardozo's opinion in *Hynes v. New York:*

The approximate and relative become the definite and absolute.

> *approximate   become   definite*
> *and   and*
> *relative   absolute*

From the brief of the appellees in *Wallace:*

The First Amendment is as simple in its language as it is majestic in its purpose.

> *as simple   as (it is) majestic*
> *in its language   in its purpose*

Also fairly common in eloquent legal writing is a related form of parallelism known as antithesis. Like balance, antithesis repeats similar parallel structures on both sides of the equation, but unlike balance, the ideas are in contrast. In other words, balance says X equals X, and antithesis says X does not equal X.

The structure of antithesis is usually quite simple and falls into one of two patterns:

> not _____ but _____
>
> _____ , not _____

Examples from the amicus brief of the United States in *Wallace:*

> The touchstone is not secularism, but pluralism.
>
> We believe that provision for a moment of silence in the public schools is not an establishment of religion, but rather a legitimate way for the government to provide an opportunity for both religious and nonreligious introspection in a setting where, experience has shown, many desire it. It is an instrument of toleration and pluralism, not of coercion or indoctrination.

Yet another variation of parallelism is the use of parallel openers. Parallel openers can start sentences, clauses, or phrases, and they often have the effect of building to a climax or suggesting that a point is well established. From the Brandeis excerpt:

If the Government becomes a lawbreaker, it breeds contempt for law; **it invites** every man to become a law unto himself; **it invites** anarchy. **To declare that** in the administration of the criminal law the end justifies the means—**to declare that** the Government may commit crimes in order to secure the conviction of a private criminal—would bring terrible retribution.

From the Scalia excerpt:

He may have thought the bill would provide jobs for his district, or **may have** wanted to make amends with a faction of his party he had alienated on another vote, or **he may have** been a close friend of the bill's sponsor, or **he may have** been repaying a favor he owed the Majority Leader, or **he may have** hoped the Governor would appreciate his vote and make a fundraising appearance for him, or **he may have** been pressured to vote for a bill he disliked by a wealthy contributor or by a flood of constituent mail, or **he may have** been seeking favorable publicity, or **he may have** been reluctant to hurt the feelings of a loyal staff member who worked on the bill, or **he may have** been settling an old score with a legislator who opposed the bill, or **he may have** been mad at his wife who opposed the bill, or **he may have** been intoxicated and utterly *un*motivated when the vote was called, or **he may have** accidentally voted "yes" instead of "no," or, of course, **he may have** had (and very likely did have) a combination of some of the above and many other motivations.

In the following excerpt from the EEOC brief in *Hishon v. King & Spaulding*, the brief writer combined parallel openers with antithesis.

But the two Senators did not obliquely approach, let alone confront, even the "employment" of lawyers at law firms. They did not mention lawyers; they spoke of doctors instead. They did not discuss law partnerships; they spoke of hospitals instead.

§25.2.6   Onomatopoeia

"Snap," "crackle," and "pop" —these words are examples of onomatopoeia; that is, they sound like what they mean. So do "sizzle," "plop," "hiss," "click," "twang," "crinkle," and a host of others. These words sound like the natural sounds they represent.

Other words have an onomatopoeic quality even though the words don't represent a sound. Consider the word "weird." Not only does it sound weird, it is even spelled weird. The word "bizarre" works the same way; it looks and sounds bizarre. The list goes on. There is something grotesque in the look and sound of "grotesque," and it is hard to imagine a word that looks and sounds more unattractive than "ugly."

Consider the sound of words like "sensual," "lascivious," and "licentious." Notice how the rolling "s" and "l" sounds combine in various ways to give the words a lazy, even erotic sound. "Sultry" works the same way.

The "slippery slope" one hears so much about in law puts the "s" and "l" together as a consonant blend and achieves a different effect. The words seem to *slide* off the tongue with slow ease. Like a judicial system that has started down that slippery slope, there are no natural brakes to stop these words once they are formed on the lips. Notice too that "slick," "slime," "slink," "slither," "slush," and "sludge" all somehow share this same slippery, even oily quality.

Should legal writers use onomatopoeia in their writing? Consider the following versions of essentially the same point.

EXAMPLES

Harris suddenly took the keys and ran out the door.

Harris snatched the keys and ran out the door.

"Snatched" says in one word—even one syllable—what the first of the examples takes two words and four syllables to say. Its quickness mirrors the quickness in the action. It *sounds* like a quick grab at those keys.

Earlier we looked at an example of alliteration, "daydream or doze," and commented that all the synonyms for "doze" — "sleep," "nap," "rest," or "snooze" —were less effective because they lacked the alliteration. Notice too that "doze" has an onomatopoetic quality. The "z" sound in it reminds us of sleep. That is also why "snooze" is the best choice among the runners-up.

§25.2.7   Simile and Metaphor

Similes are indirect comparisons.

EXAMPLE

Lowell's mental irresponsibility defense is like the toy gun he used in the robbery—spurious.

Metaphors are direct comparisons.

EXAMPLE

Our Government is the potent, the omnipresent teacher.

To be effective, similes and metaphors need to be fresh and insightful. Unfortunately, all too many metaphors used in legal writing are cliche-ridden. How often must we hear that something or other is "woven into the fabric of our society"? When was the last time you actually thought about wolves and sheep when something or someone was described as a "wolf in sheep's clothing"?

Timeworn similes and metaphors suggest that the writer's thought processes are on autopilot, and no more than that will be expected of the reader. We can all mentally coast.

A fresh simile or metaphor makes demands of the reader. It asks the reader to bring to the new subject matter all the associations it has with the other half of the metaphor.

So powerful is metaphor that metaphors have become issues themselves. Consider, for example, the same landmark Supreme Court case from which we drew earlier excerpts, *Wallace v. Jaffree,* which involved the Alabama "silent meditation or prayer" in public schools statute. Throughout that case's history, both sides argued whether there was "an absolute wall of separation" between federal government and religion.

Take particular care not to mix metaphors. The result is a confusing, sometimes ludicrous image, as in the example below.

EXAMPLE

Ms. Martinez will never forget the image of her assailant, which was forever imprinted on and burned into the pages of her memory.

---

§25.2.8   Personification

Like so many of the suggestions in this chapter, personification, or giving human traits or abilities to abstractions or inanimate objects, must be used with a light hand if it is to be used at all in legal writing.

In the brief of the appellees *in Wallace v. Jaffree,* the writer used personification to make a point about the intent of the Alabama legislature.

In 1982, in order to breathe religious life into its silent meditation statute, the Alabama legislature amended § 16-1-20 to expressly include "prayer" as the preferred activity in which the students and teachers may engage during the reverent moment of silence.

In his dissenting opinion in *Hoffa v. United States,* Chief Justice Warren uses personification to make a point about the government's actions and its witness.

> Here the Government reaches into the jailhouse to employ a man who was himself facing indictments far more serious (and later including one for perjury) than the one confronting the man against whom he offered to inform.

Eloquent language does one of two things. It creates a satisfying sound or, as in the Warren excerpt above, it creates a memorable image. The best of the best does both. Such writing is memorable, even unforgettable. It grabs the reader's attention long enough to make the reader see something new or see something old in a new way.

It takes on a life of its own.

Part V

A Guide to Correct Writing

This section of the *Handbook* was written as a review of grammar, punctuation, and mechanics. While most law students come to law school with a good command of these aspects of writing, some students complain that they have always had problems with spelling, or that they never really understood how to use a semicolon, or that they have heard about dangling modifiers but what in the world are they, anyway?

This section is designed to be a quick refresher and explanation for those students who have forgotten some of the basic rules or who, for some reason, never learned some of them. Even students who have strong backgrounds in grammar, punctuation, and mechanics may find it helpful to review some of the chapters in this section simply because legal writing puts more demands on the writer than do most other types of writing. Consequently, it may make your writing more efficient and more effective if you have all the rules, and hence all the options, at your fingertips.

Finally, although this section is entitled "A Guide to Correct Writing," the term "correct" is a slightly troubling one because it may suggest that the choices outlined in these chapters are absolutely the "right" ones in all circumstances. This is not true. In informal language, for example, certain other usage choices are not only acceptable but preferred. In legal writing, however, standard English is the norm and therefore the "correct" choice.

Chapter 26

Grammar

§26.1 BASIC SENTENCE GRAMMAR

Grammar, like law, is a system. Once you understand the basic workings of the system, you can begin to use the system effectively and efficiently.

Much of Part IV, A Guide to Effective Writing, and Part V, A Guide to Correct Writing, depends on understanding the grammar of an English sentence. This section is a quick review of basic sentence structure and the various components of most English sentences.[1]

§26.1.1 Sentence Patterns

In law, as in most other writing, most sentences are statements. These statements name someone or something (the subject) and then describe an action that that someone or something is performing (the predicate).

Smith	hit Jones.
(subject)	*(predicate)*

Smith's car	smashed into the railing.
(subject)	*(predicate)*

Occasionally, the predicate describes the state in which the subject exists, or the subject's state of being.

Smith's car	is a total loss.
(subject)	*(predicate)*

---

1. Although modern grammarians have persuasively argued that structural and transformational grammars more accurately describe the English sentence, the authors have elected to use traditional grammar, partly because it is more familiar to most readers and partly because it is sufficient for our purposes.

At the heart of every subject is a noun or a pronoun. Nouns name persons (Supreme Court Justice David Souter), places (Austin, Texas), things (savings bond), and concepts (negligence). Because pronouns are substitutes for nouns, they too can serve as subjects.

At the heart of every predicate is a verb. Some verbs express an action (sue, plead, argue, allege); others show a state of being (such as forms of the verb *to be, become, seem*). Frequently, the main verb is preceded by other verbs known as auxiliary, or helping, verbs (*might have been* assaulted), which express time relationships and shades of meaning. See section 29.1.2.

Pattern 1: Subject + Verb

To write a sentence, you will need at least one noun or pronoun for a subject and at least one verb for a predicate. This is the simplest sentence pattern.

subject	predicate
Lawyers	argue.
(noun)	*(verb)*

Pattern 2: Subject + Verb + Direct Object

Many verbs, however, cannot stand alone. They require a noun that will receive the action of the verb. We cannot, for example, simply say "lawyers make" and call that a sentence. "Make" what? To make sense, the verb needs a direct object. Notice that the direct object is part of the predicate.

subject	predicate	
Lawyers	make	arguments.
(noun)	*(verb)*	*(noun)*
		(direct object)

Direct objects "receive" the action of the verb.

Lawyers	make arguments.
Judges	deny motions.
	(direct objects)

Another way of thinking about this point is to say that the subject performs the action of the verb, and the verb "is done to" the direct object.

You can often find the direct object in a sentence by simply asking the question "what?" after the verb. Make what? Make *arguments*. Deny what? Deny *motions*.

**Pattern 3: Subject + Linking Verb +
Subject Complement**

Similarly, state of being, or linking verbs, need nouns (or sometimes adjectives) to complete the idea. Because these words do not directly receive the action of the verb in the same way as a direct object, they are not called direct objects. Instead, they are called subject complements because they complement the subject by renaming or describing it.

subject	predicate	
Lawyers	are	advocates.
(noun)	*(linking verb)*	*(noun)*
		(subject complement)

subject	predicate	
Lawyers	are	aggressive.
(noun)	*(linking verb)*	*(adjective)*
		(subject complement)

Another way of thinking about how linking verbs work is to think of them as an equals sign (=) in the sentence. Unlike action verbs, linking verbs do not describe an action; they simply say that the subject is "equal to" the subject complement.

Lawyers = advocates
Lawyers = aggressive

Note that some of the same words (am, is, are, was, were) function as linking verbs in some sentences and as auxiliary, or helping, verbs in other sentences. You can always tell whether one of these words is a linking verb or a helping verb by checking to see whether it is the only main verb in the sentence (then it is a linking verb) or whether it is followed by another main verb (then it is an auxiliary, or helping, verb).

EXAMPLE

The judge is the trier of fact.

In the preceding example, "is" is the only main verb; therefore, it is a linking verb.

EXAMPLE

The judge is speaking to the jury.

In the preceding example, "is" is followed by another main verb, "speaking"; therefore, "is" is an auxiliary, or helping, verb in this example. Notice that the combination "is speaking" is an action verb.

Pattern 4: Subject + Verb + Indirect Object + Direct Object

In another common pattern, the verb is followed by two nouns. The second noun after the verb, the direct object, receives the action of the verb. The first noun after the verb, the indirect object, identifies to whom or for whom (or what) the action is performed.

subject	predicate		
Lawyers	tell	clients	their options.
	(verb)	*(noun)*	*(noun)*
		(indirect object)	*(direct object)*

Pattern 5: Subject + Verb + Direct Object + Object Complement

In the last pattern, we also have two nouns following the verb, but in this pattern, the first noun is the direct object and the second noun is an objective complement. An objective complement renames or describes the direct object.

subject	predicate		
Smith	called	Jones	a liar.
	(verb)	*(noun)*	*(noun)*
		(direct object)	*(objective complement)*

Using these basic sentence patterns, we can now begin adding all those extras that make sentences interesting and complex.

§26.1.2   Single-Word Modifiers

Modifiers change, limit, describe, or add detail. Words that modify nouns or pronouns are, by definition, adjectives (*illogical* argument, *nervous* witness, *bearded* suspect).

Words that modify verbs, adjectives, or adverbs are adverbs (*quickly* responded, finished *soon, extremely* angry, *very* recently). Notice that adverbs often end in "-ly."

Any of our basic sentences can be expanded by using adjectives and adverbs as modifiers.

EXAMPLES

Thoughtful lawyers make very persuasive arguments.
adjective   adverb adjective

Too many lawyers are overly aggressive.
adv. adj.   adverb   adjective

---

§26.1.3   Phrases

When expanding the basic sentence patterns, we are not limited to single-word modifiers. Groups of related words, or phrases, can also serve as modifiers. A phrase is easily distinguished from other groups of related words because a phrase always lacks a subject or a verb or both.

Probably the most common type of modifying phrase is the prepositional phrase. Prepositional phrases are made up of a preposition (words that show relationships between other words, such as "about," "at," "by," "for," "in," "of," "on," "to"), its object, and any modifiers.

Preposition	Modifiers	Object
at	the same	time
by	an	affidavit
for	a new	trial
in	the	verdict
under	this	section

Prepositional phrases can modify nouns, verbs, adjectives, or adverbs.

EXAMPLE

At 10:00 p.m. on April 5, 1997, a two-truck collision occurred in Delaware between a truck driven by Ms. Constance Ruiz and a truck driven by Mr. Fred Miller.

Basic sentence patterns can also be expanded with verbals. Verbals are made from verbs, but they cannot serve as the main verb of a sentence. Instead, verbals are ways of using verb forms in other roles in a sentence. The three types of verbals—gerunds, infinitives, and participles—are described below. Notice that each can be expanded into a phrase.

a. Gerunds

Gerunds always act as nouns, so they are found in slots in the sentence that require nouns (subject, objects). They are formed by adding "-ing" to the base form of a verb.

EXAMPLES

Impeaching his testimony will be difficult.
(gerund)

Forgery includes writing a bad check.
            (gerund)

---

b. Participles

Participles act as adjectives. Present participles are formed by adding "-ing" to the base form of the verb; past participles usually add "-d" or "-ed." Irregular verbs have a special past participle form (for example, *brought, drunk, stolen*).

EXAMPLES

A television set wrapped in a blanket was found in the defendant's
            (participle)
trunk.

Applying this rule, the New York Supreme Court held that the
(participle)
appellant's constitutional rights were not violated.

Given that forgery is not a crime of dishonesty, the court found that
(participle)
evidence of the prior conviction is inadmissible.

Notice that the only way to distinguish between a gerund and a present participle is to determine the role they perform in a sentence.

c.   *Infinitives*

Infinitives can act as nouns, adjectives, or adverbs. The infinitive form is always "to" plus the base form of the verb.

EXAMPLE

To extend the all-purpose public figure standard to include all financial institutions ignores the Supreme Court's mandate to construe the standard narrowly.

---

d.   *Absolutes*

One additional type of phrase, the absolute phrase, can also be used to expand the basic sentence patterns. Absolute phrases do not modify any one word or phrase in a sentence; instead, they are whole sentence modifiers. Absolute phrases are made up of a noun (or pronoun), a participle, and their modifiers.

    attention   diverted
     noun   +   *participle*

EXAMPLE

His attention diverted by the fire, the witness is unlikely to have viewed the fleeing arsonist for more than a second.

---

§26.1.4   Clauses

A group of related words that has both a subject and a verb is a clause. There are two types of clauses: main (or independent) clauses and subordinate (or dependent) clauses. A main clause can stand alone as a sentence. A subordinate clause cannot stand alone as a sentence because a subordinate clause is introduced by a subordinating conjunction or relative pronoun.

Common subordinating conjunctions

after	if	though
although	if only	till
as	in order that	unless
as if	now that	until
as long as	once	when
as though	rather than	whenever
because	since	where
before	so that	whereas
even if	than	wherever
even though	that	while

Relative pronouns

that	which	whom
what	who	whomever
whatever	whoever	whose

Notice that in subordinate clauses introduced by a relative pronoun, the subject of the clause is often the relative pronoun (Defendants *who do not take the stand* risk having jurors infer that they are guilty.)

EXAMPLES

Main Clauses:

Martin retained full possession of the stock.

The trial court abused its discretion.

It failed to consider the statutory factors.

Subordinate Clauses:

although Martin retained full possession of the stock

that the trial court abused its discretion

when it failed to consider the statutory factors

Subordinate Clauses Attached to Main Clauses:

Although Martin retained full possession of the stock, the trial court awarded the stock to Judith.

The appellate court found that the trial court abused its discretion when it failed to consider the statutory factors.

---

§26.1.5   Appositives

Appositives are words or groups of words that follow a noun and rename it. They may also further describe or identify the noun.

EXAMPLES

Former White House aide <u>Oliver L. North</u> was the first key figure
                             (appositive)
to be prosecuted in the Iran-contra affair.

Jim Bakker, <u>television evangelist,</u> was convicted of twenty-four
                    (appositive)
counts of fraud and conspiracy.

In *Texas v. Johnson,* <u>a case about a state criminal statute forbid-
ding "the desecration of a venerated object,"</u> the Supreme Court
ruled that burning the American flag as an expression of political
discontent is protected by the First Amendment.

Appositives are frequently introduced by phrases (*that is, such as, for example*).

EXAMPLE

Evidence of some crimes, <u>such as fraud, embezzlement, and false
pretense,</u> may be probative of a defendant's credibility as a witness.

---

§26.1.6   Connecting Words

Throughout this section, we have discussed how to expand the five basic sentence patterns by adding single-word modifiers, phrases, and clauses. We can also expand these basic sentence patterns by using connecting words that allow us to combine words or word groups of equal rank. For example, we can add one or more nouns to a subject to create a compound subject (Smith and Wilson hit Jones), or we can add one or more verbs to the predicate to create a compound predicate (Smith hit and kicked Jones).

In fact, with proper use of the various types of connecting words, just about any word, phrase, or clause can be compounded.

a. Coordinating Conjunctions

The most common connecting words are the seven coordinating conjunctions.

and	nor	yet
but	for	so
or		

"And," "but," "or," and "nor" can connect any two (or more) of the same kind of word or word group. "For" and "so" connect main clauses.

EXAMPLES

Connecting Two Nouns:

Crimes of dishonesty involve **fraud** or **deceit.**

Connecting Two Verbs:

The complaint stated that the defendants had **published** but not **retracted** a defamatory article about Vashon Savings and Loan.

Connecting Three Phrases:

Copies of the article were distributed **to subscribers, to news-stands,** and **to at least three civic groups.**

Connecting Two Subordinate Clauses:

Because there are only two witnesses and **because each witness has a different version of the facts,** the jury will have to choose which one to believe.

Connecting Two Main Clauses:

Vashon Savings and Loan has not assumed a role of especial prominence in the affairs of society, nor **does it occupy a position of pervasive power or influence.**

---

b. Correlative Conjunctions

Correlative conjunctions come in pairs.

both . . . and	either . . . or	whether . . . or
not . . . but	neither . . . nor	as . . . as
not only . . . but also		

EXAMPLES

Plaintiff's contact with the community is <u>both</u> **conservative** <u>and</u> **low-key.**

The jury <u>either</u> **will not hear the defendant's testimony** <u>or</u> **will completely disregard it** if his prior convictions are admitted.

---

c. Conjunctive Adverbs

Even though conjunctive adverbs do not connect parts of the sentence grammatically, they are useful because they show the relationship between two or more ideas.

The Most Common Conjunctive Adverbs

accordingly	further	likewise	similarly
also	furthermore	meanwhile	still
anyway	hence	moreover	then
besides	however	nevertheless	thereafter
certainly	incidentally	next	therefore
consequently	indeed	nonetheless	thus
finally	instead	otherwise	undoubtedly

EXAMPLES

Mrs. Davis admits that her physician told her that she has a drinking problem. She refuses, <u>nevertheless</u>, to attend Alcoholics Anonymous. <u>Instead</u>, she claims that she drinks only an occasional glass of wine.

Mrs. Davis will have $33,872 a year to spend as she sees fit; <u>therefore</u>, she has no need for the dividend income from the stock.

Mr. Davis has no means from his present income to repurchase
the stock; <u>consequently</u>, the option to repurchase is worthless.

Notice too that because they do not connect parts of the sentence
grammatically, conjunctive adverbs can often move in the sentence.

EXAMPLES

Tom Davis owned his own business; <u>however</u>, his son did not participate in the business because the two did not get along.

Tom Davis owned his own business; his son did not participate in
the business, <u>however</u>, because the two did not get along.

---

§26.2   FRAGMENTS

Although there are a few exceptions, fragments are generally taboo in
legal writing. In fact, of the kinds of errors a writer can make, fragments
are considered one of the most egregious.

Given the strong bias against this writing error, legal writers who
are prone to writing sentence fragments should make it a priority to learn
what sentence fragments are and how to avoid them.

Simply defined, a sentence fragment is an incomplete sentence.
Theoretically, it may be missing its subject,[2] but more than likely it is
missing a main verb, or it is a subordinate clause trying to pose as a
sentence.

§26.2.1   Missing Main Verb

All verbals—gerunds, participles, and infinitives—are formed from
verbs, but they cannot fill verb slots in a sentence. Consequently, they
cannot serve as the main verb of a sentence. Some legal writers who are
prone to writing fragments mistake verbals for main verbs. See section
26.1.3 for definitions and explanations of verbals.

---

2. Imperative, or command, sentences such as "Sit down" or "Hang your
coat in the cloakroom" may appear to have a missing subject, but the subject is
always understood to be "you." Therefore, imperative sentences are not fragments
even if they are only one word long, like "Run!"

EXAMPLE   **FRAGMENT**

The attorney objecting to the line of questioning.

In the example above, "objecting" is not a verb; it is a participle modifying "attorney." Because the example has no main verb, it is a fragment, not a sentence. To make it a sentence, either add a main verb or change "objecting" from a participle to a main verb.

EXAMPLE   **POSSIBLE REVISIONS**

The attorney objecting to the line of questioning <u>rose</u> to her feet.

The attorney <u>objects</u> to the line of questioning.

The attorney <u>was objecting</u> to the line of questioning.

Notice that the same word, "objecting," can be a participle or, with an auxiliary verb added, a main verb.

§26.2.2 Subordinate Clauses Trying to Pose as Sentences

Take any main, or independent, clause and add a word like "although," "because," "if," "until," or "when" in front of it and it automatically becomes a subordinate, or dependent, clause.

until + main clause = subordinate clause

As a main clause, it is a sentence; as a subordinate clause standing alone, it is a fragment.

EXAMPLE

Main Clause:

The attorney objects to the line of questioning.

Subordinate Clause:

Until the attorney objects to the line of questioning.

Subordinate clauses must be attached to a main, or independent, clause.

EXAMPLE

Until the attorney objects to the line of questioning, the judge will
             (subordinate clause)   *(main clause)*
not rule.

"Although," "because," "if," "until," and "when" are not the only words, or subordinating conjunctions, that can change a main clause into a subordinate clause. Below is a fairly complete list of the most common subordinating conjunctions used in legal writing. Remember: If one of these words or phrases introduces a clause, that clause will be subordinate. It cannot stand alone.

Subordinating conjunctions

after	before	now that	till
although	even if	once	unless
as	even though	provided	until
as if	if	rather than	when
as long as	if only	since	whenever
as soon as	in order that	so that	where
as though	in that	than	whereas
because	no matter how	that	wherever
		though	while

Notice, too, that subordinate clauses may follow a main clause. In fact, many fragments are written because the writer should have attached a subordinate clause to the preceding main clause.

EXAMPLE

Fragment:

Kaiser's statement acknowledging our client's ownership of the land may have no effect on the hostility of his claim. Because he never acted in subordination to the true owner.

Corrected:

Kaiser's statement acknowledging our client's ownership of the land may have no effect on the hostility of his claim because Kaiser never acted in subordination to the true owner.

The relative pronouns — "who," "whoever," "whom," "whomever," "whose," "what," "whatever," "which," and "that" — also lure some writers into writing fragments.

EXAMPLE

Fragment:

The admission of a defendant's prior convictions may affect that defendant's decision to take the stand. Which would interfere with his right to testify freely on his own behalf.

Corrected:

The admission of a defendant's prior convictions may affect that defendant's decision to take the stand. Therefore, admission of his prior convictions would interfere with his right to testify freely on his own behalf.

"Who," "which," and "what" are also interrogative pronouns that introduce questions. Questions introduced by "who," "which," and "what" are not fragments.

EXAMPLE

Which witness will corroborate the defendant's alibi?

In short, to determine if you have written a sentence and not a fragment, (1) make sure you have a verb, (2) make sure you have a subject, and (3) make sure your subject and verb are not preceded by a subordinating conjunction or a relative pronoun. See Exercises 26.A and 26.B in the *Practice Book*.

§26.2.3 Permissible Uses of Incomplete Sentences

There are a handful of permissible uses for incomplete sentences in legal writing.

a. in issue statements beginning with "whether"
b. as answers to questions
c. in exclamations
d. for stylistic effect
e. as transitions

a. In Issue Statements Beginning with "Whether"

Many issue statements, or questions presented, begin with the word "whether."

EXAMPLE

Whether, under Washington tort law on wrongful death or conversion, the Hoffelmeirs may collect punitive damages for the destruction of their pet cat when the cat was impounded and when, after Mr. Janske of the Humane Society tried unsuccessfully to contact the Hoffelmeirs, the animal was destroyed before the time required by the Sequim City Ordinance.

Although a grammarian would not consider the example above to be a complete sentence, most attorneys and judges find this format acceptable in legal writing. It is as though legal readers read in an elliptical "The issue is" before "whether."

b. As Answers to Questions

Many office memos contain a brief answer section. Typically, a brief answer will begin with an incomplete sentence that is a short response to the legal question. This is an acceptable use of a fragment. The following example is the brief answer to the question presented in the preceding example.

EXAMPLE

Probably not. In Washington, there is a strong policy against the award of punitive damages and, unless there is a statutory provision allowing for punitive damages, the courts will not award them. In this instance, there is no statutory provision allowing for punitive damages.

c. In Exclamations

Exclamations rarely occur in legal writing because they make the tone of the writing appear inflammatory, effusive, or sarcastic. The one place exclamations do appear in legal writing is in quoted dialogue. On such occasions, quote exactly what the speaker said and how he or she said it, including fragments.

d. For Stylistic Effect

Sophisticated writers who are well schooled in the rules of grammar can occasionally use an intentional fragment for stylistic effect. Most writers, however, should avoid writing any fragments.

EXAMPLE

It may have been unavoidable, but it still took courage. More courage than most of us would have had.

e. As Transitions

As with fragments for stylistic effect, intentional fragments as transitions are a risk. Use them only if you are secure about and in complete control of your writing.

If you have already read sections 21.4 and 21.5 of this book, you may have noticed that the authors used two incomplete sentences as transitions to begin those sections.

EXAMPLES

First, the truth.

Again, the truth.

See Exercise 26.C in the *Practice Book*.

§26.3   VERB TENSE AND MOOD

§26.3.1   Tense

Verb tense does not pose problems for most legal writers who are native speakers of English. Native speakers tend to "hear" when the verb is right or wrong. Consequently, verb tense is one of those areas of writing that is best left alone, unless a writer is having problems.

For those native and non-native speakers of English who are having problems with verb tense in legal writing, the following is a quick review of the basic verb tense structure. See Chapter 29 for more on verbs and verb tense, particularly how auxiliary verbs create shades of meaning.

Throughout this review of verb tense, we will use a capital "X" to indicate the present on all time lines.

The term "tense" refers to the time in which the verb's action occurs in relation to the time when the writer is writing. For example, present tense is used for actions that occur in the present, that is, at the time the writer is writing.

EXAMPLE   **PRESENT TENSE**

The defendant <u>pleads</u> not guilty.

Time line: ＿＿＿＿＿＿ X ＿＿＿＿＿＿

the present
(the action is occurring
at the same time
the writer is writing)

Notice, however, that the "X" on the time line that represents "the present" may be as short as a fraction of a second or as long as several centuries, depending on what time frame the writer sets up.

Past tense refers to actions that occurred before the writer is writing.

EXAMPLE   **PAST TENSE**

Two years ago, this same prosecutor <u>charged</u> the defendant with aggravated assault.

Time line: ＿＿＿＿＿＿ X ＿＿＿＿＿＿
← **the past** →

Legal writers usually use the past tense when describing analogous cases.

EXAMPLE

In *Colorado Carpet,* the court <u>rejected</u> the argument for the specially manufactured goods exception because the carpet <u>was</u> not cut to a room size.

Future tense refers to actions that will occur after the writer is writing.

EXAMPLE   **FUTURE TENSE**

The plaintiff <u>will call</u> an expert witness.

      Time line: _____ X _____
                        ← **the future** →

The simple tenses—present, past, and future—are just that: simple and easy to use. Only the present tense offers a few noteworthy wrinkles.

In addition to its common use for actions that occur in the present, present tense is also used to express general truths and to show habitual actions.

EXAMPLES

Appellate courts <u>do</u> not <u>retry</u> a case on its facts.

The defendant <u>drinks</u> a six-pack or more of beer every Friday night before leaving the poker game.

Present tense can also be used to indicate the future when the sentence contains other words and phrases to signal a future time.

> **EXAMPLE**
>
> The court <u>hears</u> oral arguments later this afternoon.

The perfect tenses are a bit more complicated. Perfect tenses are designed to show that an action is completed before a certain time.

For example, the present perfect tense usually shows that an action is completed at the time of the statement. It is formed by using "have" or "has" before the past participle. In the sentence below, the present perfect "have tried" occurred before the present.

> **EXAMPLE**   **PRESENT PERFECT TENSE**
>
> The plaintiffs <u>have tried</u> this strategy before, but it is not working this time.
>
> Time line: _____ X _____
>   ⟶
>   (action begun in the
>   past and completed
>   before the present)

The present perfect tense is also used when the action was begun in the past and it continues on into the present.

> **EXAMPLES**
>
> The prosecutor <u>has lowered</u> his voice to a whisper in an attempt to rattle the witness.
>
> The United States Supreme Court <u>has held</u> that the "consent of one who possesses common authority over premises or effects is valid as against the absent, nonconsenting person with whom that authority is shared." *United States v. Matlock,* 415 U.S. 164, 170 (1974).
>
> Time line: _____ X _____
>   ⟶
>   (action begun in the
>   past and continues
>   on into present)

The past perfect tense is used when one past action was completed before another past action. For example, a legal writer may find it useful to use the past perfect to distinguish the time sequence of the facts of the case from the time sequence of a court's actions, both of which occurred in the past.

Note that the past perfect tense is formed by adding "had" before the past participle.

EXAMPLE　　　**PAST PERFECT TENSE**

The court <u>noted</u> that the defendant <u>had known</u> about the defective brakes for three months.

Time line: _____ x _____ x _____ X _____
　　　　　　　had　　*noted*
　　　　　　　known　*(past)*　　*(present)*
　　　　　　　(past
　　　　　　　perfect)

The past perfect tense is also useful when discussing court proceedings at different levels. For example, a writer may use the simple past tense to describe the decisions of an appellate court and the past perfect to describe the decisions of the trial court.

EXAMPLE

The Court of Appeals <u>affirmed</u> the trial court, which <u>had ruled</u> that
　　　　　　　　　　(simple past)　　　　　　　　　　*(past perfect)*
the statute did not apply.

The future perfect tense is used when an action that started in the past ends at a certain time in the future. It is formed by adding "will have" before the past participle.

EXAMPLE

By the time you finish dinner tonight, drunk drivers <u>will have</u> <u>claimed</u> five more victims on United States highways.

Time line: _____ X _____ x _____
　　　　　 _____→
　　　　　　　　　　　　　will have
　　　　　　　　　　　　　claimed

Every verb can also be progressive, that is, it can show continuing action by adding "-ing."

Present progressive: is claiming
Past progressive: was claiming
Future progressive: will be claiming
Present perfect progressive: has been claiming
Past perfect progressive: had been claiming
Future perfect progressive: will have been claiming

One last word about verb tense: One common myth is that writers have to maintain a consistent verb tense. Although writers should avoid needless shifts in verb tense, shifts in verb tense are required when there is a shift in time. Such a shift in time may even occur within the same sentence. See Exercises 26.D and 26.E in the *Practice Book.*

EXAMPLES

Her landlord <u>knows</u> that she <u>will be</u> unable to pay her rent.
      (present)   *(future)*

Although Mr. Henderson <u>built</u> the shed on the northwest corner of
               (past)
the property in 1992, he <u>admits</u> that Ms. Kyte <u>has owned</u> that
          (present)   *(present perfect)*
corner since 1989.

Smith <u>will argue</u> that he <u>did</u> not knowingly or willingly <u>consent</u> to a
    (future)   *(past)*   *(past)*
search of his wallet.

---

§26.3.2   Mood

In grammar, the term "mood" refers to the approach the writer gives the verb. English has three moods: indicative, imperative, and subjunctive. The indicative mood is used for statements of facts or questions.

EXAMPLE   **INDICATIVE MOOD**

The defendant <u>pleaded</u> "not guilty."

The imperative mood is used for sentences that are orders or commands. The subject of a sentence in the imperative mood is understood to be "you," the reader or listener.

EXAMPLE   **IMPERATIVE MOOD**

<u>Plead</u> "not guilty."

The subjunctive mood is the only mood that is a bit tricky. Although grammarians are constantly discussing its demise, the subjunctive mood is still used in a variety of situations.

     1. The subjunctive is used to express ideas contrary to fact.

EXAMPLE

If I <u>were</u> the defendant, I would plead "not guilty."

---

     2. The subjunctive is used to express a requirement.

EXAMPLE

The law requires that contracts <u>be signed</u> willingly, not under duress.

---

     3. The subjunctive is used to express a suggestion or recommendation.

EXAMPLE

His attorney recommended that he <u>be allowed</u> to give his own closing argument.

---

     4. The subjunctive is used to express a wish.

EXAMPLE

The clerk asked that the check <u>be post-dated.</u>

Note that the contrary-to-fact clauses begin with "if" and the requirement, suggestion, recommendation, or wish clauses all begin with an expressed or elliptical "that."

In addition, there are a few idioms such as "far be it from me" and "suffice it to say" that use the subjunctive mood.

The subjunctive mood is formed slightly differently depending on how it is used. For present conditions that are contrary to fact, it is formed from the past tense of the verb. For the verb "to be," it uses "were."

EXAMPLES

If I <u>took</u> a reading on the toxic particles being emitted right now, it would show that the factory has completely disregarded EPA guidelines.

If she <u>were</u> to testify, the defendant's sister would corroborate his story.

For past conditions that are contrary to fact, the subjunctive mood is formed from the past perfect.

EXAMPLE

<u>Had</u> the contract been signed, there would be no question that it is valid.

For requirements, recommendations, and suggestions, the subjunctive mood is formed from the infinitive form of the verb without the "to."

EXAMPLES

The law requires that the adverse possessor <u>prove</u> that the possession was open and notorious.

Mr. Hughes suggested that the store manager <u>notify</u> him of any discrepancies.

For wishes and desires, the subjunctive mood is formed from the past tense of the verb. For the verb "to be," "were" is used.

EXAMPLE

My client wishes that you <u>were</u> her attorney.

---

§26.4   AGREEMENT

Simply put, agreement is matching the form of one word to another. In legal writing, agreement can be a problem in two areas: (1) the agreement in number between a subject and verb and (2) the agreement in number between a pronoun and its antecedent.

§26.4.1   Subject-Verb Agreement

Singular subjects take singular verbs, and plural subjects take plural verbs.

For most native speakers of English, this kind of subject-verb agreement comes almost as naturally as breathing, as long as the sentence is short and simple.

EXAMPLES

The law requires that all drivers wear seat belts.

singular subject = law
singular verb = requires

The immigration laws require that all workers provide proof of citizenship before starting a job.

plural subject = laws
plural verb = require

In English, we often think that adding "s" makes the plural form of words. This is true for nouns but not for verbs. We add an "s" to the singular form of present tense verbs (except the verb "to be") when they are matched with a singular noun or the pronouns "he," "she," or "it." For example, we say "a client maintains," "he rejects," "she alleges," or "it confirms."

In simple sentences, a writer can usually make subjects and verbs agree by listening to the way the sentences sound. The writer's ear tells him or her what matches and what doesn't. In longer, more complicated sentences, like those that often occur in legal writing, the ear is more likely to be misled. The following rules cover those situations.

| **Rule 1** | **A Subject and Its Verb Must Agree Even When They Are Separated by Other Words** |

When other words, particularly nouns, come between a subject and its verb, the writer may inadvertently match the verb to a word other than the subject. The following example demonstrates this error in agreement.

EXAMPLE   **INCORRECT**

Custom-made <u>towels</u> imprinted with the hotel's logo <u>satisfies</u> the
          (subject)   *(verb)*
requirement that the goods be specially manufactured.

The writer has mistakenly chosen the singular verb "satisfies" to match with the intervening noun "logo" when the verb should be the plural form "satisfy" to agree with the plural subject "towels." One way writers can check for this kind of agreement error is to read their subjects and verbs together without the intervening words. "Towels satisfy" will sound right to native speakers.

The number of the subject is not changed by adding intervening words that begin with expressions such as "accompanied by," "as well as," "in addition to," "with," "together with," or "along with." These expressions are considered prepositions and not coordinating conjunctions (see section 26.1), so they modify the subject. They do not change its number.

In the following example, the verb "suggests" correctly agrees with the subject "statement."

EXAMPLE

The defendant's <u>statement</u> to the police, as well as her testimony at trial, <u>suggests</u> that her actions were premeditated.

| **Rule 2** | **Two or More Subjects Joined by "And" Usually Take a Plural Verb** |

Subjects joined by "and" are plural. This rule does not change even if one or all of the subjects are singular.

EXAMPLE

North Star Cinema and Highland Heights Theater question the validity of the admissions tax.

Unfortunately, writers sometimes hear only the second half of the subject with the verb and mistakenly select a singular verb ("Highland Heights Theater questions"). To correct this agreement error, you may find it easier to mentally substitute the word "they" for plural subjects when trying to use your ear to find the correct form of the verb ("they question").

Exception A

Occasionally two or more parts of the subject make up one idea or refer to one person or thing. In such cases, use a singular verb.

EXAMPLE

His wife and beneficiary was the only person mentioned in the will.

Exception B

Occasionally the words "each" or "every" precede one or more of the parts of a plural subject. In such cases, use a singular verb.

EXAMPLE

Every juror and spectator in the courtroom expects the defendant to testify.

Rule 3	**Subjects Joined by "Or" or "Nor" Take Verbs That Agree with the Part of the Subject Closest to the Verb**

To check subject-verb agreement in sentences with subjects joined by "or" or "nor," simply read only the second half of the subject with the verb and let your ear help you select the correct verb form. In the following examples, read "Lazar Television is" and "her older sisters have."

EXAMPLES

Neither Horizon Telecommunications nor Lazar Television is the type of enterprise that the bulk sales statutes seek to regulate.

The child's mother or her older sisters have been caring for her after school.

In a verb phrase like "have been caring" in the preceding example, the helping, or auxiliary, verbs are the ones that change.

> singular: has been caring
> plural: have been caring

Rule 4	**Most Indefinite Pronouns Take Singular Verbs**

Indefinite pronouns are ones that do not refer to any definite person or thing, or they do not specify definite limits. The following is a list of the most common indefinite pronouns:

all	each	everything	none
any	either	neither	somebody
anyone	everyone	nobody	someone
anybody	everybody	no one	something

Usually these pronouns refer to a single, indefinite person or thing, so they take singular verbs.

EXAMPLE

Everyone who takes the stand swears to tell the truth.

A few indefinite pronouns—"none," "all," "most," "some," "any," and "half"—may take either a singular or a plural verb depending on the noun to which they refer.

EXAMPLES

All of the jewelry was recovered.

All of the rings were recovered.

Rule 5   **Collective Nouns Take Singular Verbs When the Group Acts as One Unit; Collective Nouns Take Plural Verbs When the Members of the Group Act Separately**

The following is a list of the most common collective nouns in legal writing:

jury	committee	board
audience	team	majority
family	crowd	number
Supreme Court	appellate court	fractions (when used
names of companies/		as nouns)
corporations		

The following examples all use collective nouns that are acting as one unit, so the verbs are singular.

EXAMPLES

The jury has reached its verdict.

The appellate court affirms the conviction.

Two thirds of the board is absent.

The following example uses a collective noun whose members are acting separately, so the verb is plural.

EXAMPLE

The jury have all had an opportunity to state whether they believe in capital punishment.

Even though it is correct to use a plural verb with a collective noun when the members are acting separately, it usually sounds awkward. Consequently, many writers prefer to revise their sentences so that they don't have collective nouns that require plural verbs.

EXAMPLE   **REVISED**

The jurors have all had an opportunity to state whether they believe in capital punishment.

An easy way to tell if the collective noun "number" is singular or plural is to check whether "number" is preceded by "a" or "the." "A number" requires a plural verb; "the number" requires a singular verb.

EXAMPLES

A number of witnesses are willing to testify that they saw the defendant drive out of the parking lot.

The number of union members who are seeking early retirement is growing.

| **Rule 6** | **Nouns Ending in "s" That Are Singular in Meaning Take Singular Verbs** |

Despite their "s" ending, words like "aesthetics," "athletics," "economics," "mathematics," "news," "physics," "politics," "statistics," and "tactics" are usually considered singular because they describe a whole concept or body of knowledge.

EXAMPLE

Politics is inappropriate in a court of law.

When "statistics" refers to individual facts, it takes a plural verb.

EXAMPLE

The enrollment statistics show that the university has consistently discriminated against Asian students.

| **Rule 7** | **Linking Verbs Agree with Their Subjects, Not Their Subject Complements** |

In the following example, the linking verb "was" agrees with "testimony," not the subject complement "contradictory and intentionally misleading."

EXAMPLE

The defendant's testimony was contradictory and intentionally mis-leading.

In the next example, the linking verb "is" agrees with "part," not "arguments."

EXAMPLE

The best part of any trial is the closing arguments.

See section 26.1 for more on subject complements.

Rule 8   **Verbs Agree with Their Subjects Even When the Subjects Come After the Verb**

Subjects follow verbs after expletive constructions such as "there is" and "there are."

EXAMPLE

There is a possibility that the defendant will plead "temporary in-sanity."

There are several options for ensuring that your loan is repaid.

Subjects may also follow verbs when normal word order is changed for emphasis.

EXAMPLE

At no time was Brown aware that his conversations were being tape recorded.

At no time were Brown and Smith aware that their conversations were being tape recorded.

| **Rule 9** | **The Title of a Work or a Word Used as a Word Takes a Singular Verb** |

EXAMPLE

Tactics in Legal Reasoning is an excellent resource for both law students and practitioners.

When a word is used as a word, it is often enclosed in quotation marks or preceded by "the word."

EXAMPLES

"Premises" has at least two different meanings: (1) the introductory propositions to a syllogism or (2) the area of land surrounding a building.

The word "premises" has two different meanings.

Compare the previous examples, both of which used the singular verb "has," with the following example, which requires the plural verb form "have."

EXAMPLE

The premises have been searched by the police.

Rule 10	When Used as Subjects of Relative Clauses, the Relative Pronouns "That," "Which," and "Who" Agree in Number with Their Noun Antecedents; Consequently, Their Verbs Must Also Agree in Number with Their Noun Antecedents

In the following example, "who" refers back to the plural "attorneys"; consequently, the verb "are" agrees in number with "attorneys."

EXAMPLE

The attorneys who are representing the plaintiff are Linda Rhodes-Lines and Malcolm S. Hanover.

The phrase "one of the _____" can cause confusing agreement problems when it is followed by a relative pronoun. Decide whether the relative pronoun refers to "one" or to the noun in the blank before selecting the verb for the relative clause. One test for determining the relative pronoun's antecedent is to try omitting "of the _____." If the meaning of the sentence does not change, then the relative pronoun refers back to "one."

EXAMPLE

Our client is one of the several board members who are accused of price fixing.

In the preceding example, the writer intends to say that several board members are accused of price fixing and that the client is one of this group. Consequently, "who" refers to "several board members," so the verb "are accused" must be plural.

EXAMPLE

Our client is the only one of several board members who is accused of price fixing.

In the preceding example, the writer intends to say that the client is one of several board members, but he or she is the only one accused of price fixing. Consequently, "who" refers to "one," so the verb "is accused" must be singular.

Rule 11	Money, Distance, and Measurement Subjects Usually Take Singular Verbs

---

EXAMPLE

Twenty thousand dollars is a reasonable fee for a case of this complexity.

See Exercise 26.F in the *Practice Book*.

§26.4.2 Pronoun-Antecedent Agreement

A pronoun must agree with its antecedent. The noun a pronoun refers to is known as its antecedent.

Pronouns are substitutes for nouns. They have no independent meanings. Consequently, they must refer to a noun and be consistent with that noun in gender, person, and number.

Legal writers usually do not have problems making their pronouns and antecedents agree in gender or person. Agreement in number, however, can be a bit more difficult.

Rule 1	Singular Antecedents Require Singular Pronouns; Plural Antecedents Require Plural Pronouns

---

EXAMPLES

William MacDonald may claim that his constitutional rights were
    (antecedent)   *(pronoun)*
violated.

William MacDonald and Grace Yessler may claim that their con-
    (antecedent)   *(antecedent)*   *(pronoun)*
stitutional rights were violated.

This rule, although simple on the surface, becomes a little trickier when the pronoun substitutes for a generic noun that is singular. Because English does not have a singular generic pronoun to fit these situations, writers are left with less-than-ideal choices.

For example, in informal writing and oral language, you may frequently see or hear a plural pronoun used as a substitute for a singular generic noun, as in the ungrammatical example below. In formal writing, such as legal writing, this practice is unacceptable.

EXAMPLE   UNGRAMMATICAL

The <u>defendant</u> may claim that <u>their</u> constitutional rights were vio-
    (antecedent)   *(pronoun)*
lated.

Some writers try to solve the problem by resorting to the traditional masculine pronoun for all generic nouns. This practice is unacceptable to many modern writers who believe that language should be gender-neutral. (See section 24.4.)

EXAMPLE   MASCULINE PRONOUN

The <u>defendant</u> may claim that <u>his</u> constitutional rights were vio-
    (antecedent)   *(pronoun)*
lated.

Occasionally, the problem can be solved by making the generic noun plural. Unfortunately, not all sentences will allow this quick fix.

EXAMPLE   PLURAL NOUN

<u>Defendants</u> may claim that <u>their</u> constitutional rights were violated.
(antecedent)   *(pronoun)*

Even fewer sentences will allow a writer to remove the pronoun altogether without substantial revision or loss in meaning.

EXAMPLE   **REMOVED PRONOUN**

The defendant may claim that the constitutional rights were violated.

The example above avoids the grammatical problem but with a significant loss in meaning: The belief that one actually possesses constitutional rights is no longer included in the sentence's meaning.

What is left, then, is the option of using the slightly awkward "he or she," "his or her," "himself or herself."

EXAMPLE

The <u>defendant</u> may claim that <u>his or her</u> constitutional rights were
    (antecedent)   *(pronouns)*
violated.

While not perfect, this option seems to be the best choice, provided the writer doesn't put more than one "he or she," "his or her," or "himself or herself" in a sentence.

Exception to Rule 1:

Occasionally the word "each" or "every" precedes one or more of the parts of a plural antecedent. In such cases, use a singular pronoun.

EXAMPLE

Every girl and woman in the community feared for her safety.

Rule 2	When a Pronoun Refers to Two or More Antecedents Joined by "Or" or "Nor," the Pronoun Agrees with the Nearer Antecedent

EXAMPLE

Either <u>David Wilson</u> or <u>Donald Wilson</u> left <u>his</u> keys in the car.
     (antecedent)   *(antecedent)* *(pronoun)*

Notice that this rule for pronoun agreement is similar to Rule 3 for subject-verb agreement.

When a singular and a plural antecedent are joined by "or" or "nor," place the plural antecedent last so that the pronoun can be plural.

EXAMPLE

Neither the <u>defendant</u> nor his <u>brothers</u> admit knowing where <u>their</u> neighbors keep items of value.

Rule 3	When an Indefinite Pronoun Is the Antecedent, Use the Singular Pronoun

Indefinite pronouns are ones that do not refer to any definite person or thing, or they do not specify definite limits. The most common indefinite pronouns are "all," "any," "anyone," "anybody," "each," "either," "everyone," "everybody," "everything," "neither," "nobody," "no one," "none," "somebody," "someone," and "something."

EXAMPLE

<u>Anyone</u> would have noticed that <u>his</u> or <u>her</u> license plate was removed.

Notice that this rule for pronoun agreement is similar to Rule 4 for subject-verb agreement (see Section 26.4.1).

As with Rule 1, writers must take care not to use the informal and ungrammatical plural pronoun or the traditional generic "he" as a pronoun substitute for an indefinite pronoun.

EXAMPLES

Ungrammatical:

Somebody must have used their phone to call the police.

Masculine pronoun:

Somebody must have used his phone to call the police.

Corrected:

Somebody must have used his or her phone to call the police.
OR
Somebody must have used the phone to call the police.

Rule 4	**When a Collective Noun Is the Antecedent, Use a Singular Pronoun If You Are Referring to the Group as One Unit and a Plural Pronoun If You Are Referring to the Individual Members of the Group**

Some common collective nouns are "jury," "committee," "appellate court," "Supreme Court," "majority," "board," "team," "family," "audience," "crowd," "number," and the names of companies and corporations. See Exercise 26.G in the *Practice Book*.

EXAMPLES

The jury must not be misled about Jason Richardson's credibility when it is considering his testimony.

Shopping Haven discriminated against John Adams when it failed to issue him a new credit card for an existing account.

---

§26.5   Pronoun Reference

Pronouns are substitutes for nouns. Consequently, pronouns usually[3] refer back to a noun, and that noun is known as the antecedent.

EXAMPLE

Marino moved for reconsideration, but her motion was denied.
(antecedent)   *(pronoun)*

Legal writers tend to have two kinds of problems with pronouns and their antecedents: (1) they use plural pronouns to refer back to singular antecedents; and (2) they use pronouns that have unclear or ambiguous antecedents. The first problem is one of grammatical agreement, and it is discussed in the second half of section 26.4 on agreement. The second problem is the focus of this section.

§26.5.1   Each Pronoun Should Clearly Refer Back to Its Antecedent

Consider the following sentence:

EXAMPLE

Officer Robert O'Malley, who arrested Howard Davis, said that he was drunk at the time.

As it stands, the sentence has two possible readings because the pronoun "he" has two possible antecedents: Officer Robert O'Malley and Howard Davis. To clear up the ambiguity, do one of two things:

1. repeat the noun rather than use a pronoun, or
2. revise so that the pronoun is no longer ambiguous.

---

3. Indefinite pronouns such as "someone," "anybody," "everything," and "neither" do not refer back to nouns. Also, some pronouns that are parts of idioms ("it is likely that . . . ," "it is clear that . . . ," "it is raining") do not have antecedents.

EXAMPLE   POSSIBLE REVISIONS

Officer Robert O'Malley, who arrested Howard Davis, said that Davis was drunk at the time.

Howard Davis was drunk when he was arrested by Officer O'Malley.

Officer O'Malley was drunk when he arrested Howard Davis.

According to the arresting officer, Robert O'Malley, Howard Davis was drunk at the time of the arrest.

Officer Robert O'Malley, who arrested Howard Davis, admitted being drunk at the time of the arrest.

See Exercise 26.H in the *Practice Book.*

§26.5.2   Avoid the Use of "It," "This," "That," "Such," and "Which" to Refer Broadly to a General Idea in a Preceding Sentence

Consider the following sentences:

EXAMPLE

Even if Mr. Smith's testimony about possible embarrassment caused by Acme is adequate to justify a damage award, emotional harm is difficult to quantify. This makes it unlikely that Mr. Smith will receive any substantial recovery.

To what does "this" in the second sentence refer? Because it does not seem to refer back to any specific noun in the preceding sentence, the reader is left to guess exactly how much or how little of the preceding discussion "this" is supposed to encompass.

The solution to many broad pronoun reference problems is often a rather simple one: Add a summarizing noun after the pronoun to show the limits of the reference.

EXAMPLE   **CORRECTED**

This difficulty makes it unlikely that Mr. Smith will receive any substantial recovery.

The same technique often works well with "that" and "such."

EXAMPLE

Mrs. Marquette has testified that Mr. Marquette has beaten her and their children on at least three occasions, that he has locked them out of their home twice, and that he has threatened to "cut their throats" if they told anyone. According to Mr. Marquette, that is a lie.

Corrected:

Mrs. Marquette has testified that Mr. Marquette has beaten her and their children on at least three occasions, that he has locked them out of their home twice, and that he has threatened to "cut their throats" if they told anyone. According to Mr. Marquette, that testimony is a lie.

Sometimes it is better to omit "that" and "such" and use only a summarizing noun.

EXAMPLE

A court will consider modifying child custody arrangements if both parents request a modification or if there has been a substantial change in the circumstances. Such has occurred in this case.

Corrected:

A court will consider modifying child custody arrangements if both parents request a modification or if there has been a substantial change in the circumstances. A substantial change in the circumstances has occurred in this case.

The use of the pronoun "which" to refer broadly to a preceding idea is a trickier problem to correct. Look at the following example and see if you can determine what the "which" stands for. Keep in mind the basic rule that a pronoun is a substitute for a noun.

EXAMPLE

In *Boone v. Mullendore,* Dr. Mullendore failed to remove Mrs. Boone's fallopian tube, which resulted in the birth of a baby.

The only nouns that "which" could possibly refer to are the case name, "Dr. Mullendore," and "fallopian tube." Obviously none of these nouns resulted in the birth of a baby. Instead, the writer seems to suggest that "which" is a substitute for the following idea: Dr. Mullendore's failure to remove Mrs. Boone's fallopian tube. Notice that in expressing what the "which" referred to, we had to use the noun "failure" rather than the verb "failed." To correct the error, then, we must add the noun "failure" to the sentence.

EXAMPLE   **CORRECTED**

In *Bonne v. Mullendore,* Dr. Mullendore's failure to remove Mrs. Boone's fallopian tube resulted in the birth of a baby.

Notice that in correcting the broad pronoun "which," the writer often omits the word "which."

Sometimes the pronoun "which" appears to refer broadly to a preceding idea but, on closer examination, refers to a noun that appears much earlier in the sentence. To clear up any potential confusion about the "which," the writer can often repeat the previous noun and change the "which" to "that." See Exercise 26.I in the *Practice Book.*

EXAMPLE

Admission of Moore's prior conviction will adversely affect his constitutional right to testify in his own defense, which is central to this case.

Corrected:

Admission of Moore's prior conviction will adversely affect his constitutional right to testify in his own defense, a right that is central to this case.

Be sure to distinguish between the incorrect use of "which" to refer broadly to a previously stated idea and the correct use of "which" to introduce nonrestrictive clauses.

§26.5.3   Pronouns Should Refer Back to Nouns, Not Adjectives

Occasionally a word that appears to be a noun is actually an adjective because it modifies a noun.

EXAMPLE

the <u>Rheams</u> <u>building</u>
    (adjective) (noun)

Often the possessive form of a noun is used as an adjective in a sentence.

EXAMPLE

the <u>defendant's</u> <u>alibi</u>
    (adjective) (noun)

But because a pronoun must always refer to a noun, adjectives that are noun look-alikes cannot serve as antecedents for pronouns.

EXAMPLES

Incorrect:

The Rheams building has undergone as many facelifts as he has.

Corrected:

The Rheams building has undergone as many facelifts as Rheams himself has.

Incorrect:

After hearing the defendant's alibi, the jurors seemed to change their opinion of him.

Corrected:

The jurors seemed to change their opinion of the defendant after they heard his alibi.

Admittedly, this rule is a grammatical technicality. Infractions rarely create ambiguity. Even so, because correctness and precision are required in legal writing, it is best to heed the rule. See Exercises 26.J and 26.K in the *Practice Book.*

§26.6   MODIFIERS

Using modifiers correctly is simple. All one has to do is (1) remember to keep modifiers close to the word or words they modify and (2) make sure the words they modify are in the same sentence as the modifiers.

§26.6.1   Misplaced Modifiers

Forgetting to keep modifiers close to the word or words they modify leads to misplaced modifiers. Some words—"almost," "also," "even," "ever," "exactly," "hardly," "just," "merely," "nearly," "not," "only," "scarcely," "simply"—are particularly prone to being misplaced. Place these words immediately before the words they modify.

Notice, for example, how the placement of "only" changes the meaning in the following sentences.

EXAMPLES

Only the defendant thought that the car was rented.
No one but the defendant thought that.

The defendant only thought that the car was rented.
He did not know for sure.

The defendant thought only that the car was rented.
He thought one thing, nothing else.

The defendant thought that the only car was rented.
Only one car was available, and it was rented.

The defendant thought that the car was only rented.
He did not think it was leased or sold.

In speech, such single-word modifiers are often put before the verb even when the speaker does not intend them to modify the verb. Some authorities accept placing "only" immediately before the verb if it modifies the whole sentence.

> Speech: He only drove ten miles.
> Writing: He drove only ten miles.

Phrases, particularly prepositional phrases, can also be easily misplaced in sentences. The result can be imprecise writing, an awkward construction, and unintentional humor.

The writer of the following example was surprised to find out that because of a misplaced modifier he had inaccurately placed the brother instead of the cabin in New Hampshire.

EXAMPLE

The defendant owned a cabin with his brother in New Hampshire.

Revised:

The defendant and his brother owned a cabin in New Hampshire.

In the following example, the phrase "contrary to the wishes of his wife" is both awkward and misleading; it seems to be modifying "form."

EXAMPLE

Mr. Barry mailed the form contrary to the wishes of his wife to the home office in Toronto.

The sentence can be made a bit clearer by treating the phrase "contrary to the wishes of his wife" as an interrupter and setting it off from the rest of the sentence with commas. Now the phrase does not appear to modify "form." Better still, to improve the sentence construction and to show that the phrase modifies the entire clause "Mr. Barry mailed the form to the home office in Toronto," revise the sentence as follows.

EXAMPLE　　**REVISED**

Contrary to the wishes of his wife, Mr. Barry mailed the form to the home office in Toronto.

The misplaced modifier in the following example gave the writer a meaning she never intended.

EXAMPLE

The witness to the events may be unavailable after the accident.

Although there are contexts in which this sentence is correctly written, the writer intended to say, "The witness to the events after the accident may be unavailable." Her version made it sound like an intentional "accident" was being planned for the specific purpose of making the witness "unavailable"!

Take care to place clauses that begin with "who," "which," and "that" immediately after the noun they modify.

EXAMPLE

The victim described her attacker as having a tattoo on his right buttock, which was shaped like a peace sign.

This sentence suggests that the attacker's right buttock, not his tattoo, was shaped like a peace sign.

EXAMPLE   REVISED

The victim described her attacker as having a tattoo that was shaped like a peace sign on his right buttock.

See Exercises 26.L, 26.M, and 26.N in the *Practice Book.*

§26.6.2   Dangling Modifiers

Dangling modifiers are those modifiers that do not have a noun in the sentence that they can modify; hence, they are "dangling," or unattached to an appropriate noun. Legal writers tend to write dangling modifiers for one of two reasons: (1) the noun or pronoun the modifier is intended to modify is in the mind of the writer but inadvertently omitted from the sentence; or (2) the writer wanted to avoid the first person pronouns "I" or "we"[4] and, in doing so, left a modifier dangling.

EXAMPLE   DANGLING MODIFIER

By calling attention to the defendant's post-arrest silence, the jury was allowed to make prejudicial and false inferences.

In the example above, the modifier "by calling attention to the defendant's post-arrest silence" should modify the noun "the prosecutor," which does not appear in the sentence. Unfortunately, it seems to be modifying the noun closest to it: "the jury."

EXAMPLE   REVISED

By calling attention to the defendant's post-arrest silence, the prosecutor encouraged the jury to make prejudicial and false inferences.

---

4. Many authorities in legal writing still advise legal writers to avoid using first-person references.

Notice how in the following example the dangling modifier can be corrected by including the pronoun it modifies, "we," or by revising the sentence so that the dangling modifier is no longer a modifier.

EXAMPLE

In deciding whether to attempt to quash service, more than the technical merits of the case have to be considered.

Revised:

In deciding whether to attempt to quash service, we must consider more than the technical merits of the case. *OR*

A decision about whether to attempt to quash service must be based on more than the technical merits of the case.

You can see that the majority of dangling modifiers occur at the beginnings of sentences. One way to avoid writing this type of dangling modifier is to remember to place the noun the modifier modifies right after the comma separating the modifier from the main clause.

Modifier,　　　Main Clause
　　　　　(noun)

By calling attention . . . silence, the prosecutor . . . .

If you are having difficulty deciding what noun the modifier should modify, ask yourself who or what is doing the action described in that modifier. Then place the answer to that question right after the comma separating the modifier from the main clause.

In deciding . . . service, we must consider . . . .

Notice too that when the real actor in a sentence is in the subject position, the problem of dangling modifiers is usually solved. (See section 23.2 for more on using effective subjects in sentences.)

Many kinds of grammatical structures can be dangling. The most common are participles (marked by the "-ing," "-ed," or past endings), infinitives (to + verb, "to show"), and prepositional phrases.

Some dangling modifiers can also be corrected by adding a subject to the modifier.

EXAMPLE

While petitioning for a permit, zoning regulations in the area were changed.

Revised:

While the mental institution was petitioning for a permit, zoning regulations in the area were changed.

Subordinate clauses, like the one in the revision above, are not dangling modifiers.

Dangling modifiers can also occur at the ends of sentences. Again, the problem is that the noun the modifier modifies does not appear in the sentence.

EXAMPLE   DANGLING MODIFIER

This motion was denied in the interest of judicial economy, reasoning that there was evidence that raised a question regarding Anderson's knowledge of the relationship.

Who or what is doing the reasoning that there is evidence? Most certainly the court, but the noun "court" does not appear in the sentence.

EXAMPLE   REVISED

Reasoning that there was evidence that raised a question regarding Anderson's knowledge of the relationship, the court denied this motion in the interest of judicial economy.

It is also permissible to leave the modifier at the end of the sentence, as long as it modifies the subject of the sentence.

EXAMPLE   **REVISED**

The court denied this motion in the interest of judicial economy, reasoning that there was evidence that raised a question regarding Anderson's knowledge of the relationship.

The example could also be correctly revised by changing the modifier to a subordinate clause. See Exercise 26.O in the *Practice Book.*

EXAMPLE   **REVISED**

The court denied this motion in the interest of judicial economy because there was evidence that raised a question regarding Anderson's knowledge of the relationship.

---

§26.6.3   Squinting Modifiers

Squinting modifiers are labeled as such because they appear to be looking both backward and forward in a sentence; that is, they appear to be modifying both the word that precedes them and the word that follows them.

EXAMPLE

The bridge inspection that was done frequently suggested that the drawbridge electrical system was beginning to fail.

This sentence has two possible interpretations: Are the inspections themselves done frequently, or are there frequent suggestions throughout the inspection report?

EXAMPLE   **REVISED**

The bridge inspection that was frequently done suggested that the drawbridge electrical system was beginning to fail. *OR*

The bridge inspection that was done suggested frequently that the drawbridge electrical system was beginning to fail.

---

§26.7   PARALLELISM

Consider the following pairs of sentences. What is it about version B of each pair that makes it easier to read?

EXAMPLE

1A.   The defendant claims that on the day of the murder he was at home alone washing his car, he mowed his lawn, and his dog needed a bath so he gave him one.

1B.   The defendant claims that on the day of the murder he was at home alone washing his car, mowing his lawn, and bathing his dog.

2A.   Dr. Stewart is a competent surgeon with over twenty years of experience and who is respected in the local medical community.

2B.   Dr. Stewart is a competent surgeon who has over twenty years of experience and who is respected in the local medical community.

3A.   The defendant claimed the evidence was prejudicial and that it lacked relevance.

3B.   The defendant claimed the evidence was prejudicial and irrelevant.

In all the preceding pairs, the version A sentences lack parallelism and, as a result, are grammatically incorrect, as well as clumsy and unsophisticated. The version B sentences do not change the content significantly; they simply use the structure of the sentence to make that content more apparent and more accessible. Specifically, they use parallelism.

In grammar, parallelism is defined as "the use of similar grammatical form for coordinated elements." This definition may seem overly abstract or vague until it is broken into its components.

"Coordinated elements" are parts of a sentence joined by conjunctions, such as "and," "but," "or," "nor," and "yet." Sometimes they are pairs, but often they are a series or a list.

"Similar grammatical form" simply means that a noun is matched with other nouns, verbs are matched with other verbs, prepositional phrases are matched with other prepositional phrases, and so on.

For example, look at the poorly coordinated elements in sentence 1A above.

washing his car,
he mowed his lawn, and
his dog needed a bath so he gave him one

Even without analyzing exactly what kind of phrase or clause each one of these elements is, we can see that they do not have similar grammatical form. Now look at the coordinated elements of sentence 1B. Note how the "-ing" endings make the items parallel.

washing his car
mowing his lawn, and
bathing his dog

Matching endings of the first key word in each of the elements is one way to make elements parallel.

Now compare the coordinated elements in 2A and 2B.

2A.　with over twenty years of experience and
　　　who is respected in the local medical community

2B.　who has over twenty years of experience and
　　　who is respected in the local medical community

Again, without doing an analysis of the grammar of each element, we can see, or perhaps hear, that 2B is parallel, but this time the parallelism is signaled by using the same word, "who," to introduce each element.

In some cases, however, you will not be able to rely on matching endings to key words or matching introductory words; you will have to find the same grammatical form in order to make the elements parallel.

In 3A, for example, the writer has tried to match an adjective, "prejudicial," with a relative clause, "that it lacked relevance." The writer could have used the second tip—matching introductory words—and created the following parallel elements:

that the evidence was prejudicial and
that it lacked relevance

The more concise and better choice is to find the appropriate adjective to match "prejudicial."

prejudicial and
irrelevant

Because many sentences in legal writing are long and complicated, parallelism is critical for keeping the content and its presentation manageable. In the following sentence, for example, the defendant's two concessions are easier for the reader to see because they are set out using parallel constructions.

EXAMPLE

Counsel for the defendant conceded that she did assault Coachman and that a trial would determine only the degree of the assault.

$$\text{conceded} \left\langle \begin{array}{l} \underline{\text{that she did assault Coachman}} \\ \underline{\text{that a trial would determine only the degree}} \\ \text{of the assault} \end{array} \right.$$

Notice too in both the preceding and subsequent examples that by repeating the introductory word "that," the writer has made the parallelism more obvious, which, in turn, makes the sentence easier to read.

EXAMPLE

When questioned at the parole hearing, Robinson claimed that it was wrong to tell only one side of the story, that he had not received permission but felt he had a right to write what he wanted, and that people had a right to hear the other side of the story.

$$\text{claimed} \left\langle \begin{array}{l} \underline{\text{that it was wrong to tell only one side of the story,}} \\ \underline{\text{that he had not received permission but felt he had a right}} \\ \text{to write what he wanted, and} \\ \underline{\text{that people had a right to hear the other side of the story.}} \end{array} \right.$$

Writing parallel elements is required for grammatical sentences; repeating an introductory word to heighten the parallelism is not required, but rather recommended for making the parallelism more obvious to the reader.

Issue statements can also become much more manageable when the legally significant facts are laid out using parallel construction. The following example uses "when" as the introductory word to each element. Notice too how the legally significant facts are not only written using parallel construction but also grouped according to those that favor the defendant and those that favor the plaintiff. The conjunction "but" helps the reader see the two groupings.

EXAMPLE

Under Federal Rule of Civil Procedure 4(d)(1), is service of process valid when process was left with defendant's husband at his home in California, when defendant and her husband maintain separate residences, when defendant intends to maintain a separate residence from her husband, but when defendant regularly visits her husband in California, when defendant keeps some personal belongings in the California house, when defendant receives some mail in California, and when defendant received actual notice when her husband mailed the summons and complaint to her?

---

when process was left with defendant's husband at his home in
     California
when defendant and her husband maintain separate residences
when defendant intends to maintain separate residence from her
     husband, BUT
when defendant regularly visits her husband in California
when the defendant keeps some personal belongings in the Califor-
     nia house
when defendant receives some mail in California
when defendant received actual notice when her husband mailed
     the summons and complaint to her

Parallelism is also critical, indeed required, when setting out lists.

EXAMPLE

Wilson challenges the admission of three photographs, which he claims are gruesome: (1) the photograph of Melissa Reed as she appeared when discovered at the crime scene; (2) the photograph of Melinda Reed as she appeared when discovered at the crime scene; and (3) a photograph of Wilson wearing dental retractors to hold his lips back while exposing his teeth.

Lists require parallelism when they are incorporated into the writer's text, as in the example above, and when they are indented and tabulated, as in the example below.

EXAMPLE

The school district will probably be liable for the following:

1. the cost of restoring the Archers' rose bushes, as well as the lost use value of their property during restoration;
2. the cost of replacing Mr. Baker's windows and the market value of his vase; and
3. compensation to the Carlisles for the annoyance and inconvenience they have experienced.

To create parallelism, match the *key* words in each element; the parallelism is not destroyed if all the modifying words and phrases do not match exactly.

In the following examples, the key words "received" and "released" match, and the key words "for . . . harm" and "for . . . expenses" match.

EXAMPLES

In *Pepper,* the injured plaintiff <u>received</u> medical treatment and <u>released</u> the defendant from liability.

The Bells are seeking damages <u>for severe emotional and financial harm</u> and <u>for substantial medical expenses related to the pregnancy.</u>

To summarize, then, writers can correct problems in parallelism in one of three ways:

1. match the endings of key words,
2. match introductory words, or
3. use the same grammatical form.

See Exercise 26.P in the *Practice Book.*

Earlier we said that parallelism is required for coordinated elements joined by "and," "but," "or," "nor," and "yet." Parallelism is also required for elements joined by correlative conjunctions, which are conjunctions that come in pairs.

The most common correlative conjunctions are "either . . . or," "neither . . . nor," "not only . . . but also," "both . . . and," "whether . . . or," and "as . . . as."

To make the elements joined by one of these pairs parallel, simply match what follows the first half with what follows the second half.

    either _____   either <u>similar</u>
    or _____   or <u>identical</u>

EXAMPLE

Campbell's prior convictions are either similar or identical.

    neither _____   neither <u>the photographs</u>
    nor _____   nor <u>the testimony</u>

EXAMPLE

Neither the photographs nor the testimony can prove who actually committed the alleged assault.

    not only _____   not only <u>verbally</u>
    but also _____   but also <u>physically</u>

EXAMPLE

The defendant admits that she not only verbally but also physically abused her children.

Take care when using these pairs. All too frequently legal writers lose the parallelism in their sentences by misplacing one of the words in these pairs.

EXAMPLE   **LACK OF PARALLELISM**

The purpose of the rule is to ensure that actual notice is provided either by personal or constructive service.

either _____   either by personal
or   _____   or constructive

Note that "by personal" is not parallel with "constructive."

EXAMPLES   REVISED

The purpose of the rule is to ensure that actual notice is provided either by personal or by constructive service. *OR*

The purpose of the rule is to ensure that actual notice is provided by either personal or constructive service.

Parallelism is also required when elements are compared or contrasted. Many of the comparing and contrasting expressions use "than." Notice in each of the following pairs where the blanks are for the parallel elements.

more _____ than _____
less _____ than _____
_____ rather than _____

EXAMPLES

Wilson's attention was centered more on the assailant's gun than on his face.

The court applied the "clearly erroneous" standard rather than the arbitrary and capricious standard.

See Exercise 26.Q in the *Practice Book.*

Chapter 27

Punctuation

§27.1 THE COMMA

Commas are everywhere. They are the most frequently used punctuation mark and, unfortunately, the most frequently misused punctuation mark. They give most legal writers fits. Few writers seem to be able to control the little buzzards, and most seem to be more than a bit controlled by them. Many fairly good legal writers admit that they punctuate by feel, especially when it comes to commas. They rely on the "rule" that one should use a comma whenever the reader should pause—advice that works only about 70 percent of the time.

It is no wonder that few legal writers know and apply all the rules for commas. There are too many of them. In this section, we will have no fewer than twenty rules, all designed to govern one little punctuation mark. Even so, these twenty rules don't cover every conceivable use of the comma, just the high spots.

The good news, however, is that not all of these rules are equally important. Some are critical; misapplication of these rules will either mis-cue the reader or change the meaning of a sentence as significantly as a misplaced decimal can change the meaning of a number. The critical rules are listed under the heading "Critical Commas: Those That Affect Meaning and Clarity."

The next section, "Basic Commas: Those That Educated Readers Expect," includes all the commonly known comma rules. Using these rules incorrectly probably will not affect meaning, but it may distract the reader and even cause him or her to wonder about the writer's professionalism.

There are other comma rules, though, that the average reader will not know, and he or she will not notice whether they are applied correctly. Still, these rules are helpful to writers who not only care about writing correctly but also recognize that knowing the more esoteric

EXHIBIT 27.1   Overview of the Comma Rules

OVERVIEW OF THE COMMA RULES

CRITICAL COMMAS: Those That Affect Meaning and Clarity

Rule 1:   Use a comma before a coordinating conjunction joining two main clauses.

The prosecutor spoke about the defendant's motive, and the jury listened carefully.

Rule 2:   Use a comma to set off long introductory phrases or clauses from the main clause.

Using their overhead lights and sirens, the police followed the defendant out of the area.

Rule 3:   Use a comma to prevent a possible misreading.

At the time, the prosecution informed Jones that it would recommend a sentence of eighteen months.

Rule 4:   Use a comma to set off nonrestrictive phrases or clauses.

Officer Bates, acting as a decoy, remained outside on the sidewalk.

BASIC COMMAS: Those That Educated Readers Expect

Rule 5:   Set off nonrestrictive appositives with commas.

A corrections officer called Diane Cummins, the defendant's girlfriend.

Rule 6:   Set off nonrestrictive participial phrases with a comma or commas.

The trial court denied the motion, finding that the seizure fell under the plain view doctrine.

Rule 7:   Use a comma or commas to set off transitional or interrupting words and phrases.

The trial court, however, imposed an exceptional sentence of thirty months.

Rule 8:   Use commas according to convention with quotation marks.

Corbin said, "I never saw the other car."

EXHIBIT 27.1   *(continued)*

Rule 9:   Use a comma or commas to set off phrases of contrast.

Adams initially indicated that he, not Wilson, was involved in the robbery.

Rule 10:   Use commas between items in a series.

Wong had no money, identification, or jewelry.

Rule 11:   Use a comma between coordinate adjectives not joined by a conjunction.

The contract was written in concise, precise language.

Rule 12:   Use commas according to convention with dates, addresses, and names of geographical locations.

The land in Roswell, New Mexico, was surveyed on October 4, 1991, and purchased less than a month later.

Esoteric Commas: Those That Are Required in Sophisticated Sentence Structures

Rule 13:   Use commas to set off absolutes.

His career destroyed, Williams lapsed into a state of depression.

Rule 14:   Use a comma to indicate an omission of a word or words that can be understood from the context.

The first witness said the attacker was "hairy"; the second, bald.

Rule 15:   Use commas to set off expressions that introduce examples or explanations.

Collins testified that Adams had participated in the robbery and had fenced some of the items, namely, a camera, stereo, and silver.

Unnecessary Commas: Those That Should Be Omitted

Rule 16:   Do not use a comma to set off restrictive adverbial clauses that follow the main clause.

Complicity may be found if a defendant participates in the early states of an activity that results in the attack on the victim.

EXHIBIT 27.1	*(continued)*

Rule 17:   Do not use a comma to separate a subject from its verb or a verb from its object.

The idea that an individual can obtain another person's property through adverse possession is difficult for many people to accept.

Rule 18:   Do not use a comma to separate correlative pairs unless the correlatives introduce main clauses.

Neither the United States Supreme Court nor this court has ever ruled that a defendant has a due process right to an instruction on lesser included offenses.

*Rule 19:   Do not use a comma between a conjunction and introductory modifiers or clauses.

The fire had completely destroyed the trailer, and according to the fire chief, there was some concern that the overhead structure of the barn would collapse.

*Rule 20:   Do not use a comma between "that" and introductory modifiers or clauses.

He testified that when they returned to his hotel room, Wells demanded a $150 fee.

*Some authorities disagree on these comma rules.

---

comma rules allows them to add to their repertoire those sentence structures that require using these rules.

Finally, the last group of comma rules includes those situations in which commas are inserted unnecessarily. Please notice, too, that some of the last rules are marked with an asterisk (*). The asterisk indicates those few comma rules about which some authorities disagree. See Exhibit 27.1.

One final comment before launching into this comma extravaganza: More and more editors and writers favor what has come to be called "open punctuation." Open punctuation means using only as much punctuation as is necessary to make the meaning clear. "Close punctuation" is just the opposite; using as much punctuation as the rules will allow. Given the current preference for open punctuation, then, you may want to omit the comma when the rules and context make it optional simply because every unnecessary pause breaks up the flow of the writing.

§27.1.1   Critical Commas: Those That Affect Meaning and Clarity

Rule 1	Use a Comma Before a Coordinating Conjunction Joining Two Main, or Independent, Clauses

Reminder

There are seven coordinating conjunctions: "and," "but," "or," "for," "nor," "yet," and "so."[1]

Reminder

A main, or independent, clause has its own subject and verb, and it can stand alone as a sentence.

coordinating

_____,   conjunction   _____

[*main clause*]   [*main clause*]

Brackets mark the main clauses in the following examples.

EXAMPLES

[The prosecutor spoke about the defendant's motive], and [the jury listened carefully.]

[The corrections officer contacted several other persons], but [none knew of Wilson's disappearance.]

When applying Rule 1, be sure that you are not mistakenly assuming that a comma must precede every coordinating conjunction. It precedes those coordinating conjunctions that join two main clauses.

In the next example, "but" is preceded by a comma because it joins two main clauses. "And," on the other hand, joins two noun phrases ("the motion to sever" and "the motion for a new trial"), not two main clauses, so it is not preceded by a comma.

---

1. Some writers prefer to use a semicolon before "yet" and "so." The semicolon signals a longer pause.

EXAMPLE

[The trial court did not err in denying the motion to sever and the motion for a new trial], but [it did err in giving the accomplice liability instruction.]

In addition, be sure to distinguish between sentences with two main clauses (subject-verb, and subject-verb), which require a comma before the conjunction, and sentences with compound verbs (subject-verb and verb), which do not require a comma before the conjunction.

EXAMPLES

Two Main Clauses:

The defendant's girlfriend denied that she knew where he was, and she refused to answer any more questions.

Compound Verbs:

The defendant's girlfriend denied that she knew where he was and refused to answer any more questions.

Writers who omit the comma before a coordinating conjunction joining two main clauses miscue their readers. No comma before a coordinating conjunction signals the second half of a pair of structures other than main clauses. This error is often labeled a fused sentence or run-on sentence. When the main clauses are short and closely related, however, the comma before the coordinating conjunction may be omitted.

EXAMPLE

The prosecutor spoke and the jury listened.

Exception to Rule 1

When the main clauses are long or when they have internal punctuation, use a semicolon before the coordinating conjunction.

EXAMPLE

After analyzing the defendant's claim under ER 401, the court rejected it, explaining that the evidence at issue was relevant to the question of falsity; and because falsity was an element to be proved by the plaintiff, the evidence met the ER 401 requirements of probative value and materiality.

See Exercise 27.A in the *Practice Book.*

Rule 2   Use a Comma to Set Off Long Introductory Clauses or Phrases From the Main, or Independent, Clause

If a main, or independent, clause is preceded by introductory material, the reader will need a comma to signal where the introductory material ends and where the independent clause begins.

———————————, ———————————————————

[*long introductory*   [*main clause*]
clause or phrase]

Long introductory clauses that must be set off with a comma are easy to spot. Because they are clauses, they will have a subject and a verb. Because they are subordinate, not main, clauses, they will also begin with a subordinating conjunction such as "after," "although," "as," "because," "before," "if," "unless," "until," "when," or "where." See section 26.1 for more on subordinate clauses and subordinating conjunctions.

EXAMPLES

As the Court of Appeals noted, delivery would require actual or constructive possession by the accused.

If the accident were unavoidable, Smith's intoxication was not "a cause . . . without which the death would not have occurred."

When Abbott failed to return to the work release facility, a corrections officer called his mother's home.

Of the many kinds of introductory phrases used in legal writing, the most common are prepositional phrases, infinitive phrases, and participial phrases. (Section 26.1 defines and explains prepositions, infinitives, and participles. It is not critical, however, to be able to identify the types of introductory phrases to punctuate them correctly.)

EXAMPLES

Introductory Prepositional Phrase:

In the present case, the record shows that Thompson initially assaulted Blevins.

Introductory Infinitive Phrase:

To support an argument that the trial court abused its discretion, a defendant must point to specific prejudice.

Introductory Participial Phrase:

Using their overhead lights and sirens, the police followed the defendant out of the area.

Be sure to distinguish between introductory participial phrases, which modify the subject, and gerunds that are the subject. (See section 26.1 for more on gerunds.) A gerund subject should not be followed by a comma. To do so would separate a subject from its verb. (See Rule 17 in this section.) Compare the use of the phrase "using their overhead lights and sirens" in the preceding and subsequent examples. Both are punctuated correctly.

EXAMPLE   GERUND SUBJECT

Using their overhead lights and sirens was routine procedure.

Notice that long introductory phrases are often made up of several prepositional phrases or a combination of prepositional, infinitive, and participial phrases.

EXAMPLES

Two Introductory Prepositional Phrases:

[On the evening] [of August 13, 1998], Larry Utter was robbed at gunpoint while making a deposit at a local bank.

Introductory Prepositional and Infinitive Phrases:

[At the hearing] [on McDonald's motion] [to dismiss], the parties stipulated to the admission of an incident report prepared by McDonald's probation officer.

Furthermore, there is no specific rule for what constitutes a "long" phrase or clause. An introductory phrase or clause of four or more words is usually set off with a comma, but writers have some discretion, particularly with introductory phrases.

Short prepositional phrases, for example, are often set off by a comma, especially when the writer wants to emphasize the information in the phrase, as with dates or case names.

EXAMPLES

In 1997, the Oltmans removed the fence separating their property from the farm.

In *Harris,* the defendant was charged with first degree robbery.

Short, introductory transitional expressions, such as "consequently," "for example," "however," "nevertheless," "therefore," and "on the other hand," are almost always set off by a comma.

EXAMPLES

Consequently, unlawful restraint is invariably an element of the greater offense of attempted kidnapping.

Nevertheless, the defendant maintains that he was in Boston when the robbery occurred.

See Exercise 27.B in the *Practice Book.*

Rule 3	Use a Comma to Prevent a Possible Misreading

A reader should be able to read your sentences correctly the first time. If a comma can prevent a possible misreading, it should be included.

EXAMPLES

Confusing:

People who can usually hire their own lawyer.

Revised:

People who can, usually hire their own lawyer.

Although under Rule 2 you have the discretion to omit a comma after a short introductory material, you must use the comma if a reader might at first mistakenly assume that part of the main clause is part of the introductory material.

EXAMPLES

Confusing:

At the time the prosecution informed Jones that it would recommend a sentence of eighteen months.

Revised:

At the time, the prosecution informed Jones that it would recommend a sentence of eighteen months.

See Exercise 27.C in the *Practice Book*.

Rule 4	Use a Comma to Set Off Nonrestrictive Phrases or Clauses

Nonrestrictive phrases or clauses do not restrict or limit the words they modify. They give additional information.

Restrictive phrases or clauses restrict or limit the words they modify. They add essential information.

EXAMPLES

Nonrestrictive Phrase:

Officer Bates, <u>acting as a decoy</u>, remained outside on the sidewalk.

Nonrestrictive Clause:

Officer Bates, <u>who acted as a decoy</u>, remained outside on the sidewalk.

In both of the examples above, "Officer Bates" is completely identified by her name. "Acting as a decoy" or "who acted as a decoy" does not give restricting or limiting information, so both are set off by commas.

If the name of the officer were unknown, the writer may need to use the phrase or clause as a way to identify the officer. The phrase or clause would then be restrictive because it would limit the meaning of "officer." When used as a restrictive phrase or clause, the same words are not set off by commas.

EXAMPLES

Restrictive Phrase:

An officer acting as a decoy remained outside on the sidewalk.

Restrictive Clause:

An officer who acted as a decoy remained outside on the sidewalk.

A few more examples may be helpful in learning to distinguish which phrases and clauses are nonrestrictive and therefore set off by commas.

EXAMPLE   NONRESTRICTIVE CLAUSE

The child's father, who is six months behind in his child support payments, has fled the state.

"The child's father" clearly identifies the individual in question; "who is six months behind in his child support payments" does not restrict or limit the meaning of "the child's father," even though it is important information for understanding the sentence.

EXAMPLE **RESTRICTIVE CLAUSE**

The uncle who lives in Oklahoma has agreed to care for the child until an appropriate foster home is found.

This sentence suggests that the child has more than one uncle. "Who lives in Oklahoma" restricts or limits the meaning of "the uncle." It is the uncle in Oklahoma, not the one in Arkansas, who has agreed to care for the child.

Notice that whether a phrase or clause is punctuated as restrictive or nonrestrictive can significantly change the meaning of a sentence.

EXAMPLE

Attorneys who intentionally prolong litigation for personal gain misuse the legal system.

The preceding sentence says that there is a restricted or limited group of attorneys—those who intentionally prolong litigation for personal gain—who misuse the legal system.

EXAMPLE

Attorneys, who intentionally prolong litigation for personal gain, misuse the legal system.

The preceding sentence does not refer to a restricted or limited group of attorneys. It says that all attorneys misuse the legal system and that all attorneys intentionally prolong litigation for personal gain.

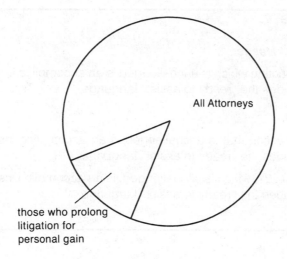

Restrictive and nonrestrictive clauses that modify people begin with "who" or "whom." Careful writers still observe the usage rule that restrictive clauses that modify things or objects use "that" and nonrestrictive clauses that modify things or objects use "which." See the Glossary of Usage for an extended explanation and more examples of the distinction between "that" and "which."

EXAMPLES

Incorrect Usage:

The instruction which is unchallenged is an accomplice instruction that includes the "ready to assist" language.

Revised:

The instruction that is unchallenged is an accomplice instruction that includes the "ready to assist" language. *OR*

Instruction 21, which is unchallenged, is an accomplice instruction that includes the "ready to assist" language.

The following chart sums up the key points in Rule 4.

Restrictive	restricts the word it modifies	no commas	who/whom that
Nonrestrictive	does not restrict the word it modifies	commas	who/whom which

See Exercises 27.D and 27.E in the *Practice Book.*

§27.1.2   Basic Commas: Those That Educated Readers Expect

Rule 5   **Set Off Nonrestrictive Appositives With Commas**

Reminder

Appositives are nouns or noun substitutes that follow another noun to identify it or further describe it.

EXAMPLE

A corrections officer called <u>Diane Cummins</u>, <u>the defendant's girl</u>
                                (noun)   *(appositive)*
<u>friend</u>.

Because most appositives are nonrestrictive, they need to be set off with commas. However, restrictive appositives, like the restrictive phrases and clauses in Rule 4, add information that restricts or limits the preceding noun; therefore, restrictive appositives are not set off with commas.

EXAMPLE   NONRESTRICTIVE APPOSITIVE

The court sentenced the defendant, a juvenile, to a term outside the standard range.

There is only one defendant; "a juvenile" adds information, but it does not restrict or limit the meaning of "defendant."

EXAMPLE   RESTRICTIVE APPOSITIVE

The defendant's brother Joseph contradicted the story another brother Daniel told to the police.

The defendant has more than one brother, so the noun phrases "defendant's brother" and "another brother" must be restricted or limited by the brothers' names.

Some appositives are introduced by the word "or." Be sure to distinguish between the appositional "or," which is a restatement of or explanation for the preceding noun, and the disjunctive "or," which introduces an alternative to the preceding noun.

EXAMPLE

Appositional "Or":

You may designate an attorney-in-fact, or agent, to make your health care decisions in the event you are unable to do so. ("Attorney-in-fact" and "agent" are the same thing.)

Disjunctive "Or":

The girl's father or uncle always accompanied her on dates. ("Father" and "uncle" are alternatives.)

Rule 6	Set Off Nonrestrictive Participial Phrases with a Comma or Commas

Reminder

Participles, which are formed from verbs, can serve as adjectives. Present participles have an "-ing" ending; past participles have a variety of endings, depending on whether the verb is regular or irregular. Common past participle endings include "-d," "-ed," "-t," "-n," and "-en."

verb	*present participle*	*past participle*
reason	reasoning	reasoned
find	finding	found

Many sentences in legal writing use a beginning or an ending participial phrase to describe the rationale for the action expressed in the main verb. Such participial phrases are not dangling or misplaced (see section 26.6.2) if, as in the following examples, they modify the subject of the sentence.

EXAMPLES

Reasoning that the sentence imposed was disproportionate to the gravity of the offense, the State Supreme Court reversed and remanded for resentencing.

The State Supreme Court reversed and remanded for resentencing, reasoning that the sentence imposed was disproportionate to the gravity of the offense.

Finding that the seizure fell under the plain view doctrine, the trial court denied the motion.

The trial court denied the motion, finding that the seizure fell under the plain view doctrine.

Restrictive participial phrases should not be set off with commas. In the following example, "washing his hands" restricts or limits the meaning of "the man." See Exercise 27.F in the *Practice Book*.

EXAMPLE

The attendant noticed blood on the shirt of the man washing his hands.

Rule 7	**Use a Comma or Commas to Set Off Transitional or Interrupting Words and Phrases**

Legal writers frequently break the flow of a sentence intentionally by inserting a word or phrase in the middle of a main clause. Readers have no trouble understanding what the main clause is and what the transitional or interrupting word or phrase is as long as those transitions or interrupters are set off with commas.

$$\underline{\qquad\qquad}, \text{ interrupter, } \underline{\qquad\qquad}$$
$$\quad\textit{(main)}\qquad\qquad\qquad\qquad\textit{(clause)}$$

EXAMPLES

The trial court, however, imposed an exceptional sentence of thirty months.

The Court of Appeals held that Wells, through her own fault and connivance, caused the delay between the time the State filed the information and the time of Wells's arraignment.

Note, however, that many of the same transitional words and phrases (for example, "however," "therefore," "on the other hand," "for example") that interrupt a main clause can also be used between two main clauses. Be sure to distinguish between the two and punctuate accordingly.

EXAMPLES

Interrupter:

His vision, therefore, was blurred.

Transition between two main clauses:

The driver lost his contact lenses; therefore, his vision was blurred.

Rule 8	Use Commas According to Convention with Quotation Marks

Commas are frequently used to separate short or informal quotations from words in the same sentence that introduce, interrupt, or follow the quotation.

EXAMPLES

Corbin said, "I never saw the other car."

"I never saw the other car," Corbin said, "until it was right on top of me."

"I never saw the other car," said Corbin.

Commas are placed inside closing quotation marks,[2] outside closing parentheses or brackets.

EXAMPLES

Inside Closing Quotation Marks:

Identification searches are valid if limited to wallets or other "common repositories of identification papers," and the examination is confined to locating a driver's license or similar document. 4 Wayne LaFave, *Search and Seizure* § 9.5(g), at 307 (3d ed. 1996).

A 24-month sentence does not appear to be "clearly excessive," especially when the presumptive range of 12-14 months could

---

2. In Great Britain a comma is placed inside closing quotation marks only if it is part of the quotation.

have been increased by 12 months under Wash. Rev. Code § 9.94A.310 (1996).

Outside Closing Parentheses:

Both of the defendants are young (nineteen and twenty), and both of them are first-time offenders.

Quotations that are immediately preceded by "that" do not have a comma between the quotation and "that."

EXAMPLE

In *Herron v. King,* the court stated that "actual malice can be inferred from circumstantial evidence including . . . the reporter's knowledge that his sources are hostile to the plaintiff . . . ." 109 Wash. 2d at 524, 746 P.2d at 302.

See Exercise 27.G in the *Practice Book.*

Rule 9	**Use a Comma or Commas to Set Off Phrases of Contrast**

Phrases of contrast usually begin with "not," "but," or "yet."

EXAMPLES

Adams initially indicated that he, not Wilson, was involved in the robbery.

The court of appeals affirmed the trial court, but on different grounds.

Some writers occasionally omit commas with phrases of contrast that begin with "but." These writers would omit the comma before the "but" in the preceding example. Either way is correct. In addition, commas are usually omitted between elements joined by the paired conjunctions "not only . . . but also . . . ."

EXAMPLES

The trial court not only overruled defense counsel's repeated objections but also accused the defendant's attorney of intentionally delaying the proceedings.

The memorandum suggested that interviewers not only look more favorably at applicants who are thirty-five or under but also disregard applicants who are fifty or over.

| **Rule 10** | **Use Commas Between Items in a Series** |

Reminder

A series is three or more items that are grouped together and that are in the same grammatical form. Each item may be as short as one word or as long as a clause.

EXAMPLES

Series of Single Words:

Wong had no money, identification, or jewelry.

Series of Verb Phrases:

Mason moved at least twice during the period of his escape, changed his name and his appearance, and held four or five jobs.

Series of Clauses:

Jones could not remember who he was, where he lived, what he did for a living, or what he had done during the last two weeks.

Even a series composed of short main clauses can use commas to separate the items.

EXAMPLE

Matthews pulled a knife on O'Hara, she screamed, and he turned and ran away.

Although the comma before the final "and" in a series is sometimes described as "optional," legal writers should make it a habit to include it because some sentences become ambiguous when that comma is omitted.

EXAMPLE

Mrs. Corsini wants her property divided equally among the following relatives: Michael Corsini, Glenda Corsini, Ralph Meyers, Joanna Mitchem, Louis Mitchem, Donna Mitchem and Donald Mitchem.

Should the property be divided six or seven ways? Assume Donna Mitchem and Donald Mitchem are married. Did Grandmother Corsini intend for the couple to get one-sixth of her property, or did she intend for each of them to receive one-seventh?

Adding a comma before the final "and" tells the reader that the property should be divided seven ways. Adding another "and" before "Donna Mitchem" says that it should be divided six ways and that Donna and Donald should, as a couple, receive a one-sixth share.

Ordinarily, commas are not used to separate pairs of words, phrases, or clauses that are joined by coordinating conjunctions.

EXAMPLES

Pair of Words:

Lundquist was <u>arrested</u> and <u>charged</u> with negligent homicide.

Pair of Phrases:

The Supreme Court is remarkably free <u>to emphasize certain issues of the case over others</u> or <u>to stress completely new issues</u>.

Pair of Clauses:

The trial court asked the defendant whether he understood his right to a jury trial and whether he received any promises of better treatment if he waived that right.

When a writer does use a comma before a coordinating conjunction joining a pair, the comma forces an unusual pause. Writers should use such a forced pause only when trying to suggest a bit of drama.

EXAMPLE

The gunman smiled at Kellogg, and then shot him.

Commas are not used between items in a series when all the items are joined by coordinating conjunctions. As a stylistic technique, joining all the items in a series with conjunctions has the effect of slowing down a series, which may be desirable on rare occasions when the writer wants the reader to focus special attention on each of the individual items in the series. See section 24.2.2 and Exercise 27.H in the *Practice Book.*

EXAMPLE

There is no indication that the delay was negligent or deliberate or unusual.

Rule 11   Use a Comma Between Coordinate Adjectives Not Joined by a Conjunction

Coordinate adjectives are two or more adjectives that independently modify the same noun.

concise, precise language
(adjective) (adjective) (noun)

The test for whether adjectives are coordinate is simple: (1) reverse the order of the adjectives; or (2) add an "and" between the adjectives. If the adjectives are modifying the noun independently, then changing their order or adding an "and" will not change the meaning.

1. precise, concise language
2. concise, precise language
3. precise and concise language

The following example does not contain coordinate adjectives. Instead, "black" modifies "leather" and "leather" modifies "briefcase." Notice that you can tell that the adjectives are not coordinate by applying either part of the test. Both create awkward constructions.

EXAMPLE

black leather briefcase

Reverse Order:

leather, black briefcase

Add "and":

black and leather briefcase

| **Rule 12** | **Use Commas According to Convention with Dates, Addresses, and Names of Geographical Locations** |

When a full date is written out in the month-day-year order, use a comma after the day so that a reader can easily see the correct groupings of the digits.

July 4, 1776

Dates in this order also require a comma (or other punctuation) after the year when the sentence continues after the date.

EXAMPLE

The land was surveyed on October 4, 1996, and purchased less than a month later.

If the day is omitted or if the full date has the month and date reversed, omit commas because there are no adjacent groupings of digits.

July 1776   4 July 1776

EXAMPLE

Martin and Hughes were arrested on 21 December 1988 and charged with first-degree assault.

Use commas to set off individual elements in addresses and geographical names. Note that the state and zip code are considered one element and therefore not separated by a comma. When addresses or geographical names are followed by the remainder of a sentence, they should be followed by a comma.

Chicago, Illinois   Ontario, Canada

EXAMPLES

Send the bill to Mr. and Mrs. Arthur Meiering, 3000 La Jolla Lane, Roswell, New Mexico 88201, before Tuesday.

The string of robberies began in San Diego, California, and ended in Oakland, California, after the police arrested the defendant.

When possible, rephrase a date or geographical name used as a modifier when the date or geographical name will have to be followed by a comma.

Awkward:

the June 21, 1998, meeting

Revised:

the meeting on June 21, 1998

Awkward:

the Atlanta, Georgia, public health official

Revised:

the public health official from Atlanta, Georgia

See Exercise 27.I in the *Practice Book.*

§27.1.3   Esoteric Commas: Those That Are Required in Sophisticated Sentence Structures

---

Rule 13   **Use Commas to Set Off Absolutes**

Reminder

Absolutes are made up of either a noun or pronoun followed by a participle. They modify an entire sentence or main clause and can appear at the beginning, at the end, or within a sentence.

his <u>career</u> <u>destroyed</u>	their <u>lights</u> <u>flashing</u>
(noun) (participle)	*(noun) (participle)*

his <u>gun</u> <u>drawn and loaded</u>	the <u>last</u> <u>being</u> a year ago
(noun) (participles)	*(noun) (participle)*

EXAMPLES

His career destroyed, Williams lapsed into a state of depression.

The police followed the defendant for less than one mile, their lights flashing.

The defendant reentered the tavern, his gun drawn and loaded, and proceeded to order the tavern's patrons to line up against the wall.

She testified that on four or five occasions, the last being a year ago, he demanded that she rewrite her will.

Rule 14   Use a Comma to Indicate an Omission of a Word or Words That Can Be Understood from the Context

EXAMPLE

The first witness said the attacker was "hairy"; the second, bald.

In Texas there are five elements to the crime; in Delaware, four.

Rule 15   Use Commas to Set Off Expressions That Introduce Examples or Explanations

"For example," "for instance," "that is," "namely," "*i.e.,*" "*e.g.,*" and "*viz.*" are usually followed by a comma. A comma can also be used before these expressions if the break in the flow of the sentence is slight. Dashes or semicolons are used before these expressions if the break is substantial. See Exercise 27.J in the *Practice Book*.

EXAMPLES

Collins testified that Adams had participated in the robbery and had fenced some of the items, namely, a camera, stereo, and silver.

The State must prove that the defendant acted by color or aid of deception—that is, that he operated to bring about the acquisition of the property or services by either creating or confirming another's false impression, which he knew to be false, or by failing to correct another's impression, which he had previously created.

Our company will accept all standard forms of identification, *e.g.,* birth certificate, driver's license, or military identification.

Some authorities suggest that writers avoid the abbreviations *"i.e.,"* *"e.g.,"* and *"viz."* in the text of their writing and use their English equivalents instead ("that is," "for example," and "namely" respectively). The rationale for this suggestion is that many readers misunderstand the abbreviations. If you decide to use the abbreviations, remember to italicize or underline them.

§27.1.4 Unnecessary Commas: Those That Should Be Omitted

Rule 16	**Do Not Use a Comma to Set Off Restrictive Adverbial Clauses That Follow the Main Clause**

Reminder

Adverbial clauses have their own subject and verb, and they are introduced by an adverb such as "although," "because," "before," "when," and "while."

A restrictive adverbial clause restricts or limits the action of the verb to a time, manner, or circumstance. Nonrestrictive adverbial clauses give additional information.

Clauses introduced by the adverb "if" are always restrictive, so they are not set off by commas.

EXAMPLE

Complicity may be found if a defendant participates in the early stages of an activity that results in the attack on the victim.

Clauses introduced by the adverbs "because" and "unless" are usually restrictive, although they can be nonrestrictive.

EXAMPLES

Summary judgment was granted because the plaintiff failed to establish the prima facie elements.

Special damages may not be presumed without proof unless actual malice is proved.

When clauses beginning with "after," "as," "before," "since," "when," and "while" restrict the time of the main verb, they should not be set off with commas.

EXAMPLES

The tractor trailer entered the parking lot as the game was ending and the crowd was beginning to leave the stadium.

Morton was drinking beer while he was driving the boat.

When adverbial clauses beginning with "as," "since," or "while" do not restrict the time of the verb but rather express cause or condition, they are nonrestrictive and should be set off by commas. (But see the Glossary of Usage on use of "as" and "since" for causation.)

EXAMPLES

Southworth returned to the scene of the assault, as he feared that he had lost his neck chain in the scuffle.

Vereen was unable to read the contract, since she had had eye surgery only two days earlier.

Clauses introduced by the adverbs "although" and "though" are always nonrestrictive, so they must be set off with commas.

EXAMPLES

Del Barker admits that he received his 1995 tax statement, although he claims that the only notice he received of the filing requirements was from general news articles in the newspaper.

Each physician received compensation and paid expenses in direct proportion to his production of the gross income of the partnership, even though the partnership was an equal partnership.

See Exercise 27.K in the *Practice Book*.

Rule 17	**Do Not Use a Comma to Separate a Subject from Its Verb or a Verb from Its Object**

Legal writers are often inclined to write long subjects. When they do, it is tempting to insert a comma after the subject and before the verb because the reader will need a pause. The comma is the wrong solution; instead, the writer should revise the sentence.

In the following example, the subject is enclosed in brackets.

EXAMPLES

Incorrect:

[The idea that an individual can obtain another person's property through adverse possession], is difficult for many people to accept.

Revised:

Many people find it difficult to accept the idea that an individual can obtain another person's property through adverse possession.

In the following example, the verb "received" is incorrectly separated from its object, "the note," by a comma.

EXAMPLES

Incorrect:

Bloomquist had received from a fellow employee at Landover Mills, a note describing where the "crack house" was located.

Revised:

A fellow employee at Landover Mills sent Bloomquist a note describing where the "crack house" was located.

Exception

Nonrestrictive modifiers and interrupters that separate a subject from its verb should be preceded and followed by commas, even though the commas separate the subject from its verb. See Rules 4, 5, and 7 in this section.

Rule 18	**Do Not Use a Comma to Separate Correlative Pairs Unless the Correlatives Introduce Main Clauses**

Reminder

Correlative pairs include "either . . . or," "neither . . . nor," "both . . . and," and "not only . . . but also."

EXAMPLES

Incorrect:

Neither the United States Supreme Court, nor this court has ever ruled that a defendant has a due process right to an instruction on lesser included offenses.

Revised:

Neither the United States Supreme Court nor this court has ever ruled that a defendant has a due process right to an instruction on lesser included offenses.

Main Clauses:

Either the manager will have to describe the damage done to the apartment, or he will have to return your deposit.

The correlative pair "not only . . . but also" connects two elements, so a separating comma is inappropriate. Some authorities, however, do

recommend a comma to separate the "not . . . but" pair because it is used
to contrast elements.

| Rule 19 | Do Not Use a Comma Between a Conjunction and Introductory Modifiers or Clauses |

When a coordinating conjunction joins two main clauses, the second main clause frequently begins with introductory modifiers or its own subordinate clause. Although some writers add a comma after the conjunction and before the introductory modifier or clause, this extra comma is needless; it merely slows the sentence down.

_____, and _____

[*main clause*]   [*introductory*   [*main clause*]
                         modifiers/clause]

EXAMPLES

Incorrect:

The fire had completely destroyed the trailer, and, according to the fire chief, there was some concern that the overhead structure of the barn would collapse.

Revised:

The fire had completely destroyed the trailer, and according to the fire chief, there was some concern that the overhead structure of the barn would collapse.

Incorrect:

The woman demanded that Thomas hand over his wallet, but, when Thomas replied that he did not have his wallet, the woman shot him in the chest.

Revised:

The woman demanded that Thomas hand over his wallet, but when Thomas replied that he did not have his wallet, the woman shot him in the chest.

Rule 20	**Do Not Use a Comma Between "That" and Introductory Modifiers or Clauses**

EXAMPLES

Incorrect:

He testified that, when they returned to his hotel room, Wells demanded a $150 fee.

Revised:

He testified that when they returned to his hotel room, Wells demanded a $150 fee.

See Exercises 27.L, 27.M, and 27.N in the *Practice Book*.

§27.2   THE SEMICOLON

The semicolon is one of the easiest punctuation marks to learn how to use. Unfortunately, some legal writers avoid using semicolons because they believe semicolons are quite complicated and will require learning numerous rules. Exactly the opposite is true. There are only two general rules for using semicolons; all other uses are variations or exceptions to these two rules.

Rule 1	**Use a Semicolon to Separate Main, or Independent, Clauses Not Joined by a Coordinating Conjunction**

main clause   ;   main clause

Reminder

Main clauses contain a subject and verb. They can stand alone as a sentence. There are only seven coordinating conjunctions: "and," "but," "or," "for," "nor," "yet," and "so."

EXAMPLES

Officer Thompson administered the breathalyzer test; the results showed that the defendant's blood alcohol level was over the maximum allowed by the state.

The plaintiff is a Nevada resident; the defendant is a California resident.

If you use a comma or no punctuation between main clauses, you will produce a comma splice or run-on sentence. See section 27.6.

Main clauses joined by a semicolon should be closely related in meaning. Often the semicolon suggests that the ideas in the connected main clauses work together as a larger idea. (See the first example above.) The semicolon can also be used to balance one idea against another. (See the second example above.) In all cases, the semicolon signals to the reader to pause slightly longer than a comma but shorter than a period. This length of pause helps the reader to see the ideas in the main clauses as more closely related to each other than the ideas would be in two separate sentences.

Variation on Rule 1

To show the relationship between the main clauses, a conjunctive adverb frequently follows the semicolon separating main clauses. The conjunctive adverb is usually followed by a comma. The most commonly used conjunctive adverbs are "accordingly," "also," "besides," "consequently," "furthermore," "hence," "however," "indeed," "instead," "likewise," "meanwhile," "moreover," "nevertheless," "still," "then," "therefore," and "thus." See section 26.1.

main clause   ;   *therefore*, main clause
_____
[*conjunctive
adverb*]

EXAMPLES

The summons was not delivered to his usual place of abode; therefore, service was not effected in the manner prescribed by law.

The elements of the test have not been completely defined; however, the court has clarified the policies underlying the rule.

Conjunctive adverbs may also occur in the middle of main clauses. In such cases, they are usually preceded and followed by a comma.

<u>main, *therefore,* clause</u>

EXAMPLE

The motor was not running, however, because of a problem with the distributor cap.

Compare the preceding example and the following example.

EXAMPLE

The motor was not running because of a problem with the distributor cap; however, the inoperability of the vehicle was irrelevant.

See Exercises 27.O and 27.P in the *Practice Book.*

Rule 2   **Use Semicolons to Separate Items in a Series If the Items Are Long or If One or More of the Items Has Internal Commas**

Reminder

A series is three or more items of equal importance. If the items in a series are relatively short or if they do not have internal commas, then the items can be separated by commas.

<u>item 1, item 2, and item 3</u>

Typical series with items separated by commas

<u>item 1   ;   item 2   ;   and item 3</u>

long items separated by semicolons

item 1   ;   ,   item 2   ,   ;   and item 3

internal commas in one or more
items separated by semicolons

EXAMPLES

Long Items:

The Montana court has applied these definitions to cases with the following fact patterns: the driver was asleep and intoxicated; the driver was positioned behind the steering wheel; the vehicle's motor was running; and the vehicle was parked.

Long Items:

The court must determine the following issues to resolve your claim:

1. whether your ex-landlord sent you a written statement within thirty days of termination;
2. whether your ex-landlord withheld your deposit in bad faith; and
3. whether the court wishes to include attorneys' fees as part of a possible damage award.

Internal Commas:

The prosecutor called the following witnesses: Linda Hastings, an advertising executive; Samuel Hedges, an accountant; and Timothy Lessor, president of the company.

Internal Commas:

The defendant claims to reside in Maryland, even though (1) his car is registered in California; (2) he is registered to vote in California; and (3) all of his financial assets, including stocks, bonds, and a savings and checking account, are in a California bank.

See Exercise 27.Q in the *Practice Book.*

§27.2.1   Use of the Semicolon with "Yet" or "So"

Some writers prefer to use a semicolon rather than a comma before the coordinating conjunctions "yet" and "so" when they join two main clauses. Either the comma or the semicolon is correct in the following examples, but note that the longer pause suggested by the semicolon adds a bit more emphasis to the conjunction and to the words that immediately follow the semicolon.

EXAMPLES

Our client was legally intoxicated at the time of the arrest, so being asleep or unconscious is not a defense.

Our client was legally intoxicated at the time of the arrest; so being asleep or unconscious is not a defense.

---

§27.2.2   Use of the Semicolon with Coordinating Conjunctions

Usually main clauses joined by a coordinating conjunction require only a comma before the conjunction. See section 27.1, Rule 1. However, when the main clauses are long and grammatically complicated or when they have internal commas, it is helpful for the reader if a semicolon rather than a comma precedes the coordinating conjunction. The semicolon makes it easier to spot the break between the main clauses.

$$\underbrace{\hspace{3cm}}_{\textit{main clause}}\text{; but}\underbrace{\quad,\qquad,\hspace{2cm}}_{\textit{main clause}}$$

EXAMPLE

Your landlord can withhold a reasonable amount to cover the cost of repairing the window; but if he failed to send you a check for the remainder of the deposit, or if he failed to state why he withheld the deposit, or if he failed to do both within thirty days of termination of the lease, then he forfeited his right to withhold any part of the deposit.

---

§27.2.3   Use of the Semicolon with Citations

Because citations are either sentences or clauses, they should be treated as main clauses. Consequently, multiple citations are separated with semicolons. See Exercises 27.R and 27.S in the *Practice Book.*

EXAMPLE

Oklahoma courts have consistently held that if an intoxicated driver is in his or her vehicle and is capable of exercising actual physical control over it, then all the elements required for a section 11-902 conviction are satisfied: *Houston v. State,* 615 P.2d 305 (Okla. Crim. App. 1980); *Mason v. State,* 603 P.2d 1146; *Hughes v. State,* 535 P.2d 1023 (Okla. Crim. App. 1975).

---

§27.3   THE COLON

Colons are useful to legal writers for a number of reasons. They are regularly used to introduce quotations or lists, and they are often the best way to set up explanations or elaborations.

EXAMPLES

Quotation:

In support of this result, the court noted that the limitation on the use of the corpus delicti rule is based on the "suspect nature" of out-of-court confessions: "Corroboration of the confession is required as a safeguard against the conviction of the innocent persons through the use of a false confession of guilt." *Id.* at 419.

List:

There are three ways to measure a plaintiff's recovery for personal property damage: 1) if the destroyed personal property has a market value, the measure is that market value; 2) if the destroyed property has no market value but can be replaced, then the measure is the replacement cost; or 3) if the destroyed property has no market value and cannot be replaced, then the measure is the property's intrinsic value.

Explanation/Elaboration:

The periodic polygraph examinations are arguably connected logically to the ultimate goal of Nyles's rehabilitation: to deter him from molesting children.

Mr. Baker has sustained personal property damage: his picture windows and valuable vase were smashed.

The main function of a colon is to introduce what will follow. For this reason, a colon requires a lead-in main clause that is grammatically complete.

grammatically complete main clause: _____

In the example that follows, "the subsections that do not apply are" is not grammatically complete; therefore, the colon is used incorrectly.

EXAMPLE   INCORRECT

The subsections that do not apply are: 201-1, 201-1(3)(b), and 201-1(3)(c).

One way to correct the example is to omit the colon.

EXAMPLE   REVISED

The subsections that do not apply are 201-1, 201-1(3)(b), and 201-1(3)(c).

Another option is to add filler expressions, such as "the following" or "as follows," to make the lead-in main clause grammatically complete.

EXAMPLE   REVISED

The subsections that do not apply are the following: 201-1, 201-1(3)(b), and 201-1(3)(c).

What follows the colon may or may not be a main clause. If a complete sentence follows a colon, the writer has the option of capitalizing the first word of that sentence.

Quotations that are integrated into the writer's own sentences are not introduced by a colon.

EXAMPLES

The first letter the Bakers received stated that "permits are issued subject to existing water rights."

Fair market value is "the amount of money a purchaser willing, but not obligated, to buy the property would pay an owner willing, but not obligated, to sell it, taking into consideration all uses to which the property is adapted and might in reason be applied." *Dillon v. O'Connor,* 412 P.2d 126, 128 (Wash. 1966).

Because colons set up the endings of sentences, they can be used effectively and stylistically to create emphasis. See section 23.6.4. Notice how the writers of the following sentences used colons to highlight a point.

EXAMPLES

Orlando's trial was originally scheduled for May 15, 1995: ninety-three days after his arraignment.

The legislature has already determined the standard range for Norris's offense: fourteen to eighteen months.

Gibson claimed that his intent was to do a lawful act: administer parental discipline.

Remember to doublespace after a colon. See Exercise 27.T in the *Practice Book.*

§27.4   THE APOSTROPHE

Apostrophes determine possession—who owns what. If you and your clients care about who owns what and about whether ownership is clearly stated, then apostrophes are worth the few minutes it takes to learn how to use them correctly.

All the apostrophe rules are important, but take special note of Rules 5 and 6. Misusing these two rules can create either ambiguity or the appearance of incompetence.

Rule 1	Use "'s" to Form the Possessive of Singular or Plural Nouns or Indefinite Pronouns Not Ending in "-s"

defendant's alibi   expert's testimony
family's income   children's guardian
a day's wages   a year's revenue
anybody's guess   everyone's concern

Rule 2	Use "'s" to Form the Possessive of Singular Nouns Ending in "-s"[3] as Long as the Resulting Word Is Not Difficult to Pronounce

James's contract   Congress's authority
business's license   witness's testimony

Three or more "s" sounds together are difficult to pronounce. When necessary, avoid three "s" sounds together by dropping the "s" after the apostrophe.

In the examples above, the double "s" ending in "business" or "witness" makes only one "s" sound, so when the "'s" is added, as in "business's" and "witness's," only two "s" sounds are required. However, when these same words are followed by words that begin with "s," then the "s" after the apostrophe is dropped for ease in pronunciation.

business' sales   witness' signature

For the same reason, many idioms that include the word "sake" drop the "s" after the apostrophe.

for goodness' sake   for righteousness' sake
for appearance' sake   for conscience' sake

Although almost all singular proper names follow the standard rule and form their possessive by adding "'s," those few proper names with internal and ending "s" sounds also drop the "s" after the apostrophe for

---

3. A few recognized authorities, including *The Associated Press Stylebook and Libel Manual,* recommend using only an apostrophe with singular proper names.

ease in pronunciation. Note that the "s" sound may be made by a "z" or an "x" as well as an "s."

> Jesus' teaching   Moses' laws
> Velasquez' hearing   Alexis' prior conviction
> Kansas' case law

> **But**   Arkansas's case law (because the final "s"
>   in Arkansas is silent)

Exception

When forming the possessive of ancient classical names, add only the apostrophe.

> Achilles' heel   Hercules' labors

Rule 3   Use Only an Apostrophe to Form the Possessive of Plural Nouns Ending in "-s"

> framers' intent   workers' rights
> four cities' plan   two agencies' concern
> ten dollars' worth   thirty days' notice

Plural proper nouns follow the same rule.

> Smiths' attorney   Thomases' dog

It is easier to form plural possessives correctly if you form the plural first and then apply the rules for possessives.

> *Singular   Plural   Plural Possessive*
> day ———→ days ————→ two days' labor
> family ——→ families ——→ families' petition
> Jones ——→ Joneses ———→ Joneses' pre-nuptial agreement

Occasionally a singular idea is expressed in words that are technically plural, for example, "United States," "General Motors," or "Olson Brothers." In such cases, apply the rule for forming plural possessives and add just an apostrophe.

> United States' commitment   General Motors' lobbyists

Rule 4	Use "'s" After the Last Word to Form the Possessive of a Compound Word or Word Group

mother-in-law's statement   district manager's idea
attorney general's office   somebody else's problem
the Governor of Florida's
recommendation

Don't use "'s" to form the possessive of a long word group, such as "The American Association of Lovers of Dogs and Cats." Use "of" or "for" instead: attorney of (or for) The American Association of Lovers of Dogs and Cats.

Rule 5	To Show Joint Possession, Use "'s" Only After the Last Noun in a Group of Two or More Nouns; to Show Individual Possession, Use "'s" After Each of the Nouns in a Group of Two or More Nouns

John and Mary's stocks ⟶ stocks are jointly owned

John's and Mary's stocks ⟶ some stocks are owned by John; some are owned by Mary

the governor and legislature's report ⟶ one report from both

the governor and legislature's reports ⟶ more than one report but still from both

the governor's and legislature's reports ⟶ one or more reports from the governor; one or more reports from the legislature

Rule 6	To Form the Possessive of Personal Pronouns, Do Not Use the Apostrophe

hers   its   ours   theirs   whose   yours

Many writers confuse the contractions "it's," "they're," and "who's" with the possessive of the personal pronouns "its," "their," and "whose."

it's = it is	its = possessive of "it"
they're = they are	their = possessive of "they"
who's = who is	whose = possessive of "who"

Besides showing possession, the apostrophe has a few other uses, including the formation of contractions and some plurals.

Rule 7	**To Form Contractions, Use the Apostrophe to Substitute for One or More Omitted Letters or Numbers**

it's = it is	ma'am = madam
they're = they are	class of '68 = class of 1968
who's = who is	

Note that contractions are used rarely in formal writing, including most legal writing.

Rule 8	**To Form the Plural of Numbers, Letters, or Words Referred to as Words, Add " 's"**

seven 0's	cross all the t's and dot all the i's
1950's	replace all the and's with or's
two Boeing 767's	

Some authorities recommend adding just "s" to make numbers plural: 1950s, two Boeing 767s. See Exercises 27.U, 27.V, and 27.W in the *Practice Book.*

§27.5   OTHER MARKS OF PUNCTUATION

§27.5.1   Quotation Marks

a.   *Identification of Another's Written or Spoken Words*

There is nothing mysterious about quotation marks; they do just what their name suggests: They mark where something is quoted.

Although many legal writers have a problem with excessive quoting (see section 24.2.3), there are still several occasions, most notably statutes and memorable phrasing, where quoting is necessary or appropriate. For these occasions, use quotation marks around those words that are not your own and that you have taken from the cited source.

EXAMPLE 1

The relationship between Southwestern Insurers and each of its agents is governed by an agreement that includes the following statement: "The location of the agent's office cannot unduly interfere with the business established by another agent."

EXAMPLE 2

In the *Ryan* case, the Court of Appeals ruled that the plaintiff's choice in not swerving was "prudent under the circumstances." *Id.* at 508.

EXAMPLE 3

The bartender testified that he overheard the defendant say he would "permanently get even" with Meyers.

Take care to quote the source's words exactly; use the ellipsis (see section 27.5.2) to indicate any omissions you have made to the wording and brackets (see section 27.5.3) to indicate changes in capitalization and additions for clarity and readability.

EXAMPLE 4

In his *Roviaro* dissent, Justice Clark observed that "[e]xperience teaches that once this policy [of confidentiality] is relaxed . . . its effectiveness is destroyed. Once an informant is known, the drug traffickers are quick to retaliate." *Id.* at 67.

Notice that in Examples 2, 3, and 4 the quotation is integrated into the writer's own sentence. When you integrate a quotation into one of your own sentences, be sure that the parts fit. The grammar of your sentence must be compatible with the grammar of the quotation.

EXAMPLE

Incorrect:

An actionable nuisance is "an obstruction to the free use of property, so as to essentially interfere with the comfortable enjoyment of life and property, is a nuisance and the subject of an action for damages and other further relief." Wash. Rev. Code § 7.48.010 (1996).

Revised:

An actionable nuisance is "an obstruction to the free use of property, so as to essentially interfere with the comfortable enjoyment of life and property . . . ." Wash. Rev. Code § 7.48.010 (1996).

---

b. Block Quotations

According to Rule 5.1(a) in the *Bluebook,* writers should not use quotation marks around quotations of fifty words or more. A quotation of this length should be set up as a block quotation, that is, single-spaced, indented left and right, and without quotation marks.

Unfortunately, some court rules require quotation marks for block quotations. As a writer, then, determine which method your reader prefers and then apply it. Know too that the trend seems to be toward using block quotations for long quotations that are not quite fifty words. The rationale seems to be that it is easier for the reader to see where the quotation begins and ends.

EXAMPLE 5

Davis argues that the trial court erred in giving instruction 19, which read as follows:

> Evidence has been introduced in this case regarding the fact that stop signs were installed in the neighborhood of Ohio and Texas

> Streets approximately one and one-half years after the accident of December 24, 1989. You are not to consider this evidence as proof of negligence nor as an admission of negligence on the part of the City.

EXAMPLE 6

The *Sholund* court held that no contract arose between the insured and the insurance company:

> [W]here the agent represents two or more companies, no one of them can be bound until the agent allocates the risk, or some portion thereof, to it by some word or act. Until that is done, there is no contract, because of failure of parties . . . . In the present case, the record is totally devoid of any act or word on the part of the agent to designate the appellant as the company to take the risk until after the property was destroyed by fire. He merely thought the appellant would take it. Thoughts can become binding as contracts only when transformed into acts or words.

Id. at 113-15.

Block quotations also tend to highlight the quoted material; consequently, some writers use them for persuasive reasons even when the quotation is fairly short.

c. *Effective Lead-ins for Quotations*

In Examples 1, 4, and 5, the quotations are not integrated into the writer's own sentences; instead, they are formally introduced and set up as separate statements.

Notice how the lead-ins to these formally introduced quotations are written. The language in the lead-ins prepares the reader for the quotation, sometimes by summarizing or paraphrasing the quotation, sometimes by explaining in advance why the quotation is significant.

Compare the lead-ins in the following pairs. Notice how the ineffective lead-ins do little more than indicate that a quotation will follow. In contrast, the effective lead-ins guide the reader into the quotation and suggest what the reader should look for in it.

Ineffective Lead-in:

The court found the following:

> The juvenile has an extensive record of adjudications and diver-
> sions for a variety of criminal offenses . . . . The court concludes
> that a sentence within the standard range would constitute a man-
> ifest injustice . . . . [C]ommitment . . . for a period of fifty-two (52)
> weeks is a more appropriate and reasonable sentence, taking into
> consideration the age of the defendant, his level of criminal sophis-
> tication and lack of success in rehabilitation . . . .

Effective Lead-in:

The court found a "manifest injustice" and increased Boyd's sentence because of his criminal history:

> The juvenile has an extensive record of adjudications and diver-
> sions for a variety of criminal offenses . . . . The court concludes
> that a sentence within the standard range would constitute a man-
> ifest injustice . . . . [C]ommitment . . . for a period of fifty-two (52)
> weeks is a more appropriate and reasonable sentence, taking into
> consideration the age of the defendant, his level of criminal sophis-
> tication and lack of success in rehabilitation . . . .

Ineffective Lead-in:

In *Curtis v. Blacklaw,* the court said the following:

Effective Lead-in:

In *Curtis v. Blacklaw,* the court explained the relationship between
the standard of ordinary care and the emergency doctrine:

> [T]he existence of a legally defined emergency does not alter or
> diminish the standards of care imposed by law upon the actors . . . .
> With or without an emergency instruction, the jury must determine
> what choice a reasonably prudent and careful person would have
> made in the same situation.

Id. at 363.

Ineffective Lead-in:

In the present case, the trial court made the following finding:

Effective Lead-in:

In the present case, the trial court found that the community had
not sustained its burden: "Although there is evidence of miscel-
laneous improvements made to the property, there is a failure of

evidence that it was these improvements that enhanced and caused the property to appreciate." CP 72.

Notice too that when a quotation is formally introduced and preceded by a colon, the portion of the sentence before the colon—the lead-in—must be grammatically complete. (See section 27.3.)

EXAMPLES

Incorrect:

It is a cardinal rule of statutory construction that a court must: "ascertain and give effect to legislative intent and purpose, as expressed in the act."

Correct:

It is a cardinal rule of statutory construction that a court must do the following: "ascertain and give effect to legislative intent and purpose, as expressed in the act."

Also Correct:

It is a cardinal rule of statutory construction that a court must "ascertain and give effect to legislative intent and purpose, as expressed in the act."

---

d.   Quotations Within Quotations

Occasionally, something you want to quote will already have quotation marks in it, either because your source quoted someone else or because your source used a term in a special way. For a quotation within a quotation, use single quotation marks (an apostrophe on most keyboards).

EXAMPLES

Baxter argues that the trial court erred when it included the following in an instruction on accomplice liability: "The word 'aid' means all assistance whether given by words, acts of encouragement, support, or presence."

"Police must discover incriminating evidence 'inadvertently,' which is to say, they may not 'know in advance the location of [certain] evidence and intend to seize it,' relying on the plain view doctrine as a pretext." *Texas v. Brown,* 460 U.S. 730, 743 (1983) (quoting *Coolidge,* 403 U.S. at 370).

---

e.   Quotation Marks with Other Marks of Punctuation

Periods and commas go inside closing quotation marks; semicolons and colons go outside closing quotation marks. Dashes, question marks, and exclamation points go inside closing quotation marks when they are part of the quotation and outside closing quotation marks when they are part of the larger sentence.

EXAMPLES

Davis's employer described him as a "street-smart youngster who knew what not to get involved with."

The jury could have arguably considered Wilson's insulting remarks to Harris as "unlawful," thereby depriving Harris of her self-defense claim.

Parole is a "variation on imprisonment"; therefore, parole and its possible revocation are a continuing form of custody relating back to the criminal act.

---

f.   Other Uses for Quotation Marks

Quotation marks may also indicate that a word is being used in some special way.

EXAMPLES

Mrs. Hartley claims that her husband played "mind games" with her to get her to sign the agreement.

Taylor approached Zimp about the possibility of obtaining an "umbrella" policy that would provide coverage in excess of his underlying automobile and homeowner's policies.

The Court of Appeals held that the attorney's phrasing was calculated to imply that Morris was a "hired gun" for insurance carriers.

Special terms are often introduced by phrases like "the word" or "the term." Put the words that follow these phrases in quotation marks, but do not use quotation marks around words that follow "so-called."

EXAMPLE

The words "beyond a reasonable doubt" in the constitutional error test created confusion in the Arizona courts for some time.

Quotation marks should also be used around words that follow the terms "signed," "endorsed," or "entitled."

EXAMPLE

The contract was signed "Miss Cathryn Smith," not "Ms. Kathryn Smith."

Do not use quotation marks around the single words *yes* and *no;* do not use quotation marks around a paraphrase.

EXAMPLE

When the officer asked her if she needed a ride home, she said yes.

---

§27.5.2   Ellipses

Use the ellipsis (three spaced periods) to indicate an omission in a quotation. The ellipsis allows you to trim quotations down and focus the reader's attention on the parts of the quotation that are relevant to your case.

EXAMPLE

Helen signed a quitclaim deed to Richard, disclaiming "an interest
in the . . . property."

Space before the first period and after the last period in an ellipsis.
When the omission occurs in the middle of a quoted sentence, retain any necessary punctuation. Notice, for example, that the comma after
"union" is retained in the following quotation because it is necessary
punctuation for the sentence as it is quoted.

EXAMPLE

"We the people of the United States, in order to form a more perfect
union, . . . do ordain and establish this Constitution for the United
States of America."

When the omission occurs at the end of a quoted sentence, use the
ellipsis (three spaced periods) to indicate that omission and then space
and add a fourth period for the punctuation to end the sentence.

EXAMPLE

"We the people of the United States, in order to form a more perfect
union, . . . do ordain and establish this Constitution . . . ."

When the omission occurs after the end of a quoted sentence, punctuate the quoted sentence and then insert the ellipsis. In such a case, the
sentence period is closed up to the last word in the sentence. This is
demonstrated in the next two examples, both of which are quotations
from the following original material.

EXAMPLE

Original Material:

The hostility/claim of right element of adverse possession requires
only that the claimant treat the land as his own as against

the world throughout the statutory period. The nature of his possession will be determined solely on the basis of the manner in which he treats the property. His subjective belief regarding his true interest in the land and his intent to dispossess or not dispossess another is irrelevant to this determination.

Id. at 860-61.

Quotation from the Preceding Material:

The hostility/claim of right element of adverse possession requires only that the claimant treat the land as his own as against the world throughout the statutory period. . . . His subjective belief regarding his true interest in the land and his intent to dispossess or not dispossess another is irrelevant to this determination.

Id. at 860-61.

Another Quotation from the Same Original:

"The hostility/claim of right element of adverse possession requires only that the claimant treat the land as his own as against the world throughout the statutory period. . . . [H]is intent to dispossess or not dispossess another is irrelevant to this determination." *Id.* at 860-61.

When the omission occurs at the beginning of the quotation, do not use an ellipsis. The reader will be able to tell that the original quotation did not begin at that point because the quotation begins with a lower case letter.

EXAMPLE

Incorrect:

In 1970, King granted to the State a ". . . permanent easement assignable in whole or in part" over King's property. CP 106.

Correct:

In 1970, King granted to the State a "permanent easement assignable in whole or in part" over King's property. CP 106.

When the quoted material is just a phrase or clause, no ellipsis is needed before or after the quoted material.

EXAMPLE

An omission, to be actionable, must show "tacit authorization" or "deliberate indifference." *Wellington v. Daniels,* 717 F.2d 932, 936 (4th Cir. 1983).

When a paragraph or more is omitted, indent and use the ellipsis plus the fourth period for the end punctuation.

EXAMPLE

The Safe Drivers' Insurance policy contains the following relevant provisions:

Definitions

. . . .

A car is a 4-wheel motor vehicle licensed for use on public roads. It includes any motor home that is not used for business purposes and any utility trailer.

. . . .

A motor vehicle is a land motor vehicle designed for use on public roads. It includes cars and trailers. It also includes any other land motor vehicle while used on public roads.

Like all good things, ellipsis marks can be misused. Never use the ellipsis to change the original intent in the quotation. Also, take care not to overuse the ellipsis in any one quotation. Too many omissions make the quotation difficult to read.

§27.5.3   Brackets

Brackets are used to show changes in quotations. The most common are additions of clarifying material and changes in capitalization and verb tense.

EXAMPLES

Addition of Clarifying Material:

"The privilege [of nondisclosure] recognizes the obligation of citizens to communicate their knowledge of the commission of crimes to law enforcement officials and, by preserving their anonymity, encourages them to perform that obligation." *Lewandowski v. State,* 389 N.E.2d 706, 708 (Ind. 1979) (quoting *Roviaro v. United States,* 353 U.S. 53, 62 (1957)).

Capitalization Change:

"[A] municipality may be held liable under 1983 for the intentional conduct of its governing body, . . . [b]ut we have held city police chiefs *not* to be such officials, . . . as they are almost uniformly subordinate to the city's governing body." *Languirand,* 717 F.2d at 227 (emphasis in original).

Change in Verb Tense:

The Council authorized the construction of a twelve-story tower, finding that reducing the tower to this height "substantially mitigate[s] adverse impacts on the land use pattern in the vicinity."

Use empty brackets [] to indicate where a single letter is omitted.

In some cases, a pronoun in a quotation may be ambiguous in the new context, so for clarity the writer substitutes the appropriate noun in brackets. In such cases, the omission of the pronoun does not need to be indicated.

EXAMPLE

At the time of her medical release, Wainwright made the following admission: "I did continue to have some pain and discomfort in my back, neck, and arms, but [Dr. Rodgers] felt this was normal pain and discomfort and that it would go away."

Occasionally, something that you want to quote has a significant error in it. In such cases, use a bracketed *sic* immediately after the error to indicate that the error was in the original and not inadvertently added.

EXAMPLE

On the day after the union vote was held, the shop foreman issued a memo to all machinists stating that how they voted "would not effect [*sic*] their performance reviews."

---

§27.5.4 Parentheses

In everyday writing, parentheses are used to add additional information to sentences. They are one way to signal that that information is of lesser importance.

EXAMPLE

Newcombe wrested a half a gram of marijuana (worth $10) from Tyson's pocket.

Because conciseness is a cardinal virtue in legal writing, legal writers usually edit out any information that is of lesser importance. As a natural consequence, you will rarely encounter parenthetical inserts in legal writing.

This does not mean that parentheses themselves do not appear anywhere in legal documents. They are frequently used in the following ways.

a.   To Enclose Short Explanations of Cases Within Citations

EXAMPLE

Washington courts have held the emergency doctrine inapplicable when only a sudden increase in degree of an already existing condition has placed the actor in a position of peril. *Mills v. Park,* 409 P.2d 646 (Wash. 1966) (where the defendant's vision in a snowstorm was further obscured by a snowplow throwing snow on defendant's car). *See also Hinkel v. Weyerhaeuser Co.,* 494 P.2d 1008 (Wash. Ct. App. 1972) (where the defendant was warned of a cloud of dense smoke ahead).

---

b.   To Refer Readers to Attached or Appended Documents

EXAMPLE

Before signing the agreement, Jones crossed out the language "at time of closing" in paragraph 12 and inserted the language "pro ratio as received by sellers" in paragraph 24. (See appendix 1.)

When a parenthetical reference is set up as a separate sentence, as in the example above, the period goes inside the closing parentheses. When the parenthetical reference is inserted in the middle of a sentence, place any punctuation required for the sentence outside the closing parenthesis.

EXAMPLE

Before signing the agreement, Jones crossed out the language "at time of closing" (paragraph 12, appendix 1), and Smith inserted the language "pro ratio as received by sellers" (paragraph 24, appendix 2).

---

c.   To Confirm Numbers

EXAMPLE

In 1997, Patrick and Rose Milton borrowed five thousand dollars ($5,000) from Southern Security Company.

---

d. To Enclose Numerals That Introduce the Individual Items in a List

---

EXAMPLES

To decide whether the same claim for relief is involved in both cases, a court must determine (1) whether the same primary right is involved in both cases and (2) whether the evidence needed to support the second action would have sustained the first action.

The company's regulations list seven circumstances under which an employee may be separated from his or her job: (1) resignation, (2) release, (3) death, (4) retirement, (5) failure to return from a leave of absence, (6) failure to return from a layoff, and (7) discharge or suspension for cause.

---

e. To Announce Changes to a Quotation That Cannot Be Shown by Ellipses or Brackets

---

EXAMPLE

"[I]solated incidents are normally insufficient to establish supervisory inaction upon which to predicate § 1983 liability." *Wellington,* 717 F.2d at 936 (footnote omitted).

The court held that "[a]n instruction, *when requested,* defining intent is required when intent is an element of the crime charged." *Id.* (emphasis added).

---

f. To Introduce Abbreviations after a Full Name Is Given

EXAMPLE

Beaver Custom Carpets (BCC) has been in business for one year.

See Exercise 27.X in the *Practice Book.*

§27.5.5   The Hyphen

The two principal uses of hyphens are to divide words at line breaks and to combine words to form compound modifiers or compound nouns.

a.   Word Division

Use a hyphen to divide a word at the end of a line only under the following circumstances:

a.   The break occurs between syllables (one-syllable words must not be divided);

b.   Enough of the word appears on both of the lines for the reader to identify the word easily (do not leave one letter at the end of a line or fewer than three letters at the beginning of a line, such as "a-part" or "abrupt-ly"); and

c.   Both parts of the word appear on the same page.

b.   Compound Modifiers and Compound Nouns

Somewhat more problematic for legal writers is deciding when a pair or grouping of modifiers or nouns should be joined by hyphens to show that they are acting as one unit.

The first step is a simple one: If the modifiers do not precede the noun they modify, then they are not hyphenated.

EXAMPLES

Owens's argument ignores other rules of statutory construction that are <u>well established</u>.

Owens's argument ignores other <u>well-established</u> rules of statutory construction.

This case has set precedents that are <u>far reaching</u>.

The case has set <u>far-reaching</u> precedents.

Notice that legal writers use many compound modifiers that begin with "well." As long as these modifiers precede the noun they modify, they will be hyphenated.

a well-reasoned opinion   a well-defined test
a well-known fact   a well-founded argument

Obviously, though, not all compound modifiers begin with "well," and unfortunately, often the only way to know whether to hyphenate is to consult a good dictionary with a recent publication date. The recent publication date is important because our language changes: What was once two or more separate words may later be hyphenated and eventually combined into one word.

air plane ⟶ air-plane ⟶ airplane

Still separate

trier of fact	sudden emergency doctrine
stop payment order	pyramid sales scheme
profit and loss statement	prima facie case
leave of absence	lame duck session
hit and run accident	family car doctrine

Hyphenated

price-fixing contract	take-home pay
out-of-pocket expenses	stop-limit order
out-of-date certificate	court-martial
cross-examination	

Combined

wraparound mortgage	quitclaim deed
counterclaim	

Our changing language also gives us new hyphenated nouns.

frame-up   split-off   squeeze-out

Many words are in transition. For example, you may notice that "line-up" is spelled with a hyphen in some cases and as the combined word "lineup" in others. The same is true for "pre-trial" and "pretrial." In such instances, consult your most recent authority and try to be consistent within the document you are writing. (Be sure to use all variations of a word when doing computer-assisted research.)

In addition to using the dictionary as a guide to hyphen use, there are a few general rules about when to use hyphens.

1. Always hyphenate modifiers and nouns that begin with the prefixes "all," "ex," and "self."

all-American	all-purpose
ex-partner	ex-judge
self-defense	self-incrimination

2. Other prefixes, including "anti," "co," "de," "inter," "intra," "multi," "non," "para," "pro," "re," "semi," and "super," generally should not be used with a hyphen.

antibiotic	multinational
antitrust	noncommissioned
codefendant	nonpayment
coheir	paralegal
degenerate	prorate
dehydrate	reactionary
interagency	reallocate
interbank	reassert
interstate	semiannual
intrastate	supersede

Unfortunately, however, there are enough exceptions to this general rule that you may often have to look up the word you need. The following exceptions apply to larger categories of words:

a.   Use the hyphen when it is needed for clarity ("re-create" and not "recreate");
b.   Use the hyphen when it is needed to prevent a doubled vowel ("re-enact," "de-emphasize") or a tripled consonant;
c.   Use the hyphen when it is needed because the second element is capitalized ("post-World War II," "un-American," or "anti-Semitic").

3. "Elect" is the one suffix that usually requires a hyphen.

governor-elect   president-elect

4. Hyphens are used to form compound numbers from twenty-one to ninety-nine. Hyphens are also used with fractions functioning as adjectives, but not with fractions functioning as nouns.

the twenty-fourth amendment
the seventy-second Congress
one-half acre *but*
    one half of the employees
two-thirds majority *but*
    two thirds of the board

5. Hyphens are often used to join a number and a noun to make a compound modifier.

twenty-year-old appellant	ten-year lease
three-mile limit	three-judge court
thirty-day letter	ten-acre tract
nine-year-old conviction	first-year student

6. Do not use a hyphen in the following instances:

    a.   when the first word in a two-word modifier is an adverb ending in "-ly" ("previously taxed income," "clearly erroneous view," "jointly acquired property");

    b.   when the compound modifier contains a foreign phrase ("bona fide purchaser," "per se violation");

    c.   when a civil or military title denotes one office ("justice of the peace" but "secretary-treasurer").

Sometimes two or more compound modifiers share the same second element. In such cases, use hyphens after each first element and do not use the second element twice.

    high- and low-test gasoline
    nine- and ten-acre parcels

7. Hyphens are also frequently used to combine two parties into one modifier.

    attorney-client privilege   husband-wife tort actions

8. Writers have the option of using hyphens when the hyphen will prevent a misreading.

    "re-cover the sofa" as opposed to "recover the sofa"

See Exercises 27.Y and 27.Z in the *Practice Book*.

§27.5.6   The Dash

Dashes are rarely used in legal writing. The consensus seems to be that dashes are too breezy and informal for the serious work of law.

Still, there are a few occasions when the dash is useful. For example, in sentences in which a list is an appositive, a pair of dashes can be used to signal the beginning and end of the list.

EXAMPLES

By 1996, the defendant had opened up bank accounts in several foreign countries—Switzerland, Brazil, South Africa, and Spain—all under different names.

The conservative bloc—Rehnquist, O'Connor, Scalia, and Kennedy—controlled the major cases of the 1988-1989 term.

Similarly, a dash is needed to set off an introductory list containing commas.

EXAMPLE

Name-calling, threats, and repeated beatings—these were the ways Wilson gave attention to his son.

When used with discretion, dashes can also be an effective way to create emphasis (see section 23.6.4). Notice how in the following pair of sentences, the dashes do more than the commas to highlight what they enclose.

EXAMPLES

Commas:

The prosecution's questions, over repeated objections, about Ms. Patten's religious beliefs cannot be deemed inadvertent.

Dashes:

The prosecution's questions—over repeated objections—about Ms. Patten's religious beliefs cannot be deemed inadvertent.

Commas:

The victim's age, eighteen months, made him particularly vulnerable.

Dashes:

The victim's age—eighteen months—made him particularly vulnerable.

Dashes can also be used to show abrupt shifts or to cue the reader that the words that follow are shocking or surprising.

EXAMPLE

Several witnesses—including the defendant's mother—testified that they believed Willie was capable of committing such a heinous crime.

On most keyboards, the dash is formed by hitting the hyphen key twice. There is no space before or after the dash.

§27.6   COMMA SPLICES AND FUSED SENTENCES

§27.6.1   Comma Splices

Perhaps the most common punctuation error in all writing, not just legal writing, is the comma splice. Simply put, a comma splice is the joining of two main, or independent, clauses with just a comma. This is the pattern for a comma splice:

main clause	,	main clause

Reminder

A main clause has both a subject and verb and can stand alone as a sentence.

EXAMPLE   **COMMA SPLICES**

The prosecutor spoke about the defendant's motive, the jury listened carefully.

The corrections officer contacted several other persons, none knew of Wilson's disappearance.

Mr. Baker sustained personal property damage, his picture windows and valuable vase were smashed.

There are five simple methods for correcting a comma splice. When correcting a comma splice, use the method that best suits the context.

1. Make each main clause a separate sentence.

EXAMPLE

The prosecutor spoke about the defendant's motive. The jury listened carefully.

---

2. Add a coordinating conjunction ("and," "but," "or," "for," "nor," "yet," "so") after the comma separating the two main clauses. (See Rule 1 in section 27.1.)

EXAMPLE

The corrections officer contacted several other persons, but none knew of Wilson's disappearance.

---

3. Change the comma separating the two main clauses to a semi-colon. (See section 27.2.)

EXAMPLE

The corrections officer contacted several other persons; none knew of Wilson's disappearance.

---

4. Change one of the main clauses to a subordinate clause.

EXAMPLES

While the prosecutor spoke about the defendant's motive, the jury listened carefully.

Although the corrections officer contacted several other persons, none knew of Wilson's disappearance.

---

5. If the second main clause is an explanation or illustration of the first main clause, use a colon to separate the two main clauses. (See section 27.3.)

EXAMPLE

Mr. Baker sustained personal property damage: His picture windows and valuable vase were smashed.

Comma splices often occur in sentences that have two main clauses and a conjunctive adverb introducing the second main clause. This is incorrect:

main clause,   therefore,   main clause

Reminder

The most commonly used conjunctive adverbs are "accordingly," "also," "besides," "consequently," "furthermore," "hence," "however," "indeed," "instead," "likewise," "meanwhile," "moreover," "nevertheless," "still," "then," "therefore," and "thus."

EXAMPLE   INCORRECT

The summons was not delivered to his usual place of abode, therefore, service was not effected in the manner prescribed by law.

Such comma splices are usually best corrected by using the third method, changing the comma to a semicolon.

EXAMPLE   CORRECTED

The summons was not delivered to his usual place of abode; therefore, service was not effected in the manner prescribed by law.

They can also be corrected by changing the comma to a period.

EXAMPLE   CORRECTED

The summons was not delivered to his usual place of abode. Therefore, service was not effected in the manner prescribed by law.

Conjunctive adverbs can also interrupt a main clause. In such cases, the conjunctive adverb is correctly preceded and followed by commas.

main,   therefore,   clause

EXAMPLE

The defendant, therefore, was not judged by a jury of his peers.

---

§27.6.2   Fused Sentences

Fused sentences, also known as run-on sentences, are a less frequent but even more serious writing error than comma splices. A fused sentence has no punctuation or coordinating conjunction between two main clauses. This is the pattern for a fused sentence:

main clause   main clause

EXAMPLE   **FUSED SENTENCE**

The prosecutor spoke about the defendant's motive the jury listened carefully.

Fused sentences can be corrected using the same methods for correcting comma splices.

Occasionally, one hears an overly long, rambling sentence described as a "run-on sentence." This is an incorrect use of the term. A run-on sentence is the same thing as a fused sentence: Either the punctuation or the coordinating conjunction is omitted between two main clauses. See Exercises 27.AA and 27.BB in the *Practice Book.*

Chapter 28

Mechanics

§28.1 SPELLING

Correct spelling. That's a given in legal writing. Unfortunately, though, it is not a given for each individual legal writer. We have not all been blessed with the same rigorous training, the same interest, and the same aptitude for any of the areas related to writing. Nowhere is this more evident than in spelling.

So, what does a law student, a practitioner, a paralegal, a clerk, or even a Supreme Court Justice do if he or she is a terrible speller? Certainly not resign oneself to a lifetime of poor spelling. Such a defeatist attitude is unworthy of a legal professional. But changing, indeed reversing, a lifelong habit or trend is never easy. Such a change almost always requires that we first change what we think or believe.

If we think spelling doesn't really matter, then we will never give it the sustained effort it requires. If we think we don't have the time to work at it, then we certainly won't find the time it takes to improve. (Fortunately, a few minutes a day is all it takes.) And if we are firmly convinced that "once a poor speller, always a poor speller," then we will undoubtedly fall victim to that self-fulfilling prophesy.

In short, the right attitude is a critical prerequisite to becoming a good speller. Once you decide that spelling is important and that you can be good at it, then you are ready to try some of the approaches discussed later in the section. But first you have to begin with your own attitude about spelling. And that is where we will begin.

§28.1.1 Getting Motivated

Most of us realize that spelling correctly is no great intellectual achievement. The ability to create and develop a good argument is certainly more significant than knowing how to spell the word "argument." Consequently, many of us neglect spelling, believing that our time should be spent on "more important things." This is a mistake. For in neglecting to learn how to spell "argument," we may in fact be hampering our ability to make an argument. Why? Poor spelling, even an occasional misspelling, is a distraction for readers.

Take the sentence you just read. Suppose you had read: "Por speling, even an occassionall mispeling, is a detraction for reders." What happened to you as you read that sentence? Did you think about the point the sentence was making, or was your attention on how the words were spelled?

Most readers, particularly ones who are good spellers, cannot help but mentally correct misspelled words as they read. Their attention is drawn away from what the writer is saying and, ironically, toward the very thing the writer least wants to emphasize: his or her ability to spell.

Some readers are particularly annoyed by spelling errors. These are the people who tend to equate good spelling with a virtue and poor spelling with a character flaw. Rightly or wrongly, this group of readers seems to assume that poor spelling is indicative of other, less apparent weaknesses. The inference seems to be that "if this writer can't or didn't bother to spell correctly, he or she is probably lax about other matters as well."

Whether or not you agree with this view, the fact remains that legal writers who are poor spellers are at a disadvantage. Their readers—whether friend or foe, self-righteous or forgiving—have a needless obstacle to communication: misspelled words. So, unless you are willing to accept working with a self-imposed disadvantage, improving your spelling is a goal worthy of every legal writer.

Of course, there is no one best way to improve your spelling. Everyone learns differently, so you should be the one to decide which of the methods discussed below will work best for you. Some people find it helpful to use two or more methods together. The important point is to decide what you are going to do and stick with it.

§28.1.2   Spelling Crutches

It is possible to improve the spelling in the end product of your writing without actually learning how to spell a single new word. The methods discussed in this section all require that you rely on someone or something besides yourself for checking your spelling. These spelling crutches get the job done, but they do have drawbacks.

a.   Computer Software

Most software companies offer programs that will correct spelling. If you always have access to a computer for writing, these spelling programs can be a godsend. Their disadvantage is obvious, though. Computer spelling programs check spelling by making a blind match between the words you have typed and the words in the program's memory. The program does not consider context. Consequently, it will read "torte" as spelled correctly without knowing whether the writer intended a wrongful act or a cake with rich frosting.

b. Dictionaries

The time-honored method of checking spelling has always been to "look it up in the dictionary." Even the best speller needs to double-check spelling in the dictionary from time to time.

Dictionaries are undoubtedly valuable resources for spelling, but they do have drawbacks. One needs to have a fairly good idea of how a word is spelled before it can be double-checked in the dictionary. Even then, the writer may have to scan numerous pages before locating the word. If the same word has to be looked up frequently, using the dictionary can become a time-consuming process.

A more efficient way of using the dictionary for spelling is to look up a word once and then use one of the other spelling methods to reinforce learning.

c. Legal Spellers

Rather than scan numerous pages in a standard dictionary, some legal writers find that it is faster to check spelling in a legal speller. These handy, pocket-sized books contain alphabetical lists (without definitions) of legal words and words that frequently occur in legal contexts. They also show correct word divisions. The disadvantage of legal spellers is that there are occasions (law school exams, the bar exam) when they, as well as dictionaries, cannot be used.

d. Secretaries and Typists

Many legal professionals who are poor spellers rely on their secretaries or typists to correct spelling errors. If you can find an individual who is 100 percent reliable as a speller and who understands the content of what you are writing, then you may have found the best spelling crutch of all. Even so, the perfect secretary or typist has many of the same drawbacks as dictionaries and legal spellers (they cannot be used in law school exams or for the bar), and they have one disadvantage that is unique — they can be hired away!

§28.1.3   Spelling Strategies

Without a doubt, all the best methods for improving your spelling have you learning to spell the words yourself. This may seem like a formidable task, especially if you truly are a terrible speller, but it can be done in just a few minutes a day. In fact, learning to spell the words you use frequently will save you time in the long run because you won't have to keep checking how those words are spelled.

Before applying the spelling strategies discussed below, begin by analyzing the spelling errors you tend to make. For a designated period of time, perhaps one week, keep track of the words you have to look up.

The chart below was designed to help you categorize your misspellings. From the chart, you can determine whether there is a pattern to your misspellings; if so, you can focus your attention on that specific type of spelling problem and choose a spelling strategy that specifically addresses that problem. Notice too that in the second column you are asked to write the word with the trouble spot circled or enlarged. This simple technique in itself reinforces visual memory of the part of the word that is difficult to remember. Use the category numbers in the following list in the last column. One is done for you.

Categories of Spelling Errors

1. when to use "ei" and when to use "ie" (receive, achieve, seize, their, thief)
2. when to and when not to drop the silent "e" (admire, admiration; judge, judgment; admissible, admissibility)
3. when to and when not to change the "y" to "i" (try, tries, tried; defy, defiance; delay, delays; pay, paid; deputy, deputize)
4. when to and when not to double the final consonant (occur, occurred, occurrence; commit, commitment, committed)
5. getting the middle right (accommodate, rescind, rescission, injunction)
6. guessing the schwa (the vowel sound in unaccented syllables) (separate, independence, severance, benefit)
7. pronunciation — omitting letters in pronunciation often leads to omitting letters in spelling (quantity, probably), and the same is true if you add letters in pronunciation (athletic, disastrous)
8. sound-alikes — learning the difference in meaning between the sound-alikes (its, it's; too, to, two; then, than; pendant, pendent; hale, hail; principal, principle)
9. other — any other misspelling that doesn't fall into the first eight groups

Word (spelled correctly)	Word (spelled correctly with trouble spot circled or enlarged)	Category of error
receive	reCEIve	1

a.   Spelling Rules

Using "ei" or "ie" (category 1)

There are two rules that you can use to distinguish between the "ei" and "ie" words.

1. Use "i" before "e," except after "c" when the two vowels are pronounced as "ē" (as in "see").

bel*ie*ve	rec*ei*ve
n*ie*ce	perc*ei*ve
br*ie*f	dec*ei*ve
f*ie*ld	conc*ei*ve
rel*ie*f	dec*ei*t
gr*ie*vance	rec*ei*pt

2. Use "ei" if pronounced as "ā" (as in "day").

eight	vein	neighbor
freight	weigh	heinous

There are several exceptions. Note that most of the exceptions do not pronounce "ie" or "ei" as either "ē" or "ā." If you have trouble spelling any of the exceptions, use the mnemonic strategy (memory trigger) that is discussed later in this section. Here are some examples of mnemonics to help you remember these exceptions.

neither	not difficult to remember if you can spell "either"
weird	this word is weird and an exception to the rule
foreign	another one foreign to the system
sheik	yet another one foreign to the system
their	"their" is the possessive form of "they," so keep the "e" where it belongs and change "y" to "i"
height	because of the "-ight" ending, it is like "right," "night," and "light"
conscience, science	because of the "-ence" ending, it is like "independence" and "convenience"
forfeit	with this one you forfeit the rule
seize, seizure, leisure	remember to "seize your leisure" or have a "leisure seizure"
financier	easy to remember this exception because another rule (add "-er" to mean "one who") takes precedence; plus, "A financier is fancier than a banker."

This poem is an easy way to remember the "ei/ie" rule and some of its exceptions:

Use i before e except after c
Or when sounded as a
As in neighbor and weigh;
But their, weird, and either,
Foreign, seize, neither,
Leisure, forfeit, and height,
Are exceptions spelled right.

The following sentence is another way to remember the exceptions:

> At his height, the financier for the weird foreign sheik
> neither seizes nor forfeits his leisure.

Dropping the Silent "e" (category 2)

Adding suffixes to words is usually not a problem unless the word ends in a silent "e." When the silent "e" occurs, here are the rules to apply.

1. Does the suffix begin with a vowel? If so, drop the "e."

kindle + ed = kindled	nerve + ous = nervous
admire + ation = admiration	blue + ish = bluish
abide + ing = abiding	imagine + able = imaginable

2. However, if the silent "e" is preceded by a soft "c" or "g" and the suffix begins with a vowel, the "e" is not usually dropped.

manage + able = manageable
notice + able = noticeable
courage + ous = courageous
advantage + ous = advantageous

3. If the suffix begins with a consonant, the final "e" is usually kept.

extreme + ly = extremely	retire + ment = retirement
force + ful = forceful	safe + ty = safety
one + self = oneself	use + less = useless

The exceptions to the dropping-the-silent-"e" rule include some words commonly used in legal writing. These five exceptions retain the silent "e."

foresee + able = foreseeable
dye + ing = dyeing (to distinguish it from "dying")
singe + ing = singeing (to distinguish it from "singing")
shoe + ing = shoeing (to prevent mispronunciation)
mile + age = mileage (to prevent mispronunciation)

These five exceptions drop the final "e" even though the suffix begins with a consonant.

argue + ment = argument	true + ly = truly
judge + ment = judgment	due + ly = duly
acknowledge + ment = acknowledgment	

Changing "y" to "i" (category 3)

One rather consistent rule of English spelling is to change the "y" to an "i" before adding a suffix. However, there are a few additional criteria to consider if you want that rule to work properly.

1. Does the word end in a consonant + y? If so, then change the "y" to "i" and add the suffix <u>unless</u> the suffix is "<u>-ing</u>."

rel<u>y</u> + ance = reliance   tr<u>y</u> + ed = tried
rel<u>y</u> + ing = relying   tr<u>y</u> + ing = trying

2. If a vowel precedes the "y," there is no change.

del<u>a</u>y + ed = delayed   empl<u>oy</u> + ment = employment

There are a few exceptions to this rule—five of them have a vowel before the "y" and still change it to "i," and one has a consonant before the "y" and does not change it to "i":

pay, paid   shy + ness = shyness
say, said
lay, laid
day, daily
slay, slain

If you have changed the "y" to "i" and want to form the plural, add "es" instead of just "s."

duty + es = duties

Doubling the Final Consonant (category 4)

When adding a suffix to a word, you double the final consonant *only if* the following conditions exist.

1. The suffix begins with a vowel.
2. The root word contains only one syllable, or
3. the root word contains more than one syllable and its primary accent is on the last syllable of the root word once the suffix is added.
4. Only one vowel precedes the final consonant (the final consonant cannot be preceded by another consonant).

plan + ing = planning   drop + ed = dropped
run + ing = running   omit + ed = omitted
occur + ed = occurred   admit + ing = admitting
occur + ence = occurrence   submit + ed = submitted
defer + ed = deferred   forgot + en = forgotten

In the following examples, the final consonant is not doubled because one of the required conditions does not exist.

1. The suffix does not begin with a vowel.

commit + <u>m</u>ent = commitment

Note that when "commit" takes a suffix that begins with a vowel, the final "t" is doubled: committed, committing.

2. A consonant, rather than one vowel, precedes the final consonant.

rele<u>n</u>t + ed = relented

3. Two vowels, rather than the required one vowel, precede the final consonant.

fe<u>ar</u> + ing = fearing
discl<u>ai</u>m + er = disclaimer

4. The accent is not on the final syllable of the root word once the suffix is added.

benefit + ed = benefited
differ + ed = differed
refer + ence = reference

Note that when "refer" takes other suffixes, the accent is on the final syllable of the root word; consequently the final consonant is doubled: refe<u>rr</u>ed, refe<u>rr</u>ing, refe<u>rr</u>al.

Using Flash Cards and Personal Spelling Lists to Get the Middle Right (category 5)

Most people, particularly fast readers, rarely focus on the middles of words. Consequently, when these people write, they don't have a strong mental image of how the middle of a given word looks.

To solve this kind of spelling problem, then, we need a spelling strategy that highlights that part of each word.

In the second column of the chart earlier in this section, the trouble spot in a word was enlarged or circled. This same highlighting technique can be used when making a set of flash cards or a personal spelling list.

Suppose, for example, that you have difficulty remembering how to spell "foreseeable." If the problem is with the first "e," your highlighted area should make that "e" dominant. Of course, there are several ways to do this, so you should choose whichever way makes you "see" the word in your mind.

> forEseeable
> FOREseeable
> foRESeeable

This highlighting technique works particularly well with flash cards that have only one word printed on each card. By isolating the word and then highlighting the trouble spot, you can be sure that your attention is on not only that word but the part of that word that causes you problems.

Flash cards have other simple but invaluable advantages. Law students can keep a dozen or so index cards in each law textbook for quickly jotting down key words or terms of art that they predict they will have difficulty spelling. These flash cards, which can double as bookmarks, can be quickly reviewed in spare moments before or after class. Once a word is memorized, it can be filed away and pulled out again only if the word becomes a problem in the future. The beauty of the flash card method, then, is that it involves a bare minimum of time invested.

Personal spelling lists that use the highlighting technique work reasonably well, but they have a few noteworthy disadvantages. First of all, the person reviewing the list has to work at focusing on individual words; the list format tends to encourage the eye to move down the list too quickly. Second, lists tend to be somewhere else when you need them. If it becomes inconvenient to write down a word, the odds increase that it won't be recorded. The list may also be elsewhere when you have that spare minute to review spelling.

Using Mnemonics (categories 5, 6, and 9, in particular, but useful for all categories)

Mnemonics, or memory triggers, are useful gimmicks for remembering almost anything. In the section on the "ei/ie" spelling rule, several mnemonics were suggested for remembering the exceptions to that rule. Here are some other examples of mnemonics that can be used for spelling.

For the word "believe": Never believe a lie.
For the word "separate": Remember "separate" is par for the course. Also, "separate" has a rat in it.
For the word "defendant": All defendants are ants.

A good mnemonic, then, is memorable, not necessarily true. Obviously all defendants are not ants; the point is to remember the "-ant" ending.

Often the more absurd the connection you create between the word and its spelling, the easier it will be to remember. You may also find that the mnemonics that you make up yourself stick with you best.

Sometimes mnemonics can be combined with flash cards or personal spelling lists so that the highlighted area corresponds with the memory gimmick. For example, to remember the "n" in "environment" try making a flash card that highlights the "on me" in "environment": envirONMEnt.

Emphasizing and Overemphasizing Pronunciation (categories 6 and 7)

If you tend to pronounce "privilege" with a "d" sound in the last syllable, you are likely to spell it with a "d." If you say "athletic" with four syllables rather than the correct three, you are apt to add an extra vowel after the "th." Consequently, some spelling problems can be corrected simply by checking a dictionary for the correct pronunciation and learning to say the word properly.

Schwa sounds (the vowel sound in an unaccented syllable) present a slightly different problem. By definition, schwa sounds are indistinguishable; when they are pronounced correctly, you can't tell whether they represent an "a," "e," "i," "o," or "u." For purposes of spelling, not speaking, then, you can overemphasize pronunciation in words that contain difficult-to-spell schwa sounds. "Permissible" becomes "permissIBle"; "existence" becomes "exisTENce"; and "warrant" becomes "war-RANT."

Distinguishing Between Sound-Alikes (category 8)

Unfortunately, the English language is full of pairs and trios of words that have similar pronunciation but distinct meanings. If you have trouble with affect/effect, principle/principal, discrete/discreet, all together/altogether, ensure/insure, counsel/council, compliment/complement, farther/further, lose/loose, it's/its, their/there/they're, to/too/two, cite/sight/site, elicit/illicit, or any of the other sound-alikes, refer to the Glossary of Usage at the end of this book.

Additional Strategies for Spelling (category 9)

Prefixes. Prefixes do not change the spelling of a word when they are added. Do not drop a letter from or add a letter to the prefix or the original word.

dis + satisfied = dissatisfied
mis + spell = misspell
ir + revocable = irrevocable
un + necessary = unnecessary
im + moral = immoral

Remember too that knowing what a prefix means can be a clue to correct spelling. For example, if you have trouble remembering whether a word begins with "pre" or "per," consider whether the word's definition includes the notion of "before," which is the meaning of "pre."

> precedent—something done or said before
> precede—to go before
> premeditate—to think about before

Plurals.   Most nouns form their plural by adding just "s."

> case ⟶ cases
> statute ⟶ statutes

Some nouns ending in "f" or "fe" change the ending to "ve" before adding the "s" for the plural.

> wife ⟶ wives
> shelf ⟶ shelves

Nouns ending in "s," "sh," "ch," or "x" add "es" to form the plural.

> loss ⟶ losses
> bush ⟶ bushes
> switch ⟶ switches
> tax ⟶ taxes

Note that the "es" ending, unlike the "s" ending, usually adds an extra syllable to these words. Also note that verbs ending in "s," "sh," "ch," or "x" form the third-person singular in the same way.

> clutch ⟶ clutches
> kiss ⟶ kisses

Nouns ending in "o" preceded by a vowel usually add just "s" to form the plural.

> folio ⟶ folios

But nouns ending in "o" preceded by a consonant usually add "es" to form the plural.

> zero ⟶ zeroes

Nouns that have changed the "y" to "i" add "es" to form the plural.

> copy ⟶ copies
> reply ⟶ replies

The formation of some plurals is borrowed from another language.

crisis ⟶ crises

analysis ⟶ analyses

hypothesis ⟶ hypotheses

basis ⟶ bases

alumna (feminine) ⟶ alumnae

alumnus (masculine) ⟶ alumni

datum ⟶ data

stratum ⟶ strata

phenomenon ⟶ phenomena

medium ⟶ media

criterion ⟶ criteria

Notice the tendency to give such words anglicized plurals. For words that have two plural forms, either is correct, but the older forms (the second column) are more commonly seen in law. In fact, most legal readers would consider "memorandums" or "dictums" an error.

Singular	*Older Plural*	*Anglicized Plural*
memorandum	memoranda	memorandums
dictum	dicta	dictums
appendix	appendices	appendixes
index	indices	indexes
focus	foci	focuses

Compound nouns form plurals by adding "s" to the last word if all the words of the compound noun are equally significant.

booby trap ⟶ booby traps

If one word is more significant than the others, the "s" is added to that word.

brother-in-law ⟶ brothers-in-law

passerby ⟶ passersby

mile-per-hour ⟶ miles-per-hour

See section 27.5.5 for more information on the use of hyphens.

To form the plural of dates, figures, or symbols, you can add either "s" or " 's."

the 1940s *or* the 1940's

To form the plural of letters, abbreviations, numbers, and words used as words, add " 's."

The *i*'s must be dotted and the *t*'s crossed.

M.D.'s

One of the *5*'s was omitted.

The disjunctive *or*'s in that law make it ambiguous.

Note that the letters, numbers, and words used as words are italicized (or underlined), but the " 's" is not.

Possessives. See section 27.4 on the apostrophe for a complete discussion of how the possessive forms of words are spelled.

Variant Spellings. Many dictionaries show more than one spelling for a given word. The first spelling shown will be the preferred spelling and the one you should use.

Unless you are practicing law in Great Britain, use American and not British spellings.

British	*American*
judgement	judgment
acknowledgement	acknowledgment
theatre	theater
criticise	criticize
realise	realize
humour	humor
colour	color
jewellery	jewelry
cancelled	canceled
travelled	traveled

b.   Spelling Lists

Many handbooks and books about writing offer lists of commonly misspelled words. When using such a list, study only a few words at a time.

The following chart contains some commonly misspelled words that occur frequently in legal writing. You should supplement this list with a study of the sound-alike words in the Glossary of Usage and the formation of the possessive.

1. paid
   forty
   their

2. coming
   writing
   across

3. receive
   believe
   achieve

4. judgment
   argument
   separate

5. appellate
   appellant
   appellee

6. statute
   statutory
   statutorily

7. omitting
   omission
   omitted

8. committed
   committing
   committee
   commitment

9. occurred
   occurring
   occurrence

10. referred
    referral
    reference

11. analyze
    criticize
    recognize

12. allege
    allegation
    acknowledge
    privilege

13. consistent
    pertinent
    convenient
    efficient

14. apparent
    independent
    analogous
    unnecessary

15. permissible
    reversible
    admissibility

16. occasional
    accommodate
    foreseeable
    among

17. government
    environment
    harassment
    fundamental

18. warrant
    hearsay
    injunction
    subpoena

19. carefully
    accidentally
    basically

20. physically
    undoubtedly
    entirely

21. liaison
    rescission
    recision

22. supersede
    succeed
    aggravate
    exaggerate

23. evidentiary
    contributorily
    nuisance
    negligence

24. existence
    absence
    license

25. defendant
    appearance
    attendance
    descendant

26. benefited
    beneficial
    recommend

27. category
    bureaucracy
    probably
    representative

28. develop
    certain
    against

29. condemn
    guaranteed
    mortgage
    illiterate

30. definite
    maneuver
    possession
    unanimous

31. perform
    precede
    prejudice

32. proceed
    procedure
    seize

33. similar
    familiar
    sincerely
    truly

34. eighth
    height
    paroled
    questionnaire

35. irrelevant
    respondent

One Final Note About Spelling

Always spell people's names correctly. Make a point of checking whether it is Stephen with a "ph" or Steven with a "v," Schmitt with a "t" or Schmidt with a "d." There is no quicker way to annoy or even alienate a reader than to misspell his or her name.

§28.2   CAPITALIZATION

§28.2.1   General Rules

In English, there are two general rules for capitalization: (1) to mark the beginning of a sentence, and (2) to signal a proper name or adjective.

a.   *Beginning of a Sentence*

The first word of a sentence is always capitalized. Even sentence fragments such as those that begin brief answers in legal memoranda have their first word capitalized.

A complete sentence enclosed in parentheses starts with a capital letter, unless the parenthetical sentence occurs within another sentence.

EXAMPLE

The Wilsons extended their garden beyond the property line and onto the disputed strip. (See Attachment A.) *but*

The Wilsons extended their garden beyond the property line (see Attachment A) and onto the disputed strip.

---

1.   Quotations

Capitalize the first word of a direct quotation when the quotation is formally introduced and set up as a separate sentence.

EXAMPLE

The Supreme Court unanimously struck down a policy banning women of child-bearing age from hazardous but top-paying jobs: "Decisions about the welfare of future children must be left to the parents who conceive, bear, support, and raise them rather than to the employers who hire those parents."

Do not capitalize the first word of a direct quotation when the quotation is integrated into the writer's sentence. See section 27.5.3 for discussion of the use of brackets when making a change to a quotation.

EXAMPLE

The Supreme Court unanimously struck down a policy banning women of child-bearing age from hazardous but top-paying jobs, stating that "[d]ecisions about the welfare of future children must be left to the parents who conceive, bear, support, and raise them rather than to the employers who hire those parents."

Do not capitalize the beginning of the second segment of a split direct quotation.

EXAMPLE

"Concern for a woman's existing or potential offspring," wrote Justice Blackmun for the majority, "historically has been the excuse for denying women equal employment opportunities."

---

2.   Sentence Following a Colon

When a full sentence follows a colon, the writer has the option to capitalize the first word of the sentence following the colon.

EXAMPLES

Correct:

The company has evidence that Mrs. McKibbin accepted the written proposal: She made a telephone call to place the order for the rugs.

Also Correct:

The company has evidence that Mrs. McKibbin accepted the written proposal: she made a telephone call to place the order for the rugs.

Do not capitalize the first word after the colon if what follows the colon is less than a complete sentence.

EXAMPLE

In *Traweek,* the court found that the appearance of the defendants differed from the witness's description in just one detail: the color of the shirts worn by the defendants.

If the items in a series following a colon are not complete sentences, do not capitalize the first word in each item.

EXAMPLE

The parties will dispute whether three of the four elements of the sudden emergency doctrine are met: (1) whether Mr. Short was confronted by a sudden and unexpected emergency, (2) whether his own negligence created or contributed to that emergency, and (3) whether he made a choice such as a reasonable person placed in the same situation might make.

---

b.   Proper Nouns and Adjectives

As a general rule, capitalize a word used to name someone or something specific; use lowercase when the same word is used as a general reference.

the President of Shell Oil
a president of a company

Stanford Law School
a law school

Environmental Protection Agency
an agency of the federal government

Unfortunately, there is disagreement about whether to apply this rule to the words "defendant" and "plaintiff" (and similar terms such as "appellant," "appellee," "respondent," and "petitioner"). Some authorities apply this rule and capitalize these words when they refer to the parties in the matter that is the subject of the document.[1] Others simply say not

---

1. See the *Bluebook* (16th ed.), *Practitioners' Notes.*

to capitalize the terms at all[2] or not to capitalize them when they appear before a name[3] as in the example "defendant Smith." All agree that these words should be capitalized on cover sheets for briefs.

Even with this general rule as a guide, legal writers often find it difficult to determine when certain words that commonly occur in legal writing ("act," "amendment," "bill," "circuit," "code," "constitution," "court," "federal," "national," "statute," and "the") should be capitalized. Use the following list as a quick reference.

"Act"

Capitalize the word "act" when it is part of a full title.

the Clean Air Act
the Controlled Substance Act of 1970, *but*
an act passed by the legislature

"Act" is also capitalized when it is used as the short form of a proper name.

the Clean Air Act ———→ the Act

"Amendment"

Despite the general rule to capitalize names of specific nouns, several authorities[4] insist that the word "amendment" is not capitalized when it is used to designate one of the specific amendments to the Constitution. Perhaps because this practice defies logic, other authorities[5] insist that it should be. Whichever course a writer selects, it is important to be consistent throughout the same document.

fifth amendment   *or*   Fifth Amendment

All agree that a general reference to an amendment should not be capitalized.

an amendment to the tax laws

---

2. See *The Texas Law Review Manual on Style* (5th ed. 1987).
3. See *The Chicago Manual of Style* (14th ed. 1993).
4. See *Webster's Legal Speller,* the *Bluebook* (16th ed. 1996), and *The Texas Law Review Manual on Style* (5th ed. 1987).
5. See *Webster's Legal Secretaries Handbook* (2d ed. 1996), *The New York Times Manual on Style and Usage* (1976) and *The Chicago Manual of Style* (14th ed. 1993).

Notice that when referring to one of the amendments to the Constitution, most writers spell out ordinals through nine and use figures for 10 and above.

fifth amendment   14th amendment

When two or more amendments are mentioned together, use figures if either is for 10 or above.

the 5th amendment and the 14th amendment

"Bill"

With the exception of the Bill of Rights, "bill" should be written in lowercase. This practice does seem to be an exception to the general rule of capitalizing words that are part of a full title.

Senate bill 47   House bill 11

"Circuit"

Capitalize "circuit" when it is used as part of a full title. Use lowercase when "circuit" is part of a general reference.

United States Court of Appeals for the Second Circuit, *but*
circuit courts

"Code"

Capitalize "code" when it is part of a full title. Use lowercase for all general references.

The United States Internal Revenue Code
United States Code, *but*
the tax code
state codes
unofficial code

"Constitution"

Capitalize "constitution" when used as part of the full title of any constitution or when used as a short form reference to the United States Constitution.

    the United States Constitution
    the Constitution (short for United States Constitution), *but*
    a new state constitution

"Court"

Probably the most common capitalization question in legal writing is when should "court" be capitalized.

1. The official and full names of all international and higher courts are capitalized.

    International Court of Justice
    United States Court of Appeals for the Third Circuit
    Texas Court of Appeals
    Arizona Supreme Court

2. Always capitalize "court" when referring to the United States Supreme Court. Note that even the short forms for referring to the United States Supreme Court are capitalized.

    the Supreme Court of the United States
    the United States Supreme Court
    the Supreme Court
    the Court (short form for Supreme Court)

3. Do not capitalize "court" if part of the name of a city or county court.

    the Phoenix night court
    Hampton municipal court
    juvenile court

Despite the agreement among the authorities about not capitalizing "court" if it is part of the name of a city or county court, most practitioners seem to ignore the rule and capitalize "court" in such instances.

4. Capitalize "court" in a document when referring to the very court that will receive that document.

5. Capitalize "court" when the term specifically refers to the judge or presiding officer.

    It is the opinion of this Court . . . .

Other personifications such as "Your Honor" and "the Bench" are also capitalized.

"Federal"

The word "federal" is capitalized only when it is part of a specific name.

> Federal Bureau of Investigation
> Federal Deposit Insurance Corporation
> Federal Energy Regulatory Commission, *but*
> federal government
> federal agents
> federal court

"National"

The word "national" is capitalized only when it is part of a specific name.

> National Security Council, *but*
> national security interests

Another test for whether to capitalize "federal" or "national" is whether the word following those terms is capitalized. If it is, then capitalize "federal" or "national" because it is part of a specific name.

"Statute"

Use lowercase for "statute," unless it is part of a title.

> federal statutes
> state statutes
> statute of limitations, *but*
> Statute of Frauds

"The"

In names and titles, capitalize "the" only if it is part of an official name.

> The Hague, *but*
> the *Bluebook*
> the United States Supreme Court
> the American Bar Association

§28.2.2   Headings

The most important thing to remember about capitalization in headings is consistency. If local rules or convention dictates that certain types of headings require all capital letters, be consistent with that rule or convention. If there are no rules governing capitalization in the type of headings you are writing, develop a system that can be used consistently throughout the document.

Elaine C. Maier, in her book *How to Prepare a Legal Citation,* outlines the following suggested scheme "in descending order of subordination":

1. All letters of all words in the heading are capitalized.
2. All initial letters of all words in the heading are capitalized.
3. All initial letters of all words in the heading except articles, conjunctions, and prepositions of four letters or fewer are capitalized.
4. The sentence style of capitalization is used; that is, only the first letter of the first word and proper nouns are capitalized.[6]

Use the same capitalization level to indicate comparable levels in your text. (Boldface, underlining, and other typefaces may also be used to create levels in text.)

In situations where you are developing your own scheme of capitalization in headings, remember that having more than five words typed in all capitals slows your reader down. For this reason, it may be best to use all capitals at a level where you have only relatively short headings.

§28.2.3   Miscellaneous Rules for Capitalization

Academic Degrees

Academic degrees are capitalized, but some have lowercase internal letters.

J.D.   LL.M.   M.D.   Ph.D.

Acronyms

Most acronyms are written in all capitals (OPEC, NASA, CERCLA). Abbreviations of government agencies, corporations, and military organizations are also in all capital letters (EEOC, FCC, IBM, USMC).

---

6. Elaine C. Maier, *How to Prepare a Legal Citation* 158 (Barron's Educational Series, Inc. 1986).

Compass Points and Geographical Names

Compass points are capitalized when they refer to a geographical region; adjectives derived from compass points are also capitalized.

the Middle West
the Northeast
Southern hospitality
Southwestern cuisine, *but*
the car was heading west
the fence runs along the northern boundary

Topographical Names

Capitalize topographical names when they are part of a proper name.

Lake Superior	a lake
the Mississippi River	the river
the Rocky Mountains	those mountains

In legal documents, words such as "state," "county," or "city" are capitalized when they are part of a specific name.

Washington State
Chaves County
the City of Spokane
the State of Florida
Commonwealth of Virginia

Similarly, capitalize words such as "bridge," "square," "building," "park," and "hotel" when they are part of a place name.

Brooklyn Bridge	Central Park
Transamerica Building	Tiananmen Square

Judges' Names

The Supreme Court has a tradition of spelling judges' names in all capitals when the names are referred to in opinions.

Rules of Law

Despite efforts at uniformity, several rules of law are known by several versions of their name, all with differing capitalization. The common issue is whether a certain phrase is part of the title of the rule. The general guideline is to capitalize the words that are essential to the rule's name. Another reasonable guideline is to use the most common form of the rule's name.

Is it, for example, "the rule in Shelley's case," "the Rule in Shelley's case," "the Rule in Shelley's Case," or "The Rule in Shelley's Case"? Using the guideline of capitalizing those words that are essential to the rule's name, "rule" and "case" should be capitalized because they are commonly treated as part of the name. "The," on the other hand, should probably be lowercase to avoid making the phrase look like a book title.

Is it the "rule against perpetuities," the "Rule against Perpetuities," or the "Rule Against Perpetuities"? Professor Dukeminier asked this question in his article *Perpetuities: Contagious Capitalization*[7] and determined that "Rule against Perpetuities" and "rule against perpetuities" were both commonly used and therefore acceptable. "Rule against Perpetuities" is preferable, according to Dukeminier, for historical reasons.

What should a legal writer do, then, when faced with a similar question? Consider the following factors:

1. What words are essential to the rule's name?
2. What capitalization is most common?
3. Is there a historical reason for preferring one version over another?

The most important consideration of all, though, is consistency. Once you have determined which version you will use, use it consistently throughout the document.

Titles

Capitalize titles of court documents. Use all capitals for titles on the documents themselves.

Trademarks

Use all capitals to distinguish a trademark from the name of a company or corporation.

XEROX (trademark)	Xerox (corporation)
EXXON (trademark)	Exxon (corporation)

---

7. Jesse Dukeminier, *Perpetuities: Contagious Capitalization,* 20 J. Legal Educ. 341 (1968).

Vessels

Although one occasionally sees all capitals used for the name of a vessel, capitalizing only the first letter is preferred.

Titanic   Valdez

§28.3   ABBREVIATIONS AND SYMBOLS

§28.3.1   General Rules for Abbreviations

Abbreviations, or shortened forms, should be used primarily for the convenience of the reader. Properly used, an abbreviation saves *reader* time and energy. It gets across the same message in less space.

The temptation for writers, of course, is to use abbreviations that are convenient for them. A writer who fails to adopt the reader's perspective may use an abbreviation to save writer time and energy only to find that the reader is unsure, confused, or even frustrated by the abbreviation.

One source of abbreviation confusion is the sheer number of specialized abbreviations used in some legal documents.[8] The result of such overuse is obvious: a harried reader who has to keep turning back in the document to keep the abbreviations straight. The solution to the problem is equally obvious: Avoid using numerous specialized abbreviations in the same document.

All of the abbreviation rules that follow apply to abbreviations in textual sentences, not in citations.

Rule 1.   Abbreviate only when the abbreviation will be clear for the reader.

Rule 2.   If an abbreviation will be initially unfamiliar to the reader, use the full form first and then follow with the abbreviation in parentheses.

EXAMPLES

Mrs. Kearney telephoned Beaver Custom Carpets (BCC) and asked if it manufactured custom-made carpets. BCC's representative took down a description of the carpets she wanted made.

---

8. Writing about a case in which no fewer than seven different groups of initials were used, Justice Rehnquist complained that "the 'alphabet soup' of the New Deal era was, by comparison, a clear broth." *Chrysler Corp. v. Brown,* 441 U.S. 281, 284, 286-87 (1979).

Mr. Washburn wants to know whether the Oregon Wilderness Watchers (OWW) can create a prescriptive easement across his land. OWW has been using a path across Washburn's property to reach its property.

Abbreviations created for a specific document, such as BCC and OWW in the examples above, are usually written in all capitals. Notice that common abbreviations that are acronyms (ERIC, SARA, ERISTA) are also written in all capitals, unless they have been fully incorporated into the language (radar, sonar, scuba, and zip code).

§28.3.2   Miscellaneous Rules for Abbreviation

Geographical Names

U.S. Postal Service abbreviations are acceptable when used on envelopes and in other situations when an address is written in block form. Note that state abbreviations are all capitalized without end periods.

> Professor Mary Brown
> 8990 6th Ave. NE
> Tacoma, WA 98498

The same words (avenue, street, northeast, Washington) should be spelled out when they appear in text. Note that all compass points (northeast, southwest) are also lower case, unless they are used as the name of a region (the Pacific Northwest, the South).

"Saint" may be abbreviated when it is part of a name of a city (St. Louis); follow the bearer's preference when it is part of a person's name (David Saint-Johns, Ruth St. Denis).

Foreign Phrases

Some Latin words commonly used in legal texts and citations are abbreviations, so they should be followed by periods *(id., i.e., e.g.)*. Others are complete words (the *ex* in *ex parte* or *re*), so a period should not be used.

Names of Laws

The first time a law is mentioned in text, its title should be typed out in full; thereafter, abbreviations can be used. (See the *Bluebook* for how to write the names of laws in citations.)

first mention: Article II, Section 3
later references: Art. II, Sec. 3

Academic Degrees

Academic degrees are abbreviated. Note too that capitalization should be checked with a dictionary.

Ph.D.   LL.D.   M.B.A.   C.P.A.
J.D.   LL.B.   LL.M.   M.D.

Time

The abbreviations for *ante meridiem* and *post meridiem* are most commonly written as unspaced, lowercase letters with periods.

9:00 a.m.   *or*   9:00 A.M.

Measures and Weights

When the numeral is written out,[9] the unit must also be written out. When the figure is used, the unit may be abbreviated.

one hundred square miles   *or*   100 sq. mi.
one hundred eighty pounds   *or*   180 lbs.

Double Punctuation

Occasionally, an abbreviation will be the last word in a sentence. In such cases, do not add an additional period after the period for the abbreviation.

The officer had checked in at 8:00 p.m.

Clark claimed she had a Ph.D.

A period for an abbreviation can be used with a question mark or an exclamation point.

Did the officer check in at 8:00 p.m.?

---

9. According to the *Bluebook* Rule 6.2(a), numbers from zero to ninety-nine are written out and larger numbers use numerals, unless the number begins a sentence. Numbers used at the beginning of a sentence must be written out.

§28.3.3 Inappropriate Abbreviations

Informal abbreviations

Avoid informal abbreviations such as "ad," "cite," "exam," "memo," "phone," "quote" (as a noun), and "&" in formal legal writing. Use the more formal, full name: "advertisement," "citation," "examination," "memorandum," "telephone," "quotation," and "and."

Dates

Do not abbreviate dates. Write them out in full.

Monday, February 11, 1991, *not*
Mon. Feb. 11, '91

Abbreviations Between Lines or Pages

Do not separate parts of an abbreviation. The full abbreviation should be on one line on one page.

Beginnings of Sentences

Avoid beginning a sentence with an abbreviation unless the abbreviation is a courtesy title (Mr., Mrs., Ms., Dr., Messrs.).

Titles

Most titles other than Mr., Mrs., Ms., Dr., and Messrs. are not abbreviated.

Professor John Q. LaFond
Dean James E. Bond
General Colin Powell

When "Honorable" and "Reverend" are preceded by "the," then "honorable" and "reverend" are spelled out; when used without "the," they can be abbreviated.

The Reverend James P. Coyne	*but*	Rev. James P. Coyne
The Honorable Walter Jackson	*but*	Hon. Walter Jackson

§28.3.4   General Rules for Symbols

Rule 1.   Do not begin a sentence with a symbol.
"Section" and "paragraph" are always spelled out at the beginning of a sentence.

Section 289 was amended in 1989, *not*
§ 289 was amended in 1989.

The symbol for "section," §, or §§ for "sections," must be used in footnotes or citations as long as it does not begin a sentence. Be sure to separate the symbol from the number following it with a space.

Rule 2.   Use the symbol for dollar ($) and percent (%) with numerals. Spell out the words if the numbers are spelled out.

fifteen dollars	*or*	$15.00
sixty percent	*or*	60%

There is no space between $ or % and their accompanying numerals.

§28.4   ITALICS

In legal writing, italics are most commonly used for case names, titles of publications, foreign phrases, introductory signals, and, occasionally, emphasis. When a particular typewriter or computer does not have italics, underlining is an acceptable substitute.

Rule 1.   All case names, including the *v.,*[10] should be in italics.

Smith v. Jones
United States v. Foster

If underlining is used, underline the blank spaces between the words.

Smith v. Jones
United States v. Foster

---

10. Some attorneys do not italicize the *v.,* presumably because the Supreme Court of the United States does not. *Bluebook* rules, however, require that the *v.* be italicized.

Rule 2. Italicize all introductory signals, phrases introducing related authority, and explanatory phrases in citations. (See the *Bluebook* for a complete list.)

Accord	*See also*	*Cf.*	*E.g.,*
aff'd	*cert. denied*	*rev'd*	*withdrawn*
cited with		*construed in*	
approval in			

"See" is not italicized when it is used in text, rather than as part of the citation, to introduce an authority.

Rule 3. Italicize all titles of publications when they appear in text. (See the *Bluebook* for titles in citations.)

Titles of books, reports, periodicals, newspapers, and plays are all italicized when they appear in textual sentences. Even titles of nonprint media such as television and radio programs, musical works, and works of visual art are italicized.

Handbook of Federal Indian Law
Index to Legal Periodicals
Yale Law Review
New York Times
Presumed Innocent
Law and Order

The Bible, however, is not italicized.

Rule 4. Italicize names of aircraft, ships, and trains.

Hindenburg   *Nimitz*   *Orient Express*

Rule 5. Italicize foreign words that are not incorporated into the English language.

carpe diem
qua
infra
supra

Rule 6. Italics can be used to indicate that a word is being used as a word.

Article 6 is silent about what constitutes *service* as opposed to *merchandise.*

Rule 7.   If used sparingly, italics can be used for emphasis.

Fremont's coach insists that he *asked* all of his players to participate in the drug-testing program.

Use of italics or underlining for emphasis occurs most commonly in
long quotations. In such cases, the writer must indicate whether the emphasis was added or whether it was part of the original quotation.

EXAMPLE

The Soldiers' and Sailors' Civil Relief Act does not operate to extend the time period during which the defendant must be served:

> The period of military service shall not be included in computing any
> period now or hereafter to be limited by any law, regulation, or order
> for the bringing of any action or proceeding in any court, board,
> bureau, commission, department, or other agency of government
> by or against any person in military service or by or against his heirs,
> executors, administrators, or assigns, whether such cause of action
> or the right or privileges to institute such action or proceeding shall
> have accrued *prior to or during* the period of such service . . . .

50 U.S.C. § 525 (1976) (emphasis added).

---

§28.5   CONVENTIONS OF FORMAL WRITING

The conventions of formal writing apply to legal writing, particularly
briefs and memoranda. Consequently, some practices that are acceptable
in informal writing or oral language are generally considered inappropriate in formal legal documents.

§28.5.1   Use of First-Person Pronouns

Although in recent years there has been a bit more acceptance of
first-person pronouns (I, me, my, we, our, us) in legal writing, most legal
writers still use only third person in legal memoranda and briefs.

"Our" is fairly well accepted when used in office memos to refer to
the client's case ("in our case"), although purists still prefer that the client's name be used ("in Brown's case"). "My" is well accepted in client
letters ("in my opinion"), and many attorneys use other first-person

pronouns throughout client letters ("I received your letter," "please call me if you have any questions").

§28.5.2   Use of Contractions

Contractions are closely associated with the informality of most oral language. For this reason, there has been strong resistance to the use of contractions in legal writing. Occasionally, you will see a contraction used in a client letter, but these instances are not the norm. As a general rule, avoid contractions in all legal writing.

§28.5.3   Numbers

The *Bluebook,* also known as *A Uniform System of Citation,* sets the standard for what is the acceptable way to write numbers in legal writing. In a nutshell, the rule is to spell out numbers from zero to ninety-nine in text and from zero to nine in footnotes. For larger numbers, use numerals unless the number begins a sentence or the number is a round number (hundred, thousand).

If a series of numbers includes one or more numbers that should be written with numerals, then numerals should be used for the entire series.

The dispatch operator received 104 calls on Friday, 72 calls on Saturday, and 11 calls on Sunday.

Numerals should be used with numbers that contain a decimal point, with numbers used for sections or subdivisions, and in contexts in which numbers are used frequently to refer to percentages and dollar amounts.

§28.5.4   Use of Questions and Exclamations

As a general rule, avoid questions in legal writing. With the exception of the question presented, or issue statement, sentences in legal writing are almost always statements, not questions or exclamations.

When you want to use a question, revise the question into a statement that says, in effect, this question exists.

EXAMPLE

Question:

Will the court apply the center of activity test or the nerve center test?

Revised:

The question is whether the court will apply the center of activity test or the nerve center test.

When you are tempted to use a rhetorical question, revise that point into a positive assertion or statement.

EXAMPLE

Question:

How can the police do their job if they are not allowed to stop suspects who match an eyewitness's description?

Revised:

The police will be unable to do their job if they are not allowed to stop suspects who match an eyewitness's description.

Exclamatory statements may appear to be forceful and therefore persuasive, but they often achieve the opposite effect. Instead of strengthening a position, exclamatory statements may weaken it because they make the writer appear unsophisticated, immature, or inflammatory. As a general rule, then, unless you are quoting another person, do not use exclamatory sentences.

Chapter 29

Legal Writing for English-as-a-Second-Language Students

Legal writing courses are challenging for native speakers of English who have spent their lives immersed in a culture heavily influenced by the United States legal system. Even for these law students, some of the terminology of legal prose is new, and many of the conventions are unfamiliar.

If you are an English-as-a-second-language (ESL) law student, you have two additional language-related challenges. First, there are numerous grammatical rules that native speakers have internalized but that non-native speakers must still learn. The first half of this chapter focuses on three grammatical areas that many ESL law students find difficult: articles, verbs, and prepositions.

Second, if you are an ESL law student who was raised in a different culture, you will have naturally internalized your native culture's approach to writing. Consequently, as an ESL law student, you will face a second challenge: learning how native speakers of English, particularly those in the United States legal culture, approach writing. These different approaches to writing, or what we will call "rhetorical preferences," tend to affect the whole piece of writing and include such things as what is assumed about the writer-reader relationship, how direct and explicit writers are when they explain and support their arguments, and what writing patterns are commonplace and expected. The second half of this chapter addresses how the rhetorical preferences in the United States and particularly in the legal culture may differ from the rhetorical preferences of other cultures.

§29.1   Grammar Rules for Non-Native Speakers of English

This section will address the most common grammatical problems for ESL law students: (1) how articles are used; (2) how auxiliary, or helping, verbs change meaning; (3) which form of the verb to match with certain auxiliary verbs; (4) which verb tense to use in certain sentence structures; (5) which verbs commonly used in law are followed by objects, gerunds, or infinitives; and (6) which prepositions follow certain verbs, adjectives, and nouns commonly used in law.

§29.1.1   Articles

Errors in the use of articles ("a," "an," and "the") are distracting to many readers. Too many missing or incorrect articles draw attention away from content and toward the errors. Consequently, most ESL law students find that if they want their writing to be considered professional, they must devote time and energy to mastering the use of articles in English.

One of the simplest and most effective strategies for learning the correct use of articles is to note how they are used in judicial opinions and other writing about law. Many ESL law students simply memorize phrases and law terminology, including how articles are used in these phrases and with these terms, from the writing of capable native speakers.

A second strategy is to learn the rules governing the use of articles in English. Unfortunately for most ESL law students, many of their native languages do not use articles, and others use articles in ways that are different from English. As a result, most ESL law students cannot rely on their native languages to help them with the rules of English articles. Instead they must learn the general rules and then be aware that there are still many exceptions.

Exhibit 29.1 is a decision tree that summarizes the following discussion about how to use articles with common nouns in English.

a.   *"A" and "An"*

Rule 1.   Use the indefinite articles "a" and "an"[1] with count nouns when the noun is singular and when the reader does not know the specific identity of the noun.

---

1. "A" is used before consonant sounds; "an" is used before vowel sounds. Examples: "A jury," "a contract," "an assault," "an incident," "an unusual request," "an alleged victim," "an hour," "an honest man," ("h" is silent in "hour" and "honest") "a unique opportunity," "a university," "a unit" "a unanimous jury" ("u" has consonant "y" sound in "unique," "university," "unit," and "unanimous") and "a one-hour delay" ("o" has "w" sound in "one"). See Glossary of Usage on **a/an.**

Count nouns[2] refer to persons, places, or things that can be counted. Count nouns have both a singular and plural form.

EXAMPLES

Singular form of count nouns

a contract　　an easement　　a trial court　　an appellate court
one juror

Plural form of count nouns

contracts　　easements　　trial courts　　appellate courts
twelve jurors

Non-count nouns

anger　　equipment　　pollution　　science　　wealth

Remember that "a" and "an" are only used (1) with the singular form of a count noun (2) when the reader does not know the specific identity of that noun. The second part of the rule usually applies when a particular noun is mentioned for the first time in the writing because at that point the reader does not know the specific identity of the noun.

EXAMPLE

(assume "truck" is being mentioned for the first time)
A truck slowly approached.

Rule 1 also applies when the specific identity of the noun is unknown to the writer or when the writer intends to name a general member of a class or group.

---

2. Many nouns like "paper" can be used as count or non-count nouns depending upon the particular sense in which they are used. Most ESL dictionaries indicate whether a noun is a count or non-count noun and, for nouns that can be both, under which meanings the noun is a count or non-count noun.

EXAMPLES

(writer does not know the specific identity of the officer)
An officer observed a truck slowly approach.

(writer intends a general member of the class of cellular phones)
A cellular phone is often a good safety precaution.

Exception to Rule 1:   Do not use "a" or "an" with a singular count noun that is preceded by another noun marker.

Noun markers include possessive nouns like "Kelly's" or "Florida's," numbers, and pronouns such as "his," "her," "its," "their," "this," "that," "these," "those," "every," "few," "many," "more," "most," "much," "either," "neither," "each," "any," "all," "no," "several," and "some."

EXAMPLES

Incorrect examples

A this officer observed a truck slowly approach.
("this" is a noun marker, so "a" should be omitted)

An one officer observed a truck slowly approach.
("one" is a noun marker, so "an" should be omitted)

Corrected examples

This officer observed a truck slowly approach.

One officer observed a truck slowly approach.

Other common exceptions to Rule 1 include many prepositional phrases that are idiomatic expressions.

on vacation	by plane	by car	at home	in school
to bed	to college	in class	at night	at school
in bed				

EXAMPLE

The defendant testified that he was at home by 8 p.m. and in bed by 8:30 p.m.

Rule 2.   Do not use "a" or "an" with non-count nouns.

Non-count nouns refer to abstractions that cannot be counted. Non-count nouns do not have a plural form.

EXAMPLES

negligence   evidence   violence   arson   discretion

However, if an amount of a non-count noun is expressed by adding a quantifier, then an article is used before the quantifier.

> a piece of evidence   an act of violence

In most instances, the following words are non-count nouns.

Nouns naming drinks and food

> water, milk, coffee, tea, wine, juice
> fruit, fish, beef, chicken, meat

Nouns naming generalized objects

> ammunition, clothing, equipment, freight, furniture, jewelry, luggage, lumber, machinery, mail, money, propaganda, scenery, stationery, traffic, vegetation

nouns naming substances, matter, or material

> (asterisks indicate the substance, not an object)
> air, coal, dirt, electricity, gasoline, gold, grass, hair, ice, iron*, oil, oxygen, paper*, plastic, steel, wood

Nouns related to weather

> fog, ice, rain, snow

Nouns naming subject matter

> architecture, art, chemistry, civics, economics, engineering, gcology, grammar, history, literature, mathematics, music, philosophy, physics, science, and all names of languages (Arabic, Chinese, English, French, German, Italian, Japanese, etc.) when they are used as nouns

Nouns related to games, sports, and recreation

(asterisks indicate the game, not an object)
baseball*, basketball*, bowling, bridge, camping, chess, dancing, football*, golf, hiking, hockey, hunting, opera, sailing, singing, soccer, swimming, tennis, television*, volleyball*

abstract nouns

advice, anger, beauty, capitalism, communism, confidence, democracy, education, employment, energy, fun, happiness, health, help, homework, honesty, ignorance, information, intelligence, justice, kindness, knowledge, laughter, liberty, life, love, merchandise, nature, news, pollution, poverty, recreation, research, satisfaction, society (in the sense of people in general), strength, technology, transportation, trouble, truth, violence, virtue, wealth, wisdom, work

Law-related nouns

abandonment, abatement, access, acquiescence, adultery, alimony, arson, authentication, capital (in the sense of money or property), commerce, conduct, depreciation, discretion, duress, evidence, extortion, housing, insolvency, insurance, intent, land, malice, negligence, privacy, real estate

---

EXAMPLES

The detective found a weapon and ammunition in the defendant's trunk.
(no article before non-count noun "ammunition")

Magistrates must exercise discretion when determining whether to authorize hidden recording devices.
(no article before non-count noun "discretion")

Gerunds[3] and gerund phrases are non-count nouns and therefore do not require "a" or "an."

EXAMPLES

Drowning was the cause of death.
(gerund)

---

3. Gerunds are verbals that end in "-ing" and that function as nouns. Gerunds with modifying phrases fall under Rule 3 and are preceded by "the." Example: "The drowning of her second child raised the prosecutor's suspicions."

Most attorneys enjoy <u>making arguments</u>.
(gerund phrase)

---

b.　"The"

Rule 3.　Use the definite article "the" with count[4] and non-count nouns when the specific identity of the noun is clear to the reader.

The specific identity of a noun can be clear to the reader for a number of reasons.

Reason #1:　Readers know the specific identity of a noun after it has already been used once in a given context.

EXAMPLE

<u>A</u> truck slowly approached. An officer noticed <u>the</u> truck contained several garbage cans.

(Use "a" before "truck" when it is first mentioned; use "the" before "truck" for subsequent references.)

Reason #2:　Readers know the specific identity of a noun when it is followed by a phrase or clause that restricts or limits its identity.

EXAMPLE

<u>The</u> driver of the truck appeared nervous.
(Use "the" before "driver" because "of the truck" is a phrase that restricts or limits the meaning of "driver.")

Many but not all modifying phrases and clauses that follow a noun restrict or limit the noun's identity thereby making it specific. You can determine which "of" prepositional phrases restrict or limit the identity of a noun by testing to see if they can be changed to the possessive form. If they can be changed to the possessive form, they are restricting or limiting thc noun, so "the" should precede the noun.

---

4. Notice that this rule applies to both singular and plural count nouns.

EXAMPLES

the driver of the truck → the truck's driver
the cost of a trial → a trial's cost
the length of the skidmarks → the skidmarks' length

Other "of" phrases, however, do not restrict or limit the identity of a noun; they show that only a part or a measured amount of the noun is intended. These "of" phrases cannot be changed to the possessive form. Use "a" or "an" before these nouns.

EXAMPLES

| a pound of marijuana | a third of her salary |
| a slice of bread | a gallon of gasoline |

Similarly, when a noun is followed by a phrase or clause that defines rather than restricts or limits, use "a" or "an" before the noun.

EXAMPLE

A contract that has all of its terms in writing is a formal contract.
*("a" used before "contract" because "that has all of its terms in writing"
defines it)*

Reason #3:   Readers know the specific identity of a noun when it is is preceded by a superlative[5] or ranking adjective.[6]

---

5. Superlatives compare the thing modified with two or more things. Superlatives include "best," "worst," words ending in -est ("biggest," "smallest," "tallest," "shortest," "wisest," "fastest," "slowest," "luckiest," "loudest") and comparisons that use "most" or "least" ("the most beautiful," "the most egregious," "the least responsible," "the least humilitating"). Be sure not to use comparative or superlative forms with things that cannot be compared ("perfect," "unique," "pregnant," "dead," "impossible," and "infinite").

6. Ranking adjectives include sequential adjectives like "first," "second," "third," and "next" and adjectives that show the noun is one of a kind ("unique").

The best example of a public figure is a film star.
(Use "the" because "example" is preceded by the superlative "best.")

The defendant was the tallest man in the line-up.
(Use "the" because "man" is preceded by the superlative "tallest.")

The plaintiff will be unable to satisfy the third element.
(Use "the" before the ranking adjective "third.")

Reason #4:　　Readers know the specific identity of a noun when both the writer and the reader have shared knowledge about the identity of the noun. Shared knowledge can be universal, like knowledge of the sun, and it can be local, like knowledge of a local landmark.

The moon provided enough light for the officers to see the defendant open his trunk.
(use "the" before "moon" because the writer and the reader have shared knowledge about its identity)

Numerous gang-related activities have occurred at the shopping mall.
(use "the" before "shopping mall" if the writer and reader have shared knowledge about its identity as a local landmark)

One way to determine whether a noun is specific is to ask "which one (or ones)?" For specific nouns, you will have a specific answer. When you have a specific answer, use "the." For example, if the test is applied to some of the earlier example sentences, the questions and answers are as follows:

Question: Which driver?	Answer: The driver of the truck
Question: Which example?	Answer: The best example
Question: Which element?	Answer: The third element
Question: Which moon?	Answer: The moon we all know about
Question: Which shopping mall?	Answer: The shopping mall that is a local landmark

If the answer to the "which one (or ones)?" question is "any one" or "all" or "I don't know which one" or "one that has not been mentioned before," then the noun is general.

Rule 4. Do not use "the" before plural nouns meaning all in a class, all of a group, or "in general."

EXAMPLES

Defendants have the right to an attorney.
(no "the" before "defendants" because it is plural and all defendants are intended, but "an" before "attorney" because it is singular and no specific attorney is intended.)

Appellate courts do not re-try the facts of a case.
(no "the" before "appellate courts" because it is plural and the intended meaning is appellate courts "in general"; "the" before "facts" because the restricting phrase "of a case" makes it specific, and "a" before "case" because it is singular and no specific case is intended.)

Rule 5. Do not use "the" before most singular proper nouns, including names of persons, streets, parks, cities, states, continents, and most countries.

EXAMPLES

Smith was last seen in Yellowstone National Park.

Jones offered trips to New York City, Florida, Germany, and Africa as sales incentives.

The possessive form of a singular name is also not preceded by "the."

EXAMPLE

Mr. Hempstead learned of the affair by reading Carol's diary.
(no "the" before possessive "Carol's")

Notice, however, that the plural form of proper nouns that are family names is preceded by "the." See Rule 7.

EXAMPLE

The Smiths were last seen in Yellowstone National Park.

Rule 6.   Use "the" with proper nouns containing the word "of," a political word like "kingdom," "union," or "republic," or organizational words like "institute," "foundation," or "corporation."

EXAMPLES

the city[7] of Los Angeles	the Republic of Korea
the University of Notre Dame	the Ford Foundation
the Boeing Corporation	the Commonwealth of Virginia

Notice that many things have two proper noun names and that "the" is only used with the form containing "of" or the political or organizational word.

the city of Los Angeles	*but*	Los Angeles
the Republic of Korea	*but*	Korea
the University of Notre Dame	*but*	Notre Dame
the Ford Foundation	*but*	Ford
the Boeing Corporation	*but*	Boeing
the Commonwealth of Virginia	*but*	Virginia

Do not use "the" with names of universities, colleges, or schools unless the name is written with an "of."

---

7. Words like "city" are usually, but not always, written in lowercase when they precede the noun and when they appear in text. In citations, however, capitalize geographic terms like "city." See Rule 10.2.1(f) in the *Bluebook*.

EXAMPLES

Harvard University Law School   the School of Law
Smith College   the College of Engineering

Rule 7.   Use "the" before most plural proper nouns, including the plural form of a family name.

EXAMPLES

the United States   the United Nations   the Bahamas
the Rockies   the Philippines   the Cayman Islands
the Smiths   the Joneses

Rule 8.   Use "the" before the names of most bodies of water and the names of specific geographic regions.

EXAMPLES

the Atlantic Ocean   the Mississippi River   the Persian Gulf
the Southwest   the Midwest   the Middle East

---

c.   No Article

Rule 9.   Do not use "a," "an," or "the" before non-count nouns used in a general sense or plural common nouns used in a general sense.

EXAMPLES

Information can lead to justice.
(No article before non-count nouns "information" and "justice.")

Expert witnesses have become common in courtrooms.
(No article before plural nouns "expert witnesses" or "courtrooms.")

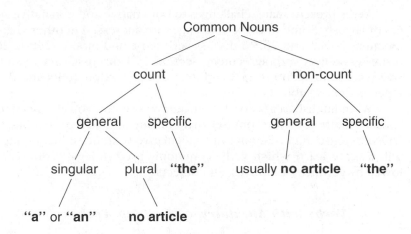

Step 1: Decide if the noun is a count or non-count noun.

Step 2: If the noun is a count noun, decide if the use of the noun is general or specific. If the use is specific, usually "the" is the correct article. Rule 3.

Step 3: If the use of a count noun is general, decide if the noun is singular or plural. If the noun is singular, usually "a" or "an" is the correct article. Rule 1. If the noun is plural, usually no article is needed. Rule 4.

Step 4: If the noun is a non-count noun, decide if its use is general or specific. If the use is general, usually no article is needed. Rule 2. If the use is specific, use "the." Rule 3.

Count nouns refer to persons, places, or things that can be counted. Count nouns have both a singular and plural form.

a contract	contracts	an appellate	appellate courts
an easement	easements	court	
a trial court	trial courts	one juror	twelve jurors

Non-count nouns refer to entities or abstractions that cannot be counted.

> negligence   evidence   violence   arson   discretion

General use of a noun usually occurs the first time a noun is used in a given context. General use of a noun also occurs when the writer intends any one of a group or class.

Specific use of a noun usually occurs for any one of the following reasons:

1. The noun has already been used once in a given context;
2. The noun is followed by a phrase or clause that restricts its identity;
3. The noun is preceded by a superlative or a ranking adjective;
4. The writer and the reader have shared knowledge about the identity of the noun.

Specific nouns will have a specific answer to the question "which one (or ones)?"

§29.1.2   Verbs

Verbs present many challenges to both native and non-native speakers of English. Some of these challenges are addressed in other chapters. (Sections 26.3.1 and 26.3.2 discuss verb tense and mood, section 26.4.1 discusses subject-verb agreement, section 23.1 discusses active and passive voice, and sections 23.3 and 23.4 discuss action verbs and the distance between subjects and verbs.)

As an English-as-a-second-language law student, you also need to pay special attention to verb phrases that contain auxiliary, or helping, verbs and verb tense in conditional and speculative sentences. In addition, you will need to learn which verbs commonly used in legal writing are followed by gerunds, infinitives, and objects.

a.   Verbs with Auxiliary, or Helping, Verbs

Unlike article errors, errors in verbs often change the meaning and are therefore much more serious. Fortunately, few ESL law students have difficulty with the main verbs in English verb phrases. The challenge is to learn the subtle yet often significant differences in meanings that auxiliary, or helping, verbs add to the main part of the verb phrase.

For example, "can" (or "cannot") before a verb shows ability or knowledge.

EXAMPLE

Despite his back injury, the plaintiff can still drive a semi-truck.
("can" indicates the ability to drive)

"Can" is also used to suggest that the action is a possibility or an option.

EXAMPLE

The defendant can argue that *Smith* applies.
("can" indicates the possibility of the defendant arguing that Smith *applies)*

Exhibit 29.2 lists the most common meanings for many auxiliary, or helping, verbs.

In addition to learning how meanings change based on auxiliary, or

EXHIBIT 29.2	Common Meanings for Auxiliary, or Helping, Verbs

Auxiliary Verb	Meanings	Example Sentences
can	shows ability or knowledge	Despite his back injury, the plaintiff can still drive a semi-truck.
	suggests possibility	The defendant can argue that *Smith* applies.
	gives an option	The prosecutor can charge the defendant with first- or second-degree murder.
could	shows past ability	Before his back injury, the plaintiff could drive a semi-truck.
	shows possibility	The defendant could argue that *Smith* applies.
could have	suggests past opportunity that was missed	The plaintiff could have learned to drive a semi-truck, but he cannot now because of his back injury.
may	asks or gives permission	Students may leave the campus during the lunch hour.
	shows possibility	The court may grant a motion to dismiss.
might	shows possibility	The court might grant a motion to dismiss.
should	shows advisability or expectation	The court should grant a motion to continue when the State amends a change the day before trial.
	shows obligation	The court should instruct the jury to disregard that remark.
	shows expectation	You should receive the signed agreement in tomorrow's mail.
should have	shows obligation that was not met	The court should have instructed the jury to disregard that remark, but it failed to do so.
	shows expectation that was not met	You should have already received the signed agreement in the mail; I do not know why it is late.
	shows advisability after the fact	The officer should have handcuffed the suspect, but he did not.

EXHIBIT 29.2	*(continued)*

Auxiliary Verb	Meanings	Example Sentences
ought to	shows advisability or expectation	The court ought to grant a motion to continue when the State amends a change the day before trial.
	shows obligation	The court ought to instruct the jury to disregard that remark.
	shows expectation	You ought to receive the signed agreement in tomorrow's mail.
ought to have	shows obligation that was not met	The court ought to have instructed the jury to disregard that remark, but it failed to do so.
	shows expectation that was not met	You ought to have received the signed agreement in yesterday's mail, I do not know why it is late.
	shows advisability after the fact	The officer ought to have handcuffed the suspect, but he did not.
must	shows requirement	The court must ask the defendant how she pleads.
	shows probablity	The defendant must be considering a plea bargain.
must not	shows prohibition	The prosecution must not suggest that the defendant's post-arrest silence implies guilt.
will	shows future	The verdict will be announced after the parties return to the courtroom.
	shows a promise or willingness	Acme will clean up the toxic waste site.
would	indicates a repeated past action	The arsonist would often warn his victims.
	indicates a future act in a past tense sentence	The arsonist warned his victims that he would set fire to the building.

helping, verbs, ESL law students have to master which form of the verb is used with various helping verbs.

Auxiliary, or helping, verbs that are followed by the base form

Use the base form of a verb after the following auxiliary, or helping, verbs: "can," "could," "do, "does," "did," "may," "might," "must," "shall," "should," "will," and "would."

EXAMPLES

can argue	could deny	did object	may plead
might consider	must rely	should admit	will determine

Auxiliary, or helping, verbs that are followed by objects and then the base form

A few verbs ("make," "let," and "have") must be followed by a noun or pronoun object and then by the base form of a verb.

EXAMPLES

The children's father lets <u>them</u> <u>leave</u> for school without eating
         (pronoun) (base form)
breakfast.

The mother makes the <u>children</u> <u>do</u> their homework.
        (noun) (base form)

The verb "help" can be followed by a noun or pronoun and then a base form or the infinitive form of a verb.

EXAMPLES

Both parents helped the children <u>learn</u> different sports.
        (base form)

Both parents helped the children to learn different sports.
(infinitive)

Auxiliary, or helping, verbs that are followed by the past participle of the verb

Use the past participle of a verb with "have," "has," or "had."

EXAMPLES

have determined   has begun   had stolen   has written

Auxiliary, or helping, verbs that are followed by the present participle of the verb

Use the present participle of a verb after forms of "be," including "am," "are," "is," "was," "were," "have been," and "had been."

EXAMPLES

are relying   is considering   was driving

---

b.   Verb Tense in Conditional Sentences

Lawyers frequently use conditional sentences to express possibilities or to suggest what might happen in the future. "If" and "unless" clauses are commonly used either before or after the main clause. Use present tense in the "if" or "unless" clause and future tense in the main clause.

EXAMPLES

If the court applies the *Reed* test, it will find that the element is
     (present tense)   *(future tense)*
met.

The prosecutor <u>will charge</u> the defendant with arson unless she
    (future tense)
<u>has</u> an alibi.
(present tense)

---

c.   *Verb Tense in Speculative Sentences*

To show that an outcome is possible but unlikely, use past tense in an "if" clause and "would" "could," or "might" as the auxiliary, or helping, verb in the main clause.

EXAMPLES

If the witness <u>saw</u> the defendant's car at the accident scene, he
   (past tense)
would have also seen the defendant.

The jury might ignore its instructions if it <u>believed</u> the police fabri-
       (past tense)
cated the evidence.

To speculate about something that did not happen, use the past perfect tense in an "if" clause and "would have," "could have," or "might have" as auxiliary, or helping, verbs with the past participle. Remember that "had" is the helping verb that creates the past perfect tense.

EXAMPLES

If the defendant had spoken to Mr. Torres, he would have apologized to him, not threatened him.

The tenants could have complained to the building superintendent if he had been accessible.

To express conditions that are contrary to fact, use "were" in an "if" clause and "would," "could," or "might" in the main clause.

EXAMPLES

If I were you, I might try apologizing to the plaintiff.

If Mrs. Henderson were alive, she would not want the jury to find the defendant guilty of manslaughter.

---

d.   Verbs + gerunds, infinitives, or objects

Some verbs should be followed by gerunds (a verb form ending in -ing and used as a noun); other verbs should be followed by infinitives (a verb form made up of "to" plus the base form of the verb); others require objects (nouns or pronouns); and some verbs can be followed by either a gerund or an infinitive.[8] Some ESL law students may find that the most effective strategy for determining whether to use an infinitive or gerund after a certain verb is to apply the "Bolinger principle," which is to use infinitives to express something "hypothetical, future, unfulfilled" and to use gerunds to express something "real, vivid, fulfilled." (Bolinger, 1968)

EXAMPLES

The defendant wants <u>to enter</u> a plea of not guilty.
(the sentence expresses an as yet unfulfilled action so the infinitive is used)

The defendant admits <u>hitting</u> the pedestrian.
(the sentence expresses a past action so the gerund is used)

The neighbors hope <u>to obtain</u> an easement.
(the sentence expresses a future action so the infinitive is used)

His responsibilities include <u>hiring</u> employees.
(the sentence expresses a real, not a hypothetical action)

Exceptions

Unfortunately, the Bolinger principle does not apply to approximately one-fourth of the verbs in question, including the following verbs:

---

8. Most verbs can also be followed by "that" clauses.

Verbs that are exceptions to the Bolinger principle and use gerunds:

> anticipate, consider, delay, envision, imagine, keep, mind, postpone, recommend, risk, suggest, understand

Verbs that are exceptions to the Bolinger principle and use infinitives:

> claim, continue, fail, get, have, hire, manage, teach, tell

---

EXAMPLES

Her attorney will recommend <u>accepting</u> the offer.
(gerund)
(sentence expresses a future action but still uses a gerund after the verb)

The officer managed <u>to distract</u> the gunman.
(infinitive)
(sentence expresses a past action but still uses an infinitive after the verb)

Consequently, many ESL law students may prefer using lists that group verbs according to what must follow them. Below are lists of verbs commonly used in law grouped by what follows them. The patterns for each combination are in boldface type.

Verbs that are usually followed by a gerund rather than an infinitive[9]

(<u>verb</u> + _____ -ing)

acknowledge	defend
admit	delay
advocate	deny
anticipate	detest
appreciate	disclaim
approve	discuss
avoid	dislike
begrudge	enjoy
cannot help	entail
complete	escape
condemn	evade
consider	facilitate
contemplate	finish
defer	get through

---

9. Although gerunds rather than infinitives often follow these verbs, using a gerund is not required. Many of these verbs are often followed by "that" clauses.

give up	relinquish
imagine	relish
involve	renounce
justify	report
keep	resent
keep on	resist
mention	resume
mind	risk
miss	sanction
necessitate	shirk
postpone	suggest
practice	tolerate
put off	understand
quit	visualize
recall	withhold
recollect	witness
recommend	

EXAMPLE

The defendant admits <u>knowing</u> the victim, but he denies <u>killing</u> him.
                (gerund)   *(gerund)*

Some verbs can be immediately followed by an infinitive; others are followed by an object and then an infinitive; still other verbs can be followed by either an object or an infinitive. When an object is between the verb and the infinitive, the object performs the action of the infinitive.

Verbs that can be followed by either an infinitive or a "that" clause with little or no change in meaning are indicated by an asterisk.

<u>Verbs that are usually followed by an infinitive rather than a gerund</u>

    (**verb** + **to** _____)

agree*	consent
appear	decide*
arrange	demand
ask	deserve
attempt	desire
bother	endeavor
care	expect
claim	fail
condescend	happen

have	refuse
hesitate	say
hope*	seem
know how	struggle
learn	swear
manage	tend
need	threaten
offer	venture
plan	volunteer
prepare	want
pretend*	wait
promise*	wish

EXAMPLES

The workers expect <u>to reconcile</u> their differences with management.   *(infinitive)*

Management plans <u>to offer</u> them a contract with a 5% salary increase.   *(infinitive)*

The mediator hoped to extend the negotiation deadline.
(verb followed by infinitive "to extend")

The mediator hoped that the negotiation deadline would be extended.
(verb followed by "that" clause)

Verbs that can be followed by either a gerund or an infinitive

A few verbs can be followed by either a gerund or infinitive with little change in meaning.

(**verb** + _____ -ing *OR* verb + to _____)

abhor	disdain
afford	dread
attempt	endure
bear	go
begin	hate
cannot bear	intend
cannot stand	like
cease	love
choose	neglect
commence	propose
continue	scorn
decline	start

EXAMPLES

Landowners continue <u>to assert</u> their rights.
           (infinitive)

Landowners continue <u>asserting</u> their rights.
         (gerund)

A few verbs can be followed by a gerund or infinitive but with a significant change in meaning. One common pattern, which is supported by the Bolinger principle (infinitive expresses fulfilled action, gerund expresses unfulfilled action), is that when the verb is followed by a gerund, past time is indicated; when the verb is followed by an infinitive, future time is indicated.

forget   prefer   regret   remember   sense   stop   try

EXAMPLES

Mrs. Warren remembered <u>locking</u> the safe.
        (gerund)
(She has a past memory of locking the safe.)

Mrs. Warren remembered <u>to lock</u> the safe.
        (infinitive)
(She did not forget to lock the safe.)

Mrs. Warren must remember <u>to lock</u> the safe.
        (infinitive)
(She must remember this for the future.)

<u>Verbs usually followed by objects, then infinitives (except in the passive[10] voice) (**verb + (object) + to** _____)</u>

---

10. In passive voice the action of the verb is done to the subject. Example: The motion was denied. In the example, "was denied" is done to "the motion." In active voice, the subject performs the action in the verb. Example: The judge denied the motion. In this example, the judge is doing the denying. See section 23.1 for an extensive discussion of passive and active voice.

advise	oblige
allow	order
appoint	permit
authorize	persuade
cause	remind
challenge	request
command	require
convince	select
encourage	teach
forbid	tell
force	tempt
get	train
hire	trust
instruct	urge
invite	warn

EXAMPLES

Opposing counsel <u>will advise</u> her <u>client</u> <u>to settle</u>.
                (verb)   *(object) (infinitive)*

The judge <u>permitted</u> the <u>prosecutor</u> <u>to ask</u> questions about prior
        (verb)   *(object)*   *(infinitive)*
convictions.

Acme <u>encouraged</u> its <u>employees</u> <u>to participate</u> in the political
        (verb)   *(object)*   *(infinitive)*
campaign.

Acme <u>instructed</u> <u>them</u> <u>to use</u> their lunch hour stuffing envelopes.
      (verb)   *(object)(infinitive)*

Employees <u>were permitted</u> <u>to attend</u> the rally.
       (passive verb)   *(infinitive)*
(no noun or pronoun before infinitive because verb is in passive voice)

<u>Verbs that can be followed by either an object or an infinitive</u>

    (<u>verb</u> + (object)) OR (<u>verb</u> + to _____)

ask	dare
beg	expect
choose	help

intend	promise
like	want
need	wish
prefer	would like
prepare	

EXAMPLES

The landlord expected the tenants to check the batteries in the smoke detectors.
(object "the tenants" follows "expected")

The landlord expected to hear tenants complain about the rent increase.
(infinitive "to hear" follows "expected")

Verbs followed by "too," "enough," and "how" expressions and an infinitive

Use infinitives when expressions with "too," "enough," or "how" follow a verb.

EXAMPLES

The police arrived too late to apprehend the burglar.
("too" expression followed by infinitve "to apprehend")

The defendant is not strong enough to kick that door down.
("enough" expression followed by infinitive "to kick")

A twenty-year-old woman knows how to protect herself.
("how" expression followed by infinitive "to protect")

---

e. Two- or Three-Word Verbs

Learning which prepositions[11] to use in two- or three-word verbs, or phrasal verbs, is crucial because the prepositions in these verbs often completely change the meaning of the verb.

---

11. The prepositions in phrasal verbs are often called particles.

EXAMPLE

One-Word Verb	Meaning of One-Word Verb
catch	"find and stop"

Two-Word Verb	Meaning of Two-Word Verb
catch up	"to improve and reach the same standard"

Three-Word Verb	Meaning of Three-Word Verb
catch up with	"to come from behind and reach" *or* "to find someone doing something illegal and punish that person"

Because there are so many two- or three-word verbs in English and because several of them (like "catch up with") have different meanings for different contexts, the best strategy for learning them is note how they are used in native speakers' oral and written language. In addition, note that most of these verbs have more formal synonyms that are preferred in legal writing.

EXAMPLES

The brief must be *turned in* by 5:00. → The brief must be *submitted* by 5:00.

The protester *handed out* leaflets. → The protester *distributed* leaflets.

The attorney *put off* the meeting. → The attorney *postponed* the meeting.

Firefighters *put out* the blaze. → Firefighters *extinguished* the blaze.

---

§29.1.3　Prepositions

The preceding section discussed two- or three-word verbs in which the addition of one or more prepositions made a significant change to the base verb's meaning. Other English verbs, adjectives, and nouns must also be followed by specific prepositions. Unfortunately, prepositional use is idiomatic and not based on rules. Consequently, we have resorted to alphabetical lists of verbs, adjectives, and nouns commonly used in legal writing and their correct prepositions. When more than one preposition can be used with a given verb, adjective, or noun, the different preposition choices are separated by slash (/) marks. Parentheses show the types of words that may follow a given preposition. Brackets indicate meaning. Some verbs are in their present tense form; others are in their past tense form.

a.   Prepositions That Follow Verbs Commonly Used in Law

absolved from (wrongdoing)
absolved of (financial liability)
accompanied by
accused of
acquainted with
acquiesced in/to
adhered to
affected by
agree on (a contract, a date)
agree to [means "to acquiesce"]
agree with [means "to be in accord with" or "have the same opinion]
allude to
apply for (a position)
apply to
approve of [means to find something good or suitable]
attribute to
based on/upon
blamed for
caused by
charge at/toward/into
charge with (murder)
comment on
commit to
communicate to [means to express thoughts or feelings]
communicate with [used when two people understand thoughts or feelings]
compare to [used with similarities]
compare with [used with similarities and differences]
compensate for
compete for/against

compete with
composed of
confined to
consent to
contrast with [used with differences]
convicted of (crimes)
convicted on (counts)
cooperate with
covered with
decide for/against (the plaintiff)
decide in favor of (the plaintiff)
decide on (a date)
derived from
discriminate against
distinguish between/from
divided into
divorced from
experiment with (drugs)
fill in (a hole or crack)
filled out (an application)
filled up (a tank)
filled with (sound, light, emotion)
finished with
founded by (a person)
founded in (a date)
founded on [means the main idea that something else develops from]
free from/to
gain access to
impressed by/with
informed about/or [means to give information]
informed on [used when information is given to police or an enemy]

interfere with
object to
participate in
prevent from
prohibit from
protect against/from
questioned about/concerning
reach (a conclusion) about
reach for (a gun)
recover from
refer to

rely on/upon
rescue from
resigned from
respond to
save for [means to keep money to
    use for a specific purpose]
save from (harm or danger)
suffer from
suspected of
worry about

b. Prepositions That Follow Adjectives Commonly Used in Law

accustomed to
afraid of
amazed at
angry about/at/over/with
anxious about
appreciative of
appropriate for
ashamed of
averse to
aware of
bad at
bored with
capable of
careful about/with
certain about/of
clever at
comparable to/with
concerned about/with
confident about
confused about
conscious of
consistent with
critical of/to
dedicated to
delighted at/by/with
dependent on/upon
different from
eager for/to
enthusiastic about
excited about/by
experienced in
familiar to/with
famous for

far above/below/from
fearful of
fond of
glad about
good at/for
grateful for
guilty of
happy about/with
hopeful about/of
inconsistent with
innocent of
interested in
jealous of
known for
liable for (damages)
    [means "to be legally
    responsible for"]
liable to [means "to be likely to"]
married to
nervous about
oblivious of/to (danger)
opposed to
proud of
qualified for
quick to
regardless of
related to
responsible for
satisfied with
sensitive to/about
similar to
sorry about/for
suitable for

tired of   upset about/by/over
tolerant of   used to

c. Prepositions That Follow Nouns Commonly Used in Law

access to   liability for
amendment to   means of
approval of   need for
attempt at   in need of
authority on [area of expertise]   objection to
belief in   opposition to
choice between/of   participation in
commitment to   possibility for/of
complaint about/against   preference for
concern about/for/over   prevention of
confidence in   process of
confusion about/as to/over   protection against/from
dedication of/to   reason for
difference among (three or more)   reference to
difference between (two)   reliance on
division between/of   respect for/of
doubt about/as to   response to
effect of/on   responsibility for
experience in/of/with   satisfaction from/in/of
explanation for/of   search for
fear for/of   skill at/in
idea about/for/of   success as/in
knowledge about/of

d. Prepositions in Idioms

during the course of (his employment)
in circumstances like (our case)
in contrast
in favor of
in light of
on the contrary

§29.2   RHETORICAL PREFERENCES IN WRITING[12]

Discourse patterns vary from language to language and from culture to culture. The way an expert writer makes a point in one culture is often

---

12. This section concerns expository and argumentative writing, not literary prose.

quite different from how an expert writer in another culture would make the same point. Indeed, what one culture may consider a good point in a given context, another culture might consider irrelevant in the same context.

What is particularly fascinating about this phenomenon, though, is that it often goes unnoticed. In fact, most writers have internalized their own culture's rhetorical preferences to the point that these preferences are subconscious choices. Most people seem to assume that their culture's world view and how it is expressed in writing is the way all human beings "naturally" think and write.

Because these cultural differences in discourse are so deeply embedded in language and in our subconscious, they are rarely taught to students. Most ESL law students report that their foreign language classes concentrated only on vocabulary and sentence grammar; they stopped short of addressing the larger cultural issues that affect the overall approach to writing. If this was true of your language classes, you may be unconsciously assuming that what was appropriate and conventional when writing in your native language is also appropriate and conventional when writing in English.

This section examines the rhetorical preferences in expository and argumentative writing in the U.S. culture, with a particular emphasis on how those preferences are manifested in legal writing. The section also compares and contrasts these preferences with some of the more common rhetorical preferences from other cultures in hopes of giving ESL law students insights about writing in English.

Remember, however, that this is a discussion of what is generally true about writing in the discourse community of U.S. lawyers and judges, and that in certain instances, the generalizations will not apply. For example, while it is generally true that writing that is direct is preferred in the U.S. legal culture, there are occasions when vagueness or indirection better serves the writer's purposes. The discussion makes similar generalizations about writing preferences in other cultures based on the research done by contrastive rhetoricians.[13] Again, like all generalizations, they may not be true in every instance, and unfortunately, the research available on rhetorical preferences in other cultures is somewhat incomplete.

---

13. The sources for the information in the following section are in two bibliographies: one for ESL law students at the end of this chapter and one for legal writing professors at the end of the teaching notes for Chapter 29 in the Professor's Edition. Students who are interested in reading the source material that applies to their specific native language and culture should consult the bibliography at the end of the chapter.

§29.2.1   Cultural Assumptions about Readers and the Purposes for Writing

All cultures treat writing as an act of communication, but they differ widely in their assumptions about that communication. Some operate under the assumption that the reader bears the heavier responsibility; it is the reader who must strive to understand the writer. Other cultures operate under the assumption that the writer has the heavier responsibility; it is the writer who must strive to be understood by the reader. (Hinds, 1987) In reader-responsible cultures, writers may intentionally obscure meaning. Good writing often has an element of mystery to it. Readers are expected to work at understanding what is written. If they fail to understand, it is their fault.

In writer-responsible cultures, writers are expected to work at being clear. Good writing is not mysterious. Writers are expected to present their ideas in ways that can be easily understood. If the reader has trouble understanding, it is the writer's fault.

a.   Assumptions and Expectations in the United States and in the United States Legal Culture

Because English is a writer-responsible language, the primary responsibility for successful communication lies with the writer. Writing clear sentences that can be understood the first time they are read is expected.[14] Being able to make a complicated topic easy for a reader to understand is admired.

The Reader's Time is Valuable

An underlying assumption of the U.S. legal culture is that the reader's time is more valuable than the writer's time. Legal readers — including judges and partners in law firms — tend to have positions of power over the writers of legal prose: lawyers writing briefs for the court, interns and associates writing memoranda for supervising attorneys. Consequently, writers are expected to expend their time and energy writing clearly so that readers do not have to spend extra time and energy understanding.

In addition, U.S. readers tend to be far less patient than readers from other cultures. Consequently, beginnings in writing in the United States tend to get to the point quickly. They answer the question, "What is this about?"

---

14. Clarity has not always been a top priority in legal writing. In the past, consumer contracts and statutes were often written in long, complex sentences that were difficult to understand because they were filled with abstractions and other legalese. See section 24.3.

U.S. legal readers tend to expect a quick overview at the beginning of a piece of writing that sets out its content and structure. Many prefer statements of facts with an overview paragraph that introduces the parties, the legal problem, and the source of the facts. Discussion sections in legal memoranda are almost always begun by giving an overview of the law and a roadmap to its application. Even when writers must describe how the law developed over a period of time, such historical discussions tend to be brief, hitting only the high points and moving rapidly toward the current state of the law. Giving some background and context for understanding the policy underlying the law is also common, but these discussions tend to be short and to the point. In general, U.S. legal readers want only enough background and context for the law to deal with the case before them.

As a rule, judges are even more impatient than other U.S. legal readers. They are eager for brief writers to get to the application of the law to the facts. Long-winded introductions or treatises on the applicable law are likely to irritate judges who are already knowledgeable about the law and who are reading the brief with the primary purpose of thinking through how that law applies to the case before them.

Introductory paragraphs in letters to clients also tend to have some features of an overview. They may include a short, polite beginning that helps establish or reinforce the relationship between the writer and reader, but then they usually move rather quickly to stating the purpose of the letter. In many cases that means stating the legal question the client brought to the attorney and, particularly when the answer to that question is one the client will like, introducing the answer the attorney found after researching the problem.

The Reader Wants to Know What You are Thinking; Be Direct and Explicit

To ensure that their meaning is clearly conveyed to their readers throughout a document, attorneys use two common features of the prose style in the United States: directness and explicitness. In office memos, writers are expected to be direct and candid with their readers. Writers should lay out the facts, the rules, the relevant cases, and the arguments each side is likely to make. Writers should tell their readers when, in the writer's opinion, the court will probably find an argument weak or persuasive. Some firms also want office memoranda to include some candid strategic advice, such as whether the firm should take the case or whether settling out of court might be the client's best option.

Unfavorable facts, rules, analogous cases, and weaknesses in the client's case are dealt with openly. In most (but not all) instances, office memoranda are in-house documents that are read only by members of the firm, who want a frank and honest assessment of the situation.

Directness manifests itself in briefs when the writer tells the court exactly what he or she wants from the court (for example, denial of summary judgment, admission of some evidence). Directness may lead a brief writer to concede a point, but it does not mean that a brief writer should be neutral or lay out the opponent's arguments in a favorable light.

It is possible, of course, to be too direct with a court. Some judges and justices admit that they do not like being told by an attorney that they "must" do something even when that something is required law. Using "should" rather than "must" in sentences like "The court should grant the motion to suppress . . ." or "This court should find that the trial court abused its discretion . . ." allows the writer to be direct without seeming to be ordering the court around. Passive voice is another way to avoid sounding like the writer is bossing the court around. Revising "The court must grant the motion . . ." to "The motion should be granted . . ." is less likely to elicit a negative reaction from a judge.

In letters to clients, directness tends to be most obvious when an attorney writer is telling the client about his or her options. Attorneys writing to clients also find that it is effective to be direct about any instructions or deadlines they must convey to the client, even though these instructions and deadlines may be softened a bit with a word like "please" (for example, "Please sign and return the enclosed documents to my office by Tuesday, December 30, 1997."). Attorney writers are also invariably direct in pointing out that their predictions are their professional opinions and not guarantees of a certain outcome. On the other hand, attorneys writing to clients tend to be slightly less direct about conveying bad or disappointing news. While the writer may save unhappy news for the end of a letter or soften the blow with an empathetic word like "unfortunately," the attorney writer will still be clear about what the bad news is.

Despite the preference for directness, most attorneys avoid first and second person references ("I" and "you") in both legal memoranda and briefs. Rather than write "I think the court will find the first element is met" in an office memorandum, most attorneys write "the court will probably find that the first element is met." Rather than write "you should consider" when addressing the court, virtually all attorneys write "the court should consider." Use of "I" and "you" is more common in letters to clients, but even there many attorneys prefer "in my opinion" to "I think" or "I believe." Even though the use of "you" is commonplace in letters to clients, indiscriminate use of "you" can make a letter seem bossy or too informal. Many attorneys prefer using "we" in letters to clients to mean both the client and the attorney. "We" conveys the impression that the two are or will be working together as a team.

Explicitness is most evident when legal memo and brief writers construct their arguments. Facts are analogized and distinguished explicitly. Little is left to the imagination as the writer makes explicit connections between points and draws explicit conclusions from the points he or she has made. Summaries that synthesize and repeat earlier points are admired. Indeed, explicitly drawn conclusions are hallmarks of U.S. legal writing.

Writing Has to Get a Job Done

Another assumption of the U.S. legal culture is that writing is primarily functional; it has a job to do—explain, persuade, or both—and its value is judged almost exclusively by whether it accomplishes its purpose. Legal writers would not create prose that is aesthetically pleasing for its own sake. Eloquence is admired only when it serves the underlying purposes of explaining or persuading. Further, excessive elaboration is not considered eloquent writing; rather, it is treated as fluff or padding.

Writers Should State and Support a Position

Writing is assumed to be the writer's own view or opinion. Readers in the United States expect writers to state a position and then defend it. Other people's writing is considered "fair game," that is, it is completely acceptable to challenge, disagree with, or criticize the writing of another, including an expert in the field or even a court, as long as the challenge, disagreement, or criticism is well supported and directed at the ideas and arguments and not at the individual. Attacking the arguments of one's opponents is expected, but once again the criticism should address the weaknesses in the arguments and not become personal.

Support for one's ideas can take a number of forms. In U.S. writing in general, facts, statistics, and other "hard data" are favorite forms of support. Readers expect concrete support for most of a writer's points. The use of detail as evidence supporting one's position is considered persuasive. Simple assertions that are not backed up by supporting evidence are widely criticized as unpersuasive.

In the U.S. legal culture, support for one's ideas or arguments generally falls into three categories: plain language arguments, analogous case arguments, and policy arguments. (See section 3.9.2.) U.S. legal readers expect that most of a legal writer's points will be supported by cited authority. A plain language argument relies on the authority of the law and a common sense reading of it. An analogous case argument relies on the authority of another court and how it ruled in a similar case. Policy arguments often cite legislative history as the authority for statements about the policy underlying a rule. Citing to the record and using detailed facts from the case to support one's arguments are all considered effective advocacy. Conversely, assertions without support are considered poor advocacy.

When an attorney uses facts and cases to support an argument, the expectation is that attorneys will be meticulously accurate. If an attorney is caught misrepresenting a fact or a case, he or she loses credibility. Legal readers would become suspicious of that attorney's other representations of fact and law. What is also expected in the U.S. legal culture, however, is that attorneys writing as advocates will "characterize" the facts and case law in a light that is favorable to their client. Attorneys disagree about where the line is drawn between characterizing and misstating facts. Most agree that characterization includes emphasis. For example, favorable facts are highlighted and discussed in detail; unfavorable facts are down-played and only mentioned briefly. (See section 8.13.3.) Most agree that omitting key facts or cases that are unfavorable is not only dishonest and ineffective advocacy, but also a probable violation of the rules. Virtually all agree that misstating key facts or cases is totally unacceptable and possibly even malpractice.

One way to determine whether a given way of expressing a fact or discussing a case is just a favorable characterization or an outright mis-statement is to ask what the opponent would say in response. If an opponent would be inclined to say something like "I wouldn't put it that way," then the attorney can assume he or she has stayed within the legit-imate boundaries of characterization. If an opponent would say "that's not true," then the attorney can assume he or she has stepped over the line into misstatement.

Assuming then that misstatement is not an option, what is still con-fusing is whether it is better to err on the side of understatement or on the side of overstatement. Many lawyers would argue that understatement is safer and better for building one's reputation with other attorneys and judges. Even so, a quick survey of writing in the profession would prob-ably show that, if an attorney is erring on one side or the other, most err on the side of overstatement.

Writing is Like Personal Property; Avoid Plagiarism

An added complication to the U.S. culture's views about writing and support for ideas is its notion of plagiarism. Because people in the United States place a high value on originality, an original idea or an original expression in words is considered a valuable possession. Consequently, people in the U.S. culture tend to think that a writer's ideas, and especially the words a writer uses to express those ideas, are that writer's personal property. Using someone's ideas or words *without attribution* is treated like stealing that person's ideas or words. Using someone's ideas or words *with attribution*,[15] however, is a commonplace and respectable form of supporting one's own points. In fact, use of attributed quotations from experts and other authorities is considered effective support as long as the writer is selective about what he or she quotes. Overquoting, while not nearly as serious a mistake as plagiarism, is frowned upon because it suggests the writer has borrowed too heavily from other sources and has not contributed any original thinking.

Concerns about plagiarism also appear in legal writing, but they are somewhat overshadowed by the heavy emphasis on having authority for one's arguments. Citing cases, statutes, books, law review articles, and other secondary sources is considered of paramount importance. These

---

15. In some instances, writers also need the original author's express per-mission.

citations show that the writer has the support of the law, other courts, and other legal minds behind his or her arguments. There is universal agreement about not only the need for citations to authority but also the use of quotation marks[16] to show that a writer has set out the exact language of a rule.[17]

There is a difference of opinion, however, in the U.S. legal culture about whether legal writers need to use quotation marks as well as the citation when they are using the exact language of a court. Some legal writers and readers seem to feel that court opinions are almost like public property. Others continue to be careful to use quotation marks around exact language from another court. The safe choice is to apply the same standards in legal writing as in other writing in the United States and use quotation marks around another's words.

An additional important point concerns plagiarism in law school settings: In all U.S. law schools, plagiarizing is considered a serious ethical offense. Despite the recent shift to encouraging some limited collaboration in legal writing classes, virtually every U.S. law school has a student code of conduct that strictly forbids copying another student's work and representing it as one's own. Plagiarizing the words, ideas, or even the key organizational features of another student's writing has serious consequences, often including expulsion from law school. Similarly, law students writing seminar papers and law review articles must be conscientous about citing their sources and using quotation marks when they are using the language of an authority. The penalties for plagiarizing the work of a published author are usually identical to the penalties for plagiarizing the work of another student.

In U.S. law firms, however, very different standards apply. Attorneys who are members of the same firm often share sample forms, in-house memoranda, and even rule sections from briefs. Using the writing of another member of the firm as a model is common. Some firms even have memo and brief "banks," which are copies of office memoranda and briefs written by firm members that other firm members can use when they are writing about similar legal problems. This sharing within a firm is not considered plagiarism; rather, it is considered a practical way to save time and resources.

b. Assumptions and Expectations in Other Cultures

Most East Asian and Middle Eastern languages are reader-responsible languages. Consequently, not fully grasping a writer's intended meaning does not frustrate these readers. They do not expect sentences that can

---

16. Long quotations of 50 words or more are written as block quotations. No quotation marks are used with block quotations even though the wording is exactly the same as the original. See *The Bluebook: A Uniform System of Citation* rule 5.1 and section 27.5.1b.

17. Using ellipses to omit parts of the rule that are not applicable to the matter at hand is completely acceptable.

be automatically understood the first time they are read. Japanese readers, for example, assume that the writer may have deliberately hidden some of the meaning. Even though a Japanese writer may continually return to the theme of an article, the theme may not be stated explicitly. Similarly, Hebrew and Arabic readers expect to "read between the lines" and draw the appropriate conclusion on their own.

A few cultures and their written languages seem to be in a transition period. Experts in contrastive rhetoric believe, for example, that modern Chinese (Mandarin) is in the process of changing from a reader-responsible to a writer-responsible approach.

In some cultures, the best way to begin a piece of expository writing is with an appropriate proverb, parable, or anecdote. This sets a tone for the discussion that follows and also underscores the "truth" of what will be said. Thai writing, for example, tends to begin with an anecdote, followed by specific detail, and then ended by an overall statement of the main point in the very last sentence. Other cultures favor a personal approach to beginnings. Relating how the topic is connected to the writer is a common way to introduce a topic. Still others rely heavily on beginnings that develop an historical context. Arabic speakers tend to set the stage for their topics by broad statements about the general state of affairs.

The length of the introduction or how much of the total piece of writing should be taken up by the introduction also varies greatly from culture to culture. Lengthy introductions are a noteworthy feature of Spanish writing. An introduction that takes up to a third of the total pages would not be uncommon.

Rather than introducing the main point quickly, Chinese writers use a "brush clearing" or "clearing the terrain" approach. In this approach, the writer begins by discussing all the ideas related to his or her main idea. Once this is done (the brush is cleared), the main idea is ready to be explored.

As a general rule, writers in East Asian languages prefer indirectness to directness and inferring meaning rather than writing explicitly. Stating one's point baldly is equated with a lack of sophistication. Chinese writers, for example, may give concrete examples but the cultural preference is to stop after listing the examples and allow the reader to make the connections and draw the inevitable conclusion. Explicit conclusions are considered repetitious and possibly even insulting to educated readers. Japanese writers may, as a general rule, be even more indirect than Chinese writers. Good Japanese writing implies or alludes to rather than explicitly states its points. Making a point indirectly, or hinting at meaning is regarded as a sign of intelligence and sensitivity. Directness is equated with brashness. Korean writers rarely use direct persuasion and explicit description. Arguing directly or explicitly is apt to have a negative effect on readers. The preference to be indirect is not limited, however, to writers of Asian languages. Finnish writers also tend to leave things unsaid that seem obvious.

In many cultures, writing is treated as received wisdom. Writers strive to pass along the insights of the past; consequently, readers do not assume that a writer is expressing his or her own opinion. Instead, students are encouraged first to memorize and later to repeat in their own writing the words of the respected authorities from the past. The purpose of writing in these cultures is to create harmony between writer and reader, not to debate or explicate a point of view. In China, for example, being a writer is equated with being a scholar and therefore one who knows and writes the truth.

In Japanese writing, there is a tendency to use a mix of arguments for and against a position. Japanese writers also may end an argument taking a different position from their beginning position. Even in argumentative essays, Japanese writers tend to be somewhat tentative and use more hedges and qualifiers than do writers from other cultures. Korean writers may use a formulaic expression like "some people say" as a way to introduce their own point of view, particularly when the position they are taking is a controversial one. The formula expression allows the writer to avoid being too direct and to suggest that there is other support for the position the writer states.

Other cultures treat writing more as an art than as a functional skill. Japanese writers, for example, tend to be very concerned about the aesthetics of their writing. Writers of Romance languages like Spanish or French pride themselves in using the language beautifully. Writers in Arabic also tend to place a stronger emphasis on the form of language.

The best support for one's points varies from culture to culture. Some cultures support points through analogies, appeals to intuition, beautiful language, or references to sages from the past. Chinese writers prefer elaborate metaphors and literary references. They also use numerous references to historical events. Rather than using different pieces of evidence as support, some cultures prefer to argue the same point in many different ways. Different cultures also disagree about what is understatement and overstatement. Middle Eastern law students, particularly those who were educated in Classical Arabic, may consider a supporting statement as neutral that a typical person from the United States would consider an exaggeration. What native speakers would consider neutral, they would tend to view as examples of understatement.

§29.2.2   Culturally Determined Patterns in Writing

a.   Preferences in the United States

As a general rule, students in the United States receive more direct instruction in rhetorical patterns in writing than do students in most other school systems. Composition textbooks stress paragraphs that use a general topic sentence, specific supporting sentences, and a general concluding sentence. The five-paragraph essay taught in junior high and high school expands this same general → specific → general structure over a slightly longer piece of prose. The typical term paper or research paper with its thesis statement expands the structure over a still longer piece of writing. In other words, U.S. students internalize a hierarchical approach with numerous levels of subordination as the appropriate way to present ideas. In fact, the degree to which a writer uses a hierarchical approach to writing is often the basis for judging whether that writer's work is mature. Conversely, frequent use of coordination (this point "and" this point "and" this point "and" this point) is considered a sign of an immature prose style. One-sentence paragraphs are also generally frowned upon and thought to be the mark of undeveloped ideas.

Writing in the U.S. legal culture emulates this same hierarchical approach. An effective prose style in law typically uses an overview → analysis → synthesis organizational strategy. In fact, successful attorney writers deliberately use topic sentences, signposts, and enumeration to reveal the hierarchical organization of their line of reasoning.

Writing that is deemed "coherent" prose in the United States usually has very explicit language links to guide readers across the levels of generality and specificity. Indeed, lexical ties are the primary ways native speakers of English create coherence in their prose. These sentence-to-sentence connections result in a linear prose style. Narratives in English also tend to be linear because speakers of English perceive time as linear. Temporal-causal sequencing is typical.

English sentences tend to be written in an old information → new information pattern. Topics tend to be in the first half of sentences.

b.   Preferences in Other Cultures

Several cultures, particularly Arabic speaking cultures, do not particularly value hierarchy and subordination in ideas. As a rule, Arabic writers are inclined to restate their positions, often with warnings, rather than support them with examples. In fact, most Arabic languages have relatively few markers for subordination. Coordination and balance are the hallmarks of sophisticated Arabic prose. Parallelism is a key ingredient for conveying a rich array of parallel ideas. Writers in many other languages, including Chinese, also favor additive conjunctions to connect ideas.

Unlike U.S. writers who tend to move from the general to the specific, Japanese writers prefer to move from the specific to the general. Many other cultures prefer to hide the underlying organization of a piece of writing. Numbering one's points or reasons is not favored. In general, writers in most other cultures use fewer language links than do their U.S. counterparts. In a few languages, most notably Puerto Rican Spanish, one- or two-sentence paragraphs are common.

Native speakers of Chinese tend to use centrifugal organizational patterns, and native speakers of Spanish tend to use linear organizational patterns but with tangential breaks.

Because both Chinese and Japanese are languages that rely heavily on the concept of topic, the typical sentence structure in these languages is a topic-comment structure. Consequently, ESL law students who have Chinese or Japanese as their first language may be inclined to replicate this sentence structure preference in English and produce what native speakers of English would consider too many sentences that begin with "as for," "in regards to," "there is," or "there are."

§29.2.3   Conciseness v. Repetition

a. Preferences in the United States

In all types of expository prose in the United States, conciseness is heralded as a writing virtue. Saying a great deal in a few words is considered a sign of the writer's intelligence and respect for his or her readers. In the U.S. legal culture, conciseness is even more highly prized as lawyers fight to keep their heads about the paper blizzard created by complex litigation. Courts require lawyers to write within page limits. Judges admonish attorneys "to be brief." Supervising attorneys chastise young lawyers to "get to the point."

In the U.S. legal culture, writers are expected to be concise in two different ways: They are expected to edit their sentences of all excess verbiage (see section 24.2), and they are expected to stay on track and focused on points that are central to developing a line of reasoning. Straying, even slightly, from the point puzzles and irritates legal readers in the United States, who are likely to view writing with digressions as disorganized, unfocused, and a waste of their time. In fact, one of the strongest condemnations of any part of a piece of legal writing is to label it "irrelevant."

Only in law review articles is exploration of a related side issue encouraged, and even in law review articles, this type of digression must be done in footnotes and not in the main body of the text. A few writers have borrowed the law review footnote system as a means for exploring tangetial points in memoranda and briefs, but this practice is the exception, not the norm. Many more memoranda and brief writers use appendices when they believe that some but not all of their readers might appreciate extensive supporting, background, or related information. In any case, the virtually unanimous view is that anything in the body of the text of any memorandum or brief must be directly "on point."

Although writing textbooks, including legal writing textbooks, often advise writers to be concise and denounce "needless" repetition, at least two kinds of repetition are favored in legal prose style. First, legal writers tend to repeat their conclusions. In legal memoranda, the overall conclusion may appear in both the brief answer and in the separate conclusion section. In addition, legal writers often state mini-conclusions after an extended discussion of a significant point and then draw these mini-conclusions together into an overall conclusion.

Second, when writing as advocates, lawyers tend to repeat points, albeit subtly, that are favorable to their case. In fact, many effective advocates expend a great deal of effort finding slightly different ways to emphasize essentially the same point. Brief writers who write an argumentative point heading and then open the next section with a positive assertion are often making exactly the same point but choosing a different sentence structure and slightly different words. The net effect of deliberate but subtle repetition is to create an overall theme, or theory of the case, that the writer hopes the reader will adopt. Lawyers in the U.S. who use subtle repetition as a form of advocacy generally know that they must use this technique selectively and carefully because they are aware that they risk annoying legal readers, particularly judges, if the repetition becomes too obvious.

b.   *Preferences in Other Cultures*

In many other cultures, elaborate and extended prose is greatly admired. In most Romance languages, for example, sophisticated writers use frills and flourishes to embellish their points. The very kinds of digressions that U.S. legal readers find irritating and irrelevant are also admired in many other cultures. Spanish readers, for example, consider the exploration of side points a sign that the writer is highly intelligent and well versed in the topic. French writers also have much more freedom to digress and introduce related material. Japanese writers often use an organizational framework called *ki-shoo-ten-ketsu. Ten*, the third element, is a sub-theme that most readers in the United States would consider an unexpected digression.

Many cultures prefer to argue the same point in many different ways. Paragraph after paragraph says essentially the same thing with only modest additions or changes. Arabic writers, for example, pride themselves in saying the same thing in many different ways.

BIBLIOGRAPHY FOR ESL LAW STUDENTS

For more information on reader-responsible and writer-responsible languages

John Hinds, *Reader Versus Writer Responsibility: A New Typology* in WRITING ACROSS LANGUAGES: Analysis of L2 Text (Ulla Connor & Robert B. Kaplan eds. 1987).

For an excellent synthesis of the difference between the rhetorical preferences in the United States and many other cultures

Ilona Leki, UNDERSTANDING ESL WRITERS: A GUIDE FOR TEACHERS (1992).

For other common problem areas that appear in ESL students' writing

Diane Hacker, *ESL Trouble Spots,* in A WRITER'S REFERENCE (2d ed. 1992).
Raymond C. Clark, Patrick R. Moran, Arthur A. Burrows, THE ESL MISCELLANY: A TREASURY OF CULTURAL & LINGUISTIC INFORMATION (2d ed. 1981).

The remaining sources are grouped by country or language.

Arabic:

Shirley E. Ostler, *English in Parallels: A Comparison of English & Arabic Prose* in Writing Across Languages: An Analysis of L2 Text (Ulla Connor & Robert B. Kaplan eds. 1987). (Note that Ostler's research has subsequently been criticized by John Swales because Ostler compared student essays written in Arabic with published texts in English. Swales believes that contrastive rhetoricians must compare writing in the same genre.)

Terry Prothro, *Arab-American Differences in the Judgment of Written Messages*, 42 J. Soc. Psychol., 3-11 (1955).

English for Specific Purposes in the Arab World, (John Swales & Hassan Mustafa eds., 1984).

Richard Yorkey, *Practical EFL Techniques for Teaching Arabic-Speaking Students* in The Human Factors in ESL (J. Alatis & R. Crymes eds. 1977).

Japan:

John Hinds, *Japanese Expository Prose,* 13 Papers in Linguistics: Int'l J. of Human Comm. 158 (1980).

John Hinds, *Linguistics & Written Discourse in Particular Languages: Contrastive studies: English & Japanese,* in Ann. Rev. Applied Linguistics, (Robert B. Kaplan et al. eds. 1979).

H. Kobayashi, *Rhetorical Patterns in English and Japanese*, Dissertation Abstracts Int'l 45(8):2425A.

Hebrew:

Michael Zellermayer, *An Analysis of Oral & Literate Texts: Two Types of Reader-Writer Relationships in Hebrew & English* in The Social Construction of Written Communication (Bennett A. Rafoth & Donald L. Rubin eds. 1988).

China:

Carolyn Matalene, *Contrastive Rhetoric: An American Writing Teacher in China*, 47 Coll. Eng. 789 (1985).

Robert T. Oliver, Communication & Culture in Ancient India & China (1971).

B.A. Mohan and A.Y. Lo, *Academic Writing & Chinese Students: Transfer & Developmental Factors*, TESOL Q. 19:515-534.

Shelley D. Wong, *Contrastive Rhetoric: An Exploration of Proverbial References in Chinese Student L1 & L2 Writing*, 6 J. Intensive Eng. Stud. 71 (1992).

India:

Robert T. Oliver, Communication & Culture in Ancient India & China (1971).

Korea:

William G. Eggington, *Written Academic Discourse in Korean: Implications for Effective Communication* in Writing Across Languages: Analysis of L2 Text (Ulla Connor & Robert B. Kaplan, eds., 1987).

Thai:

Indrasuta Chantanee, *Narrative Styles in the Writing of Thai & American Students,* in Writing Across Languages & Cultures: Issues in Contrastive Rhetoric 206 (Alan C. Purves ed., 1988).

In addition to this bibliography, which was designed for students who may wish to read the source material relevant to a particular language or culture, *The Teaching Notes for The Legal Writing Handbook, 2d ed.* contains a bibliography for legal writing professors at the end of the teaching notes for Chapter 29 that lists other source material.

Glossary of Usage

In grammar, "usage" simply means what word or phrase a native speaker of the language would use in certain situations. In legal writing, appropriate usage will typically be that of the educated professional. Choices will usually reflect a conservative, more traditional view of language.

Even in law, though, usage is not static. The language of law may be traditional and formal, but it is still living and changing. As a consequence, "correct" usage varies from time to time. What was once unacceptable may, in a decade, become the appropriate choice. For this reason, astute legal writers should consider the date of publication for any authority they consult about usage and, as always, they should consider the reader and purposes of the document they are producing.

In addition, all usage errors are not created equal. Some are egregious errors; others, more forgiveable. While it is certainly best to master all the usage questions in the following glossary, those marked with an asterisk (*) are important to learn first either because they appear frequently in legal writing or because they represent an error that would distract most readers.

*A/An. Use "a" before words that begin with a consonant sound, and use "an" before words that begin with a vowel sound. Notice that some words begin with a vowel but still use "a" because the initial sound in the word is a consonant sound. This situation occurs when the word begins with a long "u" or "eu" and before the word "one" (a university, a one-hour delay). A few words (usually silent "h" words) begin with a consonant but still use "an" because the initial sound in the word is a vowel sound (an honor, an heir).

*A lot. "A lot" as in the expression "a lot of time" is always spelled as two words. "Alot" as one word is never correct. Notice, however, that "a lot" tends to sound rather informal and may also be imprecise. For these reasons, "a lot" is often not the best choice in legal writing ("a lot of time" → "a great deal of time"; "a lot of prior convictions" → "numerous prior convictions"; "a lot of experience" → "considerable experience").

*Adverse/Averse. "Adverse" means "unfavorable," "opposed," or "hostile." One can get an "adverse verdict" or "adverse criticism." "Averse" means "disinclined" or "reluctant." Use "averse" to show a distaste for something or a tendency to avoid something. One may be averse to representing certain types of clients.

*Advice/Advise. "Advice" is the noun; "advise" is the verb. One can advise a client, or one can give advice to a client.

*Affect/Effect. Generally, "affect" is used as a verb meaning "to influence, impress, or sway": "The jury did not seem to be affected by the defendant's emotional appeal for mercy." "Affect" may also be used as a verb meaning "to pretend or feign": "The witness affected surprise when she was told that the signature was forged." Less common is "affect" used as a noun in psychology meaning "emotion."

The most common use of "effect" is as a noun meaning "the result, consequence, or outcome." "Effect" is also used to mean "goods," as in "one's personal effects," and "impression" as in "done for effect."

"Effect" is used as a verb meaning "to bring about or accomplish": "The mediator successfully effected an agreement between labor and management." Had the preceding example been "the mediator affected an agreement between labor and management" the meaning would have been significantly different. "Effected an agreement" means the agreement was reached; "affected an agreement" means the mediator had some influence on the agreement.

Study Aid

Part of what seems to confuse writers about "affect" and "effect" is that "affect" as a verb means "to have an effect on." For this reason, it may be helpful to analyze the grammar of a sentence in which "affect" or "effect" would appear. If the sentence needs a verb and you cannot substitute "to bring about," then use "affect." If the choice requires a noun, use "effect."

*Among/Between. Use "among" when discussing three or more objects or people; use "between" when discussing two objects or people: "The members of the Board of Directors could not agree among themselves." "Attorney-client privilege refers to those confidential communications that occur between a client and her attorney."

Amount/Number. Use "amount" with nouns that cannot be counted and "number" with nouns that can be counted: "The amount of grief this mother has suffered cannot be measured by the number of dollars a jury awards her."

And/or. Many authorities consider this usage cumbersome; others point out that it can be ambiguous, unless you use "and/or" to show that three possibilities exist (for example, husband and/or wife can mean (1) husband, (2) wife, or (3) both). Consequently, because the reader has to stop and sort through the three possibilities, it is easier on the reader to present each of the three possibilities separately (for example, "husband or wife or both").

Anxious/Eager.   "Anxious" comes from the root word "anxiety." Consequently, if one is "anxious," one is "concerned or worried": "I feel anxious about the interview." "Eager," on the other hand, means "looking forward to": "When asked what happened, the defendant was eager to talk to the police."

Study Aid

Use "anxious about," but "eager to." A defendant may be "anxious about" (worried about) testifying or "eager to" (looking forward to) testify.

As/Because/Since.   Because "since" has at least two meanings—"from some time in the past" and "because"—some sentences that begin with "since" may be ambiguous: "Since you have made these improvements, you have used the property almost daily during the summer months." The example sentence may mean that you have used the property almost daily since the time when you made the improvements, or it may mean that you have used the property almost daily because you made the improvements. For this reason, it is better to use "since" only for time references and "because" for cause-and-effect references. Similarly, avoid using "as" in cause-and-effect sentences because it may also be ambiguous and misunderstood to mean "while."

As/Like.   "Like" can be used as a preposition, not just as a conjunction. Consequently, if a full clause follows, use "as" or "as if": The defendant looked as if she were lying.

A While/Awhile.   "A while" is an article plus a noun; "awhile" is an adverb. Use "awhile" only when it modifies a verb, not as an object of a preposition: "The shopkeeper waited awhile before answering the officer's question; then he paused for a while before showing the officer the safe."

Bad/Badly.   "Bad" is an adjective; "badly" is an adverb. When the verb "feel" is used as a linking verb (a state of being, a state of mind), it must be followed by an adjective. Consequently, one "feels bad": "Olsen claims that he felt bad when he fired Baxter."

But however/But yet.   These phrases are redundant; avoid them. Use just "but" or just "however" or just "yet" alone.

Compare to/Compare with/Contrast.   Use "compare to" when pointing out only similarities; use "compare with" when pointing out similarities and differences; use "contrast" when pointing out only differences.

Complement/Compliment.   A complement completes something: "Ajax, Inc. considered Smith to be the perfect complement to its sales department." A compliment is a flattering remark.

Comprise/Compose/Include. "Comprise" means "to contain": The panel comprises three judges. Notice that "is composed of" can substitute for "comprise." For precision's sake, do not substitute "include" for "comprise." "Comprise" denotes a complete listing; "include" may mean a partial listing.

Study Aid

The whole comprises all the parts. The whole is composed of all the parts. The whole includes some or all of the parts.

Contact. In informal English, "contact" is frequently used as a verb to mean to telephone, write, or talk face-to-face. In formal writing, it is better to use the precise choice.

Continual/Continuous. "Continual" means "frequently repeated"; "continuous" means "unceasing": "His clients' continual complaint was that he never returned telephone calls." "Continuous water flow cools the reactor."

Convince/Persuade. To convince someone means to change that person's mind; to persuade someone means to move that person to action: "Ms. O'Brien's goal was to convince Mr. Taylor that she was hardworking and then persuade him to give her a raise."

Study Aid

Use "convince of" or "convince that" but "persuade (object) to."

Criteria/Criterion. "Criteria" is the plural form; "criterion" is the singular form. "Acme published the following criteria for the new position: a four-year college degree, experience in sales, and willingness to travel. It waived the first criterion for applicants who had completed Acme's own in-house training program."

Different from/Different than. Use "different from" unless the resulting sentence would be awkward.

Disinterested/Uninterested. "Disinterested" means "neutral, unbiased"; "uninterested" means "bored": "We want judges to be disinterested, not uninterested, in the cases before them."

Due to/Because of. Purists use "due to" only as a noun or adjective, not as a preposition. Consequently, "due to" can be used in those sentence slots that call for an adjective, such as the subject complement, and as modifiers of nouns: "The damage was due to faulty wiring" (subject complement). "The deterioration due to severe weather conditions makes the bridge unsafe" (modifier of a noun). Although some authorities on usage point to the wide acceptance of "due to" as a preposition, most recommend that "because of" be used instead in preposition slots: "Because of his poor health, Justice Brennan resigned his position on the Supreme Court."

Study Aid

Because "due to" is always acceptable as a subject complement, look for a form of the verb "to be" as the main verb to determine whether "due to" can be used. Also, one test of whether "due to" is being used as an adjective is to substitute the phrase "attributed to."

e.g./i.e.   In textual sentences, the English equivalents for "e.g." (for example) and "i.e." (that is, or namely) are generally preferable to the Latin abbreviations, although "i.e." and "e.g." are appropriate in footnotes and parenthetical matter. When the Latin abbreviations are used, they should be italicized and followed by a comma. Some writers mistakenly use "i.e." to mean "for example." In citations, use the signal "e.g." according to Rule 1.2(a) in the *Bluebook*.

Eminent/Imminent.   "Eminent" means "distinguished," "prominent," or "high ranking." An expert witness may be an "eminent scholar." "Imminent" means "about to happen" or "impending." "Imminent" is often used with danger or misfortune as in the phrases "imminent attack," "imminent disaster," or "imminent harm."

Etc.   Avoid using "etc." in legal writing. Whenever possible, replace "etc." with specifics, or use the appropriate English equivalent ("and so forth" or "and others") instead. Never use "and etc." This phrase is redundant; it means "and and so forth."

Farther/Further.   Use "farther" for geographical distances and "further" for showing other additions: "The placement of the fence suggested that the property line was farther north." "We can discuss this matter further after we have more facts."

Fewer/Less.   Use "fewer" for objects that can be counted; use "less" for generalized quantities or sums that cannot be counted: "Elaine used fewer sick days than any other employee. She also had less work."

*Good/Well.   Use "good" as an adjective and "well" as an adverb, except when referring to health: "The prosecutor is a good lawyer who prepares well for trial. Will the witness be well enough to testify in court?"

Hanged/Hung.   Use "hung" as the past tense for "hang" in all situations except executions: "The counterfeit bill was framed and hung in the lobby." "The whistleblower was hanged by the members as a warning to others."

*Have/Of.   "Have," not "of," should be used after the auxiliary verbs "could," "should," and "would": "The plaintiff could have offered a compromise before initiating the lawsuit."

Hopefully.   In the last two decades, "hopefully" has been widely used to mean "I hope" or "we hope" as in the sentence "Hopefully, we will win this case." Several purists launched a highly publicized campaign to point out that "hopefully" originally meant "to be filled with hope"; therefore, the "correct" way to use "hopefully" was in sentences like this: "Hopefully, the client began reading the opinion letter from his attorney." This sentence meant the client was "filled with hope" as he read the attorney's opinion about his case, not that anyone was hoping the client would begin reading the letter. Perhaps the best solution to the "hopefully" problem for legal writers is to revise the sentence: "We hope we will win this case." "The client was hopeful as he began reading the opinion letter from his attorney."

*Imply/Infer.   "To imply" means "to indicate, suggest, or express indirectly": "At the show-up, the police officer implied that the defendant was the assailant when he said, 'Don't you think that's him?' " "To infer" means "to deduce, conclude, or gather": "The jury may infer that the defendant is guilty if it hears about her prior convictions."

Study Aid

Use "infer" when the actors in the sentence are drawing inferences *from* something.

Is when/Is where.   Do not use these constructions in sentences that are definitions. A well-crafted definition should have a noun following "is": "An endowment is the transfer of money or property to an institution." Not: "An endowment is when someone transfers money or property to an institution."

*Its/It's.   "Its" is the possessive form of "it." Like many other pronouns, "it" forms the possessive by simply adding "s," not " 's" (hers, yours, ours). "It's" is a contraction for "it is" or sometimes "it has." Because contractions are generally avoided in legal writing, "its" or spelling out the words "it is" will be the correct choice in most legal writing.

Lay/Lie.   "Lay" is a transitive verb, which means it must have an object. "Lay" means to "put, place, or set down": "Just lay the file on my desk." "Lie" is an intransitive verb, which means it does not have an object. "To lie" means "to recline or remain": "The file will lie unopened on my desk until the bill is paid."

Study Aid

The confusion over "lay/lie" stems from the conjugation of these verbs. "Lay" is a regular verb (lay, laid, laid), but "lie" is an irregular verb (lie, lay, lain) with a past tense that matches the present tense of "lay." The simplest way to determine which word to use is to (1) decide which verb you need ("lay" or "lie") and then (2) decide which tense is required.

Literally. "Literally" is not an all-purpose intensifier. It has a specific meaning: "exactly what the words say." The sentence "The defendant was literally on pins and needles waiting to hear the verdict" means that somehow the defendant was positioned atop pins and needles.

***Lose/Loose.** "Lose" is the opposite of "win": "I am afraid you will lose in court." It can also mean "to mislay." "Loose" is the opposite of "tight": "The victim described his attacker as wearing loose clothing."

On/Upon. In almost every instance, "upon" is just a more stilted way of saying "on." Some writers still prefer "upon" when they want to convey an upward motion, but in most other circumstances, "on" is preferable.

***Principal/Principle.** "Principle" is a noun meaning a "rule, truth, or doctrine": "The principle of negligence per se may make the plaintiff's evidentiary burden easier." "Principal" can be a noun meaning "the head person or official." In finance, "principal" also means "the capital sum," as distinguished from interest: "The principal of Lincoln High School authorized an investment that earned less than one percent on the principal." In criminal law, a principal is the chief actor or perpetrator or aider and abettor present at the commission of the crime. In real estate, a principal is a person who empowers another to act as his or her representative: "The broker owes his principal, the seller, loyalty and good faith."

"Principal" as an adjective means "main" or "chief": "The principal question before the jury is whether the eyewitness is credible."

Proved/Proven. Use "proved" as the past participle of the verb and "proven" as an adjective. "The defendant has proved that he was at work at the time of the murder."

The reason is because. Do not use this construction. Replace with "the reason is that."

Supposed to/Used to. Be sure to include the final "d" in both expressions.

Sure and/Sure to. Always use "be sure to."

Try and/Try to. Always use "try to."

***Than/Then** Use "than" for comparisons, such as "taller than," "greater than," "more than," and "rather than." Use "then" to denote a time.

That (When it cannot be omitted). Do not omit the subordinate conjunction "that" when it will prevent a possible misreading. This problem occurs when a noun clause is used as the direct object. In such cases, the subject of the noun clause alone can be misread as the direct object. *Incorrect:* "Florida courts found a woman who had attempted three suicides and had been committed to a state mental hospital was an unfit and improper person." *Corrected:* "Florida courts found that a woman who had attempted three suicides and had been committed to a state mental hospital was an unfit and improper person."

That/Which/Who. Use "that" and "which" for things; use "who" for people. Use "that" for restrictive clauses and "which" for nonrestrictive clauses: "The defendant's truck, which does not have oversized tires, was identified by the victim as the vehicle that hit him." The clause "which does not have oversized tires" is nonrestrictive because it does not restrict or limit the meaning of "defendant's truck." Unless the defendant has more than one truck and the reader needs the clause to determine which truck is meant, the phrase "defendant's truck" is already clearly identified. The clause "that hit him," on the other hand, restricts or limits the meaning of the noun "vehicle."

Exception: "Which" is used in restrictive clauses that use the constructions "that which," "of which," or "in which."

*Their/There/They're. "Their" is the possessive form of "they." "There" denotes a place ("stay there"), or it can be used as an expletive ("There is one last point I want to make"). "They're" is a contraction for "they are."

Through/Thru. Always use "through."

Thus/Thusly. Always use "thus."

*To/Too/Two. "To" is a preposition with a great number of functional and idiomatic uses: "The defendant drove back to the city. To his surprise, the police had set up a roadblock. Ultimately, he was sentenced to death." "Too" is an adverb meaning "also," "very," or "excessively": "His story was too implausible." "Two" is the number.

Toward/Towards. Both are acceptable; "toward" is preferred in the United States because it is shorter.

Use/Utilize. Whenever possible, use "use."

When/Where. "When" denotes a time; "where" denotes a place. When indicating a particular situation, choose "when" or "in which," not "where." Avoid the expression "a case where . . . ." A case is not a place. Replace with "a case in which . . . ." Common practice, however, seems to be to use "where" in parentheticals after citations.

Which/Who. "Which" should not be used to refer to people.

Who/Whom. Use "who" in most subject positions and "whom" in most object positions. (See below for the exception.)

This rule of thumb means, however, that you will have to analyze a sentence before you can determine whether "who" or "whom" is correct. One easy way to analyze question sentences is to answer the question. If in the answer you use the subjective form ("I," "we," "he," "she," or "they"), then use *who* in the question. If in the answer you use the objective form ("me," "us," "him," "her," or "them"), then use *whom* in the question.

Who is calling? (He is calling.)
(subject)

To whom does the clerk report? (The clerk reports to her.)
(object)

For some questions, you may find it easier to determine whether to use "who" or "whom" if you recast the sentence in normal subject/verb/object order.

Whom should I pay?
(object)

I should pay whom? (I should pay them.)

The greatest confusion concerning "who/whom" occurs in sentences in which the same pronoun appears to be the object of one part of the sentence and the subject of another part of the sentence.

The police questioned a woman who they thought matched the victim's description.

The sentence above is correct. Although "who" may appear to be the object of "they thought," it is actually the subject of "matched the victim's description." A simple way to determine which form of the pronoun is correct in such situations is to mentally delete the subject/verb immediately after the "who" or "whom." If the sentence still makes sense, use "who"; if not, use "whom."

The police questioned a woman who ~~they thought~~ matched the victim's description.

Use the same method to determine that "whom" is the correct choice in the following example.

The man whom the police questioned matched the victim's description of her assailant.

The man whom ~~the police questioned~~ matched the victim's description of her assailant.

When the subject and verb following the "who/whom" slot are deleted, the sentence no longer makes sense. Notice too that you can isolate the clause "whom the police questioned," put it in normal order, "the police questioned whom," and answer the question ("the police questioned him") to determine that "whom" is the correct form.

Exception: The one exception to the rule is that "whom" is used for subjects of infinitives.

Whom does our client want to represent him?

Our client wants whom to represent him? (normal word order)

Our client wants her to represent him. (Answer the question or substitute another pronoun.)

Your/You're.   "Your" is the possessive form of "you." "You're" is the contraction for "you are."

Glossary of Terms

Active voice.   Active voice is the quality of a transitive verb in which the action of the verb is performed by the subject: "Judges decide cases." (See passive voice.)

Advance Sheets.   Advance sheets contain the most recent court decisions. Advance sheets are provided for most reporters, for example, for *United States Reports,* West's regional reporters, and official state reporters. Advance sheets are usually published bimonthly in soft bound pamphlets.

Alliteration.   Alliteration is the repetition of consonant sounds as in "Peter Piper picked a peck of pickled peppers."

Analogous case.   An analogous case is a case that is factually similar to the client's case. An argument based on an analogous case is an argument in which the attorney compares or contrasts the facts in a factually similar case with the facts in the client's case.

Analysis.   When you analyze something, you examine it closely, identifying each part and determining how the parts are related. In law, there are two types of analysis: statutory analysis, which involves the close examination of a statute, and case analysis, which involves the close examination of a case.

Assonance.   Assonance is the repetition of vowel sounds.

Bias-free language.   Bias-free language is language that suggests that persons from minority racial, religious, and ethnic groups are valued members of society. The term is also used to refer to language that is sensitive to perceptions about the poor, the elderly, the disabled, and homosexuals.

Bluebook.   The name is commonly used for *A Uniform System of Citation.* The *Bluebook* sets forth the conventions for citing legal materials (preferred resources to cite, the information that must be contained in a cite, abbreviations, typeface, etc.). Its citation system has been adopted to some degree by most law reviews and many courts.

Case law. Although the term "case law" is often used to refer to common law, in fact its meaning is broader. It refers to all court decisions including those interpreting or applying enacted law.

Case briefing. Case briefing is a technique used to analyze a court's written opinion. A case brief usually contains a summary of the facts, a statement of the issue(s), the court's holding, and the court's rationale.

Citation (also Cite). The convention for identifying legal (and nonlegal) resources. Typically, a citation has some numerical components (*e.g.,* volume numbers and pages for cases and secondary sources; titles and sections for statutes and regulations), as well as an alphabetic abbreviation (usually identifying the case reporter, book title or code name). A complete citation should identify for the user what governing body made the law, when it made the law, and where the law can be located.

Cite checking. Cite checking is the process used to determine the current status of an authority and to locate sources that have cited that authority. The two most common systems for cite checking an authority are *Shepard's,* which is available both in print and on LEXIS and Westlaw, and KeyCite, an on-line service available on Westlaw.

Code. A compilation of legislative or quasi-legislative acts (statutes, regulations or ordinances). A code reviser arranges laws by subject matter, inserts amendatory language into preexisting enactments, and deletes repealed language. The code reviser usually also compiles an index that is published as part of the code.

Common law. The common law is a system of law created by the judicial branch. For example, much of tort law is common law: the causes of action and rules were created by the courts rather than by the legislature.

Concluding sentence. A concluding sentence in a paragraph is the sentence that sums up the main point of the paragraph. Although not every paragraph will have a concluding sentence, in those that do the concluding sentence is invariably the last sentence in the paragraph.

Connotation. The connotation of a word is all the associations the word carries with it. For example, the word "lawyer" may have positive connotations for individuals who respect lawyers or who aspire to be lawyers, but it may have negative connotations for people who have had bad experiences with lawyers. (Compare with **Denotation.**)

Denotation. The denotation of a word is its dictionary definition. (Compare with **Connotation.**)

Dicta. Comments made by a court that are not directly related to the issue before it or that are not necessary to its holding are dicta. Such comments are often preceded by the word "if": "If the evidence had established . . . ." Although in some cases dicta are easily identifiable, in other cases they may not be. If the issue is broadly defined, the statement may be part of the court's holding; if the issue is narrowly defined, the statement is dicta. Compare with **Holding.**

Digest (specifically a **West digest**).   A collection of headnotes from judicial decisions. The headnotes are arranged by topic and key number and indexed. Digests also allow access to case law by case name, defendant and plaintiff name, and words and phrases. West publishes digests for individual states, regions, courts, and specific topics. There are some non-West digests, but they do not contain key numbers.

Dovetailing.   Dovetailing is the overlap of language between two sentences that creates a bridge between those two sentences. Dovetails are often created by moving the connecting idea to the end of the first sentence and the beginning of the second sentence, repeating key words, using pronouns to refer back to nouns in an earlier sentence, and using "hook words" (this, that, these, such) and a summarizing noun.

Elements analysis.   When you do an elements analysis, you systematically analyze a set of requirements set out either in a statute or as part of a common law doctrine by determining whether, given a particular set of facts, each requirement is met.

Emotionally significant fact.   An emotionally significant fact is one that, while not legally significant, may affect the way the judge or jury decides the case.

Enacted law.   Enacted law is law created by the legislative or executive branches. Statutes and regulations are enacted law.

ESL.   The acronym "ESL" stands for English-as-a-second-language.

Finding.   A finding is a decision on a question of fact. For example, a trial court judge may find a defendant incompetent to stand trial, or a jury may find that a police officer acted in good faith. (Compare with **Holding.**)

Gender-neutral language.   Gender-neutral language is language that treats males and females as having equal value. It does not assume being male is the norm or that certain jobs or positions are primarily filled by males or females.

Generic transition.   Generic transitions are those transitions that are commonly used in writing to describe standard mental moves, such as "consequently" to show cause/effect or "however" to show contrast.

Headnote.   A headnote is a one-sentence summary of a rule of law found at the beginning of a court's opinion. Because headnotes are written by an attorney employed by the company publishing the reporter in which the opinion appears and not the court, they cannot be cited as authority.

Holding.   A holding is the court's decision in a particular case. "When the court applied the rule to the facts of the case, it held that . . . ." Thus, a holding has two components: a reference to the applicable rule of law and a reference to the specific facts to which that rule was applied. Because the holding is the answer to the legal question, it can be formulated by turning the issue (a question) into a statement. Compare with **Dicta.**

Hypertext.   The capability to move from one part of a text to another part of the text or to an entirely separate text. Moving is done by clicking on links. Links are created by the designer and/or publisher of the text (often a Web page).

Integrated format.   The phrase "integrated format" refers to a method of organizing the discussion section of an objective memorandum. Instead of using the script format, in which the discussion section is organized around the arguments that each side makes, the writer organizes the discussion around legal principles or points.

Internet.   An international network of computers. The network allows a computer user to access information on remote computers linked to the Internet. Components of the Internet include the World Wide Web and electronic mail.

KeyCite.   KeyCite is an on-line cite checking service offered by Westlaw.

Key number.   An indexing tag assigned by West to the headnotes of cases published in its reporters. A key number consists of two components: a topic (the broader subject area components) and the key number (a narrow issue within the topic). Topics are identified by word; key numbers, by number. A West digest is an alphabetical arrangement of topics and key numbers containing the headnotes indexed under those key numbers.

Legalese.   Legalese is a broad term used to describe several common features of legal writing such as the use of archaic language, Latin terms, boilerplate language, and long and convoluted sentences. "Legalese" is usually a pejorative term.

Legally significant fact.   A legally significant fact is a fact that a court would consider significant either in deciding that a statute or rule is applicable or in applying that statute or rule.

Legislative history.   A legislative history is the collection of documents that were created during the enactment of a statute. Typically it consists of transcripts of hearings on a particular bill, reports produced by the committees that considered the bill, and records of comments made by legislators during debates on the bill.

Mandatory authority.   Mandatory authority is law that a court must apply in deciding the case before it.

Metaphor.   Metaphor is a direct comparison. For example, a journey is often a metaphor for life.

Nominalization.   Nominalization is the process of converting verbs into nouns (determine → determination).

Onmatopoeia.   Onomatopoeia is the quality some words have when they sound like what they mean. For example, "plop" and "slap" both tend to sound like what they mean.

Orienting transitions.   Orienting transitions are transitions that provide a context for the information that follows. They locate the reader physically, logically, or chronologically.

Paragraph block.   A paragraph block is a group of two or more paragraphs that together develop a point within a larger document.

Paragraph coherence.   A paragraph has coherence when the various points raised in the paragraph are connected to each other. Common connecting devices include repetition of key words, transitional phrases, parallelism, and pronouns.

Paragraph unity.   A paragraph has unity when all the points raised in the paragraph are related to one larger point, the paragraph's topic.

Parallel citation.   An alternative cite for a case citation. Many state decisions are published in a state reporter as well as a regional reporter. The two citations for the same case are considered "parallel." Some decisions (such as those of the United States Supreme Court) have more than one parallel cite. Other decisions have no parallel cite.

Passive voice.   Passive voice is the quality of a transitive verb in which the subject receives rather than performs the action of the verb: "Cases are decided by judges." (See active voice.)

Personification.   Personification is the attribution of human qualities or characteristics to abstractions or inanimate objects.

Persuasive authority.   Persuasive authority is law or commentary that a court may consider in deciding the case before it.

Plain English.   Plain English is the term used to describe a movement to encourage the use of simple, straightforward language (in professions such as law) that is readily understandable by lay people. In other countries, the same movement is referred to as the "Plain Language Movement."

Policy argument.   A policy argument is one in which the attorney argues that a particular interpretation of a statute, regulation, or common law rule is (or is not) consistent with current public policy, that is, the objective underlying a particular law. For example, child custody laws usually seek to provide stability for children; environmental laws usually try to balance the interests of developers and preservationists.

Primary authority.   The law itself. Primary authority includes constitutions, statutes, cases, regulations, and other government created law. Primary authority can be contrasted with secondary authority, which is description of or comment on the law.

Purple prose.   Purple prose is the overuse of flowery language that draws attention to itself.

Raise and dismiss.   You can raise and dismiss issues, elements, and arguments. In each case, both sides will agree on the point; therefore, extensive analysis is not necessary. However, a writer goes through the raise-and-dismiss process to assure the reader that the point was considered.

Regulation.   A law enacted by an administrative agency. Regulations are also sometimes called administrative "rules." Regulations are similar in form and substance to statutes and are usually compiled into codes.

Reporter.   A set of volumes containing judicial decisions. The reporter is the final form of publication for judicial decisions (the first being the slip opinion; the second, the advance sheet). The decisions in a reporter are published chronologically.

Roadmap.   Roadmaps are introductory paragraphs that give readers an overview of an entire document or a section of a document.

Rule.   The rule is the legal standard that the court applies in deciding the issue before it. In some cases, the rule will be enacted law (a constitutional provision, statute, or regulation); in other cases, it will be a court rule (one of the Federal Rules of Civil Procedure); and in still other cases, it will be a common law rule or doctrine. Although in the latter case the rule may be announced in the context of a particular case, rules are not case-specific. They are the general standards that are applied in all cases. (Compare with **Test.**)

Search engine.   A device for seeking out and retrieving items on the Internet (or other computer databases).

Secondary authority.   Description of or comment on the law (primary authority). Sources of secondary authority include treatises, law review articles, legal encyclopedias, and restatements. Secondary authority never has binding effect, but it can be used as persuasive authority based on its reasoning or the eminence of its author.

Session laws.   The laws enacted during a particular legislative session. Session laws are published in chronological order (as opposed to the topical format of codes). They may be published periodically in pamphlets throughout the session, or compiled and published in a bound volume after the close of a session.

***Shepard's* citators.**   *Shepard's* citators are books containing the information needed to update various authorities and to locate authorities that have cited particular sources. There are *Shepard's* citators for most state and regional reporters, state and federal statutes, law reviews, uniform laws, restatements, and a number of other sources. (See cite checking.)

Shepardizing.   Shepardizing is the process used to determine the current status of an authority and to locate sources that have cited that authority. For example, an attorney would shepardize a court's opinion to determine whether it had been reversed, overruled, questioned, or followed and to locate other, more recent authorities that have cited the case as authority.

Signposts.   Signposts are words and phrases that keep readers oriented as they move through a document. Transitional phrases, particularly ones like "first," "second," and "third," are the most common signposts. Topic sentences can also be considered a type of signpost.

Simile.   Similes are indirect comparisons that use "like" or "as," such as "his mind is like a steel trap."

Slip opinion.   A slip opinion is a court's written opinion in the form originally released by the court. For example, many state courts originally release their opinions in typed form. Slip opinions are not generally available to researchers.

Standard of review.   "Standard of review" refers to the level of scrutiny an appellate court will use to review a trial court's decision. For example, in *de novo* review the appellate court does not give any deference to the decision of the trial court; it decides the issue independently. In contrast, when the standard of review is abuse of discretion, the appellate court defers to the trial court, reversing its decision only when there is not evidence to support it.

Statute.   A law enacted by the legislative branch of federal and state governments (municipal and county enactments are called ordinances). Statutes can be contrasted with common law (or case law), which is made by decisions of the judicial branch.

Substantive transitions.   Substantive transitions are connecting words and phrases that also add content. Unlike generic transitions, which signal standard mental moves, substantive transitions tend to be document-specific. (See also **Dovetailing.**)

Synthesis.   When you synthesize, you bring the pieces together into a coherent whole. For example, when you synthesize a series of cases, you identify the unifying principle or principles.

Term of art.   Although sometimes used to describe any word or phrase that has a "legal ring" to it, "term of art" means a technical word or phrase with a specific meaning. "Certiorari" is a true term of art; "reasonable person" is not.

Test.   Although the words "rule" and "test" are sometimes used interchangeably, they are not the same. A test is used to determine whether a rule is met. (Compare with **Rule.**)

Topic sentence.   A topic sentence is the sentence in a paragraph that introduces the key point in the paragraph or that states the topic of the paragraph. Topic sentences are often the first sentence in a paragraph.

URL (Uniform Resource Locator).   The label given to each particular Web page. Through it, a computer user can access the information on the page.

Voice.   Voice is the active or passive quality of a transitive verb.

Website.   A place on the World Wide Web where information is posted (published).

World Wide Web (Web).   A component of the Internet that allows a computer user to move from site to site by way of hypertext links. The World Wide Web also allows for graphical representations (for example, graphs or photographs) unlike other Internet systems.

Index

"A" and "an," 862–867
Abbreviations, 817, 852–855
  inappropriate, 855
  names of laws, 853–854
Absolute phrases, 709
  commas with, 785–786
Academic degrees, style for, 865, 870
"Act," capitalization of, 845
Active voice, 161–164, 295, 587–593
  effective use, 587–590
  identifying, 587–588
  in persuasive writing, 295
  mixing with passive voice, 592
Adjectives, 707
Administrative decisions, 420
Advance sheets, 422
Adverbs, 707
  conjunctive, 713
Advocacy
  introduction, 253–255
After-the-fact outlines, 154–156, 518–519
Agreement, 727–747
  pronoun, 737–741
  subject-verb, 727–737
"Airtime," 290–291
Alliteration, 685–687
Ambiguity
  grammatical, 635–638
"Amendment," capitalization of, 845–846
American Law Reports, 445–451
Analogous cases
  arguments based on, 60–62
  descriptions of analogous cases, 135–137, 214–228
  introducing cases, 135, 222–224

  placement of case descriptions, using script format, 132
  placement of case descriptions, using integrated format, 214–219
  using parentheticals, 219–221
Analysis of research results, 103–109
"And," to start sentence, 524
Annotated codes, 401
Apostrophes, 799–803
Appellate briefs, *See also* Sample Briefs
  appendix, 330
  argument, 307–329
  argumentative headings, 300–306
  assignments of error, 276–277
  audience, 259–260
  conclusion, 329–330
  conventions, 260–263
  court rules governing, 261–262
  cover, 275
  issues (questions presented), 277–283
  organizing the argument, 308–315
  planning, 270–275
  purpose, 260
  prayer for relief, 329–330
  question presented, 277–283
  reviewing record for error, 264–265
  sample briefs, 332–367
  selecting and ordering arguments, 265–268
  signature, 330
  statement of the case, 283–299
  summary of the argument, 300
  table of authorities, 276
  table of contents, 276
  theory of the case, 271–272
Appendix
  in appellate brief, 330

Appositives, 711
Archaic language, 663–665
Argot, 667–668
Argumentative headings
    checklist, 306
    conventions, 305–306
    functions, 300–301
    persuasive techniques, 301–305
    positive assertion, 301
Arguing the law
    legislative intent, 52–54, 138
    plain language, 51–52, 138
    public policy, 54–57, 138
Arguing the application of the law
    analogous case arguments, 60–61,
        138
    plain language arguments, 55–60, 138
    policy arguments, 61–62, 138
Articles
    correct use of, 862–873
    decision tree, 873
    no article, 872
Assignments of error
    in appellate brief, 276–277
Assonance, 685–687

Background facts, 113
Background reading, 439–440
"Because," to start sentence, 524
Bias-free language, 679–682
    minority references, 681–682
    preferred terms, 680–681
Bibliography for ESL students, 902–904
"Bill," capitalization of, 846
Bills (congressional), 409
Block of paragraphs, 557–563
Block quotations, 805–806
Bolinger principle, 880–881
Brackets, 642, 813–815, 817
Brief answer
    checklist, 123–124
    content, 123, 200
    format, 123, 200
    purpose, 123, 200
Broad pronoun reference, 743–746
"But," to start sentence, 524

Cadence, 687–690
Capitalization, 842–852
    following colon, 843–844
    proper nouns and adjectives, 844–
        845
    quotations, 842–843

Cases
    analysis of, 36–40, 98–100, 103–109
    cite checking, 100–102, 457–466
    locating, 36–40, 94–97
    presenting persuasively, 318–323
    reading, 98–100, 188–195
    selecting, 120
    synthesis, 40–42
Charters, 396
Checklists
    argumentative headings in appellate
        briefs, 306
    brief answer in objective
        memorandum, 123–124
    conclusion in objective
        memorandum, 151–152
    discussion section in objective
        memorandum, 149–150
    questions presented in appellate
        briefs, 282–283
    question presented in objective
        memorandum, 122–123
    statement of the case in appellate
        briefs, 299
    statement of facts in objective
        memorandum, 117–118
"Circuit," capitalization of, 862
Circuits, judicial
    map of, 9
Cite checking, 100–102, 457–466
Clauses, 709–710
"Clearly," overuse of, 614–615
Client letters. *See* Opinion letters
Clustering, as drafting method, 514–515
"Code," capitalization of, 846
Code of Federal Regulations, 415–419
Codes
    annotated, 401
    codification tables, 405
    legislative histories, 411–412
    popular name tables, 405
    official, 400
    subject index, 401, 405
    unannotated, 401
    unofficial, 400
    updating, 401
Codification tables, 405
Coherence in paragraphs, 519–520,
        537–542
    devices for, 540–542
Collective nouns, 731–733
    pronouns for, 741
Colloquial language, 625

Colons, 797–799
Commas, 761–792
  before coordinating conjunction,
    765–767
  between coordinate adjectives, 782–
    783
  between items in a series, 780–782
  overview of the rules, 762–764
  to introduce examples, 786
  to prevent misreading, 770
  to set off absolutes, 785–786
  to set off nonrestrictive appositives,
    774–775
  to set off nonrestrictive phrases or
    clauses, 770–774
  to set off nonrestrictive participles,
    776–777
  to show omission, 786
  unnecessary, 787–792
  with addresses, 783–785
  with dates, 783–785
  with geographical locations, 783–785
  with long introductory clauses or
    phrases, 767–769
  with phrases of contrast, 779–780
  with quotation marks, 778–779
  with transitions and interrupters,
    777–778
Comma splices, 823–826
Common law, sources of, 21–23
Comparisons
  imprecise, 632
Compound modifiers, 818–821
Compound nouns, 818–821
Computer-assisted legal research
  capitalization of search words, 475
  cite checking, 483–485
  connectors, 475–480
  costs, 485–486
  field searching, 481–483
  full text searching, 468
  hyphenation, 474–475
  indices, 468
  Internet, 487–491
  LEXIS, generally, 468–470
  natural language, 483
  noise words, 475
  plurals, 475
  search words, 470–471
  segment searching, 481–483
  strategies, 491–493
  truncation and root expansion, 472–
    474
  Westlaw, generally, 468–470

Conciseness, 237–238, 638–660, 901–
    902
  clutter, 651–653
  combining sentences, 653–659
  excessive, 659–660
  overuse of quotations, 641–643
  repetition, 648–651
  starting too far back, 640–641
  stating the obvious, 639–640
  throat-clearing expressions, 645–647
Concluding sentences, 552–556
Conclusion in objective memorandum,
    151–152
Conclusory analysis, 146–148, 230–236
Congressional Record, 410
Conjunctions
  coordinating, 712, 765–767
  correlative, 713, 759
  subordinating, 710
Conjunctive adverbs, 713
Connections in writing, 527–534, 537–
    542, 565–586. *See also* Roadmaps;
    Signposts; Transitions
Constructing arguments, 137–140, 195–
    198, 307
Consistent terminology, 148, 628–629
"Constitution," capitalization of, 846–
    847
Constitutions
  state, 396
  United States, 393–395
Constructing arguments, 137–140, 195–
    198
Contractions, 859
Conventions of formal writing, 858–860
Correlative conjunctions, 713
  parallelism for, 759
"Court"
  as collective noun, 731–732
  capitalization of, 847
  pronoun for, 741
Court rules
  governing appellate briefs, 260–262
  in general, 431–432
Court system, 7–13
Cover for appellate brief, 275
Cultural assumptions about writing,
    892–899
Current Index to Legal Periodicals, 454
Current Law Index, 454

Dangling modifiers, 165–166, 635–637,
    750–753

Dashes, use of, 617–619, 821–823
Decision tree for articles, 873
Defendant-plaintiff tables, in digests, 437
Detail
  effective use of in persuasive writing,
    291–292
Determining issues on appeal, 264–270
  abstract of the record, 268–269
  harmless error, 266–267
  preserving errors, 266
  reviewing the record, 264–265
  standard of review, 267–268
Diction, 623–638
Dictionaries, legal, 456
Digests, 432–437
Direct object, 706
Discussion section in objective
    memorandum
  arguments, 137–142, 225–230
  balancing competing interests, 201–
    203
  checklist, 149–150
  common problems, 144–149, 230–
    236
  components of, 124
  descriptions of analogous cases, 134–
    137, 214–225
  disputed elements, 132–150
  elements analysis, 125–126
  general rules, 126–131, 207–214
  integrated format, 203–236
  issue of first impression, 202–203
  mini-conclusions, 143
  planning, 170–174
  script format, 132–150
  specific rules, 133–134
  undisputed elements, 131–132
Disputed elements, 132–150
Distance between subject and verb,
    597–599
Double punctuation, 854
Dovetailing, 159–160, 541, 574–586
Drafting a document, 516–517

Editing, 160–169, 520–521
Elements
  disputed, 132–150
  undisputed, 131–132
Ellipses, 642, 810–813, 817
Eloquence, 683–699
  common features of, 685–699
Emotionally significant facts, 112–113,
    285

Emphasis, 606–622
  positions of, 292–294, 607, 608–612,
    619–622
  single-word, 614–615
  punctuating for, 611–614
Enacted law, sources of, 23–25
Encyclopedias, legal, 440–442
English-as-a-second language, 861–904
  bibliography, 902–904
  correct use of articles, 862–863
  cultural assumptions about writing,
    892–899
  prepositions in idioms, 890
  prepositions that follow adjective,
    889–890
  prepositions that follow nouns, 890
  prepositions that follow verbs, 888–
    889
  rhetorical preferences, 890–902
  two- or three-word verbs, 886–887
  verbs generally, 874–887
  verbs with gerunds, 880–882, 883–
    884
  verbs with infinitives, 882–886
  verbs with objects and infinitives,
    884–886
Ethnic bias in language, 680–682
Exclamatory sentences, 859–860
Executive branch, 6, 413–414
Expectations of readers, 625–627
Expletive constructions, 165, 644

Facts
  identifying legally and emotionally
    significant, 49–51
"Federal," capitalization of, 848
Federal courts, 9–12
Federal Register, 415
Federal regulations, 415
First-person pronouns, 670–672, 858–
    859
Foreign phrases, 665–667
Form books, 456
Formal writing, conventions of, 858–
    860
Fractions, 820
Fragments, 714–719
  permissible uses of, 718–719
Fused sentences, 826

Gender-neutral language, 673–679, 738
General rule, presenting, 126–131
Generic transitions, 565–570 581–582

Gerunds, 708
 articles with, 866-867
 verbs with, 880-884
Grammar
 basic, 703-714

Harmless error, 266-267
"He," generic use of, 675-677, 738
Headings
 capitalization in, 849
 in general, 527-530
"Henceforth," use of, 664
"Herein," use of, 664
"Herewith," use of, 664
"Hook" words, 576
Hornbooks, 440-445
"However," to start sentence, 524
Hyphen, use of, 818-821

"I," use of, 670-672
Idioms, 625-627
 with prepositions, 890
Index to Foreign Legal Periodicals, 454
Index to Legal Periodicals, 454
*Index to Periodical Articles Related to
 Law,* 454
Indirect objects, 706
Inductive reasoning, 544
Infinitives, 709
 split, 523-524
Informal language, 625
Internet for research, 487-491
IRAC, 520, 538
Issues on appeal, 265-270
Italics, use of, 856-858
Integrated format for discussion section,
 203-230

Job titles, gender-neutral, 685-686
Judicial branch, 5-12
Jump cites, 498
"Jury"
 as collective noun, 741-742
 pronoun for, 751-752

Key terms, for coherence, 148, 539-
 540, 617-618, 619-622, 628-630
KeyCite, 465-466

Latin words and phrases, 665-667
Law reviews, 453-454
 locating, 102-103
Lead-ins for quotations, 806-808

Legal dictionaries, 456
Legal encyclopedias
 in general, 440-442
Legalese, 660-673
Legally significant facts
 question presented, 120-122
 statement of facts, 111-112
Legal periodicals
 in general, 453-454
Legislative branch, 6-7
Legislative histories
 compiled, 411
 federal, 411
 legislative process, 409-411
 state, 411-412
Legislative intent
 arguments based on, 52-54
Legislative process, 409
LEXIS
 capitalization, 475
 cite checking, 483-485
 connectors, 475-480
 costs, 485-486
 full text searching, 468
 hyphenation, 474-475
 indices, 468
 noise words, 475
 plurals, 475
 search words, 470-471
 segment searching, 481-483
 strategies, 491-493
 truncation and root expansion, 472-
  474
Looseleaf services, 451-452

"Man," generic use of, 674-675
Mandatory authority, 25-30
Measurements, agreement with verbs,
 737
Memoranda, *See* objective memoranda
Metaphor, 697-698
Mini-conclusions in objective
 memorandum
 integrated format, 225-226
 script format, 143-144
Mismatch, subject-verb-object, 630-635
Model acts, 455
Modifiers, 747-754
 dangling, 162, 636-637, 750-753
 misplaced, 635-636, 747-750
 sexist, 678
 single-word, 706-707
 squinting, 737, 753

Money, agreement with verbs, 737
Mood, 724-727
    subjunctive, 725-727
Myths about writing, 522-525

"National," capitalization of, 848
National reporter system, 423-425
Nominalizations, 162, 597, 643-644
Nonrestrictive constructions
    appositives, 774-775
    phrases and clauses, 770-774
Nouns
    count, 862-864
    non-count, 862-867
Numbers, 816, 859

Objective complements, 706
Objective memoranda
    analyzing statutes and cases, 103-109,
        184-195
    audience, 65
    brief answer, 123-124, 200
    conclusion, 150-152
    conventions, 65
    discussion section, 124-150, 201-234
    editing, 160-169
    heading, 110-111
    integrated format, 203-207
    proofreading, 169-170
    purpose, 65
    question presented, 118-123, 199-
        200
    researching, 82-103, 179-184
    revising, 152-161, 236-240
    sample memos, 66-77, 170-175
    script format, 132-150
    statement of facts, 111-118, 198-199
    synthesizing statutes and cases, 103-
        109, 184-195
Official codes, 400-401
One-sentence paragraphs, 525-547
Onomatopoeia, 696-697
Opinion letters
    advice in, 246-247
    audience, 241
    checklist, 250-251
    concluding paragraph, 247
    conventions, 243
    explanation of law, 245-246
    facts, summary of, 245
    introductory paragraph, 243-244
    issue, statement of, 244-245
    opinion in, 245

    purpose, 241
    tone of, 248-249
    warnings, 247
"Or," to start sentence, 524
Oral argument
    argument, 375-376
    audience, 369-370
    checklist, 382-384
    closing, 377
    courtroom procedures and etiquette,
        372-373
    delivery, 378-379
    eye contact, 378-379
    facts, summary of, 374-375
    gestures, 379
    handling problems, 380-382
    introductions, 373
    issues, statement of, 374
    opening, 374
    persuasiveness, 379-380
    posture, 379
    preparation for, 370-372
    purpose, 370
    questions, answering, 376-377
    rebuttal, 377-378
    references to the record, 375
Ordering issues and arguments, 272-
    275
Organizing writing, 509-514
Orienting transitions, 570-574
Outlines
    after-the-fact, 154-156, 518-519
    in general, 509-510
Overuse of quotations, 555, 641-643

Paragraph block, 563
Paragraphs
    coherence, 537-542
    function of, 535-536
    length, 547
    one-sentence, 525, 544, 546
    patterns, 542-544
    unity, 536-537
Parallelism, 541, 694-696, 754-760
Parentheses, 815-817
Parenthetical explanations, 210-221
Participles, 708-709
Passive voice, 587-593, 644-645
    effective use, 590-593
    mixing with active voice, 592
    persuasive writing, 295
Patterns in sentences, 703-706
Personification, 698-699

Persuasive authority, 25–30
Persuasive writing
    active and passive voice, 295, 587–
        593
    airtime, 290–291
    context, creating, 286–289
    detail, 291–292
    point of view, 289–290
    positions of emphasis, 292–294, 608–
        612, 619–622
    presenting arguments, 323–329
    presenting cases, 318–323
    presenting rules, 315–318
    sentence construction, 294–295
    word choice, 295–298
Phrases, 707–709
    absolute, 709
    participial, 708–709
    prepositional, 707–708
Plagiarism, 896–899
"Plain English," 660–663
Plain language argument, 55–60, 138
Point of view, 289–290
Policy arguments, 61–62, 138
Pompous language, 647–648
Popular name tables, 405
Positions of emphasis, 292–294, 607,
    608–612, 619–622
Possessive, correct use of, 799–803
Practice books, 445
Precision, 238–239, 623–638
    subject-verb-object mismatch, 630–
        635
Predicates, 703–706
Prepositions
    at end of sentence, 524–525
    in idioms, 890
    that follow adjectives, 889–890
    that follow nouns, 890
    that follow verbs, 888–889
Presidential documents, 413–414
Pronouns
    agreement, 737–741
    as devices for achieving coherence,
        541
    broad reference, 743–746
    first-person, 670–672
    indefinite, 730–731, 740–741
    in substantive transitions, 576
    relative, 710
    reference, 742–747
    second-person, 670–672
Proofreading, 169–170, 521–522

Psychology of writing, 507
Punctuation. *See* specific punctuation
    mark, *e.g.,* Comma
Punctuation for emphasis, 611–614
Purple prose, 684–685
"Pursuant to," usage of, 664

Question presented in brief
    checklist, 282–283
    format, 278–279
    making the question persuasive,
        279–282
Question presented in objective memo
    checklist, 122–123
    number and order, 118
    revising and editing, 160–162
    under-does-when format, 118–122
    whether format, 199–200
Questions in text, 859–860
Quotation marks, 803–810
    other uses, 809–810
    with other marks of punctuation,
        778–779, 809
Quotations
    block, 805–806
    lead-ins for, 806–808
    overuse of, 144, 555, 641–643
    within quotations, 808–809

Racial bias in language, 679–682
Raise and dismiss, 131–132
Readers
    expectations, 625–627
    sentence length determined by
        audience, 599–603
Reading cases, 98–100, 188–195
Record on appeal, 258
Redundancy, 648–651
Regulations
    Code of Federal Regulations, 415–
        419
    federal, 415
    state, 420
Relationship between federal and state
    governments, 13–16
Relationship between state and federal
    courts, 16–17
Relative pronouns, 710
Repetition
    in persuasive writing, 901–902
    needless, 648–651, 901–902
    of key words, 148, 617–618, 619–
        622, 628–630

Reporters
  advance sheets, 422
  bound reporters, 422
  generally, 96–97
  National Reporter System, 423–425
  slip opinions, 421–422
  West Key Number System, 424–425
Research plans, 82–85, 179–184, 495–504
Restatements, 455
Restrictive phrases or clauses, 770–777
Reviewing the record for error, 264–265
Revising
  in general, 518
  objective memoranda, 152–160, 236–240
Rhetorical preferences, 890–902
Rhetorical questions, 859–860
Roadmaps, 157, 530–532
Rule section in objective memorandum
  general rules, 126–131, 207–214
  multiple statutory sections, 128–129
  rules plus policy, 208–209
  single statutory section, 127–128
  specific rules, 133–134
  statutes plus cases, 129–130
Run-on sentences, 826

"Said," as an adjective, 668–669
"Same," as a pronoun, 669–670
Sample briefs, 332–367
Sample memoranda, 66–77, 170–175
Schedules for writing, 508
Scope of review, 256–257
Script format, 132–150
Search terms, 97, 181
Second-person pronouns, 670–672
Secondary sources
  American Law Reports, 445–451
  form books, 456
  hornbooks, 440–445
  law reviews, 453–454
  legal dictionaries, 456
  legal encyclopedias, 440–442
  legal periodicals, 453–454
  looseleaf services, 451–452
  model acts, 455
  practice books, 445
  restatements, 455
  treatises, 453
  uniform laws, 455
  words and phrases, 456

Selecting cases, 94–96, 134–135
Semicolons, 792–797
  to separate items in a series, 794–795
  with citations, 796–797
  with coordinating conjunctions, 796
  with "yet" or "so," 795–796
Sentence openers
  throat-clearing expressions, 645–647
  variety in, 692–693
  weak, 596
Sentence patterns, 703–706
Sentences
  active and passive voice, 161–166, 295, 587–593
  concluding, 552–556
  editing techniques, 161–169
  emphasis in, 606–622
  length, 599–606
    variety in, 168, 690–692
  new information at beginning, 167
  patterns within, 703–706
  persuasive writing, 294–295
  short, 605–606
  subject-verb distance, 166–167, 597–599
  topic, 547–563
Session laws, 397–399
Sexist modifiers, 678
Shepard's citators
  coverage, 458–463
  how they work, 457–458
  shepardizing cases, 100–102
  tips on using, 463–464
  types, 458
Short sentences, 605–606
Signing a brief, 330
Signposts, 158–159, 532–534
Simile, 697–699
Single-word emphasizers, 614–615
Slip opinions, 421–422
Spelling, 827–841
  crutches, 828–829
  strategies, 829–841
Split infinitives, 523–524
Standard of review, 267–268
State constitutions, 396
State courts, 12
Statement of facts in objective memorandum
  checklist, 117–118
  fact selection, 111–114, 198–199
  organizational patterns, 114–116, 199
  presentation of facts, 116–117, 199

Statement of the case in brief
  checklist, 299
  creating context, 286–289
  fact selection, 285
  organization, 286
  persuasive techniques, 290–298
  point of view, 289–290
  procedural history, 284
  references to the record, 284
  rules governing, 283–284
"Statute," capitalization of, 848
Statutes
  analysis, 35–36, 92–94
  annotated codes, 401
  codes, 400–405
  codification tables, 405
  computer databases, 405, 409
  locating, 32–35, 86–92, 397–400
  official codes, 400
  popular name table, 405
  research strategies, 401–405
  session laws, 397–400
  unannotated codes, 401
  unofficial codes, 400
  updating, 91–92, 401
Stressed and unstressed syllables, 687–688
Subject complements, 705, 733–734
Subjects, 703–706
  concrete, 593–595
  distance from, 166–167, 597–599
Subject-verb agreement, 727–737
Subject-verb-object combinations, 643–645
Subject-verb-object mismatch, 630–635
Subjunctive mood, 725–727
Subordinating conjunctions, 710
Substantive transitions, 574–586
"Such," as an adjective, 668–669
Summary of argument in appellate brief, 300
Symbols, 856
Synonyms, 627–628
Synthesis, 103–109, 184–198

Table of authorities
  for appellate brief, 276
Table of cases, 437
Table of contents for appellate brief, 276
Tense, 720–724
Terms of art, 667–668
"That" vs. "which," 773–774

"The"
  capitalization of, 848
  correct use of, 867–873
  omission of, 669
"The fact that," 658
Theory of the case, 271–272, 516
Three-column chart, 510–513
Throat-clearing expressions, 595, 645–647
Time management, 508
Titles of works, 735, 857
Tone, 248–250
  pompous language, 647–648
Topic sentences, 158–160, 547–563
  implied, 551–552
  stated, 548–551
Transitions, 157–158, 565–586
  generic, 565–570, 581–582
  orienting, 570–574, 580
  substantive, 574–586
Treatises, 453

Unannotated codes, 401
Underlining, 607–608
Undisputed elements, 131–132
Uniform laws, 455
Uniform Laws Annotated, 455
United States Code, 86, 400
United States Code Annotated, 86–96, 400–401
United States Code Congressional and Administrative News, 411
United States Constitution, 393–395
United States Statutes at Large, 86, 397–398
Unity in paragraphs, 519–520, 536–537
Unknown facts, 113–114
Unofficial codes, 400

Variety
  in sentence length, 168, 690–692
  in sentence openers, 692–693
Verbs, 704–706
  action, 595–597
  auxiliary, 704, 874–878
  auxiliary or helping verb chart, 875–876
  distance from subject, 167–168, 597–599
  helping, 704, 874, 878
  linking, 596, 703
  mixing active and passive, 592
  with gerunds, 880–882, 883–884

Verbs (*continued*)
  with infinitives, 882–886
  with objects and infinitives, 884–886
  with prepositions, 888–889
Verb tense, 720–724, 878–880
Voice, 587–593
  effective use of active voice, 587–590
  effective use of passive voice, 590–593

Westlaw
  capitalization, 475
  cite checking, 483–485
  connectors, 475–480
  costs, 485–486
  field searching, 481–483
  full text searching, 468
  hyphenation, 474–475
  indices, 468

noise words, 475
plurals, 475
search words, 470–471
strategies, 491–493
truncation and root expansion, 472–474
"Whereas," 664
"Which" vs. "that," 773–774
Word choice, 623–638
  in persuasive writing, 296–298
Wordiness, 638–660
Word order, changing, 616–617
Words and phrases, 456
  table in digest, 437
Writer's block, 516–517
Writing lists, 509
Writing plans, 509–510

"You," use of, 670–672